The law of Landlord and Tenant in Pennsylvania

THE LAW

OF

LANDLORD AND TENANT

IN

PENNSYLVANIA

BY

WILLIAM TRICKETT, LL D.

DEAN OF THE DICKINSON SCHOOL OF LAW.

ROCHESTER N Y.

THE LAWYERS' CO-OPERATIVE   BLISHING COMPANY

1904

THE E R ANDREWS PRINTING CO , ROCHESTER, N Y.

PREFACE.

The law of landlord and tenant is important, and occasions for applications of it are extremely frequent. In this book the subjects of distress, and the statutory remedies of the landlord for the recovery of the possession of the premises within or after the expiration of the term, have been exhaustively treated. Other topics have been discussed with due fullness. Interesting and important chapters on Mining Leases, and Oil and Gas Leases, have been included.

The writer here acknowledges his indebtedness to Prof. Sylvester B. Sadler. A M, LL B, for indispensable assistance.

He also recognizes his obligation to Paul Willis, LL B., for material aid

WILLIAM TRICKETT.

Carlisle, Pa.

CONTENTS.

CHAPTER I.

AGREEMENT TO LEASE.

CHAPTER II.

CONTRACTS DISTINGUISHABLE FROM LEASES.

CHAPTER III.

THE LEASE

CONTENTS.

CHAPTER IV.

THE SUBJECT OF THE LEASE

CHAPTER V.

MODIFYING OR ANNULLING LEASE

CHAPTER VI.

SURETIES IN LEASES

CHAPTER VII.

THE LESSOR'S COVENANTS.

CHAPTER VIII

LESSEE'S COVENANTS AS TO PREMISES

CHAPTER IX

RELATIONS OF LESSEES OF DIFFERENT PARTS OF BUILDING

CHAPTER X.

RENT

CHAPTER XI.

RENT PAYABLE IN KIND

CHAPTER XII.

ACTIONS FOR RENT.

CHAPTER XIII.

THE RIGHT OF DISTRESS.

CHAPTER XIV.

WHAT GOODS ARE DISTRAINABLE

CHAPTER XV.

THE PLACE OF THE DISTRESS.

CHAPTER XVI.

DISTRESS; PROCEDURE.

CHAPTER XVII.

REMEDIES FOR IMPROPER DISTRESS

CHAPTER XVIII.

LANDLORD'S PREFERENCE WITH RESPECT TO EXECUTION SALES

CHAPTER XIX

TENANCY AT WILL AND FROM YEAR TO YEAR

CHAPTER XX.

TERMINATION OF THE LESSEE'S INTEREST BY SURRENDER

CHAPTER XXI.

EVICTION.

CHAPTER XXII.

ASSIGNMENT OF TERM

CHAPTER XXIII.

SUBLEASES.

CHAPTER XXIV.

CONDITIONS SUBSEQUENT.

CHAPTER XXV.

STATUTORY FORFEITURE FOR NONPAYMENT OF RENT

CHAPTER XXVI

REPETITION AND PROTRACTION OF TERM

CHAPTER XXVII.

FIXTURES

CHAPTER XXVIII

THE WAY-GOING CROP AND EMBLEMENTS

CHAPTER XXIX.

TRANSFER OF REVERSION DURING THE TERM.

CHAPTER XXX.

RECOVERY OF POSSESSION AT END OF TERM ACT OF MARCH
21st, 1772

CHAPTER XXXI.

RECOVERY OF POSSESSION   ACT OF DECEMBER 14 1863

CHAPTER XXXII.

ACT DECEMBER 14, 1863   REVIEW ON CERTIORARI AND APPEAL

CHAPTER XXXIII.

RECOVERING POSSESSION ACT MARCH 25, 1825.

CHAPTER XXXIV.

PROCEEDINGS IN PHILADELPHIA ON LOST LEASE

CHAPTER XXXV

ESTOPPEL AGAINST DENYING LESSOR'S TITLE

CHAPTER XXXVI

LANDLORD'S AND TENANT'S LIABILITY AS TO OTHERS.

CHAPTER XXXVII.

MINES AND MINERAL LEASES.

CHAPTER XXXVIII.

MINES AND MINERAL LEASES—CONTINUED

CHAPTER XXXIX.

OIL AND GAS LEASES.

CHAPTER XL.

OIL AND GAS LEASES—CONTINUED

TABLE OF CASES CITED.

B.

D

E.

F.

G.

H

L

N

O.

Q.

Q

S

T.

U

THE LAW

OF

LANDLORD AND TENANT.

CHAPTER I.

AGREEMENT TO LEASE.

1. **Lessee's option.**—An agreement to grant a lease or to ac-cept a lease is enforceable in the same mode in which other con-tracts are enforceable, and subject to the same restrictions The owner may bind himself to make a lease on the demand of X, or on the demand of X after certain things shall have been per-formed, whether by X or others It does not follow that X is bound to accept a lease If he has obtained an option, it rests with him to determine whether he will or will not accept the lease. A, in consideration of one dollar, agreed in writing with B that, on the completion of a railroad by B within one year, "I will lease to said B all my iron ore interests and rights . . . for the term of twenty years . . . at a royalty of not ex-ceeding twenty-five cents per gross ton of 2240 pounds of the iron ore raised by said B," and that "I shall execute unto the said B the lease of mineral interests and rights above men-tioned. But in the case of failure on the part of the said B to

LAND & TEN 1.

complete said road within the time above stated, this agreement
shall be null and of no effect." The instrument was signed by
both A and B   Though the railroad was built within the time,
B not having asked for a lease nor gone into possession of the
premises, A could not recover royalties stipulated for in the
agreement. The contract was not a lease, but, at most, an option.[1]

2 **Agreement on the terms.**—An agreement between A and B
as to all the terms which are to be incorporated into a written
lease neither forms a lease nor any relation between them that
would support an action by A for the use and occupation of the
premises.   B may change his mind, and, though A has drawn up
the lease, may decline to accept it, or to occupy the premises   If
no possession is taken, no action for use and occupation can be
sustained.[2] "An arrangement of terms," says Lewis, J., "in contemplation of a written contract, is not a perfect agreement upon
which an action can be maintained." But if a written "agreement to rent" is executed by A, the owner, and accepted by B,
the person named in it as lessee, with the intention that it shall
regulate his rights to the premises and his obligations towards
A, it will be a lease, and not a mere proposal, although B was
already in possession of the premises under an earlier lease with
different provisions, and with a different period of termination.[3]

3. **Owner's breach of contract to lease.**—A contract to make a
lease is enforceable as other contracts. It may be specifically

---

[1]*Proctor* v *Benson*, 149 Pa 254, 24
Atl. 279 If B orally agrees with A
to accept from A a lease for five
years, and then refuses, A cannot recover, as damages, the rent agreed
upon for the first year during which
he is unable to obtain another tenant, in the absence of proof that he
would have been able to obtain another tenant at the same rent, nor
can he recover for improvements
made to fit the buildings to serve the
uses of B unless such improvements
are useless for other purposes and

have not increased the general rental
value of the premises   A may recover nominal damages, however, in any
case *Sausser* v *Steinmetz* 88 Pa.
324   An instrument wherein   A
"doth grant and lease the exclusive
right to mine, dig, and take away
iron ore" for eleven years is a lease,
and not an agreement to lease.
Kemble Coal & I Co v *Scott*, 90 Pa.
332

[2]*Maitland* v *Wilcox*, 17 Pa 231.

[3]*Bergner* v *Palethorp*, 2 W. N C.
297.

executed by a court of equity compelling the making of the lease and enjoining the lessor or one to whom, with knowledge of the contract, he has conveyed the premises in fee, from interfering with the lessee's taking and retaining the possession [4] It may probably be specifically enforced by the action of ejectment It may be indirectly enforced by compensating the expectant lessee in damages.[5] The oral promise to make the lease may be shown though the consideration of it was, in part, the surrender by a writing of an existing term which recites, as its consideration, the sum of $1 and a release from the obligation of the lease, but not the making of a new lease.[6] The promise may be enforced, although it defines the rent to be payable only as a "fair rent," because a fair rent can be reduced to certainty by recourse to extrinsic circumstances. But an omission to define the length of the term would probably make the enforcement of the contract by an action for damages impossible [7] An agreement to make a lease of coal land "for as long as coal was in the hill" is enforceable.[8]

4 Excuse for nonperformance.—The making of a contract to let land, or the making of a lease for the land, from a certain date, binds the lessor to make the lease and deliver the possession; or, having made the lease, to deliver the possession, and this obligation is not contingent on the continuance of his ownership to the time when the lease is to be made or possession given,[9]

---

[4] *Farley* v *Stokes,* 1 Phila 30

[5] *Heilman* v *Weinman,* 139 Pa 143, 21 Atl 29, *Weaver* v *Wood,* 9 Pa 221, *McCafferty* v *Griswold,* 99 Pa 270

[6] *Ibid*

[7] *Ibid* It is said that the expectant lessee would have to tender a lease naming a rent that would be fair, before bringing the action

[8] *Heilman* v *Weinman,* 139 Pa 143, 21 Atl 29

The owner will not be compelled specifically to perform if, the agreement being that the other party will, before a certain date, bore for the purpose of discovering whether coal in paying quantities is in the land, the latter fails to bore within the time The owner may regard the option as lapsed, and bore himself The court, at least, will refuse a preliminary injunction against the owner *Dawes* v *Maxwell,* 5 Kulp, 351. The court observed that the owner's boring did not prevent the other party's boring also

[9] *M'Cloury* v *Croghan,* 31 Pa 22

or upon his ability to give the possession.[10]   Though, *e g.,* A, a
life tenant, having contracted to make a lease, before the time
for performance arrives, dies, and the remainderman refuses to
make the lease, A's executor will be liable in damages.[11]   And
the lessor is not discharged from liability for not giving possession because he has been unable to give it on account of the refusal of a prior tenant to surrender the possession [12]   Whether,
if this refusal was without right, and unexpected, the lessor
would be liable, is, perhaps, doubtful.   In *Cozens* v *Stevenson*[13]
a written lease for two years described the property as "now occupied by G W H ," a tenant   G W H improperly refused
to give up possession until he was evicted under landlord and
tenant proceedings, nine months after the commencement of the
term   It was held that there was no implied covenant of the lessor to give the lessee possession at the beginning of the term.   On
the other hand, in *Steel* v *Frick*[14] Buffington, P. J., told the
jury that if the tenant could not obtain possession of the premises "either by the act of Steel (the lessor) or the want of right
or power to give possession," the tenant could recover damages.
In *Yeager* v *Weaver*[15] the same result was reached, when the
tenant of the preceding year refused to vacate, as also in *Allegaert* v. *Smart,*[16] where the preceding tenant was ultimately dispossessed by proceedings under the landlord and tenant act.
Damages can be recovered for breach of an oral promise to make
a lease exceeding three years, *viz ,* damages for work done and
expense incurred under the direction of the intending lessor in
developing the coal on the land, the discovery of which was the
condition on which the lease was to be made.[17]

[10]*Allegaert* v *Smart,* 10 W N C   [13] 5 Serg & R 421.
29   *Yeager* v *Weaver,* 64 Pa 425,   [11] 56 Pa 172
Steel v *Frick,* 56 Pa 172   [15] 64 Pa 425
   [11]*M'Cloury* v *Croghan,* 31 Pa 22   [16] 10 W N C 29
   [12]*Steel* v *Frick,* 56 Pa 172, *Yeager*   [17]*Heilman* v. *Weinman,* 139 Pa.
v. *Weaver,* 64 Pa 425.   143, 21 Atl. 29.

5. Measure of damages.—For the omission to execute the lease, or, having executed it, for the failure to give the tenant possession, the tenant may recover damages. The proper measure of damages will not be the worth of the bargain, *i. e*, what the tenant could have made on the farm, in the absence of bad faith or of a refusal to perform the promisor's covenant when he might do so,[18] nor even, apparently, if the promise to lease is oral, when the promissor could carry out his promise [18½] When the lessee has paid money to the lessor or another with the consent of the latter, in order to procure the lease, he will be entitled, on disappointment, to recover it with interest.[19] The lessee, expecting to get possession, but being refused it, has to haul his goods away and store them in a barn, and put his family in an almost untenantable house at another place [20] The premises being a hotel, the lessee, after taking the lease, the term under which began three months later, sold his house and his personal property at a vendue for the purpose of preparing to occupy the hotel. He bought furniture for the hotel, but was compelled, after some months, failing to gain possession, to sell it. He was then without a house, and was compelled to board [21] In these cases, compensation was allowed for the facts stated In *Smart* v. *Allegaert* [22] however, the court refused to allow the tenant to show that, expecting to get possession of the desired premises, he had laid in a stock of goods which his failure to gain possession compelled him to sell at a loss; that he had been obliged to store

---

[18] *M'Clowry* v *Croghan*, 31 Pa 22

[18½] *McCafferty* v *Griswold*, 99 Pa 270

[19] *M'Clowry* v *Croghan*, 31 Pa 22, *McCafferty* v *Griswold*, 99 Pa 270

[20] *Steel* v *Frick*, 56 Pa 172 Damages recovered, $315 91

[21] *Yeager* v *Weaver*, 64 Pa 425 Damages, *viz*, $910, were recovered The value of the lease was proved in this case but apparently without objection by the defendant In *Wolf v. Studebaker*, 65 Pa 460, the value of the bargain was laid down as the measure of damages for refusal to allow the tenant for one year under a verbal lease to take possession, but that measure was not controverted by the defendant

[22] 8 W N C 217, *Allegaert* v. *Smart*, 10 W N C 29

them; that they fell in price, and were damaged by storing. If B accepts a lease from A for tract X, on A's verbal promise to make a lease for the adjoining tract Y, and B puts down an oil well on X, only because he expects the lease of Y, he will be entitled to nominal damages only for A's refusal to make the lease of tract Y, if he has made as much money by the operation of X as he has expended.[23] When the lease or agreement is in writing, and the lessor is guilty of a fraud, the measure of damages will be the value of the bargain[24] But if the promise to lease is oral, the voluntary refusal to keep it will not expose the promissor to liability for the value of the bargain.[25] The defendant, sued for refusing to give possession to his lessee, cannot show, in mitigation of damages, that the plaintiff obtained another farm, or another occupation, which paid him better than the farm in question would have done.[26] No action can be brought against the lessor for his announced decision not to allow the tenant to take possession, until the commencement of the term[27]

6. **Merger of agreement in the lease** —Ordinarily the written lease will be assumed to express the final form of the intentions of the parties, and anterior different intentions will be understood to have been abandoned. If, *e. g*, the oral contract is for a lease of two years, and the written lease actually made, and accepted by the lessee, is for one year, and no explanation of the inconsistency is offered except that the written lease was a mistake, it will be presumed to express the final intent of the parties[28] When the court, however, discovers that the lease is not "the legal equivalent—the formal embodiment—of the previous

---

[23]*McCafferty* v. *Griswold*, 99 Pa 270

[24]*Smart* v *Allegaert*, 8 W N C 217 In *Hoy* v *Gronoble*, 34 Pa 9, the profits which the plaintiff would have made were stated to be the measure of the damages.

[25]*McCafferty* v *Griswold*, 99 Pa. 270

[26]*Wolf* v *Studebaker*, 65 Pa 460

[27]*Flickinger* v *Forry*, 6 Del Co Rep 154

[28]*Lea* v *Love*, 14 W N C 75   Cf *McCafferty* v *Griswold*, 99 Pa 270.

agreement," and that it was not intended to supersede that agreement, the agreement will be enforced, after the making of the lease. A orally agreed with B that, with a view to B's accepting a lease of the premises for iron works, he would erect a building on his lot, according to plans furnished by B, and B agreed to accept the lease for ten years, at an annual rent equal to 9 per cent of the cost of the building. The building was erected and the lease made Within thirteen months, B became insolvent, assigning for the benefit of creditors, and, shortly afterwards, the assignee gave up the premises. On account of the special arrangement of the building made to accommodate B, it was impossible to let it except for a small rent. The loss to A during the remainder of the ten years of the term would be $40,000 It was held that the original contract survived; that for its breach, A was entitled to $40,000 damages, and that he was entitled to claim a dividend on this sum, from the assigned estate.[20]

[20]Re Reading Iron Works, 150 Pa.
369, 25 Atl. 617.

CHAPTER II.

CONTRACTS DISTINGUISHABLE FROM LEASES.

7. Lease and contract to convey.—It sometimes happens that the contract between the parties is both a lease and an agreement to convey the fee within or at the end of the term, at the option of the lessee, and upon his performing certain stipulations. A lease, *e g.,* for forty-nine years, authorized the tenant to erect buildings and improvements, and provided that, at the expiration of the term, the parties should choose seven appraisers, who should appraise the land, and, separately, the buildings and improvements. It provided further, that if the lessor paid the lessee the appraised value of the latter, they should become his, but, if he refused to pay for them, the tenant might pay him the appraised value of the land, and he should then convey the premises to the tenant, his heirs, and assigns This contract gave not only a leasehold to the tenant, but an equitable interest in the fee.[1] The tenant, under a lease

---

[1] *Ely* v *Beaumont,* 5 Serg & R 124 This equitable interest could be bound by the lien of a judgment against the lessee

A lease for one year by A to B and so from year to year so long as A and B should please, which provides that, on the termination of the tenancy by A's act, he should compensate B for all his improvements gives to B no freehold interest on which a judgment becomes a lien *Krause's Appeal,* 2 Whart 398.

for seven years, had the right to take, at a stipulated price, a portion of the premises on ground-rent during the first three years. Before he exercised this right, he erected buildings on the premises Materialmen acquired a mechanics' lien on the fee, which was afterwards conveyed to him by the lessor [5] The right of purchase, under a lease, passes to the assignee of it. and is enforceable by the latter against the lessor or a grantee of the reversion, who has notice by the possession of the premises by the tenant or his assignee, or otherwise, of the lessee's right of purchase.[3] But no interest in the reversion is created by a stipulation in the lease that, when the land shall be offered for sale. the first opportunity to purchase shall be given to the lessee, on terms as favorable as those given to any one. The lessee has no right to purchase valid against the lessor's grantee.[4] A lessee who has an option to purchase is, when the purchase is made, to be regarded as owner *ab initio* so far that, if he has, agreeably to his contract with his lessor, taken out a policy of insurance "payable to him as his interest may appear," and, a fire occurring before the exercise of his option, the insurance money is paid to the lessor, he will be entitled to receive it from the lessor.[5]

8. Conveyance, and not lease.—An instrument calling itself a "lease" of all the coal beneath the surface, declaring itself "perpetual" until all the coal shall be mined, securing all rights and privileges conferred in it to the heirs and assigns of the respective parties, is a conveyance in fee of the coal, and not a lease, though it provides for a periodic payment of a royalty, authorizes distress for default in such payment, and

---

[2]*Gaule* v *Bilyeav*, 25 Pa 521 A mechanics lien entered during the period of the option will not be struck off, after the expiration of that period. unless it appears that it lapsed without exercise of the option *Morgan* v *Bloecker*, 6 Pa Dist R 659 Cf *Barnett* v. *Plummer*, 19 W. N. C. 117.

[3]*Kerr* v. *Day*, 14 Pa 112, 53 Am Dec 526, *Napier* v *Darlington*, 70 Pa 64

[4]*Elder* v *Robinson*, 19 Pa 364

[5]*People's Street R Co* v *Spencer*, 156 Pa 85, 36 Am St. Rep 22, 27 Atl. 113.

makes the grantee's rights forfeitable for the absence of sufficient personalty on the premises to satisfy, by distress, the
royalty due.[6] The use of the word "lease" and the presence of
stipulations in the instrument which are often found in leases
do not make it a conveyance of a term, which a lease is, but of
the fee[7] An agreement by A to "let" his farm to B, with the
ordinary stipulation in leases concerning good husbandry, and
reserving to A one half of the crops, followed by a provision
that if B shall perform the stipulations, and in addition do
such work as A and his wife may request him to do, furnishing
fuel, provisions, and nurses, in case of sickness, "then I, the
said A, and wife, do hereby grant to him, the said B, one day
after my and my wife's death, the farm, . . . his heirs
and assigns forever, and free of all encumbrances," is a conveyance in fee, with conditions subsequent, or a contract for
such a conveyance, enforceable in equity.[8]

9.   **Lease, and not conveyance** —A grant for a limited time,
e g, for fifteen years, of the right to take stones from a tract,
is a lease, and not a sale of the coal. The stone not actually
taken within the fifteen years would be the property of the
lessor as before the lease was made[9] A demise for a term of
years of land "with the sole and exclusive right and privilege,
during said period, of digging and boring for oil and other
minerals, and of gathering and collecting the same therefrom,"
is a lease, and not a sale.[10] The leasehold interest, however

[6]*Delaware, L & W R Co* v *Sanderson*, 109 Pa 583, 58 Am Rep 743,
1 Atl 394, *Sanderson* v. *Scranton*
105 Pa 469   The coal as a separate
estate in fee, was taxable, independently of the surface

[7] Cf *Krider* v *Lafferty*, 1 Whart
303   Where the use of the word
"let" was deemed consistent with the
creation of a fee   The words were A
"hath let unto the said B, his legal
heirs and representatives, a certain

piece of meadow . . . at the rate
of $15 per acre, to be paid by the said
B or his legal heirs annually, to the
said A, his heirs and assigns"

[8]*Fritz* v. *Menges*, 179 Pa 122, 36
Atl 213

[9]*Duncan* v *Hartman*, 143 Pa 595,
24 Am St Rep 570, 22 Atl 1009

[10]*Brown* v *Beecher*, 120 Pa 590, 15
Atl. 608, *Duke* v *Hague*, 107 Pa 57,
Kile v. *Giebner*, 114 Pa 381, 7 Atl
154.

long, is a chattel real, *i. e.*, personalty,[11]—not bound by the lien of a judgment,[12] and vendible on a "fi. fa " and without a sheriff's deed.[13]

10. A cropper.—A distinction must be observed between a tenant and a cropper. A tenant has a right of occupancy and possession of land for a term, which is valid against the landlord and against all other persons. He is, for the time being, an owner of the land, and as such entitled to the ordinary remedies of an owner for the defense or recovery of his possession; *e. g.*, trespass, ejectment. Nor is he the less a tenant because the rent which he is to pay consists of a fraction of the crop which he is to raise.[14] The crop usually belongs to him until he divides and sets apart the lessor's share from his own. And he is more than the owner of the crop. He is the owner of the soil itself for the period of his term. On the other hand, a cropper is one who acquires no right of continuous and exclusive possession of the soil; no interest in it which the law vindicates by trespass or ejectment [15] He is a mere employee of the owner of the land, whose work is to till the soil and harvest the crop, and whose distinctive name, "cropper," is bestowed on him because he receives compensation for his labor and skill in a share of the crop which they produce. The crop belongs to the person to whom the soil belongs until he divides and sets apart to the employee the share which they have agreed he shall receive. Hence, the owner of land, R, agreeing verbally with F "to put out from 25 to 30 acres of the farm in wheat, F to have two thirds of the crop, and R one third," the whole crop, it was held, passed with a sheriff's sale of the land while it was in the ground, to the pur-

[11]*Brown* v. *Beecher,* 120 Pa 590, 15 Atl 608

[12]*Krause's Appeal,* 2 Whart 398

[13]*Dalzell* v *Lynch,* 4 Watts & S 255, *Williams* v *Downing,* 18 Pa 60, *Lereu* v *Rinehart,* 3 Pa Co Ct 50 *Sterling* v *Com* 2 Grant Cas 162.

[14]*Steel* v *Frick,* 56 Pa 172, *Brown* v *Jaquette,* 94 Pa 113, 39 Am Rep 770, *King* v *Bosserman,* 13 Pa Su per Ct 480

[15]*Adams* v *McKesson,* 53 Pa 81 91 Am Dec 183, *Fry* v *Jones,* 2 Rawle, 12, *Steel* v *Frick,* 56 Pa 172

chaser. F owned and had a right to take away none of it [16]
On the other hand, when B is put in possession of a grist mill by
the owner, A, for a term, he undertaking to deliver to A one
third of the tolls taken, in kind, B is a tenant of the mill.[17]   An
agreement whereby A agreed to "let" to B "part of the Worden
farm" for one year, B to put one field in corn, and work it well,
to put another field in oats in the spring, to sow so much of the
land in wheat and rye in the fall as A may wish, to haul out all
the manure, and put it on the ground before sowing, to keep the
fences in good repair, to pay the taxes for the year, and to deliver to A one half of all the grain at market when ready for
delivery, B to have all the hay and all the pasture during the
year,—constituted B a tenant, not a cropper, because these
stipulations indicated that B was intended to have the possession.[18]

11. Lease for the raising of a crop.—The fact that the owner of
land confers on A, for a money consideration, the right to one
field for the purpose of raising crops, does not make him a cropper.   He becomes tenant of the field from the time when he
is, according to the agreement, to take control of it, until he cuts
and removes the crop.   If the agreement is that he is to have
the land "for the raising of two crops," his tenancy does not end
with the taking away of the first crop, and, in the interval between the taking away of this crop and the planting of the second, he may turn his cattle into the field,[19] in order that they
may feed on the damaged part of the crop which has been left,
or may otherwise occupy it

12. Lessee, and not partner—A partnership for the purpose of

[16]*Adams* v *McKesson*, 53 Pa 81, 91
Am Dec 183
  [17]*Fry* v *Jones*, 2 Rawle, 12
  [8]*Steel* v *Frick*, 56 Pa 172
  The tenant farming on the shares,
and agreeing to do all labor in good,
workmanlike manner, his wife, who
does manual labor on the farm, with

no expectation of compensation from
the lessor, the tenant's father, cannot
subsequently, on being divorced, recover compensation from the lessor
Rathbone v *Rathbone*, 23 Pa Super.
Ct 207
  [19]*Irwin* v *Mattox*, 138 Pa. 467, 21
Atl 209.

farming, to which the owner of the farm contributes the farm
for a term, and the farmer his time, skill, and instruments of
husbandry, is possible; but the court refused to find that a partnership was produced by an agreement between A, owner of
land, and B, that B, for one year, in consideration of one half
of the crop, should "farm for" A his land on the following
terms: Each party was to find one half of the stock, including
cattle, poultry, hogs, and one half of the seeds for crops; B was
to find all the farming implements, and all the working stock,
and all the requisite labor, to pay all the road tax, and one half
of other taxes; to submit to A, every three months, an account
of receipts, to keep the fences in repair, to cut no timber, to
keep the farm in good order   A was to pay one half of the
wheelwright's and the blacksmith's bill, and might keep one horse
on the premises for his own use.   This agreement lacked the
features of a partnership.   It provided for no division of profits, no responsibility on A's part for losses, and no joint ownership of anything   One half of the crop was to be delivered to
A, though it had been raised at a loss to B   The contribution
of stock by A to the work did not make the stock joint property.
B was merely a tenant of the farm, having the use of the farm
and of the property of the landlord, and making compensation
for the use of both kinds of property by one half of the crops
Hence, A had no partner's lien on the personalty on the farm
for a balance due him by the tenant [20]

13. Employee, and not lessee—The owner of land may employ one to move on it with his family, in order to do the farm
work, take care of the cattle, milk the cows, deliver the milk,
etc., stipulating to pay him $1 per day and allow him the occu-
pancy for himself and family of the house on the premises
Such a person is not a cropper, nor a tenant paying rent.   His

---

[20]*Broun* v *Jaquette,* 94 **Pa** 113, 39
Am Rep 770   Having made no distress nor claimed rent from the proceeds of an execution, the tenant's
property passed to the sheriff's ven
dee without liability to A   Cf *Fritz*
v *Menges,* 179 **Pa** 122, 36 Atl 213

possession of the land and the cows, and the farm implements
is that of his employer, the owner   Whenever, therefore, the
owner has a right to terminate the employment, he has a right
to terminate the occupancy of the farm and house of the employee   Hence, when for sufficient cause under the contract
the employ is terminated, if the employee refuses to vacate the
house, his goods can be lawfully removed by the owner.   It is
error to allow the jury to find that, although the employee can
be properly dismissed from the service within a year, he cannot
be properly expelled from the house until its expiration.[21]

14. Practical consequences of distinction—The distinction between tenant and cropper is important because of the different
legal incidents of the two relations   To the former, but not to
the latter, attaches the landlord's right of distress,[22] of claiming
for rent from the proceeds of an execution, of resorting to the
special remedies for the recovery of possession.   The tenant, having a right to take possession, may sustain an action on the landlord's implied covenant if prevented from taking possession.[23]
The cropper would have no such right   The tenant may retain
his share of the crop despite a sheriff's sale of the reversion.   The
cropper would have no share in the crop until it was set apart
to him, and the whole crop would pass to the sheriff's vendee [24]
The tenant could defend his possession, even against the landlord;[25] the cropper, or the employee could sustain no action,
trespass or otherwise, for this purpose, since his right is only

[21]*Bowman* v *Bradley,* 151 Pa 351,
17 L R A 213, 24 Atl 1062
   A leased one half of a culm bank to
B for the purpose of screening the
coal and conveying it to market. B
paying a certain price per ton of coal
sold   B made a contract with C to
clean and prepare the coal for the
market   C was to deliver three hundred tons of coal daily to the cars
and was to be paid 20 cents per ton
C was to provide, erect, and maintain
the necessary buildings and machinery   C was not a sublessee or assignee of the lease, but a mere employee of B, and acquired no interest
in the culm bank   or the coal   *Advance Coal Co* v *Miller,* 7 Kulp, 541.

[22]*Fry* v *Jones,* 2 Rawle, 12.

[23]*Steel* v *Frick,* 56 Pa 172

[24] Cf *Dunn* v *Mattox,* 138 Pa 466,
21 Atl 209

[25]*Adams* v *McKesson,* 53 Pa. 81,
91 Am Dec 183

to a quasi-possession, the true possession belonging to the owner of the soil.[26]

15. License to live on land.—A distinction is drawn in *Callen* v. *Hilty*[27] between a lease of land and a "mere license to live upon land and to do certain acts thereon." The latter, it is said, "may be granted without creating the relation of land-lord and tenant, or giving any other rights to the occupant than those conceded or granted by the license." An agreement un-der seal witnessed that A "doth let or give" B, "privilege of living four years on his farm" from April 1st. B was to clear 35 acres, build fences, put up such buildings as might suit his convenience; A furnishing the boards, nails, and lath. The clearing was to be at designated places, 4 acres of the clearing to be put in grass. One third of the plowland was not to be seeded when B left the premises. A reserved the use of all the timber except what might be necessary for the buildings, rails, and firewood of B. This, said Coulter, J., was no grant of the farm for any time. The inference drawn was that A could enter to take cut timber away. Hence, B suing A for failure to furnish boards, nails, and laths, A could set off the value of timber cut by B, and sold by him. The timber cut in the pro-cess of clearing, if not used on the premises for fences, for build-ing the house, and for firewood, belonged to A, and he had a right to enter in order to take it away.

[26]*Bowman* v *Bradley*, 151 Pa. 351,   [27] 14 Pa. 286.
17 L R. A. 213, 24 Atl. 1062.

CHAPTER III.

THE LEASE.

16. Who may be lessor.—Any owner of land, if of sound mind, and adult, may make a lease of it The guardian of a minor, or other trustee, if the character of the trust allows, may make the lease. The lessor may be a county,[1] a city,[2] a borough. It

---

[1]*Juergen* v *Allegheny County*, 204 Pa 501, 54 Atl 281 As to lease of state land by forestry commission, *ride Re Forestry Commission Powers* 28 Pa Co Ct 465

[2]*Gumpert* v *Hay*, 202 Pa 340, 51 Atl 968, *Mihlbauer* v *Infantry Corps*, 205 Pa 180, 54 Atl 776. Wilkes-Barre could lease to Luzerne county for 999 years a tract of land

16

may be any non-municipal corporation [3]   One of several tenants in common may make a lease of his undivided interest in the land   If he makes a lease intended to be of the whole interest in the land, and receives rent from the lessee, he will be compellable to account to the other cotenants for their proper share, under the statute of 4 and 5 Anne, chap. 16, § 27.[4]   A firm may make a lease [5]   A lessee,[6] or his assignee of the lease[7] may lease the same premises, or a part of them.

17. **Lease to two or more.**—A lease may be made to two or more persons, who become tenants in common for the period of the lease. They may change this relation subsequently. One of two may assign his interest to the other, who thereupon will become the sole owner of the leasehold. After such an assignment, the former colessees may form a partnership to conduct operations on the leased premises without the leasehold becoming the property of the firm.[8] Colessees will be presumed to have equal rights; but evidence *dehors* the lease will be heard to show that their interests are unequal.[9] The lessor's implied covenant in a lease to two or more persons will be considered to be joint or several, as the tenants are joint lessees or in common   A covenant for quiet enjoyment, *e. g.*, will follow the nature of the estate   Hence, if the lessees take as tenants in

for a court house Cf *Mahon* v *Luzerne County*, 107 Pa 1, 46 Atl 894, *Mahon* v *Morton*, 175 Pa 279, 34 Atl 660, *Bennett* v *Norton*, 171 Pa 221, 32 Atl 1112

[3]*Ardesco Oil Co* v *North American Oil & Min Co* 66 Pa 375   The corporation was one for manufacturing and refining oil   Such a corporation can absolutely convey its property or can lease it.

[4]*Kline* v *Jacobs*, 68 Pa. 57; *Enterprise Oil & Gas Co* v *National Transit Co* 172 Pa 421, 51 Am St Rep. 746, 33 Atl 687, *Lancaster* v *Flowers*, 11 Pa Dist R 495 If one cotenant is himself in sole possession,

LAND & TEN 2.

he may be made to account to the other cotenants under the act of June 24th, 1903, P L 237 Cf *Norris* v *Gould*, 15 W N C 187, *Luch* v *Luck*, 113 Pa 256, 6 Atl 142 *Baker* v *Lewis*, 150 Pa 251, 24 Atl 616

[5]*Bewley* v *Tams*, 17 Pa 485

[6]*Ardesco Oil Co* v *North American Oil & Min Co* 66 Pa 375

[7]*Bewley* v *Tams*, 17 Pa 485

[8]*Douty* v *Bird*, 60 Pa 48 The partners may, however, have a joint possession, and therefore bring a joint trespass *q c f*

[9]*Smiley* v. *Gallagher*, 164 Pa. 498, 30 Atl. 713.

common, a release of this covenant by one of them will not be
binding on the other [10]

18. Rival claimants of leasehold.—The membership and the
purposes of an incorporated "Infantry Corps of State Fenci-
bles" and of an unincorporated military body being nearly
identical, their names being confused, a lease naming the former as lessee, and executed by its president and secretary, and
sealed with its corporate seal, will be deemed the property of
the corporation, and not of the other body, which has been attached to a regiment of the National Guards of Pennsylvania [11]

19. Phrases sufficient.—"It is an established rule of law that
whatever words are sufficient to explain the intent of the parties, that the one should devest himself of the property and the
other come into it for a determinate time, whether they run in
the form of a license, covenant, or agreement, will, in construction of law, amount to a lease as effectually as if the most
proper and pertinent words were made use of for that purpose.
. . . A license to inhabit amounts to a lease . . . Words
in an agreement that A shall hold and enjoy, if not accompanied by restraining words, operate as words of present demise." [12]   The word "lease" is unnecessary to make a lease [13]
The compensation for the use of the land may be a lump sum
paid at the beginning, or to be paid at the end of a term of
several years [14]   It may be payable in money, in grain, in
ore [15]   It may be a determinate sum of money or a sum to be
fixed by the quantities of ore, coal, [16] oil, or stone to be extracted
during the term.   The compensation may be made in the less

[10]*Eisenhart* v *Slaymaker*, 14 Serg
& R 153

[11]*Mühlbauer* v *Infantry Corps*, 205
Pa 180, 54 Atl 776, Affirming 10 Pa.
Dist R 585

[1] *Watson* v *O'Hern*, 6 Watts, 362;
Kunkle v *Philadelphia Rifle Club*, 10
Phila 52, *Bussman* v *Ganster*, 72
Pa 285

[12]*Moore* v *Miller*, 8 Pa 272, *Bussman* v *Ganster*, 72 Pa 285

[14]*Stover* v *Cadwallader*, 2 Pennyp.
117

[15]*Kunkle* v *Philadelphia Rifle Club*,
10 Phila 52

[12]*Greenough's Appeal*, 9 Pa 19.

than ordinary rate at which the lessee is to sell to the lessor articles of the manufacture of the former, such as lumber.[17] An agreement letting premises to X for one year, X paying "a rent of 75 cents per thousand for all bricks made and burnt during the term, as soon as each kiln is counted" is a lease.[18] The rent may take the form of a building to be erected on the premises and left there at the expiration of the term [19]

20. What makes a lease.—An agreement that B "may have the privilege of taking coal out of the P mine, he paying . . . the sum of 25 cents per cubic yard of coal so taken out, as rent for the privilege" was held to be a lease.[20] An agreement witnessing that A "doth . . let on a lease of six years" unto B and C, stone cutters, "the privilege of quarrying and hauling away all the stone they may be able to find use for, during the said term of six years . . . provided they fulfil the following conditions, viz they agree to pay unto the said A . . . a quarry rent of 7 cents for every perch . . . of common building stone they take out, etc. They also engage to fulfil any and all of the contracts A may agree for in such materials and workmanship as the conditions of such contracts call for," —is a lease, not a mere privilege, of which B could avail himself or not, as he chose As it deprived A of control of the quarry, it was B's and C's duty to operate it so as to yield to A a compensation for the loss of his possession [21] The Philadelphia Rifle Club agreed March 24th, 1873, with K, that he was to be permitted to occupy, for himself and family, such rooms in the main building and such piece of ground within the closed property as the committee might designate until March 31st, 1876, the club reserving the right to make alter-

[17] *Mitchell* v *Com* 37 Pa 187

[18] *Noll* v *Kline,* 2 York Legal Record, 118

[19] *Gregg* v *Irish,* 6 Serg & R 211

[20] *Greenough's Appeal,* 9 Pa 19 Cf *Oram's Estate,* 5 Kulp 423 'Hath demised, leased, and let unto the party of the second part the right to mine and take away coal from the S vein,' made a lease, and not a mere license *Offerman* v *Starr,* 2 Pa St 394, 44 Am Dec 211

[21] *Watson* v *O'Hern,* 6 Watts, 362

ations and repairs for a restaurant or otherwise. K, in consideration of $500 per year, payable quarterly "during said term," was to enjoy the privilege of selling certain articles upon the premises. He agreed to furnish glasses, light, fuel, and servants, music, and the service of conducting the restaurant in a proper manner. He was to have the ten-pin alley and keep it in good condition. In default of his removing at the "expiration of his term," the club reserved the right to take possession, K authorizing an amicable action of ejectment, a confession of judgment, and the issue of *habere facias possessionem* This created a tenancy, some of the *indicia* that it did being the mention of a term, the provision for compensation quarterly to the club, and for the entry of a judgment of ejectment. It did not create a mere personal license which ended with the death of K shortly after he entered into possession [22] An agreement for the use of the roof and the north wall of a building for the purpose of displaying stereopticon views, on the roof and wall, for nine months, and providing for a rent, for distress, and that, if the tenant holds over, it shall be for a year, and on the same terms, and so on from year to year, is a lease.[23]

21. Noncontractual relation.—If the owner of a farm devises a life estate in it to B, and to C the remainder, and also "the refusal of renting the farm" during B's lifetime at a certain rent, the taking of the land by C under this refusal establishes the relation between B and him of landlord and tenant. It

[22] *Kunkle* v *Philadelphia Rifle Club,* 10 Phila 52 The club was enjoined against interfering with the possession of the administratrix

[23] *Oulford* v *Nudhuger,* 196 Pa 162, 46 Atl 374 The tenant could not remove within the term of nine months and escape rent, nor within any hold-over year, but could remove at the end of such hold-over year

An agreement giving to B the right to plant posts in a vacant lot and stretch signs upon them, for advertising purposes, is a lease, whatever the language used It matters not whether it is termed a privilege, or license, or lease Any language by which the possession is transferred for a limited time, for the stipulated return, creates a tenancy and is, in fact, a lease *Pickering* v. *O'Brien,* 23 Pa Super Ct 125

does not determine B's life estate, or give C any other interest in the land than that of a lessee during B's lifetime. Payment of the rent could be compelled, not by the orphans' court, but by the modes open to the ordinary landlord.[24]

22. **Lease of sawmill.**—A, owning a sawmill and timber land, contracted with B that B should stock and saw and manufacture boards at the sawmill for "the term of three years." B bound himself to keep the mills running, to saw and manufacture good, merchantable lumber, to deliver it to A at Allegheny, to keep the mills in good repair. B was to have the privilege of stocking the mills from land of A, taking all the sound timber from it. He was to have the use and occupancy of all the houses, stables, and out-houses, with the cleared land attached to the mills, free from rent or charge. B was to manufacture the lumber and boards in such thicknesses as A should direct. On the failure of B to observe his contract, it was to end, and A to have the right to "take possession" A bound himself to pay to B $7 per thousand for boards and lumber delivered at Allegheny. This contract made a lease of the mills, and not a mere bailment of them. The lumber after manufacture, but before delivery, was the property of B, and, as such, subject to a sale in execution for his debt. The exemption from rent, the use of the word "term," the stipulation for keeping the premises in repair at the expense of B, and for his surrender at the "termination of the contract," were indications that B was to be a tenant.[25]

23. **Lease or mortgage.**—A lease might be made as the equivalent of a mortgage, with the right of possession in the mortgagee; but the fact that the lessor is indebted to the lessee, and that the agreement is that the rent agreed upon is to be retained by the lessee as payment *"pro tanto"* of the debt, does not con-

[24]*Springer's Appeal*, 111 Pa. 274, 2 Atl 352 In the absence of any different agreement, a tenancy from year to year was created.

[25]*Mitchell v. Com* 37 Pa 187.

stitute the agreement a mortgage. A, owing $1,000 to B, lets his land to B for the term of ten years, at a yearly rental of $300, of which $132 is to be paid by B to the ground-rent land-lord, and from the residue of which taxes and water rents are to be paid, and any balance is to be applied to the debt. The lease not being defeasible on its face, the court found no evidence *dehors* that it was agreed to be subject to a defeas-ance [26]

24. Vendee, not lessee —One who enters into possession under a contract to sell, and who continues in possession without com-pleting the purchase, on account of the vendor's inability to make a title clear of encumbrances, does not become a lessee, and as such liable for use and occupation [27] The sale of an interest in the nature of an easement does not make the vendee a lessee of the vendor. A and B, owning adjoining land, agreed that, at their joint expense, a boiler, engine, and stack should be put up on B's land, and be used by both as a common source of power. B did not thereby become landlord of A, and A's denial of his right to the use of the boiler, etc , would not cause a forfeiture of his right [28]

25. Not a lessee.—An agreement by A, who is in possession of land, with B, an adverse claimant, to abandon it by a certain day, does not make A the tenant of B.[29] An agreement by X, who becomes lessee of a vendee of land, or by his assignee of the lease, with the vendee to pay the rent to the vendor, does not create a tenancy between the vendor and X, or X's assignee, nor does it constitute the vendor the vendee's assignee of the

---

[26]*Halo v Schick*, 57 Pa 319 Hence, a purchaser of the reversion at a sheriff's sale on a lien posterior to the lease, could not disturb the les-see's possession during the term

A lease may stipulate that the les-see shall erect, during the five years term, a building, and that, in addi-tion to the use of the premises rent free, the lessor will pay $1,500 for the building Though this is a lease, it subjects the lessor's fee to a me-chanic's lien for the building *Wood-ward v Leiby*, 36 Pa 437

[27]*Bardsley's Appeal*, 20 W N C 90.
[28]*Hall v Hall*, 43 Pa 528
[29]*Miller v. M'Brier*, 14 Serg & R 382.

lease [30] An agreement in the midst of a term between lessor and lessee, to increase the rent, does not make a new lease or tenancy [31] Under an ordinance of a city, the office of superintendent of the market was let out to the highest bidder, he having the right to collect and keep the rents of market stalls A cellar under the market house had never been used for the storage of meat and vegetables. The city fitted up a portion of it for the confinement of tramps This use of it caused odors and effluvia to pervade the entire cellar, so that it could not be used for storage of produce and meat The inability of renters of stalls to use the cellar made renting of some of the stalls impossible. This was no ground of recovery by the superintendent against the city, since he had not obtained a lease of the cellar. [32]

26 Existence of lease —Whether a lease has been made or not is a question of fact, which must, in jury trials, be determined by the jury, and not by the court A writing intended to be a lease becomes such only when signed by the parties or otherwise adopted. If it purports to be signed, whether the parties actually did the signing is a question of fact. If it is not signed, whether the parties have assented to it, and so adopted it, is also for the jury [33] If B, who has been in possession under a former lease, accepts a receipt for rent paid, which contains the terms of a lease, and fixes a different period for the beginning of the year, whether it constitutes a new lease or changes the point of commencement of the year under the old, or does neither, depends on the intention of the parties. The lessee may prove that he accepted the receipt with the understanding that his position under the former lease should in no respect be altered. Whether he did so, or whether a new commencement for the year was agreed upon, and the receipt was the expression of this agreement, is for the jury to decide. [34]

[30]*Helser* v *Pott,* 3 Pa St 179   '*Rothermel* v *Dumn,* 119 Pa 632,
[31]*Taylor* v. *Winters,* 6 Phila 126   13 Atl 509
[32]*Meadville* v *Boush,* 92 Pa 327
[33]*Iolsom* v *Cook,* 115 Pa 539. 9
Atl 93

A tenant already in possession under a lease procures from the lessor a written agreement to lease for a longer term. Whether the lessee accepts it as a substitute for the existing lease is a question of fact.[35] There being a writing containing the term of a lease for ten years, it is for the court to say whether it is binding on the lessor, who has not signed it, nor authorized in writing the person who does, to sign for him, and whether it is, according to its terms, a lease, or only the proposal of terms to be further canvassed, or whether, the writing not being a lease, there was an oral lease made, and if so, whether, reliance being had upon improvements by the lessee to take it out of the operation of the statute of frauds, the proven improvements would do so.[36] If the lease is oral, the jury must decide all its terms, whether, e g, it was for one year or longer, etc.[37]

27 Construction of written lease.—The construction of a written contract of lease is for the court. The court may state to the jury what its construction is, or, referring to them the question whether the unsigned writing has been adopted by the parties as the lease, may reserve the question of its proper interpretation.[38] It is error, therefore, to allow the jury to say that an additional wood floor, put by the tenant onto a skating rink, was not an "improvement," the lease stipulating that all improvements were to remain in the building.[39] But if the court allows the jury to construe the lease, no reversible error will have been committed, if the jury puts the proper construction upon it [40] When the lease is ambiguous, the intentions of the parties should be sought in the entire instrument. If that intention remains doubtful after exploring the whole instrument,

[35]*Bergner* v *Palethorp*, 2 W N C 297

[36]*Dumn* v *Rothermel*, 112 Pa 632, 3 Atl 800

[37]*Shoemaker* v. *Beaver*, 42 Phila Leg Int 511.

[38]*Folsom* v. *Cook*, 115 Pa 530, 9 Atl 93

[39]*Harris* v *Kelly* (Pa) 13 Atl 523

[40]*Jones* v *Kroll*, 116 Pa 85, 8 Atl. 457 The question was whether the will created a lease for five years, with a right of renewal for another equal term, or whether it created a term of one year with a right of renewal for five The lease was considered by the trial court as ambiguous

the circumstances of the parties when the lease was made, and their subsequent acts, may assist in discovering it,[41] and even the previous parol negotiations and agreement to make the lease may be considered [42] Occasionally the principle that the stipulations favorable to the lessor are to be construed most strongly against him is invoked. The lease, for a term of five years, *e g.*, containing the words "and said parties of the first part reserve the right absolutely to terminate this lease at any time by giving 30 days' notice in writing to second party to that effect," it was held that their right to cut off the term within the five years did not pass to the grantee of the reversion.[43]

28. Execution of lease.—A lease for a term not exceeding three years does not need to be in writing. If it is put in writing, it does not need to be signed by the lessor, unless his signature is, by the agreement of the parties, the precondition to its going into effect. If the lessee signing takes possession, the assent to the lease manifested by word or act will make the lease operative   If the lessor, accepting the lease drawn up and signed by the lessee, but not himself signing it, demands the rent or enters judgment in an amicable action, according to its terms, the lessee will be bound to pay the rent or to submit to eviction by the *habere facias* that may be issued on the judgment,[44] and the lessee, after the lessor's parol adoption of the lease, may recover damages for not being put in possession of the premises.[44½]   A lease for a term exceeding three years does not become binding, as such, upon the lessor by a parol adoption of it.[45]   The signature of the lessor at the place where witnesses usually sign will be a valid execution, if it was there made as

[41]*Berridge* v *Glassey*, 112 Pa 442, 56 Am Rep 322, 3 Atl 583

[42]*Re Reading Iron Works*, 150 Pa. 369, 24 Atl 617, *Cadwalader* v *United States Exp Co* 147 Pa 455, 23 Atl 775.

[43]*McClintock* v. *Loveless*, 5 Pa. Dist. R 417.

[44]*Schultz* v *Burlock*, 6 Pa Super Ct 573

[44½]*Flickinger* v *Forry*, 6 Del Co. Rep 154, 8 York Legal Record, 84

[45]*Jennings* v *McComb*, 112 Pa 518, 4 Atl. 812.

lessor, and not as witness.[46] When a lease is signed by A, as lessor, but with the understanding between him and the lessee that it is not to operate until A's wife signs it, the refusal of A's wife to sign it prevents its ever becoming binding, either on the lessee or on A, and A may therefore destroy it.[47] The lessee need not sign a written lease, even when, being for more than three years, it is within the statute of frauds.[48] Hence, a lease to a county may bind it, when accepted for it by the commissioners, although they have signed it and sealed it with their private seals, and not with the county seal.[49] The written lease being made to B, it may be shown in a controversy between C and a creditor of B, with respect to the ownership of the crops on the premises, that B was merely the agent of C, to whom, therefore, the crops belong.[50]

29 Delivery.—A delivery of the paper on which the lease is written may be made to the lessor or lessee only conditionally, to be void unless a certain thing happens. The lessee who physically delivers the lease to the lessor may show that he did so with the understanding that a copy of the lease was to be submitted to counsel for his judgment as to the legal effect of its stipulations, and that if he should think they would have certain legal effects, the lease should be "declared off," that the counsel put this interpretation on them, and that he, the lessee, thereupon notified the lessor that he would not abide by the lease.[51] When it is so understood, the lease may be kept by the lessor. A physical delivery of it to the lessee would be unnecessary. If the lease is signed by the tenant and his surety, and is then returned to the lessor, it is necessary, if it be understood that he is to sign it, that he should sign it with their knowledge and assent. If the lessor does not sign it until several days after

[46]*Benz* v *Langan,* 5 Northampton Co Rep 139

[47]*Tatham* v *Lewis,* 65 Pa 65

[48]*Grove* v. *Hodges,* 55 Pa 504, *Jennings* v *McComb,* 112 Pa 518, 4 Atl 812

[49]*Dauphin County* v *Bridenhart,* 16 Pa 458

[50]*Galbraith* v *Bridges,* 108 Pa 325, 32 Atl 20

[51]*Guernsey* v *Froude,* 13 Pa Super. Ct 405. Lease of a chattel.

its return to him, and then signs it in the absence of the lessee, to whom no notice of the signing is given, the lease can not be deemed operative "Delivery," says Agnew, J , "in its legal acceptation, was as necessary on part of the lessor, even though he should retain possession of the paper, as it was on part of the lessee " [52] A having made a lease of a strip of land 10 feet wide for the construction of an inclined railway by the lessee, at the request of the latter, agreed to extend it for five additional years, and to sign any proper writing, at the same time indorsing on the original lease in his possession a statement that it was extended for five years. Shortly afterwards, when spoken to about drawing up a formal lease, A replied, "It don't matter I indorsed it on the other lease the same as before " To this the lessee assented, and proceeded to erect machinery It was held that physical delivery of the writing to the lessee was, under the circumstances, unnecessary.[53]

30 Execution by agent —The lessee may be represented by an agent, and the right of the former, at least as against third persons, may be established, though the agent only is named in the lease, and the fact that he is agent for anybody is not disclosed.[54] But a lease to a partnership composed of A and B, which is signed and sealed by A alone, without written and sealed authority of the firm, will not bind the firm [55] And though B applies to A for a lease, stating that he wishes the premises for two young men, he is himself the lessee, and not the young men (whom he does not name).[56] The lessor may be

[52]*Kelsey* v *Tourtelotte,* 59 Pa 184 The lessee had not taken possession nor paid rent The action was for rent

[53]*Witman* v *Reading,* 191 Pa 134, 43 Atl 140

[54]*Galbraith* v *Bridges,* 168 Pa 325, 32 Atl 20

The lessor who has leased to the county through its commissioners may recover rent even though the lease was taken by them for a resi dence for the sheriff, and they had no power to furnish him with such resi dence, if the lessor knew no more than that the house was intended for the sheriff He could properly pre sume that the commissioners were acting in the line of their duty *Dauphin County* v *Bridenhart,* 16 Pa 458

[55]*Snyder* v *May,* 19 Pa 235

[56]*Smith* v *Clark,* 1 W N C 445 The fact that rent is received from

represented in the making of a lease by an agent. The authority of this agent, when the lease is for not more than three
years, may be proved by parol[57] and by the testimony of the
agent.[58] The proprietors of a town appointing three men as a
committee, and authorizing them to lease public lands, a lease
executed by two of them was so well executed that, after possession and payment of rent under it for eighty years, the court
would not order the cancelation of it.[59] The owners of land
by writing under seal declared that they "do hereby employ
X to act as our agent for our properties, situated in Bedford
and Blair counties, Pennsylvania, and if the said X shall
honestly and diligently manage said properties, we do hereby
agree to pay him the sum of $700 for a period of one year,"
X made a lease for fifteen years of the right to quarry, take,
and sell all the ganister stone, the lease purporting to be "by
and between X, agent for the Duncan heirs of the one part, and
B   .   .   , of the other part," and witnessing that "the said X,
agent, doth lease or let" to the said B, a certain tract   B agreed
to pay the said Duncan heirs or their agent $70 per year   B
entering and taking stones, the Duncan heirs brought trespass
against him, denying the authority of X to make the lease.   It
was held that, prima facie, the power of attorney was not wide
enough to cover such a lease, but that it might be shown to be
wide enough by proving that such leases were usual in that locality, or that a previous course of dealing between the principals
and the agent had shown that such a lease was understood by them
to be within the power. It might also be shown that the owners
had knowingly received the rent paid by B, and had therefore
estopped themselves from denying the goodness of the lease.[60]

and a receipt given to the young
men, does not preclude the lessor
from asserting that B is his tenant

[57]*Lewis v Bradford*, 10 Watts, 67
[58]*M'Gunnagle v Thornton*, 10 Serg
& R 251, *M'Dowell v Simpson*, 3
Watts, 129, 27 Am Dec 338

[59]*Providence Trustees' Appeal* 2
Walk (Pa) 37, 6 Kulp. 251, Cf
Griffin v Fellows 81* Pa 114.
[60]*Duncan v Hartman*, 143 Pa 595
24 Am St Rep 570, 22 Atl 1099.
Land was granted to the proprietors
of land in a town "to be applied only

31. Mode of execution.—A written lease made by the lessor in his own name, not indicating that he was agent for anybody, may probably be treated by the principal as a nullity,[61] but one wherein the lessor styles himself "agent for the Duncan heirs," and reserves rent, payable to the heirs or to himself, and which he signs "X, agent," is sufficient to bind the principals, if they have conferred authority on X to make it[62]

32. Undisclosed principal.—A lease executed by A, in which he describes himself as "agent," naming no principal, is so far his, and not his principal's lease, that the lessee cannot question his right to recover the possession,[63] or his right, to the exclusion of the principal, to distrain for the rent[64]

33. Lease by two or more owners.—If a lease is made by a firm, the firm name being signed and the firm seal affixed, by one of the partners, the signature as subscribing witness of all the members of the firm will make the execution binding on the firm.[65] An oral lease by one partner, made in his own name, of land belonging to and used by the partnership, will be treated as a partnership lease, and the partnership can sue on it for the rent.[66] An oral lease for a year, made by one of two cotenants, but with the authority of the other, and for both, is the

---

for public uses," to be applied or improved as a majority of the said inhabitants may from time to time order and direct, and for no other purpose whatsoever The council of the town, with the consent of a majority of the inhabitants, could lease a part of the land for ten years to X, who was to erect a warehouse on it which, at the end of the term, should become the town's, the lot being a water lot, and a warehouse being the best way of improving it Gregg v. Irish, 6 Serg & R 211

[61] Cf *Bassett* v *Hawk*, 114 Pa 502, 8 Atl. 18.

[62] *Duncan* v *Hartman*, 143 Pa 595, 24 Am St Rep 570, 22 Atl 1099

As to the revocation of the author-

ity of the agent after making the lease, Cf *Barrett* v *Bemelmans*, 155 Pa 204, 26 Atl 307.

[63] *Bedford* v *Kelly*, 61 Pa 491

The revocation of his authority cannot be shown by the tenant, to prevent his recovery of possession *Holt* v *Martin*, 51 Pa. 499

[64] *Seybert* v *Bean*, 83 Pa 450 Cf *Barrett* v *Bemelmans*, 155 Pa. 204, 26 Atl 307

[65] *Bussman* v *Ganster*, 72 Pa 285 Cf *Bewley* v. *Tams*, 17 Pa 485, where A made a sealed lease in the name of the firm, A and B, without B s knowledge Its validity was not in question

[66] *Moderwell* v. *Mullison*, 21 Pa. 257.

lease of both, not of the one who makes it.[67]   One partner may,
in the name of and for the firm, make a written lease of its
land [68]

34 Ratification by owner by estoppel —The owner of land
which has been leased, whether for him or not, by another without authority, may estop himself from denying the right of the
tenant under the lease   The husband of A, the owner of land,
makes a lease of it, in her presence and with her knowledge, to
B, who puts improvements on it, in order to obtain the ad-
vantages contemplated by the lease. After the husband's death
A continues to receive rent   Though she was not estopped
before, she now precludes herself from subsequently challenging
B's right [69] If an agent to manage land makes a lease in excess
of his authority, the receipt of rent with knowledge that it
comes from the tenant will estop the owner [70] Owners, by receiving rent after reaching majority, will estop themselves from
denying the validity of a lease made by their guardians [71] A's
will devises his land to B, C, and D, in trust, to make leases,
collect the rents, pay one third of the net income to B during
her life, and the rest, during the life of B, to X, and after the
death of B, all of the net income to X, and in trust at the death
of X to convey in fee to his issue. With the acquiescence of C
and D, B undertook the renting of the land, and made a lease
to Z for six years at a certain rental, agreeing to allow $300 to
Z for certain improvements, to be deducted in annual instalments of $50. After the death of B, X, a married woman, with
her husband, gave a receipt to Z for rent   The lease was binding on X for the remainder of the term   Her long acquiescence justified the tenant in believing that B was, in leasing the

[67]*Wenger* v *Raymond*, 104 Pa 33
Apparently, he cannot oust the ten
ant by landlord and tenant proceedings, without the consent of the other

[68]*Moderwell* v. *Mullison*, 21 Pa
237.

[69]*Trout* v *McDonald*, 83 Pa 144
[70]*Duncan* v *Hartman*, 143 Pa 595.
24 Am St Rep 570, 22 Atl 1099
[71]*Myers* v *Kingston Coal Co* 126
Pa 582, 17 Atl 891, *Myers's Appeal,*
16 W. N C 137.

premises, acting with the approbation of all concerned   Hence,
the orphans' court would not, at the instance of X, order a sale
of the premises, free from the residue of Z's term [72]

35. Ratification by the lessee.—For the period during which
the lessee has had possession of the premises, he cannot escape
paying rent on the ground that the lessor was a minor when he
made the lease, and that, since reaching his majority he has,
prior to suing for the rent, done no act of ratification,[73] or that
the lessor was a married woman and did not separately acknowl-
edge the lease,[74] or that the lease had been made by the commissioners of a county for a marble manufactory, of a portion of a tract which had been conveyed to trustees in trust for
the county, for the erection thereon of a common jail or prison,
and "for no other purpose whatever."[75]

36 Statute of frauds.—The 1st section of the act of March
21st, 1772,[76] declares that all leases, etc , of lands made "by
parol, and not put in writing and signed by the parties so making or creating the same, or their agents thereunto lawfully
authorized by writing, shall have the force and effect of leases
or estates at will only   . .   except, nevertheless, all leases
not exceeding the term of three years from the making thereof."
A lease for not more than three years, if made prior to the designated inception of the term,—if made, e g., March 10th, for
three years which are to commence on the following first day
of April, [77] is within the statute   Within it are leases for four
years,[78] seven years,[79] ten years.[80]

[72]*Vanleer's Appeal,* 24 Pa 224
[73]*Harris* v *Knowles,* 26 W N C
249
[74]*Robison* v *Inman,* 35 Phila Leg
Int 263
[75]*Northampton County's Appeal,* 30
Pa 305
[76]1 P & L 2190, 1 Smith's Laws,
389
[77]*Jennings* v *McComb,* 112 Pa 518,
4 Atl 812, *Wheeler* v *Conrad,* 6
Phila 209, *Whiting* v *Pittsburgh
Opera House Co* 88 Pa 100

[78]*Stover* v *Cadwallader,* 2 Pennyp.
117
[79]*M'Dowell* v *Simpson,* 3 Watts,
139 27 Am Dec 338
[80]*Dumn* v *Rothermel,* 112 Pa 272,
3 Atl 800, *Loran's Estate,* 10 Pa Co.
Ct 554
    A sublease for the remainder, ex-
ceeding three years, of a term of
seven years is within the statute
Jones v *Peterman,* 3 Serg & R 543,
8 Am Dec 672

37. Signature.—The lease for more than three years must be signed by the party making the same,—that is, by the lessor or by his properly authorized agent. Signature by the lessee is unnecessary.[81] The signing of the lessor's name by his agent is insufficient unless he had written authority to sign it [82] The agent's signature of the lessor's name may subsequently be ratified in writing by the lessor.[83] A ratification, however, by the lessor signing the lease, or by other writing, is too late, if, the lessee having died, his executor has given notice of his intention to vacate the premises at the end of the current year, and if he accordingly vacates. He cannot be held for subsequently accruing rent.[84] A parol ratification will be ineffectual. The lessor's reception of rent from the tenant, or suffering the tenant in possession to do the repairing which a tenant should ordinarily do, is not a ratification which makes the lease more than one from year to year.[85] A letter written by the husband of the lessor, in his own name, and signed by him, stating what terms he thinks will "do," with the approval of the other party, inviting him if there is anything else to be put in, to write, and also to write whether all contained therein suits him, is only a part of the preliminary negotiation, and, even if duly authorized in writing by the owner of the premises, would not indicate the terms of a final agreement [86]

38. Oral contract to make a lease.—An oral contract to make and accept a lease for more than three years is subject to

---

[81]*Tripp* v *Bishop,* 56 Pa 424, *Bergner* v *Palethorp,* 2 W N C 297, *Johnston* v *Cowan,* 59 Pa 275, *Carnegie Natural Gas Co* v *Philadelphia Co* 158 Pa 317, 27 Atl 951, *Witman* v *Reading,* 191 Pa 134, 43 Atl. 140 Cf *Schultz* v. *Burlock,* 6 Pa Super Ct 573

[82]*Jennings* v *McComb,* 112 Pa 518, 4 Atl 812, *Loran's Estate,* 10 Pa Co Ct 554

[83]*Jennings* v. *McComb,* 112 Pa 518, 4 Atl 812.

[84]*Loran's Estate,* 10 Pa Co. Ct 554

[85]*M'Dowell* v *Simpson,* 3 Watts, 129, 27 Am Dec 338

Ratification by the lessor after he has conveyed the reversion will be ineffectual *Dumn* v *Rothermel,* 112 Pa 272, 3 Atl 800

[86]*Dumn* v *Rothermel,* 112 Pa 272, 3 Atl. 800.

the same infirmity as an oral lease It could not be enforced specifically by the lessee, nor could he do the equivalent, *viz ,* compel the payment to him of a sum of money representing the loss of his bargain , nor, on the other hand, though the owner of the premises is willing to make the lease in writing, can he compel the tenant to accept it, or, the equivalent, to pay the rent named in it [87]

39. Exception from operation of statute.—Taking possession under the lease, and making improvements which cannot be compensated in damages, will enable the lessee to insist on the lease according to its terms, though it be oral. The mere being in possession of the tenant, he having gone into possession under some earlier lease, will not exempt the oral lease for more than three years from the statutory infirmity,[88] nor will replacing a large pane of glass and building an elevator, in accordance with the requirements of the lease, the tenant having taken possession before the lease [89] It is intimated by Kennedy, J., that making improvements not stipulated for in the lease will be at the risk of the tenant, in the sense that he cannot, by reason of them, preclude the lessor from invoking the statute of frauds Making ordinary repairs, *e. g ,* to the pavement in front of the house, will not confer on him a right to hold the premises during the term orally stipulated for, nor will the fact that the rent is larger on account of the length of the term than it would have been for a term of not exceeding three years, and that the lessor has received instalments of it [90]

[87]*Sausser* v *Steinmetz*, 88 Pa 324
[88]*Jones* v *Peterman* 3 Serg & R 543, 8 Am Dec 672 Tilghman, Ch J , intimates that, though the lessee had gone into possession before the lease was made, his making important improvements would give it validity
[89]*Whiting* v *Pittsburgh Opera House Co* 88 Pa 100
[90]*M'Dowell* v *Simpson*, 3 Watts, 129, 27 Am Dec 338. It is said by LAND & TEN 3.

Dean, J , in *Witman* v *Reading*, 191 Pa 134, 43 Atl 140, where a tenant in possession under a two-years lease obtained an extension for five years, the agreement for which was indorsed on the lease in the possession of the lessor, and never delivered to the lessee, that, even if the extension could be treated as oral, the landlord could not plead the statute of frauds, because, with his assent, the tenant had retained possession and expend-

40. Effect of statute on lease —The statute of frauds does not
make a parol lease for more than three years wholly void That
lease is capable of being made obligatory on the landlord by
acts of the lessee, subsequent to its making The lessee is a
tenant at will. He can be kept from taking possession, or, if
he has taken possession, can be at any time put off, until the
lessor has done some act additional to the making of the lease
and the giving of possession. If the lessor recognizes him
when in possession, as a tenant, by receiving rent from him,
or otherwise, the lessee will be regarded henceforth as a tenant
from year to year,[91] who, on receiving the proper notice, may
be required to vacate the premises at the end of any year.[92]
The covenants of the lessee, *e g.*, to pay the rent mentioned,
cannot be enforced by the lessor since the consideration of
these covenants has failed,[93] but the rent named in the lease
may be considered by the jury in an action for use and occupation, as a guide to the value of the occupation [94] A parol lease,
or a parol contract to make a lease, for more than three years,
is not so far void that nominal damages, at least, cannot be
recovered for violating its terms. The lessor may probably
recover from X the rent he has failed to get from others, on
account of his reliance on the promise of X to accept the lease.
He will not be entitled to the stipulated rent for the time during
which he is unable to obtain another tenant. If he has expended money in preparing the premises for X, he will not be
entitled to reimbursement of this money unless the improvements made have added nothing to the general rental value of

ed a large amount of money in improvements Cf *Dumn v Rother-*
mel, 112 Pa 272, 3 Atl. 800, as to
effect of improvements

[91]*Dumn* v *Rothermel,* 112 Pa 272,
3 Atl 800, *Loran's Estate,* 10 Pa
Co Ct 554, *M'Douell* v *Simpson,*
3 Watts, 129, 27 Am Dec 338

Whiting v *Pittsburgh Opera*
House Co 88 Pa 100.

[93]*Jennings* v *McComb,* 112 Pa.
518, 4 Atl 812, *Stover* v *Cadualla-*
der, 2 Pennyp 117

[94]*Ibid* In *Sausser* v *Steinmetz,*
88 Pa 324, Gordon, J, says that, the
lease being void, it cannot be used to
ascertain the value of the use of the
premises.

the premises, and were unnecessary for their improvement or repair [95] If the owner declines to make the lease to X according to his oral contract, X may, as damages, recover money paid, or expenses incurred, on the faith of the contract [96]

41.- Necessity of recording.—The first section of the act of May 19th, 1893,[97] requires all deeds and conveyances of land to be acknowledged or proved, and recorded in the office of the recorder of deeds of the county within ninety days after the execution of such deeds and conveyances, and adjudges such of them fraudulent and void against any subsequent purchaser or mortgagee as shall not be so acknowledged or proved, and recorded   It was said in 1851[98] by Chambers, J , that it had not been the practice to record leases for terms of years, and that the acts of assembly do not require them to be recorded when the possession accompanies the lease unless the lease is for a term exceeding twenty-one years   But it has been understood that even conveyances in fee do not need to be recorded if the grantee or his tenant is in possession   If the lessee neither records his lease nor takes possession of the premises, the lease will be valid as against another lessee or grantee of the same land, who has actual notice of it, but it will not be valid as against a grantee or lessee without notice, or against an assignee without notice of the lessee who had notice [99]   When a lease of oil land is made to B, who covenants to put a test well down on a tract in the vicinity, the putting down of the test well is not a taking of possession of the leased premises, so far as notice to others of the lease is concerned[100] but, if the lessee takes open, notorious, visible, and exclusive possession of the land, such possession is sufficient notice to a subsequent mortgagee[101] or grantee

[95]*Sausser* v *Steinmetz*, 88 Pa 324
[96]*McCafferty* v *Griswold*, 99 Pa 270 Cf *Heilman* v. *Weinman*, 139 Pa 143, 21 Atl 29
[97]1 P & L 1571 , P L 108
[98]*Williams* v *Downing*, 18 Pa 60

[99]*Aye* v *Philadelphia Co* 193 Pa. 457, 44 Atl 556
[100]*Aye* v *Philadelphia Co* 193 Pa. 457 44 Atl 556
[101]*Marsh* v *Nelson*, 101 Pa 51   As to the necessity of recording a

of the premises, although the lessor, the tenant's father, is allowed to continue to reside on them.

lease of any colliery, mining land, manufactory, etc in order to make valid a mortgage of the leasehold, under the acts of April 27th, 1875 (1 Pepper & L Digest, 1607, P L 308), and of May 13th, 1876 (1 Pepper & L Digest, 1612, P. L 160), *vide Hilton's Appeal*, 116 Pa 351, 9 Atl. 342, *Speer's Estate*, 8 Pa Dist R 212, *Gill* v *Weston*, 110 Pa. 305, 1 Atl 917, *Brown* v. *Beecher*, 120 Pa. 590, 15 Atl. 608.

CHAPTER IV.

THE SUBJECT OF THE LEASE.

42. Generally.—The lease may be of any sort of land; of land of any size, shape, or situation, and for all kinds of uses: to extract oil, coal, stones, iron ore, chrome from it, to use it for pasture, for the display of signboards and other advertisements. It may be of land without a house, or of a house, of stores, or rooms of a house, of the roof of a house, of the superficies of the wall of a house

43. The area of the leasehold—The lease of "that certain plantation . . . containing about 230 acres, be the same more or less, now in the possession of T. H ," covers all the land then in the possession of T. H. in the described locality, although it may be larger than 230 acres; the occupancy and not the magnitude, of the land, being the defining fact.[1] A lease for twelve years described the premises by the words "being all the land which may or can be flooded or covered with water by a dam to be made at a certain place across the aforesaid creek, to be built so high as to raise the water to the top of a certain rock or fixed stone on the north bank of said creek, near the place of said dam." Under this lease the lessee had a right to erect a dam so high as to raise the water to the

---

[1] *Hall* v *Powell*, 4 Serg & R 456, 8 Am Dec 722

top of the rock in the ordinary stage of the water,
and though in extraordinary stages more than the leased
land would be overflowed, he would not be liable for such
overflow.[2] The lease describing the land so as to exclude from
it an alley, over which the upper stories of the building on
the premises project, and stating that it is understood "that
the lessee takes the buildings as they now stand," it does not
embrace the soil of the alley, and, under a provision in the
lease that the lessee may purchase the premises, he will not be
entitled to a deed which will embrace the soil of the alley.[3]
A demise of a messuage, tenement, or tavern house, barn, sheds,
. . . known by the name of "Spread Eagle Tavern," did
not embrace a lot of 11 acres, in which the barn stood[4] There
can be a lease of a piece of land however small, e. g , of a strip
10 feet wide,[5] of a strip 15½ inches wide and 49 feet long, or
10½ inches wide and 27 feet long.[6]

44. Building, and not ground—A house belonging to A, and
standing on the land of B, may be the subject of a lease. Should
B become the lessee, or the assignee of the lessee, he would be
liable to pay the rent reserved in the lease;[7] but an agreement
by C with D to erect for D on a certain lot a stone house, to be
ready by a certain date, at the rent of $600 until April 1st,
1869, and thereafter for five years at the rate of $800, "and
to have stable room during the term for two horses, and the
parties of the second part to have the option of continuing in
the said premises for five additional years, at the same rent,
payable as aforesaid," and if C wishes "to sell the property,"
D to have the first offer,—was a lease, not of the building only,
but of the soil on which it was to stand.[8]

[·]*Wallace* v *Headley*, 23 Pa 106   [6]*Berridge* v *Glassey*, 112 Pa 442,
[2]*Barnett* v *Plummer*, 19 W N C 56 Am Rep 322, 3 Atl 583
117   [7]*Lockard* v *Robbins* (Pa) 10 Atl.
[4]*Bennett* v *Bittle*, 4 Rawle, 239   120
[5]*Witman* v *Reading*, 191 Pa 134,   [8]*Bussman* v *Ganster*, 72 Pa. 285.
43 Atl 140.

45. Rights to water.—The lease of a "furnace, gristmill, saw-mill, dwelling house, etc., and the tract or piece of land belong-ing thereto . . . on the south side and near the mouth of the Swatara creek," passes with the land a right to the use of the water power of the creek, although the words "with the appurtenances" are not in it[9] A lease to B of land with the privilege of erecting a tanyard, and taking from a neighboring creek, at a point not on the leased premises, as much water as necessary, provided that any water so taken, in excess of what shall be consumed, shall be conducted without unnecessary loss or waste to the creek. does not authorize the tenant to empty the contents of his tanyard into the stream, or otherwise pollute its water.[10]

46. Easements.—The lessee takes the premises subject to any permanent servitudes to which it is visibly subject, and cannot defend an action for rent by alleging their existence. Over the land the elevated viaduct of a railroad, e. g., extended when the lease was made Within the term, the railroad company was obliged to make repairs to it, and the lessee was deprived, for a time, of the use of a portion of the premises. This was no excuse for the nonpayment of the rent in full If the railroad company, to an unnecessary degree, for an unnecessary time, inconvenienced him, his redress must be sought from it[11] If the owner of a building creates a permanent servitude on one part for the benefit of another part, the lessee of the former would take it charged with the servitude. When, however, gas is introduced into the building through the cellar, pipes to the various stories conducting the gas thence,—while the lessee of the cellar would take it with the duty of suffering the pres-ence of the pipes, he is not bound to allow the meters for the measurement of the gas furnished to the upper stories to remain

The burning of the building did not discharge the lessee from future rent

[9]*Peters* v *Grubb*, 21 Pa 455

[10]*Howell* v *M'Coy*, 3 Rawle, 256
[11]*Friend* v *Oil Well Supply Co* 179 Pa 290, 36 Atl 219

in the cellar, and to be there periodically inspected by the
servants of the gas company. He will not be enjoined from removing them, at the suit of the gas company. "Although visible
when the defendant leased," says Rice, P. J., "they seem to us
to lack that characteristic of permanency which, even in the
absence of strict necessity, has been held to be evidence in
certain classes of cases, of an intent to subject one part of land
to a servitude in favor of another, and notice thereof to a purchaser or lessee of the servient tenement. For it is to be observed, they do not belong to the landlord, nor to the tenants
(of the upper stories), are not a part of the structure, and are
not essential to the supplying of gas to the upper floors."[12] A
release by a lessee of his right to use an alley appurtenant to
the premises, the releasee agreeing at the end of the term to
reopen it, is binding for the term only Should the lessee
accept a renewal lease, he will have a right to the use of the
alley.[13]

47. Restriction on use of premises —The lessee may accept the
premises for certain uses only, so as to entitle the lessor to forfeit the lease, or its privileges, on account of any different use.
If, e. g., the lessee is to use the premises for a store and dwelling house only, he cannot complain if, introducing machinery
to commence a manufacturing business, he is temporarily denied
the use of water.[14] and if the lease so provides, should the tenant become obnoxious or objectionable for any cause, he may
be required to quit the premises after twenty days' notice.[15]

[12]*Wilkes Barre Gas Co* v *Turner*,
7 Kulp, 399

Miners' houses are ordinary ap-
purtenants to coal mines, and when
they are on the premises, and included in the lease of mines, they constitute part of the estate, and all the
remedies of the landlord attach to
them without stipulation in the
lease. For rent accruing from houses
or mines} there can be a distress on
goods found anywhere on the prem-

ises *Spencer* v *Kunkle*, 2 Grant
Cas 406

[13]*Hacke's Appeal*, 101 Pa 245

[14]*Ladomus* v *McCormick*, 5 Del
Co Rep 147

The lease of an office may require
all furniture to be carried on the
freight elevator If it does, the tenant may be prevented from carrying
it on the stairway *Walsh* v *The
Bourse*, 15 Pa Super Ct 219

[15]*Adam* v *Clark*, 2 W N C 429.

A lease of land authorizing the tenant to take possession as soon as he commenced to build an iron furnace thereon, and to "hold the same and enjoy and use all the rights and privileges of real ownership as in fee simple" as long as he should carry on the furnace, and requiring him to pay royalty for every ton of iron ore mined, confers the right to take limestone for the use of the furnace without charge [16] A lease giving to the lessee the right to take out all the coal he could reach beneath the surface for a royalty of 30 cents per ton, he working the mine so as to do the least possible damage to the land, would permit him to sink as many shafts as would conduce to the profitable working of the mine, and that sinking one of them would probably destroy a spring would be no reason for restraining him from sinking it.[17]

48 Use of outside of wall for signs —When a building is let for a dwelling, there is no implied right of the lessee to occupy the outer walls with signs, and advertisements,[18] but if a building or a part of a building is let for business purposes, there is an implied right of the occupant of a room to use so much of the wall as can be used without interfering with a similar right in occupants of other rooms, for the display of signs A, a dentist, was, when he leased a room to B, occupying with his professional sign, and with hooks on which to suspend a box of exhibits, the space between the hall door and the rear window of B's room B could, at the instance of A, be restrained from placing signs on the outer wall of his room where they would interfere with A's signs and box, but not from placing them elsewhere on that wall.[19]

[16]*Watterson v Reynolds,* 95 Pa 474, 40 Am Rep 672

[17]*Trout v McDonald,* 83 Pa 144

[18]*Scott v Fox Optical Co* 38 Pittsb L J 368

[19]*Scott v Fox Optical Co* 38 Pittsb L J 368 But in *Hele v Stewart,* 19 W. N. C 129, Allison, J, reached the conclusion, apparently, that a tenant of the third and fourth floors of a business building had no right to use the outer walls of these stores for advertising, nor to prevent the use of them, with the lessor's consent, by the tenants of the lower floors.

CHAPTER V.

MODIFYING OR ANNULLING LEASE.

49. Deception of tenant.—In a suit on the lease for rent, the tenant may show that representations were made as to the condition of the building and premises, whereby he was induced to accept the lease, and that these representations were known to be untrue by the lessor when they were made. The lessee, *e. g.,* may show that he was deterred from employing a plumber to examine the premises, that he was induced, without the examination such plumber would have made, to accept the lease by representations that the plumbing and drainage were very good, and that a plumber had been employed to put them in perfect order, that the well was newly dug, and that these representations were grossly false [1] The lessee may defend, by

[1] *Wolfe* v *Arrott*, 109 Pa. 473, 1 Co Ct 271, *Crump* v. *Morrell*, 12 Atl 333, *Shoutaker* v *Boyer*, 3 Pa Phila 249

showing that he was induced to accept the lease through the false representations of the lessor that a railroad siding belonged to him and would pass to the lessee under the lease, and that the leasehold premises were valueless to him without the siding [2]

50 Affidavit of defense —The statements alleged to be false, and to have been an inducement to enter into the lease, should be stated in the affidavit of defense with reasonable precision It should appear when, relatively to the making of the lease, they were made. They should appear to be of such definite facts that the lessee might reasonably rely on them The tenant's averment that, relying on an advertisement in the Ledger, and on a statement to the same effect, that the premises were well known, that they had been arranged for, and in use as, a first-class summer boarding house, and that there was a never-failing supply of pure, soft, spring water on them, that in fact the supply of water had entirely stopped, that the place was not known as a summer resort, and had been used only by a private family, and that the lessee had spent much money in fitting up the place for boarders, and had, for the reasons stated, failed to secure any,—was insufficient to prevent judgment [3]

51 Action of deceit —If a tenant is induced, by the false representations of the lessor that the roof of a bow-window of the premises is new and water tight, to accept a lease and to place millinery in the window for exhibition, and the goods are destroyed by a rain, on account of the bad condition of the roof, the lessee may sustain an action of trespass for the deceit, although the lease contained a covenant on the lessee's part to repair. [4]

---

[2] *Morris* v *Shakespeare* (Pa) 12 Atl 414

[3] *Lockwood* v *McNamara*, 6 W N. C 367.

A representation by the landlord that the house is completely furnished cannot be a defense to an action for rent, if the lessee, before accepting the lease, knew the fact that one room was not furnished *Hess* v *Weingartner,* 5 Pa. Dist R. 451 Cf *Johnson* v *Mathues*, 4 Del Co Rep 305

[4] *Sachs* v. *Schimmel*, 3 Pa Super

52. Lease does not express intention of lessee.—A written lease may be modified by evidence that its language was adopted in mistake as to its import, or that, it being understood by the parties that it was to bear one interpretation, one of the parties is attempting to enforce it in a different sense A, under a devise, being entitled to the profits of land during his minority, and B entitled to the remainder, A's guardians, when he is twelve years and nine months old, lease the premises to B. The intention of both parties, expressed at the conference at which the lease was written, was that it was to be for the period of A's minority and ownership The period named in it was for nine years; the scrivener stating to both parties that A could claim no rent after he came of age Evidence of these facts should have been received. If not mistake, there was fraud Fraud consists in the fraudulent use of the instrument by A, though no fraud existed in the procuring of the lease [5] B, while in possession under a verbal lease, in which the lessor promised to make certain necessary repairs, accepts and signs a written lease containing a statement that the premises are in good repair Sued for the rent, B may show the oral promise, and account for his acceptance of the written lease by a statement of the lessor that the written lease was a mere matter of form, and should not affect the agreement for repairs. [6]

Ct 426 Although the action was not on the contract the court said that the same kind and degree of evidence was necessary as to reform a contract for omissions The evidence must be clear, precise, and indubitable. One of the two lessees, who did not sign the lease, could, nevertheless, unite with the other in an action for the deceit, they being joint owners of the goods

[5]*Hultz* v *Wright*, 16 Serg & R 345 16 Am Dec 575

The written lease expressly saying that the premises are rented with the "distinct understanding that the landlord shall not be put to any expense for repairs, and that neither the condition of the premises nor any other cause shall excuse from paying the rent," an affidavit alleging that the lessor verbally agreed prior to the signing of the lease, to make repairs will not prevent a recovery of rent, or a forfeiture of the lease for nonpayment   *Gates* v. *Adinolfi*, 11 Kulp, 100

A parol agreement contemporaneous with the written lease which induced the execution of it, must be proved by clear, precise, and indubitable evidence *Replogle* v *Singer*, 19 Pa Super Ct 442

[6]*Lansdale* v *Richardson*, 1 W N. C 413

The lease for five years providing

53. Error in written lease —A mistake in a written lease may be shown by the lessee. The lease reserving a "semiannual rent of $300," he may prove that the agreement of the parties had been that the annual rent should be $300, payable in equal semi-annual instalments; and he may thus reform the lease as against an assignee of the lessor's interest in it, and of the reversion [7]

54 Duress.—A purchaser at a sheriff's sale of X's land, in proceedings to eject him, informs him that he will be put out unless he accepts a lease from the purchaser This is not such a duress as avoids the lease, and deprives the lessor of the right to maintain proceedings under the landlord and tenant acts for the recovery of possession.[8]

55 Insanity of lessor.—The unsoundness of mind of the lessor may be a defense to an action upon the lease by the lessee. The smallness of the rent reserved, e. g , 8 cents per ton for all coal mined, would be important only in conjunction with other facts, e. g , the feebleness of mind of the lessor, imposition, etc. It would not, of itself, preclude the enforcement of the lease [9]

56. Misrepresentations to lessor.—The lessor may avoid a lease signed by him, by showing that it was procured from him by false representations of facts the correct apprehension of which would have deterred him from making it A lease, e. g , for one year from April 1st, 1886, may be shown by the lessor, when sued for not giving possession to the lessee, to have been made by him on the lessee's assurance that he had, for a price, procured the consent of the tenant already in possession, and having a right to continue in possession until April 1st, 1887,

that the lessor could terminate it by giving one year's notice, at the end of any year, the tenant cannot prevent an eviction by showing that it was agreed that this provision should not take effect unless the lessor sold the property and the purchaser required the possession. *Hertzler* v *Worman*, 1 W N C 153 In *Martin* v *Berens*, 67 Pa 459,

an affidavit of defense alleging an oral agreement that, in case of fire, the rent should cease, was insufficient to prevent judgment for the rent accruing after a fire.

[7]*Snyder* v *May*, 19 Pa 235
[8]*Pottsville Bank* v *Oake*, 12 Pa. Super Ct 61
[9]*Grotz* v *Coal Co.* 1 Kulp, 53.

to vacate the premises on April 1st, 1886, whereas he had in
fact not done so [10] The lessor may prove that the lessee
obtained the lease by declaring that he was seeking it for himself and that he was worth $45,000, whereas he was getting it
for X, to whom he immediately assigned it, and who sues the
lessor for refusing to give him possession [11]

57. Misreading lease.—An illiterate lessor, the lease stipulating for rent of $1,000 for each well for the whole term of
twenty years, may prove in ejectment by the tenant that the
agreement was that $1,000 for each well should be paid annually
during the term, and that, being unable to read, the lessee
read it as if it contained a provision accordant with the agreement, and thus procured his acceptance of it.[12]

58 Lessee's oral promise.—Probably if a lessor refrains from
requiring, in a lease of coal land, reserving as rent so much
per bushel of coal mined, a stipulation that the lessee will mine
as much coal as he can dispose of, on account of his request
that it be omitted, and promise to perform it, it will be enforceable. But if such an agreement is not declared on, it cannot be
proven as a ground of recovery for the rental of coal that was
not mined.[13]

59 Promissory statements by lessor.—The mere fact that a
promise by the lessor, by which the tenant is known by him
to be induced to accept the lease, is not carried out, will not,
in the absence of fraud, be a defense to the rent. An affidavit
of defense, e. g , which alleges, that, to induce the defendant to
accept the lease, the lessor represented that objectionable houses
on the opposite side of the street, under his control, would be
demolished, and that, on this representation, the defendant ac-

[10]*Thudium* v. *Yost,* 20 W N C
217
[11]*Harvey* v *Guneberg,* 148 Pa 294,
23 Atl 1005
[12]*Christie* v *Blakeley* 2 Monaghan (Pa) 118 15 Atl 874
[13]*Lyon* v *Miller,* 24 Pa 392   Ap
parently there was in fact a recovery The measure of damages was
the difference between the stipulat-
rate of compensation per bushel and
the value of the coal, per bushel, in
place.

cepted the lease, but not averring that it was "false" [it was averred that it had not been carried out] or that there was any fraud in the making of it, or in the failure to perform it,[14] or an affidavit alleging that the defendant "was led to believe by representations made to him" that no building would be erected between the leased lot and another building owned by the plaintiff, that he would not have accepted the lease had he not believed these representations, and that the plaintiff had leased the intervening ground for the erection of a bowling alley and shooting-gallery[15] is insufficient to prevent judgment In replevin by the tenant under a sealed lease the plea to the avowry averred that the lessor had agreed orally, when the lease was made, that he would not let the adjoining premises as a liquor store, and that, in violation of his promise, he had done so. A demurrer of the landlord was sustained.[16] An offer of the tenant, when sued for the rent, to show that the lessor agreed orally when the lease was signed that he would put the roof of the building in good condition and that he would make other repairs, and that the lease would not have been accepted but for such an agreement, was properly rejected because it did not tend to show "fraud, mistake, or trust;"[17] and, the lessee covenanting to keep the premises in good order and repair, and to deliver them in such condition at the expiration of the term, the tenant's declaration, in an action for personal injury for the breaking through of the kitchen floor, will be demurrable, which alleges that the lessor promised to repair the floor, unless it also alleges that the

[14]*Wilcox* v *Palmer,* 163 Pa 109 29 Atl 757

An affidavit of defense that, at the time of the executing of the lease, the lessor agreed to furnish the premises with water but he had not furnished it and that the tenant had never read the lease, relying on the lessor's representations, was insufficient *Loley* v *Heller,* 1 W N C 613

[15]*Tischner* v. *Bambrick,* 3 W. N C

94 A verbal agreement, inducing the tenant to sign the lease, that the tenant should have the straw and hay left by the outgoing tenant, was shown in *Plumstead* v *Conway,* 2 Del Co Rep 43, as a defense to an action for rent

[16]*Hood* v *McDonald,* 1 W N C 299

[17]*Eberle* v *Bonafon,* 17 W N C 335, *Ker* v *Hunt,* 1 W N C 115

lease was accepted by him in its actual form as the result of fraud, accident, or mistake.[18] The lessee, on failing to get punctual possession of the premises on account of the refusal of the former tenant to retire, cannot recover damages from the lessor on a parol promise made the day before the execution of the lease, that the tenant should have immediate possession, no mistake of the scrivener, no trick or artifice of the lessor being shown.[19] A promise to deepen and widen the tailrace of the mill, the subject of the lease, being omitted from the written contract, if the lessee is induced to assent to the lease by an assurance that the omission is of no consequence, that the lessor is a man of honor and will punctually perform his promise, the tenant, on showing these facts, may set off against the rent the damage arising from the lessor's nonperformance.[20]

60 **Promissory statements, continued**—If the lease, when presented to the tenant for acceptance, does not contain a promise, orally made, of the lessor to build a barn on the premises by harvest, and for this omission the lessee declines to accept it, until the lessor says that the insertion of the promise in the lease is unnecessary, that he will do as he has promised,—the lessee may enforce the promise by an action for damages for its nonperformance [21] The lease containing the covenant that the lessee shall keep the premises in repair, an oral promise of the lessor to keep them in tenantable state must be averred directly, and not inferentially, in an affidavit of defense to an action for the rent.[22]

[18]*Wodock* v *Robinson*, 28 W N C 288

[19]*Cozens* v *Stevenson*, 5 Serg & R 421

A written lease for a portion of the lessor's land does not preclude proof of a later oral lease of another contiguous portion of that land *Heilman* v *Weinman*, 139 Pa 143 21 Atl 29

[20]*Christ* v *Diffenbach*, 1 Serg & R 464, 7 Am Dec 624

[21]*Shughart* v *Moore*, 78 Pa 469 Cf *Weaver* v *Wood*, 9 Pa 220, *Poulton Coal Co* v *McShain* 75 Pa 238 A written lease for one tract does not prevent a parol lease of an adjacent tract, between the same parties *Heilman* v *Weinman*, 139 Pa 143, 21 Atl 29

[22]*Cochran* v *Ward*, 8 Del Co Rep 423 The lease being from month to month, the continuance in the possession by the tenant many months

61. Proving custom.—A custom may be proved, for the purpose of creating a right or a duty not expressed in the lease, nor inconsistent with what is therein stipulated   The written lease, *e. g.,* being silent as to the way-going crop, and specifying the time when the lessee is to surrender the premises, he may prove the custom according to which tenants take the way-going crop after the expiration of the lease [23]   A lease of a hall for theatrical purposes being silent as to the lessee's right to terminate it on a month's notice, the custom of the theatrical profession to exercise the right thus to cancel a lease may be shown.[24]   Nothing being said in the lease concerning the payment of water rent, the lessee may, when sued for the rent, prove a custom of landlords, when the lease is silent, to pay this water rent [25]   Custom may be proved to explain a vague phrase in a lease   The lease, *e g ,* requiring the tenant to cultivate the land in a "workmanlike manner," it may be shown that in the locality in which the land is it is the custom for the tenant who is about to occupy a farm in the spring, to prepare the ground the previous fall, if he can procure the consent of the person in possession.[26]

62. Proving habit.—Evidence of the habit of an individual is not so readily admissible as is that of a custom.   In a suit for the rent, after the tenant, claiming that his term was from month to month, had vacated the premises against the will of the lessor, who insisted that the letting was from year to year, the lessor cannot show the habit of the former owner or of himself in letting the premises to the lessee or others, for the purpose of making a letting from year to year probable.[27]   The terms of

after the lessor's failure to repair would preclude a defense to the rent landlord made the promise
[23]*Stultz* v *Dickey*, 5 Binn 285, 6 Am Dec 411
[24]*American Academy of Music* v *Bert*, 8 Pa Co Ct 223
[25]*Stone* v *Van Nort*, 3 Law Times N S 84
LAND & TEN. 4

[26]*Aughinbaugh* v *Coppenheffer*, 55 Pa 347
[27]*Arrott Steam Power Mills Co* v. *Way Mfg Co* 143 Pa 435, 22 Atl. 699
But when the evidence indicates that an oral lease was on the same terms as a former written lease of the same premises between different parties, the lease may be put in evi-

a destroyed lease being in dispute between the lessor and the
lessee, the latter, in an action for rent, cannot, in order to sustain his version of its contents, prove that he acquired a very
large number of leases of oil land, and that he had a standard
to which they all conformed, for it would not follow that this
particular lease was made to conform to that standard.[28]

63. **Value of premises as test of probability.**—The rental value
of the premises may be appealed to when there is a dispute concerning the duration of the term, the area of land embraced in
the lease, etc.   An agreement for a lease being made between
A and B, X, who was present, wrote a lease, which the tenant,
however, never signed or accepted, or, so far as appears, saw   B
taking possession and refusing to vacate the premises at the end
of a year, alleging that he had leased for three years, A brought
an ejectment against him.   The evidence being in conflict, B
could prove that the rent, *viz* , $100 per year, was greatly exces-
sive if the term was but for one year, since he had been obliged
to make valuable and permanent improvements; but would
have been a fair rent for a term of three years.[29]   A lease of a
tract described it as containing 138 acres   On one side of the
farm, fronting a public road, were three tenant houses, occupied
by persons not employed on the farm   The tenant defended a
claim for rent by showing that he had not been allowed to have
possession of the tenant houses, and that the lessor had collected
rents from their occupants.   It was allowable for the lessor to
show that the rent reserved in the lease would have been a fair
rent for the farm without the houses, and that the rental value
of the houses was equal to half the rent reserved, for the purpose of giving probability to the lessor's version of the boundaries of the subject-matter of the lease.[30]

dence   *Pancoast* v *Coon,* 20 W. N
C 89
   [28]*Morris* v *Guffey,* 188 Pa 534, 41
Atl 731   Cf. *Schoneman* v *Fegley,*
14 Pa 376   The defendant attempted to show that he had a book of

blanks printed, and that it was used
by the recorder of deeds
   [29]*Sennett* v *Bucher,* 3 Penr & W
392
   [30]*Boice* v *Zimmerman* 3 Pa Super Ct 181.   It was allowable to

64. Explaining the terms.—In an action for the rent, a lease for oil land was shown which provided that work should commence within three months, or that thereafter $180 per year should be paid until the work commenced, and that a failure of the lessee to make any one of the payments when due would render the lease null and void and not binding on either party The lesssee, not commencing within the three months or ever, it was not permissible for him to prove that his agents informed the lessor that the words of the lease meant that the lessee would have the power to terminate it at any time, by declining to pay the rental.[31] The lease requiring the tenant to relinquish possession after a six months' notice, when the lessor should have occasion for a part of the premises, letters and negotiations previous to the execution of the lease cannot be employed by the tenant to show that the occasion was a special one, upon which he was to be required to vacate the premises [32] A lease for two years, at an annual rent of $1,400, provided that if the tenant should fail to secure a retail liquor license, the lessor agreed to receive $400 for the term of one year only The tenant failing to obtain a license for the second year, insisted that his rent was but $400 He was not permitted to ask a witness "what took place when the lease was signed or before it was signed," or to prove by the witness that the agreement for a $400 rent expressly applied to the second as well as to the first year The offers "were not comprehensive enough to justify their admission for the purpose of reforming the lease."[33]

65. Later oral modifications.—After a lease is made in writing,

show that, in the preliminary negotiation, the tenant houses were excluded and that the scrivener was directed to exclude them from the written lease Such evidence, though not enough to justify a reformation of the lease, was pertinent with respect to the application of the written description to the premises

[31] *Hall* v *Phillips*, 164 Pa 484, 30 Atl 353

[32] *Woodland Cemetery Co* v. *Carville* 9 Phila Leg Int 98

[33] *Rea* v *Ganter*, 152 Pa 512, 25 Atl 539 But the court put the same interpretation on the lease, without the evidence.

and even under seal, the parties may orally modify it, *e. g ,* with respect to the time for paying the rent[34] or with respect to the rental. The rent reserved in the lease being $500 per year, the lessor, *e. g ,* may agree, in order to dissuade the lessee from abandoning the premises, as he has a right, under existing circumstances, to do, that no rent shall be paid, but that the lessee shall allow the lessor all the gas from the well, needed by him, and shall have the residue for himself without charge[35] The written lease providing that the way-going crop should belong to the landlord, the parties may afterwards agree, for a consideration, that it shall belong to the tenant.[36] It is not necessary that such modifications should be proved by two witnesses, nor does proof by two witnesses become necessary because the modification is expressed by an erasure of a part of the original lease, and by interlineations upon it, made with the concurrence of both parties.[36½]

[34]*Wilgus* v *Whitehead,* 89 Pa 131.

[35]*Crauford* v *Bellevue & G Natural Gas Co* 183 Pa 227, 38 Atl 595

[36]*Yeager* v *Cassidy,* 12 Pa Super. Ct 232

[36½]*Yeager* v *Cassidy,* 12 Pa Super Ct 232 The change of terms of the lease, if not with a fraudulent intent, will bind a subsequent purchaser at a sheriff's sale of the reversion An alteration in a lease to the advantage of a lessee prevents his putting the lease in evidence to support a right, even one not affected by the alteration, until it is explained The lease for 27 months containing a covenant to allow the lessee to renew it for three additional years, and also a covenant by the lessee to keep the water pipes and hydrant in good repair, the lease cannot be put in evidence by the lessee to support his action for the lessor's breach of the former covenant, if the second covenant is erased, and no explanation is offered. *Burgun* v *Bishop,* 91 Pa 336

CHAPTER VI.

SURETIES IN LEASES.

66. Form of contract.—Since the distinction between a suretyship and a guarantee is important, it is profitable to note the phraseology that has been considered to create the former, and not the latter, contract Instances of suretyship are: "I do hereby agree to become surety for the faithful performance of all or any of the conditions . .   which are to be kept, done, and performed" by the tenant, and "in default thereof on the part of said lessees, to be liable therefor to the lessor as fully . . . as if I was the lessee."[1] "We do hereby agree to be responsible to the lessor for the true and faithful performance of the above contract" on the part of the lessee.[2] "I do

---

[1] *Scott v Swain*, 19 W N C 547 "I hereby become surety for rent of house 111 Strawberry, at $1,200 per annum payable monthly from this date (Signed) David Giltinan,' was held capable of being understood to make Giltinan a princi-pal, *i e*, a lessee, **in** *Giltinan* v. *Strong* 64 Pa 242

[2] *Coe v Vogdes* 71 Pa 383, *Korn v Hohl* 80 Pa 333, *Frechie v Drinkhouse* 4 W N C 298, *Miller v Keller*, 1 W N C 27, *Pleasonton's Appeal*, 75 Pa 344 Similar

53

hereby guarantee to the lessor the true and punctual payment of the rent . . at the times mentioned" in the lease.[3] "I hereby guarantee and become security for the faithful performance" of "the tenant."[4] "For consideration received, I hereby agree to become security for the faithful performance of the above agreement "[5] "We do hereby guarantee the faithful performance of all the covenants of the foregoing lease" of the lessee "and in case he fails to pay the rent and keep the covenants as to repairs and improvements . . . we will do it for him "[6]

67. Must be in writing.—Being an assumption for the debt or default of another, the suretyship must be expressed in writing, and all its terms must be written[7] unless it be the consideration If, *e. g ,* the lessor, being about to evict the tenant for a year, before the expiration of the term, for nonpayment of rent, X agrees to pay the future rent if the tenant be allowed to remain, and fails to pay, the agreement, if oral, will be invalid. Apparently the assumption can be by telegraph [8]

68. Consideration necessary—Ordinarily the contract of the surety is before or simultaneous with that of lease, and the making of the lease is the consideration for the assumption of the surety If the making of the suretyship is posterior to that of the lease, some other consideration will be necessary[9] unless the

language was understood by Lowrie, Ch J , to make a guarantee in *Gilbert* v *Henck*, 30 Pa 205, but the result would have been the same had the words been thought to make a suretyship Cf *Allen* v *Hubert*, 49 Pa 259

[3]*Haynes* v *Synnott*, 160 Pa 180, 28 Atl 832

[4]*Smeidel* v *Lewellyn*, 3 Phila 70 Held to be a suretyship because of the word "security" and because "faithful performance" is equivalent to "punctual performance."

[5]*Allen* v *Hubert*, 49 Pa 259
[6]*Kennedy* v *Duggan*, 23 Pa Co Ct 625

[7]*Riegelman* v *Focht*, 141 Pa 380, 23 Am St Rep 293 21 Atl 601 *Supplee* v *Hermann*, 9 Pa Dist R 27

[8]*Booth* v *Hoenig*, 7 Pa Dist R 529

[9]*Booth* v *Hoenig*, 7 Pa. Dist R 529, *Underwood's Estate,* 5 Pa. Co. Ct 621.

suretyship is under seal. A seal will, when no consideration is intended to exist by the surety and the lessor, dispense with it.[10]

69. Connection of surety's contract with the lease.—The surety's contract may be separate from the lease, whether written on the same paper, below the lease, or on the back of the paper on which the lease is written, or on a different paper[11] If the surety signs his contract before the tenant has signed the lease, but with the intention that the lease shall be signed by the tenant, he will not be bound, unless the tenant signs it.[12] The lease may name the lessor and the lessee alone as parties, but if it is signed by another, along with the lessee, with the intention to assume the liability of surety, he will become so liable.[13] He may write the word "bail" before[14] or after, or the word "surety" after[15] or before his name to indicate in what capacity he has signed. When the surety signs the lease, he may be sued jointly with the lessee[16] A lease contained the statement, "The lessee and the sureties J C & S J R. covenant with the lessor to pay the rent punctually, as above provided for," and was signed by the lessee and the sureties Their engagement was joint, and not several, and the sureties could not be sued apart from the lessee The fact that the sureties are so named in the covenant does not make them separately suable[17] A lease signed by the lessee and also by the surety, who designates himself as such, is several as well as joint, and the surety can be separately sued.[18] If the surety becomes such in a

[10]*Meek* v *Frantz* 171 Pa 632, 33 Atl 413

[11]*Scott* v *Swain*, 19 W. N C 547, *Meek* v *Frantz*. 171 Pa. 632, 33 Atl 413, *Riley* v *Cullen*, 7 W N C 114 *Duffee* v *Mansfield*, 141 Pa 507, 21 Atl 675, *Frank* v *Maguire* 42 Pa 77, *Krauss* v *McGlone*, 3 W N C 272

[12]*Cooney* v *Biggerstaff* 34 Pittsb L J 381

[13]*Fidler* v *Hershey*. 90 Pa 363 The surety who signs with lessee is liable, although the lessor does not sign. *Duffee* v *Mansfield*, 141 Pa 507, 21 Atl 675

[14]*Brown* v *Peters*, 2 Kulp, 518

[15]*Klapp* v *Kleckner*, 3 Watts & S 519 Cf *Kleckner* v *Klapp* 2 Watts & S 44

[16]*Fidler* v *Hershey* 90 Pa 363, *Brown* v *Peters*, 2 Kulp, 518

[17]*Philadelphia* v *Reeves*, 48 Pa 472

[18]*Klapp* v *Kleckner*, 3 Watts & S 519.

separate contract, he is liable separately, and not jointly with the lessee [19]

70. Things to be performed—When the surety signs the lease he engages for the performance of all the duties imposed by it upon the lessee The separate assumption may be made to apply to all the terms of the lease, *e. g ,* to the duty of keeping the premises in good condition, ordinary wear and tear excepted [20] Usually the surety's covenant is enforced for the payment of rent. Besides undertaking to be responsible for the rent, the surety may agree to be security for "the taxes and water taxes payable" on the premises during the term Under such a contract, the term expiring June 1st, 1891, and taxes being assessed in May, 1891, for the years 1891, 1892, the surety would be liable for the taxes assessed in May, 1891, though of the year for which they were assessed the term embraced only one month [21]

71. Suretyship arising subsequently to lease.—One may, for a consideration, become surety pending the term, for the rent to become due, or already due. If, *e. g ,* the lessor has distrained on goods, and X is known for some reason to desire their release, and if, in answer to the lessor's telegram, stating that he would not permit the goods to be taken away unless X would agree to pay the balance of the rent due upon the Hoenig leases, X telegraphs the reply, "I will be responsible for Hoenig leases," X will be liable for the rent, if the lessor releases the goods from the distress [22] A landlord being about to evict the tenant for failure to pay the rent, may consent to his remaining in possession on B's promising to pay the rent if he is allowed to remain If the tenant is understood to continue liable, and B's

---

[19]*Krauss* v *McGlone,* 3 W N C 272 Cf *Frank* v *Maguire,* 42 **Pa** 77
[20]*Hillary* v *Rose,* 9 Phila 139

[21]*Haynes* v *Synnott,* 160 Pa 180, 28 Atl 832
[22]*Booth* v *Hoenig,* 7 Pa Dist R. 529.

undertaking is not that of a lessee, B's promise will, as a promise to pay the debt of another, need to be in writing.[23]

72 Qualifications of liability of surety.—The surety agrees to do the same things that the tenant agrees to do, and at the same time, and on the same conditions   The guarantor's liability is subject to conditions of various sorts additional to these, which qualify the liability of the tenant or principal debtor   In the ordinary case, the guarantor becomes bound to do the acts to which he obliges himself, not at the time when the tenant is to do them, but later, and only after the tenant's failure to do them; and, further, he becomes bound to do them only in case the lessor fails to secure satisfaction from the tenant for his nonperformance of the contract, after due and unsuccessful diligence to obtain it, or in case there are circumstances which excuse this diligence.   It is enough for the lessor, there being two tenants, to sue both, although the sheriff returns *nihil habet* as to one, if, judgment being obtained against the other, a fi. fa. issues, to which the sheriff returns *nulla bona,* unless it is shown that the defendant in the judgment had property real or personal in some other county that was known to the lessor, or ought to have been, and that could have been reached by ordinary execution process.   A return of *nulla bona* to a justice's execution is not sufficient, because it does not negative the existence of real property of the defendant in the county.[24]   These measures to obtain satisfaction from the tenant should precede the commencement of the action against the guarantor   It is not enough for them to be adopted between its commencement and the trial.[25]   The fact that the lessor has attempted, by distress or otherwise, to collect the rent from the lessee, does not convert the surety's liability into that of a guarantor.[26]

[23]*Riegelman v Focht*, 141 Pa 380, 23 Am St Rep 293 21 Atl 601
[24]*Gilbert v Hench*, 30 Pa 205, *Allen v Hubert*, 40 Pa 259
[25] But the taking of the steps after the beginning of the action against the guarantor would be a matter in abatement, and not in bar
[26]*Scott v Swain*, 19 W. N. C. 547.

73. Further qualifications of surety's liability —Notice to the surety of the lessor's acceptance of his written suretyship is not necessary to bind him.[27] Seeking payment of the rent from the lessee is not a condition precedent to the right to sue the surety, nor does failure to seek payment from the lessee discharge him,[28] and an affidavit of defense alleging a want of due diligence in collecting the rent from the lessee will not prevent judgment[29] The act of May 14th, 1874,[30] enacts that the sureties in any written instrument for the forbearance or payment of money at any future time shall not be discharged from their liability upon the same, by reason of notice from them, to the creditor, to collect the amount thereof from the principal, unless such notice shall be in writing, and signed by the party giving it. The notice must not be given before the rent has become due.[31] It must be a positive and explicit declaration by the surety that he will hold himself discharged unless the lessor brings suit against the lessee[32] A notice to the lessor, before the rent is due, to push for it as soon as due, and that the surety "wants out of it," is not enough to discharge the surety, though there is enough property of the tenant on the premises to pay the rent.[33] It is hardly necessary to observe that a notice from the surety, during the term, that he will not be longer responsible for rent, does not disengage him from his contractual obligation[34] An agreement, after the lease is made, between the lessor and the lessee, which simply reduces the rent of the tenant for the future, does not discharge the surety, though he did not participate in it.[35] Merely giving time to a tenant to repay to

[27] *Baker* v *Robb*, 2 Del Co Rep 439

[28] *Haynes* v *Synnott*, 160 Pa 180 28 Atl 832, *Supplee* v *Hermann*, 9 Pa Dist R 27

[29] *Miller* v *Keller*, 1 W N C 27

[30] 2 Pepper & L Digest, 4425, P. L 157

[31] *Fidler* v *Hershey*, 90 Pa 363.

[32] *Fidler* v *Hershey*, 90 Pa 363

[33] *Fidler* v *Hershey*, 90 Pa 363 Cf *Loftus* v *Corles*, 9 W N C 333

[34] *Coe* v *Vogdes*, 71 Pa 383, *Pleasonton's Appeal*, 75 Pa 344

[35] *Dickson* v *Wolf*, 5 W N C 37, *Flanigan* v *Rossiter*, 7 W N C 180, *Barns* v. *Carney*, 6 W. N. C. 448.

the landlord taxes which the landlord has, but the tenant should have, paid, does not discharge the surety [36] The surety may take a stipulation from the lessor that the latter shall notify the former, quarterly, of any nonpayment of rent, which is payable quarterly. For one quarter's rent there could be no recovery from the surety unless, before suit, this notice had been given [37] The death of the surety within the term does not relieve his estate from liability for the rent subsequently accruing [38] One of two administrators of the surety may, with the lessor and the lessee, agree to terminate the term (originally of five years) at the end of the second year, so as to escape the liability for the rent of the other three years [39] An offer by the surety, who has obtained control of the premises, to surrender the term, will not relieve him from the rent, unless it is accepted by the lessor,[40] nor will the abandonment of the possession by the tenant [41] The untenantableness of the premises will not discharge the surety, if the tenant keeps possession, nor if, though he leaves in the midst of the term, he does not do so on account of the condition of the premises.[12]

74. Effect of unenforceableness of lessor's contract.—The fact that the lease, made by a married woman, is not separately acknowledged by her, should that acknowledgment be necessary in order to bind her, will not discharge the surety from liability for the tenant's rent, if the tenant in fact has enjoyed possession [43] A lease for five years was signed by the lessee, but not by the lessor. The surety executed a writing agreeing to be responsible for the true and faithful performance of the

[36]*Haynes* v *Synnott*, 160 Pa 180, 28 Atl 832

[37]*Hillary* v *Rose*, 9 Phila 139, *Pleasonton's Appeal*, 75 Pa. 344

[38]*De Morat* v *Howard*, 6 Pa Dist R 761

[39]*Reber* v *Gilson*, 1 Pa St 54

[40]*Booth* v *Hoenig*, 7 Pa Dist R 529

[41]*Meek* v *Frantz*, 171 Pa 632, 33 Atl 413

[42]*Coe* v *Vogdes*, 71 Pa 383

The landlord's want of diligence in collecting rent does not discharge the surety *Lightner* v *Axe*, 3 Del Co Rep 110; *Johnson's Appeal*, 19 W N C 98

[43]*Riley* v *Cullen*, 7 W N C 114

lessee's contract "for the full time in which he may retain possession of said premises." The liability of the surety, under this contract, was dependent simply upon the continuance of the tenant in possession, and not upon the enforceableness of the lease for the five years.[44]

75 Duration of the obligation.—If the lease is for a definite term, with provision for a renewal from year to year if the tenant holds over or unless legal notice of removal be given, the surety becomes responsible for the rent of a renewal year if the tenant holds over,[45] or if no notice to quit has been given Under such a lease for one year, beginning Nov. 15th, 1865, the tenant continued in possession in 1870 The surety was liable for the rent of 1870.[46] And even if notice to quit has been given, under a lease for one year, which provides that, if the tenant remains on the premises after the termination of the year, the contract is to continue in force another year, and so on from year to year, until legal notice shall be given for a removal, if the tenant actually continues in possession, despite the notice, for a second year, the surety will be liable for the rents of the second year[47] But if, after the notice to quit, a new lease is made with the lessee, and not with the surety, the lessee's continuance in possession will be referred to it, and not to the former lease, and the surety will not be liable for rent accruing subsequently to the expiration of the original term[48] The lease providing that, for nonpayment of rent, it should become void, the surety remains liable for rent accruing until the exercise by the lessor of his power to avoid the lease. One default in pay-

---

[44]*Duffee* v *Mansfield,* 141 Pa 507, 21 Atl 675

[45]*Oakford* v *Nirdlinger,* 196 Pa 162, 46 Atl 374

[46]*Coe* v *Vogdes* 71 Pa 383 Cf *Oalford* v *Nirdlinger,* 196 Pa 162, 46 Atl 374

[47]*McNamee* v *Cresson,* 3 W N C 450 "The notice of 1873," says the

supreme court, "did not terminate the lease, the tenant holding over in 1874 by its terms"

[48]*Reading Trust Co* v *Jackson* 22 Pa Supei Ct 69 This case intimates that the mere notice terminated the first lease and exempted the surety from liability for rent for the time following its expiration

ment does not, *ipso facto,* extinguish the duty of the lessee or his surety to pay the future instalments.[49]

76 Surety's right to prevent a renewal of lease.—If the lease is for a term, with provision for holding over from year to year, unless notice is given by lessor or lessee of the intention to demand or to relinquish the possession the surety may escape liability for the rent for any renewal period, by giving notice the proper time before its inception, that he will not continue bound. A lease for one month, commencing May 1st, 1883, contained the usual clause that, in the event of a holding over, the lessee should be considered tenant for another month, and so on from month to month, and provided that either party could terminate it at the end of any month by giving the other twenty days' notice of his intention. A notice by the surety on April 5th, 1884, to the lessor that he would not be surety any longer, would discharge him from liability for rent for the following month of May and later months.[50] In *Pleasonton's Appeal*[51] a lease for one year from January 1, 1867, was to continue from year to year until one month's notice was given of the intention to terminate it. On June 4th, 1869, the surety notified the lessor that he would not be such after the 31st of December, 1869 The tenant continued in possession until February, 1871. The surety died September 10th, 1870. His estate was not liable for the rent of August, 1870, or for future rent. "Had De Silver suffered the lease to begin again for 1870," says Agnew, Ch. J., "his estate would have been liable But his notice and death were facts probing the conscience of the landlords, who could not in equity

---

[49]*English* v *Yates,* 205 Pa 106, 54 Atl 503

[50]*Traeger* v *Hartnett,* 15 W N C. 300

[51]75 Pa 344 The opinion of the court does not apprehend the facts as they are presented in the history of the case. The court's remarks seem to assume that the renewal of the lease had taken place after the death of the surety Only one month's rent for the year beginning after his death was claimed The rest was for the year that began prior to his death, but after his notice to the lessor.

permit a renewal of the lease on the credit of the surety, when
they had it in their power to compel the tenant to give a new
surety or terminate the lease" Perhaps, the death of the
surety, known to the landlord, and other circumstances, may be
the equivalent of notice from him not to renew the term in reliance on his suretyship, but no such equivalence to notice was
found, when, the term being for three years, with provision for
renewal from year to year unless notice was given, the surety
died in the midst of the term, and the tenant was allowed to continue in possession beyond the term, and the administratrix of
the surety, who was his widow and the mother-in-law of the tenant, continued to dwell with the latter on the premises. The
widow, it was said, in effect affirmed the propriety of the lessor's
act in allowing the tenant to hold over.[52]

77 Discharge of surety.—If the lessor, having made a distress on goods, allows the tenant to remove them on his promising
to pay the rent in instalments, the surety will be discharged to
the extent of the value of the goods[53] If, an execution being
levied on the tenant's goods, the surety in the lease notifies the
landlord to apply to the constable who is making the sale, for the
rent of the term, and he declines to do so, but, as agent for the
lessor of the same premises for the preceding year, demands and
receives the rent of that year, relying on the surety for the rent
under the lease in which he is lessor, the surety will be *pro tanto*
discharged.[54] The surety is not discharged if a distress is rendered abortive by the clandestine removal of the goods after they
were distrained upon, which the lessor's want of care and diligence did not make practicable, nor possible, the goods being
taken from the constable by the tenant himself[55] The lease
stipulating against assigning or subletting, an assignment with

[52]*De Morat v Howard*, 6 Pa Dist.
R 761

[53]*McNamee v Cresson*, 3 W. N. C.
450.

[54]*Lachtenthaler v Thompson*, 13
Serg & R 157, 15 Am Dec 581.

[55]*Myers v. Hulseman*, 3 W. N. C.
487.

the consent of the lessor will free the surety from liability for subsequent rent,[56] but when the lease stipulates against assignment, not absolutely, but only when made without the lessor's consent, the surety will be liable for rent accruing after an assignment is made with the lessor's consent [57] "This provision is for the benefit of the lessor, and not of the guarantors,"[58] says Lowrie, Ch. J., "and an assignment according to it is not inconsistent with their guaranty." A landlord's eviction of the tenant discharges him and his surety from liability for rent subsequently falling due,[59] and if, the lessee dying, his widow is allowed by the lessor to continue in possession and to pay some rent, though no letters of administration are granted to any one, these acts of the lessor will be "analogous to the eviction of the prior tenant" and the lessee's surety will not be liable for the rent which accrues during the widow's occupancy, although he orally urges the widow to continue the possession. Even his oral promise to pay the rent would not make him liable [60]

78. Defenses of surety —A surrender of the term accepted by the lessor will end the liability of the surety for rent that would have subsequently accrued [61] As the surety has no right to the possession of the premises on the lessee's vacating them without assigning the lease to him, he will not be discharged by the lessor's refusal to allow him to take possession [62] To the extent to which the tenant could protect himself from the payment of the rent, on account of the failure of the landlord to perform his covenant to make repairs, *viz ,* to the extent of the diminution of the value of the premises to the tenant, but no farther, the surety will be excused from paying the rent [63] If

[56]*Bedford* v *Jones,* 5 Legal Gaz 230.

[57]*Gilbert* v *Henck,* 30 Pa 205

[58] The parties were really sureties

[59]*Duff* v *Wilson,* 69 Pa 316

A married woman cannot become surety *Underwood's Estate,* 5 Pa Co Ct 621.

[60]*Supplee* v *Hermann,* 9 Pa Dist R 27

[61]*Frank* v *Maguire,* 42 Pa 77

[62]*Goodman* v *Rothaker,* 17 Phila 245

[63]*Medary* v *Cathers,* 161 Pa 87, 28 Atl 1012

the lessor refuses for some weeks to give possession to the tenant, the surety is discharged though the lessee himself waives
the refusal; but the continuance of the lessor in some of the
rooms of the house for two months after the term began, with
the consent of the lessee, ne change having been made in the
contract, would not discharge the surety [64] If the surety was
induced to become such by the fraud of the lessor, if, e g , he is
falsely told by the lessor that the lessee, his brother-in-law, desires him to become surety, he will be discharged   The false-
hood is material, since if he became surety without the request
or consent of the tenant, he would have no action against the
tenant for reimbursement for rent paid [65] The surety's erroneous impression when he signed the lease, that it was for but
one year, when in fact it was for three years, is no defense, there
being no obstacle to his reading it, and no misrepresentation by
which he was deceived.[66] It is no defense for the surety that
before she signed the lease, one, not an agent of the lessor, but
an agent of the lessee, asked her to sign, and stated that the
lessor, who was then occupying the premises, was going to give
up entire possession; that she then said she would "go security,
but Mrs Medary (the lessor) must give up full possession," and
that, notwithstanding, the lessor continued on the premises for
two months after the term began, no ground being laid for the
introduction of the oral agreement into the lease, no representation having been made by any one to induce the surety to sign,
and the lessor not having authorized, or been informed of, the
statement made to the surety before signing.[67] A change of
ownership of the reversion does not terminate the surety's liabil-

[64]Medary v Cathers, 161 Pa 87,
28 Atl 1012
[65]Meek v Frantz, 171 Pa. 632, 33
Atl 413
[66]Meek v Frantz, 171 Pa 632, 33
Atl 413
[67]Medary v Cathers, 161 Pa 87,
28 Atl 1012.

A judgment against the tenant,
and a sheriff's return to an execution
on it of nulla bona, could not be put
in evidence, in a suit for the rent
against the surety   Gultinan v
Strong, 64 Pa 242   But see Reber
v Gilson, 1 Pa St. 54.

ity for rent afterwards accruing, when the tenant's promise is
to pay the rent "as long as the said premises shall be held or occupied" by him, and the surety has made himself responsible
for the tenant's performance.[68] A statement by the lessor to
the lessee (who informs the former that he will pay a portion of
the rent due), that he will not accept such payment, does not
pro tanto discharge the surety, there having been no tender of
any part of the rent, nor clear offer of any [69]

79. Liability of surety to competitor of lessor.—Pending an
ejectment by A, claiming to be a cotenant with B against B,
B made a lease of the premises to C, A refusing to join in it,
and announcing his intention to claim mesne profits in the
ejectment. The lease provided that should A succeed in the
ejectment, one half of the rent only should thereafter be paid
to B, until it should be legally determined to whom the other
half was due, and in case C should be legally required to pay one
half of the rent to A during the entire term, he, C, should be allowed to apply all the rent to the payment of A until A should
receive as much as had been paid to B On this contract A,
who had recovered a judgment for mesne profits, could not maintain an action against the sureties on the lease. The lease did
not admit of the construction that the stipulation was made for
the benefit of A if he succeeded in establishing his right. It
was intended to protect the lessee from loss.[70]

[68]*Taylor* v *Kennelly*, 14 W N C   [70]*Kennedy* v *Duggan*, 200 Pa. 284,
124.   49 Atl 781   Cf *Kennedy* v *Duggan*,
[69]*English* v *Yates*, 205 **Pa.** 106, 23 Pa Co Ct. 625.
54 Atl 503.

CHAPTER VII.

THE LESSOR'S COVENANTS.

80. Kinds of covenants—Covenants of various sorts with respect to the premises to be demised may be made by the landlord, and the appropriate remedies for the breach of them by him may be resorted to by the tenant. He may agree, *e g.,* to

66

erect stabling on premises leased as a furnace,[1] to build a house and improve the mill on the premises;[2] to build a barn[3] The covenant to put up the dam and wing dams "so as to drive at least two saws in low water" is a stipulation for the effect, and is not carried out by putting up a dam and wing dams which, in low water, will not drive at least two saws.[4] The shop being on the Board-Walk at Atlantic City, the moving of which towards the sea is in contemplation, the lessor may agree that if the Board-Walk is moved, he will move the shop so that it will continue to be upon the walk.[5] He may stipulate to repair a break in a kiln, to build a counting house and a weigh-house, to plank the wharf,[6] to repair a porch floor,[7] to keep the fences of the premises—a dairy farm—in repair,[8] to keep in repair the roof of a hotel,[9] to lay cinders and gravel in the yard of the tavern,[10] to make alterations and improvements,[11] to make an addition to the dwelling house and improvements to the mill,[12] to deepen and widen the tail race.[13] He may covenant that the tenant shall have the free use of the road and well upon other premises than those leased [14] The lease may authorize the tenant to make repairs at his discretion at the expense of the lessor, five per cent of the expense to be added to the rent. One employed by the tenant to make these repairs could not collect the cost from the tenant, if he knew that the tenant was acting under the authority of the landlord, and was intending to bind the

[1]*Gray* v *Wilson*, 4 Watts, 39.
[2]*Obermyer* v *Nichols*, 6 Binn 159, 6 Am Dec 439
[3]*Shughart* v *Moore*, 78 Pa 469.
[4]*Lomis* v *Ruetter*, 9 Watts, 516.
[5]*Jackson* v *Farrell*, 6 Pa Super. Ct 31
[6]*Warner* v *Caulk*, 3 Whart 193
[7]*Hahn* v *Roach*, 7 Northampton Co Rep 21
[8]*Brimner* v *Reed*, 23 Pa Super Ct. 318
[9]*Forrest* v *Buchanan*, 203 Pa 454, 53 Atl 267

[10]*Fairman* v *Fluck*, 5 Watts, 516.
[11]*Block* v *Dowling*, 7 Pa Dist R. 261
[12]*Obermyer* v *Nichols*, 6 Binn 159, 6 Am Dec 439 Cf *Prescott* v. *Otterstatter*, 85 Pa 534
[13]*Christ* v *Diffenbach*, 1 Serg & R. 464, 7 Am Dec 624
[14]*Depuy* v *Silver*, 1 Clark (Pa.) 385 Damages from the breach may be set off in an action for the rent.

landlord, and not himself. If he did not know of this right of
the tenant to bind the lessor, and gave credit to the tenant, he
could recover from the latter. If the lessor and lessee agree on
the erection of a cold storage room, and the former makes a contract with X to do the work, in which he names the tenant as
architect and agent, and authorizes changes and additions at the
discretion of the tenant, for any alterations and additions to the
work specified in the contract, the lessor would be liable, and not
the tenant, to X.[15] If the promise is omitted from the written
lease, which is accepted by the tenant on the lessor's assurance
that it shall be performed, it will be enforceable.[16]

81. Covenant as to existing state —The landlord may covenant as to the existing state, or fitness for certain purposes, of
the premises, *e. g.,* that they are adapted to a certain business,
that they are suitable for residence, but there is no implied
promise on the part of the lessor that they are fit for any particular purpose, *e g ,* for the purpose of making and selling
hats,[17] of serving as a vault for the storing of beer,[18] of manufacturing morocco,[19] of being a boarding house[20] or an inn,[21]
of being a residence [22] Though it is said by Finletter, J., that
"the supreme court has said that there is an implied covenant
that the house [the subject of the lease] is habitable,"[23] it is understood that, except in special cases, *e g.,* when an examination
of the premises by the tenant before he accepts a lease is, owing
to his distance from them or other causes, impracticable, or
when, by representation or artifice, he is dissuaded from exam-
ining them, it is the business of the tenant to examine them, and

[15]*Schaetzle* v *Christman,* 16 Pa
Super Ct 294
[16]*Christ* v *Diffenbach,* 1 Serg & R.
464, 7 Am Dec 624, *Shughart* v
Moore, 78 Pa. 469
[17]*Moore* v *Weber,* 71 Pa 429, 10
Am Rep 708
[18]*Schleppi* v *Gindele,* 14 W. N. C.
31.

[19]*Huber* v *Baum,* 152 Pa. 626, 26
Atl 101
[19]*Samuel* v *Scott,* 13 Phila 64
[21]*Wheeler* v *Crawford,* 86 Pa 327
[22]*Druckenmiller* v *Young,* 27 Pa
97
[23]*Showaker* v *Boyer,* 3 Pa Co Ct.
271

to judge for himself of their fitness, and if he wants the covenant of the landlord that they are and shall be fit for his purposes, to insist upon getting an express covenant. His eyes are said to be his bargain or his market.[24] There is no implied promise or warranty that the premises, a residence, are in sufficiently good repair to be tenantable,[25] or that, let with its furniture, all the rooms of the house are completely furnished,[26] or that the heating plant and apparatus are in such order that steam will not escape and injure goods in the store [27] There is no implied covenant that the premises, rented as a drinking saloon, are free from the reputation of being an opium joint and a bawdy house [28] A lease of the "right and privilege to mine and take away" coal, though a lease of the coal itself, and not a mere license, does not imply a warranty that there is sufficient coal to work profitably and compensate for expenditures in making preparations for carrying on the business [29] Nor does the lessor of a part of a building covenant impliedly that the heating apparatus in another portion is, or will remain, in good order, and not, by escaping steam, etc., injure the tenant's goods in the leased portion.[30]

82. Leasing for particular use —The fact that the lessor knows to what use the lessee intends to put the premises, or mentions the use in the lease, or even prescribes it, does not imply a covenant on his part that they are adapted to the use. The

[24]*Huber* v *Baum*, 152 Pa 626, 26 Atl 101, *Moore* v *Weber*, 71 Pa 429, 10 Am Rep 708, *Hess* v *Weingartner*, 5 Pa Dist R 451, *Johnson* v *Mathues*, 4 Del Co Rep 365, *Wien* v *Simpson*, 2 Phila 158 *Dillon* v. *Carrol*, 2 Luzerne Legal Reg 89

[25]*Druckenmiller* v *Young*, 27 Pa 97 *Hess* v *Weingartner*, 5 Pa Dist R 451, *Wien* v *Simpson*, 2 Phila 158, *Kline* v *Jacobs*, 68 Pa 57

[26]*Hess* v. *Weingartner*, 5 Pa Dist. R 451.

[27]*Krohn* v *Wolf*, 7 Del Co Rep 420

[28]*Turbill* v *Brown*, 17 W. N C. 221

[29]*Harlan* v *Lehigh Coal & Nav Co* 35 Pa 287. Action by the lessee on the alleged implied covenant

[30]*Krohn* v *Wolf*, 7 Northampton Co Rep 18 The action for damages to the tenant's goods would be founded, not on contract, but on the negligence of the lessor.

thing leased may be a dwelling house, and the lessee's intention to use it as such be well known to the lessor.[31] The lease may specify that it is to be used as a boarding house[32] or hotel.[33] But, in all these cases, the tenant must exercise his own judgment as to the fitness of the premises now and the probable continuance of their fitness hereafter, for his uses and needs, and he must rely on this judgment, unless he obtains an express covenant from the lessor, or unless the landlord's representations are intended to dissuade, and do dissuade, the tenant from investigation.[34]

83 Covenant that premises are "perfectly dry"—A representation, or covenant, by the lessor, that the premises are "perfectly dry," must not be understood to mean that they are not so far damp as the tenant, on inspection, sees them to be, nor that they will not become damp by the action of neighbors, or the negligence of the tenant himself in not keeping the spouts from the roof in good condition or preventing the cesspool from overflowing so that its contents reach the cellar. When the lease was made, there was a damp spot on the wall, caused by a neighbor's ice-box, but the dampness did not loosen the paper. The house subsequently grew damp from the bad order of the spouting and the overflow of the privy. The covenant that the house was "perfectly dry" was not violated by the slight dampness at the time it was made, which was visible to the tenant, nor by the dampness which subsequently arose from the neglect of the lessee, nor from improper acts of neighbors, which the lessee could have taken measures to prevent.[35]

---

[31] E g , Wien v Simpson, 2 Phila 158 Cf Carson v Godley, 26 Pa. 111, 67 Am Dec 404, Schleppi v. Gindele, 14 W N C 31

In Wolfe v Arrott, 109 Pa 473, 1 Atl 333 it was intimated that the lease stipulating that the premises should not be used otherwise than as a dwelling house, it fairly represent-ed and declared the house to be in all respects fit and suitable for that purpose

[32] Samuel v Scott, 13 Phila 64

[33] Hazlett v Powell, 30 Pa 293

[34] Wolfe v. Arrott, 109 Pa 473, 1 Atl 333

[35] Johnson v. Mathues, 4 Del. Co Rep 365.

84. Covenant as to neighborhood.—A covenant that the lessor will cause objectionable houses in the neighborhood to be demolished and better houses erected instead is merely collateral, and the nonperformance of it will not suspend or discharge the rent. *A fortiori,* a mere representation *dehors* the lease, by the agent of the lessor, made to induce the acceptance of the lease, that the houses opposite were controlled by him and would be demolished, and better houses erected, not averred to be false or fraudulent, and being contrary to the terms of the lease, would not defeat the rent.[36]

85. Covenant as to safety of stairway.—When the rooms or floors of a house are let to different parties, all of whom use a common stairway in control of which the lessor continues, he is bound to keep it in safe condition although he does not expressly covenant to do so, and although the respective lessees have covenanted to make repairs   They are not tenants of the stairway, and their covenants do not apply to it.   A tenant who, in descending the stairway, is hurt in consequence of its defects, will have a right to indemnity from the landlord.[37]

86. Covenant as to future state of premises—The landlord no more covenants impliedly for the future state of the premises than for their state at the time of making the lease. He does not, *e g.,* covenant that an ice-house, connected with a beer vault, shall not fall in,[38] that the wall of the adjoining house belonging to another person shall not be taken down so as to expose to the weather the wall of the demised premises,[39] that a building rented as a morocco factory shall not, after four years' use, become, by reason of age and dilapidation, so unsafe

[36]*Wilcox* v. *Palmer,* 163 Pa 109, 29 Atl. 757. But the intention, alleged by the representation to exist, was never carried out. *Prescott* v. *Otterstatter,* 79 Pa 462, *Allegaert* v *Smart,* 11 W. N. C 177, are cited.

[37]*Lewin* v *Pauli,* 19 Pa Super Ct. 447

[38]*Schleppi* v *Gindele,* 14 W. N C 31

[39]*Moore* v *Weber,* 71 Pa. 429, 10 Am Rep 708.

as to preclude the further prosecution of the business there,[40] that a house will be kept, by necessary repair, in a tenantable state;[41] that eighteen windows looking over an adjoining vacant lot, belonging to another, shall not be closed up by the erection against them of a party wall;[42] that the roof of a barn shall not so get out of repair as to leak and make the barn untenantable, and the pump so worn out as to render the well useless,[43] that the ceilings in the upper rooms of an inn shall not fall or threaten to fall, so as to render the rooms insecure and untenantable,[44] that the drainage shall be such as to make it safe for the health and lives of the lessee and his family for them to remain on the premises during the term, and as to avoid the prohibition by the board of health, of the continuance of the occupancy,[45] that the drainage shall not become so defective as to render the back buildings of a boarding house uninhabitable, and to dissuade boarders from taking rooms in them;[46] that the roof shall not leak and, by so doing, cause the cellar to be flooded and the house to be rendered untenantable,[47] that the bulk windows shall be made not to leak, a hand-rail constructed in the staircase to the second floor, terra-cotta collars put on the chimneys, and necessary plumbing done to keep the cellar dry,[48] that the roof shall not become decayed and leaky, or the spouting clogged up and out of order,[49] that the house shall not become damp by the action of the neighbors, or by the neglect of the tenant to

[40]*Huber* v *Raum*, 152 Pa 626, 26 Atl 101

[41]*Phillips* v *Monges*, 4 Whart 226, *McCloskey* v *Wiltbank*, 1 W N C 413, *Reeves* v *McComeskey*, 168 Pa 571, 32 Atl 96

[42]*Hazlett* v *Powell*, 30 Pa 293

[43]*Lukens* v *Hedley*, 1 W N C 266

[44]*Wheeler* v *Crawford*, 86 Pa 327

[45]*Hollis* v *Brown*, 159 Pa 539, 28 Atl 360

[46]*Samuel* v. *Scott*, 13 Phila 64;

Stull v *Thompson*, 154 Pa 43, 25 Atl 890

In *Brolaskey* v *Loth*, 5 Phila 81, Thompson, P J, held that a leaking roof making the house untenantable, the tenant could remove, and escape liability for future rent

[47]*Walz* v *Rhodes*, 1 W N C 49

[48]*Bradley* v Citizens' Trust & Surety Co 7 Pa Super Ct 419

[49]*Russell* v. *Rush*, 2 Pittsb. 134

cleanse the drains and conductors,[50] that a stable shall be kept
in a tenantable state for horses.[51]

87. Agreement to repair made after the lease.—An agreement
between the landlord and tenant, made after the lease
has been made, that the former will make repairs or changes,
is, like any other agreement, enforceable only if some consideration for it exists The tenant being by the lease bound to
pay the rent without repairs being made, escapes that duty only
by a posterior contract for which he has furnished a consideration [52] A tenant having the right to remove at the end of the
current year would, by holding over, and becoming liable for the
rent of another year, furnish a consideration for the lessor's
promise during the first year to make repairs if the tenant
would retain possession such another year. But if the lease
requires the tenant to remain another year unless he gives notice
prior to the close of the current year, and if, such notice not being given and the time to give it having gone by, the lessor's
grantee promises to make the repairs if the tenant will continue
in possession the next year, the grantee is not legally bound to
make the repairs, and whether he makes them or not, the tenant
will be liable for the whole of the next year's rent,[53] and if a
tenant, who has held over for a second term, but, removing from
the premises before its expiration, desires to escape the rent,
alleges that the lessor promised to make repairs, he must show
that the promise was made before, by holding over, he had already become liable for the whole year's rent [54] The surety of
the lessee sued for the rent may set off moneys paid by him for
repairs to the premises, at the instance and request of the

[50]*Johnson* v *Mathues,* 4 Del Co 226, *Lukens* v *Hedley,* 1 W N C.
Rep 365
266, *Druckenmiller* v *Young,* 27 Pa
[51]*Cochran* v *Ward,* 8 Del Co Rep 97
423
[53]*White* v *Campion,* 1 W. N. C
[52]*Dillon* v *Carrol,* 2 Luzerne Legal 130
Reg 89, *Phillips* v *Monges,* 4 Whart.
[54]*Hoban* v *Lawall,* 3 Lack Jur. 38.

lessor [55]   The term being for a year, the tenant cannot properly infer from the lessor's having, during the year, told him, repairs to the mill being needed, to have them made, and from the lessor's having subsequently paid for them, that he might, during the second year, have repairs made to the dam at the cost of the landlord.   If the lessor induces the tenant to make extraordinary repairs which he is not bound to make, by promising to pay for them, the lessor will be bound.   The fact that the lessor paid for repairs though he was not bound to do so, during the term, would not oblige him to pay for repairs made by the tenant during a hold-over year; the holding over not having been induced by any promise to continue in possession.[56]

88   Lessor's duty to repair.—The landlord does not impliedly covenant that the premises shall continue in the state in which they are, or, if they do not, that he will bring them back to that state by repairs.   He is under no implied duty to make repairs,[57] or, if the tenant makes them, to reimburse him.[58] He is not bound, e g , to put on new shutters, the former having rotted off,[59] or to reconstruct an ice-house which has fallen,[60] or to repair a dam which breaks during the term,[61] or, the lease being of a basement in New York city, so connected with a sewer that water occasionally backs up into it, to change the connection so as to prevent this,[62] or to repair the roof of a barn, or a pig-pen.[63]

89. Covenant to repair.—The landlord does not covenant to put the house "in order," by inserting in the lease the phrase "the party of the second part [the lessee] to do all inside repairs

[55]*Kelly* v. *Duffy* (Pa) 11 Atl 244
[56]*Everhart* v *Bauer*, 1 Lehigh Valley Law Rep 157
[57]*Long* v *Fitzimmons*, 1 Watts & S 530, *Hitner* v. *Ege*, 23 Pa 305, *Schleppi* v *Gindele*, 14 W N C 31, *Wien* v *Simpson*, 2 Phila 158
[58]*Kline* v *Jacobs*, 68 Pa 57
[59]*Hess* v. *Weingartner*, 5 Pa. Dist R 451.

[60]*Schleppi* v. *Gindele*, 14 W N C 31
[61]*Everhart* v *Bauer*, 1 Lehigh Valley Law Rep 157
[62]*Plummer* v *Shulmyer*, 12 Lanc L Rev 217   For damages to the tenant's goods, the landlord is not liable
[63]*Medary* v. *Cathers*, 161 Pa. 87, 28 Atl 1012

after the house is put in order "[64]   The lease being silent as to repairs, it is improper to infer that there was a duty to repair sufficiently to keep the house tenantable from the fact that the lessor has, at the request of the tenant, made some repairs   An agreement of some kind must be shown.   The landlord may erroneously suppose himself bound, or he may do the repairs for the benefit of the property, and that it may not fall into dilapidation [65]   Though the lease is in writing, an oral agreement, made at the time, that the tenant may make the necessary repairs and be credited for the expense of them upon the rent[66] will be enforced if the agreement is omitted by inadvertence from the written lease, and is repeated immediately before the execution of the lease, as an inducement to the lessee to accept it, and again, after the tenant has taken possession.[67]   When repairs are made by the tenant, "with the assent and by the authority of the landlord," he is liable for the cost of them without any express promise to pay.[68]   If the ordinary repairs are made by the tenant, the lessor will not be obliged to reimburse him unless they were made at the lessor's request, or in conformity with an agreement.[69]   If the landlord covenants that "he is to pay all repairs exceeding two dollars," he does not bind himself to make repairs, but only to compensate the tenant for such repairs as

---

[64]*Frey* v *Zabinski*, 10 Kulp, 36 Even if it was a covenant to put 'in order" it would not follow that it obliged the lessor to repair the furnace, leaking pipes, bad roof spigots without washers, fire places without grates

[65]*Moore* v *Weber*, 71 Pa 429, 10 Am Rep 708

[66]*Johnson* v *Blair*, 126 Pa 426, 17 Atl 663   No explanation was given of the omission of the agreement from the writing

[67]*Caulk* v *Everly*, 6 Whart 303 Cf *Shughart* v *Moore*, 78 Pa 469 The mere fact that the oral agree-

ment was made is not sufficient reason for giving effect to it. *Moore* v *Gardiner*, 161 Pa 175, 28 Atl 1018

[68]*Cornell* v *Vanartsdalen*, 4 Pa 364   What amounts to an assent or authority of the lessor will depend on circumstances, of which the jury will judge   If the lessor, under a promise to give the farm to the lessee (his son-in-law) and wife, encourages him to erect a new building and to make repairs, and then he devises the farm to another, the law implies an obligation to pay

[69]*Hitner* v. *Ege*, 23 Pa. 305.

he shall have made [70] The lease stipulating "said Lockhart (lessee) to put mills and race in complete order for running, and keep a correct account of the same, which is to apply towards paying the rent on the second year of the lease, and all after-repairs at the expense of Lockhart," the cost of the repairs, between $2,000 and $4,000, could be set off not only against the second year's rent, which was but $1,050, but against any subsequently accruing rent The landlord was liable for all.[71] The agreement of the lessor to reimburse the tenant for the cost of the repairs may be conditioned on his sale of the premises within one year. "The said lessor," says the lease, "agrees to refund any amount, not exceeding $300, which the said lessee may expend on the premises towards putting it in habitable condition, and for which he shall produce vouchers, in case the property is sold within said period. The lessee agreeing to allow access to the property for the purpose of effecting a sale " The phrase "in case the property" etc. was understood to be connected with the preceding words [72] The lessor may agree in the lease that the tenant may make such repairs as, in his judgment, are needed, and that he shall be repaid out of the rent [73] The fact that the written lease says that the inside repairs are to be done by the tenant, in conjunction with the fact that the landlord made, some outside repairs after the tenant went into possession, would require the submission to the jury of the question whether he did not agree to make outside repairs, e. g., to the roof and spouting [74]

---

[70]*Lomis* v *Ruetter*, 9 Watts, 516 The contract really was that the tenants "are to pay all repairs that shall not exceed $2 each " The lower court assumed that this imposed the duty on the lessor of paying for all repairs above $2, if they were made by the tenant

[71]*Mattocks* v *Cullum*, 6 Pa 454.

[72]*Wright* v. *Milne*, 9 Pa Dist R 170.

[73]*Johnson* v *Blair* 126 Pa 426. 17 Atl 663 The tenant, if sued for the rent, can set off the sums expended for repairs

[74]*Russell* v *Rush*, 2 Pittsb 134 It would, however not be the lessor s duty, if he had made such an agreement, to so make the roof and spouting that there could be no leakage during and after an extraordinary storm and freezing For temporary

90 Destruction by fire.—There may be a provision in the lease with respect to injury or destruction of the building by fire, and defining the rights or duties, upon the happening of a fire, of the landlord or of the tenant. In the absence of such provision, there is no implied condition to the tenant's duty of continuing to occupy the premises and of paying rent, that they shall not be destroyed or seriously injured by fire, or that, if they are, the landlord will restore them. "Equity," said Gibson, Ch J., "refuses to relieve against such a covenant [e g. to pay rent] though the premises be consumed by fire, destroyed by the elements, or encroached on by the sea "[75] Hence, the destruction of a barn on a leased farm,[76] of a leased store,[77] a store house[78] or house,[79] does not excuse the tenant from continuing to pay the rent. The value of a tavern depended largely on the neighboring ferry bridge over which travelers came to it. The destruction of the bridge, and consequent serious reduction of the patronage of the tavern, did not excuse from paying the full rent.[80] The tenant cannot set off against the rent damages from the loss of nuts from shell-bark trees which have been destroyed by fire occasioned by locomotives on a neighboring railroad.[81] If the lessor has had an insurance on the property, the fact that he has received the money from the insurance company does not relieve the tenant from the rent. "It is impossible to see," says the court, "what payment of the loss by the insurance company had to do with the payment of the rent by the tenant. It was not the rent which was insured, but the

and accidental obstructions to the spouts the lessor would not be responsible, but the lessee

[77]*Fisher* v *Milliken*, 8 Pa 111, 49 Am Rep 497, *Camp* v *Casey*, 7 Pa Co Ct 160

[78]*Maberry* v *Dudley*, 2 Pennyp 367

[79]*Phillips* v *Epp*, 4 Del Co Rep 426, 2 Lack Jur 41

[79]*Bussman* v. *Gansler*, 72 Pa 285

[77]*Hoeveler* v *Fleming*, 91 Pa 322, *Magaw* v *Lambert*, 3 Pa St 444, *Mannerbach* v *Keppleman*, 2 Woodw. Dec 137

[80]*Smith* v *Ankrim*, 13 Serg & R 39 Even had the bridge been a part of the demised premises, the legal result of its destruction would have been the same

[81]*Jenkins* v *Stone*, 14 Montg Co. L Rep 27.

premises out of which it issued, and the tenant could not say that the company had paid it for him."[82] Nor, the insurance company offering to rebuild in lieu of paying the money, is the tenant relieved from the rent because the landlord declines the offer and takes the money, or because he declines the offer of the tenant to rebuild with the money.[83]

91 Destruction by fire, upper story demised.—When the subject of the lease is apartments in the upper story of a building, if there is no covenant by either landlord or tenant to rebuild, the lessee is discharged from his covenant to pay rent by the burning of the building which makes the enjoyment of the space demised to him impracticable   Hence, all the rooms on the second story of a stone building being demised, the destruction of the building terminated the accruing of rent.   The tenant ceased to be liable for any accruing in the future.[84]

92. Fire, insurance by tenant—If the tenant, agreeably to the lease, maintains insurance on the landlord's interest in the premises, and is bound to pay the insurance money to the landlord, or, if he shall prefer, to rebuild, the payment of the insurance money to the landlord, who does not rebuild, will excuse the tenant, who withdraws from the possession, from further rent. "It is well established," remarks Hare, P. J., "that the destruction of the building by fire does not discharge the tenant. The reason is, that he impliedly assumes the risk; and moreover, as the land remains, the failure of consideration is only partial.

[82]*Magaw* v *Lambert*, 3 Pa St 444

[83]*Bussman* v. *Ganster*, 72 Pa 285

[84]*Camp* v *Casey*, 7 Pa Co Ct 160 The fact that the use of a cistern in a cellar, in common with other tenants, was given in the lease, did not prevent the application of the principle Cf *Phillips* v. *Epp*, 2 Lack Jur 41, 4 Del Co Rep 426, where it is held that the stipulation in the lease that if the tenant's goods are removed from the premises the whole rent for the rest of the term shall become at once payable was enforceable although the removal was made necessary by a fire   A stipulation that the rent shall cease if the building be destroyed by fire will not exempt the tenant from rent, if the building is only injured, though the part of it occupied by the tenant is rendered untenantable.

When, however, it is agreed that the premises shall be insured, and the amount due on the policy employed to rebuild them in the event of loss, or paid to the lessor, at his option, and he chooses the latter alternative, the presumption is strong, if not irresistible, in favor of an agreement to discharge the tenant. The money stands, under these circumstances, in lieu of the house, and the effect of the payment of it to the landlord is to replace him in the possession of a part at least, of that which he granted by the lease Accordingly, when such a transaction is followed by the withdrawal of the tenant, a jury may, and perhaps ought to, find a surrender by him and an acceptance of it by the landlord."[85]

93. Stipulations with respect to fire.—The lease may stipulate that a destruction of the premises by fire shall unconditionally or conditionally relieve the tenant from future rent. It may, *e. g.*, provide that should a fire occur without the tenant's negligence, the tenant may require the lessor to rebuild, and, if when so required, the lessor shall not within three months commence to rebuild and shall not duly prosecute the rebuilding, the tenant may relinquish the premises and escape liability for the rent. Under such a lease, it would be the duty of the lessor to rebuild in case of fire not caused by the tenant's negligence, should the tenant require, or to forego future rent. That the fire was not caused by the tenant's negligence, he could show by the statements of the lessor to the insurance company, for the purpose of procuring the money on the policy [86] But if the written lease expressly says that the tenant shall continue liable for the rent, notwithstanding any accident making rebuilding necessary, and that he will rebuild at his own expense and without any reduction of the rent, he cannot escape the liability

[85]*Boyer* v *Dickson,* 7 Phila 191. A note for the rent of two years having been given in advance, the occurrence of the fire within the two years, and the payment to the lessor of the insurance money, would be a partial defense

[86]*Philadelphia Trust, S D & Ins. Co* v *Purves* (Pa) 12 Cent Rep. 659, 13 Atl 936.

to pay the rent on the allegation that it was agreed between him and the lessor that he should not be liable, unless he accounts for the appearance of the actual stipulation in the lease by fraud, accident, or mistake, and establishes this fraud, accident, or mistake by clear, precise, and indubitable evidence.[87]

94. Stipulations after the fire.—The lessor, after a fire has occurred, may. although he is not bound by the lease to rebuild, and although the tenant is not excused by the lease from paying the rent, obtain control of the property for the purpose of rebuilding, by agreeing with the tenant that he shall pay no rent for the time he shall be out of possession. If, under such an agreement, the tenant gives up the possession, the lessor cannot compel him to pay rent for the period of his absence from the premises [88] If the landlord, after the destruction of one of the two barns on the demised premises, agrees to rebuild it by harvest time, and in fact rebuilds, but not by that time, so that the tenant is obliged to stack a large part of his crops, he will have a right to set off the damages arising (not, apparently, from the nonfulfilment of the contract in time, but) from the occupancy of a portion of the farm during the process of rebuilding, and from the nonusableness of the burnt barn until it was rebuilt, although the landlord did not promise to reduce the rent.[89]   The damages are the difference between the rental

[87]*Martin* v *Berens,* 67 Pa 459

[88]*Re Holmes,* 30 Pittsb L J N S 309 Hence, the lessor, being a trustee, cannot be compelled to account for the rent which he could not collect from the tenant

[89]*Wayne* v *Lapp,* 180 Pa 278, 36 Atl 723   The fire occurred between the making of the lease, January 31st, and the commencement of the term, April 1st Waddell, P J , says that possibly the fire would have excused the tenant from taking possession, but that, taking possession, he could not claim an abatement from the rent, but for the landlord's inducing him to take possession by promising to rebuild Being thus induced to waive his right to refrain from taking possession, the tenant was entitled to a reduction from the rent on account of the interference with his possession caused by the rebuilding, although the landlord did not agree that there should be any reduction   In *Hoeveler* v *Fleming* 91 Pa 322, the lessor rebuilt the house without the consent of the lessee This was treated as an eviction, suspending the rent.

value of the premises in the state in which they would have been had the fire not occurred, and the state in which they were, during the rebuilding.

95. Landlord's right to make repairs.—The lease may reserve to the landlord the right of "doing any repairing." Under such a reservation, the landlord has a right to enter on the premises for the purpose of tearing away the *debris* and tearing down the walls of a barn which is destroyed by fire, without the consent of the tenant, although the barn is not rebuilt during his term, and the exercise of this right will not exempt the tenant from rent for the term.[90]

96. Landlord's covenant to buy tenant's improvement.—A lease of a tannery for three years gives to the lessee the privilege of building a bark-shed and of obliging the lessor to pay for it at the end of the term, at a price to be fixed by three carpenters. A week or two before the end of the term the tenant may, despite the objection of the landlord, build the shed, though his only object in building it is to compel the lessor to pay the arbiters' price for it, and though his motive is dissatisfaction with the refusal of the lessor to reduce the rent for the last year of the term.[91]

97. Independent agreements.—The lease of a foundry for so much per year may contain the separate stipulation: "It is further agreed" that the tenant "shall pay 15 cents an hour for the steam furnished to his engine by the lessor, and he shall have the right to use the tools in the pattern shop, but in consideration therefor, the first party hereto shall have the use, without charge, of the power of the engine of the second party whenever they shall require it in the pattern shop" These words are not an agreement by the lessor to furnish any steam, but of the lessee to pay for it if it should be furnished, and if the latter should take any. The tenant is entitled to no damages for the failure of the lessor to furnish him a sufficient supply [92]

98. Landlord's covenant to procure right to a switch —A's lease to B of a quarry gave B the right to use an existing switch, and also the right to construct another switch from the main track of a certain railroad   It further stipulated that if the charges of the railroad company should exceed 25 cents per car, such excess should stand as a credit upon the royalty. The railroad company refused to permit the second switch except on the condition that the lessor should surrender her right to use the first switch at the rate of 25 cents per car. There was no covenant on the lessor's part to procure the use of the second switch for the lessee [93]

99. What is breach of covenant to repair.—The lessor's covenant that he will, during the term, "keep in good repair the roofs upon the buildings hereby demised," is not broken if, living in another town, he authorizes the tenant to have any repairs done by a tin-roofer named, whenever they are needed, and the tenant, though former repairs have been made with reasonable promptness, has neglected to cause the roofer to make the repairs in question [94]

100. Defense of tenant for breach of landlord's covenant.— The tenant, alleging a right to have the premises tenantable, or to answer his purpose, or to have them kept tenantable, or adaptable to his purposes, may set off the damages which he has sustained by the violation of this right, against the claim for rent. This he may do, in an action by the landlord for the rent,[95] or in replevin by himself, for goods distrained upon by the

[92]*Penn Iron Co v Diller*, 113 Pa. 635, 6 Atl 272

[93]*Skillen v. Logan*, 21 Pa Super Ct 106

[94]*Forrest v Buchanan*, 203 Pa 454, 53 Atl 267

[95]*Schleppi v Gindele*, 14 W N C 31, *Showaker v Boyer*, 3 Pa Co Ct

271, *Walz v Rhodes*, 1 W N C 49, *McCloskey v Wiltbank*, 1 W N C. 413, *Stull v Thompson*, 154 Pa 43, 25 Atl 890, *Hollis v Brown*, 159 Pa. 539, 28 Atl 300, *Reeves v McComoskey*, 168 Pa 571, 32 Atl 96, *Moore v Gardner*, 161 Pa 175, 28 Atl 1018 *Russell v Rush*, 2 Pittsb.

landlord.[96] The surety, sued for the rent, may attempt the same defense,[97] or creditors may defeat, *pro tanto,* the claim for the rent from the proceeds of an execution[98] A recognizance for an appeal in a landlord's proceeding to recover the possession, binding the recognizor for the tenant's rent until final judgment, in a suit on it, the defendant may show a failure of the landlord to keep his covenant to repair.[99]

101. Action for breach — The tenant, besides setting off damages for the lessor's breach of covenant against the claim for rent, may alternatively recover them in an action   If he has made no covenant, but causes damages by his negligence, *e g.,* in maintaining the heating plant in improper condition, the action would not be *ex contractu,* and therefore the claim could not be enforced by a creditor of the tenant, by foreign attachment[100]   If the lessor warrants the purity of the water on the premises, he will be liable if it is not pure, however honest he was, but he will not be liable in deceit if he believed it to be pure[101]

102. Measure of damages — In a majority of cases in which damages for breach of the lessor's covenant that the premises are, or, by means of repairs and improvements, shall be put and be preserved in a certain state, are sought, it has been held that the proper measure of damages is the difference between the worth of the premises in the condition in which they are, the covenants being unperformed, and their worth in the condition in which they would have been had the covenants been performed.[102]   The lessor having promised to improve the yard

134, *Frey* v *Zabinski,* 10 Kulp, 36; *Obermyer* v *Nichols,* 6 Binn 159, 6 Am Dec 439

[96]*Hazlett* v *Powell,* 30 Pa 293, *Christ* v *Diffenbach,* 1 Serg & R 464, 7 Am Dec 624, *Block* v *Dowling,* 7 Pa Dist R 261, *Fairman* v *Fluck,* 5 Watts, 516, *Prescott* v *Otterstatter,* 85 Pa 534

[97]*Wheeler* v *Crawford,* 86 Pa 327

[98]*Gray* v *Wilson,* 4 Watts, 39

[99]*Broad* v *Winsborough,* 1 Northampton Co Rep 330

[100]*Krohn* v *Wolf,* 7 Del Co Rep 420

[101]*Harrington* v *Hamill,* 3 Montg Co L Rep 31

[102]*Fairman* v *Fluck* 5 Watts 516; *Wayne* v *Lapp,* 180 Pa 278, 36 Atl. 723, *Warner* v *Caulk,* 3 Whart 193,

of a tavern by putting cinders and gravel on it, this rule was held applicable. The profits which the lessee might have made, the losses arising from customers actually going away because of the condition of the yard, furnished no measure.[103]   The lessor agreeing to shift the shop leased so that it should accompany the Board-Walk on which it was, in Atlantic City, N J , should that walk be moved towards the sea, the measure of damages for his failure to do so would be the difference between the value of the shop as it was left behind by the walk, and its value as it would have been had it been brought forward to the shifted walk ; but not the losses to the tenant in his business, during the season.[104]   In *Prescott* v. *Otterstatter*[105] the lease of a hotel contained an agreement by the landlord to erect an additional story, to remove the old porches and replace them with halls. The changes promised were very imperfectly made, and in the making of them, avoidable damage was done to the furniture and other property of the lessee   The measure of damages approved was that already indicated,—the difference between the value of the hotel as actually changed, and that of the hotel as it ought to have been changed   Evidence that the rental value of the barroom, which was not diminished by the imperfect alteration, was a very large percentage of the rental of the whole property, was improperly received, and evidence of

Jackson v *Farrell*, 6 Pa. Super. Ct. 31

In an action for breach of the covenant to repair, there can be no recovery of more than nominal damages unless the evidence shows the damages suffered   The jury cannot determine the damages from the character of the building, and the uses to which it is put, and the de scribed effects of the omission to repair   *Forrest* v *Buchanan*, 203 Pa 454, 53 Atl 267

[103]*Fairman* v *Fluck*, 5 Watts, 516
The lessor having promised to

erect a barn, the trial court said that the lessee's damages for his refusal to perform were the injury suffered from the want of a barn, the exposure of the stock, etc   *Shughart* v *Moore*, 78 Pa 469

[104]*Jackson* v *Farrell*, 6 Pa Super Ct 31   The court suggests that the tenant might himself have moved the shop and defalked the cost of the removal from the rent, or he might have surrendered the possession and thus escaped the duty of paying future rent

[105] 79 Pa 462, 85 Pa 534.

what would have been the rental value of the rooms was inadmissible, except as a reply to that concerning the value of the barroom. These are "items of detail selected from the body of the property," and the effect of receiving them would be to afford the jury a means of making a fresh contract between the parties, in lieu of the contract actually made by them. The value of the premises as a unit, in both states, the actual and the promised, should be shown.

103. Another measure of damages.—The measure of damages heretofore discussed is not uniformly adhered to. In *Penn Iron Co.* v. *Diller*,[106] Green, J., states that "the value of the lease or any part of it, is not the measure of the damages to which the plaintiff is entitled for a breach of a particular covenant contained in it If such a covenant was broken, the actual damage which resulted from the actual breach can be and should be shown. To ask what was the value of the lease lets in the wildest and most speculative conjectures which the friendly zeal of the party's witness may choose to indulge in. If [he adds] there was an injury done, let the witness state what it was and how it was done, and if he can express the value of that particular injury in figures, let him do so "[107] If the tenant of a farm is, by the terms of the lease, to keep the fences in repair, the landlord furnishing the material, it is the duty of the tenant, should the lessor fail to furnish the material,

---

[106] 113 Pa 635, 6 Atl 272

[107] The breaches of the lessor s contract alleged were, not furnishing steam, and not allowing the tenant the use of the tools in a pattern shop The lease was of a foundry The tenant was improperly allowed to state what was the value of the use of the pattern shop of which he was deprived, that is, make a separate estimate of the value to him of the use of different parts of the leased subject In *Bradley* v *Citizens' Trust & Surety Co* 7 Pa Super Ct 419,

in replevin by a tenant of goods distrained for rent, the court told the jury that failure of the lessor to make repairs would entitle the tenant to damages, or he might have the repairs made and deduct the cost from the rent In *Brimner* v *Reed*, 23 Pa Super Ct. 318, it is said that, if the lessor fails, as he agrees, to repair the fences of the premises, the lessee may repair them, at the lessor's expense Cf *Hahn* v *Roach*. 7 Northampton Co Rep 21.

to procure the material himself and then repair the fences.
He can recover the cost of the material, if he procures it.
Otherwise, he can recover nothing [108] The difference between
the value of the farm without the fences, and its value with the
fences, is not an admissible measure,[109] nor the injury to the
crops, and the inconvenience of farming, caused by the want
of proper fences [110] If the lessor promises to repair the porch
floor, which is known by the lessee to be insecure, the lessor is
not liable in an action of trespass for injuries suffered by the
tenant's wife in consequence of the unrepaired state of the floor
The use of the floor with knowledge of its condition would be
contributory negligence, and any action for the nonperformance
of the lessor's promise would have to be contractual [111]

104. Duties whose breach is not available in replevin.—In distress proceedings, and in the replevin to recover chattels distrained, damages may not be set off for the violation of every
duty to the landlord   The lease stipulated that the tenant
should make certain bulk-windows and doors, and have the
privilege of taking them away, or of leaving them for the lessor
at a valuation to be made in a certain mode   No valuation having been made at the expiration of the lease, the landlord sold
the premises with the improvements and distrained for rent in
arrear   The value of the tenant's interest in the improvements
could not be set off in the replevin brought by him   If the
lessor's act was a tort, the remedy would be trespass [112]

105 Breach an obstacle to recovery of any rent.—When the
contract is entire, the rent being for the enjoyment of the prem-

[104]*Wood* v *Sharpless*, 174 Pa 589,
34 Atl 319, 321, *Jenkins* v *Stone*,
14 Montg Co Law Rep 27
  [109]*Wood* v *Sharpless*, 174 Pa 589,
34 Atl 319, 321
  [110]*Jenkins* v *Stone*, 14 Montg Co.
Law Rep 27
  [111]*Hahn* v *Roach*, 7 Northampton
Co Rep 21   On the omission of the
landlord to repair, the tenant might
repair, and deduct the cost from the
rent
  [112]*Peterson* v *Haight*, 3 Whart.
150 Whether injury from the
negligence with which improvements
contracted for in the lease were made
could be a ground of set-off in replevin, not decided in *Prescott* v.
Otterstatter, 79 Pa 462.

ises, it may be a question whether the covenant of the lessor is
of such importance that the breach of it would destroy any right
of the lessor to recover rent.   A lease of the gristmill and the adjacent premises required the lessor to build an addition to the
dwelling house, to furnish boards for counters and shelves in the
storehouse, to make a husk floor in the mill, and other improvements.   The court held, the lease being in writing, that it was
for the court, and not the jury, to say whether the covenants to
be performed by the lessor were such that, without their performance, there was no obligation to pay the rent or any part of
it, and that, since the entry of the tenant was to precede the acts
to be performed by the landlord, and since the former would enjoy a considerable benefit from the lease despite the nonperformance of the lessor's covenants, it was proper to allow only such
reduction from the rent as the damages amounted to.[113]   A lease
contained the lessor's promise to make certain alterations according to plans decided by X, and the lessee undertook to pay
a specified monthly rent.   The second monthly instalment of
rent being unpaid, the landlord distrained for it.   In the lessee's
replevin, it was held that the lease being on a single consideration for the whole term, although payable in periodic instalments, constituted an entire contract, and, therefore, that the failure of the lessor to make the promised improvements prevented
any recovery of rent, as for use and occupation [114]   Courts are
disinclined to construe a promise to do certain things within a
certain time in consideration of the payment of money, as a con
dition precedent, unless compelled to do so in order to carry out
the express intention of the parties.   No condition is found in
the statement of the lessee to the lessor, at the making of the

[113]*Obermyer* v *Nichols*, 6 Binn
159, 6 Am Dec 439
[114]*Block* v *Dowling*, 7 Pa Dist R
261, citing *McClurg* v *Price*, 59 Pa
420, 98 Am Dec 356, where it is
held that if the lessor refuses to deliver possession of two of the five
stories of the building, the tenant,
though he remains in the occupancy
of the rest of the building, will not
be liable for any rent.

lease, that he would pay one month's rent then, and no more
until repairs were done, and in the reply of the lessor that
"everything should be done before any more rent was due," but
only a promise to make repairs before the next instalment of
rent fell due. The repairs never being made, but the lessee remaining in possession for more than four years, he could not refuse to pay all rent on the allegation that the making of the repairs was a condition precedent to the duty of paying rent. For
the lessor's failure to make repairs, the remedy was an action
for damages, or deduction from the rent.[115] If the lease is
from month to month or quarter to quarter, etc., the continuance
in possession by the tenant after the month or quarter in which
the lessor has broken his covenant will preclude a defense against
the rent for the new months or quarters.[116]

106. **Duty imposed on lessor as trustee.**—A will devising land
to a trustee may impose various duties upon him,—e g, "to
keep the said houses in repair, and rented; to collect the rents,
to pay taxes and for repairs, and to pay and distribute the net
income thereof" between a son and a daughter The duty thus
imposed on the trustee to make repairs is not one towards any
lessee, but towards the *cestui que trust*. The tenant must stand
on the terms of his lease. He cannot, the lease not imposing the
duty to repair on the lessor, insist that the lessor shall make
repairs or suffer an abatement from the rent [117]

107. **Repairs imposed on the tenant**—When repairs or alterations are made by the tenant which the landlord might be
compelled to make for the welfare of the public, the tenant is
entitled to reimbursement for making them although the lessor
has not covenanted to make these repairs or to reimburse him.
The privy of the premises being in a "shocking condition," it

[115]*Bradley* v *Citizens' Trust &*   [117]*Wheeler* v *Crawford,* 86 Pa 327.
Surety Co 7 Pa Super Ct 419
[116]*Cochran* v *Ward,* 8 Del Co Rep.
423

must be cleansed "It would be unjust to hold that a tenant who might occupy the house but a month or year should be compelled to bear the expense of cleaning the privy well, the expense is one which becomes as necessary to be paid at times as the substantial repairs to a roof or other parts of a house Ordinary repairs must be paid by a tenant unless he covenants otherwise; but that which is extraordinary ought to be paid by the landlord, and not the tenant. The jury were informed that the tenant might have complained to the Board of Health, and that body would undoubtedly have removed the nuisance at the cost of the landlord "[118] Under the 4th section of the act of April 11th, 1856, it is made the duty of the building inspectors of the city of Philadelphia, at the request of any two citizens, to examine all walls and their supports, deemed dangerous, and to order their removal, if requisite, at the expense of the owner A fire having destroyed a building and made its walls dangerous, so that their demolition is necessary for the safety of the public, the tenant may tear them down, and compel the lessor to reimburse him.[119] "That the premises," says Hare, P. J , "which he [the tenant] holds are destroyed by fire or devastated by a flood, will not, it is true, entitle him to call on the landlord for aid, or even suspend the rent If he restores the dykes or rebuilds the walls, it must be at his own cost If, however, under these circumstances, a duty is imposed by the law, which, though primarily that of the lessor, is yet obligatory on the tenant, and actually performed by him, the right to indemnity or contribution will be as clear as in the instances already cited,[120] and

[118]*Scheerer* v *Dickson*, 7 Phila 472 Neither ground for the decisions is entirely satisfactory A reference is made to a custom in the county of Philadelphia for the landlord to pay the expense of cleaning the privy

[119]*French* v *Richards*, 6 Phila 547.

[120] A shipowner bound to contribute to a loss occasioned by a jettison of the cargo, the landlord compelled to refund taxes paid by his tenants, a tenant for life or a cotenant entitled to require that the cotenant or remainderman shall bear his due proportion of the charge on the land etc.

such, in effect, is the case now in hand; because the walls being, according to the evidence, in a condition dangerous to all around, were a nuisance requiring instant measures for its abatement. The obligation to do this devolved, in the first instance, upon the tenants, as the persons in possession, and who would have been liable civilly and criminally if injury had ensued " An ordinance of a borough ordering a pavement to be laid at the cost of the occupier, a tenant for a term of less than three years, having laid it, was entitled to reimbursement by the landlord, by deduction from the rent.[121]

108 Negligence, of tenant; injury to tenant.— For the negligence of one tenant, or of a stranger, whereby damage is caused to another tenant, the landlord is not responsible. A leased a farm for dairy purposes to B, reserving the right to lease for oil, gas, and coal, and providing for paying certain damages to B in case such oil, gas, and coal lease were made. The lease of the oil right, being made, operations under it impregnated a field of 30 acres with salt water, so as to unfit it for pasturage B was then compelled to keep his cattle in another field Some one let down the bars separating the two fields, and the cattle entered the 30-acre field, ate the grass and drank the water, and some of them died. The lessor, A, was not liable, in the absence of evidence that he or one acting for him, let down the bars The risks attending the operations under the oil lease were visible, and known to B. A was under no obligation to pay for the negligence of the oil operator, his employees or strangers [122] After A had leased a piece of land to B for the pasture of cattle, he, at the request of a stranger, permitted him to bury a dead horse in the field, but took no part in the burial, gave no directions, and did not know that the horse had had any infectious disease. Several of B s cows subsequently died from the anthrax.

[121]*Hitner* v *Ege*, 23 Pa 305
[122]*Brimner* v *Reed*, 23 Pa Super.
Ct 318.

A was not liable to B. His mere permission to the stranger to bury the horse, followed by the burial, did not make him guilty of trespass. Besides, the death of the cows, A being ignorant of the disease of the horse, was not the natural and probable consequence of the act.[123]

109. Waiver of defects in premises.— The defects may be so waived by the tenant that he cannot take advantage of them, as a defense to the payment of the rent. The heating arrangements being unsatisfactory, if the tenant, nevertheless, remains in possession during the cold season, paying the rent, he has no justification for abandoning the premises during the warm season, when the house is no longer uninhabitable, and he cannot, by abandoning them, escape the duty of paying the rent.[124] The tenant remaining in possession for five months, paying the monthly rent as it fell due, cannot refuse to pay for the remainder of the term, on the ground that the house was, when leased, in bad order, and that the lessor agreed to put it in order, the lessee repairing afterwards "Defendant, by moving into the premises with the written lease in her hand, and remaining there during the whole of the time, paying rent as it fell due, cannot, in my opinion," says Lynch, J, "set up the failure of the landlord to put the house in order as a bar to recovery in this action" for the rent for the rest of the term [125] Having been tenant for a year, and discovered the defective condition of the cellar, the lessee cannot, holding over for the next year, escape paying the rent of that year by leaving before the close, because of this condition [126] Having remained in possession during the continuance of the defect, e g., an overflowing water-closet, the tenant cannot, after it is corrected, remove, and evade the payment of the subsequently accruing rent [127] For

[123]*Fitzwater* v *Fassett,* 199 Pa 442, 49 Atl 310

[124]*Moore* v *Gardiner,* 161 Pa 175, 28 Atl 1018

[125]*Frey* v *Zabinski,* 10 Kulp, 36.

[126]*Hoban* v *Lawall,* 3 Lack Jur 38

[127]*Hess* v. *Weingartner,* 5 Pa Dist R 451.

dampness of the house, continuing through a number of years, the tenant cannot escape liability to pay the rent if he continues in possession, making important changes in the building, tearing down partitions. He should act promptly if he intends to rescind the contract [128]

110. Covenant running with the land — The covenant may run with the land, and cease to be binding on the lessor at his death. A leases a mill and for himself and his heirs, covenants at his own cost to keep the dam, the race, and other reservoirs of water for the supply of the mill, in good repair. He dies and the land passes to his devisees Three fifths of the land are acquired by the lessee. Repairs becoming necessary, he makes them. He cannot maintain an action against the executor of the lessor, because the latter must be understood not to have intended to bind his executor, but to bind only his heirs or his assignees, and his devisees are assignees An action on the covenant would lie against the owners of two thirds of the reversion for their proper share of the expenses of the repair [129]

[128]*Johnson* v. *Mathues,* 4 Del Co Rep. 365.

[129]*Kershaw* v. *Supplee,* 1 Rawle, 131.

CHAPTER VIII.

LESSEE'S COVENANTS AS TO PREMISES.

111. Implied duty to repair — If nothing is said in the lease concerning repairs, the tenant is bound to keep the premises in repair, to "make fair and tenantable repairs, such as putting in windows or doors that have been broken by him, so as to prevent waste and decay of the premises"[1] If the grate which covers the opening into a vault or cellar below the sidewalk breaks, the tenant is bound to repair it.[2] If the tenant puts a new trough on the premises in lieu of the former one, it will belong to his landlord, and not to him, and he cannot recover its value from the landlord, who on the expiration of the lease retains it[3] Since it is the tenant's duty to the landlord to make

[1]*Long* v *Fitzsimmons,* 1 Watts & S 530
[2]*Bears* v *Ambler,* 9 Pa 193 The tenant is liable to the passenger who is injured by the broken grate, and not the lessor, if the grate was sound when the lease was made
[3]*Rawle* v. *Balfour,* 16 W. N. C. 195.

93

repairs, he is, of course, entitled to no compensation for making them,[4] and this is true though he is a tenant in common with his lessor   By becoming tenant as to the undivided interest of the other, he becomes bound to make the repairs at his own expense[5]   It is the tenant's duty to cleanse the cesspool on premises which he has occupied for a number of years, and to keep in order the drains and spouts.[6]   The tenant is not bound, in the absence of a covenant, to make "substantial and lasting repairs, such as putting on new roofing, or restoring premises that have been burnt down or have become ruinous by any other accident," without fault on his part,[7] or to put the premises in better condition than when he got them[8]   Hence, if, despite the exercise of reasonable care, an explosion of a tank in a soap factory occurs, whereby the building is greatly injured, the tenant will not be liable to the landlord to make good the injury, in the absence of an express covenant imposing such liability upon him   The want of reasonable care on the tenant's part must be shown by the landlord in an action of trespass for the injury to the property.[9]   If the tenant chooses to make permanent[10] or other repairs without the consent of the landlord, he cannot require reimbursement from the latter by set-off against the rent, or otherwise.

112 Express covenants — The tenant may, by the covenants of the lease, impose upon himself duties with respect to the premises, which would not, but for these covenants, exist.   The lessee may covenant to "deliver up the premises in good order

[4]*Long* v *Fitzimmons*, 1 Watts & S 530, *Kline* v *Jacobs*, 68 Pa 57

[5]*Laney's Estate*. 14 Pa Co Ct 4

[6]*Johnson* v *Mathues*, 4 Del Co Rep 365, cf *Russell* v *Rush* 2 Pittsb 134

[7]*Long* v *Fitzimmons*, 1 Watts & S 530, *Brolaskey* v *Loth*, 5 Phila 81, *Faile* v *Arbogast*, 180 Pa 409, 36 Atl 923

[8]*Medary* v *Cathers*, 161 Pa. 87, 28 Atl 1012

[9]*Earle* v *Arbogast*, 180 Pa 409, 36 Atl 923

[10]*Kline* v *Jacobs*, 68 Pa 57, *Long* v *Fitzimmons*, 1 Watts & S 530, *Cornell* v *Vanartsdalen*, 4 Pa. 364; *Hitner* v. *Ege*, 23 Pa 305.

and repair."[11]   A sale of the timber on a tract of land was accompanied with a lease of a portable steam sawmill.   When all the timber was manufactured into shingles the lessee covenanted "to deliver said sawmill to said Hoy [the lessor] in reasonably good condition and repair "   This covenant was broken by the nondelivery of the mill in good condition, notwithstanding its destruction by fire   "It has always been considered," says Paxson, J., "that where in a lease there is an express and unconditional agreement to repair and keep in repair, the tenant is bound to do so though the premises be destroyed by fire or other accident."[12]   If the covenant is at the expiration of the lease to surrender the premises in as good order and condition as they were at any time during the term, ordinary decay and inevitable casualty excepted, the tenant assumes no duty to return the property in good condition, if its bad condition is due to a fire which was not caused by his negligence, and which, with proper efforts, could not have been arrested before it destroyed the building.[13]   The lessee's covenant for himself, his executors, administrators, and assigns, to deliver up the premises in good repair, will be subject to the exception (unless such exception is expressly excluded), that the lessee will not be liable for the waste and spoliation of a public enemy, or the destruction wrought by an act of God.[14]

113 Mortgage to secure performance of covenants.—The lessee—a corporation—may execute a mortgage upon all its property, real and personal, to secure the performance of all the covenants of the lease, *viz*, to repair, to supply electric power to

[11]*Hollis* v *Brown*, 159 Pa 539, 28 Atl 300, Cf. *Huston* v *Springer*, 2 Rawle, 97

[12]*Hoy* v *Holt*, 91 Pa 88, 36 Am Rep 659, *Gettysburg Electric R Co* v *Electric Light, Heat & Power Co* 200 Pa 372, 49 Atl 952   The non liability to rebuild after a fire does not imply a nonliability to continue,

after the fire, to pay the accruing rent   *Phillips* v *Epp*, 2 Lack Jur 41

[13]*Kelly* v *Duffy* (Pa) 11 Atl 244.

[14]*Pollard* v *Shaaffer*, 1 Dall 210, 1 Am Dec 239, 1 L ed 104, *Hoy* v *Holt*, 91 Pa 88, 36 Am Rep 659   This covenant binds the assignee of the lease.

the lessor,—a railway company, to pay the net receipts of its business to the satisfaction of certain debts of the lessor; to pay the taxes. For breach of any of these covenants the mortgage, made to a trustee in trust, may be foreclosed in equity.[15]

114　Covenant to put in machinery and not remove it.—The lessee of premises—*e g ,* of a building in which slate is to be milled—may covenant to put in the requisite machinery and not to remove it during the term. The lessee, having put in the machinery, will not be restrained by injunction from removing it during the term, although such removal is a violation of a negative covenant, unless the lessor in his bill avers and proves that the removal would inflict irreparable injury on him, nor even then, unless there is a mutuality of remedy between lessor and lessee. The lease required the lessee to mill all the slate furnished him by the lessor. The lessor was to furnish such slate as a certain quarry would produce, not suitable for roofing slate, school slate, or blackboards. Because no one was named in the lease who was to decide what slate was thus unsuitable, and because it was silent as to the quantities of slate to be delivered by the lessor, and the times of delivery, the lessor's covenant was said to be too vague The lessee's covenant concerning the removal of machinery was said to lack mutuality. The court refused to continue a preliminary injunction [16]

115　Covenant to restore premises to former condition.—The lease may authorize the tenant to make important changes in the buildings, but require him, "at the expiration of said lease, to place the buildings in the same shape and condition as they were" at the commencement of the term, "if required so to do by the lessor." Under this stipulation the tenant could be re-

[15]*Gettysburg Electric R Co* v *Electric Light, Heat & Power Co* 200 Pa 372, 49 Atl 952.　Cf *Reed* v *Harrison*, 196 Pa 337, 46 Atl 415, where the tenant deposited shares of stock in a railroad company as se

curity for the performance of his covenant to restore the premises to the condition in which he received them

[16]*Bangor Excelsior Slate Co* v *Shimer*, 8 Northampton Co Rep 409

quired, after the expiration of the lease, though not notified be
fore, to restore the two buildings by replacing a partition wall
between them, which, in part, he had removed; and the landlord
could refuse to surrender a collateral security for the performance by the tenant of his covenant, until he had restored the partition wall [17]

116 Covenant to deliver the premises in good condition —The
lease often stipulates that at the end of the term the lessee will
deliver the premises to the lessor in as good condition as he received them, ordinary wear and tear excepted. If the tenant
makes changes and repairs for his own accommodation, he is
bound by this covenant to put them in good repair at the expiration of the lease. All he has to do is to return the building in
the condition in which he received it. For breach of this covenant, the measure of damages is not "the value of the injury
to the reversion," but the reasonable cost of the repairs necessary to bring the premises back to the state in which they were
when the tenant received them   The landlord may himself
make the repairs, and if he does so, and also improves the building beyond its original condition, he will be entitled to recover,
not the cost of all the repairs and improvements, but the reasonable cost of such of them as were needed to restore the building
to its former state [18]

117. Covenant to keep in good, tenantable repair.—A covenant by the lessee of a forge "to keep the said forge in good, tenantable repair during the term," in the absence of *indicia* in
the lease, or circumstances, of a contrary intention, contemplates
only the ordinary repairs which shall become necessary by natural wear and decay   This interpretation is corroborated, when
the lease, which is of an undivided half of the premises for two

---

[17] *Reed* v *Harrison*, 106 Pa 337, 46
Atl 415
[18] *Darlington* v *De Wald*, 194 Pa
305, 43 Atl 57   The fact that the
LAND & TEN 7.

landlord made the repairs during the
term, but with the consent of the tenant, does not prevent his recovering
the cost of the repairs

years, makes the distinction between the classes of repairs by
specifying that considerable new work and repairs must be done
to the forge, such as roofing, repairing the forebay and trunks,
the hammer and bellows wheels, so far as may be agreed on by
the lessor and his cotenant, not a party to the lease, and by agreeing to deduct from the rent one half of the cost of these repairs.
Hence, apparently, the tenant is not precluded by his covenant
concerning "good, tenantable repairs" from compelling the lessor
to reimburse him for the cost of rebuilding the forge within the
term [19]

118. Covenant concerning fences.— The tenant agreeing "to
keep the fences in proper repair, the material for which to be
furnished by the lessor," his covenant is not conditional upon
the latter's furnishing the material, in the sense that the tenant
will have an action against the lessor, who neglects to furnish
the material for damages arising from the nonrepair of the
fences. The tenant, if he wishes to avoid the damages from
nonrepair, should procure the material at the cost of the lessor,
and repair the fences.[20]

119. Scope of covenant to repair.—"Repairs do not include
new buildings, but they are a restoration, to a sound state, of
what had gone into partial decay or dilapidation, or bettering of
what had been destroyed in part" By "repairs on the farm,"
in a covenant to pay for them, would not be meant improvements
of the soil arising from liming and fertilizing. "It would be
little less than nonsense to say that a farm was repaired, when

---

[19]*Huston* v *Springer*, 2 Rawle, 97
But the decision is not distinct as to
whether the contribution could be
compelled from the lessor as landlord or as cotenant, the lessee having, by devise from the lessor's cotenant, become cotenant with the
landlord before the repairs were
made

If in consequence of the tenant's
failure to repair according to covenant the landlord is compelled by
the building inspector to put the
building into proper condition, the
landlord may recover from the tenant
the cost of the repairs and the rental
value of the premises for the time
during which they are unoccupied
while the repairs are being made.
Loughlin v *Carey*, 21 Pa Super Ct
477

[20]*Wood* v *Sharpless*, 174 Pa 588,
34 Atl 319, 321.

you intended it had been increased in value by an improved cultivation of the soil."[21] "Repair," says Read, J , "means to restore to its former condition, not to change either the form or the material. If you are to repair a wooden building, you are not to make it brick, stone, or iron, but you are to repair wood with wood " An oil tank with a capacity of 13,000 gallons was built with sides of iron, but with a wooden bottom. A rise in the water of the Ohio river had forced the bottom upwards. In this condition the tank was leased to X for two years in consideration of his agreeing to put it "in perfectly good repair," and leaving it in that condition at the expiration of the lease. The lessee caused the bottom to be repaired at an expense of $1,000, but, the leaking continuing, he caused a new wooden bottom to be put over the old, at an expense of $2,000. The tank continuing to leak, an action was brought by the lessor, after the expiration of the term, for breach of the lessee's agreement. It was held that it was not the duty of the lessee to put an iron bottom on the tank because that would have prevented the leaking. "All that the lessee's agreement would naturally mean, would be, at the outside, to put a new wooden bottom in, and then it would be as good as it ever was, when originally furnished for use by the plaintiffs "[22]

120. Covenant to leave improvements.—A covenant that the

---

[21]*Cornell* v *Vanartsdalen*, 4 Pa 364 The tenant's covenant "to make all necessary improvements and repairs" refutes his contention that, the building being too weak and rickety to permit of the continuance of his business in it, he had a right to abandon it, and escape the payment of future rent *Huber* v *Baum*, 152 Pa 626, 26 Atl 101

[22]*Ardesco Oil Co* v *Richardson*, 63 Pa 162 A statement by the president of the plaintiff company, made when defendant was about to make the repairs, that the cost of them would not exceed from $200 to $500, was evidence to show that the plaintiff did not think of an iron bottom, which would cost several thousand dollars, as within the terms of defendant's promise The president's presence while repairs were being made and his expression of satisfaction with them, were admissible facts "To repair means to put the premises in their former condition."

The right to repair includes the right, on the destruction of a barn by fire, to rebuild it *Maberry* v *Dudley* 2 Pennyp 367.

lessee will leave the premises "in as good condition as the same now is or may be made by improvements, natural wear and decay and casualties by the elements excepted," will require the tenant to let remain, at the expiration of his lease, a new kitchen costing several hundred dollars, and a house in which to cure tobacco, 62 by 24 feet, resting on stone walls, and costing $1,200, which he has erected, notwithstanding that, having been long in possession, he expected to be allowed to remain there during life, but in this hope was disappointed by the death of the owner of the premises, and notwithstanding that he had insured the buildings in his own name, with the knowledge and consent of the lessor. The covenant could be enforced by an injunction.[23]

121. Covenant to make additions.— The tenant may covenant to construct a building The lease, being for one year at a rent of $500, with the option to extend it to five years upon giving notice to the lessor sixty days before the end of the year, required the construction of a building, and stipulated for a credit of $100 on the first year's rent The tenant held over for seven months, but did not elect to extend the lease to five years, and the lessor's interest was then sold by the sheriff Deciding that the construction was intended to be made within the first year, the court held that the lessor could recover the rent that accrued prior to the sheriff's sale, and damages for the nonerection of the building.[24] The lease, being for five years, with the privilege of ten years, provided that the lessee should bring the first two stories of the building out to a certain line No time for doing this being indicated, the tenant would not be in default until the expiration of the five years The declaration by the tenant of a purpose not to perform the covenant would not en

[23]*Carver* v *Gough*, 153 Pa 225, 25 Atl 1124 The lessor, suggests the court, might be willing that the tenant should get the insurance money   in case of destruction by fire of the buildings, and not be willing that he should remove them
[24]*Pollman* v *Morgester*, 99 Pa 611.

title the landlord to require him to begin the work either five months or other time shorter than five years, nor would the declared purpose of the tenant not to perform, provoked by the lessor's insisting on his doing things that the contract did not require him to do, shorten the period of performance, or make him liable at once to action.[25]

122. Covenant; performance made illegal.— If the tenant is prevented from performing his contract to erect a frame building by the enactment of an ordinance of the city prohibiting frame buildings in the locality of the premises, the landlord may rescind and recover possession by ejectment before the expiration of the term, or he may sustain an action upon the covenant for nonperformance. He will be entitled to damages for nonperformance, or for omission to build a brick house in lieu of a frame, if the lessee refuses to surrender the possession. If both ejectment and an action on the covenant are brought at the same time, the court, after execution of the judgment in one will prevent the execution of the judgment in the other [26]

123. Covenant to use the premises properly.— There is an implied promise in every lease, arising out of the relation of landlord and tenant, to use the premises in an ordinary and proper manner.[27] This duty may be expressly covenanted for The lessee of a farm, e. g., may agree to "take all proper care of said premises, the same as a careful and prudent farmer should of his own property, and return the same at the end of said lease in as good condition as the same is received, except natural wear and unavoidable accidents" He may agree to leave as many acres of the farm seeded down at the end of the term as there were at the date of the lease, and to work it as a careful and prudent farmer. These covenants would be broken by permitting Canada thistles to grow and go to seed upon the farm, or by destroying the meadow by pasturing sheep upon it, or

---

[25]*Palethorp* v *Bergner,* 52 Pa 149   [27]*Long* v *Fitzimmons,* 1 Watts &
[26]*Rooks* v *Seaton,* 1 Phila 106   S 530

by not leaving as much ground seeded down as the tenant agreed
to leave.[28] The tenant covenants to "cultivate and farm said
land in a workmanlike manner He shall put out all the crops
in good season and in proper order, of such kind of grain and
in such fields" as the lessor shall designate In the fall before
the commencement of his lease, he, with the permission of the
lessor, plows a field and spreads it with lime for corn to be
planted in, in the spring, the lessor purchasing the lime. In an
action by the tenant against the lessor for compensation for his
labor in thus working the field, it was proper to allow the defendant to prove that good husbandry and custom made it
proper for the tenant to prepare the ground for the spring crop
the preceding fall or winter, whenever he could do so, and that
he should spread all the lime or other fertilizers which the landlord would furnish for that purpose, without any stipulation to
that effect in the lease, and without entitling him to charge the
landlord therefor.[29]

124. Waste by tenant — The covenant of the tenant not to
remove machinery will be enforced by an injunction if irreparable injury will result to the lessor from the removal [30] The
assignee of a lease for a farm tract, the premises being designed
for playing golf and other games, would have no right to grant
a license to construct a single railroad track across a portion
of the land, the making of which would require certain cuttings
and fillings which would inconvenience other tenants of the
lessor and seriously damage and interfere with the sale of the

---

[28]*McBride* **v** *Daniels*, 92 Pa 332.
The damages could be set off against
a claim of the tenant against the
landlord

The lessee promised to leave the
premises in as good condition as he
found them This would include all
the duties of good husbandry, and
would be broken by putting wheat
and rye in an undue area of the land,
at the expense of timothy and other
grasses But for a breach of this
covenant no action can be brought
until the close of the term *Hoskinson* v *Bradford,* 1 Pittsb 165

[29]*Aughinbaugh* v *Coppenheffer,* 55
Pa 347

[30]*Bangor Excelsior Slate Co* v
Shimer, 8 Northampton Co. Rep.
409.

property The assignee of the lease would be enjoined from granting the license by injunction [31]

125. Covenant respecting hay, corn, etc.— The lease may contain a stipulation that all the hay, straw, and corn fodder shall be consumed upon the premises, except that the tenant shall have the right to remove as much as he brings upon the premises, and that, for the violation of this agreement, the tenant "shall forfeit and pay the sum of $15 for every ton of hay, straw, or corn fodder so sold or removed, as liquidated damages, fairly ascertained and determined, for breach of the contract in this particular." Notwithstanding this provision, if it appears that the only value to the farm of a ton of good hay is from $2 to $3, the tenant, who in violation of his covenant sells 25 tons of hay, will be liable, not for $15 per ton, but for from $2 to $3.[32]

---

[31] *Christ Church* v *Bala Golf Club,* 10 Pa Dist R 666 The club had no authority in its charter to grant the license, or make a sublease for the purpose

[32] *Sharpless* v. *Murphy,* 7 Del. Co Rep. 22. The value of the hay was $14 to $15 per ton, of straw not more than $8, and of corn fodder not more than $3 to $4 These values were not allowed, but only that of the manure which would have been made from them had they been consumed on the place.

CHAPTER IX.

RELATIONS OF LESSEES OF DIFFERENT PARTS OF BUILDING.

126. Right to stairway.— The different stories of a house may be let to different tenants, and the lease to the tenant of each of the upper stories may reserve to the party on the other "the privilege of front and back stairs, each party to take turns in keeping said stairs clean " Under such a lease, in the absence of a custom in the city or neighborhood, the tenant of the second floor has no right to keep the front door leading to the stairway locked during the daytime, the result being that the tenant of the third floor, and the members of his family, would have to unlock it when they wished to enter, and also to descend the two flights of stairs and unlock it in order to admit visitors As to the front door, hall, and first flight of stairs, the tenants of the second and third stories stand upon an equality, having a common right of way Each must exercise this right reasonably, he must refrain from unreasonable or unnecessary obstruction of their use. The court may defend the right of the tenant of the third floor by enjoining the tenant of the second floor from keeping locked the front door between the hours of half-past six in the morning and half-past eight in the evening [1]

[1] *Kleeman* v. *Kemmerer*, 3 Kulp, 481. The fact that the front door is supplied with separate bells, communicating with each suite of rooms, and that each tenant is furnished with keys to the locks, does not indicate that any tenant is at liberty to keep the door locked whenever he chooses, despite the dissent of the other As to duty of landlord to re-

104

127. Use of pavement.—When different stories or rooms are let to different tenants, he who rents the first story has no more ownership of the sidewalk than the occupant of the upper stories or rooms   None has more than a right to an uninterrupted passage way in common with the public. The tenant of the first floor may object to obstructions to convenient access to the street door; but the occupant of the first floor being a merchant tailor, and that of the second, a photographer, the latter may station a show-case by the side of the front door for the exhibition of his pictures, if it does not obstruct the passage in or out of the building, and is not otherwise injurious or inconvenient to anyone.[2]

128. Negligent use of upper story.—The tenant of an upper story is bound to the use of due care so as to avoid injury to the occupants of the lower story. He is bound, *e. g.,* to take proper precautions against the water cock being left open over night, with the effect that the water runs on and through the floor, and descends on goods in the lower stories, injuring them. He is liable for injury arising from such an act, whether done by himself, or his servants, or one who visits his premises and makes use of the water cock with his implied or express authority.[3]

129. Right to use entrance for show-cases.—The lease of the second, third, and fourth stories of a building, together with "the north side of the entrance" for the purpose of exhibiting a show-case, with the appurtenances thereto belonging, being made to A, a lease of the first story of the building was subsequently

pair the stairway, *vide Lewin* v *Pauli*, 19 Pa Super Ct 447

[2]*Cunningham* v *Entrekin*, 3 Pa Dist R. 291   An injunction at the suit of the tenant of the first floor was refused   He had once expressed approval of the presence of the case at the door   The tenant of the second floor could put an awning over the door, if it was not an inconvenience to anyone, but was a convenience to people entering the building, as well as a necessary protection of the defendant's pictures   Cf *Brown* v *Weaver*, 17 W N C 230

[3]*Killion* v *Power*, 51 Pa. 429, 91 Am Dec 127.

made to B   This story had bow windows and a large front, on two streets. B placed a wooden sign perpendicular to the wall extending out into the street to a line beyond the show-case, and reaching above the top of it, obstructing the view of the whole of it and making useless one side of it   This was a violation of the right of A, whose continuance might be enjoined. The second lessee took the lease subject to the anterior right of the first lessee   The lessor was precluded from depriving the first lessee of the use of the space described in the lease for show-cases, and from rendering this use of no avail by obstruction of the view of the case, and the second lessee was subject to the same disability.[4]

130 Right to carry on business noxious to tenants of other parts — The tenant of one part of a building, *e. g ,* for the manufacture of boots and shoes, has a right not to be injured by the carrying on, by the tenant of another part of it, of a noxious business, *e. g.,* the grinding of marble, coal, etc., the dust and effluvia created by which pervade the rest of the building   This right will be protected by an injunction.[5]

[4]*Snyder* v *Hersberg,* 11 Phila. 200
As to putting up signs, *vide Scott* v
Fox Optical Co 38 Pittsb L J 368,
Hele v. *Stewart,* 19 W. N. C. 129.

[5]*Richardson* **v. Oberholtzer,** 2 W.
N. C. 332.

CHAPTER X.

RENT.

131 For land and personalty — Land and personalty upon it, *e g*, cattle and utensils, may be let together for a given rent "The ordinary definition of rent as a profit issuing yearly out of lands and tenements corporeal is defective in overlooking some of the cases that belong to the class; as, where a furnished house or a stocked farm is leased, which are common cases . In such cases the personal property is really a part of the consideration of the rent, and it is only by a fictitious accommodation of the case to the defective definition, that it can be said that the rent issues exclusively out of the land.[1] Rent can be reserved in a grant of a right of way; or of a right to take water from the lessor's land [2] A granted to a railroad company a perpetual right to take water from a spring by means of a pipe. The pipe lay across the land of B. A subse-

---

[1] *Mickle* v *Miles*, 31 Pa 20, *Vetter's Appeal*, 99 Pa 52 In the former of these cases distress for the entire rent was allowed In *Com* v *Contner*, 18 Pa 439, the right to the landlord's preference with respect to proceeds of an execution was conceded only with respect to so much of the gross rent as represented the realty

[2] *Williams* v. *Ladew*, 171 Pa. 369, 33 Atl. 329.

107

quently granted to B the right to attach a pipe on his own land, to the railroad company's pi] 2, for a compensation of $5 a year for each house that he might thus supply with water   This compensation, says Gordon, J , is "a profit issuing yearly out of lands; a rent *redilus* to the landlord for their annual use."[3]

132. Repayment, in instalments, of a loan — In addition to rent proper, as consideration for the use and occupation of the premises, the lease may provide for a loan of money to the lessee, and for the repayment of this loan by instalments, which it terms rent. A lease, *e g.,* of veins of coal, at a rental of 25 cents per ton for all coal mined except chestnut coal, for which the rent was to be 15 cents per ton, provided for a loan to the lessee of $12,000 to be repaid with interest "by an additional rent" of 10 cents per ton on all coal taken out.   This "additional rent," though so called, was not rent but simply a repayment of a loan of money "True," says Woodward, Ch J , "it is called rent in the lease, but you do not alter the essential nature of a thing by misnaming it   In Philadelphia it is common for ground-rent landlords to advance improvement funds to their tenants, which are usually secured by mortgage, and repaid like any other debt. But such payments are never called rent. No two things are more easily distinguished. Repayments of borrowed money cannot be that annual profit issuing out of lands and tenements, which rent is, and no false nomenclature can make them identical."[4]

133 Assessments on property.—A covenant of the lessee that he will pay all assessments upon the property will oblige him to pay assessments for grading and paving,[5] or for paving and curbing[6] streets, made by the municipality during the term, and,

[3]*Manderbach* v *Bethany Orphans'*   [5]*Miller* v *Lankard,* 1 Pittsb 75.
Home, 109 Pa 231, 2 Atl 422   The   [6]*Griffin* v *Phœnix Pottery Co* 14
grantee of the reversion became en- W. N. C. 266.
titled to the rent
[4]*Miners' Bank* v. *Heilner,* 47 Pa
452.

if the lessor pays them, he may recover them from the lessee. A covenant to pay taxes only will not embrace such assessments. A covenant, *e. g.,* to pay all the taxes that may be levied and assessed upon the premises, except such tax as may be assessed to pay city or county railroad subscriptions, will not impose on the tenant the duty of paying assessments for grading and paving the streets on which the premises abut.[7] A lessee for fifteen years of coal, who has covenanted to pay "all and every the United States, state, and local taxes, duties, and imposts on the coal mined, the mining improvements of every kind, and the surface and coal land itself," is not bound to pay assessments for a sewer.[8]

134. Taxes—Taxes are included in "all charges and assessments whatsoever," and if the lessee covenants to pay the named rent "clear" of such charges and assessments, he must pay the rent and the taxes that are assessed on the premises during his term, and the assignee of the term must pay such as are assessed during his ownership of it.[9] When the lessees undertake to pay all "taxes, charges, and assessments whatsoever" imposed by the United States, the state, the county, township, or school district, "as well on their improvements as on the coal mined" during the term, and they build a coal breaker, and make other improvements which increase the assessable value of the land, they are bound to pay such part of the taxes as represents the increase of value of the premises, caused by their improvements[10] If, before a lease or a renewal of it is accepted by the lessee, a law is passed enacting a new and special tax, the lessee is bound to pay one half of a tax assessed in pursuance of the law during his term, he having covenanted to pay one half the

[7]*Longmore* v *Tiernan,* 3 Pittsb 62 *Petroleum Co* v *Stanton Oil Co* 23
[8]*Pettibone* v *Smith,* 150 Pa. 118, Pa Co Ct 153
17 L R A. 423, 24 Atl 693   [10]*Hoeckscher* v *Sheafer,* 17 W N
[9]*Sandwith* v *De Silver,* 1 Browne C 323, Cf *Delaware, L & W R Co*
(Pa) 221   The duty of the lessee v *Sanderson,* 109 Pa. 583, 58 Am
to pay the tax passes to the assignee Rep 743, 1 Atl. 394.
of the lease. *Oil Creek & C Branch*

taxes assessed or to be assessed,[11] but a covenant to pay "all
taxes . . . that may be assessed" did not embrace a bounty
tax, such a tax being unknown when the lease was made,
being often greater than the rental value of the land, and the
benefit of it accruing to the owner of the land.[12] When the
lessee agreed, in addition to the rent, to "pay city and state
taxes" assessed during the term, and subsequently, the lessor, a
charitable society, with the assent of the lessee to the declared
object of "adding the sum paid in taxes to their income for
charitable expenditures," obtained an act of assembly exempting
its property from taxation,—it was held that the lessee was
bound to pay the taxes that would have been assessed, but for
the exempting statute, to the lessor.[13] The lessee covenanting to
pay the taxes assessed within his term, he must pay a tax assessed within a month of the close of the term, though the tax be
for the year beginning with the assessment.[14]

135. Tenants' statutory liability for taxes.—The 6th section
of the act of April 3, 1804,[15] enacts that every tenant in possession of lands shall be liable to pay all the taxes which, during
his possession, may become due and payable, and that, having so
paid such taxes or any part of them, he may recover them from
the landlord, or defalcate them in the payment of the rent due
the landlord, unless the contract between them imposes the
duty of payment upon the tenant. If the leasehold itself should
be the subject of taxation, the lessee could not, on paying a tax
assessed on it, compel the lessor to reimburse him.[16] If the
lessor's fee is assessed, and the interest of the lessee in improvements put by him on the premises—a state quarry—is separately
assessed, and the lessee pays the tax assessed against his interest,

[11]*Brown* v *Wagner,* 1 Pearson
(Pa) 254.

[12]*Focht's Estate,* 2 Woodw Dec.
269

[13]*German Society* v. *Philadelphia,*
9 Phila 245.

[14]*Haynes* v. *Synnott,* 160 Pa 180,
28 Atl 832

[15] 1 Pepper & L. 2636, 4 Sm L 201.

[16] Cf *Franciscus* v. *Reigart,* 4
Watts, 98.

he cannot compel the lessor to refund the sum paid [17] Taxes improperly assessed against the landlord the tenant may not pay, with hope of obtaining reimbursement [18]

136 Road taxes.— The 8th section of the act of April 6, 1802,[19] enacts that the tenant or tenants or other persons residing on lands owned by persons not residing in the township, his, her, or their goods, shall be liable to be levied on for the payment of road taxes; and if any tenant or tenants shall be in possession under a lease for one or more years, when the tax is assessed or levied, and shall pay the tax, they may deduct the tax thus paid out of the rent due, or recover it by action from the lessor.

137. Interest on rent.— Rent payable at a fixed time, if not paid at that time, carries interest unless from the conduct of the landlord it might be inferred that he meant not to insist on interest, or unless he acted in an oppressive manner by demanding more than was due, the tenant being willing to pay the proper sum, or unless there are other circumstances making the charge of interest improper.[20] If the tenant, having a set-off against the rent, tenders the difference between the rent and the set-off to the landlord, which the latter refuses to receive except as payment on account, the tenant may refuse to pay on these terms; and if, sued for the rent, he establishes the set-off, he will not be liable for interest [21]

[17]*Flory* v *Heller*, 1 Monaghan (Pa) 478

[18]*Kitchen* v *Smith*, 101 Pa 452

[19] 1 Pepper & L 2636; 3 Sm L 512

[20]*Obermyer* v *Nichols*, 6 Binn 159, 6 Am Dec 439 The trial court left the question to the jury, and, thought Tilghman, Ch J , "properly " Interest was allowed as a matter of course in *M'Clure* v *M'Clure*, 1 Grant Cas 222, *Spackman's Appeal*, 16 W N C 79, *Lane* v *Nelson*, 167 Pa. 602, 31 Atl 864 Cf *Buck* v *Fisher*, 4 Whart 516, *Naglee* v *Ingersoll*, 7 Pa. 185, *Chew's Estate*, 4 Phila 186, *Buchanan* v *Montgomery*, 2 Yeates, 72, *Society* v *Swindell*, 2 W N C 560, *McQuesney* v *Hiester*, 33 Pa 435, *Re Makinson*, 8 Phila 381, *Bantleon* v *Smith*, 2 Binn 146, 4 Am Dec 430, *Doughe ty's Estate*, 9 Watts & S 189, 42 Am Dec 326, *Ter Hoven* v *Kerns* 2 Pa St 96, *Pancoast's Appeal*, 8 Watts & S 381

[21]*Nickols* v *Jones*, 166 Pa 599, 31 Atl 329

138. When rent is payable.— The lease usually prescribes the time at which rent is to be paid   Though the lease is for one or more years, it may require payments quarterly, monthly, weekly, or at any other interval.   If the lease is for one year[22] or more, and nothing is said as to the time for paying the rent, it is payable at the end of the year, whether it be payable in money,[23] or in products of the ground [24]   The rent is payable at any moment after midnight of the last day of the term or subdivision of the term for which the rent is payable   If that day is Sunday, the rent will be payable on Monday following [25]   A demise, *e. g ,* being made for one year, on May 1, 1842, the last quarter's rent is due on May 1, 1843,[26] and can be sued for on that day.[27]   It may be made, by the term of the lease, payable in advance for the year, the quarter, the month, the week, and that the rent is to be paid in advance may appear from the lease, the circumstances, and the testimony, though the lease does not expressly state that it is to be so paid.   A lease for four years, the term under which was to commence September 15, was made September 12.   The first month's rent was paid when the lease was executed.   The second payment of a month's rent was made December 2.   The lease provided that the lessee should pay for the first two years a yearly rent of $800, and for the last two a yearly rent of $1,000, "in monthly payments of $66.67 and $83 33 respectively, commencing the first day of November"   It was concluded that the monthly rent was payable at the beginning of each month [28]   The lease may provide that on

[22]*Menough's Appeal,* 5 Watts & S 432, *Boyd* v *McCombs,* 4 Pa 146, *Sharpless's Estate,* 8 Lanc Bar, 125
[23]*Menough's Appeal,* 5 Watts & S 432
[24]*Boyd* v *McCombs,* 4 Pa 146, *King* v *Bosserman,* 13 Pa Super Ct 480
[25]*Marys* v *Anderson,* 24 Pa 272, *Gregg* v *Krebs,* 5 Pa Dist R 779

[26]*Prentiss* v *Kingsley,* 10 Pa 120 Cf *Negley* v *Morgan,* 46 Pa 281
[27]*Donaldson* v *Smith,* 1 Ashm (Pa) 197 Cf *Duffy* v *Ogden,* 64 Pa 240
[28]*Ellis* v *Rice,* 195 Pa 42, 45 Atl 655 Rent originally payable in advance may be made payable at the end of the period *Wilgus* v *Whitehead,* 89 Pa. 131.

the happening of various events,—*e. g.,* the removal or attempted removal of goods from the premises,[29] the lessee's removal before the end of the term,[30] the lessee's becoming embarrassed, or making an assignment for the benefit of creditors,[31] the lessee's failure to pay, for five days after it becomes due, any monthly instalment,[32]—the whole rent shall become payable Though the lease is made June 27, 1848, for five years from the first day of April, 1848, it may be orally shown that possession was taken of the premises on April 1, 1848, and that the rent being payable semiannually in advance one half year's rent was payable on April 1, 1848.[33]

139. Rent contingently payable — The lessor may suspend the duty of the lessee to pay rent upon the success of the former in defending his title to the land against an adverse claimant.[34] The rent becomes due at the intervals specified. Nothing is due between. A having assigned the lease to B in the midst of a quarter, and B paying the rent from the time of the assignment, A would remain liable for so much of the rent of the quarter as the assignee did not pay, but it would not be correct for the lessor's declaration to describe the rent as due on the day on which the assignment was made [35]

140 Commuting rent; assignment for creditors.—If, in order to adapt the premises to the special needs of B, to whom a lease is to be made, A, the owner, expends much money, and B agrees,

---

[29]*Excelsior Shirt Co v Miller,* 4 Lack Legal News 332

[30]*Goodwin v Sharkey,* 80 Pa 149, *Yanko v Leizerouitz,* 8 Del Co Rep 107. 18 Lanc. L Rev 1, *McAnniny v Miller,* 19 Pa Super Ct 406

[31]*Platt v Johnson,* 168 Pa 47, 47 Am St Rep 877, 31 Atl 935, cf *Ouens v Shovlin,* 116 Pa 371, 9 Atl 484

[32]*Teufel v Rouan,* 179 Pa 408, 36 Atl 224, *Halluood Cash Register Co v Hefferman,* 12 Pa Dist R 515 The landlord does not waive this provision by accepting payment of the overdue instalments Cf *Merrill v Trimmer,* 2 Pa Co Ct 49

[33]*Com ex rel Irwin v Contner,* 21 Pa 266

[34]*Sassaman v Feagly,* 4 Watts, 268

[35]*Ghegan v Young,* 23 Pa 18 The affidavit of defense not denying that the rent then became due, two of the four judges of the supreme court favored the affirmance of the judgment for the lessor.

in the lease, to pay a rent which in ten years, the term, will repay nine tenths of the outlay, A may, B assigning subsequently for creditors, claim from the assigned estate the present worth of the instalments of rent which are to accrue under the lease, less the present worth of the rental which, for the remainder of the term, he will be able to get from another tenant.[36]

[36]*Re Reading Iron Works,* 150 **Pa.** 369, 24 Atl. 617.

CHAPTER XI.

RENT PAYABLE IN KIND.

141. Rent in crops — The rent reserved may be, instead of money, a share of the produce of the land, expressed in some ratio; e g , one half[1] or one third[2] or two fifths of spring grain and one third of fall grain,[3] or some definite number of bushels of grain may be reserved, or such a number, as, at a certain price per bushel, will produce a certain sum of money,—e g., lease of land at 12s. and 6d per acre, payable in wheat at 4s., rye at 3s and corn at 2s. and 6d per bushel[4] The lease being of a grist-mill, the rent reserved may be two thirds,[5] or any other fraction, of the tolls; that is, of the share of the grain taken by the lessee from his customer as compensation for the service of grinding. If the rent reserved is one half of the grain, the lessor is entitled only to one half of the straw, the other half being the tenant's, of which he may dispose as of any other property unless the lease requires its use on the premises[6] If the lease requires the tenant to cut the grain, thresh it, clean it, and deliver one third of it to the landlord, the other two thirds of the

---

[1]*Borrell* v *Dewart,* 37 Pa 134, *Hoover* v *Hoover,* 10 Pa Co. Ct 563, *Rank* v *Rank,* 5 Pa 211, *Lehr* v *Taylor,* 90 Pa. 381

[2]*Price* v. *Wright,* 4 Lanc Bar 32, *Iddings* v *Nagle,* 2 Watts & S 22. Evidence of a custom to the contrary will not be heard

[3]*Borie* v *Crissman,* 82 Pa. 125

[4]*Meason* v *Philips,* Addison (Pa.) 346

[5]*Long* v *Fitzimmons,* 1 Watts & S 530, *Fry* v *Jones,* 2 Rawle, 11

[6]*Rank* v *Rank,* 5 Pa 211 If the grain is corn, the tenant is entitled to one half of the fodder *Kauffman* v *Schaeffer,* 2 Walk (Pa) 331

115

grain, and all the straw, belong to the tenant,[7] as it does when the rent reserved is one half or other fraction of the grain "in the bushel "[8]

142 Ownership of the grain.— When the rent reserved in a lease is a share of the grain or other products of the farm, such grain and products, while growing, belong wholly to the tenant The landlord has "no right whatever to an interest in the grain sold by" the tenant "and growing upon the land "[9] The tenant may sell the whole of it, and a good title will pass to his vendee, and this vendee, though it be the lessor himself, or the purchaser of his reversion, or the agent of such purchaser, will be compellable to pay the price.[10] Says Rogers, J.. "Then as to the title of a tenant to the grain in the ground, where by the terms of the lease the landlord is entitled to a share of it, deliverable in the bushel. The better opinion seems to be that it is the property of the tenant, and until the grain is severed and delivered to the landlord, he has no interest in the thing itself. If he [the tenant] sells it, it goes to his vendee, and the landlord cannot pursue it in his hands. The only remedy of the landlord is by distress [or action on the promise] as in the case of money rent." Nor can any part of the crop become the lessor's, until a share is separated for him from the remainder and is appropriated to him by the tenant. Doubtless this separation and appropriation might take place while the crop is still standing in the grounds; but ordinarily they do not occur until it has been cut down, after maturity. Until this division and appropria-

[7] *Iddings* v. *Nagle*, 2 Watts & S. 496, 24 Am Dec 339 Hence, a 22

[8] *Iddings* v *Nagle*, 2 Watts & S 22, *Burns* v *Cooper*, 31 Pa 426, *Borrell* v *Deuart*, 37 Pa 134, *Hoover* v *Hoover*, 10 Pa Co Ct 563, *Ream* v *Harnish*, 45 Pa 376, *Rinehart* v. *Oluine*, 5 Watts & S 157

[9] *Johnston* v. *Smith*, 3 Penr. & W

fieii facias levied on the lessoi's interest in growing grain on the tenant's premises passes nothing as against a subsequent purchaser of the reversion *Long* v *Seavers*, 103 Pa 517

[10] *Rinehart* v *Oluine*, 5 Watts & S. 157; *Long* v *Seavers*, 103 Pa 517.

tion, the landlord owns no part of the crop. A creditor of the lessor who levies on and sells any part of it, and the vendee, will be guilty of trespass [11] If the lessee sells all the crop before division the landlord can recover none of it from the vendee, in replevin.[12] Though a day has been appointed by the tenant and landlord for the making of the division, e g., of hay, but, the day arriving, the division is not made, the landlord has no right to take the hay. If he does, and he refuses to give it up, the tenant may retake all of it without being a trespasser The landlord's only remedy, says Coulter, J., is "by an action on the contract of lease."[13] And if the landlord takes any part of the grain without a previous division by the tenant, the latter may recover the full value of all taken.[14] But, after the tenant divides the grain in his barn, designating the landlord's share in the presence of the landlord's son and agent, and takes his own share away, the property in the other share passes to the landlord, though he does not take possession of it. If any person, whether the tenant or another, should subsequently take it away without his consent, he can recover it in replevin.[15]

[11]Ream v Harnish, 45 Pa 376 Cf McCormick v Skiles, 163 Pa 590, 30 Atl 195, where it is held that a cropper who is to receive, as compensation, a share of tobacco cultivated by him on premises in the possession of the owner acquires no property in any part of the tobacco until a division is made Johnston v Smith, 3 Penr & W 496, 24 Am Dec 339 Yet, in Stafford v Ames, 9 Pa 343, the owner having cut the crop and refused to deliver any part of it to the cropper, it was held that the latter had the right of immediate possession and could maintain trover against the former

[12]Price v Wright, 4 Lanc Bar, 32

[13]Briggs v Thompson, 9 Pa 338 In Rank v Rank, 5 Pa 211, it was assumed that the landlord and tenant were tenants in common of the crop and for this reason it was intimated that trover by the tenant against the landlord for taking all the crop would not lie Trover was unsuccessfully brought by the landlord against the tenant for all the straw, in Iddings v Nagle, 2 Watts & S 22

[14]Rank v Rank, 5 Pa 211 If after suit is brought the landlord allows the tenant to take the grain the tenant may recover the value of the grain at the time of taking, less the depreciated value of the grain when it was given back Kauffman v Schaeffer, 2 Walk (Pa) 331. Albright, P J, instructed the jury that if the landlord had asked for a division, and it was improperly refused, he would have a right to take his proper share.

[15]Burns v Cooper, 31 Pa 426.

143 Landlord's remedies.— If the tenant fails to deliver to the landlord his share he may distrain for it,[16] or bring an action of account-render,[17] or an action of assumpsit on the covenant in the lease [18] The action would be, not replevin, nor trespass, nor trover and conversion, presupposing an ownership of the grain, but assumpsit or some other action founded on the breach of contract. If the tenant has sold the landlord's share, he will be obliged to account for the price, though he may have failed to collect it, on account of the insolvency of the buyer, inasmuch as he has sold it without right. If the tenant of a mill has agreed to deliver to the landlord two thirds of the tolls he receives, and he agrees with some customers to grind for cash instead of tolls, he must account for two thirds of this cash Should he fail to collect the money, because of his negligently spoiling the flour made out of the grain of the customer, he will be bound, nevertheless, to pay two thirds of the contract price of the grinding to the lessor [19] If the rent agreed on is so many bushels of wheat, rye, and corn at designated prices per bushel as would produce a given sum of money, this number of bushels must be delivered, notwithstanding the larger price per bushel prevailing when the rent is due, and in an action of covenant the value of these bushels at the time when they should have been delivered must be allowed, with interest from that time.[20] If the declaration of the lessor alleges that the rent was $60, there can be no recovery on evidence showing that the rent was a share of crops.[21]

[16]*Fry v Jones,* 2 Rawle, 11, *Rinehart v Ohune,* 5 Watts & S 157.

[17]*Long v. Fitzimmons,* 1 Watts & S 530

[18]*Briggs v Thompson,* 9 Pa 338. Formerly covenant, when the lease was sealed *Meason v Philips,* Addison (Pa.) 346 Cf *Lehr v Taylor,* 90 Pa 381.

[19]*Long v Fitzimmons,* 1 Watts & S 530.

[20]*Meason v Philips,* Addison (Pa) 346

[21]*Conable v Van Housen,* 11 Pa. Super Ct 497 Even if the declaration alleged that the rent was payable in kind, which the tenant had refused to deliver, there could be no recovery, without proof of the value of the landlord's share of the crops.

144-5. Exceptional right of landlord.—The lease, and the custom of the county where the land is situated, may make a crop wholly the landlord's. It may, *e. g.,* be a custom that the tenant on entering in the spring is to become owner of the away-going crop, and that when he leaves the premises at the expiration of the term, the fall crop sown by him is to become wholly the landlord's.[22] The lease may stipulate that the right of possession of the grain grown, whether while it is in the fields or after it is in the barn, shall be in the lessor until division and delivery by the landlord to the tenant of the share of the latter. Under such a lease the tenant moving off at the end of his term, April 1, and the landlord taking possession of the away-going crop which ripens the following summer, the former could not maintain trover for his share, the possession being in the landlord. The reason of the landlord's refusal to give to the tenant his share of the away-going crop being the tenant's having taken an undue share of the corn crop which, while in possession of the term, he had cut, the value of the landlord's share of the corn thus improperly kept would be properly deducted, even if trover lay, from the value of the tenant's share of the winter crop.[23]

[22]*Loose* v *Scharff*, 6 Pa. Super. Ct.   [23]*Lehr* v. *Taylor*, 90 Pa. 381. 153.

CHAPTER XII.

ACTIONS FOR RENT.

120

146. Account render — As a general rule, account render will not lie for rent reserved in a lease, but this must be understood of a certain rent, and not where the amount reserved is uncertain, and, consequently, where an account on oath may be necessary to ascertain the amount received. The rent for a mill being two thirds of all the tolls received during the term, an action of account render was proper.[1]

147. Assumpsit not local action — The action for rent is not local necessarily. The fact that the land lies, *e. g*, in New Jersey,[2] or in New York,[3] or in Massachusetts,[4] or in Delaware,[5] will not make it impossible to sue for rent in Pennsylvania, and assumpsit[6] and debt[7] have been used. It is said in *Henwood* v. *Cheeseman*[8] that the suit by the lessor himself against the lessee will always be transitory, because it will be upon the contract. But if the lessor assigns the reversion, and the assignee sues in debt at common law, the action, being founded only on privity of estate, is local. If he sues in covenant, by virtue of the statute, 32 Hen. viii. chap. 34, which transfers the privity of contract from the assignor to the assignee, the action will be transitory. The lessee being dead, rent may be claimed in the distribution of his estate.[9]

[1]*Long* v *Fitzimmons*, 1 Watts & S 530

[2]*Henwood* v *Cheeseman*, 3 Serg & R 500

[6]*Pratt* v *Richards Jewelry Co* 69 Pa 53, *Philadelphia Fire Extinguisher Co* v. *Brainerd*, 2 W N C. 473

[4]*Hoynes* v *Synott*, 160 Pa. 180, 28 Atl. 832

[5]*Kline* v *Jacobs*, 68 Pa 57.

[8]*Henwood* v *Cheeseman*, 3 Serg & R 500

[7]*Pratt* v. *Richards Jewelry Co.* 69 Pa 53 55 Atl 539

[8]3 Serg & R 500

[9]*Thompson's Estate*, 205 Pa 553,

148. Assumpsit for use and occupation —It was said by Dun-can, J., in 1823, in *M'Gunnagle* v. *Thornton*,[10] that assumpsit, for use and occupation "has lately been frequently used, and is a very convenient action;" and in that case and several others it was used to compel the payment of rent reserved in a lease for a definite term, specifying the rent [11] An assignee for the bene-fit of creditors, who paid rent for a quarter following the as-signment, was held in one case to have become by that and other acts a tenant for the remainder of the term, and to be liable in assumpsit for the rent, according to the contract, at the end of the next quarter, though he did not retain possession during that quarter Holding that his liability arose from privity of con-tract, and not as assignee of the term, the court said that he could not annul the contract for the running year at any time that suited him, he was bound till the end of the year, if the lessor insisted on it, he, in legal contemplation, used and occupied the premises, though he was not in possession.[12] A tenant for one year, who leaves the premises in the midst of the year, without the acceptance of a surrender by the landlord, is liable in as-sumpsit for use and occupation for the rent for the remainder of the year, less such rent as may be obtained from some other oc-cupant.[13] B accepted from A a lease of a house for one year from April 1st There was already a tenant in the house, who agreed with the lessee, before the lease was made, to vacate the premises on May 1st. B, subsequently changing his mind, never occupied the house, and, four months after the lease was made, notified the lessor He was liable in assumpsit for use and occupation for the rent of the year. Though no actual oc-

---

[10]10 Serg & R 251.

[11]*Grant* v *Gill*, 2 Whart 42, *Mar-seilles* v *Kerr*, 6 Whart 500, *Mait-land* v *Wilcox*, 17 Pa. 231.

[12]*Grant* v *Gill*, 2 Whart 42

[13]*Marseilles* v. *Kerr*, 6 Whart. 500.

The declaration should show whether the claim is for a definite rent, or for a reasonable rent for use and oc-cupation *Diehl* v. *Bookius*, 1 Pa. Dist. R. 479.

cupation of the premises was taken, the tenant could have taken it.[14]

149. When action for use and occupation is inapplicable — If there has been a contract for a definite rent, or for the ascertainment of the rent in a prescribed mode, there can be no recovery of what the occupation of the land is reasonably worth The recovery must be of the definite rent, or of the rent that shall be ascertained in the prescribed mode. A lease for five years provided for its renewal for another two and a half years, at a rent to be determined by arbiters. These arbiters, or referees, were to be chosen, two by the lessor, and two by the lessee, who were to call in a fifth. The determination of a majority of these arbiters was to decide the rent The lessee continued in possession, after the expiration of five years, for six weeks, when he called on the lessor to appoint referees After their appointment and the selection of a fifth by them, the lessor revoked the reference He could not, it was held, recover for use and occupation, until the rent had been fixed by the referees, or until the tenant declined further to proceed for the submission of the question.[15] If A had leased the land to B by a sealed instrument, and B assigned the lease to C, the action against C formerly could not be in assumpsit for use and occupation. The existence of the lease and the assignment excluded the hypothesis of a different tacit or oral contract.[16]

[14]*M'Gunnagle* v *Thornton*, 10 Serg & R 251

[15]*Abbot* v *Shepherd*, 4 Phila 90 An express contract to pay a definite rent or a reasonable rent may be shown under a count for use and occupation *Kline* v *Jacobs*, 68 Pa. 57; *Pott* v. *Lesher*, 1 Yeates, 576, *Henwood* v. *Cheeseman*, 3 Serg & R 500 The terms of the statute of 11 Geo II , chap. 19, are too clear to admit of controversy on this point, says Sharswood. J., in *Kline* v

Jacobs Cf *Mackey* v *Robinson*, 12 Pa 170

[16]*Blume* v *M'Clurken*, 10 Watts, 380 If A of the firm of A & B makes a sealed lease in the name of both, and, B retiring, a new firm of A & C is formed, the payment of the rent reserved to this new firm will not justify the inference of the abandonment of the lease and of the tacit substitution of another *Bewley* v *Tams*, 17 Pa 485 A person in possession of land sells stones

150. No agreement to pay rent presumable — The act of April 2, 1872,[17] provides that the receiver of taxes of the city of Wilkesbarre may have his office in such place as may be approved by the council. This does not authorize the council to decide not to approve of any places other than the city building If they notify the receiver that they will not approve of any office except one in the city building, and he thereupon occupies it, a resolution of council, subsequently passed, that he be charged an annual rental of $300, imposes no obligation on him to pay it. There is no express or implied contract on the part of the receiver to pay it.[18]

151. When no rent is specified; void lease.— The action of assumpsit for use and occupation is generally resorted to only when there is a duty upon the occupant to pay for the occupation of the land, but no binding contract defines the amount of the compensation to be paid There may, e g , be a lease, but, because of the statute of frauds or other cause, it may be invalid If possession is taken under it, compensation for the use may be recovered If, under a lease for a term lasting more than three years beyond the time of making it, made by an agent whose authority is not in writing, and therefore invalid under the statute, possession is taken and retained for ten months, compensation can be recovered by assumpsit, not upon the lease, but upon the implied contract to pay it And if the contract implied is not one to pay the rent mentioned in the lease, the rent mentioned is at least a guide to the jury in determining the value of the occupation The defendant, says Trunkey, J , "is liable in assumpsit for the rental value of the premises he occupied. The writing was admissible on the question of value,—it

from it to X He can compel X to pay the price though he is not the owner of the premises for X is not liable to the owner, either in trespass or assumpsit *Rhoades* v *Patrick*, 27 Pa 323

[17] P L 740
[18] *Wilkes-Barre* v. *Chase*, 7 Pa. Super Ct 343.

was not offered in evidence as the foundation of the action."[19] The oral lease being for four years for $400, payable at the end of the term, assumpsit could be brought for the recovery of the value of an occupation for three years, and the jury could take three fourths of the sum mentioned in the lease as a proper measure of value.[20]

152. Express contract, but no rent named.— There may be a covenant to pay "a reasonable rent" or compensation without defining the rent. Assumpsit for use and occupation may be employed to recover it.[21] And one tenant in common who makes the express promise to pay a reasonable rent to his cotenant may be compelled to pay it, though without such promise to pay either a definite rent or a reasonable rent, he could not be made to pay at all.[22] One tenant in common may agree with the others to pay as rent an amount to be "hereafter agreed upon, or to be otherwise determined." The parties not subsequently agreeing, assumpsit may be sustained for use and occupation.[23]

[19]*Jennings* v *McComb*, 112 Pa 518, 4 Atl 812

[20]*Stover* v *Cadwallader*, 2 Pennyp 117. In *Dauphin County* v *Bridenhart*, 16 Pa 458 it is said that if the sheriff to whom the county is not bound to furnish a house, occupies one without actual contract between the owner and the county for it, the county is not liable as for use and occupation

[21]*Henwood* v *Cheeseman*, 3 Serg & R 500, *Pott* v *Lesher*, 1 Yeates, 576.

[22]*Kline* v *Jacobs*, 68 Pa 57 An occupation may be maintained by allowing heavy machinery to remain in a building after it has become the property of another *Grove* v *Barclay*, 106 Pa 155 Simply visiting a house to inspect it before making a lease is not an occupation of it. *Maitland* v *Wilcox*, 17 Pa 231.

[23]*Peirce* v *Peirce*, 199 Pa 4, 48 Atl 689 A testator devised his houses to his widow and children, giving the executor power to rent them The widow had possession of one of them for a series of years The executor rendered to her and the other devisees, semi-annually, an account of the rents collected and distributed In these accounts he charged the widow with a rent of $300 per annum The reception of these accounts by her, without objection within a reasonable time, would have been an acquiescence in the charge of $300, that would have been binding on her. Her objection, resulting in an agreement that, while she would pay rent, the amount of it should be determined in the future prevented them from becoming stated accounts.

153. No express contract at all.— There may be no express contract, either to pay a determinate rent or to pay rent; yet the facts may warrant the inference of promise to pay a reasonable rent. If they do, the action of assumpsit upon this inferred or implied promise, for the value of the use or occupation, may be sustained. If they do not, the only remedy of the owner is an ejectment of the occupant, and a recovery therein of mesne profits, or, after judgment therein, an action of trespass for mesne profits In *Mackey* v. *Robinson*[24] a father, with the consent of three adult children, leased for his own benefit the land belonging to them and to four minor children, and died in the midst of the term The tenant continued in possession, and the children sued in debt for the rent. Holding that the defendant was in no privity of contract with the plaintiffs, that he remained in possession after the death of the lessor,—practically a life tenant,—"under circumstances, to say the least. no better than those of tenants holding over without permission, whom the law calls tort feasors," Gibson, Ch J, decides that neither in debt nor in assumpsit for use and occupation, the use of which latter is permissible "only where the defendant has held by the plaintiff's demise, or at least by his permission, not inferred from mere inactivity" in not expelling him, could compensation be recovered. "As the defendants have left the premises, the plaintiffs cannot recover in any form of action."[25] In *Brolasky* v. *Ferguson*,[26] B had had possession of land prior to

---

[24] 12 Pa 170

[25] *Mackey* v *Robinson*, 12 Pa 170 Cf *Pott* v *Lesher*, 1 Yeates, 576, where the only remedy for the use of land by a trespasser is said to be ejectment and an action for mesne profits

[26] 48 Pa 434 If the defendant entered as a trespasser, a contract to pay rent cannot be inferred *Henwood* v *Cheeseman*, 3 Serg & R 500 The remark of Gordon, J, in *National Oil Ref Co* v *Bush*, 88

Pa 335, that the action for use and occupation is founded on the "use of the premises,   that the occupant may be in fact a trespasser, but the owner of the tenement may waive the trespass and recover in assumpsit, and it does not lie with the tortfeasor to defeat him by interposing his own wrong."—abandons the doctrine that the action reposes on a contract, express or implied, and is inconsistent with the cases cited

April, 1862, and again from July 26, 1862, when he reoccupied it under an agreement with A, the owner of an undivided interest in it, to pay $50 per month for it. B was not liable for use and occupation before April, 1862, in the absence of any contract made before that time, or any acknowledgment by B that the relation of landlord and tenant existed between him and A, or any understanding with the owner and without his knowledge B, claiming land on demise of his mother, takes and retains possession, refusing to pay rent to his father, the tenant by the curtesy. No contract could be inferred, and no action by the father for use and occupation sustained.[27] If coal underlying land is sold, to be taken out in forty years, and, together with it, a right to use the surface for the purpose of removing this coal, a use of the surface for any other purpose could not be supposed to be permissive, and assumpsit for it would not be a proper remedy [28] A vendee of land takes possession of the land, but the sale is never consummated on account of the inability of the vendor to make a clear title. For the continuance in possession of the vendee for seven years, no compensation as for use and occupation can be recovered The circumstances repel the inference of any contract to pay rent.[29] One who occupies under a claim of ownership cannot be held to have impliedly contracted to pay rent.[30]

154 Implied contract.— The action for the use and occupation of land is founded upon privity of contract, not privity of estate The plaintiff must prove a contract to pay either a stipulated compensation for the use of the land, or such a sum as the use is reasonably worth. But the proof of this contract may

[27]*Marlatt* v. *Marlatt,* 4 Pennyp 91
[28]*McCloskey* v *Miller,* 72 Pa 151
[29]*Bardsley's Appeal,* 20 W N C 90 But, in *Grove* v *Barclay,* 106 Pa 155, it is said by Gordon, J, that a claim of right does not destroy the right to maintain assumpsit unless the claim is substantial The theory of an implied contract, as distinguished from a quasi-contract, seems to be abandoned
[30]*Newlin* v *Brinton,* 1 Chester Co Rep 233, *Carroll* v. *Carroll,* 2 Chester Co Rep 119.

be direct or presumptive   If the possession is taken with the knowledge and the permission of the plaintiff, a promise to pay a reasonable rent is inferred.   The contract to pay rent is deduced from the assent of the plaintiff and the action of the defendant under it.[31]   If B has been in possession of A's land as a tenant, or otherwise, with his consent, a notice to quit by a certain day, while it tends to show that B's possession continued after that day is in defiance of A, is not conclusive   A may nevertheless consent to that continuance,[32] and if he does, he may recover for the value of the use and occupation, until the consent is withdrawn.

155 Holding possession despite notice from sheriff's vendee — If after notice to the tenant to vacate the premises in three months, given by the purchaser of the reversion at a sheriff's sale, the tenant retires at the end of the three months, he will be liable for the occupation of the premises during the period;[33] and, *a fortiori,* if, disregarding the notice, he remains in possession beyond the three months, though not liable for the rent specified in the lease he will be compelled to give compensation for the use and occupation of the land.[34]

156. Landlord's permission — If the occupant does not expect and intend to pay rent, and the circumstances indicate to the owner of the premises that he does not, no contract can be inferred, either by the owner or by the courts.   The contract cannot be deduced from the mere expectation of the owner that

[31]*Brolasky* v *Ferguson,* 48 Pa 434, *Bressler's Appeal.* 2 York Legal Record, 57, *Seitzinger* v *Alspach,* 42 Phila Leg Int 68, *Kline* v *Jacobs,* 68 Pa 57; *Henwood* v *Cheeseman,* 3 Serg & R 500, *Wells* v *Hornish,* 3 Penr & W 30, *Pott* v *Leshei,* 1 Yeates, 576, *Marlatt* v *Marlatt,* 4 Pennyp 91, *Bardsley's Appeal,* 20 W N C 90, *Grove* v *Barclay,* 106 Pa 155

[32]*National Oil Ref Co* v *Bush,* 88

Pa. 335, *Seitzinger* v *Alspach* 42 Phila Leg Int 68, cf *Stockton's Appeal,* 64 Pa 58

[33]*Stockton's Appeal.* 64 Pa 58   It matters not, says Read, J, whether the compensation is called mesne profits, or damages or for use and occupation   Cf *Mozart Bldg Assn* v *Friedjen,* 12 Phila 515, 5 W N C 318

[34]*Hemphill* v *Tevis,* 4 Watts & S. 535

he will be paid. Nor, even when the occupant manifests that he expects to pay rent, is the simple acquiescence of the owner, the mere refraining from positive dissent, or from active steps to expel the occupant, sufficient to support an inference of a contract The owner's permission to occupy neither is, nor is to be deduced from, mere inactivity,[35] though his silently suffering the possession may, in conjunction with other facts, justify the inference of a contract to pay rent on the occupant's part, and to receive it, on the owner's.[36]

157. What relations negative a contract — The relationship of the parties may preclude the inference of a contract to pay for the occupation of the land, when the other circumstances alone would require that inference. The fact, *e g ,* that the occupant is the only child of the owner, his mother, will negative any contract on the part of the child to pay for an occupancy of seventeen years, no rent being shown to have been demanded or promised.[37] The occupancy of his wife's land, for his business, by a husband, in the absence of other indications, will not support the inference that he agreed to pay rent for it It must be presumed that he was permitted by her to occupy the premises as a means of livelihood for the family, without any intention on the part of the wife ever to claim rent.[38] There is no prima facie presumption that, when a son-in-law occupies the land of his wife's father, he does so with the assent of the latter, gratuitously. The burden is on the former to show that the use of the land is a gift The relationship would facilitate,

[35]*Mackey* v *Robinson,* 12 Pa 170
[36] If an agent of a railroad company is retained, with the understanding that he is gratuitously to furnish a warehouse for goods, he cannot recover from the company for its use and occupation *Pennsylvania R Co* v *Brisbin,* 35 Phila Leg Int 317
[37]*Thompson's Estate,* 1 Kulp, 235.

Cf *Albright's Estate,* 1 York Legal Record, 121
[38]*Gilman's Estate,* 9 Pa Co Ct 111 Cf *M'Glinsey's Appeal,* 14 Serg & R. 64, *Bardsley's Estate,* 7 W N C 48, *Cogley's Estate,* 13 Phila 308, *Metz's Estate,* 1 Legal Record Rep 201.

LAND & TEN 9.

but not dispense with, this proof.[39] The relation between niece
and uncle is not such as to justify the inference that the occupancy by the latter of the house of the former was intended to
be gratuitous   Having at his request come to his house, and
lived there some years, she keeping house and he (a bachelor)
paying all the living expenses, he at length sold the house to
her, saying, "I will expect a home here as long as I live, and I
will pay all expenses, as I have been doing."   During the sixteen following years, he continued to occupy the house and to
pay the expenses of the family. It was held that he was liable
also to pay rent.[40] The circumstances may indicate, however,
that, while a nephew and family occupy the uncle's house, there
is no contract to pay rent   The nephew came, as a single man
over twenty-one years of age, to live in the family of his uncle,
and continued there for fourteen years, during several of which
he was married, having several children   The two families
lived as one, the products of the farm being used without division, and no account being kept, by uncle or nephew, of his con-
tributions.   The evidence was held insufficient to show that the
nephew was under any obligation to pay rent.[41]

   158 Tenants in common.—Although when one tenant in common alone occupies the premises, the nonoccupying tenant has
been allowed to recover in assumpsit compensation for the use
and occupation of his share of the land,[42] without evidence of
an express promise to pay rent, it has been held that the occupying tenant cannot be supposed, from the fact alone that he occupies, to intend and to promise to pay rent, but that he must
expressly promise to pay it, in order to be liable to pay it [43]

[39]*Sierrett* v *Wright*, 27 Pa 259.   [10]*Spackman's Appeal*, 16 W. N C
The condition in life of the parties   79
may also render it easier for the son-   [41]*Walker* v *Marion*, 148 Pa 1, 23
in law to prove that a gift of the use   Atl 1002
of the land was intended   A rich   [4]*Borrell* v *Borrell*, 33 Pa 492;
father in law could more easily be   *M'Clure* v *M'Clure*, 1 Giant Cas
believed to have intended a gift, than   222
a poor one   [43]*Kline* v. *Jacobs*, 68 Pa 57   Nor

If, however, he expressly agrees to pay a "reasonable rent," an action of assumpsit for use and occupation may be sustained on this agreement [44] In the absence of an express contract the law possibly implies a promise by an occupant of land belonging to several tenants in common, to pay each severally his proper share of the rental value.[45]

159. Tenant at sufferance — The occupancy which follows the termination of the lease, and which, at the election of the lessors, may be treated as a trespass, gives rise, until he chooses so to treat it, or the tenant expressly negatives the intention to pay rent, to liability for use and occupation. "At common law," says Mitchell, J., "tenants at sufferance appear not to have been liable for rent, and some expressions to that effect are to be found in our own earlier cases. But in *Bush* v. *National Oil Ref. Co.* 5 W N C 143, it was expressly held that such tenant is liable in assumpsit for use and occupation for the interval between the termination of the lease and the election of the lessor to treat him as a trespasser."[46] Hence, a lessee of a right to use water for fifteen years, which expired April 15, 1892, but who continued to use it until May, 1893, was liable for the value of the use, in assumpsit for use and occupation. A notice to withdraw from the premises at once[47] or at a designated future time[48] does not make the future occupation in such sense a trespass as to preclude an action for compensation for such occupation, unless the notice is followed by some act indicating the lessor's purpose to treat the occupant as a trespasser.

160. Other remedies besides assumpsit.—The owner of land may be a defendant in an action for money. He may set off a

could there be a recovery in account render or by bill in equity *Norris* v *Gould,* 15 W N C. 187

[44]*Peirce* v *Peirce,* 199 Pa. 4, 48 Atl 689

[45]*Marys* v *Anderson,* 24 Pa 272

[46]*Williams* v. *Ladew,* 171 Pa 369, Atl 329

[47]*Grove* v *Barclay,* 106 Pa 155

[48]*Bush* v *National Oil Ref Co* 5 W N C 143, *National Oil Ref Co.* v. *Bush,* 88 Pa 335

claim which he has against the plaintiff for the use and occupation by the latter of his land,[49] and the owner's claim can be made in the distribution of the estate of the occupant in the orphans' court [50] When sued by the tenant, the landlord can set off rent due. But if the action is in tort, e g , for converting the personal property of the lessee on the premises, set-off will not be allowed [51]

161. Warrant of attorney —The lease may authorize the confession of a judgment for the rent,[52] and, in addition, the confession of a judgment in ejectment.[53] A judgment entered on confession, for the rent, may be set off against a judgment recovered by the lessee against the lessor [54] Where the rent appears on the face of the lease, the prothonotary may enter judgment without appearance of an attorney, though the terms of the warrant are that "any practising attorney of any court of record of Pennsylvania," or the "lessee," may appear and confess judgment. The prothonotary may properly assume that the whole rent is unpaid The possibility that some of it has been paid does not take from him the power to enter judgment If the warrant authorizes judgment for rent "due or to become due," judgment can be entered for all the rent that is yet to accrue, as well as that which has accrued, and execution can issue from time to time as the instalments become payable The judgment will be opened if it is for more rent than remains unpaid.[55]

162. The measure of compensation.— In the action for use and occupation, the sum recoverable represents, not the value

[49]Seitzinger v Alspach, 42 Phila Leg Int 68, Bressler's Appeal, 2 York Legal Record, 57
[50]Bardsley's Appeal, 20 W N C 90
[51]Lykens Valley Coal Co v Dock, 62 Pa 232
[52]Fahey v. Howley, 22 Pa Super Ct 472.
[53]Yanko v Leizerowitz, 18 Lanc L Rev 1
[54]Yanko v Leizerowitz, 18 Lanc L Rev 1
[55]Yanko v Leizerowitz, 18 Lanc L Rev 1.

of the use of the premises to the defendant, but the value of it
to the owner, that is, what the owner could have got for it from
others had the defendant not been in possession. A having let
to B the right to take water from his premises, and B having
continued, after the expiration of the lease, to take it, A's compensation should be measured, not by the worth of the water
to B, not by the sum that B would have had to pay for the
same amount of water had he procured it elsewhere, or by the
loss he would have suffered had he failed to get a supply, but
by what A could reasonably and probably have got for the use
of the water from other parties had the defendant given up
possession at the end of the lease.[56] It is intimated in *Kline* v
Jacobs[57] that the defendant, occupying a farm belonging to
another, without having expressly agreed to pay any rent,
might show, when sued for the use and occupation, the expenses
and products of the farm, and expenditures for repairs without
which the premises would not have been tenantable and rentable,
and that it would be an answer to the plaintiff's claim to show
that the occupation had not been beneficial; but it was held that,
when there was an express agreement to pay a "reasonable rent,"
the occupant, like an ordinary tenant, could not set up that the
premises were untenantable, could not reduce the rent on account of repairs made by him, and that the bad condition of
the premises could only be shown as bearing on the question of
what would be a reasonable rent   If an executor having charge
of the realty of the decedent renders an account to the widow,
who is entitled to one third of the rents, and who is in possession
of a house, and in this account charges her with $300, the an-
nual rent of the house, there having been no agreement between
them as to the proper rent, and if she objects to the rent, and

[56] *Williams* v *Ladeu,* 171 Pa 369,
33 Atl 329
[57] 68 Pa 57   The occupant may
reduce the amount to be recovered
by showing the plaintiff's interfer-
ences with his possession   *Harris*
v *Watson* 1 Phila Leg Int May 8,
1844.

it is then agreed that the rent shall be thereafter agreed upon
or otherwise determined,—the reception by her of semi-annual
accounts for five years thereafter, charging her with the same
rent, without provoking dissent from her, will not make them
accounts stated, and determine the amount of rent for which
she shall be liable. Some agreement is necessary, or a jury must
determine [58]

163. Lease by tenants in common.— When a lease is made by
several tenants in common, and the lessee promises to pay, not
to each his individual part of the rent, but to them all the gross
sum, the action must be by all for the whole rent. It cannot be
brought by one for his fractional share of the rent.[59] But in
Swint v *McCalmont Oil Co ,*[60] where, a lease having been made
by two, the rent had been paid to one, and the other then
brought an action against the tenant for his share of it, Williams, J., said that while a payment to the other colessor of all
the rent, without notice from the plaintiff to pay his share to
him, was, as against the plaintiff, a good payment, the plaintiff
could notify the tenant thereafter to pay his share to him, and
that a payment, in disregard of the notice, to his colessor, would
not be valid as against him.

164. Action by stranger to lease.— If a lease provides that,
since the title to an undivided half of the land is in dispute,
the tenant may retain one half of the rent, after the success of
the claimant in ejectment, until it shall be determined to whom
the other one half shall be due and payable, and that, should
the tenant be legally required to pay one half of the rent to the
claimant for the entire term, he shall be allowed to apply all
the rent to the claimant until he has received as much as the
lessor, and that, if the dispute between the claimant and the
lessor should not be determined by June 1, 1898, the tenant

[58]*Peirce* v *Peirce,* 199 Pa. 4, 48   [60] 184 Pa 202, 63 Am St. Rep.
Atl 689   791, 38 Atl. 1021.
[59]*Marys* v *Anderson,* 24 Pa. 272.

shall withhold all the rent until the dispute is determined,—the claimant, on succeeding, may maintain an action on this covenant, though not a party to it, for the rent retained by the tenant, and also on the contract of X whereby he guaranteed the faithful performance of the tenant's duties [61]

165. Agent, principal.—The lease being made by A, agent for X, the action is properly brought by A, agent for X.[62] When the lease is in the name of the principal, but is executed by an agent, and the declaration so states, it should further state, under the practice of Luzerne county, the nature of the agency or how it was constituted, in order to entitle the plaintiff to a judgment for want of a sufficient affidavit of defense.[63]

166 Privity with lessor — There must be privity of contract or estate to support the action of assumpsit (or, formerly, debt) by the plaintiff. If he did not make the lease, and is not privy to the lessor by grant, devise, or inheritance, he cannot sue on it [64] After an assignment by B, the lessee, to X, B, a corporation, was consolidated with corporations C and D, and the debts of B, C, and D were by statute imposed on the consolidated company. As no transfer from X was shown to this company, the company was not liable in an action on the lease by the lessor or his alienee [65]

167. Declaration.—The court on rule will require a more specific statement, if the one filed does not clearly show whether a determinate rent is claimed, or only compensation for use and occupation.[66]

168. Affidavit of defense.— A written lease is an instrument,

[61]*Kennedy* v. *Duggan*, 23 Pa Co Ct. 625

[62]*Philadelphia Fire Extinguisher Co.* v. *Brainerd*, 2 W N C 473

[63]*Lane* v *Nelson*, 2 Pa Dist R 18

[64]*Mackey* v *Robinson*, 12 Pa 170

[65]*Acheson* v *Kittanning Consolidated Natural Gas Co* 8 Pa Super Ct 477. But B continued liable under the lease, notwithstanding his assignment of it Why this liability did not devolve on the consolidated company does not appear

[66]*Diehl* v *Bockius*, 1 Pa. Dist R 479 Cf *Lomis* v *Ruetter*, 9 Watts, 51b, as to filing statement under act March 21, 1806, § 5.

in a suit on which judgment can be taken for want of an affidavit, or of a sufficient affidavit, of defense.[67]   If the affidavit admits the rent to be due, but denies the right of the plaintiff,— *e g ,* claiming the land under a will of the lessor, whose validity is contested, judgment will be entered for the sum admitted to be due, and the defendant will be allowed to pay it into court.[68] The affidavit is, for the purpose of preventing judgment, assumed to be true, and though it avers that a clause is in the lease which, on the exhibition of what purports to be the lease by the plaintiff, is not found in it, its verity must be assumed.[69]   The plaintiff's claim being for $117.04, with interest from August 8, 1886, and not specifying the period during which it accrued, an affidavit alleging that on August 8, 1886, only $83 25 rent for five months remained unpaid, all previous rent having been paid, is sufficient   No greater particularity in it than is observed by the plaintiff in his affidavit of claim will be required.[70] The affidavit alleged that three months before the close of the term of one year, the lessor leased the premises to the affiant for another year, but six weeks afterwards the lease was revoked, and he was notified to quit at the end of the current year, that he did so; that he had, during his occupancy, spent $7 for windows and a door, that he had been obliged to take another house which was unsuited for his business, had incurred $6 expense in moving and loss of time, that he had spent $12 for blinds and carpets to make the new place tenantable; that he had suffered a loss in his cigar trade, and had been specially damaged $50,— an amount exceeding the rent   The affidavit was held to be insufficient.[71]   The lease granting to the tenant the free use of a road to a point beyond the premises, and of water in lessor's well, an affidavit simply saying that the lessee "had not the free

[67]*Frank* v *Maguire,* 42 Pa 77 , *Maull* v *Lowery,* 1 W N C 169
[68]*Dietrich* v *Dietrich,* 154 Pa 92, 25 Atl 1080
[69]*Knerr* v *Bradley,* 105 Pa 190
[70]*Cochran* v *Emmeretz,* 3 Del Co Rep 433
[71]*Smith* v *Mishler,* 7 Lanc L Rev 169.

use" of the road and water, without saying that this want of use was due to acts for which the lessor was responsible on the covenant, is insufficient to prevent judgment [72]

Under a lease in which the lessor reserved the right to take iron ore from the premises, and also a certain royalty, and stipulating for a settlement at the end of every year, the plaintiff filed a statement claiming the amount stated by the lessee's bookkeeper to be due. An affidavit that defendant did not think that he owed so much, and that he could not know without consulting the bookkeeper, who was sick, was insufficient.[73] It need not be said that the facts averred in the affidavit must constitute a valid defense, otherwise, it will be insufficient [74] When the grounds set up in the affidavit of defense do not traverse the obligation declared in the statement, but are in the nature of confession and avoidance, in reduction of or set-off to the payment sued for, the averment in the affidavit must be specific as to the amounts claimed in reduction, so that plaintiff may, if he choose, elect to admit them and take judgment for the balance.[75]

169. Proof of execution of lease; oyer — Under a rule of court that the execution of a written instrument need not be proved, unless it has been denied by the affidavit of the defendant, filed before the trial, the execution of a lease need not be proved, in the absence of such affidavit.[76] The defendant might, in covenant on a lease, pray oyer of the original lease, and a rule to show cause why the demand for oyer should not be stricken off will be discharged.[77]

170. Exemption — The tenant may retain $300 worth of property against an execution for rent, and also against distress. He

[72]*Dewey* v *Dupuy,* 2 Watts & S 553

[73]*Evans* v. *Lanigan,* 1 W N C. 299

[74]*Maull* v *Lowery,* 1 W N C 169, *Evans* v. *Lanigan,* 1 W N. C. 299, *Dewey* v *Dupuy,* 2 Watts & S 553;

Chambers v *Smith,* 183 Pa 122, 38 Atl 522

[75]*Cosgrave* v *Hammill,* 173 Pa 207, 33 Atl 1045

[76]*Ahrns* v *Chartiers Valley Gas Co* 188 Pa 249, 41 Atl 739

[77]*Frick* v *Hugle,* 1 Pa Co Ct 572.

may waive this privilege in the lease,[78] or elsewhere; and if he does, his claim for exemption against a fi. fa. issued by the land-lord,[79] or against an attachment of a debt due him by a third person,[80] will be disallowed   A stipulation by the lessee that all personal property on the premises shall be liable to distress and may be destrained and sold for rent, and that the lessee waives all right under the exemption law to exemption of such property from levy and sale, will be understood to waive the ex-emption only with respect to a distress, and not to an execution, or to an attachment execution.[81] But the words, "And the lessee hereby expressly waives the benefit of all laws and usages exempting any property from distress or execution for rent, the lessor not waiving any remedies given by existing laws," waive the exemption as respects not only a distress, but also an execu-tion, or an execution attachment [82] To get advantage of the waiver it is not necessary that the judgment should recite a waiver. A waiver in the contract will control the execution, and it may be proved either by the judgment, when the judgment recites it, or by proof *aliunde*.[83]

171. Jurisdiction of justice.— A justice of the peace may en-tertain a suit for rent, when it does not exceed $300. The 6th section of the act of March 22, 1814,[84] expressly conferred ju-risdiction in all cases of rent not exceeding $100, and the amount was increased to $300 by the act of May 29, 1879.[85] If the defendant makes oath before the hearing that the title to the

---

[78]*Mitchell* v *Coates,* 47 Pa 202, *Beatty* v *Rankin,* 139 Pa 358, 21 Atl 74, *Smith* v *Mishler,* 7 Lanc L Rev 169

[79]*Smith* v. *Mishler,* 7 Lanc L Rev. 169

[80]*Beatty* v. *Rankin,* 139 Pa 358, 21 Atl 74, *Mitchell* v. *Coates,* 47 Pa 202

[81]*Mitchell* v. *Coates,* 47 Pa 202

[82]*Beatty* v. *Rankin,* 139 Pa. 258, 21 Atl 74

[83]*Beatty* v *Rankin,* 139 Pa 258, 21 Atl 74   The fact that the judg-ment of a justice recites the waiver is not material

[84]1 Pepper & L Digest, 2550, 6 Smith's Laws, 182

[85]P L 194, *Beatty* v *Rankin,* 139 Pa 358, 21 Atl 74, *Royer* v *Ake,* 3 Penr & W 461, *Lower* v. *Hummel,* 21 Pa 450.

land will come in question, the justice should dismiss the proceedings, according to the 2d section of the act of March 22,
1814,[86] though ordinarily the lessee cannot question the title
when sued for the rent.[87] The tenant is entitled to appeal from
the justice's judgment, unless he has waived the right; the denial of the appeal to the tenant under the 12th section of the act
of March 28, 1804, applying only to proceedings to defalk
against rent.[88] The lease, however, may contain a waiver of "all
right to an appeal, writ of error, or certiorari to any judgment,
order, or decree that may be given or entered by any court, alderman, or justice of the peace" against the lessee When the
lease contains this or a similar provision, the justice will not be
compelled to allow an appeal,[89] and if he does allow it, it will be
stricken off.[90]

172. Limitations.— The action for rent must be brought within the time prescribed by the statute of limitations. All rent
becoming payable within six years of the issue of the summons
is free from the bar, although the period for possession during
which it, or some of it, is the consideration, precedes the commencement of the six years Thus, if rent is payable for a
year, at the end of the year, the rent for a year whose termination is not more than six years before the issue of the writ may be
recovered.[91] If for a term of four years the rent was payable,
in one sum, at the end of that time, and the end of that time was
within six years prior to suit, the rent for the whole term is recoverable [92] The statute has no application to any rent falling
due under a sealed lease,[93] but it has been held that, the definite

[86]*Williams* v *Smith,* 3 Clark
(Pa) 22
[87]*Jacobs* v *Haney,* 18 Pa 240
[88]*Ingersol* v *Gibbons,* 1 Browne
(Pa) 69
[89]*Lippincott* v *Cooper,* 19 W N
C 130
[90]*Strojny* v *Merofchinski,* 9 Kulp,
444.

[91]*M'Clure* v *M'Clure,* 1 Grant Cas
222 An acknowledgment of the
principal rent, though accompanied
by a denial of liability for interest,
tolls the statute. *Henwood* v
Cheescman, 3 Serg & R 500
[92]*Stover* v *Cadwallader,* 2 Pennyp
117
[93]*Davis* v *Shoemaker,* 1 Rawle,

term under a sealed lease having expired, the duty of paying
rent for the possession retained thereafter arises out of a parol
contract, and the action for such rent is subject to the statute of
limitations [94] A parol lease for four years reserving rent for
the whole term in one sum payable at its expiration, being void
by the statute of frauds, unless possession is actually enjoyed
by the tenant for the whole term, if the tenant remains in possession three years only, he is liable for the rent at the end of
each year, and if the action is not brought within six years from
the close of the third year, it is barred [95]

173 Set-off — The tenant may set off contractual claims which
he has against the lessor, e. g , a book account,[96] a claim for
work done for the lessor,[97] or payments made at his request,[98]
although there was no agreement between them that such claim
might be set off.[99]   The prohibition against setting off against
rent in distress proceedings, or in the tenant's replevin of goods
taken in distress, does not apply to other remedies for the rent,
—e. g , to a feigned issue to determine the right of the landlord
to claim as such, out of the proceeds of a sale in execution of the
lessee's goods on the premises.[100]   Unliquidated damages arising
from the landlord's tort—e g , from his improper distraining
upon goods of the tenant—cannot be set off,[101] but damages arising from the breach by the lessor of his covenant in the lease may
be set off,—e g , for breach of covenant that the lessee should
have the free use of a cart road to a certain point beyond the
premises, and of the water of a well in the vicinity,[102] or of a
covenant that the plumbing and drainage of the house are, or will

135; *Ahrns* v *Chartiers Valley Gas
Co* 188 Pa 249 41 Atl 739
    [94]*Davis's Estate*, 1 Phila 360
    [95]*Stover* v *Cadwallader*, 2 Pennyp
117
    [96]*M'Clure* v *M'Clure*, 1 Grant Cas
222
    [97]*Nichols* v *Jones*, 166 Pa 599, 31
Atl 329

    [98]*Mooney* v   *Reynolds* (Pa.) 12
Atl 481
    [99]*Nichols* v *Jones*, 166 Pa 599, 31
Atl 329
    [100]*Gray* v *Wilson*, 4 Watts, 39
    [101]*Groetzinger* v *Latimer*, 146 Pa.
628 23 Atl 393
    [102]*Depuy* v *Silver*, 1 Clark (Pa)
385

be made to be, in first-class order,[103] or of a covenant to furnish steam for carrying on the lessee's business,[104] or of a covenant not to let the lessor's neighboring property for the same business that the tenant is going to conduct on the leased property,[105] or of a covenant for quiet enjoyment. But if A, who has granted the coal in a tract to B, reserving the right to drill three oil wells through the coal, and who has leased the surface to C, not reserving the right to drill oil wells, grants his right to drill three wells to D, A is not responsible for any interference with his operation by B, as to whom D has a right   If D pays money to B to buy off his obstructiveness, D cannot set off the money thus paid against A's claim for royalty.[106] The expense of making repairs, under the authority of the lease, may be set off[107] If the tenant of an executor is also one of the persons entitled to a share of the profits of the whole estate of the deceased, when sued for the rent, he cannot, probably, set off against the rent his share of the profits, since to do so would be to settle the account of the executor in a court having no jurisdiction.   But, if the executor has himself stated accounts showing his receipts and disbursements, to the accuracy of which the tenant excepts only with respect to the amount of rent with which he is charged, he can, when sued for the full rent, deduct from it the credit to which, according to the account of the executor, the plaintiff, he is entitled.[108] If, to induce B to accept a lease of A's premises, A agrees to satisfy B's present landlord for the remainder of

[103]*Wolfe* v *Arrott*, 109 Pa 473, 1 Atl 333   The tenant, having corrected the defects, was allowed to set off the cost against the rent

[104]*Devlin* v *Burns*, 147 Pa 168, 23 Atl. 375   The damages were the loss of the price of the lessee's labor, and what he had had to pay to his customers for being unable to properly fulfil his contracts.

[105]*Allegaert* v. *Smart*, 2 Pennyp 320.

[106]*Chambers* v *Smith*, 183 Pa 122, 38 Atl 522

[107]*Mooney* v *Reynolds* (Pa) 12 Atl 481   A tenant who has denied the tenancy in his plea cannot shift his ground at the trial, and set up liens for his improvements   *Reed* v *Reed*, 1 Am L J 263

[108]*Peirce* v. *Peirce*, 199 Pa 4, 48 Atl 689.

B's term, and B, nevertheless, after removing into A's premises, is compelled to pay his former landlord, he will be entitled to set off the amount thus paid, less so much of it as represents a period during which B improperly retained possession of his original premises. It is B's duty to retain them no longer than is reasonably necessary to fit up A's premises for his, B's, needs. After this time, B should allow A to have control of them, and if he has failed to do so he must himself pay the rent [109]

174. Defenses to payment of rent, possession not taken.— The lease having been made, and no obstacle existing to the lessee's taking possession according to its terms, his refraining from taking possession is no defense to a suit for the rent, nor is the fact that, getting into possession under the tenant by a former lease, a short time before his own term begins, he gives up the possession before his term begins, never resuming it [110] A lessee for a period—e. g, a month—cannot, by abandoning the possession within the period, and tendering an apportioned part of the rent, escape from the duty of paying the rent for the whole period, the lessor not accepting a surrender.[111] Nor is it a defense that, after the lessee has quit the premises within the term, the lessor has neglected to procure another tenant [112]

175. Want of title.— The lessor's want of title to the premises cannot, as is elsewhere shown, be set up to defeat a recovery of the rent, the lessee being estopped from denying, for this purpose, the lessor's title. The court properly excludes, therefore, an offer of evidence that the lessor "had no interest in the property leased at the time he leased it, and had no right to lease," etc.[113] Yet in *Kunkle* v *People's Natural Gas Co.,*[114] where A

[109]*Cadwalader* v *United States Exp Co* 147 Pa 455 23 Atl 775

[110]*Howard* v *Murphy*, 23 Pa 173

[111]*Willing* v *Becker* 96 Pa 182, *Teller* v *Boyle* 132 Pa 56, 18 Atl 1069

[112]*Willing* v. *Becker* 96 Pa 182,

Lipper v *Bouvé*, 6 Pa Super Ct. 452

[113]*Howard* v *Murphy*, 23 Pa 173

[114] 165 Pa 133, 33 L R. A 847 30 Atl 719 The lease describing the premises as containing "60 acres, more or less," the fact that they con-

leased land for oil and gas extraction, to B, and, after default in making the development of the land during the first six months, whereupon B became liable to pay $630, A, while demanding that sum, revealed the fact that his wife, who was not a party to the lease, had an interest in the land, it was said by Dean, J., that if B had commenced operations within the six months and taken from the land oil or gas, equity, on his complaint of peril to his rights from the wife's outstanding interest, would probably have decreed that payment of royalty be not compelled until she should join in the lease. But since B was guilty of complete default during the six months, and since, on the disclosure of the wife's interest, the lessor tendered his wife's signature, but B declined to accept it and insisted on surrendering the lease on condition that all his liability should be released, and then, after suit for the royalty was brought, made an unconditional surrender of it, B was held liable to pay the $630.

176 Payment by distress — The lessee may defend an action for rent by showing payment of it by means of distress   If goods enough to satisfy the rent are taken and not appraised, nor their proceeds, if a sale takes place, accounted for to the lessee, the rent may be treated as paid, at the election of the tenant;[115] but if the lessee sues the lessor for an illegal distress and recovers judgment and satisfaction thereof, he cannot defeat an action for the same rent by alleging the distress [116]

177. Appropriation of payments.— The tenant, when he makes a payment, may appropriate it to the rent of any portion of the term which he chooses. If the lessor refuses to allow such appropriation, he should decline to receive it or to retain it [117] If he makes no appropriation, the lessor may make it He may, e. g ,

tain only 54 acres is no defense to rent *Caveat emptor* applies, the lessee having had an opportunity to examine the land and ascertain its contents *Harnish* v. *Musser,* 19 Lanc L Rev 283

[115]*Cochran* v *Emmertz,* 3 Del Co Rep 433
[116]*Robinson* v *White,* 39 Pa 255
[117]Cf *Washington Natural Gas Co* v *Johnson,* 123 Pa 576, 10 Am. St Rep 553, 16 Atl 799

apply a monthly payment to rent due for a month prior to that in which it was made, and safely distrain for the subsequently accruing rent, without risk of having the application changed, in replevin of the distrained goods, to the rent for which the distress was made.[118] Numerous payments of rent being made without appropriation by the tenant to any particular year, in replevin by the tenant of goods taken in distress these payments ought to be applied to the extinguishment of the rents which first accrued.[119] In *Garrett's Appeal*[120] the lessee owed money to the lessor, and was also in arrears for rent. Payments of money made but not appropriated by him could, it was held, be applied by the landlord to the debt at any time before a controversy arose, so that he could issue a distress for the rent. A levy in execution being made on the goods distrained, and they being sold by the sheriff on both processes, the rent was payable from the proceeds.

178. Presumption of payment.— A payment of rent for a certain period is prima facie evidence that the rent for all prior periods in the same term has been paid[121] A recovery in an action brought in 1837 for one year's rent due October 1, 1837, is prima facie evidence, in an action brought in 1838 for a year's rent due October 1, 1836, that such rent had been paid[122] The presumption of the payment of earlier instalments may be rebutted; *e g*, by showing that the lessor gave the receipt as of payment of the later instalment, under the mistaken impression that the earlier had been paid.[123] If, after a distress, and replevin by the tenant, payment is made of an instalment falling due later than that for which the distress was made, and a receipt for it is given, this receipt is not prima facie evidence that

[118]*Underhill* v *Wynkoop*, 15 Pa Super Ct 230

[119]*Reed* v *Ward*, 22 Pa 144

[120] 100 Pa 597

[121]*Saving Fund* v *Marks*, 3 Phila 278, *Underhill* v *Wynkoop*, 15 Pa Super Ct 230, *Young's Estate*, 16 Phila 215

[122]*Hemphill* v *Eckfeldt*, 5 Whart 274

[123]*Saving Fund* v *Marks*, 3 Phila 278.

the rent for which the distress was levied has been paid.[124] The presumption may be strengthened, *e. g.,* when the payment was made under the compulsion of a distress, and it will be presumed that a distress is for all rent then due [125] A receipt for rent, generally, not indicating for what period, furnishes no ground for presuming instalments earlier than the last due to have been paid.[126]

179 Former recovery.—A judgment for the tenant in replevin for distrained goods, grounded on a denial of the tenancy, is conclusive against the existence of a tenancy, in a subsequent action for rent growing out of a lease for the same period of time If the judgment was because there was no certain rent reserved, it would not import a denial of a demise, and would not bar a later action for the rent for the same period for which the distress had been made [127] A recovery for nonperformance by the tenant during one part of the term does not preclude a recovery in a later action for nonperformance during a later period,[128] nor for nonpayment of rent during an earlier period, of the term.[129]

180. Payment—It is needless to observe that payment is a defense to the action for rent If the lessee sends a check to the lessor, with an accompanying statement that it is in full for rent for a certain period, and a receipt is sent to him, stating that it is for a part only of the rent due, and the lessee sends back the receipt, and requests one in full, or the return of the

[124]*Underhill* v *Wynkoop,* 15 Pa Super Ct 230

[125] *Young's Estate,* 16 Phila 215

[126]*Underhill* v. *Wynkoop,* 15 Pa Super. Ct 230

[127]*Cist* v. *Zeigler,* 16 Serg & R 282, 16 Am. Dec 573.

[128]*Watson* v. *O'Hern,* 6 Watts, 362, *Stiles* v *Himmelwright,* 16 Pa Super Ct 649

[129]*Hemphill* v *Eckfeldt,* 5 Whart 274 In *Stiles* v *Himmelwright,* 16 Pa. Super. Ct. 649, it is said that the landlord is bound to bring his suit for all the instalments which have accrued at the time of bringing his action.

money, and the money is not returned, the lessor will be considered to have agreed that the payment was in full [130]

181. Nonacceptance of lease.— When sued for rent on a lease, the tenant may defend by showing that, though in possession of the premises for a series of years, he was in under an earlier lease having different terms, and that he had never accepted the lease upon which the suit has been brought.[131] An agreement that, in case the tenant shall vacate the premises, X shall have a right to occupy, gives X an option. No tenancy is created until X exercises the option.[132] A corporation which has not signed a lease as lessee may nevertheless be shown to have accepted it, by the facts that it has not, as a rule of court requires, denied the acceptance, that it took possession of the premises, operated them for oil, paid royalty according to its terms, and executed a written agreement referring to the leasehold created by the lease, as its property [133] A confession of judgment in an earlier suit for rent may be used in a later suit to show an admission by the defendant of the relation of landlord and tenant [134]

182. Inability to use premises in covenanted mode —Though the lease conditions the right of the tenant on his refraining from using the premises, or permitting them to be used, otherwise than for a saloon and dwelling, the failure of the lessee on application to procure a license from the quarter sessions, whereby it is impossible to use the premises as a saloon, will not excuse him, on vacating the premises within the term, from the rent.[135]

[130]*Washington Natural Gas Co* v. *Johnson*, 123 Pa 576, 10 Am St Rep 553, 16 Atl 799

[131]*Johnson* v *Smith*, 165 Pa 195, 30 Atl 675 Cf *Maitland* v *Wilcox*, 17 Pa 231

[132]*Fell* v *Betz*, 5 Pa Dist R 310

[133]*Ahrns* v *Chartiers Valley Gas Co* 188 Pa 249, 41 Atl 739

[134]*Weidner* v *Foster*, 2 Penr & W. 23

[135]*Teller* v *Boyle*, 132 Pa 56, 18 Atl 1069 The lease gave the lessee the right to use an existing switch, and also "to construct another switch" The railroad company refused to allow the construction of another switch unless the lessee

183. Surrender.— No rent can accrue after a surrender of the term which has been accepted by the landlord. If the lease itself concedes to the lessee "the right at any time to surrender up this lease, and be released from all moneys due and conditions unfulfilled," and provides that, from the time of such surrender, it shall be "null and void and no longer binding on either party," this right to surrender is impliedly so conditioned that it must be exercised when a demand for rent that has become due is made. If it is not then exercised, if the lease is not surrendered, and suit is brought for the rent, a surrender pending the action will not relieve from that rent. The right of action being complete when suit is brought, a subsequent surrender will not destroy it [136]

184. Mistake in description of premises — The lease may describe the property as being on the southwest corner of certain streets, whereas the premises intended are on the northwest corner. In an action for the rent, the declaration properly describing the premises intended, there can be a recovery on explaining the discrepancy between the lease as written and that described in the declaration.[137]

185. Illegality of object of lease — The fact that the county commissioners are under no duty, and therefore have no right, to furnish a residence for the sheriff, will be no defense to an action for rent for a house leased to them in order that they may put the sheriff in it, the lessor having no knowledge of the facts which would reveal the transcendence of their power by the commissioners. The lessor was not bound to inquire under what arrangement with the sheriff they had agreed to furnish

should surrender some of his rights respecting the first switch The lessee declined to surrender them This was no excuse for the nonpayment of the rent, unless the premises could not be used without a second switch *Shillen* v *Logan*, 21 Pa Super. Ct 106.

[136]*Douthett* v *Gibson*, 11 Pa Super Ct 543 Cf *Kunkle* v *People's Natural Gas Co* 165 Pa 133, 33 L R A 847, 30 Atl 719

[137]*Henry* v *Wilson*, 1 W N C. 506

him the house, or even for what purpose it was to be furnished.
If informed of the illegal purpose, he could not recover the rent,
but barely receiving information that it was for a residence for
the sheriff would not be sufficient, as he would have a right to
presume that the commissioners were acting conformably with
their duty [138]

186 Assignment of lease no defense.— The lessee does not escape his contractual liability by assigning the lease,[139] or by
suffering a sheriff's sale of the lease[140] to another. Such an
assignment destroys the privity of estate between the lessor and
the lessee, but not the privity of contract   Nor is the lessee
discharged by the additional fact that the lessor has assented to
the assignment, or has accepted rent,[141] or a note for rent[142]
falling due after the assignment, from the assignee, or that the
lessor has distrained on goods of the assignee on the premises, for
such rent.[143]   The lessor may accept the assignee in lieu of the
lessee, so that practically a surrender of the lease and a new
lease to the assignee are made.   The lessee would then be freed
from liability for future, though not for past, rent.[144]   But the
recognition of the assignee as tenant, in the modes heretofore
indicated, is not to be interpreted as an acceptance of a surrender   The lessor may even contract with the assignee for a
less rent than that in the lease, without discharging the lessee
from liability for the original rent, if he reserves all his rights
under the lease.[145]   A leasehold was sold at auction in 1874,

[138]*Dauphin County* v *Bridenhart*,
16 Pa 458

[139]*Ghegan* v *Young*, 23 Pa 18,
Bender v *George*, 92 Pa 36 , *Washington Natural Gas Co* v *Johnson*,
123 Pa 576, 10 Am St Rep 553, 16
Atl 799

[140]*Kerper* v *Booth*, 10 W N C 79

[141]*Ghegan* v *Young*, 23 Pa 18 ,
Frank v *Maguire*, 42 Pa 77. Ac
cepting rent from the assignee does
not absolve the lessee from liability
for earlier rent falling due after his
assignment   *Hall* v *Bardsley*, 5 W
N C 553

[142]*Kerper* v *Booth*, 10 W N C 79
The note being conditional payment,
if it is not paid, resort to the lessee
can be had

[143]*Manley* v *Dupuy*, 2 Whart 162
The lessee continues liable for subsequent rent

[144]*Hall* v. *Bardsley*, 5 W N C 553

[145]*Fisher* v *Milliken*, 8 Pa 111, 49
Am Rep 497.

and assigned to A, who the same year assigned to B The lessor "recognized" B as terre-tenant, who paid him rent. In January and February, 1875, the estate and the rent were, by agreement between lessor and B, reduced The lessee continued liable, notwithstanding, for the rent of 1875 and 1876, it not appearing that any agreement for the substitution of B's liability for that of the lessee had preceded the dates when these rents fell due.[146] If the assignee holds over after the expiration of the term, the lessor not having assented to the assignment, the lessee is liable for the hold-over rent [147] If the lessee is known to the lessor to be only nominally such, and to have accepted the lease for an incipient corporation to which, on its organization, he assigns the lease, according to his agreement with his coadventurers, the lessee will not be considered in fact such, nor be liable for rent that accrues [148]

187. Reduction of rent.— The lease, providing for an initial rent, may make provision for its reduction after the lapse of a certain period or upon the happening of a designated event A lease for two years, of premises for the retail liquor business, named $1,400 per annum as the rent, but stipulated that, if the lessee should fail "to secure a retail license for said Eagle House," the lessor "agrees to accept $400 per year . . . for the purpose of any merchandise business, liquor and beer business excepted, for the term of one year only." The tenant obtained a license for the first year, but failed to secure one for the second. The agreement for a reduction of rent was held applicable to the second year, since the condition of its application to the first year had not been realized.[149] The lease may reserve to the lessor the right to sell portions of the premises and to give

[146]*Hall* v *Bardsley*, 5 W N C 553
[147]*Fulmer* v *Crossman* 8 Del Co Rep 78, 2 Luzerne Leg Obs 331
Heckman's Estate, 172 Pa 185, 33 Atl 552
[149]*Rea* v *Ganter*, 152 Pa 512 25

Atl 539 There may be an agreement, in the midst of the term, for an increase of rent, but to be binding it must be supported by a consideration *Taylor* v. *Winters*, 6 Phila. 126.

immediate possession to the purchaser of the parts purchased, "on a corresponding reduction being made in the rent," and on payment to the lessee of the value of any crop in the ground sold. The reduction, under such an agreement, must not be according to the ratio of the area sold to the original area of the demised premises, but according to the ratio of the value of the parts sold to the value of the original premises The lease being made to two persons, B and C, if, after sales are made, B, with the knowledge and acquiescence of C, agrees with the landlord that the proper amount to be reduced from the rent is $50, and pays the rent less $50, and at the expiration of the lease B removes, C remaining in possession, C cannot, when sued for rent falling due after B's removal, ignore the agreement made by B with the lessor, and set off against his rent what he alleges to be an excess of rent paid by B He may, however, claim a larger reduction of the rent for the hold-over period.[150]

188 Subsequent agreement to reduce rent — The lessor may agree during the term that the rent reserved in the lease shall be reduced   If the agreement is that it shall be reduced "for the time being," the lessor may at any time retract the reduction by notifying the tenant that for the future he will demand the original rent.[151] The agreement may be to reduce the rent if it is paid promptly. If the rent is not paid promptly, the tenant cannot avail himself of the agreement. He may, however, have a right to a reduction on account of the inability of the lessor to give him possession of a portion of the leased premises, and this right he may insist on, though he cannot insist on the promise to reduce [152] If the amount of reduction is not specified, the agree-

---

[150]*Doyle v Longstreth*, 6 Pa Super Ct 475   After agreeing to reduce the rent for reasons advantageous to himself, and accepting reduced payments from time to time, the lessor cannot claim the full rent in bankruptcy proceedings against the tenant   *Evans v Lincoln Co* 204 Pa 448, 54 Atl 321

[151]*Rohrheimer v Hofman*, 103 Pa. 400

[152]*Watson v Serverson*, 1 Del. Co. Rep 87.

ment will not be enforceable,[153] nor if there is no consideration for it;[154] and if there is a simple agreement that the lessee shall pay less rent for the remainder of the term, when he is already bound to pay the originally stipulated rent, there is no consideration [155] If B is tenant from year to year, with the duty of giving three months' notice of an intention to quit, and, less than three months before the end of a year, not having given notice, he obtains a promise from the lessor that he may pay the monthly rent at the end of each month, instead of the beginning, his continuance in possession the next year, in reliance on this promise, will be sufficient consideration for it   The promise of the landlord is a waiver of the three months' notice, and a recognition of the tenant's right to treat with him as if the tenant could leave at the end of the year [156]   The agreement to reduce the rent may be made with an assignee of the term [157]

189. Reduction of rent, of right —There are various reasons for an abatement from, or a total suspension of, the rent Though the building which is the subject of the lease is not completed or delivered to the tenant till a month of the term has elapsed. any right to abatement from the rent will be regarded as waived if the lessee takes possession, pays regularly twenty-five separate month's rent thereafter without complaint, and takes for each a written receipt in full without demanding an abatement.[158]   It is elsewhere seen that destruction of or injury to the premises during the term, without the fault of the lessor, and without a covenant on his part against such destruction or injury, or

---

[153]*Smith* v *Ankrim*, 13 Serg & R 39   In *Rohrheimer* v *Hofman*, 103 Pa 409, the supreme court refrained from deciding whether the agreement was without consideration The court below found no consideration

[154]*Smith* v *Ankrim*, 13 Serg & R 39, *Taylor* v. *Winters*, 6 Phila. 126.

[155]*Taylor* v *Winters*, 6 Phila 126, *Smith* v *Ankrim*, 13 Serg & R 39

[156]*Wilgus* v *Whitehead*, 89 Pa 131

[157]*Fisher* v *Milliken*, 8 Pa 111, 49 Am Rep 497, *Rohrheimer* v *Hofman*, 103 Pa 409

[158]*Murphy* v *Marshell*, 179 Pa. 516, 36 Atl 294

against the continuance of its consequences, is no defense to the demand for rent [159]

190. Release.—The lessor may release the lessee from liability for rent that has accrued or that shall hereafter accrue, and in a suit for the rent such release can be proved without a special plea or notice of special matter; and a parol release from liability for rent falling due under a sealed lease, if supported by a consideration, will be valid, but if there be no consideration for it, even a written, but unsealed, release will be ineffectual.[160] The lessor may accept the lessee's assignee as a substitute for the lessee, agreeing to hold the lessee no longer liable, but from the lessor's receipt of rent from the assignee merely, no inference can be drawn that the lessee has been released.[161] The assignee of a term, who is under no contractual obligation to retain the ownership of the term, may be effectively released from paying a portion of the rent, on his agreeing to continue owner.[162]

191 Bankruptcy.—Under the bankruptcy act of 1841, a discharge in bankruptcy did not operate on an instalment of rent falling due between the decree of bankruptcy and the discharge. The lessee, *e g.*, being decreed a bankrupt December 30, 1842, he continued liable for an instalment of rent becoming due May 1, 1843, notwithstanding his discharge in June, 1845.[163]

192. Assignment of rent.— The lessor may assign the rent to fall due under the lease. After notice of the assignment the lessee must pay the rent to the assignee. He cannot set off against it a claim which he had against the lessor prior to the assignment.[164]

[159]*Fisher* v *Milliken*, 8 Pa 111, 49 Am Rep 497, *Smith* v *Ankrim*, 13 Serg & R 39.
[160]*Mannerbach* v *Keppleman*, 2 Woodw Dec 137, *People's Sav Bank* v *Alexander*, 140 Pa 22, 21 Atl 248 Cf *Whitehill* v *Wilson*, 3 Penn & W 405, 24 Am Dec 326
[161]*People's Sav Bank* v *Alexander*, 140 Pa 22, 21 Atl 248.

[162]*Bamsdall* v *Guild*, 32 Phila. Leg Int 152
[163]*Prentiss* v *Kingsley*, 10 Pa 120, *Bosler* v *Kuhn*, 8 Watts & S. 183.
[164]*Kiefaber* v. *Armour*, 10 Pa. Dist R 383.

CHAPTER XIII.

THE RIGHT OF DISTRESS.

153

193. At common law — The right of distress may arise from certain relations, without contract or as a result of contract. "Rent service," says Blackstone,[1] "is so called because it hath some corporeal service incident to it, as at the least, fealty or the feudal oath of fidelity   For if a tenant holds his land by fealty and ten shillings rent, or by the service of ploughing the lord's land, and five shillings rent, these pecuniary rents, being connected with personal services, are therefore called rent service And for these, in case they be behind or arrere, at the day appointed, the lord may distrain of common right, without reserving any special power of distress, provided he hath in himself the reversion or future estate of the lands and tenements after the lease or particular estate of the lessee or grantee is expired "

194. Distress by contract. — By contract the right of distress may be created where the law would not otherwise confer it The rent charge, e g , was a rent for which, apart from contract, there could be no distress, but for which the right of distress was stipulated in the deed. "In this case," says Blackstone,[2] "the land is liable to the distress, not of common right, but by virtue of the clause in the deed, and therefore it is called a rent charge, because in this manner the land is charged with a distress for the payment of it " As the right can be created by agreement of parties, when it would otherwise not be recognized, so the restrictions attending the right may be qualified or removed by agreement. If there be an agreement the lessor may distrain on goods which are not at the time upon the premises,[3] or for rent before it has become normally due,[4] or for a sum made payable as a penalty, in addition to the rent.[5] The right to

---

[1] 2 Com. 42, 3 Com 7

[2] 2 Com 42, 3 Com 7, *Ingersoll* v *Sergeant*, 1 Whart 337, *Arrison* v *Harmstead*, 2 Pa St 191, *Wallace* v *Harmstad*, 44 Pa. 492

[3] *Gold* v *Gleason*, 26 Pittsb L J N S. 10, *Dinner* v *McAndreus*, 10 Pa Dist R 221, *Owens* v *Shovlin*, 116 Pa 371, 9 Atl 484, *Goodwin* v *Sharkey*, 80 Pa 149

[4] *Owens* v *Shovlin*, 116 Pa 371, 9 Atl 484, *Goodwin* v *Sharkey*, 80 Pa 149, *Grant's Appeal*, 44 Pa 477

[5] *Latimer* v *Groetzinger*, 139 Pa

distrain may be conditioned on a previous demand of the rent.[6] The lessee, on assigning the term at a rental, retaining no reversion, may, if he contracts for the right, distrain for the rent.[7] The right of distress, as at common law, may be reduced or taken away by contract. Thus, if the landlord consents to a sublease of the premises, and agrees that the goods of the tenant, if left on the premises, in the possession of the sublessee, shall not be liable to distress, the right of distress upon such goods does not exist.[8] If goods of a stranger are on the premises and the landlord, thinking he has a right to distrain upon them, is about to do so, but, on X's request to refrain and his promising to be responsible for the rent, he refrains, X becomes liable for the rent, and his goods on the premises can be taken in distress, though otherwise not liable[9]

195. Time of distraining, relative to maturing of rent —There can be no distress until, under the terms of the lease, rent has become payable. If, *e. g.,* rent should be payable quarterly, and not in advance, there could be no distress within a quarter for a proportional part of that quarter's rent, in the absence of a justification for an apportionment of the rent.[10] The fact that rent for one period is already in arrear does not justify a distress for that rent, and for a part of the rent of the succeeding period, apportioned to the time of making the distress Thus, one quarter's rent being overdue, a distress during the next succeeding quarter cannot properly embrace any portion of the rent

---

207, 21 Atl 22 But so exceptional a right as that of distress cannot be given by implication

[6]*Helser* v *Pott,* 3 Pa St 179

[7]*Ege* v *Ege.* 5 Watts, 134, *Manuel* v *Reath,* 5 Phila 11

[8]*Perrin* v *Wells,* 155 Pa 299, 26 Atl. 543 In *Royer* v *Ake,* 3 Penr & W 461 the lease stipulated for distress after five days' default in paying rent

[9]*Booth* v *Hoenig,* 7 Pa Dist R.

529 A subsequent offer of X to give up the keys and possession of the premises to the lessor could not expunge this liability

[10]*McElroy* v *Dice,* 17 Pa 163, *Burchard* v *Rees,* 1 Whart 377, *Morris* v *Parker,* 1 Ashm (Pa) 187 If rent is payable yearly, there can be no distress for it four months before the expiration of the year *Jackson's Appeal,* 3 Montg Co L Rep 96

of this quarter [11] That the tenant is, without fraud, about to remove the goods from the premises,[12] or that he has made an assignment of all his property including the goods on the premises,
for the benefit of creditors,[13] does not make the rent for the current period distrainable. Under § 1 of the act of March 25,
1825,[14] applicable to Philadelphia, and, by the act of March 29,
1870,[15] extended to Pittsburg and Allegheny, if the tenant, before the rent becomes payable, fraudulently conveys away or
carries off from the demised premises his goods and chattels, with
intent to defraud the landlord of his remedy of distress, the
landlord may consider the rent as apportioned up to the time of
such conveying away or carrying off, and he may make a distress
for it.[16] The landlord cannot even distrain on the day on which
the rent becomes due, but must wait until the day after.[17]　If,
e g , rent falls due on January 10, there can be no distress until
January 11.[18] "As the rent was not payable until the last minute of the natural day, the distress could not be made until the
next day, for until that time it is not absolutely due "[19]

196　Computing time when rent is payable.—The rent is normally payable on the last day of the period for which it is the
consideration　If it is payable quarterly, under a lease for one
year, beginning on the 1st day of April, the first quarter's rent
becomes due on the 30th day of June.　If the rent is payable at
the end of the term beginning April 1, 1903, it falls due at midnight on the 31st day of March, 1904.[20]　A term beginning Jan-

[11]*M'Kinney* v *Reader,* 6 Watts,
34

[12]*McElroy* v *Dice,* 17 Pa 163

[13]*Morris* v *Parker,* 1 Ashm (Pa)
187

[14] 1 Pepper & L Digest, 2639, P L
114

[15] P L 669

[16]Cf *Purfel* v *Sand*, 1 Ashm
(Pa) 120

[17]*M'Kinney* v *Reader,* 6 Watts,
34, *Beyer* v *Fenstermacher,* 2
Whart 95.

[18]*Donaldson* v *Smith,* 1 Ashm
(Pa) 197

[19]*Hoskins* v *Houston,* 2 Clark
(Pa) 489　The rent falling due
January 1, the death of the tenant
on that day made distress impossible

[20]*Marys* v *Anderson,* 24 Pa 272,
Donaldson v *Smith,* 1 Ashm (Pa)
197, Taylor, Land & T § 573

uary 10, 1829, payable quarterly, the last quarter's rent was overdue on January 10, 1830, if it had not been paid.[21]

197. **Rent payable in advance.**— In *Diller* v. *Roberts*[22] the court declined to express an opinion whether rent payable in advance could be distrained for immediately upon its becoming payable The question was again presented in *Beyer* v. *Fenstermacher*,[23] where a lease for one year, beginning April 1, 1834, stipulated that the rent should be paid quarterly, *viz.,* on April 1, July 1, and October 1, 1834, and on January 1, 1835 It was held that distress could properly be made during the third quarter, for the rent of that and the two preceding quarters. The right to distrain for rent payable in advance "must be conceded "[24]

198. **Payment of rent accelerated.**— As rent may be made payable in advance, or at any time within the period during which it accrues, *e. g.,* within the year, quarter, month, etc., as well as at the end of such period, so, though the rent be made primarily payable at the end of such period, the time for paying it may be accelerated, on the happening of any contingency Thus the lease may stipulate that if the tenant shall at any time during the term remove, or manifest an intention to remove, his goods from the premises, without having paid all the rent that shall become due under the lease, the whole rent for the en-

[21]*Donaldson* v *Smith,* 1 Ashm (Pa) 197 A lease for one year commencing March 25, 1807, the 3d year's rent became due March 25, 1810. The distress was on March 26 *Kelly* v *Davenport,* 1 Browne (Pa) 231 Rent being payable on July 1, October 1, January 1, and April 1, if the tenant dies on January 1, he dies before the right of distress accrues That right does not accrue until the last minute of January 1. *Hoskins* v *Houston,* 2 Clark (Pa) 489

[22]13 Serg. & R 60, 15 Am Dec 578.

[23]2 Whart 95

[24]Mercur, J , *Seyfert* v *Bean,* 83 Pa 450, *Moss's Appeal,* 35 Pa 162, *Goodwin* v *Sharkey,* 80 Pa. 149, *Murphy* v *Marshell,* 179 Pa 516, 36 Atl 294 In *Anderson's Appeal,* 3 Pa St 218, there was a lease of Bedford Mineral Springs for five years, commencing April 1, 1840, at an annual rent of $1,250, payable September 1 of each year. It was suggested that on September 1 the entire year's rent fell due, and that it could be recovered by distress Cf *Purdy's Appeal,* 23 Pa 97.

tire term shall be deemed due and payable [25] Under such a lease, on the removal or the manifestation of the intention to remove, the landlord could distrain for the whole rent. It would not be necessary that the intention or attempt to remove should be fraudulent.[26] But such an agreement would be no warrant for a distress elsewhere than on the leased premises [27] The lease may likewise provide that, if the lessee becomes "embarrassed," or makes an assignment for the benefit of creditors, or is "sold out by sheriff's sale," then the rent "for balance of term shall at once become due and payable, as if by the terms of the lease it were all payable in advance." Under such a clause, the whole rent on the happening of a sheriff's sale would become payable, and being such, might be paid from the proceeds of the execution, in preference to the debt due the execution creditor [28] A provision that all the rent shall become due if the lessee removes or attempts to remove is not rendered operative by his simply intending to remove and notifying the landlord of that intention.[29] An agreement subsequent to the lease may provide for the prematuring of the rent on the happening of certain events Such events happening, the rent may be distrained for.[30] The lease may make all the rent pay-

[25]*Grant's Appeal*, 44 Pa 477, *Goodwin* v *Sharkey*, 80 Pa 149, *Owens* v *Shovlin*, 116 Pa 371, 9 Atl 484, *Platt* v *Johnson*, 168 Pa 47, 47 Am St Rep 877, 31 Atl 935

[26]*Goodwin* v *Sharkey*, 80 Pa 149, *Platt* v *Johnson*, 168 Pa 47, 47 Am St Rep 877, 31 Atl 935, *Owens* v *Shovlin*, 116 Pa 371, 9 Atl 484 In the cases cited the lease contained the express stipulation that, the whole rent becoming payable on the removal or manifestation of intention to remove, might be at once distrained for Probably the right to distrain would be an incident to the maturing of the rent but in *Owens* v *Shovlin*, 116 Pa 371, 9 Atl 484, Green, J, remarks "Not only did

the remaining rent for the term become due and payable, but it was also collectible by distress or otherwise because the lease so declared"

[27]*Owens* v *Shovlin*, 116 Pa 371, 9 Atl 484

[28]*Platt* v *Johnson*, 168 Pa 47, 47 Am St Rep 877, 31 Atl 935

[29]*Klein* v *McFarland*, 5 Pa Super Ct 110 The tenant notified his landlord in May that he intended to vacate the house on July 1 The landlord had no right to treat all the rent as due and distrain for it till some attempt was made to carry out the intention

[30]*Teufel* v *Rowan*, 179 Pa. 408, 36 Atl. 224.

able, on failure to pay any instalment when it becomes due. On such failure distress for all could be resorted to [31]

199 Payment of rent retarded.—It is possible for the lease to provide that, on the occurrence of a certain event, the time of paying the rent shall be postponed The event happening, the right to distrain would be adjourned But a provision in a lease for seven years, that if the lessee shall make default for three months beyond the 1st day of April of each year, the lessor may re-enter and dispossess the former "unless, for the first year, it is agreed that he shall have six months to pay up after the expiration of the first year, but three only thereafter," —does not postpone the maturing of the first year's rent six months, or that of the rent of the subsequent years three months It only conditions the right of re-entry The tenant vacating the land within the first year, distress could be at once made on the grain therein.[32]

200. Payment of rent conditioned.—If the duty of paying the rent is, by the terms of the lease, conditioned upon the landlord's making improvements, and he fails to make them, there can be no distress. A lease was for three years and five and a half months. For the entire term $1,660 were to be paid,— $20 on a day named, and thereafter $40 the last day of every month For the first instalment of $40 it was held that there could be no distress, because in the lease the landlord had contracted to make certain alterations on plans decided by a third person, and these alterations had not been made A lease, upon a single consideration for the whole term, though payable in periodical instalments, is an entire contract, and the landlord can recover no portion of it until he has fully performed, unless performance has been waived or prevented by the tenant.[33]

[31]*Merrill* v *Trimmer*, 2 Pa Co Ct 49

[32]*Smith* v. *Meanor*, 16 Serg & R. 375

[33]*Block* v *Dowling*, 7 Pa Dist R. 261.

201. Spoliation of deed.—The right to distrain for rent may be lost by the fraudulent alteration of the lease by the landlord The rent cannot be proved by other means than the deed, and the deed cannot be employed as a means of proof after the alteration   This principle applies to the right of a ground landlord to distrain for ground rent [34]

202 Rent must be certain.— A distress can be made only for a rent which is, by the lease itself, made "certain" and fixed; [35] and the reason for insisting on this certainty is stated to be "that the tenant may know, in case he be threatened with a distress, what he is to pay to prevent it, or, in case his goods shall be distrained, what sum to tender in order to retain them," [36] and that the landlord may know for what amount to distrain. [37] It follows that where there is no lease, or no lease defining the rent, there can be no distress.   Hence, if B is in possession of A's land, under no lease, but in circumstances which entitle A to compensation for B's use and occupation, A cannot distrain for any compensation [38]   Sometimes the lease undertakes to say what will be rendered as compensation for the possession, but does so too vaguely.   A lease for three years stipulated that no rent was to be paid for the first year, provided that the tenant put the dwelling-house in such order as would make it convenient for his purpose.   The rent for the other years was to be

---

[34] *Wallace* v *Harmstad*, 44 Pa 492 Cf *Arrison* v *Harmstead*, 2 Pa St 191, *Wallace* v *Harmstad*, 15 Pa 462 53 Am Dec 603

[35] *Wells* v *Hornish*, 3 Penr & W 30, *Diller* v *Roberts*, 13 Serg & R 60, 15 Am Dec 578, *Fry* v *Jones*, 2 Rawle, 11; *Com* v *Contner*, 18 Pa 439 Cf *Spencer* v *Kunkle*, 2 Grant Cas 406

[36] *Wells* v *Hornish*, 3 Penr & W 30, *Grier* v. *Cowan*, Addison (Pa) 347

[37] *Grier* v *Cowan*, Addison (Pa.) 347.

[38] *Wells* v *Hornish*, 3 Penr & W 30 Hence, in trespass for taking B's goods in distress, it is not proper to allow A's witness to give an opinion as to the reasonable rent for the period of B's occupancy   A lease to B for life, B paying the interest on a mortgage and also interest on the price paid by A for the land, makes the interest rent, for which there may be distress *Read* v. *Kitchen*, 1 Am. L. Reg 635.

£30 per annum. The rent was paid but distress was levied because the repairs had not been made. The court in replevin held the distress improper, because the value of the repairs intended by the parties was uncertain.[39] In *Diller* v. *Roberts*,[40] a lease was made by Ream to Roberts for one year, commencing April 1, 1816, of a tavern and lot of ground, for £47 rent, to be paid in advance. Roberts was also to finish a room in the house, for his expense in doing which he was to be paid at the end of the year. He was to keep a public house and obtain a license for it. He was to replace two wagon loads of dung, which, then on the premises, he was permitted to use. Ream was to have the right until August 1, 1816, to keep his horse in the stable, the roof of which he was to repair by April 5. The first year's rent being paid in advance, distress was made for £47, the second year's, on April 30, 1817. Although there was a holding over, and usually it is understood that the tenant who holds over is to pay the same rent, it could not be known what the rent for the premises, apart from the other stipulations in the lease, was. Forty-seven pounds represented, not the value of the premises only, but also that of the promises and reservations, which could not persist into the second year. Distress was therefore unallowable. "As some of the things which were to be done the first year could not be done the second year, I do not see," says Tilgham, Ch. J., "on what ground the law would imply a contract that the same money should be paid the second year, and on the first day of the year."

[39]*Grier* v *Cowan*, Addison (Pa) 347. In *Shaffer* v. *Sutton*, 5 Binn. 228, the lease was for seven months and three weeks, the lessee daubing and chinking the house, and paying the taxes of the preceding year This was held a rent certain because the justices' jury could easily assess the damages for not daubing and chinking, and last year's taxes could be readily ascertained by a reference to the assessment books In *Hohly* v *German Reformed Soc* 2 Pa St 293, the consideration of a lease to an organist was his services as organist and foresinger Such rent would be too indefinite *Shaffer* v *Sutton*, criticized

[40] 13 Serg & R 60, 15 Am. Dec. 578.

LAND. & TEN 11.

203 Hold-over tenancies.— The case just considered was one in which the holding-over tenant could not be inferred tacitly to agree to pay the money-rent mentioned in the lease. When such can be inferred, a distress for this rent becoming due after the expiration of the lease, is permissible. Thus a tenant for one year at $84 37½ quarterly rental holding over two years beyond the term, distress could be had after the expiration of the second quarter of the third year, for the two quarters of that year, and the last of the preceding year [41] A lease for one year, at $150 rent, payable quarterly in advance. The tenant paid the rent for the year, and continued in possession the next For the first three quarters' rent of that year, distress was valid [42] The rent being one half of grain, etc, under a lease for one year, rent for the second following year can be distrained for, the tenant holding over.[43] A lessee subletting for one year, and the sublessee holding over beyond the year, the former could distrain for rent accruing during the holding over.[44]

204. Rent payable in kind.— It is not necessary that the rent be payable in money in order to be recoverable by distress. When in *Warren* v. *Forney*[45] the question was first presented, the court declined to give an answer. The rent there reserved was "one half part of all the grain of every kind, and all hemp, flax, potatoes, apples, fruit, and other produce." It has since been conceded that for such rent there may be a distress [46] A grist-mill being let for "one third of the toll which the mill grinds," a distress for 160½ bushels of different kinds of grain, amounting in value to $76 58, was sustained. "If," says Rog-

---

[41] *Phillips* v *Monges,* 4 Whart 226
[42] *Beyer* v *Fenstermacher,* 2 Whart 95
[43] *Warren* v *Forney,* 13 Serg & R. 52
[44] *Ege* v *Ege,* 5 Watts, 134
[45] 13 Serg & R 52
[46] *Brown* v *Jaquette,* 2 Del Co

Rep 245, Paxson, J *Rinehart* v *Olwine,* 5 Watts & S 157 "The only remedy for the landlord is by distress, as in the case of a money rent," i e, he does not own the share till it is severed and set apart to him by the tenant, or until he takes it by distress

ers, J., "the tenant keeps an account of the toll, which it is his duty to do, the rent may be reduced to the utmost certainty."[47] A forge and connected lands were let for a term of years, in consideration of the tenant's making specified repairs, and paying 1¼ ton of bar-iron For the iron, there could be a distress[48] A lease of a furnace for five years named the rent as $800 yearly "payable in bar-iron of good merchantable quality drawn to order at $5 per 100 pounds at the works, no iron to be drawn less than one-half inch by an inch and a half " The right to distrain was tacitly conceded but only after a specific demand had been made for the bar-iron Were this not so, it was said, the landlord could exact cash in payment instead of the iron, putting the tenant in a more unfavorable position than the parties intended[49] In such cases, the distress must not be for the money which expresses the value of the articles, but for the articles themselves The tenant has a right, after the distress, to tender the amount and costs, and stop the sale. The landlord may distrain when his rent is grain, for so many bushels of grain, and name the value, in order that, if the goods should not be replevied, or the arrears tendered, the officer may know what amount in money is to be raised by the sale. The tenant may tender the arrears in grain.[50]

205 Provision for reduction of rent — The lease may provide that, on a certain contingency, the rent named in it shall be reduced to a lower specified sum This is not inconsistent with the right to distrain for the larger sum, if the event has not occurred on which it is to be lessened. The lease, e. g , may

[47]*Fry* v *Jones*, 2 Rawle, 11
[48]*Jones* v *Gundrim*, 3 Watts & S 531
[49]*Helser* v *Pott*, 3 Pa 179 With out demand and specification of the iron required the tenant could not, even after the distress, know how much, or of what size, or when to tender.

[50]*Warren* v *Forney*, 13 Serg & R 52 The warrant in *Jones* v *Gundrim*, 3 Watts & S 531, required the bailiff to distrain "the said ton and a fourth of bar iron, and in default thereof the other goods and chattels" of the tenant.

stipulate for $1,500 yearly rent, with the qualification, that if the tenant shall punctually pay the rent as it falls due quarterly, "a reduction will be made of $75 from each said quarter's rent, otherwise the rent to be and remain the full amount as above mentioned" Distress for the larger rent is allowable.[51]   A lease for five years of iron works contained the lessee's covenant to pay the annual rent of $7,000; but the lessor agreed that if, at the end of the term, "it shall not manifestly appear" that the works have cleared beyond all expenses of constructing them, the annual sum of $12,000, the rent shall be $6,000.   Holding that distress for the rent was allowable, Rogers, J., remarks· "The lease is for $7,000 a year reducible, it is true, to $6,000 in a certain contingency.   The rent is payable in money and is payable yearly, for where the rent is ascertained, a general reservation makes it payable yearly.   *Cole* v. *Surry,* Latch, 264. Besides, the rent is undoubtedly certain, to the amount of $6,000, which the tenant must pay, at all events, and the landlord limits his claim to that sum"[52]

206   Apportionment of rent — If the lease covers several tenements at a gross rent, and, for any reason, the tenant is unable to obtain possession of one of them, the landlord cannot, apportioning the rent, distrain for the rent thus found to be due for those tenements of which the lessee takes possession Four contiguous stores were leased for the gross sum of $4,250 per year.   Of one of them a prior tenant refused to give possession.   The tenant took possession of the other three   The landlord, estimating the rental of this as fairly $1,500 per year, distrained for one third of $2,750, the rent for four months, of the other three tenements in arrear.[53]   A demurrer to an

---

[51]*Fernwood Masonic Hall Asso* v *Jones,* 102 Pa 307

[52]*Ege* v *Ege,* 5 Watts, 134   The landlord claimed against the proceeds of an execution sale

[53] In *Com* v *Contner,* 18 Pa 439, rent for land and chattels on it was

$3,500, but the lease furnished indications that the parties intended $2,-500 to be the rent of the land and $1,000 that of the chattels   For the former there could therefore be a distress

avowry in replevin on the ground that there was no averment in it that the stores were rented separately was sustained [54] But, if the tenement out of which the rent issues is divided by the tenant's assignment or conveyance of a portion of it, and the landlord releases the part thus assigned or conveyed from the rent, a part of the rent proportional to the value of the part not released will continue to be payable on account of that part, and for so much of the rent there may be a distress.[55] The owner of a rent charge may divide it by will or deed, so as to make the tenant liable, without attornment, to several distresses.[56]

207 Assignee of part of reversion; apportionment.— The land which is the source of the rent may be divided by its owner, X, and a part assigned to A, and another to B, or a part retained by X, the grantor, and the other part assigned to C. By such division of the premises, an apportionment of the rent falling due in the future is effected, and in the first case, A and B, or in the second case X and C, may severally distrain for so much of the rent as represents the value of the portion of the land conveyed to or retained by him [57] So, the integral estate may be resolved into fractional parts, as by a conveyance to two or more as tenants in common, or by a descent, at the death of the lessor, upon two or more heirs. Each tenant in common would have a right to an aliquot part of the rent, and could dis-

---

[54] *Allegaert* v. *Smart*, 2 W N. C 397 But the apportioned rent could have been recovered in assumpsit. *Seabrook* v *Moyer*, 88 Pa 417

[55] *Ingersoll* v *Sergeant*, 1 Whart. 337 This was a ground-rent After releasing a part of the ground from the rent, the landlord distrained for a portion of the rent upon the goods on the residue of the ground In replevin by the ground tenant, Kennedy, J , held that the rent was apportioned, that distress was permissible, that the apportionment could be made, however, only by the jury

in the replevin suit, and, as the verdict did not ascertain the respective values of the part of the premises released, and of the other part, a new trial would be necessary, unless the parties could agree on an apportionment

[56] *DeCoursey* v *Guarantee Trust & S D Co* 81 Pa 217.

[57] *De Coursey* v *Guarantee Trust & S D Co* 81 Pa 217, *Reed* v *Ward*, 22 Pa 144, *Bank of Pennsylvania* v *Wise*, 3 Watts, 404, *Linton* v *Hart*, 25 Pa 193, 64 Am Dec 691.

train for it.[58] The apportionment of the rent will be according
to the value, not the areas, of the respective parts into which the
land may be divided [59]

208. Apportionment by agreement.—The tenant contracting
for the purchase of the reversion with the landlord may agree
with the latter that the rent for the current quarter payable in
advance shall be apportioned according to the ratio of the part
of the quarter elapsed when the conveyance is to be made, to the
residue of it. The landlord cannot distrain for more than this
part of the rent.[60]

209. Provision for increase of rent — The lease may specify a
rent and provide for an increase of it on the happening of an
event, the increase being determinable by the nature of the
event On the happening of the event distress could be resorted
to, for the unconditional rent, and also for the addition. A
lease specified $1,200, as yearly rental, payable monthly, and
provided that if the landlord should, during the term, "add to
the said premises permanent improvements or betterments,
to the amount of $500 or more," the tenant should pay "rent
in addition to the rent above reserved, at the rate of $30 per
annum for every sum of $500 or fractional part thereof that
shall be expended in such permanent improvements or betterments." The landlord spent $4,000, so that the rent was in-
creased to $1,440 per annum. For the whole of this rent in
arrear there could be distress.[61] It has even been held that if,
subsequently to the making of and occupying under the lease,
there is an agreement by the tenant, for a consideration, to pay
a larger rent for his past occupancy than that reserved in the
lease, for such increased rent distress will be lawful Thus, in
Brisben v. *Wilson*[62] a factory was let for three years at the rent

[58]*Ibid*
[59]*Ibid* , *Seabrook* v *Moyer*, 88 Pa.
417
[60]*Lyon* v *Houk*, 9 Watts, 193.

[61]*Detwiler* v *Cox*, 75 Pa 200; *Anderson's Appeal*, 3 Pa St 218.
[62] 60 Pa. 452

of $1,000 per year payable quarterly, the tenant having the right to surrender the premises at any time within the term on giving six months' notice   Fifteen months after taking possession, the tenant, owing $1,150, proposed to surrender the lease at once, and the landlord consented on his agreeing to pay $500 additional rent   The whole of the rent, *viz ,* $1,650, could be distrained for

210   Distress for penalty.—When a sum of money additional to the rent is made payable as a penalty for the breach of a covenant, enforcement of the payment of it cannot be effected by distress   A lease for two years, reserving a monthly rental of $416 67, contained an agreement by the tenants made for themselves and their assigns, that they "will not engage in the retail or wholesale business of bargaining for, buying and selling carpets and oil-cloths" upon the premises during the term "under the penalty of $10,000, to be paid by the said lessees or their assigns, in the nature of rent, in addition to the amount above mentioned, in equal monthly instalments at the times of payment of the rent aforesaid "   The assignee of the lease having engaged in selling carpets and oil-cloths, the landlord notified him that he would be required to pay rent at the rate of $1,250 per month.   Distress for this sum was not permissible   "If it, the penalty," says Green J , "is in the nature of rent or to be paid in the nature of rent, and yet in fact is not rent, it cannot have the incident of distress, because that incident pertains only to that which, in strict legal contemplation, is rent."[63]

211   Taxes, gas, steam heat.— The duty of paying for all gas consumed may be so assumed by the tenant as to make it a part of the rent.   In *Fernwood Masonic Hall Asso.* v. *Jones*[64] a lease

[63]*Latimer* v *Groetzinger,* 139 Pa. 207, 21 Atl 22

[64] 102 Pa 307   An indorsement on the lease provided that the rent to be paid should be "$3,000, with the addition of taxes upon the additional valuation which may be assessed upon this property for the year 1887 "   This made the additional tax a part of the rent, of which the landlord was entitled to preferential payment from the estate of the de-

of a summer hotel or boarding-house, which was lighted by gas
manufactured on the premises from gasoline, named the yearly
rental as $1,500, payable quarterly. The lessee covenanted to pay
this rent, and to pay for all gas consumed at the rate of $3 per
1,000 feet. Rent proper, to the extent of $700 being in arrear,
and $105 worth of gas not being paid for, there could be a dis-
tress for $805. Says Trunkey, J., "the covenant to pay for the
gas is as much a part of the rent as would be a covenant to pay
taxes upon the premises during the term." Taxes already assessed when the lease is made, e. g., for the year preceding the
making of the lease, could be recovered by distress [65] A lease
of a dwelling-house and nine green-houses for the term of two
years and three months, at a rental of $1,600 for the whole
term, gave the privilege of an additional term at the rental of
$1,025 payable quarterly, the lessor furnishing steam heat at
75 cents per 1,000 units to be paid for monthly. The price of
the steam heat as well as arrears of the other rent could be properly distrained for [66] While water rent may be made part of
the rent, and, when it is so made, may be distrained for, it is not
made a part of the rent by the lessee's mere covenant that "he
will pay for any gas used on said premises, and all water taxes
assessed thereon," the water not being furnished by the lessor
nor the water rent payable to him, and under such a lease there
can be no distress by the landlord for the unpaid water rent.[67]

212. Relation of landlord and tenant; ground rent.—The
right to distress, when it is not the subject of a contract, depends on the relation of landlord and tenant, lessor and lessee [68]
The lord may distrain of common right, says Blackstone,[69]

ceased tenant *Morgan's Estate*, 1
Pa Dist R 402, *Scott's Estate*, 35
Pittsb L J 443
   [65]*Shaffer* v *Sutton*, 5 Binn 228
The proceeding was to recover pos-
session
   [66]*Conroy* v. *Bitner*, 10 Lanc. L.
Rev 185.

   [67]*Evans* v *Lincoln Co* 204 Pa 448,
54 Atl 321
   [68]*Fry* v *Jones*, 2 Rawle, 11, *Helser* v *Pott*, 3 Pa St 179.
   [69] 2 Bl Com 42

"without reserving any special power of distress, provided he hath in himself the reversion or future estate of the lands and tenements, after the lease or particular estate of the lessee or grantee is expired." The statute, *Quia emptores terrarum,* which breaks all *nexus* between the grantor and grantee of lands in fee, has not been recognized in Pennsylvania [70] It follows that when A enfeoffs B in fee, or conveys to B in fee, reserving a perpetual rent, the rent is a rent service, to which distress is incident,[71] while in England and other jurisdictions in which that statute operates the rent could not be collected by distress, in the absence of an agreement that it might be so collected. The rent would be, in short, a rent seck or a rent charge.

213. Term of years.— The right to distrain attaches to a lease for years, of whatever magnitude,—for a month, a quarter, four months, a year, two,[73] three,[74] four, five,[75] ninety-nine,[76] or any number of years It attaches to a tenancy at will, or from year to year. The 14th section of the act of March 21, 1772,[77] enacts that "it shall and may be lawful for any person or persons, having any rent in arrear or due upon any lease for life or lives, or for one or more years, or at will, ended or determined, to distrain for such arrears" after the end of the lease. When dower is set apart to the widow in money charged on the land, she is regarded as a quasi landlord of the land with the right of distress.[78] If in proceedings to eject the tenant on the ground

---

[70]*Ingersoll* v. *Sergeant,* 1 Whart 336

[71]*Ingersoll* v. *Sergeant,* 1 Whart 336, *Franciscus* v *Reigart,* 4 Watts, 98, *M'Curdy* v *Randolph,* 2 Clark (Pa) 323, *Arrison* v *Harmstead,* 2 Pa St 191; *Wallace* v *Harmstad,* 15 Pa 462, 53 Am Dec. 603, *Wallace* v *Harmstad,* 44 Pa 492, *Kenege* v *Elliott,* 9 Watts, 258

[73]*Latimer* v. *Groetzinger,* 139 Pa. 207, 21 Atl 22, *Hoskins* v. *Houston,* 2 Clark (Pa) 489.

[74]*Brisben* v *Wilson,* 60 Pa 452, *Grier* v *Cowan,* Addison (Pa) 347

[75]*Ege* v *Ege,* 5 Watts, 134

[76]*Moss's Appeal,* 35 Pa 162

[77] 1 Pepper & L. Digest, 2635; 1 Smith's Laws, 370

[78]*Shouffler* v *Coover,* 1 Watts & S 400, *Davis* v *Davis,* 128 Pa 100, 18 Atl 514, *Henderson* v *Boyer,* 44 Pa 220, Trickett, Partition, 162.

that his lease has expired, he defeats the landlord by causing the freeholders to disagree, by means of evidence that he has a lease for the current year, he will be estopped from denying this lease, when the landlord distrains for the rent of one of the quarters of the current year.[79]

214. Cropper.— If one hires a man to work his farm and gives him a share of the produce he is a cropper. He has no interest in the land, but receives his share as the price of his labor. The possession is still in the owner of the land, who alone can maintain trespass; nor can he distrain, for he does not maintain the relation of landlord and tenant, which is inseparable from the right of distress.[80] The tenant has possession of the land and of the crops, and the landlord must await his separation of his share of the latter, before he becomes owner of it. But the cropper has possession neither of the land nor of its crop, although his contract with the owner entitles him to a share in specie of the crops. Should he improperly take the whole crop, the landlord could not distrain for his share of it.[81]

215. Character of lessor.— The lease may be made by an owner in severalty, or by two or more cotenants,[82]—in which case each may distrain for his share of the rent,[83]—by a corporation, e. g., a railroad company,[84] a building association,[85] or any other.[86] The lessor holding the land in trust for others may

---

[79]*Hostetter* v *Hykas*, 3 Brewst. (Pa) 162

[80]*Fry* v *Jones*, 2 Rawle, 11. Cf *Steel* v *Frick*, 56 Pa 172, *Adams* v. *McKesson*, 53 Pa 81, 91 Am Dec 183

[81]*Brown* v. *Jaquette*, 2 Del Co Rep 245

[82]*Goodwin* v *Sharkey*, 80 Pa 149 In *Jones* v *Gundrim*, 3 Watts & S 531, two owners having leased land and caused a distress for rent, in replevin against the bailiff, the court declined to say whether, where the lease shows the lessors to be tenants in common, they may join in the avowry The lease was joint There was no occasion to deduce in the avowry the title to the lessors, and it was not deduced The distress was valid

[83]*De Coursey* v *Guarantee Trust & S D Co* 81 Pa 217

[84]*Pittsburg, J E & E R Co* v. *Altoona & B C R Co* 196 Pa. 452, 46 Atl 431, *Bonsall* v *Comly*, 44 Pa 442

[85]*Lengert Co.* v *Bellevue Bldg. & L Asso* 15 Pa Super Ct 380

[86]*Fernwood Masonic Hall Asso.* **v.**

distrain,[87] as may guardians of the infant owner,[88] but the *cestui que trust,* not entitled to the possession, may not.[89] The lessor may be a vendee to whom the legal title has not yet been conveyed The vendor cannot as such distrain for the rent due [90]

216. Assignee of the reversion —When the reversion is transferred from the lessor, by his own act,[91] by a sheriff's sale,[92] by his death,[93] the right to rent falling due subsequently passes to the transferee, while the right to rent already due remains with him, unless he assigns it, or at his death it devolves upon his executor or administrator. The transferee of the reversion though he be such in trust for others[94] may distrain for the rent becoming due after the transfer. If the conveyance is to several of undivided fractions of the land, they may all make distress [95]

217. Assignee of rent — From the doctrine that the relation of landlord and tenant must exist in order to authorize one party to make a distress on the premises of another, the conclusion has been drawn that, while the assignee of the lease and of the rent becomes entitled to the remedy of distress for it, the assignee of a contingent right to the rent acquires no right of distress. In *Helser* v. *Pott,*[96] A contracted to sell land to B. B leased it (a forge, furnace, and saw-mill) for five years to C, who agreed, as rent, to pay $800 yearly in bar-iron to be demanded and specified by B. C's interest in the lease and personalty on the prem-

---

Jones, 102 Pa 307, *Garrett* v *Longnecker,* 2 Legal Record Rep 174

[87]*Anderson's Appeal,* 3 Pa St 218

[88]*Warren* v *Forney,* 13 Serg & R 52

[89]*Chicago & A Oil & Min Co* v *Barnes,* 62 Pa 445

[90]*Helser* v *Pott,* 3 Pa St 179

[91]*Collender Co* v *Speer,* 29 Pittsb L J. 125, *De Coursey* v *Guarantee Trust & S D Co* 81 Pa 217

[92]*Hoskins* v *Houston,* 2 Clark (Pa) 489 *Wood* v *Custer,* 16 Montg Co L Rep 118 The point

was not decided in *Wells* v *Hornish,* 3 Penr & W 30

[93] The devisee for life may distrain for rent falling due after the devisor's death *Lewis's Appeal,* 66 Pa. 312

[94]*Collender Co* v *Speer,* 29 Pittsb L J 125

[95]*Chicago & A Oil & Min Co* v *Barnes,* 62 Pa 445

[96] 3 Pa St 179 It is to be observed that the order of B from time to time was necessary to entitle A to receive the rent from H and G.

ıses was sold by the sheriff to D, who sold it to H and G   H and
G indorsed on the lease to C a promise to comply with it, so long
as they should carry on the iron works, and to pay the rent to A
on account of B's purchase money on B's order. A subsequently
distrained for the rent which H and G had neglected to pay him.
Concluding that the stipulation indorsed by H and G, and B's
orders to deliver the iron to A, did not make an assignment of
the lease, the court adjudged the distress by A invalid. "We
see," says Rogers, J., "no indication of an intention that Bowers
should cease to be lessor, or that Pott should have control of the
rents, so as to enable him to distrain for its nonpayment   Had
an assignment of the lease been in contemplation of the parties,
it seems strange it should be drawn in its present form."   The
right of the assignee of a ground rent to distrain for arrears of
the rent has never been questioned, although the owner of the
rent has no reversion in the land and therefore neither can assign, nor professes to assign, a reversion.[97]   But it was held by
Lewis, P. J., in 1844[98] that the assignment of rent to accrue
under a two years' lease did not pass to the assignee the right of
distress; though the assignor might have distrained for the use
of the assignee, so long as he remained owner of the reversion,
and that after the later sale of the reversion by the sheriff, the
right of distress would exist only in the sheriffs vendee, and not
in the previous assignee of the rent,—a doctrine inconsistent
with that of *Kost* v *Theis*[99] where it was held that the lessor's
assignee of the lease could distrain, although the ownership of
the reversion continued in the lessor.

[97]*Ingersoll* v *Sergeant*, 1 Whart.
337, *Manuel* v *Reath*, 5 Phila 11,
Arrison v *Harmstead*, 2 Pa 191,
Wallace v *Harmstad*, 15 Pa 462, 53
Am Dec 603, *Wallace* v *Harmstad*,
44 Pa 492, *Franciscus* v *Reigart*, 4
Watts, 98. A ground rent reserved
upon a conveyance in fee is, in Pennsylvania, a rent service, and to all
rent services the right of distress is
incident of common right   The assignee of such rent has the same
right of distress [as the original
ground landlord], there being no re
version in the assignor capable of
being retained by him so as to affect
the right of distress by the assignee.
[98]*Hoskins* v *Houston*, 2 Clark
(Pa) 489
[99] 20 W N C 545, 12 Atl 262

218. Sublessor and assignor of term.—The lessee for years may assign his rights under the lease, that is, all his rights, and for the whole period of the term. If he does so, reserving a rent. he will not be able to distrain for the rent, unless the assignee has agreed that he may make distress.[100]   If, however, he retains a reversion, if, *e g*, his lease being for five years, he during the first year sublets from year to year, he will during all but the last year have a right of distress for the rent reserved by him.[101]   The lease to A was for five years from November 1, 1831. In August, 1831, A sublet to B, on the same terms, for one year, or from year to year, and B remained in possession until March 23, 1835, when his property was sold on execution. As A had a right to distrain, he also had a right to one year's rent from the proceeds of the sale.[102]

219. Quantity of rent distrainable—There is no limit to the amount of the rent for which, or to the period for whose rent, distress is permissible. The landlord may distrain not simply for the rent which has last fallen due, but for any number of instalments. Thus, rent falling due on April 1, July 1, October 1, and January 1, a distress can be levied on January 10, not merely for the rent of the quarter ending on January 1, but for that of the preceding quarters   So, if rent is payable yearly, distress can be made for one, two, three, or more years[103] not

---

[100]*Ege* v *Ege*, 5 Watts, 134, *Moulson's Estate*, 1 Brewst (Pa) 296, *Manuel* v *Reath*, 5 Phila 11

[101]*Ege* v *Ege*, 5 Watts, 134, *Goodwin* v. *Sharkey*, 80 Pa 149, *Walbridge* v *Pruden*, 102 Pa 1

[102]*Ege* v. *Ege*, 5 Watts, 134   "Was this" says Rogers, J , "a contract or assignment of the whole term, or an underletting from year to year with a reversionary interest in the lessor? For if a lessee for years assign over his whole term, reserving a rent without a special clause of distress, he cannot distrain for the rent so reserved. Bradby, Distress-es, 1 Law Lib 68   But the law is otherwise if this was a lease from year to year   The nature of the lease depends on parol testimony We cannot say the jury were wrong in finding that the lease was, in the first instance, for one year, and that the estate was held under the same terms and conditions from year to year   It follows that Peter Ege was entitled to all legal means to enable him to collect the rent by distress or otherwise, to comply with his agreement with his lessor, and to fulfil the engagements with his creditors "

[103]*Moss's Appeal*, 35 Pa 162.

exceeding six. If the lease is under seal, the rent even of eleven
or more years can be collected by distress.[104] If there is a hold-
over, distress can be made for rent accruing under the lease, and
also for that accruing during the hold-over.[105]

220. Nature of the premises.— Under a lease of land, whatever its nature, or the objects to which it is adapted, there can be
a distress for rent. Distress has been allowed when the thing
demised was a dwelling-house and lot,[106] a town lot,[107] a store,
warehouse, and factory,[108] a farm, a dairy farm with its stock
of cattle and utensils;[109] a single room on the fourth floor of a
building,[110] the first floor of a building;[111] a forge, furnace,
and saw mill;[112] a dwelling-house and green-houses;[113] a grist-
mill, house and lot;[114] a tavern-house;[115] a summer hotel or
boarding house,[116] a marble yard,[117] veins of coal below the surface, and miners' houses on the surface.[118] Rent reserved in a
coal lease of 10 cents per ton for pea coal, 15 cents per ton for
nut coal, etc., can be distrained for.[119]

221. Rent for land and chattels.— Whether, if land and chattels upon it were leased at the same time and for a gross rent
there could be distress for the rent, or for any part of it apportioned to the land, has been answered differently by different

[104]*Franciscus* v *Reigart*, 4 Watts,
98 There was distress for one
quarter's rent, in *Fairman* v *Fluck*,
5 Watts, 516, *Warner* v *Caulk*, 3
Whart 193, for three conservative
quarters, in *Beyer* v *Fenstermacher*,
2 Whart 95
[105]*Phillips* v *Monges*, 4 Whart
226
[106]*Beyer* v *Fenstermacher*, 2
Whart 95
[107]*Spencer* v *Clinefelter*, 101 Pa
219
[108]*Brisben* v *Wilson*, 60 Pa 452.
[109]*Mickle* v *Miles*, 31 Pa 20
[110]*Whitton* v *Milligan*, 153 Pa
376, 26 Atl 22, *Walsh* v *The
Bourse*, 15 Pa Super Ct. 219.

[111]*Goodwin* v *Sharkey*, 80 Pa 149
[112]*Helser* v *Pott*, 3 Pa St 179,
Jones v. *Gundrim*, 3 Watts & S
531, *Ege* v *Ege*, 5 Watts, 134
[113]*Conroy* v. *Bitner*, 10 Lanc. L.
Rev 185
[114]*Fry* v *Jones*, 2 Rawle, 11, *Detwiler* v *Cox*, 75 Pa 200
[115]*Fairman* v *Fluck*, 5 Watts, 516
[116]*Fernwood Masonic Hall Asso* v
Jones, 102 Pa 307, *Anderson's Appeal*, 3 Pa St 218
[117]*Fretton* v *Karcher*, 77 Pa 423
[118]*Spencer* v *Kunkle*, 2 Grant Cas.
406
[119]*Grier* v *McIlarney*, 148 Pa 587,
24 Atl 119.

judges. In *Com.* v. *Contner*,[120] there was a lease of a furnace and the farm connected therewith, and also of the teams and other personal property, with wood lease and ore privilege, for the annual rent of $3,500. Black, Ch. J., held that a sum of money payable periodically for the use of chattels is not rent; it cannot be distrained for, and consequently a portion of the $3,500 will not support a distress, but, if a lease so mixes the real and personal property that it cannot be determined how much of the so-called rent is to be paid for the chattels, and how much for the land, there can be no distress even for the rent of the land. Finding indications in the lease that the parties considered $2,500 of the rent as for the land, and $1,000 as for the goods, he conceded the right of distress limited to the $2,500. In *Mickle* v. *Miles*,[121] however, where the lease was of a dairy farm with its stock of cattle and utensils, at an annual rent of $495, there was nothing to show how much of this rent was for the land and how much for the chattels. A distress for the whole rent in arrear was supported, Lowrie, J., remarking that the ordinary definition of rent as a "profit issuing yearly out of lands and tenements corporeal" was defective, and that this defectiveness escaped the notice of the court in the earlier case "A rent," he averred, for which there might be a distress, "may issue out of lands and tenements corporeal, and also out of them and their furniture "

222. Rent due by assignee of term — The duty of paying rent runs to the assignee of the lease so far as instalments falling due subsequent to the assignment are concerned. Thus, a lease of a forge in consideration of making certain repairs and paying a quantity of bar-iron, being made to A, he assigned it to B. The lessor could distrain for the bar-iron falling due during B's

[120] 18 Pa 439

[121] 31 Pa 20 In *Vetter's Appeal,* 99 Pa 52, the right of a landlord to

claim from the proceeds of an execution, rent reserved in a lease of land and personalty is affirmed.

ownership of the lease,[122] and the assignment may be by means of a sheriff's sale of the tenant's interest[123] as by his own volition. And the assignee may be a corporation[124] or a married woman or any other natural person

223. Duration of right to distrain, end of term.— It has been stated elsewhere, that there is no limit of time beyond which the right of distress is lost, when the lease is not under seal, save that prescribed by the statute of limitations. There could be, *e g,* a distress on January 13, 1858, for rent becoming due in advance, on May 8, 1854 [125] Formerly, the cessation of the term terminated the right to distrain for rent that had become due during it. The statute, 8 Anne, chap 14, provided that if a tenant retained possession of the premises after the expiration of the term, the landlord, if his interest continued, might distrain within six months for rent due and unpaid.[126] The 14th section of the act of March 21, 1772,[127] enacted that landlords might distrain for arrears of rent after the determination of the leases "in the same manner as they might have done if such lease or leases had not been ended or determined; provided, that such distress be made during the continuance of such lessor's title or interest." Under this statute, therefore, the expiration of the tenancy is no bar to a distress on goods upon the premises although the tenant remains in possession under a subsequent lease.[128] K, *e g,* leased a tavern to M for one year, beginning April 1, 1868. K died in September, 1868, devising the tavern to his widow. She made a second lease to M for the year commencing April 1, 1869. She could distrain, in the fall of 1869,

---

[122]*Moss's Appeal,* 35 Pa 162, *Jones* v *Gundrim,* 3 Watts & S 531 The goods clandestinely removed from the premises could be levied on

[123]*Latimer* v *Groetzinger,* 130 Pa 207, 21 Atl 22

[124]*Moss's Appeal,* 35 Pa 162

[125]*Moss's Appeal,* 35 Pa. 162.

[126]*Lewis's Appeal,* 66 Pa 312

[127] 1 Pepper & L Digest, 2035, 1 Sm L 370, *Gandy* v. *Dickson,* 166 Pa 422, 31 Atl 127

[128] If B goes into possession of the premises by assignment or sublease from the tenant, and holds over after the term, or if B is in posses-

for rent falling due under the earlier lease.[129] The lease might be terminated by a breach of condition subsequent, and the lessor, after insisting on the condition, might nevertheless distrain   Thus a demise made on May 8, 1851, for 99 years of a tract containing ore, provided that if the lessee or his assigns should cease operations for twelve consecutive months the lease should become void and of no effect   Operations ceased on April 8, 1854, and were not resumed. Though the lease became forfeited on April 8, 1855, the landlord could distrain in 1858 on goods on the premises, for the rent of the year preceding April 8, 1855.[130] The withdrawal from possession by the tenant during the term without the landlord's assent does not terminate his obligation to pay rent for the remainder of the term, and for the rent subsequently accruing, there may be a distress.[131]

224. End of term; when distress not allowable.— The right. after the expiration of the term, to distrain the goods of the lessee, though he remains on the premises under a new lease, was affirmed, as we have just seen, in *Lewis's Appeal*. If the second lease were to a new tenant, his goods, though he had brought them from his predecessor,[132] could not be taken in distress for the rent of his predecessor.[133] If the second lease is to the first tenant, A, and another, B, jointly, the goods, even of A, found on the premises during this lease, cannot be taken in distress for the rent of A under the former lease. The legislature, says the court, did not intend to subject to distress for rent

sion after the term without authority from anyone, his goods are liable to distress for rent due by the tenant   *Whiting* v. *Lake*, 91 Pa. 349

[129]*Lewis's Appeal*, 66 Pa 312

[130]*Moss's Appeal*, 35 Pa. 162. Grain on the land was subject to distress after the end of the term, "for, although the lien lease had expired, Land & Ten 12.

yet, inasmuch as it had not been removed from the premises, it is liable for the rent." *Snyder* v. *Kunkleman*, 3 Penr & W 487

[131]*Gunnis* v *Kater*, 29 Phila Leg. Int 230

[132]*Clifford* v *Beems*, 3 Watts, 246
[133]*Whiting* v *Lake*, 91 Pa 349, *Beltzhoover* v. *Waltman*, 1 Watts & S. 416.

under a lease the property of others, brought on the premises, under a new lease, nor did it intend that the property of the first tenant should be taken in distress for back rent, if the effect would be to deprive the new cotenant of the security of the property for the old cotenant's share of the rent   "Had the lessor told the son [the new cotenant] that he meant to pounce upon the father's [the former tenant's] chattels for the back rent, and thus make the son bear the burden of the whole, it is easy to suppose the lease would not have been accepted, and we are not to give the statute [§ 14 of the act of March 21, 1772] a construction that would make it a snare."[134]

225 Death of tenant — The 21st section of the act of February 24, 1834,[135] prescribes the order in which the debts of a deceased person are to be paid. Funeral expenses, medicine furnished and medical attendance given during the last illness of the decedent, and servant's wages, not exceeding one year, are to be first paid *pro rata.* In the second rank are "rents, not exceeding one year." Below these are all other than commonwealth debts, and, last of all, are debts due the commonwealth. To allow the landlord to distrain, after the death of the tenant, might disturb this order. Besides, it is the policy of the law to cast all the personalty of the deceased, at his death, upon the administrator for administration and distribution. A distress displacing this administration would contravene this policy. For these reasons, after the death of the tenant no distress can be made for the rent, whether it accrued before,[136] on the day of,[137] or after, that death.[138] Thus, the tenant dying June 11, 1892, there could be no distress for a quarter's rent falling due

[134]*Beltzhoover* v *Waltman,* 1 Watts & S 416, *Leibert* v *Baker,* 1 Northampton Co Rep 333, 3 Del Co Rep 557, *School Fund* v *Heermans,* 2 Law Times N S 137
[135] 1 Pepper & 'L Digest, 1432, P. L 70.

[136]*Hoskins* v. *Houston,* 2 Clark (Pa) 489
[137]*Hoskins* v *Houston,* 2 Clark (Pa) 489
[138]*Gandy* v *Dickson,* 166 Pa 422, 31 Atl 127, *Stahlman's Estate,* 26 Pittsb L. J. 113.

July 24 [139] Nor does the presence in the lease of a stipulation that the goods on the premises should be liable for rent for thirty days after their removal from the premises; or that the rights and liabilities of the parties should extend to their respective "heirs, executors, administrators, successors, and assigns"—affect the applicability of this principle "The distrainors," says McCollum, J , "had no lien on the goods for rent, in the lifetime of the decedent, and, at his death, they passed to his administrator as other assets of the estate did His custody of them was lawful and for the purposes of administration. It was his duty to apply them to the payment of the decedent's debts in the order prescribed by the statute."[140] A distress after death, will be prohibited by the orphans' court, on the petition of the administrator,[141] or will be adjudged void in a replevin by him.[142]

226. Loss of landlord's estate.—At common law a landlord could make distress only during the continuance of his estate. If he conveyed it, the rent still being due, he lost the right to distrain for that rent. In this respect the law, for the most part, remains unchanged by statute The 14th section of the act of March 21, 1772,[143] which permits a distress to be made after the termination of the lease, adds the words: "Provided that such distress be made during the continuance of such lessor's title or interest." The distress will therefore be void, if, when he makes it, the former landlord has lost the reversion,[144] whether he loses it by a sheriff's sale[145] or otherwise. The re-

[139]*Gandy* v *Dickson*, 166 Pa. 422, 31 Atl. 127

[140]*Ibid*

[141]*Stahlman's Estate*, 26 Pittsb L J 113

[142]*Gandy* v *Dickson*, 166 Pa 422, 31 Atl. 127 If goods of the deceased are sold on an execution whose lien began before the death of the tenant debtor, the landlord will be denied a payment from the proceeds *Hoskins* v. *Houston*, 2 Clark (Pa) 489

[143] 1 Pepper & L Digest, 2635, 1 Sm L 370

[144]*Smoyer* v *Roth* (Pa) 13 Atl 191, *Lewis's Appeal*, 66 Pa 312, *Hoskins* v *Houston*, 2 Clark (Pa) 489

[145]*Hoskins* v *Houston*, 2 Clark

version may be simply the balance of a term of years. On the expiration of the term, the reversion would cease to exist, and with it the right to distrain. If, *e g.,* A, the lessee of land, assigns the land to B, who sublets to C, B cannot, after the expiration of the original lease and the surrender of possession to the landlord, distrain the goods of C for rent owed by him to B [146] But the grant in the lease to the lessee of a right to buy the premises at a price to be agreed upon does not divest the lessor of the reversion, and although the lessee afterwards elects to take the land, and a price is agreed upon by the parties, and the parties meet at a later day to close the transaction, when the lessor declines to sell except for cash, which the lessee does not offer to pay, the lessor may subsequently distrain for rent unpaid [147] The exception to the principle just stated must not be overlooked that, when the conveyance is in fee, with reservation of a perpetual rent, the grantor, although he parts with the reversion at the moment of creating his right to the rent, may distrain [148]

227. Loss of landlord's estate by death.—The 7th section of the act of February 24, 1834,[149] provides that if a life tenant, having made a lease, dies before the expiration of the term, the rent not then payable shall be apportioned[150] and be assets for the executor or administrator. The 8th section of the same act declares that arrearages of any "rent charge or other rent or reservation in nature of a rent, due at the death of any tenant in fee simple, fee tail, or for term of life or lives of such rent," shall go to the executor or administrator of such tenant. The

(Pa) 489, *Hampton* v *Henderson*, 4 Clark (Pa) 438 Cf *Lyon* v *Houk*, 9 Watts, 193

[146]*Walbridge* v *Pruden*, 102 Pa 1

[147]*Smoyer* v *Roth* (Pa) 13 Atl 191

[148]*Manuel* v *Reoth*, 5 Phila 11

[149]1 Pepper & L Digest, 1474, P. L 70

[150]*Borie* v *Crissman*, 82 Pa 125. Cf *Smith* v *Wistar*, 5 Phila 145, where the administrator of a life tenant was allowed to recover a portion of the rent not yet mature at her death

29th section of the same act[151] enacts that the executors or administrators of any owner of a rent charge or other rent or reservation in nature of a rent, whether in fee or otherwise, as mentioned in the 8th section, may sue for the arrears of such rent "due to the decedent at the time of his decease," "or they may distrain therefor upon the lands or tenements which were charged with the payment thereof, and liable to the distress of such decedent, so long as such lands or tenements remain and are in the seizin or possession of the tenant who ought to have paid such rent, or in the possession of any other person claiming the same, from or under the same tenant, by purchase, gift, or descent, in like manner as such decedent might have done if he had lived." Under these acts rent which is accruing, but is not yet payable at the death of the owner, cannot, in whole or part, be distrained for by the executor or administrator of the decedent.[152] So much is inferable from the word "due." Though when the landlord is a life tenant provision is made for apportionment of the rent, and also for an action of assumpsit against the under tenant for the apportioned part[153] equitably belonging to the deceased, there is no provision for distress. But for rent which is already payable at the death of any landlord, the personal representative may make distress.[154] If the land has passed under a will to the executors they may, as succeeding proprietors, distrain for the rent that, still in process of accruing at the death of the testator, becomes payable afterwards, and of course for rent which has wholly accrued since his death, whether under a lease made by him or under one made by them.[155]

228. Repetition of distress.—There may be a distress as soon

[151] 1 Pepper & L Digest, 1492, P. L 70

[152] Cf Smith v. Wistar, 5 Phila 145.

[153] Act February 24, 1834, § 30, 1 Pepper & L. Digest, 1493, P. L. 70.

[154] Cf. Herbst v. Hodgson, 23 Pittsb L J 182

[155] Gandy v Dickson, 166 Pa 422, 31 Atl 127.

as any rent becomes payable and remains unpaid, and another distress for the next instalment after it becomes payable, and so on *toties quoties*. But when any distress is made it should be made for all the rent then due and unpaid. If it is made for less than is due[156] there can be no second distress for the residue.[157] But if for part of the rent, the note of a third person is taken, "to be a credit when paid," and for the residue a distress should be made, there may be a second distress for the rent for which the note was taken, if it is subsequently not paid.[158] Though the distress is made for all that is then due, it may be abandoned before sale. If abandoned at the request of the tenant himself, another distress for the same rent, if not inconsistent with any binding promises made to him by the landlord,[159] would be permissible. If it is abandoned capriciously, or because in some respect the directions of the law have not been complied with, *e. g.,* because the appraisement was made too soon,[160] a second distress will be wholly unwarranted. If there are not sufficient distrainable goods on the premises to satisfy the rent, there may be a second distress on goods subsequently coming upon them, for the portion of the rent which the first distress failed to satisfy.[161] But if, when the first distress is made, the goods on the premises, capable of being taken, are sufficient, a second distress will not be allowed, unless the failure to take sufficient goods on the first was due to a mistaken over-estimate of their value or of the money which their sale would produce,[162] or unless, possibly, the prosecution

[156] In *Becker* v *Werner*, 98 Pa 555, the warrant was for the rent due, but not for the taxes, which, by the lease, were to be treated as rent

[157] *Quinn* v *Wallace*, 6 Whart 452

[158] *Kreiter* v *Hammer*, 1 Pearson (Pa) 559 The right of the landlord to be paid from the proceeds of an execution was affirmed That right depends on the right to distrain

[159] Cf *Pfeiffer* v *Schubmehl*, 7 Del Co Rep 575, 6 Lack Legal News, 60

[160] *Ibid* The second distress would be a trespass Cf *Lengert Co* v *Bellevue Bldg & L Asso* 15 Pa Super Ct 380

[161] *Quinn* v *Wallace*, 6 Whart 452, *Pfeiffer* v *Schubmehl*, 7 Del Co. Rep 575; 6 Lack Legal News, 60.

[162] *Ibid.*

of the first distress has been arrested by the tenant's replevin, and the delivery of the goods back to him by the sheriff,[163] or after the completion of the first distress the tenant has, in an action of trespass on the ground that it was illegal, recovered judgment[164] In replevin upon a second distress the burden is on the defendant, the landlord, or his bailiff, to prove the facts which authorized the second distress[165]

229. Other remedy no obstacle to distress — The existence of a contract on which suit can be brought for the rent is of course no obstacle to, but rather the precondition of, the right to distress. Nor are the bringing of an action founded on the contract and the recovery of a judgment therein, a bar to a distress for the same rent,[166] nor is the issue of a ca sa or of a fi fa, upon the judgment if not followed by actual payment of it,[167] nor is the giving of a special bail for stay of execution, in a suit by the landlord for the rent, which is less than $20 before a justice of the peace[168] The taking of a guaranty or surety-

[163]*King* v *Blackmore*, 72 Pa 347, 13 Am Rep 684 Agnew, J, distinguishes this case, which was an action against the surety for the rent, after a distress had been arrested by replevin, from *Quinn* v *Wallace*, by remarking "that the record of the replevin and sheriff's return show that the goods were made unproductive by the act of the tenant himself, who had them returned into his own possession, and the liability of the bond and of the sheriff substituted"

[164]*Robinson* v *White*, 39 Pa 255 The first distress thus rendered "barren," says Thompson, J, would not "preclude a second distress for the same rent" In *M'Geary* v *Raymond*, 17 Pa Super Ct 308, the replevin, after delivery of the goods to the plaintiff, was quashed Could there be a second distress?

[165]*Quinn* v *Wallace*, 6 Whart 452

If the second distress is on goods of a subtenant, he may insist on its invalidity, as could the tenant

[166]*Snyder* v *Kunkleman*, 3 Penr & W 487, *Shetsline* v *Keemle*, 1 Ashm (Pa) 29, *Kerr* v *Sharp*, 14 Serg & R 399 The last two cases were before a justice of the peace Taking of a judgment for arrears of ground rent is said, in *Bantleon* v *Smith*, 2 Binn 146, 4 Am Dec 430, not to prevent distress for the same rent Cf *Gordon* v *Correy*, 5 Binn. 552 The fact that a guardian has obtained a judgment for the rent does not preclude a distress for it by his successor, or by the ward on reaching majority *Weltner's Appeal*, 63 Pa 302

[167]*Snyder* v *Kunkleman*, 3 Penr & W 487

[168]*Shetsline* v *Keemle*, 1 Ashm. (Pa) 29.

ship, [169] or of a promissory note [170] from a third person for the debt, does not preclude distress   A novation of the rent, the absolute payment of it, e. g., by a note, would bar any distress for it, should the note not be paid.   Under a lease, rent consisting of one half of all the grain, hemp, flax, potatoes, fruit, etc , was due and was in arrear.   The landlord and tenant struck an account, in which the value of the landlord's share was estimated at $320.71.   A promissory note was given for that sum.   This was a sale of the landlord's share of the grain, etc ,to the tenant for $320.71,and the nonpayment of the note did not justify a distress [171]   After accepting a check or a draft, as payment of the rent, the lessor cannot distrain [172]   The lease may give to the landlord, for breach of the covenant to pay rent, the right to enter upon and forfeit the premises   The possession of this power to forfeit is not inconsistent with the right to distrain, whether this right be[173] or be not[174] expressly stipulated for.   Nor is the exercise of the power to forfeit

230 Tender — If the lessee or the assignee of the term tenders the rent due, and the tender is declined, the right to distrain is suspended until, demand being made later on the tenderer, the latter refuses or omits to pay the rent   The tender by the assignee of the term will suspend the right to distrain not merely his own goods, but also those of the lessee still on the premises.[175]

231. Distress as affecting other remedies.— The stipulation in a lease for a right of distress does not negative a right to bring an action on the covenant, against the original lessee or his

[169]King v Blackmore, 72 Pa 347, 13 Am Rep 684

[170]Kreiter v Hammer, 1 Pearson (Pa) 559

[171]Warren v Forney, 13 Serg & R 52

[172]Columbia Iron Co's Appeal, 114 Pa 66.

[173]Becker v Werner, 98 Pa 555.

Having distrained for the rent due, the landlord could immediately forfeit for the taxes, which the lease treated as a part of the rent

[174]Murphy v Marshell, 179 Pa. 516, 36 Atl 294, Smith v Meanor, 16 Serg & R 375

[175]Lyon v Houk, 9 Watts, 193.

assignee.[176] And a distress actually made, which has produced only a part of the rent for which it was made, will not preclude a forfeiture by the landlord under a clause in the lease authorizing such forfeiture for default in paying rent.[177] A distress which is relinquished by the lessor at the request of the tenant will release the surety of the latter, to the extent of the money which the sale of the goods thus relinquished would have brought, but no farther,[178] but if the distress has been made abortive, by the eloignment of the goods, after levy, by the tenant or others, without negligence on the part of the landlord or bailiff, the surety will remain fully answerable for the rent [179] If after levy on the tenant's goods, in distress, they are delivered to him by the sheriff, in replevin, action for the same rent can be brought successfully against the tenant's surety. "The record of the replevin and return," said Agnew, J.,[180] "therefore show that the distress was no satisfaction and consequently no bar to the independent action against the surety on his several covenant as bail absolute for the rent," and even if the distress proceeds to sale of the goods, the proceeds being received by the landlord, the tenant and surety will again become liable for the rent, if in a subsequent trespass by the tenant against the landlord, for an illegal distress, the value of the goods is recovered from the latter.[181]

[176]*Royer* v *Ake*, 3 Penr & W 461 (a ground rent)

[177]*Pennsylvania Co for Ins on Lives & G A.* v *Shanahan*, 10 Pa Super Ct. 267 The leasehold had itself been distrained and sold

[178]*McNamee* v. *Cresson*, 3 W. N. C. 450.

[179]*Myers* v. *Hulseman*, 3 W N C 487

[180]*King* v *Blackmore*, 72 Pa. 347, 13 Am Rep. 684

[181]*Robinson* v. *White*, 39 Pa. 255

CHAPTER XIV.

WHAT GOODS ARE DISTRAINABLE.

232 Goods of subtenant — The lease may or may not permit subleasing by the tenant   In either case the tenant may in fact sublet.   The goods of the sublessee, on the premises, will be liable to distress by the landlord for the rent becoming due by the tenant under the terms of the lease, during the subtenant's possession, whether the landlord has assented in the lease[1] or otherwise to the sublease[2] or not,[3] and whether the rent for which the distress is made becoming payable during the subtenancy began to accrue before the subtenancy began,[4] or not. The cessation of the term does not preclude a distress on the goods of the subtenant who remains in possession. Thus, a lease ending on March 30th, 1875, the goods of a subtenant who entered on January, 1875, but continued in possession on April 1st, 1875, could, on the latter day, be distrained for the year's rent due by the landlord the day before[5] Probably for rent which has become payable by the tenant before he sublets, the goods of his sublessee, found on the premises, may be levied upon in distress. But, if the tenant surrenders the term during the subtenancy, and the landlord, without the subtenant's consent, makes a new lease covering the remainder of the term and an additional period, the goods of the subtenant do not become liable, during the remainder of the term, to distress for the rent arising under the second lease, but during the time embraced in the first lease. A leased, in 1886, a building to B until April 1st, 1888. On October 19th, 1887, C, to whom, three days before, B had assigned the lease, surrendered it to A, the landlord, who immediately made to C a new lease commencing November 1st, 1887, but for a term extending to November 1st, 1889, at a rental payable monthly, in advance. In

---

[1]*Hessel v Johnson*, 142 Pa 8, 11 L R A 855, 21 Atl 194, 129 Pa 173, 5 L R A. 851, 15 Am St Rep 716, 18 Atl 754 Cf. *American Pig Iron Storage Warrant Co v Sinnemahoning Iron & Coal Co* 205 Pa 403, 54 Atl. 1047

[2]*Perrin v. Wells*, 155 Pa 299, 26 Atl 543

When a widow's dower is charged on land, she can distrain on the goods of the tenant of the owners in fee. *Murphy v Borland*, 92 Pa 86

[3]*Jamison v Reifsneider*, 97 Pa 136, *Rosenberger v Hallowell*, 35 Pa 369, *McCombs's Appeal*, 43 Pa 435

[4]*Whiting v Lake*, 91 Pa 349 The subtenancy began during January, 1875, and the subtenant continued in possession until April 1, 1875, when the rent for the previous year, ending March 31, was distrained for

[5]*Whiting v Lake*, 91 Pa 349

March, 1888, distress was made by A for four months' rent due by C upon the goods of D, who had entered as a subtenant of B, shortly after the lease had been made to B, and who had in no way acquiesced in the surrender by B of the lease. It was held that these goods were not liable for the rent due on the second lease, although it was the same, and payable at the same times, as the rent under the first lease. When C surrendered his lease to A, it was not merged in A's fee. It continued to subsist. The effect of the surrender was to make practically the subtenant D the tenant of A [6] When the new lease was made to C it was subject to D's rights. D did not become a subtenant of C, nor were his goods liable for C's defaults.[7] The sublease may be of the entire premises[8] or of a part only of it,[9] —e. g , one room[10] or other part of a dwelling house,[11] first floor of a building,[12] of a storeroom,[13] a part of a lot [14] The goods of the subtenant on the part sublet to him may be taken for the lessee's rent.

233. Goods of sublessee; payment of sublessee's rent.—This liability of the sublessee's goods to distress is independent of the prior payment or nonpayment of his rent to his immediate land-

---

[6] A could have distrained D's goods for the rent due by D on the sublease, but not for the rent due under the first or the second lease Williams, J Hessel v Johnson, 142 Pa 8, 11 L. R A 855, 21 Atl. 794.

[7] Hessel v Johnson, 129 Pa. 173, 5 L R. A. 851, 15 Am. St. Rep 716, 18 Atl. 754. Clark, J. In Hessel v. Johnson, 142 Pa. 8, 11 L. R A 855, 21 Atl. 794 Williams, J , reaches the same result by a different course. The surrender of the lease, he remarks 'may have passed the right to collect" the subtenant's rent from C to A, D's subtenancy surviving The new lease passed this right back to C But there was no right in A to distrain on D's goods for rent, because C's lease had been surrendered, nor could he distrain for

D's rent to C, for the right to this rent had passed back from A to C by the new lease There was no relation of landlord and tenant between A and D when the distress was made

[8] Cf Perrin v Wells, 155 Pa. 299, 26 Atl 543.

[9] Jannson v Reifsneider, 97 Pa. 136

[10] Quinn v Wallace, 6 Whart 452; Lane v Stemmetz, 9 W N C 574

[11] Smoyer v. Roth (Pa) 13 Atl 191

[12] Hessel v Johnson, 129 Pa 173, 5 L R A 851, 15 Am St Rep. 716, 18 Atl 754

[13] McCombs's Appeal, 43 Pa 435

[14] Rosenberger v. Hallowell, 35 Pa 369.

lord, the lessee. Though he has paid[15] and more than paid[16] his own rent, they are distrainable. "No doubt," says Lowrie, Ch J., "undertenants may sometimes suffer loss by the operation of the rule if they do not see that the principal rent is duly paid; because the rule and the law of distress make all goods on the premises surety for the rent for the enjoyment of them [the premises]. An undertenant can usually save himself by seeing that his own rent is duly paid over to the principal landlord."[17]

234. **Sufficient goods of tenant.**— Nor is the liability of the goods of the undertenant to be taken for the landlord's rent contingent on the absence from the premises of sufficient goods of the tenant to satisfy the rent. Of goods of the tenant there may be ample, and yet the subtenant's goods are liable. Thus, the goods of the tenant distrained may be appraised at $362, and of the subtenant, at $818, the rent being only for $257;[18] or, the rent being $675, the goods of the tenant on the premises may be worth $5,000, and of the subtenant $3,000[19] The subtenant cannot even compel the lessor who has distrained both goods of the tenant and goods of the subtenant, to agree to make sale first of the tenant's goods, and only if they should not produce enough to satisfy the rent, to proceed to sell his, the subtenant's[20] Perhaps a release before replevin by the subtenant, of the tenant's goods, would discharge, to the value of the goods released, the goods of the subtenant; but, if no such discharge of the tenant's goods occurs and a replevin is begun by the sub tenant, and his goods are delivered to him, the landlord's subsequent direction to the bailiff to surrender to the tenant his

[15]*Smoyer* v. *Rath* (Pa) 13 Atl. 191, *Quinn* v *Wallace*, 6 Whart. 452, *Jimison* v. *Reifsneider*, 97 Pa 136, *Murphy* v *Borland*, 92 Pa 86
[16]*McCombs's Appeal*, 43 Pa 435
[17]*McCombs's Appeal*, 43 Pa 435
[18]*Smoyer* v. *Roth* (Pa) 13 Atl 191.

[19]*Jimison* v. *Reifsneider*, 97 Pa 136, *American Pig Iron Storage Warrant Co* v *Sinnemahoning Iron & Coal Co* 205 Pa 403, 54 Atl 1047
[20]*Jimison* v *Reifsneider*, 97 Pa 136; *American Pig Iron Starage Warrant Co* v *Sinnemahoning Iron & Coal Co* 205 Pa 403, 54 Atl 1047

goods will not authorize a recovery by the subtenant in the replevin "They," [the landlords] says Mercur, J., "had a right
to rely on that security [the bond of the plaintiff in replevin.]
They were precluded from then proceeding further against the
goods thus replevied, and had an undoubted right to stay proceedings against the other goods distrained. In so doing, after
the writ of replevin was executed [by the sheriff's delivery of
the goods to the plaintiff therein] they did not in the least render invalid any act of theirs prior to its execution, which was
valid when performed."[21]

235. **Goods of assignee or other person in possession** —The
assignee of a term is personally liable for the rent becoming due
after the assignment, and, of course, distress for this rent can
be levied upon his goods. But if the landlord had agreed, in
order to induce him to remain longer in possession, or for some
other consideration, to accept a sum, which is paid him, in com-
mutation of the rent, there could be no subsequent distress for
the rent thus commuted.[22] For the rent that fell due before
the assignment the assignee is not personally liable, but his
goods, brought on the premises after the assignment, are probably liable to distress for it. It is even said by Sterrett, J., in
Whiting v. *Lake*[23] that if C goes into possession of A's land
under B, as tenant, and C holds over after the lapse of the
term, or if he, C, is in "without authority from anyone," it
cannot be doubted that his goods, on the premises, are liable, after the term, to distress for rent becoming due during the term.
If the person in possession after the term is a new tenant, his
goods cannot be distrained for the rent due by his predecessor.[24]

[21]*Jimison* v *Reifsneider*, 97 Pa
136
[22]*Damsdall* v. *Guild*, 32 Phila Leg
Int 152
[23]91 Pa. 349 The term closed
March 31st, 1875 The plaintiff
went in under the tenant in January, 1875, but continued in on April

1st, 1875, his goods were then distrainable for the rent of the previous year The report states that
the rent distrained for was due
April 1st, 1876,—a misprint, probably, for 1875
[24]*Clifford* v *Beems*, 3 Watts 246;
School Fund v *Heermans*, 2 Law

In *Karns* v. *McKinney*,[25] K leased to P a lot containing 12 acres of ground on which was a steam sawmill. W, a sawyer under P, sawed there some lumber of his own, and sold it to M; M, letting it remain on the premises, sent his own workmen, who built it into barges. He placed there iron, oakum, spikes, etc. In about three weeks subsequently, distress was made upon the barges, the timber and other articles belonging to M, who, whether as a "tenant or a trespasser," was in actual and exclusive possession of the yard. The distress was proper.[26]

236. **Goods of assignor of term.**—After an assignment by the lessee of his term, his goods may remain upon the premises. Unless the lessor has agreed to a substitution of the assignee for the lessee, the latter continues liable for the rent. His goods, remaining on the premises, are liable to distress for the rent subsequently accruing. But if the assignee tenders the rent and the landlord declines to receive it from him, the landlord may not distrain for it without having later made a personal demand for it, of the assignee. The tender, followed by constant readiness to pay, of the assignee, will protect the assignor's goods from distress.[27]

237. **Goods of persons not in possession of premises.**—We have seen that the goods of an assignee, a subtenant, or even of one having possession of the premises under no authority from the owner of the land or from the tenant, may be taken in distress for the rent. It is also true generally that goods of anyone who is not in possession of the premises or any part thereof may, if found on the premises, be distrained by the landlord. The common law and the act of March 21st, 1772, both allow such

Times N. S. 137; *Beltzhooer* v *Waltman*, 1 Watts & S 416, *Whiting* v *Lake*, 91 Pa 349. Goods of a person who resided with the tenant were held exempt from distress because they had been removed before the distress was made. *Scott* v. *McEwen*, 2 Phila 176.

[25] 74 Pa 387

[26] The court concludes that the property did not fall under any category of property privileged from distress

[27] *Lyon* v *Houk*, 9 Watts, 193.

distress[28] although occasionally the principle has been dis-
paraged   In 1827, Gibson, Ch J , remarked [29] "The right to
distrain the property of strangers rests on no principle of reason
or justice , it is a feudal prerogative, handed down from the
time when chattels were of little account, and when it may
have been impolitic, if not unreasonable, to embarrass the lord
with responsibility to one who had thrust his property in the
way of the remedy to compel a performance of the services;"
and in 1824, Duncan, J.,[30] pronounced the doctrine "not suited
to the transactions of men and the present state of society,"
while conceding that "it transcends judicial power to abrogate
it" The legislature has not abrogated it, and the doctrine still
finds frequent application.

238 Goods of wife, daughter, or mother of tenant —Though
a wife is expected to reside with her husband, and she will,
naturally, have articles belonging to herself with her, such
articles, on the premises demised to the husband, will be liable
to distress for his rent.[31] In *Trimble's Appeal*[32] a wife, with
the husband's consent, engaged in a business on her own account.
A lease from X, made May 8, 1876 "let unto Mrs Caroline
Williams" premises, the lease containing covenants to pay rent,
that all property on the premises should be subject to distress,
etc. She and her husband signed the lease. The covenants did
not become binding on her, but, as the lease was to the husband
as well, he became bound by them, and the wife's property, like
that of any other person, could be taken in distress. The land-

[28]*Kessler* v *M'Conachy*, 1 Rawle,
435 , *Whiting* v *Lake*, 91 Pa 349,
Price v *McCallister*, 3 Grant Cas.
248 , *Beltzhooer* v *Waltman*, 1
Watts & S 416 , *Karns* v *McKin-
ney*, 74 Pa 387 , *O'Donnel* v *Sey-
bert*, 13 Serg & R. 54 . *Adams* v *La
Comb*, 1 Dall 440, 1 L ed 214,
Murphy v *Borland*, 92 Pa 86,
Booth v *Hoenig*, 7 Pa Dist R 529,
Kensil v *Chambers*, 5 Phila 64,
Harris v *Shaw*, 17 Pa Super Ct 1,
Gilliam v. *Tobias*, 11 Phila 313

[29]*Brown* v *Sims*, 17 Serg & R
138

[30]*Weidel* v *Roseberry*, 13 Serg &
R 178

[31]*Blanche* v *Bradford*, 38 Pa 344,
80 Am Dec 489 , *Karns* v *Moore*, 5
Pa Super Ct 381, *Murphy* v *Bor-
land*, 92 Pa 86, *Ball* v *Penn*, 10 Pa.
Super Ct 544, *Balmer* v *Peiffer*, 16
Lanc L Rev 251   Cf *Murphy* v.
Rementer, 7 Del Co. Rep 203.

[32]5 W N. C 396.

lord's "right to distrain," it was said *per curiam,* "does not flow
from her covenant, or his relation as tenant, but from the common law as an incident to the lease to the husband; a right to
distrain for his rent all property found upon the leased premises, not within the well-known exceptions on account of trade,
etc."[33] In an action on the case for an excessive distress, the
tenant was not allowed, in *Fernwood Masonic Hall Asso.* v.
Jones,[34] to show that goods of his daughter had been included in
it. Goods of a mother of the tenant, on the premises, can be distrained for his rent.[35]

239. Goods lent to tenant or his wife.—Goods lent to the tenant, or to his wife for a term, either gratuitously, or for a rental
(*e. g.,* a sewing machine let for one month at the rental of $3),[36]
may be distrained for the tenant's rent due to his landlord if
found on the premises when the distress is made. So, goods
lent to the tenant or his wife[37] for a term, with provision in
the lease for the acquisition of ownership by the lessee on the
payment of all the instalments of rental, or of them and an
additional amount, are subject to distress. Instances have been
a billiard table thus let to a hotel keeper,[38] a soda water fountain to a druggist,[39] office furniture,[40] house furniture,[41] a
piano let to the wife of a tenant.[42]

---

[33] In *Saltzman* v *Hacker,* 1 W N
C 6, a demurrer to the tenant's plea
to the avowry, alleging that the
goods distrained were not his, but
his wife's, was sustained

[34] 102 Pa 307

Goods of a son *Hazlett* v. *Mangel,*
9 Pa Super Ct 139

[35] *M'Geary* v *Raymond,* 17 Pa.
Super Ct 308

[36] *Boyert* v *Batterton,* 6 Pa. Super.
Ct 468 In *Jones* v *Goldbeck,* 8 W
N C 533, a boarder's furniture was
found throughout the house of the
boarding-house keeper, as well as in
his own room. That beyond the
room could be distrained on for the
housekeeper's rent

LAND & TEN 13.

Goods leased for a year to the
tenant were distrainable *Sleeper* v.
Parrish, 7 Phila 247

[37] *Kleber* v *Ward,* 88 Pa 93.

[38] *Price* v *McCallister,* 3 Grant Cas
248

[39] *Tufts* v *Park,* 194 Pa 79, 44 Atl.
1079, *Harris* v *Shaw,* 17 Pa. Super.
Ct 1 In the former of these cases
the court failed, in trespass by the
owner of the goods for a conversion,
to find in the evidence any conversion prior to the distress The sale in
distress was not a trespass.

[40] *Walsh* v *The Bourse,* 15 Pa
Super. Ct 219

[41] *Myers* v *Esery,* 134 Pa. 177, 19
Atl 488

[42] *Kleber* v *Ward,* 88 Pa 93.

240. Piano, melodeon, lent to tenant — The act of May 13th, 1876,[43] enacts that all pianos, melodeons, and organs leased or hired by any person residing in this state shall be exempt from distress for rent due by such person; provided that the owner of such pianos, etc , or his agent, or the person hiring the same, shall give notice to the landlord or his agent, that the instrument is leased or hired. The lender of the instrument need not be a dealer.[44] Although the act confines the exemption to cases in which the tenant is the hirer of the instrument, it has been held to extend to a case in which the daughter of the tenant is the hirer [45] The notice must be given when the instrument is put on the demised premises, or, if later, at a time when no rent is due for which there is a subsequent distress. Were the notice permitted to be given after the rent is due, it might happen that the tenant would receive a credit to which he was not entitled. Hence, the term beginning April 1st, 1876, and the tenant bringing with him to the premises an organ leased by him on Sept 21st, 1875, for one year, a distress levied Aug. 23d, 1876, upon the organ, could not be annulled by replevin, no notice of the ownership of the organ having been given until Aug. 28th, 1876.[46] The notice should be clear, naming the make and style of the organ, and should be in writing; or, if oral, should be shown to have been heard and understood by the landlord. The notice may be given by the agent of the owner. If, the organ having been the tenant's, he sells it to X, who immediately lends it to the tenant's daughter, a member of his family, a notice by the tenant to the landlord that the organ is X's will be sufficient if the jury find him to have been X's

[43] 1 Pepper & L 2637 , P L 171

[44] *Rohrei* v *Cunningham,* 138 Pa. 162, 20 Atl 872

[45] *Rohrer* v *Cunningham,* 138 Pa 162, 20 Atl 872

[46] *McGeary* v. *Mellor,* 87 Pa. 401.

Finletter, J , had held a notice the day following the distress on a piano to be sufficient, in *Wireman* v *Ditson,* 5 W N C. 428.

agent. The landlord having, at the tenant's request, executed
a release of the organ from liability for rent, which mentioned the sale to X, the jury might easily find an implied
authority from X to the tenant to give the notice.[47] In the
absence of the notice, a piano let to the tenant with the right
of purchase is distrainable for his rent.[48]

241. Sewing machine, typewriter, lent to tenant.—The act
of June 25, 1895,[49] declares that all sewing machines and type-
writing machines leased or hired by any person residing in this
state shall be exempt from distress for rent due by such person
in addition to any articles or money already exempt by law, provided that the owner or his agent, or the person leasing the
same, shall give notice to the landlord or his agent that the instrument is leased or hired.

242. Soda-water apparatus.—The act of April 28th, 1899,[50]
exempts from distress for rent all soda-water apparatus and appurtenances thereto leased or hired by any person in this state,
provided that notice is given to the landlord of the fact that it
is leased or hired, by the owner, his agent, or the lessee.

243. Goods sold by tenant — Goods, once the tenant's, but
sold by him, and still on the premises, may be distrained,[51] and,
if he has become insolvent and assigned his property to trustees,
the goods remaining on the premises may, nevertheless, be distrained.[52] But if these goods remain, after sale, on the premises which are leased to another, they cannot be distrained for
the former owner's rent. Thus, the way-going crop continues
on the premises after the end of the term, until fully ripe   Being sold by the tenant to whom it belongs, it is no longer sus-

[47]*Rohrer* v *Cunningham,* 138 Pa
162, 20 Atl 872
[48]*Delp* v. *Hoffman* 7 Pa Dist R
253
[49]P L 382
[50]P L 117
[51]*Furbush* v *Fisher,* 40 Phila Leg

Int 286, *Bevan* v *Crooks,* 7 Watts
& S 452, *Rohrer* v *Cunningham,* 138
Pa 162, 20 Atl 872
[52]*O'Donnel* v *Seybert,* 13 Serg &
R 54, *Osborne's Estate,* 5 Whart
267.

ceptible of being levied on for his rent.[53]　Goods sold in execution as the tenant's, if allowed to remain on the premises an unreasonably long time become subject to distress.[54]

244　Where goods must be at time of levy.— The　owner　of goods other than the tenant is under no duty to the landlord of the latter to allow him to take his, the owner's, goods in satisfaction of rent owed by the tenant.　If the goods are on the premises, they can be so taken, but if they, having been on, have been taken off before the distress is levied, and remain off when the distress is levied, they cease to be subject to it.　The 5th section of the act of March 21st, 1772,[55] enacts that if any "lessee" shall "fraudulently or clandestinely" carry from the premises "his goods and chattels," in order to prevent a distress, the landlord may pursue and distrain upon them for the period of thirty days　This act has no application to the goods of a stranger　As soon, therefore, as a stranger's goods are removed from the premises, they cease to be liable to be taken in distress,[56] though the removal was clandestine,[57] or its object was the avoidance of a distress,[58] and the wife[59] or mother[60] of the tenant is such a stranger.　If the goods have been distrained while on the premises, they are not released from the distress by a removal therefrom by the owner, tenant, or another　They can be pursued, if clandestinely removed, and brought back to the leased premises, or to some place under the control of the lessor.[61]　If the removal constituted a "pound breach or rescous"

[53]*Worrilow* v *Sharpless,* 13 Lanc Bar, 124, 1 Del Co Rep 155
Booth v *Hoenig,* 7 Pa Dist. R 529
[55] Pepper & L Digest, 2638, 1 Smith's Laws, 370
[56]*Adams* v *LaComb,* 1 Dall 440, 1 L ed 214, *Ball* v *Penn,* 10 Pa Super Ct. 544, *M'Geary* v *Raymond,* 17 Pa Super Ct 308, *Baer* v *Kuhl,* 8 Pa Dist R 389, *Scott* v *McLucn,* 2 Phila. 176.

[57]*Murphy* v *Rementer,* 7 Del Co Rep 203, 15 Lanc L Rev 270, *Ellis* v *Lamb,* 9 Pa Dist R 491
[58]*Sleeper* v *Parrish,* 7 Phila 247
[59]*Ball* v *Penn,* 10 Pa Super Ct 544, *Ellis* v *Lamb,* 9 Pa Dist R 491, *Murphy* v *Rementer,* 7 Del Co Rep 203, 15 Lanc L Rev 270
[60]*M'Geary* v *Raymond,* 17 Pa Super Ct 308
[61]*M'Geary* v *Raymond,* 17 Pa Super Ct 308　In *Woglam* v.

a special action on the case would lie, under the 2d section of the act of March 21st, 1772, or the landlord might take the goods wherever he found them, and impound them again.[62] If a replevin by the owner results in the delivery of the goods to the plaintiff in the action, and if this delivery, notwithstanding the subsequent quashing of the writ of replevin, destroys the lien of the distress,[63] no further steps under it can be taken A new distress, the goods no longer being on the demised premises, would be unlawful, and it would be irregular for the constable, assuming the former distress to retain its lien, without making a new distress, and without an adjournment on the day of sale originally fixed, to post, on the day after the replevin was quashed, and a full month after the original distress, a bill on the house where the goods were, advertising the property for sale If the goods were a stranger's, and had been removed in good faith, and not clandestinely for the purpose of removing them from the lien of the distress, the owner could issue a second replevin after the constable had indicated his purpose to treat them as still in his power for the purpose of sale.[64]

245. Preventing the removal of goods.— As the owner of goods who is not the tenant has a right to remove them from the premises before distress, and so to escape the distress, he

---

Cowperthwaite, 2 Dall 68, 1 L ed 292, the goods were clandestinely removed on the day following the levy The officer pursued them to another house, and he there appraised them, within eight days of the distress Shortly after this, the goods being still where they were appraised, they were taken by the sheriff under process issued by another person. The landlord had a right to sell them, as against this person or the tenant

[64] M'Geary v Raymond, 17 Pa Super Ct 308, Woglam v Cowperthwaite, 2 Dall 68, 1 L ed. 292

[63] The court does not say whether the lien is destroyed or not.

[64] So the case seems to hold The distress was made Sept 12, 1899 A writ of replevin issued Sept 19th the sheriff taking the goods This writ was quashed Oct 12th Meantime the landlord abandoned the premises, taking the goods with him to another house The day after the writ was quashed the constable, not making a new distress, not having adjourned the sale, upon the day fixed for the original sale posted a bill upon the house in which the goods now were, advertising a sale. M'Geary v Raymond, 17 Pa Super. Ct. 308.

cannot be compelled by the landlord to allow them to remain. Probably, if the landlord did compel him, a subsequent distress would be inadmissible   In *Walsh v. The Bourse*[65] A let to B a room in the Philadelphia Bourse Building, and into the room, furniture belonging to X was put.   When B was in arrears for rent, A was notified that someone was surreptitiously removing the furniture by carrying it down the stairway, contrary to a rule which required all furniture to be carried on the freight elevator.   A thereupon prevented the removal of the furniture, ordering it to be returned to the room.   It was returned and was subsequently levied on for the rent, and sold.   In trespass by X he could not recover for the interference with the removal of the goods.   The regulation was reasonable.   Nor did the order that the goods be returned to the office constitute a conversion. A might have done this to protect the owner or the tenant from improper removal of the furniture by others   If no liability was incurred prior to or by the return of the goods to the office, A's subsequent seizure of them by distress was proper.

246. Liability of tenant to owner of goods.— When the goods of a stranger are taken for rent due by the tenant, the latter will be liable to the owner for the loss of the goods,[66] and, when the owner has brought replevin, and fails therein, for the costs of the replevin.[67]   It has been held to follow that an action on the case for an excessive distress upon the goods of a stranger could be brought by the tenant.[68]

247. Exemption of stranger's goods from distress.—The principle that goods, even of a stranger, are, while on the demised premises, subject to distress, is liable to exceptions whose scope has been variously described.   "Where," says Mercur, J., "the tenant, in the course of business, is necessarily put in possession of the property of those with whom he deals, or of those who em-

---

[65] 15 Pa Super Ct 219
[66] O Donnel v Seybert 13 Serg & R   54, Kessler v. M'Conachy, 1 Rawle 435

[67] *Kessler* v. *M'Conachy*, 1 Rawle, 435
[68] *O'Donnel* v. *Seybert*, 13 Serg & R. 54.

ploy him, such property, although on the demised premises, is not liable to distress for rent due thereon from the tenant."[69] In 1827, Gibson, Ch. J.,[70] observing that exceptions "in favor of trade" had been allowed, remarked: "Where the course of business must necessarily put the tenant in possession of the property of his customers, it would be against the plainest dictates of honesty and conscience to permit the landlord to use him as a decoy and pounce upon whatever should be brought within his grasp, after having received the price of its exemption in the enhanced value of the rent." "Where," said the court, "in the course of the tenant's business, he receives the property of third persons, as a means of making a livelihood, it is not subject to distress."[71] The exceptions to the principle that strangers' goods are liable in distress, Gibson, Ch. J., predicted in 1827, would "in the end eat out the rule,"[72] and in 1839 he found them to be "growing."[73] The prediction has not yet been fulfilled.[74]

248. Goods of boarder exempt.—The effects of a guest at an inn are not liable to distress for the host's rent. The principle is extended to boarding-house keepers. The boarder has no term or interest in the house. His chattels could not be distrained at common law for what he owes the keeper of the house. He is not a subtenant, and not as such can his goods be taken by the keeper's landlord for the keeper's rent. Nor can they on the principle merely that they are on the premises. Thus, a boarder occupying two rooms and boarding in a boarding house, his

[69]*Karns* v *McKinney*, 74 Pa 387, quoted by Clark, J, in *Page* v *Middleton*, 118 Pa 546, 12 Atl 415, by Sharswood, J, in *Howe Sewing Mach Co* v *Sloan*, 87 Pa 438, 30 Am Rep 376, *per curiam* in *Myers* v *Esery*, 134 Pa 177, 19 Atl 488, by Rice, P J, in *Clothier* v *Braithwaite*, 22 Pa Super Ct 521

[70]*Brown* v *Sims*, 17 Serg & R

138, *Riddle* v *Welden*, 5 Whart. 9

[71]*Cadwalader* v. *Tindall*, 20 Pa 422

[72]*Brown* v *Sims*, 17 Serg & R 138, *Myers* v *Esery*, 134 Pa 177, 19 Atl 488

[73]*Riddle* v *Welden*, 5 Whart 9

[74]*Tinware Mfg Co* v *Duff*, 15 Pa Super Ct 383.

goods in these rooms could not be taken by the landlord of the boarding-house keeper for rent.[75] The goods must be not simply in the house, but in the parts occupied by the owner, and in his possession.[76] If the boarder takes to the house sufficient furniture, not only for the room occupied by himself and wife, but also for other parts of the house, indeed, all the furniture in the house, except a few kitchen articles, so much of it as is outside of the boarder's room, and is used by all the boarders in common, and is not in his sole actual use, and necessary for his boarding and lodging as a boarder, is liable to distress.[77] A boarder whose goods will be exempt from distress must take meals in the house, from the keeper of it; "that is, he must constitute one of the family of the boarding-house keeper." If he simply rents rooms, supplying his own meals, or obtaining them elsewhere, he is a subtenant, whose goods will not be exempt.[78]

249. Commission merchant, agent — Goods consigned to an agent to be sold on commission are not liable to distress by the landlord of the agent. And apparently it is not necessary that the landlord should have had actual knowledge of the character of the business done by the tenant.[79] Thus, if the latter is in fact receiving organs, whether from one or many makers, for sale, any of the organs thus received and held for sale by him are exempt from distress. Should they be distrained, all that is necessary to visit liability on the landlord as a trespasser is that he should have been informed before the sale whose property they were, and that the owner should not have had notice

[75]*Riddle* v *Welden*, 5 Whart 9.

[76]*Erb* v *Sadler*, 8 W N C 13, *Jones* v *Goldbeck*, 8 W. N. C 533

[77]*Jones* v *Goldbeck*, 8 W. N C. 533

[78]*Lane* v. *Steinmetz*, 9 W N. C. 574. The plaintiff had rented rooms at so much per month, and was to have meals at 25 cents each, and $14 per month rent. This arrangement lasted only a short time. Having ceased "before the rent accrued," and she having become a mere "renter" of rooms, her goods were distrainable.

[79]*Howe Sewing Mach Co* v *Sloan*, 87 Pa 439, 30 Am. Rep. 376, *Brown* v. *Stackhouse*, 155 Pa 582 35 Am St Rep 908, 26 Atl 669, *Dorsh* v. *Lea*, 18 Pa Super. Ct 447

of the distress in time to replevy the goods before sale [80] So, though the landlord did not know when he made the lease, nor afterwards, that sewing machines received on the premises by the tenant were only consigned to him, and were not his own, these machines, if received on commission for sale as agent, by the tenant, cannot be properly distrained On the owner's replevin, before sale, they will be restored to him [81] The lease being made to "Lewis & Hitchcock, Managers," goods of W. delivered to them, his sales agents, as samples only, the property in them remaining in W , are not subject to the landlord's distress.[82] In *Bevan* v. *Crooks*,[83] a grocer occasionally received on commission flour and butter from the neighborhood. On one occasion only in four years he received for sale on commission another article, *viz ,* four ceroons of indigo. He sold this indigo and all the other goods in the store to X. The day after this sale the landlord distrained on the indigo. Huston, J., intimates that the indigo was not privileged from distress, suggesting that the tenant was a grocer, not a commission merchant, his receipt of the indigo for sale on commission was the only instance, in four years, of receipt for a similar purpose of anything else than the country produce, and, moreover, the indigo had in fact been sold, seemingly in conformity with the com-

[80]*Brown* v *Stackhouse*, 155 Pa 582, 35 Am. St. Rep 908, 26 Atl 669 In *Esterly Mach Co* v *Spencer*, 147 Pa. 466, 23 Atl 774 A sent agricultural machines and certain extra parts of them to B, the tenant, for sale as agent on commission They were not liable to distress by B's landlord. But the landlord was not liable in trespass to A, because A had notice of the distress before sale, and could have replevied.

[81]*Howe Sewing Mach Co* v. *Sloan*, 87 Pa 439, 30 Am Rep 376 Sharswood, J , remarks: "It is notoriously the usage for merchants not holding themselves out as commission merchants, to receive and sell goods in that way In the particular case before us, it would seem reasonable to infer that the products of sewing machine companies, the machines themselves being known by the name of the manufacturers, are usually sold by these agents on commission There was enough to put the landlord on inquiry, if notice was necessary "

[82]*Wanamaker & Brown* v. *Carter*, 22 Pa. Super Ct 625.

[83]7 Watts & S 452

mission, the day before the distress, so that it was no longer
kept by the tenant for sale [84] If the arrangement between the
owner and the tenant—a retail shoe dealer—is not that the
shoes shall be in any case returned, but that they shall be sold,
the tenant accounting only for the invoice price, the tenant is
not a commission merchant. The transaction is a sale, as to
creditors of the tenant, who are ignorant of a vendor's lien [85]
The owner's plea to the avowry in replevin, alleging that the
goods were plaintiff's, and were by him consigned and shipped
to the tenant, and put upon the premises "in the way and for
the benefit of trade," was held sufficient, on demurrer, Finletter,
J., remarking that "the terms used have a fixed meaning in
commerce."[86]

250. Warehousemen.— Goods received by a warehouseman,
for storage, are not subject to distress for his rent.[87] Nor is it
necessary that the warehouse should be used exclusively for the
storage of the goods of others than the warehouseman He may
conduct the business of a merchant, and keep his own as well
as others' goods therein.[88] The goods may be deposited directly
by the owner, or, being consigned by him to a commission merchant for sale, the latter may deposit them.[89] Tobacco,[90]

[84] The action was trover by the
owner of the indigo Another point
made was that the owner had not replevied. In *Tinware Mfg Co* v *Duff*,
15 Pa Super Ct 383, tin cans were
consigned to the tenant for sale on
commission   The tenant's business
was that of manufacturer's agent
and merchandise broker, of buying
and selling, on his own account,
grocers' supplies, and of renting
rooms for the storage of goods of
others   The tin cans were not distrainable for the tenant's rent, and
the landlord was liable in trespass
for not giving notice of the distress
before sale, so as to allow a replevin
by the owner. Cf, also, *Clothier* v

Braithwaite, 22 Pa Super Ct. 521.
   [85] *Dorsh* v *Lea*, 18 Pa Super. Ct.
447

   [86] *Biegenwald* v. *Winpenny*, 9 W
N C 542 In another case the words
of the plea were that the goods were
"the goods and chattels of the plaintiff in and upon the said premises in
the way of trade, and as such, privileged from distress" The plea was
sufficient   *Nass* v. *Winpenny*, 9 W
N C 542

   [87] *Brown* v *Sims*, 17 Serg & R
138

   [88] *Briggs* v *Large*, 30 Pa 287

   [89] *Briggs* v *Large*, 30 Pa 287;
Brown v. *Sims*, 17 Serg & R 138.

madder,[91] and other articles thus stored, cannot be properly distrained for the warehouseman's rent. When the place of storage is not kept for storage by the tenant, the goods will not be exempt from distress. A consigned to B, for thirty days' trial by B, and, if they should be found satisfactory, for sale to B, who was in the planing and sawmill business, a corundum wheel and knife grinder. B, not having used the wheel, sold out his business, and, apparently, also his lease of the premises to C, and stored the wheel with one Officer, who occupied the third story of the premises and who received it for B's accommodation, without pay. C falling in arrears for rent, his landlord distrained on the corundum wheel. It was held not to be exempt.[92] Officer, however, was not the tenant whose rent was the subject of the distress. If the warehouseman is a sublessee, the lessor may distrain on the goods on deposit, the title to which has, under the act of Sept. 24th, 1866 (P. L. 1867, p. 1363), passed to holders of warehouse warrants, unless he had notice of the character of the business of the sublessee before distraining, and of the fact that the things distrained on had been received on deposit by the sublessee.[93]

The owner brought trover in the former. In the latter, the commission merchant replevied.

[90]*Braun* v *Sims*, 17 Serg & R 138.

[91]*Briggs* v *Large*, 30 Pa. 287.

[92]*Page* v *Middleton*, 118 Pa. 546, 12 Atl 415 "Officer," says Clark, J., "was not a warehouseman at all; he was not to any extent engaged in the business of keeping goods on storage, he permitted this knife-grinding machine to be placed on his premises purely as a matter of favor, and without hope of reward In such a case the principle of exemption invoked can have no possible application."

[93]*American Pig Iron Storage Warrant Co* v *Sinnemahoning Iron & Coal Co* 205 Pa 403, 54 Atl 1047. The lease was to B of a furnace property containing coal mine, coke ovens, and blast furnace B assigned the lease to C, who sublet a small part of the premises to D At the time of making this sublease, 7,000 tons of iron, belonging to C, were stacked upon this small part C continued to make iron, and it was carried to the same place. D, a storage company, issued warrants upon all this iron to X, who had bought it from C X pledged the warrants to certain banks as collateral security Subsequently, the original lessor levied on the iron for rent due Nothing indicated to him that the iron was in the custody of D, as a warehouseman. The part sublet to D was distinguished from the rest of the premises merely by a wire fence The iron having been

251. Cattle agisted.— Cattle received on a pasture or farm, for the purpose of agistment, cannot be levied on for the farm-tenant's rent, though the tenant's own cattle are also pastured on the same premises.[94] The tenant, in *Cadwalader* v. *Tindall*,[95] received cattle to pasture, and A's cattle were on his premises in the day time, but were sent home in the evenings. They were not liable to be distrained, while on the premises, for the rent. "Certainly not," says the court, "else the law of distress would be a mere trap to catch other people's cattle "

252. Goods bailed for manufacture or repair.— Cloth left with a tailor to be converted into a garment,[96] grain sent to a mill in order to be ground,[97] an article, *e. g ,* a paper machine or roller, put with a machinist for repair,[98] will, while in the possession of the bailee, be exempt from liability for his rent. But a paper machine which was sent to a machinist in order to be repaired, but without any instructions to him concerning repair, and which remained with him for two years and five months, was, at the end of that period, distrained, not improperly.[99] "Nor is it clear," says Gibson, Ch. J., "that the machine, having been suffered to remain on the premises unclaimed for so long a time, by reason of the negligence of the owners or their agents, was in truth privileged."

253. Exemption of stranger's goods not absolute.—The privilege which, under certain circumstances, goods of a stranger on the demised premises enjoy of being exempt from distress for rent, is subject to the condition that the owner, if he is aware of the distress sufficiently early before sale to intercept the sale by

---

manufactured by C, there was no notice to the lessor of a change of its ownership   He had a right to think it still the property of C

[94]*Howe Sewing Mach Co* v *Sloan,* 87 Pa 439, 30 Am Rep 376, *Karns* v *McKinney,* 74 Pa 387.

[95] 20 Pa 422.

[96]*Karns* v. *McKinney,* 74 Pa. 387.

[97]*Korns* v *McKinney,* 74 Pa 387.

[98]*Caldcleugh* v. *Hollingsworth,* 8 Watts & S 302

[99]*Caldcleugh* v. *Hollingsworth,* 8 Watts & S 302   The action by the owner was trover, for the sale of the machine. One point made is that the owner should have brought replevin.

a replevin, shall replevy them If he does not, he cannot, after the sale, recover their value in an action of trespass, if the prescriptions of the statute of 1772, with respect to procedure, shall have been observed.[100] Nor, even if the owner is not aware of the distress, can he maintain trespass, unless the landlord learned that he was owner before the sale. When the distress is made, it is the tenant's duty to inform the distant owner, and, the landlord having no knowledge of this ownership, the owner will be bound to bring replevin, whether he is in fact informed by the tenant or not.[101] But when the landlord knows before the sale that the goods are X's, he must notify X, if X is not otherwise informed of the distress He cannot rely on the duty of the tenant to give this notice, if the tenant in fact fails to give it. In the absence of such notice to X, the landlord knowing that X is the owner before the sale, X may, after the sale, sustain trespass for the wrongful distress.[102] And, after the notice to the owner, sufficient time, by adjournment of the sale, if necessary, must be allowed to the owner to institute the replevin.[10']

254. Exemption from distress; sewing machines.—By the act of April 17th, 1869,[104] it was enacted that all sewing machines belonging to seamstresses in this state shall be exempt from distress for rent, in addition to any articles or money already ex-

[100]*Bogert* v *Batterton*, 6 Pa Super. Ct 468, *Thomas* v *Baner*, 6 Pa Dist R 177, *Lengert Co* v *Bellevue Bldg & L Asso* 15 Pa Super. Ct 380 The owner cannot recover in trespass, though the landlord knew, before the sale, that the goods were his

[101]*Caldcleugh* v. *Hollingsworth*, 8 Watts & S 302, *Bevan* v *Crooks*, 7 Watts & S 452 If he is informed by the tenant or otherwise, the owner must bring replevin, if he has a chance, before the sale. *Esterly Mach Co* v *Spencer*, 147 Pa 466, 23 Atl. 774. Notice by the tenant is

sufficient *Tinware Mfg Co.* v *Duff*, 15 Pa Super Ct 383

[102]*Brown* v *Stackhouse*, 155 Pa. 582, 35 Am St Rep 908, 26 Atl 669 In *Ellis* v *Lamb*, 9 Pa Dist R 491, it is assumed that if goods of another than the tenant are taken off the premises, the owner is not bound to replevy, but may recover damages in trespass

[103]*Brown* v *Stackhouse*, 155 Pa 582, 35 Am St Rep. 908, 26 Atl 669, *Tinware Mfg Co.* v. *Duff*, 15 Pa Super Ct 383

[104] 1 Pepper & L. Digest, 1928, P. L. 69.

empt. The act of March 4th, 1870,[105] directed that the provisions of the act of 1869 should apply to "all sewing machines
used and owned by private families in this commonwealth:
Provided, That this act shall not apply to persons who keep sewing machines for sale or hire" The machines thus exempted
must be owned by a seamstress, or be owned and used by a private family. A sewing machine leased by a dealer, who kept
such machines for hire, to a private family, is not exempt. The
hirer having abandoned the premises occupied by him as tenant,
and left the machine there, it could not be considered as "owned
and used" by his family [106] But, under the act of June 25th,
1895,[107] leased sewing machines are exempt if the owner or his
agent, or the lessee, gives notice to the landlord that they are
leased.

255. Goods of public corporation.— When one railroad corporation leases its road to another, no distress for rent can be
levied on a lot of ties, rails, or other property essential to the
performance of the function of transportation. At the instance
of the lessee, the distress will be enjoined.[108]

256. Goods in legal custody.— "It is a rule without an exception," said Gibson, Ch. J, in 1842,[109] "that a landlord cannot
distrain goods which are in the custody of the law." Of this principle there have been various applications. After a foreign attachment had been executed upon 5 acres of wheat, a landlord
of the defendant caused a distress to be made of the grain, and
sold it. He was held liable to the sheriff in an action on the

[105] 1 Pepper & L Digest, 1928, P
L 35 Doubt of the constitution-
ality of this act is expressed, because
its title gives no notice of an intention to legislate in favor of any
other than seamstresses *Bogert* v.
Batterton, 6 Pa Super Ct 468

[106] *Bogert* v *Batterton,* 6 Pa
Super Ct 468 Gunster, J, intimates that the exemption of a sewing machine could not be waived by
a seamstress, or the head of a family
owning and using it
[107] P L 282
[108] *Pittsburg, J E & E R Co* v
Altoona & B C R Co 196 Pa. 452,
46 Atl 431
[109] *Pierce* v *Scott,* 4 Watts & S.
344, *Shiles* v *Sides,* 1 Pa Super Ct.
15.

case, for the whole value of the grain.[110] If, under a replevin begun for goods on the demised premises, by an owner, the sheriff takes possession of the goods, but leaves them on the premises for a brief time, in order to allow the defendant to obtain sureties for a claim property bond, during this interval the goods are in the custody of the law, and the landlord cannot distrain on them for rent due him. The sheriff may take them despite the distress, without being liable in trespass to the landlord;[111] and if he does not, he will be liable to the plaintiff in the replevin.[112] After the appointment of a committee for a lunatic who is a tenant, the landlord loses the power of making distress for rent due before the finding of the inquisition.[113] After a levy has been made in execution against the tenant, on goods on his premises, the landlord cannot distrain upon them.[114] But if, no inventory being taken, the goods are allowed to remain for ten days on the premises, so as to make the levy invalid as against one having no knowledge of it, the goods can be levied on in distress by the landlord, if ignorant of the levy, and sold[115] When, fi fa against B being levied on goods upon the premises which B holds as tenant, a sheriff's interpleader is begun on account of a claim of the goods as his by A, under which the sheriff withdraws from the possession of the goods, they may be distrained upon by B's landlord, whether they are in fact B's or A's[116] A sale by the sheriff

[110]*Pierce* v *Scott*, 4 Watts & S. 344 As landlord, he would have been entitled to one year's rent from the proceeds of the sale of the grain at the completion of the attachment proceedings He was denied this

[111]*Skiles* v *Sides*, 1 Pa Super Ct 15, *Com* v *Lelar*, 1 Phila 173

[112]*Com* v *Lelar*, 1 Phila 173

[113]*Cochran* v. *Howes*, 3 Del Co. Rep 248

[114]*Leidich's Estate*, 161 Pa 451, 29 Atl 89, 90

The constable or sheriff who makes the levy in execution, but not the plaintiff therein, can maintain trespass against the landlord who distrains after the levy *Taylor* v *Manderson*, 1 Ashm (Pa) 130

[115]*McHugh* v *Malony*, 4 Phila 59 If the property is taken from the purchaser at the distress sale, by the deputy sheriff, in virtue of the execution, and sold, the purchaser's action is against this officer, and not against the landlord, on an implied warranty of the regularity of the distress proceedings

[116]*Gilham* v *Tobias*, 11 Phila 313 A, claiming the goods to be his in

of goods which the landlord has already distrained will be subject to the distress, and the landlord will be entitled to the rent
from the proceeds [117]

257. Goods on premises after sheriff's sale.— If the goods of
the tenant have been sold in execution upon the premises, the
purchaser must have a reasonable time in which to withdraw
them, before they can be distrained by the landlord for the rent
of the execution defendant.   Under a lease for five years, the
rent, $24,000 per year, was payable quarterly in advance, on the
first day of April, July, October, and January   On Dec 25th,
under a fi fa , the goods in the building were levied on, no rent
being then in arrear.   The sale was not effected until Jan 2d,
3d, and 4th   On Jan. 9th, the goods being still on the premises, distress was made upon them for the rent due on January
1st.   It was held, in replevin by the purchaser of the goods,
that if, under the circumstances, the time between the sale and
the distress was not sufficiently long for the removal of the
goods, had reasonable expeditiousness been observed, the distress
was improper [118]   Had the goods sold in execution been allowed
to remain an unreasonable time on the premises, they could, after the expiration of a reasonable time, have been distrained [119]

258. Receivers of tenant — If, the tenant becoming insolvent,
a receiver of his property and business is appointed, who takes

replevin against B's landlord, is estopped from saying that they are in
the custody of the law to answer the
execution by B's creditors   It is
said by Briggs, J , that even if the
distress occurred before the sheriff
had withdrawn, A could not recover   In *Power* v *Howard,* 22 W
N   C. 475, replevin by B was
quashed, though there was a discrepancy in the statement of the
deputy sheriff as to whether, under
the interpleader, there had been a
formal withdrawal from possession
by the sheriff   He had made a formal levy and locked up the place, but
put no one in possession, and had
given the key to the defendant in the
execution, who went on running the
business as before, until the distress
was levied.

[117]*Garrett's Appeal,* 100 Pa 597

[118]*Stern* v *Stanton,* 184 Pa 468,
39 Atl 404   The failure to pack
and remove any of the goods within
the time did not forfeit the right to
a reasonable time

[119]*Stern* v *Stanton,* 184 Pa. 468, 39
Atl 404, *Booth* v *Hoenig,* 7 Pa.
Dist R 529

possession of the leased premises, and of the goods and chattels thereon, the landlord cannot distrain on such goods thus in his possession. But the landlord will have a lien for the rent on the goods, and on the proceeds of their subsequent sale by the receiver.[120]

259 Things distrainable — All varieties of personalty are subject to the right of the landlord to distrain. A few of the articles that have been distrained in the reported cases are a coal barge, a lot of lumber, oak streamers, kegs of spikes, a lot of bolts, four bales of oakum,[121] twenty-six hogsheads of tobacco,[122] five casks of madder,[123] four organs,[124] a stove,[125] a soda fountain,[126] a ceroon of indigo,[127] safes,[128] household furniture,[129] coal in a coal yard,[130] a sewing machine,[131] sand, oars, in a warehouse.[132] The 7th section of the act of March 21st, 1772,[133] authorizes the taking, as a distress, of any cattle or stock of the tenant, feeding or depasturing on the demised premises, and of all sorts of corn and grass, hops, roots, fruits, pulse, or other product whatsoever which shall be growing on the premises Grain in the ground may, accordingly, be distrained.[134] So may buildings erected by the tenant under a provision in the

[120]*Lane* v *Washington Hotel Co* 190 Pa 230, 42 Atl 697, *Cooper* v *Rose Valley Mills*, 174 Pa 302, 34 Atl. 559 This lien will prevail against the receiver's commissions and his counsel fees, but will be subject to the payment of a proper share of the expenses of a necessary audit But see *Singerly* v *Fox*, 75 Pa. 112

[121]*Karns* v *McKinney*, 74 Pa 387.

[122]*Brown* v *Sims*, 17 Serg & R 138

[123]*Briggs* v *Large*, 30 Pa 287

[124]*Brown* v *Stackhouse*, 155 Pa 582, 35 Am St Rep 908, 26 Atl 669

[125]*Kessler* v. *M'Conachy*, 1 Rawle, 435

[126]*Tufts* v *Park*, 194 Pa 79, 44 Atl. 1079

[127]*Bevan* v. *Crooks*, 7 Watts & S 452

[128]*Gilham* v *Tobias*, 11 Phila 313

[129]*Blanche* v *Bradford*, 38 Pa 344, 80 Am Dec 489

[130]*Rosenberger* v *Hallowell*, 35 Pa 369

[131]*Bogert* v *Batterton*, 6 Pa Super Ct 468

[132]*Quinn* v *Wallace*, 6 Whart 452

[133] 1 Pepper & L Digest, 2636, 1 Smith's Laws, 370, *Quinn* v *Wallace*, 6 Whart 452

[134]*Snyder* v *Kunkleman*, 3 Penr & W 487, *Kerr* v *Sharp*, 14 Serg & R 399, *Pierce* v. *Scott*, 4 Watts & S 344.

lease that he may remove them at the end of the term, *e. g.*, a brick malt house,[135] two houses, a stable, and out-buildings.[136] Fixtures which are not removable by the tenant, becoming a part of the realty, are not distrainable. If they are removable, they remain personalty. A mule, 90 feet long, occupied 11 feet space in width, and had from 400 to 600 spindles. It was fastened to the floor of the mill, the demised premises, by means of screws, and was part of the machinery of the mill. The tenant, to whom it belonged, sold it to the persons from whom he had bought it, who sent their workmen to remove it. It was distrained on before they accomplished this object, and properly. It was a "chattel subject to distress."[137] The term itself is not distrainable by the landlord, unless he has contracted that it shall be.[138] If the landlord is the owner of the goods on the premises, by purchase from the tenant, or other person, they cannot be distrained,[139] but, though the lease assigns the goods of the tenant to the landlord as security for the rent, he may distrain them. If he does, he must proceed as when he distrains goods not so transferred to him.[140]

260 Exemption from distress.—The 1st section of the act of April 9th, 1849,[141] enacts that "in lieu of the property now exempt by law from levy and sale on execution issued upon any judgment obtained upon contract, and distress for rent, prop-

[135]*Spencer* v *Darlington*, 74 Pa. 286

[136]*Beeker* v *Werner*, 98 Pa 555 Cf *Chicago & A Oil & Min Co* v *Barnes*, 62 Pa 445

[137]*Furbush* v *Chappell*, 105 Pa. 187. Cf *Thropp's Appeal*, 70 Pa 395

[138]*Spencer* v *Darlington*, 74 Pa 286 Cf *Pennsylvania Co for Ins on Lives & G A* v *Shandhan*, 10 Pa Super Ct 267

[139]*Tufts* v *Park*, 194 Pa 79, 44 Atl 1079 He could not justify his taking possession of them, as against a former owner, contesting the right of the tenant, by setting up a distress upon them.

[140]*Fernwood Masonic Hall Assn* v *Jones*, 102 Pa 307; *Wyke* v *Wilson*, 173 Pa 12, 33 Atl 701

[141] 1 Pepper & L Digest, 1920, P L 533 If a chattel is set apart to the tenant, under the exemption, *e g*, wheat growing, it becomes his property His subsequent vendee or purchaser of it at an execution sale has the right to take it after it ripens *Hazlett* v *McCutcheon*, 158 Pa. 539, 27 Atl. 1086.

erty to the value of $300, exclusive of all wearing apparel of
the defendant and his family, and all Bibles and school books
in use in the family (which shall remain exempted as here
tofore), and no more, owned by or in possession of any debtor,
shall be exempt from levy and sale on execution, or by distress
for rent." All wearing apparel, whether of the tenant, or of
his family, and, probably, whether belonging to him or to them,
all Bibles and school books in use in the family, were previously
and continue to be exempt from distress. Besides these articles,
property "owned by or in possession of the tenant," to the extent, in value, of $300, is made exempt by the act of 1849. As
property not the tenant's, but in his possession, may be taken
in distress for his rent, it may be claimed by the lessee as
exempt;[142] but it does not result that the tenant can claim
$300 worth of his own property, and $300 worth of the property of another, in his possession, or that he can claim
$300 worth of his own, and the owner of other property in his
possession can claim $300 of that[143] That the wife of the
tenant could claim exemption of her property was denied in
Com. ex rel Menges v. *Huttel*,[144] though it was affirmed in
Balmer v. *Peiffer*,[145] that, despite a waiver of exemption in
the husband's lease, she could claim it as to her own goods. An
assignee of the lessee, not being contractually indebted to the
lessor, neither his goods nor those of a subtenant, distrained
on by the lessor, are exempt on the demand of their owner,
though the original tenant may claim them as exempt.[146] If

[142]*Huey's Appeal*, 29 Pa 219,
Rosenberger v *Hallowell*, 35 Pa
369.

[143] The demand to exempt the
property of other than the lessee
must be by him, "and preclude him,"
says Sharswood, P. J, "from another
demand for the exemption of other
property which may be distrained or
levied for the same debt" *Rosenberger* v *Hallowell*, 35 Pa 369.

[144] 4 Pa Super Ct 95 As to exemption of a stove under early
statute, *vide Kessler* v *M'Conachy*, 1
Rawle, 435

[145] 16 Lanc L Rev 251 But the
goods were distrained off the
premises, and this would have exempted them

[146]*Rosenberger* v. *Hallowell*, 35 Pa.
369.

the lease is made to two persons jointly, their joint property is not exempt from distress [147]

261. Waiver of the exemption.— Although it is intimated[148] that a waiver of the exemption secured by the act of 1849 is not applicable to the wearing apparel, Bibles, and school books which had been privileged from execution before that act, the validity of a waiver of the exemption of $300 worth of property is unquestionable.[149] The waiver is usually inserted in the written lease,[150] though it may be oral when the lease is oral, and it may be made subsequently to the making of the lease. To the original written lease, containing a waiver, a supplement written on the same paper was entered into, providing for the making of improvements by the landlord, and the paying of a larger rent   Though the supplement said nothing concerning a waiver of the lease, such waiver under it was implied.[151] The waiver may be of the right to take the property on the premises, or within 30 days after its removal from the premises.   It will then apply simply to a distress, and not to a judgment recovered in an action for rent.[152]   A married woman, lessee, may waive the exemption.[153]

262. Waiver of inurement.— If there is a waiver as to a debt for which, on a judgment recovered for it, an execution has issued, this waiver would inure to the advantage of an earlier distress, levied on the same goods, the sale taking place in virtue of both processes; or, upon the execution, but subject to the landlord's right to first take the proceeds.   In *Steininger v.*

[147]*Bonsall v Comly*, 44 Pa. 442 Overlooked in *Conroy v Bitner*, 10 Lanc L Rev 185

[148]*Bogert v Batterton*, 6 Pa Super Ct 468

[149]*Mitchell v Coates*, 47 Pa 202, *Beatty v Rankin*, 139 Pa 358, 21 Atl 74, *M'Kinney v. Reader*, 6 Watts, 34, *Conroy v. Bitner*, 10 Lanc L Rev 185

[150]*M'Kinney v. Reader*, 6 Watts,

34, *Temple v Gough*, 9 Pa Co Ct. 85

[151]*Conroy v. Bitner*, 10 Lanc L. Rev 185

[15]*Mitchell v Coates*, 47 Pa 202 Or the waiver may be broad enough to apply both to distress and suit. *Beatty v Rankin*, 139 Pa 358, 21 Atl 74

[153]*Lloyd v Underkoffer*, 1 Legal Rec Rep 8

Butler,[154] the tenant's goods were taken in an execution with respect to which he had waived the exemption. A few hours later, the same day, the landlord distrained the same goods. On the next day, he claimed his rent from the proceeds of sale, under § 83 of the act of June 16th, 1836,[155] which gives a preference as to one year's rent, to a landlord As the tenant had waived his right to the exemption against the creditor, it was held that he could not assert it against the landlord. But the fact that there was no exemption, as respects the execution, because the debt on which it was based originated before the going into operation of the act of April 9th, 1849, did not make a waiver in regard to rent falling due, and distrained for, subsequently to that time.[156] If the sale is on the distress alone, with respect to which there is no waiver of the exemption, and goods, to the worth of $300, are set apart to the tenant, the fact that these goods are afterwards taken in an execution, as to which there is a waiver, does not entitle the landlord to take the proceeds of their sale[157] The mere right which the landlord has to be preferred to the execution does not cause the waiver of exemption in his favor to inure to the benefit of the execution, as to which there is no waiver. If $300 worth of goods have been set apart to the debtor in the execution, the landlord's subsequent notice to the sheriff of his demand of one year's rent does not justify the court, on the application of the execution-creditor, in setting aside the appraisement of the goods for the debtor.[158] A waiver of exemption in a lease is

---

[154] 17 Pa Co Ct 97, 5 Pa Dist. R 43, *Collins's Appeal*, 35 Pa 83

[155] 1 Pepper & L Digest, 1954, P. L 755

[156] *Rowland* v *Goldsmith*, 2 Grant Cas 378   Under one execution, goods had been set apart to the debtor   They were afterwards levied on under the execution, whose debt began prior to April 9th, 1849. As

to this latter execution, the landlord had no right to preference

[157] *Frick* v. *McClain*, 12 Lanc Bar, 78.

[158] *Temple* v *Gough*, 9 Pa Co Ct 85   A waiver of the exemption is not applicable to the excess of money made by a distress sale, which excess is payable to the tenant   The landlord, though the lease contains a

valid in favor of the grantees of the lessor's reversion, by sheriff's sale[159] or otherwise.

263. Remedy to secure allowance of exemption.—The tenant makes his demand upon the bailiff, or landlord, whose duty it then becomes to select as appraisers three disinterested and competent persons. It is too late to make the demand on the day on which the bills of sale are posted or after any costs have been incurred which, by early notice, would have been avoided[160] If the demand is improperly ignored, an action of trespass lies[161] against the person on whom the demand is made and who, having the power to cause the appraisement, has refused to cause it.[162] In replevin by the tenant, if the judgment is for the landlord, no deduction will be made on account of any right of the tenant to have claimed $300 worth of the goods, against the distress.[163] And even when a selection of goods has been made by the tenant, and they have been appraised to him, he acquires no right to them which he can vindicate by a replevin for them, if subsequently, before they are removed from the premises by the tenant, the landlord directs his bailiff to disregard the claim for exemption, and the latter then advertises the goods for sale.[164] Since the remedy of trespass[165] is

waiver of the exemption, cannot, for subsequently accrued rent, attach that excess The attachment under the act of March 17th, 1869, will be quashed and the excess ordered to be paid to the tenant *Simes* v *Steadwell*, 12 W N C 292

[159]*Wood* v *Custer*, 16 Montg Co L Rep 118

[160]*Rosenberger* v *Hallowell*, 35 Pa 369 The notice of distress was given to the tenant on April 2d, 1858 On the 8th the goods were appraised with a view to sale and on the same day the sale was advertised for April 14th The demand on April 12th for the exemption was too late.

[161]*Rosenberger* v *Hallowell*, 35 Pa 369, *McDowell* v *Shotwell*, 2 Whart 26, *Moulson's Estate*, 1 Brewst (Pa) 296

[162]*Rosenberger* v *Hallowell*, 35 Pa 369

[163]*Wood* v *Custer*, 16 Montg Co L Rep 118 In *Conroy* v *Bitner*, 10 Lane L Rev 185, the court apparently instructed the jury to allow for the rent, less the exemption.

[164]*Bonsall* v *Comly*, 44 Pa 442

[165]*Com ex rel Menges* v *Huttel*, 4 Pa Super Ct. 95.

ordinarily adequate, a writ of mandamus will be refused, commanding the bailiff or landlord to allow the exemption, no peculiar facts showing that trespass is inadequate.[166]

[166] The court named trespass and replevin as the possible remedies.

264 Place where goods must normally be — At common law the chattels subject to distress were such only as were at the time of distress upon the premises for whose rent the distress was made. Goods anywhere on the premises could be taken. The tract might embrace hundreds of acres, and the goods might be found within an area of a few square yards. The rent for a building of twenty stories could, if let as one tenement, be levied on goods in a single room on one floor. If a lease is made of coal mines below, and of miners' houses upon, the surface, at an entire rent, or even at one rent for the mines, and a separate rent for the houses, any portion of either rent can be distrained on goods found anywhere within or upon the leased property. "It is of no importance," says Woodward, J , "that the rents for the coal veins and the houses were measurable by different standards. Both were certain and fixed or easily reduced to certainty."[1] The demise being of a "house, No. 420 Dewey street," the sidewalk in front of it is not to be considered a part of the premises, and goods of a stranger[2] or of

[1]*Spencer* v *Kunkle,* 2 Grant Cas   [2]*Pickering* v *Breen,* 22 Pa Super.
406   Ct 4.

the tenant, which have been taken from the house and set on the sidewalk, in process of removal to a wagon, are not subject to distress.

265. Fraudulent and clandestine removal of goods.—The 5th section of the act of March 21st, 1772,[3] authorizes the landlord or lessor to distrain goods no longer on the premises, if they shall have been "fraudulently or clandestinely" conveyed or carried off or from the premises, with intent to prevent distress for arrears of rent, if the distress is made within thirty days after such conveying or carrying away. The goods may be taken "wherever the same may be found." Proceedings are to be the same as when the goods are found on the premises   This, in the absence of a stipulation in the lease, is the only authority for the pursuit of the goods and a distress upon them, beyond the leased premises.[4] The right to distrain off the premises is by the act given in "case any lessee" shall fraudulently or clandestinely carry off "his goods and chattels " We have elsewhere seen that goods of another than the tenant may be removed clandestinely, and with a view of evading distress, without right in the landlord to pursue them.[5] And the tenant may sell his own goods, on the premises, when no rent is due, and on their removal by the purchaser they could not be taken in distress.[6] The assignee of a lease is liable for the rent falling due during his possession of the premises. His goods may, therefore, be pursued by the landlord if they are removed clandestinely or fraudulently.[7]

[3] 1 Pepper & L. Digest, 2638; 1 Smith's Laws, 370   After a sale in distress, the title of the purchaser cannot be impugned in an action by him against a third person, by showing that the goods were distrained off the demised premises   This irregularity is waived, unless the tenant or owner brings replevin before sale   *Water* v *M'Clellan*, 4 Dall 208, 1 L. ed 803.

[4] *Owens* v *Shovlin*, 116 Pa 371, 9 Atl 484; *Clifford* v. *Beems*, 3 Watts, 246

[5] *Murphy* v *Rementer*, 7 Del Co Rep 203, 15 Lanc L Rev 270

[6] *Morris* v *Parker*, 1 Ashm (Pa) 187

[7] *Jones* v *Gundrim*, 3 Watts & S 531.

266 Rent due at time of removal.— Goods of the tenant cannot be pursued beyond the premises under the act of 1772, unless, when they were removed, rent for which the landlord could distrain was in arrear. Rent payable quarterly would fall due on April 1st, 1821. On the preceding March 20th, the tenant removed his goods from demised premises to another house. On April 2d, the landlord distrained the goods. Says Tilghman, Ch J.: "The removal, to bring it within the law, must be with an intent to prevent the landlord from distraining for arrears of rent, which cannot be when there is no arrear, and there can be no arrear before the rent is due "[8] An intended sale four months before rent fell due of the goods by the tenant to a stranger, who would remove them, would not be enjoined.[9] The lease may make the act of removal of the goods, without regard to motive or mode, accelerate the maturity of the debt; it may, e g , provide that in case of removal of the goods, the whole rent unpaid shall at once become payable and collectible by distress or otherwise. Under such a lease, distress beyond the premises would be permissible, although no rent was due until the removal, if the other conditions prescribed by the act of 1772, existed, viz., the clandestinity or fraudulence of the removal [10]

267. Clandestine or fraudulent removal, continued.—The mere fact that, after rent is due, the tenant withdraws his goods from the premises, does not expose them to distress.[11] They cannot be thus distrained on while off the premises, unless their removal was clandestine or fraudulent [12] A removal of goods in the night is, in itself, clandestine,[13] but, since a clandestine is

[8]*Grace* v *Shively*, 12 Serg & R 217 Cf *Sargent* v *Matchett*, 20 W N C 96

[9]*Jackson's Appeal*, 3 Montg Co L Rep 96, 9 Atl 306

[10]*Owens* v *Shovlin*, 116 Pa 371, 9 Atl 484

[11]*Clifford* v *Beems*, 3 Watts, 246,

Owens v *Shovlin*, 116 Pa 371, 9 Atl 484

[12]*Owens* v *Shovlin*, 116 Pa 371, 9 Atl 484, *Grant's Appeal*, 44 Pa 477.

[13]*Grace* v *Shively*, 12 Serg & R 217; *Purfel* v. *Sands*, 1 Ashm (Pa) 120

a secret removal, "it is not easy to conceive," said Tilghman, Ch. J.,[14] "how a removal in broad day can be secret, although, under some circumstances, it may perhaps be fraudulent." Nor does the fact that the removal in the daytime occurs without the knowledge of the landlord make it clandestine or fraudulent. "The tenant," says Tilghman, Ch. J., "is not bound to give notice to the landlord that he is about to remove his goods, nor is he under any obligation not to remove them; it is the landlord's business to be vigilant."[15] In *Grant's Appeal*,[16] the landlord resided in a house adjoining the store occupied by his tenant. He left the town on Sept. 17th, on business, and did not return until Sept. 24th. On Sept. 19th, the wife of the tenant, his agent, began taking an inventory of the goods, and finished on Sept 20th, and on the same day, in the daytime, moved the goods to a building 60 feet distant. They were not clandestinely removed [17]

268. Fraudulent removal, continued.—Clandestineness of removal is "sufficient evidence of fraud;"[18] but there may be a fraudulent removal which is not secret. A case of this class is suggested by Tilghman, Ch. J., *viz.*, when the landlord, about to distrain, is induced to desist by the tenant's promise to pay the rent or furnish satisfactory security by a certain hour, and, meantime, to refrain from removing the goods, and, as soon as the landlord's back is turned, the tenant removes the goods.[19] But the tenant's statement to the landlord that he intends at once to remove the goods, and will pay the rent as soon as he can, and that he expects to be able to in a few days, does not make

[14]*Hoops* v *Crowley*, 12 Serg & R 219, note The removal began in the forenoon, but was not finished until after night The landlord had been told by the tenant of the intention of the latter to remove the goods

[15]*Grace* v *Shively*, 12 Serg & R 217; *Hoops* v *Crowley*, 12 Serg & R 219, note.

[16] 44 Pa 477.

[17]*Grant's Appeal*, 44 Pa 477.

[18]*Grace* v *Shively*, 12 Serg & R 217

[19]*Grace* v. *Shively*, 12 Serg & R 217.

the removal fraudulent, whether the landlord consents or not to the threatened removal[20] The mere fact that the removal is without the landlord's knowledge will not make it fraudulent, or justify an inference of fraud,[21] nor that the removal occurs during a temporary absence of the landlord from the neighborhood[22]

269. Distress must be made in thirty days after removal—The act of March 21st, 1772, authorizes distress on goods which have been clandestinely or fraudulently removed, "within the space of thirty days next ensuing" after such removal There is no right after the expiration of the thirty days to distrain, however, clandestine or fraudulent the removal may have been,[23] unless there is a stipulation in the lease allowing a longer period[24] The 6th section of the act of March 21st, 1772,[25] expressly says that nothing in that act shall empower the lessor to take or seize any goods or chattels as a distress, which shall have been, bona fide, and for a valuable consideration, sold before such taking or seizing, to any person not privy to the fraud of the tenant.

270. Fraudulent removal in Philadelphia, Pittsburg, and Allegheny.—The act of March 25th, 1825,[26] enacts that if a tenant of land in Philadelphia city or county shall, before rent becomes due and payable, fraudulently convey away or carry off from the premises his goods and chattels, with intent to defraud the landlord of the distress, the landlord may consider the rent as apportioned up to the time of such removal of the goods, and, within thirty days after such removal, may take and seize such goods wherever they may be found, as a distress for the

[20]*Hoops* v *Crowley*, 12 Serg & R 219, note

[21]*Grace* v *Shively*, 12 Serg & R 217, *Grant's Appeal*, 44 Pa 477, *Purfel* v *Sands*, 1 Ashm (Pa) 120, *Morris* v *Parker*, 1 Ashm (Pa) 187

[22]*Grant's Appeal*, 44 Pa 477.

[23]*Jackson's Appeal*, 3 Montg Co L L 114

Rep 96, 9 Atl. 306, *Clifford* v. *Beems* 3 Watts, 246.

[24]*Baer* v. *Kuhl*, 8 Pa. Dist R. 389.

[25]1 Pepper & L Digest, 2639, 1 Smiths Laws, 370, *Clifford* v. *Beems*, 3 Watts, 246

[26]1 Pepper & L. Digest, 2639, P.

rent so apportioned. Before he seizes them, however, he must make oath or affirmation before some judge, alderman, or justice of the peace, that he verily believes that the goods were removed for the purpose of defrauding him No such seizure may be made after the goods have, since their removal, been sold to a purchaser, bona fide, and for value.[27] In order to resort to this proceeding the goods must be conveyed from the premises fraudulently. Simply taking them away in the daytime, without notice to, or the knowledge of, the landlord is not, nor is it sufficient evidence of, a fraudulent taking[28] The affidavit must conform to the act. To aver that the affiant "had just cause to suspect and did believe," etc., is not a compliance. "Belief," says King, P. J.,[29] "admits of all degrees, from the slightest suspicion to the fullest assurance The legislature have thought fit to make use of the word 'verily,' and we cannot say they attached no importance to it " A distress made after so imperfect an affidavit will, in replevin by the tenant, be treated as invalid.

271 Conventional right to distrain beyond premises.—The contract between the landlord and the tenant may bestow a right on the former to distrain goods after their removal from the premises, when the circumstances do not exist under which the statutes confer such right Thus, it may stipulate that all property removed from the premises shall, for thirty days after such removal, be liable to distress and sale for rent in arrear Under such a clause, the rent must be in arrear at the time of the removal to justify pursuit and distress of the goods beyond the premises. Removed, e. g., Oct 24th, before rent is in arrear

[27] The act was extended to Pittsburg and Allegheny by the act of March 29th, 1870, P. L 669

Purfel v Sands, 1 Ashm. (Pa) 120, Morris v Parker, 1 Ashm (Pa) 187 The tenant makes an assignment for the benefit of creditors. The assignee sells the goods on the premises No rent is then in arrear There is no fraud which would justify an apportionment of the rent to the time of assignment or of sale, and a distress

[29] Purfel v. Sands, 1 Ashm (Pa) 120.

(it fell due Nov. 1st), they cannot be distrained after the rent
has become due, *e. g.*, Nov. 2d, though within the thirty days [30]
A distress made after the thirty days will be unjustifiable. [31]
A provision in the lease that "in case of removal on the part of
the lessee from the premises, during the continuance of the
lease," the whole rent shall become at once payable and "collectible by distress," does not authorize a distress on goods no
longer on the demised premises. Such distress, if proper at all,
is so because the removal was fraudulent, and because the
statute, for this reason, authorizes distress beyond the premises. [32] But if the stipulation is that, should the tenant remove
any part of the goods, they shall, "for thirty days, . . .
wherever found, be liable to distress," distress can be made anywhere. [33] If the lease provides for such pursuit and distress
of "the property of the lessee" it will not warrant the pursuit
of property of his wife, after removal. [34] The lessee covenant-

---

[30]*Conway* v *Loury*, 7 W N C 64;
Sargent v *Matchett*, 20 W N C 96,
Gold v *Gleason*, 26 Pittsb L J N
S 10   In *Kelly* v *Davenport*, 1
Browne (Pa) 231, a lessee of a
house in New Jersey, before the rent
was due, clandestinely removed his
goods to Pennsylvania   After the
rent had become due the lessor fol
lowed them and distrained them, but
meantime they had been levied on in
foreign attachment by another   The
goods being sold, the attachment
creditor was held entitled to the proceeds   New Jersey could not give a
right to a creditor to arrest either
the goods or the person of his debtor
in Pennsylvania   On Jan 2d, removal from the premises, one month's
rent being due   On Jan 12th, another month's rent fell due. There
could not be a distress on the removed goods for more than one
month's rent   *Weber* v *Loper*, 16
Montg Co L Rep 70

[31]*Dinner* v *McAndrews*, 10 Pa
Dist. R. 221; *Mather* v *Wood*, 12

Pa Co Ct 3   The plea "*hors de son
fee*" was held proper to raise the
issue whether the distress had been
made within the thirty days

[32]*Owens* v *Shovlin*, 116 Pa 371, 9
Atl 484   How, were all the goods
removed, there could be any distress
at all, is not apparent

[33]*Dinner* v   *McAndrews.* 10 Pa.
Dist R 221, *Baer* v *Kuhl*, 8 Pa
Dist R 389   In *Balmer* v *Peiffer*,
16 Lanc L Rev 251, a distress was
made on a wife's goods when off the
premises   The husband s lease allowed distress beyond the premises
The right to distrain the wife's goods
under this clause is not discussed

[34]*Baer* v *Kuhl*, 8 Pa. Dist R 389.
The lease stating that "should the
property of the lessee be removed
from the aforesaid premises" it
might be pursued for ninety days,
the court questioned whether the removal did not need to be clandestine
or fraudulent   The landlord had
consented to the removal.

ing that if, during the term, he should "attempt to remove, or manifest an intention to remove, his goods and effects out of or off from the premises" the landlord might proceed "to distrain and collect" the rent, it was said, *per curiam:* "There is nothing here requiring the intention or attempt to be fraudulent,"[35] and, the goods being shipped in the daytime, by a railroad, to another town, they could be there distrained.[36]

---

[35]*Goodwin* v. *Sharkey,* 80 Pa. 149 An intention to remove is not an attempt *Klein* v. *McFarland,* 5 Pa. Super. Ct. 110.

[36]*Gold* v *Gleason,* 26 Pittsb. L. J. N S. 10, 8 Kulp, 76.

CHAPTER XVI.

DISTRESS, PROCEDURE.

272. Entrance of house to distrain.— The landlord cannot legally break open the outer door of a house for the purpose of entering it and making a distress therein.[1] Nor may he, during the absence of the tenant, unlock the front door with a key borrowed from a neighbor, or with one of his own brought for the purpose. If he does so, he is guilty of trespass.[2] Once lawfully in the house he may proceed upstairs, even into the room of a subtenant, in order to make a levy.[3] The landlord will be a trespasser if, finding the front door locked, he enters the cellar by an outside door, and climbs up the wall, removes some boards which cover an opening in the floor, left with a view to the construction of a stairway, and thus effects an entrance into one of the rooms embraced in the lease, and there finds goods of the tenant upon which he causes a levy to be made.[4] Nor may the landlord make the distress on Sunday,[5] nor during the night, nor on the highway.[6] If, believing that the tenant has fraudulently withdrawn goods from the demised premises to the house of X, the landlord, taking a constable with him, goes to X's house, knocks at the door, and, being told to come in, enters, and causes the constable to proceed with an inventory, he is a trespasser if in fact no goods of the tenant are in the house. The leave given to enter is abused by the attempt, when in, to make a distress.[7]

---

[1] *Mayfield* v *White*, 1 Browne (Pa) 241; *Riggin* v *Becker*, 9 Pa. Dist R 439 If he thus breaks in, he is liable in the trespass *quare clausum fregit* The landlord shook and pushed the door with such violence that the bolt gave way and the door flew open Cf *Crawford* v *Evans*, 158 Pa. 390, 27 Atl 1105 A bond to secure to the tenant the use of his property, stipulating that if the landlord allowed it to remain with the tenant it should not be removed from the premises until September 1, 1892, was not broken by the fact that the tenant on that day barred his house and prevented the landlord's entrance to make the levy, the goods remaining

[2] *Com* v *Moreland*, 9 W N C 272, *Walker* v *Wiese*, 8 Del Co Rep 565, *Murray* v. *Vaughn*, 2 Dauphin Co Rep 354

[3] *Com* v *McStay*, 8 Phila 609

[4] *Walker* v *Wiese*, 8 Del Co Rep 565, 4 Lack Jur 9 Not decided whether the landlord may lift the latch of the closed front door, not otherwise fastened, or may turn the key, purposely left in the lock upon the outside, or may draw a bolt fastened to the outer woodwork

[5] *Mayfield* v. *White*, 1 Browne (Pa) 241

[6] *Riggin* v *Becker*, 9 Pa Dist. R 439

[7] *Hobbs* v *Geiss*, 13 Serg. & R 417.

LAND & TEN. 15

273. Demand for rent as precondition to distress.— Generally, no demand upon the tenant for the payment of the rent needs to precede the distress. The very taking of the distress is a legal demand. This is true, though the lease says that if the rent be behind, "being lawfully demanded," the landlord may distrain [8] But to the general rule there are exceptions. Thus, when the rent is payable at a place off the land, with a clause, "if the rent be behind, being lawfully demanded" at the place off the land, or with a clause that if the rent be behind, being lawfully demanded of the person that is to pay it, then he may distrain,— in these cases, though the remedy be by distress only, yet the grantor cannot distrain without a previous demand [9] When the rent reserved is $800, payable in bar iron drawn to order, it is plain that the lessor is not expected to distrain until an order is made on the tenant specifying the kind and amount of iron required, and until the tenant fails, after such order, to furnish the iron. "How can the tenant know when, how much iron, or of what size to tender? By the contract, within certain restrictions, the lessor himself is the sole judge of those particulars."[10]

274. Who may make the distress.— The landlord may make the distress in person.[11] He may, e. g., go to the tenant's mill and prevent the removal of a machine in it; he may lock the mill, retaining the key If this step is followed up by the proper proceedings, it will be deemed a distress. "A landlord," said the court, "may verbally distrain for the nonpayment of rent, and he may, by parol, authorize a bailiff to distrain."[12] The lessor, however, usually appoints one to make the distress. Such person is known as his bailiff.

275. Who may be bailiff.— An unofficial person[13] may be, and

[8]*Royer* v *Ake*, 3 Penr & W 461, *Robert* v *Ristine*, 2 Phila 62

[9]*Helser* v *Pott*, 3 Pa St 179.

[10]*Helser* v *Pott*, 3 Pa St 179

[11]*Wells* v. *Hornish*, 3 Penr & W.

[12]*Furbush* v *Chappell*, 105 Pa 187. The further prosecution of the distress was prevented by a replevin by the party who had been prevented from withdrawing the machine

[13]*Wells* v. *Hornish*, 3 Penr & W.

often is, appointed bailiff. The intervention of a sheriff, under sheriff, or constable is necessary only after the failure of the tenant, within five days of the distress, to replevy the goods [14] But not infrequently a constable[15] or the sheriff[16] is made bailiff.

276. How bailiff constituted—The bailiff may be appointed directly by the owner of the land or his agent to make leases and collect the rents,[17] or to collect the rents only. If A in his own name makes a lease and signs it, adding after his name "Agent," he, and not any principal, is the lessor. A warrant by the principal will not authorize a distress.[18] The grantee of the reversion may issue the warrant for rent falling due, after the conveyance to him. The original lessor, or his grantee, may hold the land as trustee for others, and may issue the warrant [19-20] A *cestui que trust* who is not entitled to the possession may not cause a distress; and if a lease is made by the heirs of A, the former owner, the executor of A, having no interest in the land, cannot authorize a distress.[21] If tenants in common are lessors, or have succeeded in ownership to the lessors, they may issue the

30, *Fry* v *Jones*, 2 Rawle, 11, *Lengert Co* v *Bellevue Bldg & L Asso* 15 Pa Super Ct 380, *Tinware Mfg Co* v *Duff*, 13 Pa Super Ct 383, *Goodwin* v *Sharkey*, 80 Pa 149; *Riggin* v *Becker*, 9 Pa Dist R 439

[14]*McElroy* v *Dice*, 17 Pa 163, *Wells* v *Hornish*, 3 Penr. & W 30 The first section of the act of March 21, 1772 (Pepper & L Digest, 2640, 1 Sm L 370), directs that when the tenant shall not, within five days after notice of the distress, replevy the goods, "the person so distraining shall or may, with the sheriff, under-sheriff, or any constable in the city or county where such distress shall be taken," cause the goods to be appraised

[15]*Karns* v *McKinney*, 74 Pa 387, *Davis* v *Davis*, 128 Pa 100, 18 Atl 514, *Holland* v *Townsend*, 136 Pa 392, 20 Atl 794, *Murphy* v *Chase*, 103 Pa 260, *Com* v *Sheppard*, 2

Clark (Pa) 393, *Brown* v *Stackhouse*, 155 Pa 582, 35 Am St Rep 908, 26 Atl 669

[16]*Weber* v *Rorer*, 151 Pa 487, 25 Atl 100, *Northampton County's Appeal*, 30 Pa 305

[17]*Riggin* v *Becker*, 9 Pa Dist R 439 The agent of the lessor may direct counsel to issue the warrant *Becker* v *Werner*, 98 Pa 555

[18]*Seyfert* v *Bean*, 83 Pa 450 Cf. *Holt* v *Martin*, 51 Pa 499

[19] [20]*Collender Co* v *Speer*, 29 Pittsb L J. 125

[21]*Grier* v *McAlarney*, 148 Pa 587, 24 Atl 119 The distress will be held invalid, in replevin by the owner of the goods *Vide Harrison* v *Van Gunten*, 15 Pa Super Ct 491, for personation of a constable by a stranger to whom a warrant addressed to the constable was given by the agent of the landlord, and who executed it himself

warrant.[22] A bailiff may distrain under a mere parol authority,[23] though usually his warrant is in writing. As the warrant
may be oral, so, if in writing, it may be entirely informal; a
letter would be sufficient,[24] as would probably a subsequent ratification of the acts of one assuming to act as bailiff without precedent authority. A corporation can appoint a bailiff without
deed or writing.[25] He must have some authority, otherwise his
distress will be quashed by replevin by the owner of the goods,[26]
and even the warrant will be no authority, if the landlord had
no right to distrain for the rent. The bailiff, though a constable,
must in trespass against him prove the facts which justified the
landlord in issuing the warrant. He cannot shelter himself behind the warrant, as he could behind that of a justice of the
peace. "There was," says Kennedy, J., "no warrant of the justice of the peace in this case, nor could a justice of the peace, as
such, have given a warrant authorizing a distress for rent due
and in arrear."[27]

277. Seizure of the goods.— There must be an assumption of
control over the goods in order to make a distress. "As a general rule," said the court in *Furbush* v. *Chappell*,[28] "to render
the distress complete, there must be a seizure of the property dis-

---

[22]*Chicago & A. Oil & Min Co* v.
Barnes, 62 Pa 445 Where several
join in the avowry, a demise by all
must be shown *Ewing* v *Vanars-
dall*, 1 Serg & R 370 The commissioners of a county, having leased
land, may issue a warrant *Northampton County's Appeal*, 30 Pa. 305

[23]*Jones* v *Gundrim*, 3 Watts & S
531, *Franciscus* v *Reigart*, 4 Watts,
98, *Kerr* v. *Sharp*, 14 Serg & R
399, *M'Geary* v *Raymond*, 17 Pa
Super Ct 308, *Furbush* v *Chappell*, 105 Pa 187, Huston, J, in
Jones v *Gundrim*, said "I would
advise, however, for the facility of
proof, that a written authority be
given to the bailiff, a short piece
of writing will suffice"

[24]*Franciscus* v *Reigart*, 4 Watts,
98 If a constable, in making a distress in the house, is resisted by the
tenant, the latter, knowing his authority, though it be simply oral,
may be indicted for assault and bat-
tery   *Com* v. *McStay*, 8 Phila.
609

[25]*Com* v. *McStay*, 8 Phila 609

[26]*Jimison* v *Reifsneider*, 97 Pa.
136, *Kerr* v *Sharp*, 14 Serg & R.
399, *Franciscus* v *Reigart*, 4 Watts,
98

[27]*Wells* v *Hornish*, 3 Penr & W
30, *Jones* v *Gundrim*, 3 Watts & S.
531

[28]105 Pa 187.

trained upon, but a very slight act is sufficient to constitute a seizure in contemplation of law It need not be an actual seizure of the particular goods. If the landlord [or his bailiff] gives notice [to the owner, tenant, or other person in custody of the goods] of his claim for rent, and declares the goods which he names shall not be removed from the premises until the rent is paid, it is a sufficient seizure." But in that case the article in question was a spinning mule in a mill, which, the tenant having sold, his vendee was detaching from the building with a view to its removal. Hearing of this, the landlord came to the mill, and, stating that rent was due him, threatened to arrest the workmen. They thereupon desisted, and the tenant locked up the mill, giving the key to the landlord, who said that he had possession and that the machine could not go until the rent was paid. The acts constituted an adequate seizure [29] If, when the bailiff visits the premises, an article is on them, and he declares that he takes all the goods on distress, makes a list, in which he mentions this article, and leaves a watchman in general charge, this article will be regarded as distrained, although later in the day it is taken off for use elsewhere, by the tenant or another, and, being thus on the street, is found by the constable who made the visit, deposited by him with an auctioneer, and later sold.[30]

278. Inventory of goods taken.—When the bailiff makes the distress, he makes a memorandum of that fact, beneath or on the back of the warrant, or on some other paper, together with a list of the things embraced in the levy. If goods in a store

---

[29] Cf *Fleming* v. *Heitshu*, 8 Pa Dist R 715, where, the tenant moving out, the landlord appeared, demanded the rent, and insisted that a piano should remain in the house until the rent was paid The tenant then quit the house, leaving the piano. It is intimated that, while this would have been a sufficient levy had the piano belonged to the tenant, it was not sufficient, since the piano belonged to another

[30] *Lengert Co* v *Bellevue Bldg & L Asso* 15 Pa Super Ct 380, where the facts are obscurely stated.

are distrained, it would be neither necessary nor practicable to enumerate them all, separately.[31]

279 Necessity of notice of the distress.— If the tenant is present, he will probably be aware of the bailiff's presence and of the distress made by him.   After it has been made, no formal notice is given to him unless the landlord subsequently proceeds to sale. "At common law," says Kennedy, J., "such notice was not required, and would seem to be necessary under the act of assembly,[32] only in order to warrant a sale of the distress agreeably to the directions thereof " If, then, no sale is made because of the discontinuance of the distress proceedings, or of a replevin begun by the tenant, the omission to give notice that the distress has been made will not make the landlord a trespasser [33] If, however, such notice not having been given, a sale shall be made, the landlord will be a trespasser,[34] and should the landlord become the purchaser thereat, he will acquire no title; and in a replevin by him, founded on his ownership as purchaser, he must affirmatively prove that the notice had been given to the tenant.[35]

280. Form of notice of distress — In order to justify a sale, notice of the distress, "with the cause of such taking," must be left "at the mansion house or other most notorious place on the premises charged with the rent distrained for."[36]   The notice must be in writing.[37] It must be sufficient to inform the tenant or the owner what goods are taken, and the amount of rent in arrear. A mere schedule of the goods levied on, which does not contain notice of the cause of taking, is not a

[31]Cf *Richards* v *McGrath*, 100 Pa 389

[32]Sec 1, act March 21, 1772 (I Pepper & L Digest, 2640)

[33]*M'Kinney* v *Reader*, 6 Watts, 34, *Richards* v *McGrath*, 100 Pa 389

[34]*Snyder* v *Boring*, 4 Pa Super Ct 196, *Richards* v *McGrath*, 100 Pa 389.

[35]*Murphy* v *Chase*, 103 Pa 260

[36] Act March 21, 1772 (1 Pepper & L Digest, 2640, Smith's Laws 370), *Quinn* v *Wallace*, 6 Whart. 452

[37]*Snyder* v *Boring*, 4 Pa Super. Ct 196

compliance with the statute.[38] This notice can be, and often is, given on the very day of making the distress[39] It may be given on the day following[40] The object of the notice is to enable and to compel the tenant or other owner of the goods to contest the propriety of the distress by the action of replevin, and thus prevent the landlord from being involved in unforeseen difficulties The statute allows it to be given to the tenant, or, when another is owner of the goods distrained, to such owner. Personal service of the notice is unnecessary. It may be left, in his absence, with the tenant's wife at the dwelling on the demised premises.[41] The tenant will be considered as the agent of the owner for the transmission of the notice,[42] unless the landlord knows whose the goods are before the sale, and unless the owner is ignorant of the distress[43] That the notice mistakenly states that the distress was made by the bailiff in behalf of Childs & Evans, executors, instead of Evans & Tarrance, does not make it void, the tenant understanding by whom the distress had been in fact authorized[44]

281. What may be done with the goods — The bailiff who distrains the goods had at common law the right, and, indeed, after a reasonable time,[45] was under a duty,[46] to remove them

[38]*Snyder* v *Boring*, 4 Pa. Super Ct 196

[39]*Whitton* v *Milligan*, 153 Pa 376, 26 Atl 22, *Davis* v *Davis*, 128 Pa 100, 18 Atl 514

[40]*Richards* v *McGrath*, 100 Pa. 389

[41]*Wood* v *Custer*, 16 Montg Co L Rep 118

[42]*Caldcleugh* v *Hollingsworth*, 8 Watts & S 302

[43] In *Whitton* v *Milligan*, 153 Pa 377, 26 Atl 22, the notice, signed by the constable and served upon the tenant, was as follows "Take notice that by authority and on behalf of your landlord, William Milligan, I have this day distrained the several goods and chattels specified in the above schedule on the premises No 1013 Chestnut street in said city, for the sum of $120, rent due him, the said William Milligan as aforesaid, or replevy the same goods and chattels according to law within five days hereafter I shall, after the expiration of the said five days from the date hereof, cause the said goods and chattels to be appraised and sold according to the act of assembly in such case made and provided. Given under my hand the 2d day of February, 1888 "

[44]*Wood* v *Custer*, 16 Montg Co L Rep 118

[45]*Woglam* v *Cowperthwaite*, 2 Dall 68, 1 L ed 292

[46]*Waitt* v *Laing*, 7 Phila 195.

from the premises for safe keeping. Various statutes were passed in England to limit the distance beyond which they should not be taken, but none forbade their removal absolutely [47] The statute of 1 & 2 Phillip and Mary, chap 12, Roberts's Digest, 172,[48] which is in force in Pennsylvania, forbids their removal out of the township, unless to an open pound within the same county, not above 3 miles from the place of the distress, and all the chattels taken in one distress must be impounded at the same place.[49] The distrainor may still remove the goods. He may, e. g , deposit a van levied on, with an auctioneer until sale.[50] Under the act of 2 Wm. & Mary, chap. 5, § 2, which conferred on the landlord the power to sell the distress, it was held that the landlord was authorized to impound the goods upon the premises Although the act of 1772 confers no such right in Pennsylvania, it has been the usage for the bailiff to allow the goods to remain on the premises [51] In *M'Kinney* v *Reader*[52] the demised premises were a tavern It was held that the landlord might impound the goods at the place the most convenient for the tenant on the premises, *viz.,* in the barroom, and that he had a right to place a young man in that room at night, in order to prevent entrance by others and removal of any of the goods It the tenant, a saloon keeper, has sublet all the premises but the room on the first floor, and the distress is upon the bar fixtures, furniture, shelves, liquor, and cigars, the landlord may let those articles remain in the room and exclude the tenant from it, taking the key, without being guilty of an actionable eviction, or of a trespass, *ab initio.* "As this was the only room the tenant occupied," remarks Green,

---

[47] Cf *Woglam* v *Cowperthwaite,* 2 Dall 68, 1 L. ed 292

[48] *M'Kinney* v *Reader,* 6 Watts, 39

[49] Whether, leaving some of the goods in the house, the bailiff could take others to another place, was not decided in *M'Kinney* v. *Reader,* 6 Watts, 34.

[50] *Lengert Co* v *Bellevue Bldg & L Asso* 15 Pa Super Ct 380

[51] *Woglam* v *Cowperthwaite,* 2 Dall 68, 1 L ed 292, *Waitt* v *Ewing,* 7 Phila 195, *M'Kinney,* v. *Reader,* 6 Watts, 34; *Hanbest* v. *Heerman,* 2 Walk (Pa) 471.

[52] 6 Watts, 34.

J., "an exclusive possession thereof could not be taken by the landlord except in the way in which it was done."[53] The time during which a portion of the leased premises may be thus converted into a pound is said to be a reasonable one,[54] and not only is the period of five days, allowed for replevying before appraisement, reasonable,[55] but the still longer time required, after the appraisement, to precede the sale,[56] and a postponement of the sale for a proper time, when the circumstances warrant, will not make wrongful the protraction of the use of the premises as a pound until the sale A distress was levied August 10th. An appraisement was waived on August 16th A sale was advertised to take place on August 24th. On August 24th the bailiff, without the knowledge of the tenant, postponed the sale until August 31st, when it took place The use of the premises as a depositary of the goods during all this time was not unlawful.[57]

282 Ending custody of goods by payment, etc.—Not only may the landlord allow the goods taken in distress to remain for five days upon the premises, but it is his duty toward the tenant to do so, so that, if the latter pays the rent, or otherwise effects a settlement with him, the tenant may at once resume his use of the goods. After such payment or settlement, e. g., acceptance of a security for the rent, it is the lessor's duty to prevent the removal of the goods by giving proper directions to the bailiff If, in consequence of his failure to give the direction at the right place or to the right person, the goods are in fact removed and

[53]*Holland* v *Townsend*, 136 Pa. 392, 20 Atl 794 Cf *Delp* v *Hoffman*, 7 Pa Dist R 256, where a piano after distress remained with the tenant

[54]*Seyfert* v *Bean*, 83 Pa 450.

[55]*M'Kinney* v *Reader*, 6 Watts, 34

[56]*Waitt* v *Ewing*, 7 Phila 195, *Murphy* v *Marshell*, 179 Pa. 516, 36 Atl 294.

[57]*Holland* v *Townsend*, 136 Pa 392, 20 Atl 794 In *Murphy* v *Marshell*, 179 Pa 516, 36 Atl 294, goods throughout the building were distrained and allowed to remain, but the tenant was not excluded from the possession This was no eviction which suspended the rent.

impounded away from the premises, the landlord will be liable in damages [58]

283. The bailiff's inventory.— Accompanying the notice of the distress should be a list of the things levied upon. When many articles of various sorts, e. g, in a store, are levied on, the landlord is not required to weigh or measure all the goods distrained, and give a full and complete inventory of every pound of such as are usually sold by weight, and of every yard or quart of such as are usually sold by measure; nor need he detail every article or notion in a stock of goods. The inventory should be so full as to inform the tenant of the goods distrained, for which he may issue a writ of replevin [59]

284. The appraisement.— The 1st section of the act of March 21, 1772,[60] directs when, within five days next after "distress taken and notice thereof," the tenant or owner neglects to replevy the goods, that after the "expiration of the said five days the person distraining shall and may, with the sheriff, under sheriff, or any constable in the city or county where such distress shall be taken (who are hereby required to be aiding and assisting therein), cause the goods and chattels so distrained to be appraised by two reputable freeholders," etc.

285. Time of appraisement.— In computing the five days, on whose expiration the appraisement is to be made, the day on which the distress is made is not counted. Five full days must follow this day, and the appraisement cannot be held properly before, and should normally be held on, the sixth day following the day of the distress [61] If the fifth day is Sunday, the next

[58]*Bale* v *Hess*, 28 Pa Co Ct 25, 11 Pa Dist R 376 The mere removal by the tenant, with the knowledge of the constable who made the distress of the goods from the house to another in the immediate neighborhood, will not be larceny At most it is "pound breach" *Com* v. *Martin*, 4 Lack Jur 93.

[59]*Richards* v *McGrath*, 100 Pa. 389

[60] 1 Pepper & L Digest, 2640, 1 Smith's Laws, 370

[61]*M'Kinney* v *Reader*, 6 Watts, 34 As to rule for computation of time, cf *Lutz's Appeal*, 124 Pa 273, 16 Atl 858, *Edmundson* v *Wragg*, 104 Pa 500, 49 Am Dec 590, *Sims* v.

day, Monday, must be counted as the fifth, and the appraisement cannot be held until Tuesday.[62] The notice being given
February 1st, the appraisement must not take place until February 7th,[63] or notice April 2d, appraisement April 8th,[64]
notice April 27th, appraisement May 3d.[65] The notice being
given January 5th, the appraisement on January 10th was too
soon,[66] as was one held on December 2d, the notice of the distress having been given November 27th[67] The notice being
given on Tuesday, July 22d, and the fifth day being Sunday,
the appraisement could not be held until Tuesday, July 29th.[68]
If the sixth day after that on which the notice of the distress
has been given is Sunday, the appraisement would not be held
until the next day If the notice of distress is actually served
on the tenant on February 1st, the appraisement held on February 7th is not too soon, though the notice mistakenly bears
date of February 2d.[69]

   286. Effect of premature appraisement and of no appraisement.
—If the appraisement is altogether omitted, and the goods are
sold by the landlord, he becomes a trespasser *ab initio,* and a
recovery can be had against him in trespass.[70] If an appraise-

Hampton, 1 Serg & R 411, *Duffy* v
Ogden, 64 Pa 240, *Ege's Appeal,* 2
Watts, 283, *Green's Appeal,* 6 Watts
& S 327, *Marks* v *Russell,* 40 Pa
372

   [63]*Ibid Waitt* v *Ewing,* 7 Phila
195

   [64]*Whitton* v *Milligan,* 153 Pa 376,
26 Atl 22

   [64]*Rosenberger* v *Hallowell,* 35 Pa
369

   [65]*Richards* v *McGrath,* 100 Pa
389

   [66]*McLean* v *McCaffrey,* 3 Pennyp
406   Written notice being given
May 25th, although there had been
earlier parol notice, the appraisement on May 30th was premature
Snyder v *Boring,* 4 Pa Super Ct
196, *Blair* v *Boring,* 200 Pa 27, 49
Atl 365.

   [67]*Brisben* v *Wilson,* 60 Pa 452
   [68]*Davis* v *Davis,* 128 Pa 100, 18
Atl 514   Cf *Re Gosweiler,* 3 Penr
& W 201
   [69]*Whitton* v *Milligan,* 153 Pa
376, 26 Atl 22
   [70]*Richards* v *McGrath,* 100 Pa
389, *Kerr* v *Sharp,* 14 Serg & R
399, *Hazlett* v *Mangel,* 9 Pa Super
Ct 139, *Christman* v *Geise,* 1
Chester Co Rep 342, *Duke* v *Wilson,* 173 Pa 12, 33 Atl 701 The distress was made on March 17th The
sale, without appraisement, took
place on March 30th The statute,
Geo II, chap 19, which mitigates
the liability of a landlord in this respect, has not been adopted in Penn
sylvania.

ment is held a day too soon, and the goods, though advertised to be sold also on a day too soon after the appraisement, are replevied before the day set for the sale, the landlord is not a trespasser *ab initio,* and the tenant cannot recover in the replevin [71] But if the sale is made on such premature appraisement, the landlord becomes a trespasser *ab initio,*[72] and is liable to the owner of the goods for their full value, and the purchaser at the sale acquires no title "The unlawful act of purchase itself is a conversion."[73] The constable who sells after a premature appraisement, after obtaining a bond of indemnity from the landlord to protect him from harm for levying on goods of a stranger, can maintain no action on this bond after being compelled to pay damages to the tenant, the landlord not having advised the premature appraisement.[74]

287. Delayed appraisement.—There may be justification for a delay beyond the minimum period prescribed in the act of 1772, in making the appraisement Thus, the tenant may eloign the goods a day or two after the distress, and they may not be found early enough to appraise them on the sixth day after the distress An appraisement, under such circumstances, on the eighth day, was apparently approved in *Woglam* v. *Cowperthwaite.*[75] Though a premature appraisement will not support a sale, it does not discharge the right of the landlord to retain the goods.[76] There must be, therefore, a right to hold a second appraisement even beyond the normal time for the first.

288. Who may be appraisers.—The 1st section of the act of March 21, 1772,[77] directs that the person distraining shall

[71]*McLean* v. *McCaffrey*, 3 Pennyp 406 The distress was on January 5th, the appraisement on January 10th, the sale was advertised to occur on January 16th, the replevin was commenced January 14th. Cf *Smoyer* v *Roth* (Pa) 13 Atl 191

[72]*Snyder* v *Boring*, 4 Pa Super Ct 196, *Davis* v *Davis*, 128 Pa. 100, 18 Atl 514

[73]*Brisben* v *Wilson*, 60 Pa 452

[74]*Blan* v *Boring*, 200 Pa 27, 49 Atl 365

[75] 2 Dall 68, 1 L ed 292

[76]*McLean* v *McCaffrey*, 3 Pennyp. 406

[77] 1 Pepper & L 2640, 1 Sm. L. 370.

"cause the goods and chattels so distrained to be appraised by two reputable freeholders, who . . . first take the following oath or affirmation I, A B., will well and truly, according to the best of my understanding, appraise the goods and chattels of C. D , distrained on for rent by E F. Which oath or affirmation such sheriff, under sheriff, or constable [aiding in the distress] are hereby empowered and required to administer." An appraisement by three persons is irregular. The appraisers must be freeholders. A tenant from year to year is not such.[78] They should not be minors. An appraisement by three who are non-freeholders, and one of whom is a minor, is not such as the law prescribes as a condition precedent to a lawful sale. The sale would be a trespass [79] The landlord is not converted into a trespasser by the appointment, without his consent or knowledge, of a non-freeholder as appraiser [80] The oath is administered by a magistrate or justice of the peace, or by the sheriff, under sheriff, or constable. The omission of the appraisers to be sworn or affirmed will not make the landlord a trespasser, he having no knowledge of that fact.

289. The appraisers' inventory.—The appraisers may adopt the list of articles, made by the bailiff, and of which a copy is embraced in the notice of distress, appending to the names of the various articles their valuations; or they may make another, identical as respects the things contained in it. The oath or affirmation of the appraisers is properly placed at the top of the inventory.

290. Waiver of appraisement — The person for whose sake the law has required the appraisement may waive it. The tenant, e. g., may, before any levy, waive it in his lease, or, informed of a distress actually made, may waive it, effectually.[81] He can-

[78]*Fretton v. Karcher*, 77 Pa 423
[79]*Snyder v Boring*, 4 Pa Super. 392, 20 Atl 794, *Briggs v Large*, 30
Ct. 196 Cf *Blair* v. *Boring*, 200 Pa. 27, 49 Atl 365
[80]*Fretton v Karcher*, 77 Pa 423.

[81]*Holland v Townsend*, 136 Pa Pa 287 Cf *Murphy* v. *Chase*, 103 Pa 260.

not, having done so, maintain that in the further retention or the sale of the goods the landlord is a trespasser But if the goods belong to another than the tenant, and the tenant has no express authority to waive the appraisement for the owner, a waiver by him will be void as to the owner, who may treat the landlord as a trespasser. Nor does the right thus to treat the landlord as a trespasser depend on his having had knowledge who the owner was. Even if he is ignorant that anyone else than the tenant is owner, he acts on the tenant's waiver at his own risk. Should someone else be owner, he is, when he subsequently sells the goods, as to such person a trespasser.[52] But it is held in *Smoyer v. Roth*[83] that, the object of the appraisement being that the owner may know the sum at which he can redeem his goods, if he resorts to replevin, this object is accomplished, and therefore the replevin is a waiver, by the plaintiff, of the omission to appraise An act which might be a waiver by A could not, unless he was authorized to do it, affect his wife Thus, his being present at the sale and assisting in it by handing out the goods would not be a waiver by her of the omitted appraisement, or an estoppel against setting it up [54] Though in the lease, the tenant, as security for rent, authorizes the landlord, when rent is unpaid, to seize all his property on the premises and sell it on three days' notice, if the landlord chooses to distrain on the property as the tenant's he must appraise according to law.[85]

291. Object of the appraisement.— The purpose of the appraisement has been variously stated. According to Thompson,

[52]*Harris* v *Shaw*, 17 Pa Super Ct. 1; *Briggs* v *Large*, 30 Pa 287, *Johnson* v *Black*, 15 Phila. 252, 9 W N C 438 In *Henkels* v *Brown*, 4 Phila 299, the court found that, the tenant claiming furniture under a conditional sale, he was as to creditors, and therefore as to the landlord the owner Hence his waiver of the appraisement was valid

[83]*Smoyer* v *Roth* (Pa) 13 Atl 191, *Johnson* v *Black*, 15 Phila 252, 9 W N C 438

[84]*Christman* v *Geise*, 1 Chester Co. Rep 342.

[85]*Wyke* v. *Wilson*, 173 Pa. 12, 33 Atl. 701.

J , it is required "so that excessive distress may not be made "[86] It is elsewhere said that its object is to enable the owner to know at what sum he can redeem the goods [87] It accomplishes neither object perfectly. The appraisement may represent the opinions of the appraisers. Their estimate may be above or below the real values, or prices that will be produced at a fair sale.[88] The landlord is not bound to stop the sale when the sum of the appraised prices of the articles already sold equals the rent and costs, if the sum of the prices actually obtained is less. So, the tenant cannot redeem the goods by tendering the appraised value, since they might, at a sale, bring more   It is only by tendering the rent in arrear, and the costs, that he can prevent the sale [89] Should it be alleged, however, that the landlord or officer has misconducted the sale so as to sacrifice the property, the appraisement will be some evidence of its value

292 The sale of the goods.— At common law the landlord had no power to sell the chattels distrained upon ; nor did he obtain this power in England until the statute of 2 Wm. & Mary, chap. 5, § 2.[90] The provisions of this statute were incorporated into the act of March 21, 1772,[91] the 1st section of which directs, after requiring an appraisement, that the person distraining, with the sheriff or other officer, "shall or may, after six days' public notice, lawfully sell the goods and chattels so distrained, for the best price that can be gotten for the same, for and towards satisfaction of the rent for which the said goods and chattels shall be distrained, and of the charges of such distress, appraisement, and sale, leaving the overplus, if any, in the hands of the said sheriff, under sheriff, or constable, for the owner's use " Prior to this provision, there was no power to sell the distress in Pennsylvania.[92]

[86]*Briggs* v *Large*, 30 Pa 287.
[87]*Smoyer* v *Roth* (Pa) 13 Atl 191; *Johnson* v *Black*, 15 Phila 252
[88] Cf *Kline* v *Lukens*, 4 Phila 296.

[89]*Richards* v *McGrath*, 100 Pa 389
[90]*Woglam* v *Couperthuaite*, 2 Dall 68 1 L ed 292
[91] 1 Pepper & L Digest, 2640, 1 Smith's Laws, 370
[92]*Davis* v *Davis*, 128 Pa 100, 18

293. Duty to sell.—The person who distrains may not be inferred, from the words "shall or may," to have an option to sell or not. He may, of course, relinquish the levy; or he may wait a reasonable time after appraising before selling; but he cannot indefinitely hold the goods, as he could before the statute, as a means of coercing payment.[93] "The duty," remarks Green, J., "to sell the distress, is imperative."[94] Of course, he is liberated from this duty if he relinquishes the distress, or if it is discharged by a replevin begun by the tenant.

294. Advertisement of sale.—The act requires that the sale shall be preceded by "six days' public notice." The notice may be given at any time after the appraisement has been made, even on the same day.[95] Thus, the distress having been made and notice thereof given on February 1st, and the appraisement having been held on February 7th, the notice of a sale to be had on February 13th was properly given on February 7th.[96] The advertisement of the sale may be given the day following that on which the notice of the distress is given, or "at any time after the appraisement."[97] Though the delay in advertising must not be capricious or unreasonable, there are circumstances which will justify it. The advertising is by means of handbills, either on the premises or in the neighborhood.[98] The law does not prescribe the form of the notice, but requires that it be given publicly and for the specified time.[99] In *Caldcleugh* v. *Hol-*

Atl 514, *Richards* v. *McGrath*, 100 Pa 389, *Hazlett* v. *Mangel*, 9 Pa. Super Ct 139

[95]*Quinn* v *Wallace*, 6 Whart 452

[96]*Holland* v *Townsend*, 136 Pa 392, 20 Atl 794, *Richards* v *McGrath*, 100 Pa 389

[96]*Whitton* v *Milligan*, 153 Pa 376, 26 Atl 22

[99]*Whitton* v. *Milligan*, 153 Pa 376, 26 Atl. 22.

[97]*Brisben* v *Wilson*, 60 Pa. 452 In *Holland* v *Townsend*, 136 Pa. 392, 20 Atl 794, the distress was levied August 10th On August 16th an appraisement was waived On August 18th a sale was advertised for August 24th The delay was caused by the request of the tenant

[98]*Briggs* v *Large*, 30 Pa 287, *Perrin* v *Wells*, 6 Kulp, 313

[99]*Perrin* v. *Wells*, 6 Kulp, 313.

lingsworth[100] a notice was put in a newspaper, and handbills were posted on the premises.

295. Length of the notice.— The act of 1772 directs that the sale may take place "after six days' public notice." It has not been understood that six full days must intervene between the close of the day on which the notice is first given and the commencement of that on which the sale is to occur. The sale can be advertised to take place, and it may take place, on the sixth day following the close of the day of the giving of the notice. Thus, notice given on February 7th of a sale on February 13th,[101] or on August 18th of a sale on August 24th,[102] was proper. If the sixth day after that on which the notice is made public is Sunday, the sale will be on the seventh day.[103]

296. Effect of omitting to advertise —The advertising of the sale is a prerequisite to its validity. Omission of it makes the landlord a trespasser if he causes a sale,[104] and it renders the sale invalid, and the purchaser thereat acquires no title as against the tenant or other owner The burden, in a replevin by the purchaser to recover the property, is upon him to show that the sale was duly advertised, since the presumption that an officer does his duty is not applicable to the bailiff, though a constable, because he acts as agent of the landlord, and not as an officer.[105]

297. Waiver of advertising or of punctuality in advertising.— The advertisement of the sale is for the benefit of the tenant or owner. It gives him a further notice of the impending loss of his property It also tends to secure the attendance of bidders, and to increase the price at which the goods will sell. The tenant may waive the advertisement altogether, as respects himself,

---

[100] 8 Watts & S 302

[101] *Whitton* v *Milligan*, 153 Pa 376, 26 Atl 22.

[102] *Holland* v *Townsend*, 136 Pa 392 20 Atl 794

[103] *Waitt* v *Ewing*, 7 Phila 195

[104] *Briggs* v *Large*, 30 Pa. 287; LAND & TEN 16.

Kerr v *Sharp*, 14 Serg & R 399; *Perrin* v *Wells*, 6 Kulp, 313, *Esterly Mach Co* v *Spencer*, 147 Pa 466, 23 Atl 774

[105] *Murphy* v. *Chase*, 103 Pa 260; *Perrin* v *Wells*, 6 Kulp, 313

though not as respects another person who is owner of the goods.[106]

298. Postponement of sale.—Various causes may prevent a sale on the day first advertised. The rent, e. g., may on that day be paid by a surety of the tenant,[107] or by the tenant himself. There may be no persons present, or, if present, none of them may bid. The sale, under such circumstances, should be adjourned [108] "The sudden and severe illness of either the tenant or the landlord, or the death of either party, or the pendency of negotiations, or the occurrence of fire in the building where the distress is impounded, at the time of the sale, or the nonattendance of bidders, or very great inadequacy of bids,—in short," says Green, J., "many quite unforeseen events may readily occur which would make an adjournment quite necessary. The act simply requires a notice of at least six days before making the sale It is therefore indispensable that a public notice of that length be given, but, beyond that, nothing is required by the act as a prerequisite to a perfect sale A power of adjournment is incident to a power to sell, unless an adjournment is prohibited by express words or necessary implication, but there is nothing of that kind in this act."[109] The sale in this case was adjourned by the bailiff without notice to, or the knowledge of, the tenant, from August 24th to August 31st This did not make the landlord a trespasser, though no cause for the adjournment was shown by him. The act of 1772 does not so peremptorily require a sale on the sixth day from the first appearance of the notice, or on the day named in the first notice, as to throw on the landlord the duty of explaining the postponement in order

[106]*Briggs* v *Large*, 30 Pa 287 Cf *Wyke* v *Wilson*, 173 Pa 12, 33 Atl 701

[107]*Guckert* v *Lowrie*, 118 Pa 289, 12 Atl 282 The landlord assigned his warrant and claim for rent to one named by the surety. The sale did not go on, but afterwards the constable readvertised a sale, which was held

[108]*Ricketts* v *Unangst*, 15 Pa 90, 53 Am Dec 572

[109]*Holland* v *Townsend*, 136 Pa 392, 20 Atl 794.

to avoid liability as a trespasser.[110] In *Perrin* v *Wells*[111] the sale was postponed from August 7th to August 14th, and in *Caldcleugh* v. *Hollingsworth*[112] it was adjourned from June 22d to June 28th. In *Bogert* v. *Batterton*[113] the landlord received notice from X on the day of sale that the goods did not belong to the tenant, but to him. The constable thereupon adjourned the sale for a week to allow X to replevy the goods. X not replevying meantime, the sale was then made. The purchaser thereat acquired a good title. If at the request of the tenant the landlord consents to a postponement of the sale for a few days, the landlord probably does not thereby postpone his distress to an intervening execution, or, if he does, he does not lose the landlord's right to take out of the proceeds of an execution sale the rent of one year.[114]

299. Preventing sale by payment.—The tenant may prevent a sale by tendering the rent due for which the distress has been made, and the costs If the sale has begun, some things having been already sold, a tender of the difference between the price at which they have been sold and the rent, and costs, will make the continuance of the sale a trespass The tender may be made at an adjourned sale, as well as at the original, with the same effect Of course the tender would be effectual if made by the agent or attorney of the owner of the goods. "A tenant," says Trunkey, J , "ought to be permitted to pay the money necessary to satisfy the warrant, whenever he can, with the same effect as if the money were made by sale of his goods The chief object of the statute is to enable the landlord to collect his rent,

---

[110]*Quinn* v *Wallace,* 6 Whart 452
[111] 6 Kulp, 313 The landlord does not become a trespasser by adjourning the sale, though he shows no cause for so doing
[112] 8 Watts & S 302
[113] 6 Pa Super Ct 468 In *Tinware Mfg. Co.* v *Duff,* 15 Pa Super.

Ct 383, notice being given at the sale that the goods belonged to a stranger, it was held to be the duty of the landlord to adjourn the sale, to give him an opportunity to replevy

[114]*Kline* v *Lukens,* 4 Phila 296

not to sacrifice his tenant's property."[115] The tender may probably be effectively made by the owner of the goods, as well as by
the tenant, and also by the surety of the tenant. The question whether if it is made by a surety and is accepted by the
landlord, the sale can proceed for the advantage of the
surety, or of another to whom, at his instance, the landlord assigns his warrant, was decided negatively by Collier, J., in
Guckert v. *Lowrie,*[116] who held that the continuance of the sale
was a trespass. If the assignee of the term in possession of the
premises should, as respects his assignor, pay the rent, his tender
of it, followed by constant readiness to pay it, will make a distress on the goods of the lessee, his assignor, unlawful. The
goods can be replevied.[117]

300 Who conducts the sale — The 1st section of the act of
March 21, 1772,[118] directs that the person distraining shall or
may, with the sheriff, under sheriff, or constable, cause an appraisement, and after such appraisement and six days' public
notice shall or may sell the goods   "If any other than the sheriff, under sheriff, or constable," says Kennedy, J., "be made
bailiff and distrain the goods of the tenant, such an officer must
be called in to the appraisement of the goods and to superintend
and conduct the sale of them in all cases, as directed by this
act."[119] Lewis, J., remarks "that the constable is not bound to
make a distress for rent, and that the law only requires his interference after the distress made, should an appraisement and sale

[115]*Richards* v *McGrath,* 100 Pa
389
[116] 118 Pa. 289, 12 Atl 282   The
supreme court reversed because it
did not appear that the assignee in
any way caused the sale to continue
In *Com* v *Sheppard,* 2 Clark (Pa)
393, money paid to a constable was
sued for on his bond
[117]*Lyon* v *Houk,* 9 Watts, 193

is the duty of one who claims to
have tendered the rent, and who has
begun replevin, to keep up the tender
or to bring the money into court
Gallagher v. *Burke,* 4 Del Co Rep
136
[118] 1 Pepper & L Digest, 2640, 1
Smith's Laws 370
[119]*Wells* v. *Hornish,* 3 Penr & W
It 30.

become necessary."[120] In *Com.* v. *Sheppard*,[121] Stroud, J , asserts that a constable may be compelled to assist in the collection of rent by distress. "Although he is not bound, perhaps, to perform the part of an auctioneer, or act as bailiff generally, yet there is nothing to disable him from so doing, and the practice has long obtained, probably before the passing of this act [of March 21, 1772], of confiding the whole conduct of a distress for rent to this class of officers." At all events, the officer takes charge of and conducts the sale [122]

301. **Conduct of the sale.**—The sale is made in the mode in which sheriffs' or constables' sales are made. Goods must be sold separately or in parcels, not the entire stock in the mass. They may be sold in such lots or parcels as shall be best calculated to bring the highest price. If sold in too large parcels, the injured party may have a remedy, formerly not in trespass, but on the case [123] A sale in the lump, of from 500 to 1,000 extra parts of harvesting machines, having in Philadelphia, the place of sale, no general value, for $65 (the owner estimating them at $1,500), did not make the landlord a trespasser.[124]

302. **The proceeds of sale**—Ordinarily, the landlord is entitled to so much of the proceeds of sale as is necessary to pay the rent in arrear They cannot be ordered to be paid into court.[125] Since labor claims are entitled by the acts of April 9, 1872,[126] and May 12, 1891,[127] to a preference to the landlord, the constable who makes the sale must pay them before the land-

[120]*McElroy* v *Dice*, 17 Pa. 163 A landlord's warrant is not legal process Until appraisement has been made, the constable is only a bailiff *Com* v. *Nichols*, 4 Pa Dist R 318, *Com* v. *Leech*, 27 Pittsb. L J 233

[121] 2 Clark (Pa) 393 Hence, if the constable fails to pay over rent paid to him by a tenant, after a distress, to avoid a sale, he and his sureties are liable on his official bond

[122]*Guckert* v. *Lowrie*, 118 Pa 289, 12 Atl. 252

[123]*Richards* v. *McGrath*, 100 Pa. 389

[124]*Esterly Mach Co* v *Spencer*, 147 Pa. 466, 23 Atl 774

[125]*Garrett* v *Longnecker*, 2 Legal Record Rep. 174.

[126] P L 47

[127] 2 Pepper & L Digest, 4787, P. L. 54.

lord [128]   The surplus, in the constable's hands, is not subject to
the execution attachment of the tenant's creditor [129]

303. Rescue of the distress —The 2d section of the act of
1772[130] authorizes the person or persons "grieved" by any
"pound-breach or rescous of goods or chattels distrained for
rent," in a special action on the case to recover for the wrong
sustained, "his, her, or their treble damages and costs of suit
against the offender or offenders in such rescous or pound-breach,
any or either of them, or against the owner or owners of the
goods distrained, in case the same be afterwards found to have
come to his or their use or possession"   Rescous is defined by
Blackstone[131] as the taking back by force of goods which have
been taken in distress, which from the first taking are considered
in the custody of the law.   For this rescous, two remedies are
mentioned, viz , the writ of rescous when the goods were going to
the pound, and the writ of pound-breach when they were actually
impounded at the time of the taking.   The statute of 2 Wm &
Mary, chap. 5, also gave a remedy similar to that subsequently
conferred in Pennsylvania by the act of 1772.   The action can be
on this statute against several, if they co-operate in the removal
of the goods, and as well against those who are not physically
present and do not actually participate in the taking, as against
those who are present and participate.[132]   Under the statute,
treble damages can be recovered; not treble the unpaid rent, or
treble the value of the property eloigned   The costs of the distress are not to be trebled , but the costs and expenses caused
by the rescous or pound-breach , e. g., the cost of recapture of
the goods, and of the taking care of them until they could be

[128] *Yeager* v *Toole*, 1 Dauphin Co
Rep 120   He will be liable if he does
not

[129] *Comfort* v *Taylor*, 1 Troubat &
H Pr § 1184, ed 1848

[130] 1 Pepper & L Digest, 2642, 1
Smith's Laws, 370.

[131] 3 Com 146

[132] *Hanbest* v. *Heerman*, 2 Walk
(Pa) 471   If any rent is due, the
fact that the distress is for too large
an amount will not justify the tenant
in taking the goods without replevying   If he takes them he will be
liable in treble damages   *McElroy*
v *Dice*, 17 Pa. 163.

made available for the payment of the rent. Cattle were distrained and impounded on the premises, in Delaware county. Three nights afterwards they were taken away secretly, and three days afterwards they were found in Philadelphia, on the premises of X The landlord reclaimed them and took them back to Leiperville, Delaware county, and there impounded them. Shortly afterwards the pound was broken and the cattle again taken, and a few days afterwards were found in X's stable. They were retaken and impounded in Chester and sold, bringing $230.50. The officers' charges were $79 31 costs, leaving $151.19 as the proceeds The landlord claimed and was allowed as damages three times the value of the property not recovered, and three times the depreciation and expense of what was recovered; the expense including the care and feeding of the cattle while in the pound at Leiperville and Chester. If the goods eloigned are equal to the rent, the eloigner is liable, in the first instance, to three times the rent. A part of the distress being recaptured and kept until sale, he cannot have an abatement for this, without paying the expense necessary to his enjoyment of it [133] If it appears that the defendant, the owner of a piano let to the tenant with an option to buy, and left in the tenant's house after levy, removed it from the house without knowledge of the distress, he will be liable in trespass only for actual damages, that is, when the value of the piano does not exceed the rent unpaid, and there are no expenses arising from an attempt at recovery of it by the landlord, the value of the piano, and not treble that value.[134] If, after levy and before appraisement, the tenant loads the goods on a wagon, and, in spite of the efforts of a constable to prevent him, carries them away,

---

[133] *McElroy* v *Dice*, 17 Pa 163
[134] *Delp* v *Hoffman*, 7 Pa Dist. R 256 Had the defendant known of the distress, Frazer, J , says he would probably have been liable for treble damages, though, "strictly speaking," he was not guilty of rescous or pound breach, because he did not take the piano while it was being taken to a pound, nor did he break into the pound and take it thence

he is not guilty of the crime of resisting the execution of legal process   A landlord's warrant is not legal process,[135] but it was larceny for the tenant, moving to another house after the distress, and taking the goods with him, to deny access to them to the sheriff when he came to appraise them.[136]

[135]*Com* v *Nichols,* 4 Pa Dist R 318, *Com* v *Leech,* 27 Pittsb L. J 233

[136]*Com* v *Shertzer,* 14 Lanc L Rev 70   But it is not larceny for the owner of the goods merely to re- move them, after levy, from the house to another in the neighbor hood, with the knowledge of the distrainor   It is at most pound breach *Com* v *Martin,* 4 Lack Jur 93, 12 Pa. Dist R 644.

CHAPTER XVII.

REMEDIES FOR IMPROPER DISTRESS.

304. Distress for too much rent.—There is a distinction between excessive distress and distress for more rent than is due. The former consists in levying on much more goods than it is necessary to sell in order to raise the rent and costs; while the latter consists in demanding too much money as rent that is due, and causing the distress to be made for this money. If, *e. g.,* the rent due is $80, and distress is made for $160,[1] or, if rent is payable half-yearly on Oct. 1st and April 1st, and the distress

---

[1] *Spencer* v *Clinefelter,* 101 Pa 219, *Thomas* v *Gibbons,* 21 Pa Super Ct 635 An amendment of a declaration by substituting for its admission that $200 rent is due and that property worth $2,000 was levied on, the averment that no rent was due, changed the cause of action from one for an excessive distress to one in which no right of distress for any sum existed *Royse* v *May,* 93 Pa 454.

249

issues in January for the half year payable in October, and for
the quarter year from October to January,[2] the distress is for
too much rent, but not excessive. If rent of $20 were distrained
on 20 cows, each of which was worth $30, the distress would be
excessive.[3] The distress is not for too much, if for the rent due,
simply because the tenant has disconnected counterclaims which,
in an action against him by the landlord, for the rent, he could
defalk. The landlord must deduct from the rent, before distraining, all payments, actual or constructive, on account of it.
But other claims of the tenant, especially claims for as yet unliquidated damages,[4] do not need to be recognized by the landlord
and subtracted by him from the rent, before distraining. For
distraining for more rent than is due, both the landlord[5] and
the bailiff,[6] whether constable or not, are liable. Nor does this
liability depend on the presence of malice or want of probable
cause, or of knowledge that the rent claimed is too large.[7] The
proper remedy for distress for too much rent, prior to the aboli-
tion of the distinction in form of action between trespass and
trespass on the case, was trespass on the case,[8] founded on the
statute of Marlbridge, 52 Hen III. chap 4.[9] Where no circumstances of aggravation are shown, and the distress has been
sold, the damages are the fair value of the goods, with the cost
of replacing them, and other actual injury. To these

---

[2]*McElroy* v *Dice*, 17 Pa 163 Rent
due, $700, distress for $805 *Fernwood Masonic Hall Asso* v *Jones*,
102 Pa 307

[3] Rent $200, goods worth $2,000
distrained on *Royse* v *May*, 93 Pa
454 Rent, $33 34, goods appraised at
$223 20 For the distinction *vide*
Weber v *Loper*, 16 Montg Co L
Rep 70

[4]*Spencer* v *Clinefelter*, 101 Pa
219

[5]*McElroy* v *Dice*, 17 Pa 163 Cf
Bair v *Warfel*, 5 Lanc L Rev 81.

[6]*McElroy* v *Dice*, 17 Pa 163
[7]*McElroy* v *Dice*, 17 Pa 163,
Fernwood Masonic Hall Asso v
Jones, 102 Pa 307

[8]*Fernwood Masonic Hall Asso* v
Jones, 102 Pa 307, *Spencer* v *Clinefelter*, 101 Pa 219

[9]*Karns* v *McKinney*, 74 Pa 387,
M'Kinney v *Reader*, 6 Watts, 34,
Jimison v *Reifsneider*, 97 Pa 136,
Richards v *McGrath*, 100 Pa 389,
Thomas v. *Gibbons*, 21 Pa. Super Ct
635.

sums interest may be added   The value of the goods is
the value at the time and place at which they were distrained, not merely what they are worth for removal,
but what they would have cost to procure others of like quality, and put them in the same place   Compensation must also
be allowed for the loss of the use of the goods during the time
that must elapse before they can be replaced, and for actual loss,
directly and clearly proved, to business [10]   The rent actually
due and unpaid at the time of the distress must be deducted from
the damages [11]   The fact that after the distress has been made
for more rent than is due, the tenant and landlord make a settlement of the account between them, and the former agrees that
the sale may proceed for the amount thus ascertained, does not
preclude recovery for damages suffered, unless such is the agreement, and though a sale may not take place, the tenant may obtain damages actually suffered.[12]   Nor, for the purpose of miti-
gating the damages, must the tenant resort to replevin[13] in order
to prevent the sale.   Indeed, replevin would not lie if, rent being due, a distress for any amount was lawful [14]

305. Excessive distress — Besides distraining for too much
rent when some is due, the landlord may act improperly in
distraining on too many articles for a rent which is due.   It
would rarely be possible to find chattels whose price at the distress sale would exactly coincide with the rent due and the costs
attending the distress   Slight excesses of the values of the
things levied on beyond the rent and costs, being unavoidable,
are to be condoned.[15]   Indeed, an excessive distress was, at the

---

[10]*Fernwood Masonic Hall Asso* v
Jones, 102 Pa 307 No damages can
be recovered by the tenant for the
seizure and sale of the goods of other
persons, in which he had no interest
[11]*Fernwood Masonic Hall Asso* v
Jones, 102 Pa 307
[12]*McElroy* v *Dice*, 17 Pa 163.

[13]*McElroy* v *Dice*, 17 Pa 163
[14]*Karns* v *McKinney*, 74 Pa 387;
Jimison v *Reifsneider*, 97 Pa 136
In replevin, evidence that the distress was for too much was irrelevant
[15] In *Spencer* v *Clinefelter*, 101 Pa
219, for rent either of $80 or $160,

early common law, "perfectly allowable, because it was more
likely [than a moderate distress] to induce or compel the payment of the rent due "[16] The statute of Marlbridge, 52 Hen
III. chap. 4, enacted however, "that distress shall be reasonable, not too great, and that he who takes great and unreasonable distresses shall be grievously amerced for the excess of
such distress " Since this statute the remedy of the person ag-
grieved by a distress which is excessive was formerly an action
on the case and not trespass.[17] It is now trespass For violation of this statute the landlord and bailiff are both liable.
In replevin, no regard can be had to the excessiveness of the
distress. The plaintiff cannot recover if any rent was due, whatever the disparity between the rent and the value of the articles
levied upon.[18] In *Jimison* v. *Reifsneider*[19] a distress for $675
rent was levied on goods of the tenant worth $5,000, and on
goods of Reifsneider worth $3,000. Although he requested the
landlord to proceed first to sell the tenant's goods, the landlord
refused, and thereupon Reifsneider brought the replevin.
Thereupon, relying on the replevin bond, he directed the bailiff
to stop proceedings against the tenant's goods, and the latter
resumed possession of them In the replevin judgment was
rendered for the bailiff. The tenant's right of action for an
excessive distress does not pass, on his becoming insolvent, to
his assignee After an assignment in insolvency he can maintain the action.[20] The fact that the tenant receives the surplus
of the money produced by the distress sale, after discharging the
rent, or that suit for it is brought to his use, against the pur-

distress was made on a house which
the tenant, having put it on the
premises, had a right to remove
  [16] *M'Kinney* v *Reader*, 6 Watts, 34
  [17] *M'Kinney* v *Reader*, 6 Watts, 34,
O Donnel v *Seybert*, 13 Serg & R
54, *Spencer* v *Clinefelter*, 101 Pa
219, *Thomas* v *Gibbons*, 21 Pa
Super Ct 635   "The statute," says

Duncan, J, in *O'Donnel* v *Seybert* 13
Serg & R 54, "has nearly superseded
the common-law action "
  [18] *Jimison* v   *Reifsneider*, 97 Pa
136
  [19] 97 Pa 136
  [20] *O'Donnel* v *Seybert,* 13 Serg &
R 54

chaser at the distress sale, is no waiver of the right to recover damages   Recovery in it would be no bar to the action on the case for excessive distress, "nor," says Duncan, J., "ought it to go in mitigation of damages."[21]

306. **When no rent is in arrear.**— The 3d section of the act of March 21, 1772,[22] provides that "in case any distress and sale" shall be made, "for rent pretended to be in arrear and due, when in truth no rent shall appear to be in arrear or due to the person or persons distraining, or to him or them in whose name or names or right such distress shall be taken, the owner of such goods and chattels distrained and sold as aforesaid, his executors or administrators, shall and may, by action of trespass, or upon the case, to be brought against the person or persons so distraining, any or either of them, his or their executors or administrators, recover double the value of the goods or chattels so distrained and sold, together with full costs of suit." This penalty can be recovered only when there has been a sale,[23] nor then if any rent at all was due, unless, perhaps, the sale was purposely for more than was due.[24] It is unnecessary to remark that the action on this statute may be brought in the common pleas   It may not be brought before a justice of the peace.[25] The person who may bring the action is the owner of the property taken, whether it be the tenant or another.   The person against whom the action can be brought is not the landlord, as such, or because he has issued a warrant, but the person who does the distraining,—who levies or directs the levy on the property.   It is the person distraining, not the

---

[21]*O'Donnel* v *Seybert*, 13 Serg & R 54   In *Royse* v. *May*, 93 Pa. 454, in trespass *vi et armis*, the declaration was for an excessive distress, i e , taking property worth $2,000 for a rent of $200   It was improper to allow an amendment denying the relation of lessor and lessee, and that there was any rent for which distress could be made.

[22] 1 Pepper & Lewis Digest, 2642, 1 Sm L. 370

[23]*Bischoff* v. *Loper,* 16 Montg Co L. Rep 73 , *Weber* v *Loper,* 16 Montg Co L Rep 70

[24]*Weber* v *Loper,* 16 Montg Co L. Rep. 70.

[25]*Ike* v *Westfield,* 10 Kulp, 510. But see *Shetsline* v *Keemle,* 1 Ashm. (Pa.) 29.

person in whose name the distress is made, that is liable.[26] In order to recover the double damages, the action must be brought on the statute The declaration must refer to the statute, and claim expressly such damages. It must conclude, "against the form of the statute "[27] It is for the jury to find the value of the goods distrained, and to return in their verdict double this sum. If they return the sum, it will be understood, unless the contrary appears in their return, that the sum is twice the value of the goods, and it will be error for the trial court to enter judgment for double the verdict [28]

307. Action not on 3d section, act of 1772 — When distress is made at a time when no rent is due, or after it has been properly tendered,[29] there is a right of action in trespass at common law. That furnished by the act of 1772 has not superseded it.[30] Hence, though in the trespass brought, there can, for any reason, be no recovery of double the value of the goods distrained, there may, nevertheless, be a recovery of compensatory, and, if the facts warrant them, exemplary, damages [31] If there has been a sale of the goods, their value, at the time and place of the sale, at least, will be recoverable If there were circumstances of aggravation for which the landlord was responsible,

[26]*Wells* v *Hornish*, 3 Penr & W 30, *Fretton* v *Karcher*, 77 Pa 423
[27]*Royse* v *May*, 93 Pa. 454, *Rees* v *Emerick*, 6 Serg & R 286, *Hughes* v *Stevens*, 36 Pa 320, *Morrison* v *Cross*, 1 Browne (Pa) 1, *Thomas* v *Gibbons*, 21 Pa Super Ct 635, *Fretton* v *Karcher*, 77 Pa 423, *Smith* v *Meanor*, 16 Serg & R 375 In the last case Duncan, J , thought that a count for trover could not be joined
[28]*Campbell* v *Finney*, 3 Watts, 84
[29]*Rees* v *Emerick*, 6 Serg & R 286 An eviction suspends rent accruing subsequently. By distraining for such rent the landlord becomes a trespasser. *Gunnis* v. *Kater,* 29 Phila. Leg. Int. 230.

[30]*Rees* v *Emerick*, 6 Serg & R 286, *Fretton* v *Karcher*, 77 Pa 423, *Franciscus* v *Reigart*, 4 Watts, 98 In the first case, double the value of the goods was $120, but the jury found the damages $290, and judgment for the latter sum was entered Cf also, *Thomas* v *Gibbons*, 21 Pa Super Ct 635
[31]A judgment in the common-law action is a bar to a recovery on the statute, though the action on the statute was begun at the same time as the action at common law Indeed, it is said by Duncan, J , that by bringing one action a party waives the other *Garvin* v. *Dawson,* 13 Serg & R. 246.

still greater damages will be allowed, *e g*, if the appraisers were not qualified; if notice of the distress was not given to the tenant or left on the premises, if the six days' public notice of sale was not given. But, if the landlord did not direct, or in any way countenance, but was ignorant of, these omissions by the bailiff, damages should not be allowed against him on account of them.[32] If any portion of the money produced at the sale has been paid to the owner of the goods, this will not preclude an action of trespass, but will reduce, *pro tanto,* the damages.[33] The landlord[34] and the bailiff[35] are both liable when distress is made when there is no rent in arrear. The bailiff[36] and the landlord have the burden of showing that there was rent in arrear.

308 Tenant's recaption of goods.— If the landlord distrains after his rent has been paid, or after a tender of it has been improperly rejected by him, "the tenant may make rescous of the goods distrained, and may maintain trespass for the injury done him in lawless intrusion into his house, seizing and carrying away his goods."[37] But, if any rent is in arrear, the tenant, though the amount claimed in the distress is excessive, cannot take the goods back without becoming liable to treble damages [38]

309. Irregularity in mode of making distress.— If the distress is conducted irregularly or oppressively, though the circumstances warranted a distress in the proper mode, the party responsible for the irregularity or oppression becomes liable in trespass. The circumstances that warrant a proper distress do not warrant an improper one, and that which was lawful when it began may lose even its past lawfulness and become a tres-

[32]*Fretton* v *Karcher,* 77 Pa 423
Wells v *Hornish,* 3 Penr & W 30, *Ingram* v *Hartz,* 48 Pa 330
[34]*Ingram* v *Hartz,* 48 Pa 380, *Fretton* v *Karcher,* 77 Pa 423
[35]*Bair* v *Warfel,* 5 Lanc L. Rev. 81.

[36]*Wells* v. *Hornish,* 3 Penr & W 30
[37]*Rees* v *Emerick,* 6 Serg & R. 286
[38]*McElroy* v. *Dice,* 17 Pa 163

pass *ab initio.* When the improper acts are done by the bailiff, he is liable as a trespasser. But the landlord is not liable unless he was present and aiding or countenancing, or unless he has antecedently directed or subsequently approved and ratified the act, or, probably, unless he was negligent in the selection of a bailiff [39] Hence, for an assault[40] on the tenant or some third person, committed by the bailiff without the participation of the landlord, or for the bailiff's breaking into the house, in order to make the distress,[41] or for unnecessary injury to the tenant's property,[42] the landlord not counseling or subsequently approving the breaking or the injury, the landlord is not liable When the landlord participates in the wrong, he is liable in trespass, *e g.,* for improperly impounding the goods on the premises, or preventing the use by the family of indispensable domestic furniture, such as cooking utensils, chairs,[43] for omitting, before the sale, to appraise[44] and give the six days' notice of the sale,[45] for appraising too soon,[46] for appraising by three persons who are not freeholders, and one of whom is a minor, and before a written notice of the distress has been given.[47] Of course, when, because no rent is due,[48] or for some reason, the goods are not distrainable, the mere distress, however regular in mode, is a trespass; irregularities in mode would be a basis for increased damages. An agent of the landlord for collecting rent, may, on his own judgment, cause a distress to issue. If he does so, he will be liable or exempt under the same cir-

[39]*Harrison v. Van Gunten,* 15 Pa Super Ct 491

[40]*Ellis* v *Lamb,* 24 Pa Co Ct 150, 9 Pa Dist R 491 But for a levy on goods of another than the tenant, off the premises, the landlord is liable It does not appear that he directed the levy

[41]*Riggin* v *Becker,* 9 Pa. Dist R 439

[42]*Harrison* v *Van Gunten,* 15 Pa. Super. Ct. 491.

[43]*M'Kinney* v *Reader,* 6 Watts, 34 Not decided

[44]*Kerr* v *Sharp,* 14 Serg & R 399, *Harris* v *Shaw,* 17 Pa Super Ct 1

[45]*Kerr* v *Sharp,* 14 Serg & R 399

[46]*Brisben* v *Wilson,* 60 Pa 452, *Snyder* v *Boring,* 4 Pa. Super Ct 196.

[47]*Snyder* v *Boring,* 4 Pa Super Ct 196

[48]*Fretton* v *Karcher,* 77 Pa. 423.

cumstances under which the landlord would have been. Where he authorizes the breaking into a house, he is liable He is not the mere channel through which, in ignorance of its contents, the order of the landlord is communicated to the bailiff,[49] but if he does not authorize the wrongful acts of the bailiff, and has not been negligent in the selection of the bailiff, he is not responsible [50]

310 When the goods are not distrainable —The goods taken in distress may, for some reason, not be distrainable. The landlord may, for a consideration, have agreed that they should not be distrained,[51] or the goods may be the property of another than the tenant, and because of some exemption,[52 3] or because no longer on the premises when taken, may not be distrainable If the bailiff and landlord know, before making the levy, that the goods should not be distrained on, they are trespassers *ab initio*.[54] If they learn before the sale that the goods are not distrainable, they will become trespassers if they go on with the sale, unless the owner is, or is made by them, aware of the distress. In that case, he should intercept the distress proceedings by replevin [55] If he does not, the sale may proceed without making the landlord or bailiff a trespasser.[56]

[49]*Riggin* v *Becker,* 9 Pa Dist R 439 An agent who issues a warrant for a distress for too great a sum is liable, and also the bailiff *McElroy* v *Dice,* 17 Pa. 163

[50]*Harrison* v *Van Gunten,* 15 Pa Super Ct 491 A, employed by a constable as a canvasser, for business, presented to the landlord's agent a blank distress warrant, and he signed it A, instead of delivering it to the constable, made the distress himself

[51]*Perrin* v *Wells,* 155 Pa 299, 26 Atl 543

[52 53]*Brown* v *Stackhouse,* 155 Pa 582, 35 Am St Rep 908, 26 Atl 669

[54]*Brown* v *Stackhouse,* 155 Pa LAND & TEN 17.

582, 35 Am St Rep 908, 26 Atl 669, *Perrin* v *Wells,* 155 Pa 299, 26 Atl 543

[55]*Tenuate Mfg Co* v *Duff,* 15 Pa Super Ct 383 Nonsuit in trespass by the tenant is improper unless it affirmatively appears that, prior to the sale, the tenant received notice of the distress, and that an appraisement was made *Sassman* v *Brisbane,* 7 Phila 159

[56]*Lengert Co* v *Bellevue Bldg & L Asso* 15 Pa Super Ct 380, *Bogert* v *Batterton,* 6 Pa Super Ct 468, *Esterly Machine Co* v *Spencer,* 147 Pa 466, 23 Atl 774, *Thomas* v *Baner,* 6 Pa Dist R 177, *Starr* v. *Simon,* 9 Pa Co Ct 15 *Lardner* v. *Mutual L Ins Co* 32 W N C 62

311 Damages — When, in any case, the bailiff or landlord is a trespasser, he will be liable for the actual, and, in proper cases, even for exemplary, damages. The distress proceedings may not advance to a sale, or they may In the latter case, the least damages would be the value of the goods at the time of the taking, with interest from that time.[57] Of course, if the court allows (as it should not) a deduction from this amount of the rent due, the landlord cannot complain.[58]

312. Set-off by justice — The 20th section of the act of March 20, 1810,[59] extends the powers of a justice to "all cases of rent not exceeding $100, so far as to compel the landlord to defalcate or set off the just account of the tenant out of the same." The object of this proceeding is to ascertain, by means of a justice, the amount of set-off which should be allowed by the landlord before proceeding with the distress, and to subject him to a penalty defined in it if he proceeds for more than the balance of rent after deducting the set-off allowed by the justice. Possibly, before the distress is begun, resort can be had to this procedure by the tenant. In the reported cases he has applied to the justice only after the distress had been begun The justice has the jurisdiction only in cases where the rent does not exceed $100,[60] or, since the act of July 7, 1879,[61] $300.[62-3] It is the amount of rent claimed, not the size of the amount asked to be set off, that defines the jurisdiction. The matters to be set off may be a book account,[64] a claim for labor done

---

[57]*Perrin* v *Wells*, 155 Pa 299, 26 Atl 543, *Esterly Machine Co* v *Spencer*, 147 Pa 466, 23 Atl 774

[58]*Pfeiffer* v *Schubmehl*, 7 Del Co Rep 575.

[59] 1 Pepper & Lewis Digest, 2549, 2643, 5 Smith's Laws, 161

[60]*Black* v *Coolbaugh*, 2 Luzerne Legal Obs 324 On appeal to the common pleas, the justice's record must show the amount of rent due. The omission will be a fatal error.

[61] P L 194

[62] [63]*Lowenstein* v *Helfrich*, 7 Kulp, 533 Under a special act, the recorder of Bradford City had jurisdiction when the rent did not exceed $400 *Fowler* v *Eddy*, 110 Pa 117, 1 Atl 789

[64]*Walsh* v *Greenwood*, 2 Pa Dist R 64, *Fowler* v *Eddy*, 110 Pa 117, 1 Atl 789.

for the landlord,[65] a claim for damages from the landlord's
breach of a covenant to repair the premises,[66] or for damages
for disturbance of the tenant's possession by hauling dirt from
the premises [67] The counterclaim may exceed the rent claimed,
but in that case, the justice sets off no more that the amount
of the rent claimed [68] The landlord is cited before the justice
in the ordinary way, and is permitted to oppose the claim of
set-off. The justice properly decides, not the amount of rent
which is due the landlord or for which he may distrain, but
simply the amount the defalcation of which he ought to permit.[69] Though sometimes, the amount of the rent claimed being
undisputed, the justice finds that a certain amount remains due,
or, if the set-off is equal to or greater than the rent claimed, he
may find that no rent is due.[70] But the finding has validity
only so far as it expressly or impliedly ascertains, not the rent
due, but the amount to be set off The decision of the justice
cannot be appealed from by the tenant,[71] but his remedy by
replevin remains as it was before the act was passed. The landlord, however, may appeal from the decision to the common
pleas.[72] But a certiorari may issue from that court at the instance of the tenant to inquire into the jurisdiction of the justice
to enter a judgment against him.[73] The justice can enter no
judgment against the tenant for the rent due If he does, and

[65]*Thomas* v *Pyle*, 2 Pa Co Ct
258

[66]*Hilke* v *Eisenbeis*, 104 Pa 514
[67]*Spencer* v *Clinefelter*, 101 Pa
219

[68]*Thomas* v *Pyle*, 2 Pa Co Ct
258

[69]*Hilke* v. *Eisenbeis* 104 Pa 514,
Fowler v *Eddy*, 110 Pa 117, 1 Atl
789, *Lowenstein* v *Helfrich*, 7 Kulp
533

[70] So, in *Spencer* v *Clinefelter*, 101
Pa 219 In *Lowenstein* v *Helfrich*,
the justice found the set off to be
$15 80, and that the balance of the
rent was $117 54 The distress war-

rant had issued for $133 34 In
Kessler v *M'Conachy*, 1 Rawle, 435,
the justice decided that there was no
rent due the landlord, but that he
was indebted to the tenant $4 48

[71]*Ingersol* v. *Gibbons*, 1 Browne
(Pa) 69

[72]*Hilke* v *Eisenbeis*, 104 Pa 514,
Thomas v *Pyle*, 2 Pa Co Ct 258,
Ingersol v *Gibbons*, 1 Browne (Pa)
69, *Spencer* v *Clinefelter*, 101 Pa
219, *Allman* v *Atwell*, 33 Pittsb L
J 258

[73]*Fowler* v. *Eddy*, 110 Pa 117, 1
Atl 789

execution thereon issues, the judgment will be reversed [74]   On
appeal the common pleas court can do only what the justice
could   It can enter no judgment for the tenant, not even for
costs.[75] The court on the appeal may find as large a set-off as
the justice, or a less sum,[76] or no set-off at all   The 20th
section of the act of March 20, 1810, directs that the landlord,
after the decision of the justice, "may waive further proceedings before the justice,"—*i. e ,* may refrain from appealing to
the common pleas,[77]—"and pursue the method of distress in
the usual manner for the balance so settled " If, not appealing,
he nevertheless proceeds for the rent, unreduced by the set-off,
and sells goods so as to produce more money than the reduced
rent, and detains the surplus in his hands, he will, if convicted
thereof in any court of record, "forfeit to the tenant four times
the amount of the sum detained,"—that is, four times the set-off
ascertained by the justice.   Thus, the set-off ascertained being
$15 80, the sum forfeited would be $63 20.[78] The suit is properly brought by the tenant in the common pleas, and the decision of the justice, as to the set-off, cannot be reinvestigated,
but is conclusive.[79] As the justice may set off an unliquidated

[74]*Fowler v Eddy*, 110 Pa 117, 1
Atl 789   Cf *Sheed v Wartman*, 4
Yeates 237, *Miller v Peters*, 1
Lack Jur 23, *Weyandt v Diehl*, 4
C P Rep 74

[75]*Thomas v Pyle*, 2 Pa Co Ct 258
Each party must pay the costs incurred by him   The costs on appeal
should be paid by the landlord   In
order to appeal, he has paid the costs
before the justice   Should he be repaid them by the tenant?

[76]*Spencer* v. *Clinefelter*, 101 Pa
219

[77] Such is the explanation of the
phrase   *Hilke v Eisenbeis*, 104 Pa
514   Cf *Mutter v Shackman*, 28
Pittsb L J 51

[78]*Lowenstein v Helfrich*, 7 Kulp,
533.

[79]*Lowenstein v Helfrich*, 7 Kulp,
533   In *Kessler v M'Conachy*, 1
Rawle, 435, after the distress the
owner of an article levied on (not the
tenant) began replevin   He had a
right to use the decision of the justice that the set-off was greater than
the rent as prima facie evidence on
the issue of no rent in arrear   If,
appealing, the landlord, nevertheless,
proceeds with the distress for his
original claim, the tenant cannot
have his liability to the penalty prescribed by the act of March 20th,
1810 adjudicated in the proceeding
on appeal   *Illman v. Atwell*, 33
Pittsb L. J 258.

claim for damages, or matters wholly disconnected with the lease, his decision is not decisive that when the distress warrant issued and was levied, the rent claimed was more than due   If the set-off was in fact of unliquidated damages, from the landlord's trespassing on the possession of the tenant, the landlord was not bound to have foreseen what they would be adjudged to be, and to have deducted them from the rent [80]   Unless the tenant has had the set-off ascertained by the justice, he cannot avail himself of it in replevin [81]

313. Replevin.— The 1st section of the act of March 21st, 1772,[82] authorizes a sale of goods distrained, when the tenant or owner shall not, within five days after notice of the distress, replevy them with sufficient surety, to be given to the sheriff The 2d section of the act of April 3d, 1779,[83] which declares irregular, erroneous, and void, all writs of replevin issued for any owner of goods levied or taken in execution or by distress or otherwise, by any sheriff, constable, or other officer, does not repeal, *pro tanto,* the act of 1772,[84] nor refer to replevins in case of distress for rent, but only in case of distress for taxes [85] In all cases in which the owner of the goods distrained[86] or the tenant, when he is not the owner,[87] thinks that they should not

[80]*Spencer* v *Clinefelter,* 101 Pa 219
[81]*Walsh* v *Greenwood,* 2 Pa Dist R 64
[82] 1 Pepper Lewis Digest, 2640, 1 Smith's Laws, 370
[83] 2 Pepper & Lewis Digest, 4109, 1 Smith's Laws, 470
[84]*Bonsall* v *Comly,* 44 Pa 442, *Starr* v *Simon,* 9 Pa Co Ct 15, *Thomas* v *Baner,* 6 Pa Dist R 177, *Lardner* v *Mutual L Ins Co* 32 W N C 62, *Quinn* v *Wallace,* 6 Whart 452
[85] Though the constable who made the distress claims to have done so as constable, the goods can be taken from him by means of replevin.

Barr v *Warfel,* 5 Lanc L Rev. 81 Though the lease contains a waiver of the right to replevy goods distrained for rent in arrear, this will not preclude a replevin when the tenant alleges that no rent was in arrear. *Repp* v *Sousman,* 9 Kulp, 180
[86]*Power* v *Howard,* 22 W N C. 475, *Scott* v *McEwen,* 2 Phila 176, *Sommer Piano Co* v *Wood,* 8 Kulp, 494, *Nass* v *Winpenny,* 9 W N C. 542, *Biegenwald* v *Winpenny,* 9 W. N C 542, *Page* v *Middleton,* 118 Pa 546, 12 Atl 415, *Clothier* v. *Braithwaite,* 22 Pa Super Ct 521.
[87]*Sleeper* v *Parish,* 7 Phila 247.

have been distrained, because there was no rent due[88] or the goods were not the tenant's, were not on the demised premises, or for some other reason were exempt from distress, replevin may be resorted to during the proceedings in distress. It can be begun not merely during five days following notice of the distress, but at any time before sale [89] We have elsewhere seen, indeed, the circumstances in which the tenant or owner must resort to replevin, and cannot wait until sale, and then begin the action of trespass or case. In these cases, the owner or tenant cannot wait until sale, and then bring replevin against the purchaser, on the theory that no title has passed to him [90] If, after a claim of $300 exemption, the bailiff selects appraisers, who appraise articles selected by the tenant, and the bailiff withdraws from the possession of them, and subsequently the landlord, the goods being still on the premises, directs the bailiff to disregard the claim for exemption, the tenant cannot, by replevin, prevent the sale of them The remedy is by trespass against the bailiff or landlord [91]

314. Replevin, procedure — The action of replevin may be brought against the landlord alone or the bailiff alone,[92] or against both together.[93] The landlord, when defendant, makes an avowry[94] and the bailiff makes cognizance. Both may avow

[88] In *Wallace* v *Harmstad*, 44 Pa 492, the alteration of the deed reserving the rent was alleged to destroy the right to rent No rent due *Diller* v *Roberts*, 13 Serg & R 60, 15 Am Dec 578 No certain rent reserved *Grier* v *Cowan*, Addison (Pa) 347

Sommer Piano Co v *Wood*, 8 Kulp, 404, *Starr* v *Simon*, 9 Pa Co Ct 15, *Brisben* v *Wilson*, 60 Pa 452, *Esterly Machine Co* v *Spencer*, 147 Pa 466, 23 Atl 774, *Tindare Mfg Co* v *Duff*, 15 Pa Super Ct 383

[90] *Bogert* v *Battleston*, 6 Pa Super. Ct 468.

[91] *Bonsall* v *Comly*, 44 Pa 442

[92] *Jones* v *Gundrim*, 3 Watts & S 531, *Warren* v *Forney*, 13 Serg & R 52

[93] *Fry* v *Jones*, 2 Rawle, 11, *Kost* v *Theis*, 20 W N C 545, 10 Cent Rep 845, 12 Atl 262, *Detwiler* v *Cox*, 75 Pa 200, *Latimer* v *Grootzinger*, 139 Pa 207, 21 Atl 22, *Bryer* v *Fenstermacher*, 2 Whart 95

[94] *Quinn* v *Wallace*, 6 Whart 452, *Chicago & A Oil & Min Co* v. *Barnes* 62 Pa 445, *Ingersoll* v. *Sergeant*, 1 Whart 337.

and make cognizance, generally, that the tenant was such under a demise at such a certain rent, during the time wherein the rent distrained for was incurred, and that this rent was, when distress was made, and still remains, due. It is not necessary to set forth the grant, tenure, demise, or title of the landlord.[95] The defendant is, by the avowry or cognizance made, virtually a plaintiff, and the burden is upon him of showing that there was rent in arrear.[96] The right of intervention of third persons, secured by the 3d section of the act of April 9th, 1901,[97] does not exist when goods which have been properly distrained for rent admittedly due have been replevied by the tenant.

315. Set-off.—Matters of set-off against the rent cannot be taken advantage of by the plaintiff in replevin,[98] but all payments, formal or virtual, can be   If, *e. g ,* the landlord has agreed that repairs may be made by the tenant, and that the cost of them, paid by the tenant, shall be a credit upon the rent,[99] or that payment by the tenant of certain debts of the landlord

[95] Section 10, act March 21, 1772, 1 Pepper & Lewis Digest, 2645, 1 Sm L 370, *M'Curdy* v *Randolph,* 2 Clark (Pa) 323, *Jones* v *Gundrim,* 3 Watts & S 531, *Manuel* v *Reath,* 5 Phila 11 The provision applies to distress for ground-rent *Franciscus* v *Reigart* 4 Watts 98

There can be no avowry or cognizance while the goods are in the landlord's possession The claim of them as owner is inconsistent with a distress If he relies on his right to distrain, as a defense, he must surrender the possession to the sheriff If he keeps them, under a claim-property bond, and he fails to show his ownership, judgment will go against him He cannot assert a right to distrain *Fleming* v *Heitshu,* 7 Northampton Co Rep 96, 16 Lanc L Rev 365 The plea to the avowry should not contain a demurrer The plea *riens in arrere* admits the tenancy described in the avowry The plea *non tenent* denies the tenancy The two are therefore inconsistent Though they can both be pleaded, they must be kept separate The denial that rent is in arrear creates a traverse upon which issue must be tendered, and the plea should conclude to the country, and not with the words ' and this the plaintiff is ready to verify " *Lutz* v *Browne,* 10 Pa Dist R 355

[96] *Wells* v *Hornish,* 3 Penr & W 30, *Hessel* v *Johnson,* 129 Pa 173, 5 L R A 851, 15 Am St Rep 716, 18 Atl 754

[97] P L 88, *Samson* v *Levy,* 12 Pa Dist R 600

[98] *Warner* v *Caulk* 3 Whart 193, *Beyer* v *Fenstermacher,* 2 Whart. 95

[99] *Kost* v *Theis,* 20 W N. C 545, 10 Cent Rep 845, 12 Atl 262

shall be a payment on account of the rent,[100]—damages to which the tenant is entitled on account of a breach of the landlord's covenant to make repairs and improvements upon the demised premises may be deducted from the rent.[101]

316. Set-off of taxes.—The 6th section of the act of April 3d, 1804,[102] enacts that every tenant "shall be liable to pay all the taxes" which, during his occupancy, became due and payable, and it shall be lawful for him, "by action of debt or otherwise, to recover said taxes from his landlord, or, at his election, to defalcate the amount thereof in the payment of the rent due to such landlord, unless such defalcation or recovery would impair any contract or agreement between them previously made." In case of ground rent, the taxes on the land are the proper burden of the ground tenant. If he pays them he pays only what he should, and he cannot set them off in replevin founded on a distress for the rent.[103]

317. Damages.—As the property is delivered by the sheriff to the tenant or owner of the goods, if he succeeds in the replevin, he should recover, as damages, a compensation for the taking and detention of the goods,[104] and for any circumstances of

---

[100]*Beyer* v *Fenstermacher*, 2 Whart 95

[101]*Fairman* v *Fluck*, 5 Watts, 516, *Warner* v *Caulk*, 3 Whart 193 The lease was for one year The distress was for the third quarter's rent The damages to be deducted would be one fourth of the difference between the value of the premises had the repairs been made, and the value of them in their actual state.

Breaches of promise of the landlord, without consideration to make repairs, could furnish no ground for reduction of the rent *Phillips* v *Monges*, 4 Whart 226

In distribution of the proceeds of a sheriff's sale, there would be a reduction from the landlord's claim, because of his nonfulfilling of his

covenant to erect sufficient stabling upon the premises *Gray* v *Wilson*, 4 Watts, 39

In *Colwell* v *Peden*, 3 Watts, 327 the tenant, denying that the landlord had a right to distrain, because he had failed to make repairs, and had caused a nuisance, paid the rent, after a distress warrant had been issued He could not recover it back in an action He should have resorted to replevin, or to trespass

[102]1 Pepper & Lewis Digest, 2036, 4 Smith's Laws, 201

[103]*Franciscus* v *Reigart*, 4 Watts 98

[104]*Franciscus* v *Reigart*, 4 Watts 98 If the defendant in replevin claims the property only in virtue of a distress, he must not claim prop-

hardship or oppression   If the landlord distrains on goods after removal from the premises, supposing them to be the tenant's, when they are a stranger's, and that they have been fraudulently removed, when they have not been, he should not be compelled to pay as damages more than what would compensate for the taking and detention.[105]   If, the property being delivered to the plaintiff by the sheriff, the defendant nevertheless succeeds in the replevin, and the jury finds the amount of rent in arrear, for which the distress was properly made, and the value of the goods distrained upon,[106] the landlord will be entitled to recover so much as the goods would have brought at the sale, less the expenses of sale avoided by the intervention of the replevin, and less the amount of the proceeds of the sale that would have exceeded the rent, and that he would have been obliged to return to the tenant.

318. Effect of replevin on lien of distress.— The delivery by the sheriff of the goods to the plaintiff in replevin discharges them from the lien of the distress.   They may, therefore, be again distrained by another landlord for other rent, and, after this distress, they cannot be returned to the defendant in the replevin, on a writ de retorno habendo [107] So they may be levied upon in execution [108] And if they are levied on in execution, the landlord cannot claim from the proceeds of sale in execution,

---

erty and give a claim property bond, but must allow the sheriff to deliver the goods to the plaintiff   Otherwise judgment must go for the plaintiff without finding any rent due the defendant   Baird v Porter, 67 Pa 105, Cassidy v Elias, 90 Pa 431, Fleming v Heitshu, 8 Pa. Dist R 715

[105]Scott v McEwen, 2 Phila 176 The court told the jury in M'Geary v Raymond, 17 Pa Super Ct 308, that the defendant was entitled to

the rent in arrear with a proper allowance for the cost of taking the goods in distress

[106]Franciscus v Reigart, 4 Watts, 98 The landlord claimed the costs of the distress and the watchman's fees and double costs, in Underhill v Wynkoop, 15 Pa Super Ct 230

[107]Woglam v Cowperthwaite, 2 Dall. 68, 1 L ed 292

[108]Frey v Leeper, 2 Dall 131, 1 L ed 319, Bair v Warfel, 5 Lanc L. Rev 81.

any of the rent for which he previously distrained, in preference to the execution-creditor.[109]

319. Assumpsit.— For the improper taking of goods in distress, because they were exempt, being a stranger's, because they were no longer upon the demised premises, the owner cannot maintain assumpsit after the sale of the goods [110] Nor, paying the rent after the distress warrant issues, can he recover back what he pays by assumpsit, on the ground that, by reason of the landlord's having failed to make repairs, as he had covenanted to do, and of his maintaining a nuisance on or near the premises, the rent was equitably not due [111]

320. Tenant's remedies adequate.— The remedies of the tenant, in replevin or trespass, are generally deemed adequate Hence, an injunction has been refused to the assignee of the lease, to prevent the taking of his goods in distress for the rent owed by the lessee prior to the assignment.[112] After a sheriff's sale on a mortgage, the mortgagor remaining in possession, the purchaser at the sale issued a distress warrant for rent alleged to be due by the former mortgagor, as tenant in possession. An injunction against prosecuting the distress was refused.[113]

321 Landlord's remedy against officer — If, after a constable, acting as bailiff in distress, has caused an inventory to be taken, he receives the rent from the tenant, and fails to pay it over, or, receiving only a part of the rent from the tenant, neglects further to prosecute the distress, he and his sureties are liable upon his official bond. Though it is not entirely clear that he is bound, on the requisition of a landlord, to perform all the duties incident to distress, he may become bailiff, and he must, if called on, aid and assist in making the appraisement and sale He is entitled to specific fees for whatever he performs Whatever he

[109]*Gray* v *Wilson,* 4 Watts, 30
[110]*Walsh* v *The Bourse,* 15 Pa
Super Ct 219
[111]*Colwell* v *Peden,* 3 Watts, 327

[112]*School Fund* v *Heermans* 2 Law Times N S 137
[113]*Williams* v *Flood,* 1 W N. C. 199

does, he does officially, and not as a mere agent of the landlord.[114] In *Baer* v. *Kuhl*[115] a constable made a levy under a landlord's warrant, left the goods on the premises where found, went away and secured appraisers, on his return with them, was locked out, and could not then or subsequently gain admission to the premises where the goods were A rule for judgment for want of a sufficient affidavit of defense in an action on the official bond was discharged, the affidavit alleging that the goods had been distrained off the demised premises, having been removed therefrom fifty-two days before, with the landlord's consent, that they belonged to the tenant's wife, and could not properly be levied off the demised premises, and that the bond tendered to the constable by the landlord was not in proper form, and did not protect him. The measure of damages would not be the rent due, unless the goods distrainable, or distrained, were sufficiently valuable to pay it.

322 Liability of surety for rent.— The replevin by the tenant of the goods distrained will not make the suit against the surety for the rent unsuccessful, the replevin remaining undetermined at the trial of the action [116] The clandestine removal of the goods, while under distress, by some person unknown to the constable or landlord, and without negligence on his part, will not be a defense for the surety to the extent of the value of the goods eloigned [117] If the distress is released, however, on the tenant's promise to pay the rent as soon as able, the surety will be discharged of liability for so much of the rent as would have been paid had the goods been sold in the distress proceeding, and the proceeds applied to it [118]

[114]*Com* v *Sheppard,* 2 Clark (Pa) 393

[115] 8 Pa Dist R 389

[116]*King* v *Blackmore,* 72 Pa. 347, 13 Am Rep 684.

[117]*Myers* v *Hulseman,* 3 W N C. 487

[118]*McNamee* v *Cresson,* 3 W N C. 450.

CHAPTER XVIII.

LANDLORD'S PREFERENCE WITH RESPECT TO EXECUTION SALES

323. The statutory provision.— The 83d section of the act of June 16, 1836,[1] enacts that "the goods and chattels being in or upon any messuage, lands, or tenements which are or shall be demised for life or years, or otherwise, taken by virtue of an execution, and liable to the distress of the landlord, shall be liable for the payment of any sums of money due for rent at the time of taking such goods in execution: Provided, That such rent shall not exceed one year's rent."

324. "Money due for rent;" apportionment— By "money due" is not meant money by the terms of the lease, now payable, for which a distress or an action could at once be levied or brought. Rent is conceived as accruing from day to day; and at the end of each day the rent apportioned to it is "due," though not yet payable. If rent is payable by the year, the quarter, the month, the week, and a levy in execution should be made upon the tenant's goods on the premises at a point of time within such year, quarter, etc., a fraction of the year's, quarter's, month's, or week's rent would be claimable from the proceeds, equal to the ratio between the part of such period already run, and the whole period. If, *e g.,* the lease being payable annually, the levy is made on the 300th day of the year, 300/365 of the rent would be claimable by the landlord.[2] Examples follow: term

---

[1] 1 Pepper & Lewis Digest, 2643; P L 755 The 3d section of the act of March 30th, 1859, applicable to Schuylkill county, restricts the landlord's preference to the rent for one month and of any fraction of a month accruing immediately before the levy in execution, or the landlord's warrant This act is constitutional, whether applied to leases made before or after its passage It does not impair the contract of lease, but only the lien and remedy for the recovery of the rent *Farmers' Bank's Appeal,* 1 Walk (Pa) 33.

[2] *Greider's Appeal,* 5 Pa 422, *Weltner's Appeal,* 63 Pa 302, *Shaw* v *Oakley,* 7 Phila 89, *West* v *Sink,* 2 Yeates 274, *Anderson's Appeal,* 3 Pa St 218, *Case* v *Davis,* 15 Pa. 80, *Collins' Appeal,* 35 Pa 83 *Oram's Estate,* 5 Kulp, 423, *West* v *Zint,* cited in 5 Binn 506, *Lichtenthaler* v *Thompson,* 13 Serg & R 157. 15 Am Dec 581, *Thropp's Appeal,* 70 Pa 395, *Timmes* v *Metz,* 156 Pa 384, 27 Atl 248, *Greenwood's Appeal,* 79 Pa 294, *Parker's Appeal,* 5 Pa 390, *Ege* v *Ege,* 5 Watts, 134 The right to apportion rent to the levy has been questioned

begins Oct. 10, 1842, levy, Dec 6, 1842; the rent, $200 quarterly   The landlord was entitled to $123 69,[3] term began April 1st, 1867, rent payable quarterly; levy May 27th, 1867; landlord entitled to $70 82,[4] term for five years began September 1st, 1811, rent payable quarterly, levy, July 25th, 1812, fraction of the rent for the current quarter, equal to that which represents the ratio of the part of the quarter run, to the whole, was payable.[5]

325. Rent payable in advance, apportionment.—Rent payable at the beginning of a period is, of course, not merely due, but payable, at the time of any levy within that period, but no apportionment will be made of the rent to fall due at the commencement of a period to begin after the levy   Thus, rent was payable quarterly, in advance, on July 1st, October 1st, January 1st   A levy was made September 15th, when the rent due July 1st had not yet been paid.   This quarter's rent could be taken from the proceeds of the execution, but not five sixths or any other portion of the succeeding quarter's.[6]   Again, term began April 1st, rent payable quarterly in advance was $62 50; levy in execution June 9th   The quarter's rent due April 1st had been paid   The court below allowed to the landlord $48.08. This was error, "for," said Lowrie, J, "it was not due, and there had been no enjoyment on which to found the allowance. To allow it would be to apportion the rent neither by the contract, nor by the time of enjoyment "[7]   When rent for a year was payable in one instalment, in the midst of the year, and a levy occurred before the arrival of the day of payment, it was held that so much of the year's rent should be paid to the landlord from the execution proceeds as represented the ratio of the time elapsed to the whole period between the inception of the

in *Prentiss* v *Kingsley*, 10 Pa 120, *Purdy's Appeal*, 23 Pa 97, *Bank of Pennsylvania* v *Wise*, 3 Watts, 394

[3]*Morgan* v *Moody*, 6 Watts & S. 333.

[4]*Wickey* v *Eyster*, 58 Pa 501
[5]*Binns* v *Hudson*, 5 Binn 505
[6]*Morris* v *Billings*, 1 Phila 464
[7]*Purdy's Appeal*, 23 Pa. 97, *Com.* v *Contner*, 18 Pa 439.

term and the contract day of payment   The term began April 1st, the rent for the year was to be paid September 1st; the levy was made August 1st   Four fifths of the time between April 1st and September 1st had then elapsed   It was held that four fifths of the rent, having been earned, should be taken by the landlord [8]

326 No rent after levy — The apportionment of rent is made, not to the day of issue of the writ of execution, but to the day of levy thereunder   A considerable period may elapse between the levy and the sale, but no part of the rent accruing in that interval can be taken by the landlord [9]   In *Minnig* v. *Sterrett,* the interval was seven months [10]   And payment of the rent between levy and sale cannot be effected indirectly by allowing the landlord to apply the rent accruing during that time in reduction of set-offs offered by the defendant against the rent accrued at the levy [11]   If the sheriff, after levy, removes the goods to another building leased to the defendant, the owner of the building cannot claim from the proceeds of sale of the goods, the compensation for the use and occupation of the building by the sheriff, between the removal and the sale [12]   If, after levy, there is a sheriff's interpleader, and he withdraws from the possession, but, subsequently, the claimant suffering a nonsuit, the sheriff resumes possession of the goods, and they are finally sold on a *vend. ex* , the landlord cannot claim rent down to the resumption of possession, but only down to the original levy.[13]

327. Successive executions. — If there are several executions issued and levied successively, upon all of which the sale of

[8]*Anderson's Appeal,* 3 Pa St 218 The court below allowed only four twelfths The premises were the Bedford Mineral Springs

[9]*Wager* v *Duke,* 1 Clark (Pa) 316

[10] 7 Pa Co. Ct 73.

[11]*Case* v *Davis,* 15 Pa 80.

[12]*Megarge* v   *Tanner,* 1   Clark (Pa) 331   The landlord must look to the sheriff for compensation

[13]*Horan* v *Barrett,* 3 Luzerne Legal Obs. 96, 5 Leg & Ins Rep. 27

the tenant's goods is made, the landlord's rent, as against the
execution on which occurred the first levy, will be apportioned
to that levy; as against the execution on which the second levy
was made, will be apportioned to the making of the second
levy.[14]   There were six executions which were levied, respectively, on the 20th, 22d, 23d, 24th, and 25th of November, and
on the 14th of December.   Sale was made on all the writs.   The
writ on which levy was made November 23d exhausted the fund.
Rent could be taken from the proceeds, apportioned to November 23d.[15]   If there are two successive executions, and, for
any cause, the earlier is postponed in the distribution to the
later, the rent will be apportioned to the day of the second
levy   A fi fa was levied March 7th, but the defendant was allowed to continue his business, buying and selling as before,
until June 2d, when a second execution was levied.   The lien
of the first was lost as to this.   Successive sales took place on
these writs   The rent apportioned to June 2d was paid from
the proceeds, and the balance to the execution levied on that
day [16]

328 Rent payable absolutely in advance.—Rent payable in
advance, the time of payment named in the lease having arrived
before the levy, is entitled to be paid from the proceeds of the
execution sale   Thus, term begins April 1st, annual rent $700,
of which half is to be paid in advance; levy May 24th.   The
landlord had a right to $350 from the proceeds [17]   Rent pay-
able in advance for the quarter beginning July 1st was still
unpaid when the levy was made September 15th   It was paid
in full from the proceeds.[18]   Lease for five years, beginning
April 1st, 1848, rent payable semiannually in advance   When
the levy was made, June 14th, 1849, only one half-year's instal-

[14]*Minnig* v *Sterrett*, 7 Pa Co Ct
73, *Worley* v *Meckley*, 1 Phila 398
[15]*Leaming's Appeal*, 5 W N C
221, *Todd* v *Ashton*, 4 W N C 347.

[16]*Earls Appeal*, 13 Pa 483
[17]*Collins' Appeal* 35 Pa 83
[18]*Morris* v *Billings*, 1 Phila 464

ment had been paid The landlord was entitled to the two semi-
annual instalments payable in advance on October 1st, 1848,
and on April 1st, 1849.[19] The rent payable in advance is payable on the first day of the period to which it is applicable
The lease beginning April 8th, 1851, the rent being payable
semiannually in advance, the seventh instalment was due
April 8th, 1854.[20] If a lease begins April 1st, 1841, and a
levy is made on the lessee's goods on the premises before that
date, he being in under a prior lease, the rent payable in advance
under the second lease cannot be taken from the proceeds[21]

329. Rent payable contingently in advance.— The lease may
require the payment of the rent in instalments, but may stipulate that, on the happening of a certain event,—*e. g ,* the tenant
becoming embarrassed, or making an assignment, or being sold
out by the sheriff, or attempting to remove, or manifestly intending to remove, the goods, at any time during the continuance of the lease,[22]—the whole rent for the term, not yet paid,
shall become due and payable. Such a stipulation is valid
Hence, a fi fa. issuing against the tenant, the entire rent, he
having become embarrassed before the attaching of the lien of
the execution, would become payable from the proceeds of the
execution sale[23] But the event which renders all the rent due
must happen before the levy. Hence, under a lease making
all the rent due on a removal of the goods, or an attempt to
remove them from the premises, if the removal is not attempted
until after the levy, though on the same day, the rent, whose
payment is thus accelerated, is not payable from the goods

[19]*Com ex rel Irwin* v *Contner*, 21
Pa 266
[20]*Moss's Appeal*, 35 Pa 162.
[21]*Martin's Appeal*, 5 Watts & S
220 Cf *Diller* v *Roberts*, 13 Serg
& R 60, 15 Am Dec 578 If the
levy is made during the term ending
April 1st, but after a lease has been
made to the same person for the fol-
LAND & TEN 18.

lowing year, no rent to accrue under
this second lease will be payable
from the proceeds *Martin's Appeal,*
5 Watts & S 220
[22]*Excelsior Shirt Co* v *Miller*, 4
Lack Legal News, 332
[23]*Platt* v *Johnson*, 168 Pa 47, 47
Am. St Rep 877, 31 Atl 935.

sold [24] The lease declaring that on failure to pay any monthly instalment within five days after it becomes due, all the rent for the term shall become immediately due, this provision is not waived by the lessor's accepting payment for a month's rent when it is more than five days overdue On any later month's rent becoming overdue for more than five days, the landlord may treat all the rent as due, and claim it from the proceeds of an execution.[25]

330. Rent; taxes; water rent.—The rent may be so reserved as to cover the taxes, and when this has been done the landlord will have a right to take not merely the rent strictly so called, but also the taxes, from the proceeds of an execution sale of the tenant's goods But, the lease stipulating for an annual rent of $1,200, payable quarterly, without any deduction on account of taxes, which the lessee covenanted to pay, together with the taxes on a lot not included in the demise, Tilghman, Ch. J., remarked: "The rent might have been reserved in such a manner as to cover the taxes, but it has not been done so in this lease The rent reserved is $1,200, payable quarterly, without any deduction on account of taxes, and the tenant covenants to pay all taxes, so that the taxes are no part of the rent reserved."[26] A covenant by the lessee to pay water rent does not make it rent On his neglect to pay it, and the landlord's paying it, the latter

[24] *Lowry* v *Evans*, 2 Lack Jur 43

[25] *Teufel* v *Rowan*, 179 Pa 408, 36 Atl 224, *Rowan* v *Rowan*, 179 Pa 411, 36 Atl 1130 In *Merrill* v *Trimmer*, 2 Pa Co Ct 49, Church, P J, held that the stipulation, that on default in paying punctually any month's rent all the rent should become due, would not be enforced, and that, if it should be, the lessor's accepting overdue rent once or twice, and failing to warn against subsequent defaults, would prevent insisting on it.

[26] *Binns* v *Hudson*, 5 Binn 505 The taxes had, apparently been paid by nobody In *Case* v *Davis*, 15 Pa 80, the tenant was to pay all taxes assessed on the premises during the term He failed to do so Had the landlord paid the tax before the levy, he could have set off the tax thus paid by him against a counterclaim by which the tenant sought to reduce the rent due Not having done so before the levy, he could make no use of it Cf *Wickersham* v *Stetson*, 34 Phila. Leg Int 248.

cannot demand the water rent from the proceeds of an execution sale [27]

331. Kind of rent.— Besides money rent of a determinate amount, the rent may take the form of a royalty, *e. g ,* a royalty on iron ore,[28] or on coal,[29] or on all limestone quarried and lime burned.[30]   If the rent is reserved in shares of crops or other commodities, it does not seem convenient to give effect to any landlord's preference over an execution creditor, with respect to money proceeds of a sale.

332 Amount of rent.— The goods of the tenant, taken in execution, are, by the 83d section of the act of June 16th, 1836, made "liable for the payment of any sums of money due for rent, at the time of taking such goods in execution   *Provided,* That such rent shall not exceed one year's rent."[31]   There is no limit to the sums   "Any sums due," if for not more than one year, must be paid to the landlord   The rent must remain "due." If it has been paid, it cannot be paid again.[32]   But the landlord's accepting the note of a third person as conditional payment of, or as collateral security for, the rent, is not equivalent to the payment.   The note would need to be itself paid. Should the note not be paid, the landlord may insist on being paid from the proceeds of sale of the tenant's goods[33]   But when the landlord accepts, for rent due, a draft at four months, drawn by the tenant or a third person, for the rent and the interest for the period of the draft, gives a receipt for the rent, and his books show the rent paid, the failure of the drawee or drawer to pay the draft will not revive the rent, so as to qualify

---

[27]*Lewin* v *Acheson,* 30 Pittsb L. J N S 215

[28]*Cambria Iron Co's Appeal,* 114 Pa 66

[29]*Oram's Estate,* 5 Kulp, 423

[30]*Kendig* v *Kendig,* 3 Pittsb 287

[31] Not rent for two years   *Stark* v *Hight,* 3 Pa Super Ct 516, *Leidich's Estate,* 161 Pa 451, 29 Atl. 89, 90.

[32] Payments can, of course, be shown in the distribution proceedings   *Case* v *Davis,* 15 Pa. 80

[33]*Kreiter* v *Hammer,* I Pearson (Pa) 559, *Snyder* v *Kunkleman,* 3 Penr & W 487, *Kendig* v *Kendig,* 2 Pearson (Pa) 89, 3 Pittsb 287.

the landlord to claim it as such.[34] If, after a levy in execution
on goods of the tenant, the landlord takes, without authority,
some of them, as a means of paying the rent due him, he cannot
claim his rent from the proceeds of the sale of the rest of the
goods.[35] If, after a distress, the tenant replevies the goods, the
landlord cannot claim for that portion of the rent for which
he properly distrained, and which the goods distrained would
have been able to satisfy So much he can recover in the replevin. But for any other portion of the rent, and for any
rent accruing after the distress, he would have a right to claim
from the proceeds of a later execution sale.[36]

333. Deductions from rent.— In the proceedings for distributing the proceeds of an execution sale, the tenant or the execution
creditor may reduce the amount of rent claimed by showing de-
falcations of various sorts Thus, if the lease has required the
landlord to build a stable, and he has neglected to do so, the tenant has the right to an abatement from the rent, and, therefore,
so has the execution creditor.[37] The landlord may have agreed
that the tenant might put in a heater, etc., and deduct the cost
from the rent The cost of such a heater, put in by the tenant,
will be deducted from the rent,[38] and counterclaims, not connected with the lease or the premises demised,—*e. g ,* a book
account existing before the levy,—may be set off[39] In *Case v
Davis,* the tenant's set-off was itself reduced by claims of the
landlord against him, having no connection with the lease, or
with the tenant's counterclaim. If the landlord has a claim
against the tenant, arising from his breach of his covenant in
the lease, and the claim was complete before the levy, it can be

[34]*Cambria Iron Co's Appeal,* 114
Pa 66 Obtaining a judgment for
the rent does not destroy the landlord's right to proceeds *Weltner's
Appeal* 63 Pa 302
    Martin's Appeal, 5 Watts & S
220
[35]*Gray* v *Wilson,* 4 Watts, 39.

[36]*Gray* v Wilson, 4 Watts, 39,
Platt v *Johnson,* 168 Pa 47, 47 Am
St Rep 877 31 Atl 935
[38]*Wilkinson* v *Kugler,* 153 Pa 238,
25 Atl 1133
[39]*Gray* v Wilson, 4 Watts, 39,
Case v *Davis,* 15 Pa 80

employed to reduce the tenant's set-off. If the landlord's right of action on account of it did not arise until after the levy, it cannot be so used. Thus, the tenant covenanting to pay the taxes, his mere omission to pay was held not to give rise to a counterclaim by the landlord; but only the landlord's payment If the landlord did not pay the taxes until after the levy, he could make no use of the taxes as an abatement from the tenant's defalcation.[40]   The execution creditor cannot require the landlord to distrain on the goods of others than the tenant on the premises, in order to diminish the amount the landlord otherwise will demand, to his detriment, from the proceeds of the sheriff's sale [41]

334. Extinction of rent.— The landlord's release of the tenant from the rent will, of course, extinguish his claim to subsequent payment from the proceeds of the sale of the tenant's goods [42] A final eviction by the landlord will extinguish any liability for rent not already payable at the time of the eviction, or already payable, but in advance, for a period within which the eviction subsequently happens; but it will not destroy the right to rent already mature.   On a fi. fa. levied on the goods of a tenant, they were sold, and immediately thereafter the landlord went into full possession of the premises.   He had already been paid the rent in advance, from the proceeds of the sale.   Had the eviction occurred after the rent became payable in advance, but before it was actually paid, the landlord could not have claimed it from the proceeds.[43]   The acceptance of a surrender of the term by the landlord will extinguish the claim for rent which was then accruing, but not yet due.   Rent for the year

---

[40]*Case* v *Davis*, 15 Pa 80

[41]*Timmes* v *Metz*, 156 Pa 384, 27 Atl. 248

[42]*Thropp's Appeal*, 70 Pa 395. The lease was also surrendered

The fact that a distress has realized a part of the rent does not prevent a claim for the residue from the proceeds of an execution   *Kreiter* v *Hammer*, 1 Pearson (Pa) 559

[43]*Com ex rel Irwin* v. *Contner*, 21 Pa. 266.

between April 1st, 1845, and April 1st, 1846, was payable on the last day of the year   On January 8th, 1846, an oral surrender of the term, which was to end March 31st, 1846, was accepted by the landlord.   On the next day, an execution against the tenant was levied on his goods.   The landlord had no right to have the rent apportioned to the levy, and receive it from the proceeds The surrender drowned the term, and the result of this drowning and extinction is, that rent reserved and issuing out of the lesser estate, and not due at the time of the surrender, is also extinguished.[44] A purchase of the leasehold, even after the levy, by the landlord, will extinguish rent then accruing, and not yet due, and prevent the allowance of an apportioned part of it to the landlord.[45]

335. **Rent for what year.**— In *Lichtenthaler v. Thompson*,[46] Gibson, J., held that only the rent of the year within which the levy was made, or, it being made after the expiration of the term, of the last year of the term, could be taken from the proceeds of an execution sale.   In that case, a term for one year began on April 1st, 1818.   A second lease to the same tenant, but with X as his surety, was made for the year commencing on April 1st, 1819   A levy was made in March, 1820.   The rent of both years being unpaid, the proceeds of the execution sale, it was held, must be applied to the rent of the second year.   The question has since been determined differently, and, there being two successive leases to the same tenant, the landlord may claim the rent due on the first,[47] or he may claim a part of the rent due on

[44]*Greider's Appeal*, 5 Pa 422.

[45]*Shaw* v *Oakley*, 7 Phila 89

[46] 13 Serg & R 157, 15 Am Dec 581

[47]*Parker's Appeal*, 5 Pa 390, *Richie* v *McCauley*, 4 Pa 471, *Platt* v *Johnson*, 168 Pa 47, 47 Am St Rep 877 31 Atl 935

A succeeds to the reversion, by devise, in the midst of the term At its expiration he relets the premises to the same tenant He may apply the money made by an execution levied during the second term, to the rent due on the first term, though, in so doing, the proceeds of the execution are exhausted. *Lewis's Appeal*, 66 Pa 312.

the current term, and a part of that due on the preceding.[48]   "It is well settled," says Williams, J., "that the landlord is not confined, in his claim for rent out of the proceeds of the sale of the tenant's goods, to the rent for the last year, or for the year immediately preceding the sale, so that no more than one year's rent be demanded and received."[49]   Three successive guardians of the same minor made three successive leases to the same tenant   During the running of the last, the guardian who made it was superseded by another.   A levy was then made on the tenant's goods   It was held that the proceeds could be applied to the portion of the current year's rent that was apportioned to the levy; and that the residue of one year's rent could be applied either to the first or to the second year, according to the rights *inter se* of the guardians.[50]   If, successive leases being made, the rent under the earlier can be claimed, *a fortiori* can rent for an earlier year under the same lease be claimed.   The entire rent for the year ending July 1st may be taken from the proceeds of an execution levied in the following December.[51]

336. Locality of the goods.—The 83d section of the act of June 16, 1836,[52] declares that "the goods or chattels being in or upon any messuage, lands, or tenements which are or shall be demised for life or years, or otherwise, taken by virtue of an execution," shall be liable for the payment of rent.   The goods, therefore, must be on the demised premises when they are taken in execution   A, by separate leases, having rented to B two adjoining houses, *m* and *n,* B, for his own convenience, tore down the partition wall, so as to make one large pool room.   A pool table belonging to B, and standing in that part of the room which was in house *m,* was seized in execution.   The rent due for *m,* but not that due for *n,* could be paid from the proceeds [53]

[48]*Ege* v *Ege,* 5 Watts, 134
[49]*Weltner's Appeal,* 63 Pa. 302
[50]*Weltner's Appeal,* 63 Pa. 302
[51]*Richie* v *McCauley,* 4 Pa. 471
[52]1 Pepper & Lewis Digest, 2643;
P L 755

[53]*Baum* v *Brown,* 11 W N C. 202, *Naylor* v *Skelly,* 1 Chester Co Rep 408.

The lessor first rented lime kilns and quarries, covering about 3 acres, and, a year later, leased to the same tenant the remainder of the farm, which was not separated from the tract first leased by fence or otherwise   From the time of the later lease, the tenant operated the quarries and kilns together with the farm, using on both the same horses and carts.   The proceeds of the tenant's property found anywhere on these premises were payable indiscriminately to the rents falling due under both leases.[54]   Though the goods are removed clandestinely or fraudulently[55] or honestly, but, the lease providing that they shall, on removal, continue liable for distress,[56] so that the landlord may by distress pursue them, he will not be preferred to the execution creditor if, he not distraining, the goods are levied on in execution.   If, under an execution, a constable takes chattels from the demised premises to another place, and there sells enough of them to satisfy the execution, leaving the residue there, this residue, if there levied on under a second execution, is not subject to the landlord's claim for rent[57]   The landlord cannot take advantage of an unlawful detention of the goods on the premises.   If, e g , he distrains on them when he has no such right, in order to hold them until a creditor may levy upon them there, and the levy is thereupon made on them there, he will have no right to payment of the rent from the proceeds[58]

337. Locality, removal after levy.— The landlord's right does

---

[54]*Hartranft's Appeal*, 17 W N. C 420

[55]*Grant's Appeal*, 44 Pa 477

[56]*Naylor* v *Shelly*, 1 Chester Co Rep 408

[57]*Allen* v *Lewis*, 1 Ashm (Pa) 184

If A, renting two stores, *l* and *m*, his goods are levied on in *l* and removed by the sheriff to *m*, and there kept until sold, the rent for *m* cannot be claimed from the proceeds *Megarge* v. *Tanner*, 1 Clark (Pa) 331.

In *Wilbur* v *Hankins*, 3 Lack Legal News, 49, most of the fund for distribution arose from the sale of the tenant's goods not on the demised premises when levied upon The fund raised from the sale of the goods on the premises was applied to the execution creditor and wage claimants   It was held that the landlord could be subrogated to their right, so as to be entitled to payment from the product of the goods not on the premises

[58]*Burchard* v *Rees*, 1 Whart 377.

not depend on the continuance of the goods on the demised premises after the levy. The sheriff or constable may remove them. "This removal," said Rogers, J., "has never been supposed to affect the right of the landlord to the rent."[59] "In Pennsylvania, under our statute, the sheriff is not estopped from removing the goods, and he is protected, provided he pays over to the landlord one year's rent, or the landlord neglects to give notice of his claim in proper time,"[60] and, if the goods are attached on the premises, under the 27th section of the act of July 12th, 1842,[61] and then removed, and, after judgment obtained, are sold, the landlord may claim the rent form the proceds [62]

338. Goods must be liable to distress.— The goods, whose proceeds may be demanded by a landlord for the rent, under the 83rd, section of the act of June 16, 1836, are described as goods which "shall be liable to the distress of the landlord" This liability to distress is the precondition to the landlord's claim upon them.[63] This liability must exist when the levy is made under the execution. Though it existed when the fi fa issued, the landlord's right will vanish if, before the levy, the right of distress is lost. Thus, the death of the tenant before the levy will make it impossible for the landlord then to distrain For that reason he loses his privilege of taking from the proceeds.[64]

[59]*Morgan v Moody*, 6 Watts & S 333

[60]*Ege v Ege*, 5 Watts, 134 Goods taken by the sheriff from a store in Allegheny City to Pittsburg, and there sold, were subject to the lien for the rent of the Allegheny City store

McCombs's Appeal, 43 Pa 435. After a levy on two safes, a stranger claiming them and the execution creditor, at the request of the sheriff, were ordered to interplead The claimant gave a forthcoming bond, and removed the goods from the premises They could no longer be liable, it was said by Briggs, J, to the claim of the landlord for rent

[61]2 Pepper & Lewis, Digest, 2577, P L 339

[62]*Morgan v Moody*, 6 Watts & S. 333

[63]*Grant's Appeal*, 44 Pa 477, *Ege v Ege*, 5 Watts, 134, *Rowland v Goldsmith*, 2 Grant, Cas 378, *Lewis's Appeal*, 66 Pa 312, *Merrill v Trimmer*, 2 Pa Co Ct 49, *Naylor v Shelly*, 1 Chester Co Rep 408

[64]*Hoskins v Houston*, 2 Clark (Pa.) 489. The landlord s loss of

For rent due by a partnership, the landlord cannot take from the proceeds of the sale of the interest of one partner.[65] The leasehold is not a source of payment of the preferred rent; but frame[66] or brick[67] buildings put on the premises by the tenant, under an agreement that he may remove them, are chattels which may be distrained.

339. **Goods of a wife, subtenant, etc** — It is not necessary that the defendant in the execution should be the debtor of the landlord   It is enough that his goods are on the premises and are liable to distress. Hence, on an execution against a married woman, whose goods are on premises demised to the husband, his landlord may claim the rent from the proceeds of the sale [68] "As to John Reber, the landlord," says the court, "all property on the premises, whether of the husband or of the wife, became liable to his distress for the rent.   His right to distrain does not flow from her covenant, or his relation as tenant, but from the common law, as an incident to the lease to the husband,—a right to distrain for his rent all property found upon the leased premises, not within the well-known exceptions on account of trade, etc.   It is this right which the legislature intended to protect when it gave to a landlord his preference in payment out of the proceeds of sale of the goods found on the premises, and liable for the rent." The lessor may take from the proceeds of the sale of the property of a subtenant in an execution against him, he being under no personal duty to the lessor to pay rent, the arrears due from the lessee, who is landlord of the subtenant.[69]

the reversion before the levy has the same result

[65]*Rundal* v *Stedge,* 2 Pa Co. Ct 608

[66]*Thropp's Appeal,* 70 Pa 395

[67]*Stark* v. *Hight,* 3 Pa. Super. Ct 516

[68]*Trimble's Appeal,* 5 W N C 396 The court treats the lease as made to the husband

If goods of a stranger are on the premises the execution creditor cannot compel the landlord to distrain on them, in exoneration of the fund to be produced by the sale of the defendant's own goods   *Timmes* **v.** *Metz,* 156 Pa 384, 27 Atl 248

[69]*McCombs's Appeal,* 43 Pa 435.

A leased a store to B for one year from April 1st, 1860, with the privilege of renewing the lease for two years longer. B sublet a store-room to C, whom A refused to recognize as tenant, looking to B and his sureties for the rent. On an execution against C, his goods in the store-room were levied on and sold. A was allowed one year's rent from the proceeds, although C had fully paid the rent to B which he had agreed to pay

340. Landlord claims the goods — The landlord cannot distrain on his own goods   If, under a fi. fa. against the tenant, goods are levied on, and the landlord, claiming them as his, notifies the sheriff, who thereupon demands a bond of indemnity from the execution creditor, and the landlord institutes trespass against the sheriff, he cannot, subsequently, claim the proceeds of the sale of the goods [70]   "It is out of all conscience," says Gordon, J., "that creditors should be thus driven to the trouble and expense of disproving title in the claimants, and when this has been successfully accomplished, that those same claimants should be permitted to pocket the fund by the interposition of the very title by which they were defeated."[71]

341   Goods exempt — If goods exempt from sale are set apart under an execution to the debtor, and are subsequently levied on under another execution, as to which also the debtor has an exemption, there can be no sale, and the landlord's claim of the proceeds would be inept and resultless; so, though the things may be liable to sale on any particular execution, if they are exempt from distress, their proceeds cannot be diverted from the execution plaintiff by the landlord.[72]   If goods are taken under an execution as to which there is no exemption, because of the fact that the act conferring exemption is not applicable to it (e   g , the debt came into existence before the passage of the exemption act of April 9th, 1849),[73] and the exemption is op-

[70] *Vetter's Appeal,* 99 Pa 52, *Edwards's Appeal,* 105 Pa 103, *Bush's Appeal,* 65 Pa 363
[71] *Edwards's Appeal,* 105 Pa 103
[72] *Morgan* v *Moody,* 6 Watts & S 333
[73] 1 Pepper & Lewis Digest, 1920, P L 533

erative as to the rent, *e g.*, it has arisen since the going into operation of that act, the rent cannot be taken from the proceeds.[74]   The waiver of the exemption in favor of the execution
creditor, *ipso facto* waives it in favor of the landlord,[75] even if,
before the execution issued. a distress by the landlord had
aborted by the tenant's claim of the exemption.[76]   The fact that
the landlord has a waiver from the tenant of his exemption will
not forfeit his right to claim from the proceeds of an execution,
as to which there is no waiver.[77]   The $300 worth of property
being set apart to the defendant, his sale of it to the landlord at
the appraisement, in satisfaction *pro tanto* of the rent, if bona
fide, would condone the failure of the landlord to prosecute a
distress.

342. Landlord's loss of reversion.— The right of a landlord to
distrain depends upon his retention, to the time of distress, of his
title or interest.   If he shall have aliened it, or it shall have been
sold from him by a judicial sale when the levy is made, he, not
then having the power to distrain, will not have the privilege of
claiming his rent from the proceeds of the execution sale.[78]   In
Lichtenthaler v. *Thompson*,[79] where there was a guardian of a
minor, who leased the land of the latter for a year, and, the minority terminating, the former ward renewed the lease for the
following year, and during the latter year an execution sale of
the tenant's goods took place, Gibson, J., assuming the guardian
to have had the reversion, and to have lost it to the ward, held,

[74]*Rouland* v *Goldsmith,* 2 Grant,
Cas 378, *Hampton* v *Henderson,* 4
Clark (Pa) 438

[75]*Collins's Appeal,* 35 Pa 83

[76]*Frick* v *McClain.* 9 W N C 32,
12 Lanc Bar, 78 In a distress the
tenant claimed the exemption, and
the goods being appraised at less
than $300, the landlord abandoned
the proceeding Subsequently a
creditor issued an execution, as to
whose claim there was a waiver.
The landlord took the rent

[77]*Kline* v *Lukens,* 4 Phila 296

[78]*Hoskins* v *Houston,* 2 Clark
(Pa) 489, *Lichtenthaler* v *Thompson,* 13 Serg & R 157, 15 Am Dec
581.

[79] 13 Serg & R 157, 15 Am Dec.
581   There was a surety in the second lease who was interested in the
appropriation of the proceeds of sale
to the payment of the second year's
rent.

for this reason, that the rent for the former year could not be taken from the proceeds   "But what is decisive in this case is, that Kline [the guardian], the landlord for the preceding year, had lost the right to distrain. His title as landlord did not continue to the time of the levy; and consequently his lien, which was originally intended to guard his right of distress whilst he chose, within a limited time, to suspend the exercise of it, was gone."   A different view was taken in *Weltner's Appeal.*[80]   A had been guardian of X, and as such, had leased X's farm for a number of years to Z.   On June 6, 1865, A was discharged from the trust, and B was appointed in his stead.   On September 6th, 1866, Z gave a judgment note to A for rent in arrear during A's guardianship   On this note judgment was entered January 7th, 1867.   On June 16th, 1868, B was superseded in the guardianship by C   Under A's judgment a levy was made on Z's chattels, September 1st, 1868, and a sale was had   It was held that the case must be considered as if the lessor had been the ward. There could have been, on September 1st, 1868, a distress for the rent of any one or of all of the years of guardianship, so that the question of distribution was one of equity.[81]

343. Close of the term.— The goods of the tenant remaining on the premises after the expiration of the term may be distrained for rent of the term; and hence this rent can be claimed from the proceeds of the judicial sale of the goods   The term may have normally expired, or it may have come to an end by a breach of a condition subsequent.[82]

344. Taken by virtue of an execution — The goods, the proceeds of which are made applicable to rent due by the 83rd sec-

---

[80] 63 Pa 302

[81] The rent of the portion of the last year preceding the levy was paid, as the money was made on an execution for the rent arising under the first guardianship, there was no equitable reason for appropriating what remained of one year's rent to the rent of the second guardianship, so as to deprive the first guardian of the value of the security which he had taken the pains to procure.

[82] *Moss's Appeal*, 35 Pa 162

tion of the act of June 16th, 1836, are goods "taken by virtue of
an execution " An attachment under the act of July 12th, 1842,
entitled "An Act to Abolish Imprisonment for Debt and to Pun-
ish Fraudulent Debtors," is such an execution, when it is followed by judgment and execution [83] An execution issued to a
constable by a justice of the peace,[84] as well as one issued to the
sheriff or coroner by the common pleas or other court of record,
is intended by the act   The judgment and the execution may
be for a portion of the rent. This will not preclude a claim for
another portion of the rent, if the claimant is not the execution
plaintiff.[85] A receiver of a partnership business makes a sale of
goods on the premises. The landlord is not entitled to his rent
from the proceeds.[86]

345. The demise.— The goods and chattels on any lands "demised for life or years or otherwise" are, by the 83rd section of
the act of June 16, 1836, subjected to the rent. A grant of land
in fee, subject to a perpetual ground rent, is not such a demise.
Goods of A on premises held by him in fee subject to two ground
rents, one of $185 per year, payable half-yearly to B, and an-
other of $259 per year, payable half-yearly to C, were levied on
in execution   Though B and C had the right to distrain on the
goods, and to re-enter for arrears, they could not take their rents
from the proceeds of the execution sale. But the ground tenant
making a demise would be the landlord entitled to the preference [87] A demise for any number of years, e g , of mining land
for 99 years, is within the act [88] The demise may be oral[89] or

---

[82]*Morgan* v *Moody*, 6 Watts & S
333   As to foreign attachment *vide*
Pierce v *Scott*, 4 Watts & S 344
   [84]*Allen* v *Lewis*, 1 Ashm (Pa)
184, *Seitzinger* v *Steinberger*, 12
Pa 379, *Lichtenthaler* v *Thompson*,
13 Serg & R. 157, 15 Am Dec 581.
   [85]*Weltner's Appeal*, 63 Pa 302
   [86]*Singerly* v *Fox*, 75 Pa   112
But, why not, on the ground that,
the landlord's right to distrain having been displaced by the law, he

should have a lien on the proceeds?
Lane v *Washington Hotel Co* 190
Pa 230, 42 Atl 697 , *Cooper* v *Rose
Valley Mills*, 174 Pa 302, 34 Atl.
359
   [87]*Pattison* v *M'Gregor*, 9 Watts &
S 180, *Stark* v *Hight*, 3 Pa Super.
Ct 516
   [88]*Moss's Appeal*, 35 Pa 162
   [89]*Greenwood's Appeal*, 79 Pa 294,
Collins's Appeal, 35 Pa 83.

in writing   The lease may be oral for a considerable time, and when reduced to writing may be antedated to the time when orally made. The right to distrain or otherwise collect rent for the period prior to the execution of the writing will depend on the establishment of the prior parol lease.[90] The lease being drawn up in writing, and orally assented to, and possession of the premises being immediately taken by the tenant, the rent from the beginning can be collected, although the tenant declined to sign it until a short time before the levy in execution against him [91]

346. Use and occupation.— Mere occupation of land, with an expectation on the occupant's part and also on the part of the owner, that the former will pay a reasonable compensation for it, does not create a demise giving rise to a right to distrain for the compensation or to claim it from the proceeds of a judicial sale of the occupant's chattels.[92]

347. A cropper.— A cropper is hired to work the land for a share of the produce   He is only a hireling   The possession of the land remains in the owner. Hence, the remedy of distress and of claim against the proceeds of an execution sale of the cropper's chattels is not applicable [93] When possession of the land is given by the owner to another, for a certain time, and he agrees to give to the owner, in consideration of its use, a certain part of its product, he is a tenant [94]

348 Sublessee.— If the lessee assign over to another his whole term, reserving a rent, without a special clause of distress, he cannot distrain for the rent, nor claim proceeds of an execution

[90]*Com ex rel Irwin v Contner,* 21 Pa 266, 18 Pa 439

[91]*Greenwood's Appeal,* 79 Pa 294

[92]*Greenwood's Appeal,* 79 Pa 294, *Com ex rel Irwin* v *Contner,* 21 Pa 266   Cf *Case* v *Davis,* 15 Pa. 80 Cf *Megarge* v *Tanner,* 1 Clark (Pa) 531, where, on making a levy, the sheriff removed the goods to the property of X, and detained them until the sale of the goods

[93]*Steel* v *Frick,* 56 Pa 172, *Fry* v *Jones,* 2 Rawle, 11, *Adams* v *McKesson,* 53 Pa 81. 91 Am Dec 183

[94]*Steel* v *Frick,* 56 Pa 172, *Rinehart* v *Olwine,* 5 Watts & S 157, *Fry* v *Jones,* 2 Rawle 11 Cf *Brown* v. *Jaquette,* 8 W N C 475

sale of the assignee's goods [95] If the lessee sub-lets, *i e.,* reserves
to himself a reversion and rent, the right of distress is incident.
Hence, when A leased July 28th, 1831, iron works to B for five
years from November 1st, 1831, and B on August 27th, 1831,
rented them for one year to C, and this sublease was renewed
from year to year, and on March 23rd, 1835, during the fourth
year of the sublease, C's personal property was sold in execution,
B was entitled to a landlord's priority in the distribution of the
proceeds.[96]

349 Interval between lease and commencement of term.—The
demise does not begin, so as to give rise to rent for which distress can be made, with the mere making of the lease   That
may precede by weeks, months, or years the commencement of
the term   A sheriff's sale of the goods of the tenant on the
premises before the inception of the term would not make payable from its proceeds any rent on account of the lease. So,
being in under one lease, a second lease may be made to the
tenant some time before the close of the first lease. If a sheriff's
levy were made between the making of the second lease and the
commencement of the term created by it, no rent arising from
that term would be payable from the proceeds of the sale.[97]

350. Change of landlord — The reversion may be sold, or pass
by inheritance or devise. The alienee, heir, or devisee will then
become landlord as to all rent falling due subsequently, and
have the landlord's right with respect to the proceeds of an execution   A lessor dying in September, his devisee could claim
for the quarter's rent becoming due on September 30th, and for
the following rent [98]   A, having leased the land for ten years
from April 1st, 1844, at an annual rent, payable at the end of
the year, conveys it to B January 2, 1845, reserving to himself

[95]*Ege* v *Ege,* 5 Watts, 134, *Mc*   [97]*Mortin's Appeal,* 5 Watts & S.
Combs's Appeal, 43 Pa 435   Cf 220 *Moss's Appeal,* 35 Pa 162
Bromley v *Hopewell,* 14 Pa 400   [98]*Lewis's Appeal,* 66 Pa. 312.
[96]*Ege* v *Ege,* 5 Watts, 134

the rent of the current year   B had the landlord's precedence for the rent of the year ending March 31st, 1846 [99]   When a sheriff's sale of the land demised took place on January 1st, 1831, the sheriff's vendee could claim the half year's rent due February 1st, following [100]   Should the lessor alien a part of the demised premises, the alienee will acquire a right to a proportional part of the rent, with the incidental remedies [101]

351 Notice of claim.— The statute does not require notice from the landlord to the officer who executes the writ, or to the execution creditor. Notice to the officer has, however, been held to be necessary   Without it, the landlord loses his right to share in the fund produced by the execution sale, and the execution creditor must be paid without diminution on account of rent in arrear [102]   It is not distinctly decided whether the notice must be in writing.   For obvious reasons, it should be, and, in the reported cases, has been, written [103]   The notice must be from the landlord, or from his attorney [104]   No adjudication defines the necessary form or contents of the notice.   It should, doubtless, refer to the execution, identifying it, should aver that the claimant is landlord of the defendant, with respect to the premises on which the goods are, that rent is due to him as such, naming the amount thereof, and that this rent is for a period not greater than one year, and should express the claim of the landlord to receive this rent from the proceeds of the execution sale [105]   The notice is not "required to contain every element of precision "

---

[99]*Greider's Appeal*, 5 Pa 422, *Mc-Combs's Appeal*, 43 Pa 435

[100]*Hoskins* v *Houston*, 2 Clark (Pa) 489, *Bank of Pennsylvania* v *Wise*, 3 Watts, 394, *Boyd* v *Mc-Combs*, 4 Pa 146

[101]*DeCoursey* v *Guarantee Trust & S D Co* 81 Pa 217

[102]*Brown* v *Jaquette*, 8 W N C. 475, *Timmes* v. *Metz*, 156 Pa 384, 27 Atl 248

[103] In *Martin's Appeal*, 5 Watts & S 220, there was an oral notice, and the day following a written notice

[104]*Martin's Appeal*, 5 Watts & S 220, *Greenwood's Appeal*, 79 Pa 294

[105]*Vide Borlin* v *Com* 110 Pa 454, 1 Atl 404, *Timmes* v *Metz*, 156 Pa 384, 27 Atl 248, *Greenwood's Appeal*, 79 Pa 294.

A mistake in the amount of rent claimed does not impair its validity, when the evidence shows that the execution creditor understood the extent, nature, and character of the claim.[106] If the sheriff accepts and acts on the notice, it is too late, in distribution of the proceeds of sale, to object to its sufficiency.[107] If, immediately after the issue of an execution and a levy, an assignment for creditors is made, and the sheriff deputizes the assignee to sell the goods, a notice to the latter will be sufficient.[108]

352. Notice, when it must be given — The notice need not be given prior to the levy, nor shortly after the levy. In several cases, it has been effectively given a few days before the sale. Thus, the fi. fa. issuing to the April term, a sale was made on March 23d. The notice on March 17th was good.[109] Given on the day of sale it has been held valid.[110] The fact that the sale is made after the return day does not make postponement of notice until sale improper [111] If no sale is made on the fi. fa. for want of buyers, and the writ is returned, a notice before the return to the *vend. ex.*, that the writ was stayed, is early enough to make the sheriff responsible to the landlord [112] Since the officer, if he sells before the return day, may keep the money until the return day, he will become liable to the landlord if, the sale occurring ten days before the return day, he pays the proceeds over to the execution creditor on the day after the

[106]*Timmes* v *Metz*, 156 Pa. 384, 27 Atl 248 At the date of sale the rent, apportioned to levy, was $1,168 88 A few days of the current month had yet to run The notice stated the rent to be $1,250 00

[107]*Greenwood's Appeal*, 79 Pa. 294.

[108]*Leidich's Estate*, 161 Pa 451, 29 Atl 89, 90

[109]*Ege* v *Ege*, 5 Watts, 134 Rogers, J, thought the notice in time, if given before the money was paid over.

[110]*Lewis's Appeal*, 66 Pa. 312. *Martin's Appeal*, 5 Watts & S 220, *Timmes* v *Metz*, 156 Pa 384, 27 Atl. 248

[111]*Ege* v. *Ege*, 5 Watts, 134

[112]*Borlin* v. *Com* 110 Pa 454, 1 Atl. 404 Levy July 23rd, 1888, notice February 22d, 1889, sale March 4th, 1889. The landlord was awarded the rent *Minnig* v. *Sterrett*, 7 Pa. Co Ct. 73.

sale and the landlord gives him notice before the return day [117]
A notice after the sale, if the landlord had no knowledge of the
proceeding before, and if the officer has not paid over the proceeds nor returned the writ, will not be too late. The constable,
if he ignores the notice, will be liable.[114] A notice after a stay
of execution, and the subsequent sale by the debtor of his goods,
is too late;[115] as is one after a sale in execution to the plaintiff in the writ, and after a settlement with the sheriff, by
the purchaser, by an exchange of receipts, though the landlord
had no knowledge of the execution.[116] In *Mitchell* v *Stewart*,[117] a levy was made May 27th, 1819   The defendant induced the sheriff to relinquish possession by giving a bond conditioned to produce the goods, or to discharge the debt   On November 1st, 1819, defendant paid $100 to the sheriff, and de-
livered goods which the sheriff subsequently sold for enough to
pay the debt. On February 7th, 1820, the proceeds of that sale
undergoing distribution, the court ordered the landlord to be
paid. No notice prior to this day had been given of the landlord's claim. It was too late, the writ having been returned,
said Gibson, J.

353 Staying the writ.—The 85th section of the act of June
16th, 1836,[118] directs that whenever goods liable to the payment
of rent shall be seized in execution, the proceedings thereupon
shall not be stayed by the plaintiff therein without the consent,
in writing, of the person entitled to the rent, first obtained. The
officer who has charge of the writ, sheriff or constable, will be
liable to the landlord on his official bond or recognizance if he
permits the writ to be stayed in violation of this command of the
statute,[119] or possibly may, on a rule granted on the landlord's

[113]*Fisher* v *Allen*, 2 Phila 115
[114]*Allen* v *Lewis*, 1 Ashm (Pa)
184
[115]*Work s Appeal*, 92 Pa 258
[116]*Schuyler* v *Philadelphia Coach*
Co 29 W N C 343.

[117] 13 Serg & R 295
[118] 1 Pepper & Lewis Digest, 2644;
P L 755
[119]*Borlin* v *Com.* 110 Pa 454, 1
Atl 404.

petition, be directed by the court having control of the execution, to pay him the rent.[120] The fi fa. being returned "unsold for want of buyers," a *vend ex.* subsequently issued. The defendant paid a portion of the debt to the plaintiff in the writ, and, at his direction, the sheriff, having notice of the landlord's claim, then returned it "stayed by order of the plaintiff." The sheriff and his sureties were responsible upon his recognizance.[121] Before the levy was made, the defendant in the execution had advertised a vendue of his property. After the levy the creditor and he agreed that this vendue might proceed, and the sheriff was notified not to advertise the sale The sheriff took no further action on the writ The vendue was held a week after the levy Three days after the vendue, which was five days after the return day of the writ, the landlord notified the sheriff of his claim to rent, and, upon his rule, the court directed the sheriff to pay the rent. Though the writ had been practically stayed by the plaintiff in it, without the consent of the landlord, it was held by the supreme court that the landlord had unduly postponed the giving of the notice, and the order of the court below was reversed Had that notice been given before the vendue, the sheriff might have resumed possession of the goods But, when it came to him, it was too late for him to retake the goods [122] If the landlord proves his whole claim for rent before the referee in bankruptcy proceedings, begun by the tenant, he thereby relinquishes his right to take the rent from the proceeds of an execution After such relinquishment the execution creditor may satisfy the judgment. The landlord, subsequently amending his claim for rent before the referee, so as to claim only the excess beyond what he was entitled to from the proceeds of the execution, cannot have the satisfaction of the judgment stricken off, in order that he may be subrogated to it, to

[120]*Work's Appeal,* 92 Pa 258   [122]*Work's Appeal,* 92 Pa 258
[121]*Borlin* v *Com* 110 Pa 454, 1
Atl 404.

the extent of the unpaid rent, even for the purpose of reaching the property set apart to the tenant under the exemption law [123]

354 Landlord's claim postponed to that of laborer.—The act of May 12th, 1891,[124] protects the wages of laborers of various classes, for any period not exceeding six months, and for any amount not exceeding $200; declaring that the wages "shall be preferred and first paid out of the proceeds of the sale" of the real and personal property of the employer, by execution or otherwise, on account of the death or insolvency of such person Similar acts had preceded it The phrase "shall be preferred and first paid," in the act of April 9th, 1872, it was held, conferred on the laborer a right to be paid in advance, not simply of the execution creditor, but of the landlord [125] The same interpretation was put on it, in the act of June 13th, 1883 [126] Under the act of Congress of July 20th, 1868, taxes on distilled liquors were declared to be "a first lien on the spirits distilled, the distillery used for distilling the same, the stills, vessels, fixtures, and tools therein," as well as on the ground on which the distillery was situated The taxes must be paid in preference to the landlord, or to the execution creditor whose writ has produced the sale.[127]

355. Bankruptcy.— When, by proceedings in bankruptcy, begun between the issue of an execution against the bankrupt and

---

[123]*Turrell* v. *Ball,* 26 Pa Co Ct. 36 The lease contained no waiver of the exemption The judgment creditor may waive the waiver of the exemption, without the consent of the landlord

[124] 2 Pepper & Lewis Digest, 4788, P L 54

[125]*Riddlesburg Coal & I Co's Appeal,* 114 Pa 58, 6 Atl 381, *Huntingdon & B T R Co's Appeal* 114 Pa 66; *Ellenwold Coal Co's Assignment,* 9 Lanc Bar, 144, *Noll* v *Kline,* 1 Del Co Rep 101, *Perrept* v. *Frankenfield,* 2 Del Co Rep 112;

Nogle v *Cumberland Ore Bank Co* 1 Chester Co Rep 491, *Woodmansie* v *Boyer,* 1 Lehigh Valley L R 106, *O'Brien* v *Hamilton.* 12 Phila 387 *Contra, Maloy's Estate,* 1 Del Co Rep 331 The principle of *Wood's Appeal,* 30 Pa 274, arising under the act of April 2d 1849, and deciding that miners got by it no preference over landlords, is not applicable to the later acts

[126] P L 116, *Timmes* v *Metz* 156 Pa 384, 27 Atl 248

[127]*Dungan's Appeal,* 68 Pa 204

the levy thereunder on the chattels of the tenant on the demised premises, the title passes to the assignee or trustee in bankruptcy, but subject to the lien of the execution, it will also pass subject to the landlord's prior right to payment from the proceeds of a sale.[128] In *Evans* v. *Lincoln Co.*[129] the trustee in bankruptcy of the tenant sold goods to the landlord, agreeing that the rent for which the latter had a preference might be set off against the price. The landlord having got possession of the premises during the term, and relet them, could claim only the difference between the rent reserved on the original lease, and that obtained under the new lease.

356. Costs.— The 84th section of the act of June 16th, 1836,[130] provides that if the proceeds of a sale in execution are insufficient to pay the landlord, together with the costs of execution, only so much of the costs shall be paid as the landlord would have been liable to had he sold under a distress. When the landlord claims from its proceeds he adopts the execution as the equivalent of a distress, hence, the sheriff is entitled to his costs in full. The costs referred to in the act are the costs mentioned in the execution. The sheriff's costs are never so mentioned [131]

357. Liability of sheriff, constable.— The officer (and his official sureties) who conducts the execution will be responsible to the landlord if he fails to perform his duty toward him. If, e g , the sheriff refrains from sale on a stay of the writ to which the landlord, who has given due notice of his claim, does not consent, he and his sureties will be liable on his recognizance [132] He

---

[128]*Barnes's Appeal,* 76 Pa 50   Cf. *Longstreth* v *Pennock,* 9 Phila 394
[129] 204 Pa 448, 54 Atl 321
[130] 1 Pepper & Lewis Digest, 1956, P. L 755
[131]*Hennis* v *Streeper,* 1 Miles (Pa 269
[132]*Borlin* v *Com.* 110 Pa 454, 1 Atl 404

In a suit by the execution creditor, upon the recognizance. the plaintiff cannot recover more than the amount of his debt, less the landlord's rent, if the goods levied on could not have yielded more *Com ex rel Irwin* v. *Contner,* 21 Pa 266

will be liable for paying the product of the execution sale over to the creditor too soon after the sale, and too long before the return day of the writ, although the landlord, not having learned of the execution, has given no notice to him [133] A constable who removes the goods after levy, and sells enough of them to pay the debt only, and then, for the first time, receives a notice from the landlord, should either return the goods to the premises, in order that the landlord may there distrain upon them, or he should make a further sale for the landlord's benefit. If he does neither he will be liable.[134] If notice of the landlord's claim comes only after the sale of all the goods and the money has been paid over, actually or virtually, the sheriff will be liable for nothing.[135] If the sheriff pays the proceeds to the landlord, when he should not, he will be liable to the execution creditor [136]

358. Landlord's preference in assignments.—The 1st section of the act of May 26th, 1891,[137] enacts that when any tenant makes an assignment for the benefit of creditors, of goods on the demised premises which are liable to distress for rent, the landlord shall receive, from the proceeds of the sale of such goods by the assignee, rent due him at the making of the assignment, not exceeding one year's. If these proceeds are not sufficient to pay the landlord and the costs of the assignment, so much of the costs[138] shall be deducted as the landlord would be liable to pay

---

[133]*Fisher* v *Allen*, 2 Phila 115

[134]*Allen* v *Lewis*, 1 Ashm. (Pa) 184. The jurisdiction of a justice in such cases is denied in *Seitzinger* v *Steinberger*, 12 Pa 379

[135]*Schuyler* v. *Philadelphia Coach Co* 29 W. N C. 343

[136]*Burchard* v. *Rees*, 1 Whart 377.

[137] 1 Pepper & Lewis Digest, 202, P L 122 This act was not retrospective. *Re Glazier*, 33 W N. C 310

Formerly, the assigned goods, so soon as they were removed from the premises, ceased to be subject to distress, and the landlord had no right to payment from the proceeds of their subsequent sale. *Morris* v *Parker*, 1 Ashm (Pa) 187, *Re Ellenwold Coal Co.* 7 Luzerne Leg Reg 19, 9 Lanc Bar, 144

The assignee might, by contract, bind the goods for the rent for which the landlord could have distrained *Osborne's Estate*, 5 Whart 267; *Maloy's Estate*, 1 Del Co Rep 331

[138] This rule was applied in *Lane* v. *Washington Hotel Co* 190 Pa

in case of a sale under distress, and the residue shall be paid to him The 31st section of the act of June 4th, 1901,[139] enacts that "any lien or claim for wages, for the rent of mechanics or materialmen, or otherwise, which, by virtue of any act of assembly, would be preferred in case of an execution, shall retain its preference in case of an assignment, and to the same extent." If goods of another are on the demised premises when the assignment is made,—*e. g.*, a cider press, lent to the tenant with a provision for its sale to him,—and such goods are sold by the assignee, the landlord, as against its owner, will be entitled to its proceeds for rent in arrear [140]

359 Landlord's preference when lessee dies — The 21st section of the act of February 24th, 1834,[141] directs that all debts owing by any person at his death shall be paid by his executors or administrators in the following order "(1) Funeral expenses, medicine furnished and medical attendance given during the last illness of the deceased, and servants' wages, not exceeding one year , (2) rents, not exceeding one year ; (3) all other debts, without regard to their quality, except debts due to the state; (4) debts due to the state " The preference thus given is not conditioned on the presence of distrainable goods on the premises at the time of the lessee's death   Payment will be allowed, though, at his death, he had no goods on the premises [142] Rent which, at the lessee's death, has become overdue, and so much of rent accruing but not yet due as represents the ratio between the portion of the rent period within which the death occurred, that

---

230, 42 Atl 697, where a receiver took charge of a leased hotel and finally sold the goods in it The landlord had a right to the proceeds less so much costs as under the rule, should be deducted No deduction was made for receiver's commissions, counsel fees, etc.

[139] P L 404

[140]*Barnhart's Estate,* 13 York Legal Record, 129

[141] 1 Pepper & Lewis Digest, 1432, P L 70

[142]*Dawson's Estate,* 4 Lanc L Rev 343 35 Pittsb L J 63 Bell P J, expressed the opinion in *Re Ralston,* 2 Clark (Pa) 224, that the preference was in aid and lieu of the distress and for rent for which the lessor might distrain at the death of the tenant

preceded the death, and the portion following, are entitled to the preference.[143]   Rent, e g., being payable quarterly, and the tenant dying one month after the commencement of one quarter, the lessor was entitled to receive, under the statutory preference, one third of the quarter's rent[144]   The rent being payable yearly, at the end of the year, and the year ending April 1st, 1842, if the tenant died Oct. 6th, 1841, rent for six months and six days was payable to the landlord before general creditors were paid [145]   So much of the rent becoming payable by the terms of the contract, after the tenant's death, as accrues likewise after his death, is entitled to no preference, though, like other debts, it is entitled to a ratable payment, if the estate is insolvent.[146]   As the rent allowed a preference does not exceed one year's, when a year's rent due before the tenant's death is claimed, interest on it will not be preferred.[147]   It would have to share ratably with other debts   The agreement between lessor and lessee stipulating that the rent shall be $3,000, with the addition of taxes upon the additional valuation which may be assessed upon this property for the year, above the assessment of 1887, this tax is a part of the rent, and, with the rent proper, may be paid from an insolvent tenant's estate, in preference to other creditors,[148] and under an agreement that the tenant should pay for any gas used on the premises and all water rents, which made the water rents a part of the rent, they were entitled to preferential payment.[149]   Several cotenants of

---

[143]*Jaquette's Estate*, I Chester Co Rep 197

[144]*Kemp's Estate*, 34 Pittsb L J 82, *Walker's Estate*, 9 Pa Co Ct 515

[145] In *Re M'Kim's Estate*, 2 Clark (Pa) 224, so the auditor decided, and no exception was taken by creditors   Bell, P J , doubted

[146]*Rainow's Estate*, 4 Kulp, 153

[147]*Vandegriff's Estate*, 3 Pa Dist. R 421.

[148]*Morgan's Estate*, 11 Pa. Co Ct. 536

A widow to whom dower has been awarded may distrain for the annual interest on the sum set apart as rent   She is entitled to a preference only for one year's interest   *Turner* v *Hauser*, 1 Watts, 420

[149]*Scott s Estate*, 35 Pittsb L. J 443   But a lien for the water rents that the tenant had neglected to pay, being filed, and an execution issued,

coal land agree that B, one of them, "may have the privilege of taking coal," he paying to the owners their proportions of the sum of 25 cents per cubic yard of coal taken out, as rent. On B's death, insolvent, the cotenants were entitled to be paid in full the rent that had become payable before.[150] The rent preferred is not more than one year's, but it does not need to be the rent of the last year of the tenancy or of any particular year.[151]

the costs which the landlord had to   [150]*Greenough's Appeal*, 9 Pa. 18
pay, in order to prevent a sale of the   [151]*Morgan's Estate*, 11 Pa. Co. Ct
premises, would not be entitled to   536.
the preference.

CHAPTER XIX.

TENANCY AT WILL AND FROM YEAR TO YEAR.

360. Tenancy at will.— The lease may be terminable at any time at the will of the lessor, the parties so contracting. It may be made terminable after giving a certain notice, the lessor being able to give this notice at any time. The lessee agreeing to remove and give peaceable possession to the lessor within fifteen days after receiving notice so to do, at the expiration of that time after the notice, the lessor may begin ejectment and recover the land [1] The lease may be made terminable upon three months' notice, in case of a sale of the reversion. The mere fact of sale and of knowledge of it by the tenant would not end his term. If in the fall he surrenders the term, on receiving knowl-

---

[1] *Matthews* v *Rising*, 31 Pittsb L. J N S. 163 The lease also contained the covenant that if the rent remained unpaid the lessor might re-enter on fifteen days' notice.

edge of the sale, without notice from the landlord to give up in three months, he does not lose the right to the way-going crop then in the ground.[2]   A lease of a house in a cemetery, by a cemetery company, provided for a six months' notice to quit when the company should have occasion for part of the house The lessor had no right to terminate the term by a six months' notice, until the house was needed for some proper purpose connected with its business   Possession could not be recovered from the tenant without proof of such need [3]

361. Will of tenant.— The lease may be terminable by the tenant on notice, _e g_, on one month's notice   The lease being of the privilege of occupying the Academy of Music upon certain nights, the lessee may show a custom under which lessees for such purposes may give a month's notice of the desire to cancel the lease, and a notice given in conformity with the custom will terminate his liabilities as respects future rent.[4]

362   Unenforceable contract — A contract which leaves some of its terms—_e g_, the rent to be paid—to be settled later is, until such settlement, unenforceable   But if possession of the premises is taken under it the lessee becomes a tenant at will, who if allowed to remain for a year and longer by the lessor will become a tenant from year to year, exactly as if the contract, though complete in all its terms, had been for more than three years, and in parol [5]

363. Lease from year to year.— A lease may be from year to year, though the rent is payable at the end of shorter intermediate periods, _e g_, quarters,[6] or months [7]   If no time is men-

---

[2]_Comfort_   v   _Duncan,_   1   Miles (Pa) 229

[3]_Woodland Cemetery Co_ v _Carville_, 9 Phila Leg Int 98

[4]_American Academy of Music_ v _Bert_, 8 Pa Co Ct 223

[5]_Walter_ v _Transue_, 22 Pa Super Ct 617   The rent was to be 25 cents per 1,000 bricks made on the premises by the tenant, or 50 bricks out of every 1,000 made, as the parties should subsequently determine

[6]_Lloyd_ v _Cozens_ 2 Ashm (Pa) 131, _Lesley_ v _Randolph_, 4 Rawle, 123   A lease "by the year" is a lease for one year only   _Pleasants_ v _Claghorn_, 2 Miles (Pa) 302

[7]_Goldsmith_ v _Smith_, 4 Phila 31;

tioned as the limit of the term, but the letting is stated to be at an annual rent, e g., of $800,[8] or at an annual rent of, e g.,$300, payable in monthly instalments,[9] the lease will be from year to year   Indeed, in *Brown* v. *Butler*,[10] Sharswood, J , says of a lease at "$12.50 per month, without specifying any time," that it was from year to year. A contract by which B is put in possession of a house, makes repairs, and has the right to remain until, at the rate of $60 per year, the rent reimburses him for the repairs,—makes him, after he has been in possession for several years, a tenant from year to year, entitled to notice to quit, if it does not (as it does), make him a tenant for a term to be defined by the expenditures in the improvements[11]   There can be no doubt when the lease expressly states that it is from year to year   In *Woelpper* v. *Philadelphia*,[12] the city, under an ordinance providing for a lease of market stalls to the highest bidders, the successful bidders becoming tenants from year to year at a fixed rent, leased stalls to X, who, as highest bidder, paid $2,240 for the lease. When, twenty years afterwards, the city tore down the market house, he was not entitled to be reimbursed this money. "He paid his money voluntarily for the privilege of becoming a tenant, and he enjoyed all the advantages of his position from 1835 to the time of the removal of the sheds." A lease of an iron-furnace to continue as long as the lessor receives a revenue of not less than $1,000 a year royalty on account of iron made, and to be voidable at the option of the lessor, if the tenant should fail to pay $1,000 per year, was

Brown v *Butler,* 4 Phila 71, *Hey* v. *McGrath,* 81* Pa 310, *Milling* v *Becker,* 96 Pa 182, *Arrott Steam Power Mills Co* v *Way Mfg Co* 143 Pa 435, 22 Atl 699

[8]*Lesley* v *Randolph,* 4 Rawle, 123

[9]*Hey* v *McGrath,* 81* Pa 310, *Jones* v. *Kroll,* 116 Pa. 85, 8 Atl. 857.

[10] 4 Phila 71

[11]*Thomas* v *Wright,* 9 Serg & R 87

[12] 38 Pa. 203   Cf *Boggs* v *Black,* 1 Binn 333   Cf *Moore* v *Miller,* 8 Pa 272, where the lease was to dig ore, but whether it was at will or from year to year was referred to the jury.

more than a lease at will. It created at least a tenancy from
year to year.[13]

364. Expiration of term.— If, after the expiration of a definite term, the tenant continues in possession, he may be treated
as a trespasser,[14] or as a tenant at will. And if he is treated as
a tenant at will, he becomes, *ipso facto,* a tenant from year to
year, and is entitled to notice to quit, notwithstanding the death
of the lessor during the hold-over year.[15]

365. Statute of frauds.— A parol lease for more than three
years,[16] or for three years which are to begin at a time future to
the making of the lease,[17] or a written lease made by an agent
of the owner, whose authority is not in writing,[18] will constitute
the lessee a mere tenant at will, who can be ejected at any time.
But one of the incidents of an estate at will is its convertibility,
upon the annual payment and acceptance of the rent, into a
tenancy from year to year. A parol demise for more than three
years is changed into a tenancy from year to year, if the lessor
allows the tenant to remain in possession a year, and receives
the prescribed rent from him for the year,[19] or otherwise mani-

---

[13]*Heck* v *Borda*, 18 W N. C. 212
The lessor could recover damages for
the breach of the covenant to give
up possession of the premises "in as
good condition as when put in blast,
wear and tear excepted"

[14] He may be ejected *Overdeer* v
Lewis, 1 Watts & S 90, 37 Am Dec
440, *Adams* v *Adams,* 7 Phila 160

[15]*Hanbest* v *Grayson*, 200 Pa 59,
11 Pa Dist R 497, 55 Atl 786

[16]*M'Dowell* v *Simpson*, 3 Watts,
129, 27 Am Dec 338, *Dumn* v
Rothermel, 112 Pa. 272, 3 Atl 800,
Jones v *Peterman*, 3 Serg & R 543,
8 Am Dec 672; *Loran's Estate*, 10
Pa Co Ct. 554.

[17]*Whiting* v *Pittsburgh Opera
House Co* 88 Pa. 100, *Jennings* v
McComb, 112 Pa. 518, 4 Atl 812.

[18]*M'Dowell* v. *Simpson*, 3 Watts,

129, 27 Am. Dec. 338, *Dumn* v
Rothermel, 112 Pa 272, 3 Atl. 800,
Jennings v *McComb*, 112 Pa 518, 4
Atl 812

[19]*Dumn* v *Rothermel*, 112 Pa 272,
3 Atl 800, *Walter* v. *Transue*, 22
Pa. Super Ct 617, *M'Dowell* v.
Simpson, 3 Watts, 129, 27 Am Dec.
338, *Phœnixville* v *Walters*, 184 Pa.
615, 39 Atl 490, *Muller's Estate*, 16
Phila 321. In *Clark* v *Smith*, 25
Pa 137, a parol gift of land to X,
followed by his possession for three
years, was said to make him a tenant from year to year so that the donor, not having the possession, could
not maintain trespass *q. c. f* In
Heartzog v *Borgel*, 7 Pa Super Ct
257, a parol donee, it was held, could
be ejected at any time by the donor
or his devisee.

fests the intention to treat the tenant as one from year to year. Hence, the tenant under a parol lease for ten years may vacate the premises, without responsibility for after-accruing rent, at the end of the first or any later year.[20]

366. Sheriff's sale of reversion.— When the reversion is sold, in execution, pending the lease, on a lien which antedated it, the purchaser may recognize the lessee as a tenant or may require the possession to be given up to him, under §§ 105,[21] 111,[22] and 119[23] of the act of June 16, 1836. The lessee becomes a tenant at will.[24] A tenant of the purchaser from a vendee of land, the purchase being subsequent to a judgment against the vendee, has no right to the possession as against the purchaser at the sheriff's sale under the judgment. The latter may enter the premises and set the goods of the tenant out upon the highway, without being liable to an action of trespass.[25]

367. Notice to quit.— When the lessee is one from year to year or has become such by holding over beyond the term, he has a right to continue in possession until he receives a notice to quit. The notice must designate the proper time to quit, *viz.*, the close of the year. A notice, *e. g.*, in the first month of the year, to leave in three months, would be ineffectual.[26] The notice must be unconditionally to quit. A notice not sufficiently unequivocal to show the landlord's intention that the premises shall be vacated,[27] *e g ,* to leave or pay an increased rent,[28] or

[20]*Loran's Estate,* 10 Pa Co Ct. 66, 554. A ratification after the death of the tenant, by the lessor, will not make the lease valid for the entire term

[21]1 Pepper & Lewis Digest, 1987; P L 755.

[22]1 Pepper & Lewis Digest, 1990, P L 755

[23]1 Pepper & Lewis Digest, 1993, P L. 755.

[24]*Duff* v *Wilson,* 69 Pa 316, *Adams* v *McKesson,* 53 Pa 81, 91 Am Dec 183, *Bittinger* v *Baker,* 29 Pa.

70 Am Dec 154 Cf. *Hemphill* v *Tevis,* 4 Watts & S 535, *Wilson* v *Hubbell,* 1 Pennyp 413

[25]*Kellam* v *Janson,* 17 Pa 467

[26]*Brown* v. *Vanhorn,* 1 Binn. 334, note, *Fahnestock* v *Faustenauer,* 5 Serg & R 174, *Dellone* v *Gerber,* 3 York Legal Record, 23

[27]*Dellone* v *Gerber,* 3 York Legal Record, 23

[28]Cf *O'Neill* v *Cahill,* 2 Brewst. (Pa) 357, *Pittfield* v *Ewing,* 6 Phila 455

to leave or pay an increased rent, or purchase the premises,[29] may be ignored by the tenant   The notice to quit must precede by three months the close of the year.[30]   Where the year began April 1 and closed at midnight of March 31 of the following year, it was held that notice given on January 1 was one day too late,[31] though where the term began January 15, a notice on October 15 of the intention to vacate the premises was assumed to be a three months' notice.[32]   But while it must be at least three months long, it may be longer   Thus a notice January 25 to vacate the premises at the end of the year, viz., June 1, was valid[33]   It matters not how the lease from year to year arose If it was an oral lease for more than three years and has become a lease from year to year, the notice must be given to terminate the tenant's right to the possession.[34]

368 Notice by tenant.— Whether a tenant from year to year must give notice, preceding by three months the close of the current year, in order to escape liability for the rent of the following year, if the landlord chooses to hold him liable, is not

[29]*Byrne* v *Funk,* 13 W N C 503 Cf   *Oakford* v *Nirdlinger,* 196 Pa 162, 46 Atl 374

[30]*Logan* v *Herron,* 8 Serg & R 459, *Pickering* v *O'Brien,* 23 Pa. Super Ct 125, *Lesley* v *Randolph,* 4 Rawle, 123, *Redford* v *M'Elherron,* 2 Serg & R 49, *Brown* v *Vanhorn,* 1 Binn 334, note, *Dunn* v *Rothermel,* 112 Pa 272, 3 Atl 800, *Rich* v *Keyser,* 54 Pa 86, *Dellone* v *Gerber,* 3 York Legal Record, 23, *Lloyd* v *Cozens,* 2 Ashm (Pa) 131, *Hey* v *McGrath,* 81* Pa 310, *Thomas* v *Wright,* 9 Serg & R 87, *Fahnestock* v *Faustenauer,* 5 Serg & R 174   A notice on September 20, 1882, was not in time if the year closed on December 4, but was in time if the year closed on December 22   *Dunn* v *Rothermel,* 112 Pa 272, 3 Atl 800   The term beginning January 15, notice on October 15 by the tenant was tacitly assumed to be

a three months' notice   The lease ending January 1, a notice on September 29 was early enough   *Fitzpatrick* v *Childs,* 2 Brewst (Pa) 365.

[31]*Parsons* v *Roumfort,* 2 Pearson (Pa) 81

[32]*Binswanger* v *Dearden,* 132 Pa 229, 19 Atl 32

[33]*Lloyd* v *Cozens,* 2 Ashm (Pa) 131   A tenant from year to year, whose term ended on March 29, was notified in February, 1800 to leave on March 29, 1801   The tenant became a trespasser after the latter date, by remaining in possession *Boggs* v *Black,* 1 Binn 333   Lease expiring March 31, 1901, notice to quit December 28, 1900 is valid *Brown* v *Montgomery,* 21 Pa Super. Ct 262

[34]*Walter* v *Transue,* 22 Pa. Super Ct 617.

entirely clear. It was declared in 1879, by Trunkey, J , to be "not wholly free from doubt."[35] In *Brown* v *Brightly*,[36] it was decided by Arnold, J., that the tenant may leave at the end of the year, without giving any notice A judgment of the district court of Philadelphia that a tenant from quarter to quarter was not required to give notice of an intention to vacate the premises was affirmed by an equally divided court in 1848, in *Cook* v. *Neilson*,[37] and that a tenant from month to month is not required to give notice to the landlord was assumed in *Hollis* v. *Burns*.[38]

369. Contractual duty to give notice—The lease may require from a tenant from year to year notice of his intention to quit. It may prescribe a period and also a mode. It may, *e. g*, require a written notice.[39] But if a verbal notice is received without objection by the lessor or his agent, a written notice will be considered to be waived   The tenant dying, an offer by his executor, in the midst of the year, to surrender possession, though not accepted, is equivalent to notice that the premises will be given up at the end of the year.[40]

370 Revocation of notice—After a notice to quit, the lessor may agree with the tenant that the latter shall continue for another year   Whether because the notice would then be revoked,[41] or on account of the new contract, the tenant would have a right to continue in possession for another year   It would be necessary to distinguish, however, between a willingness on

[35]*Wilgus* v *Whitehead*, 89 Pa 131 In *Loran's Estate*, 10 Pa Co Ct 554, 20 Phila 174, 29 W N C 115, it seems assumed that notice is necessary Knowledge of the tenant's death, and tender of the key to the landlord by the administrator, are said to be equivalent to notice

[38]14 W N C 497, 17 Phila 252 Cf *Lesley* v *Randolph*, 4 Rawle, 123, *Lane* v *Nelson*, 167 Pa 602, 31 Atl 864

LAND & TEN 20.

[37]10 Pa 41 Cf *Goldsmith* v *Smith*, 4 Phila 33

[38]100 Pa 206, 45 Am Rep 379

[39]*Smith* v *Snyder*, 168 Pa 541, 32 Atl 64

[40]*Loran's Estate*, 10 Pa Co Ct 554, 20 Phila 174, 29 W N C 115

[41] Cf *Supplee* v *Timothy*, 124 Pa. 375, 16 Atl 864

the lessor's part, after giving the notice, to treat and actually
treating with the tenant on the one hand, and coming to an
agreement on the other. The former, not resulting in an agreement, would not prolong the tenant's right of possession.[42]

371. Death of lessee.— On the death of a tenant from year to
year, possibly the lease will come to an end at the termination of
the current year without affirmative action by his administrator,
such as retention of possession. The continuance in possession
for four years of two sisters, who had resided with him, will not
be deemed a renewal from year to year of his tenancy, but the
creation of a new lease between the lessor and them [43] Undoubtedly if the administrator gives notice to the landlord that
he will surrender at the end of the current year, and he accordingly withdraws from all possession, there will be no liability
for rent for any subsequent year [44]

372 Lease from quarter to quarter.— A tenancy from quarter
to quarter may be explicitly created by the use of the phrase
It is impliedly created when, no term being defined, the rent
reserved is so much per quarter. A note dated September 24,
1844, addressed by the owner to X, running thus: "Sir. The
rent of the house you occupy will be $250 per quarter, commenc-
ing on the 10th of December next,"—was followed by X's continued possession until June 10. A tenancy from quarter to
quarter, and not from year to year, was created.[45] The tenant
cannot be compelled to leave at the end of any quarter, unless
he has received a quarter's notice to quit, but he may leave at
the end of any quarter without giving notice to the lessor of his
intention to do so.[46]

---

[42]*Brown* v *Montgomery*, 21 Pa.
Super. Ct 262

[43]*Colhoun's Estate*, 8 Pa Co Ct
550 The court, however, admits
that a term from year to year would
continue in the original lessee and
his administrator until it was ended
by surrender or assignment. An
implied surrender is assumed.

[44]*Loran's Estate*, 10 Pa. Co Ct.
554

[45]*Cook* v *Neilson*, 10 Pa. 41, *Manley* v *Dupuy*, 2 Whart 162

[46]*Cook* v *Neilson*, 10 Pa 41. Notice was given four days before the
end of the quarter. The lessee was
not liable for the next quarter's

373. Lease from month to month.— The letting may be explicitly from month to month [47] A letting "for $50 per month," nothing being said about a year, or any other duration of the letting, is a letting from month to month,[48] as is an agreement between A and B that B shall occupy A's land, and pay a rent of $25 at the end of each month, no period of occupancy being otherwise indicated.[49]   The only evidence as to the term being that the tenant of a house has paid $27.50 per month for eight months, the inference that the lease was for a year, or from year to year, or other than from month to month, is not warranted.[50] The lease, though prescribing a monthly rental, may require the tenant to leave at any time on five days' notice. It could not then constitute a tenancy from month to month,[51] and a lease of a room "by the month at $10 a month, payable in advance, to be given over to the same [the lessor] April 1, 1886," creates a term ending April 1st, 1886, and not from month to month.[52]

374. Notice to remove — The tenant under a lease from month to month is not required to vacate at the end of a month unless he has received a month's notice from the landlord that he must then remove, unless the contract provides otherwise. The contract may explicitly require the month's notice from the

rent. Cf. *Lane* v. *Nelson*, 167 Pa 602, 31 Atl 864

[47]*Williams* v *McAnany*, 1 Pa Dist R 128, *Schultz* v *Burlock*, 6 Pa Super Ct 573, *Gault* v *Neal*, 6 Phila. 61, *Vedrtz* v *Levy*, 18 Phila 328

[48]*Hollis* v *Burns*, 100 Pa 206, 45 Am Rep 379, *Jones* v *Kroll*, 116 Pa 85, 8 Atl 857.

[49]*Wall* v *Ullman*, 2 Chester Co Rep 178

[50]*Hess's Estate*, 2 Woodw Dec 339 Cf *Brown* v *Butler*, 4 Phila 71

[51]*E g , Stout Coal Co* v *O'Donell*, 4 Kulp, 495

[52]*Diehl* v *Lee* (Pa) 8 Cent Rep 867, 9 Atl 865   The tenant was lia-

ble for the rent of the whole term If the tenant for a term (which is to run from year to year, until he gives three months' notice, before the end of any year, of his intention then to leave), gives the notice but subsequently states to the lessor that he will be willing to stay on from month to month, who. being a trustee, says he will consult the *cestui que trust* and will let the tenant know in time, and, without hearing, the tenant stays on, he will not become a tenant from month to month, but will be liable to the landlord for the rent of another year *Smith* v *Snyder*, 168 Pa 541, 32 Atl 64.

lessor,[53] or it may require thirty days' written notice[54] or notice of any other duration. If the lease requires the lessor to give notice of his intention to terminate the tenancy, a notice simply requiring the tenant to remove from the premises "which you now hold as tenant under me, at the end of your current term, to wit, the third day of July, 1865," is insufficient, since, not declaring the intention to terminate the tenancy, it assumes that the term will end on the day mentioned, independently of the notice of such intention.[55] The term beginning November 26, 1886, a notice served on November 26, 1891, is insufficient to entitle the lessor to the possession on December 26. A judgment in ejectment having been entered on December 28, on warrant of attorney, the rule to open it was made absolute.[56] The lessee may remove at the end of any month, although he has given no previous notice of his intention,[57] unless he stipulates, as he may, to give thirty days' notice,[58] one month's notice,[59] or notice of any other duration.

375. Necessity of notice to terminate tenancy.—When the lease is to determine at a certain time, there is no occasion for notice from the lessor to the lessee that he must surrender the possession, because the time of termination is as well known to the tenant as to the landlord, and if the tenant wishes to renew the lease, it is his business to apply to the landlord for a renewal. If no such application is made, the landlord has a right to take for granted that the lease is to expire at the appointed time.[60] Hence, if the lease is for less than one year, viz. until April 1st, 1846,[61] or for one year,[62] or other longer time,[63] the landlord

---

[53]Peditz v Levy 18 Phila 328
[54]Gault v Neal, 6 Phila 61
[55]Gault v Neal, 6 Phila 61
[56]Williams v McAnany, 1 Pa Dist R 128
[57]Hollis v Burns, 100 Pa 206, 45 Am Rep 379, Lane v Nelson, 167 Pa 602 31 Atl 864
[58]Gault v Veal, 6 Phila 61
[59]Williams v McAnany, 1 Pa Dist R 128

[60]Logan v Herron, 8 Serg & R 459, Lesley v Randolph, 4 Rawle, 123, Bedford v M'Elherron, 2 Serg & R 49
[61]Frans v Hastings, 9 Pa 273 The notice was given on April 1, 1846 It was, however, the tenant's duty to leave without notice
[62]Logan v Herron, 8 Serg & R. 459, Overdeer v Lewis, 1 Watts & S 90, 37 Am Dec 440, Rich v Keyser,

may re-enter without being a trespasser,[64] or may recover the possession by means of ejectment[65] or the landlord's statutory remedy.[66]   If the lessee is allowed to remain in possession after the term of a series of years, *e. g.,* seventeen, under such circumstances as justify the inference that it is "with the consent" of the lessor, he becomes a tenant from year to year, and as such entitled to three months' notice;[67] but if the lease contains a provision that the lessor may "enter and repossess the premises at the end of the period, of at any time thereafter," and that the lessee shall "deliver up the possession at the expiration of the term without further notice," the landlord does not, by allowing the lessee to remain in possession nine years after the close of the term, lose the right to dispossess him at any time without notice [68]

376. **Contractual necessity to give notice** — The lease, while specifying a term, may likewise stipulate for the lessee's right to continue beyond the term, unless he receives notice from the landlord that the latter will require the possession at the end of the term.   But a clause in the lease for three years, providing that if the tenant continue on the premises beyond that time the contract shall continue in full force for another year, and so from year to year, does not entitle the tenant to remain beyond the three years, unless he receives three months' notice to quit before their expiration,[69] and a requirement of notice to quit for

54 Pa 86, *McCanna* v *Johnston*, 19 Pa 434.

[65]*Bedford* v *M'Elherron*, 2 Serg & R 49, *MacGregor* v *Rawle*, 57 Pa 184, *Williams* v. *Ladew*, 171 Pa 369, 33 Atl 329

[64]*Overdeer* v *Lewis*, 1 Watts & S 90, 37 Am Dec 440

[65]*McCanna* v. *Johnston*, 19 Pa 434, *MacGregor* v. *Rawle*, 57 Pa 184

[66]*Logan* v *Herron*, 8 Serg & R 459

[67]*Bedford* v *M'Elherron*, 2 Serg & R 49

[68]*McCanna* v *Johnston*, 19 Pa 434 In a lease for three years the lessee covenants to give up possession at the end of the term   It was agreed that if he should continue in possession after the termination of the contract, "the contract should continue in force for another year " The tenant is obliged to leave at the end of the term without three months' notice, and can be ejected by the action of ejectment   *MacGregor* v *Rawle*, 57 Pa 184

[69]*MacGregor* v *Rawle*, 57 Pa. 184,

breach of condition, before the normal expiration of the term, is not to be understood as requiring a notice to quit at the expiration of the term.[70] The lease being for eight months, to continue for a year, and so on from year to year, unless either party gives notice to the other before the end of the term that the lease is to terminate, the vendee of the reversion may, before the end of the eight months, give the notice to quit; nor will it be ineffectual, the tenant having attorned to him, because it states that the lease was made by the vendee.[71]

377. Notice by tenant.— When the lease is for one year or other definite period, the tenant, in the absence of a stipulation that unless he gives notice before the end of that period of the intention to leave, he shall be regarded as a tenant for a longer period, need give no notice of the intention to quit at the end of the term. By simply retiring from the possession, he escapes all liability as tenant, for the rent[72] or otherwise. But the lease may require a notice from the tenant, in order to determine it, at the end of the first year or other period The lease, *e. g.,* may be for eight months, and may provide that at the expiration of that time it will be continued for another year, and so from year to year, unless either party shall, before the end of the term, give legal notice to the other that the lease is to terminate.[73] The lease, being for a term of one year, added that "from and after the expiration of the term hereby created this lease shall be deemed to be renewed and in force for another year, and so on from year to year, unless either party shall have

Wilcox v *Montour Iron & Steel Co* 147 Pa 540, 23 Atl 840

[70]*Gill* v *Ogborn,* 1 W N C 28

[71]*Fitzpatrick* v *Childs,* 2 Brewst (Pa) 365 The landlord does not lose the right to end the tenant's term by his notice, by the reception of rent for the first month of the next year, if the rent is received by his agent in ignorance of the lessor's notice and intention to end the tenancy, and the lessor waits four days, in order to inquire into his rights, before tendering back to the tenant the money.

[72]*Dauphin County* v *Bridenhart,* 16 Pa. 458

[73]*Fitzpatrick* v *Childs,* 2 Brewst. (Pa.) 365.

given to the other notice of its intention to determine said tenancy sixty days prior to the expiration of any current year."
Sixty days' notice from the tenant, prior to the end of the first
year, was necessary in order to relieve him from liability for the
rent of the whole of the next year [74]   The lease being for one
year, "with the privilege of four additional years," contained
the provision that either party might determine it "at the end
of said term" by giving three months' notice, but, in default of
such notice, it should continue upon the same terms and conditions for a further period of one year, and so on from year to
year, until the three months' notice was given before the end of
the current year   The tenant could not, by retiring at the end
of the first year without the notice, escape from liability for the
rent of the next year.[75]   But if, the lease being for one year, it
provides that if three months' notice of the intention to quit be
not given before the close of the first year, "this agreement shall
be considered as renewed for the succeeding term of one year,"
it does not require notice from the tenant before the close of
the second year, and he may therefore retire, without notice, at
the end of the second year, and escape liability for rent for any
succeeding time.[76]   The lease, being for one year, provided that
if the lessee should hold over after the year, with the lessor's
consent, it should be deemed a "renewal of this lease, and all
terms, conditions, covenants, and provisos herein contained, for
the term of another year, and so on if the possession is still con-

---

[74] *Wilcox* v *Montour Iron & Steel Co* 147 Pa 540, 23 Atl 840   Paying one month's rent of the next year might be shown not to have been
intended by the tenant to recognize his duty to pay rent for the whole
year, but that duty did not depend on his recognition   It arose from
his not having given the notice. Cf. *Lane* v *Nelson*, 167 Pa 602, 31 Atl
864; *Megargee* v. *Longaker*, 10 Pa Super. Ct. 491.

[75] *Gardiner* v *Bair*, 10 Pa. Super Ct 74

[76] *Stiles* v *Himmelwright*, 16 Pa Super Ct 649   In *McCarroll* v
Clements, 2 W N. C 305, the lease was for one year, and, in default of
notice, was to be considered as re newed for the succeeding term   The
obligation of the tenant to pay the rent for the succeeding term was
treated as turning on his having been in possession after it commenced.

tinued with like consent, after the expiration of this additional
year, from year to year, unless either party shall give three
months' previous notice to the other of an intention to determine
the tenancy at the end of any year   Provided also that, if the
lessors in their option so elect, the failure of the lessee to give
said notice of its desire to determine said tenancy shall be
deemed and taken to be such renewal " The three months' notice under these terms was not required prior to the end of the
third year.   The lessee on vacating the premises at the end of
the second year without notice ceased to be liable for subsequently accruing rent.[77]   The lease for nine months stipulated
that if the lessee continued on the premises after the expiration
of that time, the lease should continue for a further period of
one year, and so on from year to year, until terminated by a
thirty days' notice from either party, prior to the expiration of
the current year.   The lessee having held over after the end of
the nine months was liable for a year's rent   The court instructed the jury that if the tenant held over after the first hold-
over year he was liable, and if he did not he was not liable, for
the rent of the second and later years, submitting also the question whether, early in the first hold-over year, the tenant informed
the lessor that he was going to vacate the premises if a certain
obstruction was not removed, whether, the obstruction not being
removed, he did remove [78]   If on the last day for giving the notice the tenant makes two attempts in business hours to serve notice on the lessor at his place of business, but finds the door locked,
and two days later he mails the notice to the lessor, who the
next day receives it, and subsequently admitting the receipt of
the notice, uses language which causes the tenant to believe that
he has accepted the notice as valid ; and if later the rent is paid

[77] Ashhurst v Eastern Pennsylva-   [78] Oakford v Nirdlinger, 196 Pa.
nia Phonograph Co 166 Pa 357, 31   162, 46 Atl 374.
Atl 116.

in full to the agent of the lessor, who receives it unconditionally and also the keys of the premises,—the notice may be considered as sufficient, or its insufficiency as waived.[79]

[79]*Binswanger* v *Dearden*, 132 Pa. 229 19 Atl 32   Cf *Binswagner* v. *Dearden*, 9 Pa Co Ct. 653.,

CHAPTER XX.

TERMINATION OF THE LESSEE'S INTEREST BY SURRENDER.

378. Surrender of term, consideration.— Like those springing from any other contract, the rights and liabilities growing out of a lease may be terminated by a later agreement between the parties for such termination. If, at the time of the agreement, the lessee has liabilities to perform, *e. g.,* the payment of rent, the release from these liabilities will be a sufficient consideration for his relinquishment of his right to possession, use, and enjoyment of the premises   The opportunity to resume possession and control will be for the landlord a sufficient consideration for his giving up his rights under the covenants of the tenant.[1] A yielding up by the lessor of a part of the rent already due would be a consideration for the tenant's surrender.[2]

---

[1] *Kiester* v *Miller*, 25 Pa 481   [2] *Thropp's Appeal*, 70 Pa 395.

The lease itself may confer the right to surrender, at any time, upon the tenant.[3] The consideration which supports the lease would then support that particular provision of it, but if the lease itself does not confer this right, it can be acquired by the tenant for the future only by a contract supported by a fresh consideration.[4]

379. Verbal surrender valid.— The agreement to surrender may be in writing. When the lease is for a term not exceeding three years, it can always be orally surrendered.[5] "What is wanting to the rescission of an executory contract," says Gibson, Ch. J., "is the assent of the parties; and it may be signified by their words or their acts. The rescission of a lease by express words is called a surrender in fact; and when by acts so irreconcilable to the continuance of the tenure as to imply the same thing, it is called a surrender in law. An implication of surrender is not precluded by the statute of frauds, which concerns a surrender by express words, and of a lease, too, which could not have been validly constituted otherwise than by writing. I take it, therefore, a lease for less than three years, whether written or not, may be surrendered or transferred by an oral expression of assent. The case of an implied surrender, however, as I have already intimated, was never imagined to be within the statute."[6] A verbal surrender of a term which is of more than three years' length, whether at the surrender it has more than three years to run[7] or less,[8] is also valid, where the possession is given

---

[3] *Hooks* v *Forst*, 165 Pa. 238, 30 Atl. 846

[4] *Mannerbach* v *Keppleman*, 2 Woodw. Dec. 137

[5] *Greider's Appeal*, 5 Pa. 422, *Frank* v *Maguire*, 42 Pa. 77, *Kiester* v *Miller*, 25 Pa. 481, *M'Kinney* v *Reader*. 7 Watts, 123, *Magaw* v *Lambert*, 3 Pa. St. 444

[6] *M'Kinney* v *Reader*, 7 Watts, 123. The desertion of the premises by the tenant he considers an implied surrender

[7] *Auer* v *Penn*, 92 Pa. 444 In *Lobach* v *Breisoh*, 8 Northampton Co. Rep. 193, on a lease for ten years, an assignment for five years with the privilege of five additional years was written, but, though the lessee agreed to it, he did not sign it He obtained the written consent of the lessor to it, and the assignee accepted the lease in writing It was held that this assignment for five years, at least, was, though oral, valid for three years, and that the

316 LANDLORD AND TENANT.

up by the tenant,[9] or where exclusive possession has never been taken by him [10] The surrender may be of the lease as to the entire premises or as to a part only."[11] A sealed lease can be surrendered orally [12]

380. **Surrender by new lease** — The execution of a new lease to the tenant for the same premises for a term coinciding in part with that of the earlier lease,[13] or of a contract of sale of the premises taking effect during the term, would be a rescission of the former lease and a surrender by the tenant of the former term. Thus, the landlord may sell the reversion to X. X, some years before the expiration of the lease, may enter into articles of agreement with the tenant, according to which the tenant is to pay him the same rent as heretofore, until a certain day, which is earlier than the termination of the lease, when X will make a deed to him This is in substance a surrender of the lease, and X must therefore be considered as having gained possession under the deed from the lessor.[14] The burden is on the party who alleges the new lease to prove it. If the landlord, in the exercise of a power in the first lease to terminate the possession of the tenant, gives a three months' notice to quit, the tenant asserting that this lease has been displaced by another, under which he has a right to continue in possession, must prove

lease was surrendered, and a new lease with the assignee substituted, at least for the three years

[9]*Pratt* v *Richards Jewelry Co* 69 Pa 53

[10]*Auer* v *Penn* 922 Pa 444 *Roh- bock* v *McCargo*, 6 Pa Super Ct 134, *Pratt* v *Richards Jewelry Co* 69 Pa 53 *West* v *Connell* 6 Montg Co L Rep 196, *Morgan* v *Luzerne Lodge*, 5 Kulp, 512 Lease for five years During the second year the surety died The lessor, lessee and administrator of the surety may agree that the lease shall

end at the close of the second year. *Reber* v *Gilson*, 1 Pa St 54

[10]*Cochran* v *Shenango Natural Gas Co* 23 Pittsb L J N S 82

[11]*Tate* v *Reynolds*, 8 Watts & S 91

[12]*Kiester* v *Miller* 25 Pa 481

[13]If, the landlord alleging a forfeiture of the old lease, the tenant accepts a new lease, he virtually surrenders the former *Carnegie Natural Gas Co* v *Philadelphia Co* 158 Pa 317, 27 Atl 951

[14]*Denison* v. *Wertz*, 7 Serg. & R. 372.

the second lease.[15] Judgment being entered for rent in arrear, under a warrant of attorney contained in the lease, the court discharged a rule to open it on the ground that the landlord had agreed to accept a surrender of the term, for the reason that the court was not convinced that such an agreement had been made.[16] Possibly the new lease, in order to work a surrender of the old term, would need to be itself valid. A lease from month to month was alleged by the tenant to have been superseded by a new lease by the secretary of the lessor, a corporation, for a term lasting until the city of Philadelphia should take the ground for a street,—an occurrence not expected for ten or twenty years. Judgment in ejectment having been entered on a warrant contained in the original lease, the court properly discharged the rule to open it, because the power of the secretary to make a lease for the corporation was not apparent, and because the alleged new lease, being in parol, "was void under the statute of frauds."[17] An agreement in the midst of the term, for the payment of increased rent for the future, is not a surrender of the existing term, and the beginning of a new term.[18]

381 Form of surrender—"To constitute an express surrender, no set form of words is necessary, nor is it required there should be a formal redelivery or cancelation of the deed or other instrument which created the estate to be surrendered. All that is requisite is the agreement and assent of the proper parties manifesting such an intent, followed by a yielding up of the possession to him who hath the greater estate; for a surrender

[15]*Gibson* v *Vetter*, 162 Pa 26, 29 Atl 292 A judgment in ejectment having been entered on the warrant of attorney, on a rule to open it the oath of the tenant and his wife, contradicted by that of the landlord, was deemed insufficient to prove the new lease

[16]*Philadelphia* v *Weaver*, 155 Pa. 74, 25 Atl 876

[17]*Ellis* v *Ambler*, 11 Pa Super Ct 406 Of course the authority of the secretary to terminate the first lease was not shown The agent who makes the new lease. must have authority *Philadelphia* v *Elvins*, 1 W N C 2

[18]*Taylor* v *Winters*, 6 Phila 126.

is nothing more than a delivery up of lands, tenements, or hereditaments, and the estate a man hath therein, unto him who hath the greater or equal estate in immediate reversion or remainder."[19]

382. **Consent of both parties necessary.**—The surrender is a contractual act. It occurs only with the consent of the tenant, and, no less, of the landlord. In most cases involving the question whether there has been a surrender, it is the tenant who alleges that it has been made. He relies on the fact that he has quitted the premises, and that he has done so with the intention to give up all right to them and to disengage himself from all liabilities springing from his contract of lease[20]. But it is uniformly held that to his acts and intention there must respond the assent of the landlord, to convert them into a surrender. The landlord must agree that from henceforth the tenant shall cease to be such, both as to his obligations and his rights[21]. When there is evidence of the verbal expression by the landlord of this consent, the case can present no difficulty except that arising from the relative credibility of witnesses, or from the uncertainty of the meaning of the expression. Disputes most frequently arise when the landlord's intention is to be inferred from what he does, or from what he refrains from saying or doing. The key of the premises belongs to the landlord. The tenant, vacating the premises, may send or carry the key to the landlord or his agent and proffer it to him. If he refuses to accept it, his assent to a surrender could scarcely be suspected.[22]

---

[19]*Greider's Appeal,* 5 Pa 422.

[20] These are not enough to make a surrender   *Teller* v *Boyle,* 132 Pa 56, 18 Atl. 1069, *Ogden* v. *Offerman,* 2 Miles (Pa) 40.

[21]*Kiester* v *Miller,* 25 Pa 481, *Lane* v *Nelson,* 167 Pa 602, 31 Atl 864, *Marseilles* v *Kerr,* 6 Whart 500, *Teller* v *Boyle,* 132 Pa 56, 18 Atl. 1069, *Ashhurst* v *Eastern Pho-*

nograph *Co.* 166 Pa 357, 31 Atl. 116, *Lipper* v *Bouvé, C & Co* 6 Pa. Super Ct 452, *Gardiner* v *Bair,* 10 Pa Super. Ct 78

[22]*Kiester* v *Miller,* 25 Pa 481; *Auer* v *Penn,* 99 Pa 370, 44 Am Rep 114, *Marseilles* v *Kerr,* 6 Whart. 500, *Gardiner* v *Bair,* 10 Pa Super Ct 78, *Dillon* v *Carrol,* 2 Luzerne Legal Reg. 89, *Hess* v.

But perhaps the tenant leaves it on the landlord's table, or elsewhere in his office or house, and there is no expressed refusal on the landlord's part. Or perhaps, though the landlord does refuse, the key is nevertheless left with him, and he does not send it back. In the latter case, the omission to return could scarcely be interpreted as an acquiescence in the escape of the tenant from the engagements of the lease.[23] Though the landlord does receive the key, if he indicates to the tenant his intention to hold him liable for rent for the remainder of the term, the receiving of the key will not signify an acceptance of a surrender,[24] nor is his mere silence when he receives the key equivalent to an acquiescence in the extinction of the lease.[25] Receiving the keys and taking possession of the premises "exclusively" of the tenant would imply acceptance,[26] and if, hearing that the tenant, B, is going to leave, A, the landlord, visits B, and inquires, and, informed that B is going to leave, asks for the keys, and if B, not then having them, promises to send them, and he subsequently sends them, and they are received, and the premises are rented to another person, acceptance of the surrender is a necessary inference.[27] In March, B, the tenant, calls on A, the landlord, and informs the latter that he intends to vacate the premises in May. A's reply is that he thinks he has a tenant and that there will be no difficulty in obtaining a tenant. He soon after places a sign "to let" on the house, and instructs B to let people know

Weingartner, 5 Pa Dist R 451, *Jenkins* v *Stone*, 14 Montg Co L Rep 27.

[23]*Harvey* v *Gunzberg*, 148 Pa 294, 23 Atl. 1005, *Hess* v *Weingartner*, 5 Pa Dist R. 451; *Carson* v *Shiffer*, 1 Lack Legal News, 399, *Snyder* v *Middleton*, 4 Phila. 343, *Auer* v *Penn*, 99 Pa 370, *Diehl* v *Lee*, 9 Allen, 865.

[24]*Auer* v *Penn*, 99 Pa 370, 44 Am Rep 114, *Lane* v *Velson*, 167 Pa 602, 31 Atl. 864, *Hess* v *Weingart-*

ner, 5 Pa Dist R 451, *Reeves* v. *McComeskey*, 168 Pa 571, 32 Atl. 96

[25]*Gardiner* v *Bair*, 10 Pa Super. Ct 74, *Milling* v *Becker*, 96 Pa. 182, *Pier* v *Carr*, 69 Pa 326; *Carson* v *Shiffer*, 1 Lack Legal News, 399

[26]*Frank* v *Maguire*, 42 Pa 77

[27]*Reaney* v *Fannessy*, 14 W N C 91 The affidavit of defense alleging these facts was sufficient.

that it is to let and that the rent will be \$50 per month, \$5 more
than under the existing lease. On April 29, B pays A the rent
to May 1, having, as he informed A, already left the house. He
also hands the key to A, who takes it without saying a word.
These facts justify B in believing that A has accepted his surrender.[28] The tenant tenders the key for the purpose of surrendering the house. The landlord takes it, but returns it, in
order that the tenant may make some repairs When the repairs are completed, the key is returned. From this the jury
may properly infer an acceptance of the surrender. If the
tenant to the knowledge of the landlord gives up the control of
the house to the latter, in order that the latter may discharge
him from the contract, the landlord cannot accept it for a different purpose. He must accept it as the tenant offers it or not
at all [29]

383. Consent not manifested by acts on premises.—Besides
acts or omissions with respect to the key there may be acts done
with respect to the leased premises,—acts indicating a resumption of control, inconsistent with the continuance of rights in

---

[28] *Weightman* v *Harley,* 20 W N
C. 470   In *Suplee* v *Harley,* 3 W
N C 240, the affidavit was held
sufficient which said that B had
rented the premises as a boarding-
house, that on a day named he "surrendered" it to A, the landlord, who
took possession and conducted therein a boarding-house, that the taking
possession was without qualification,
and with no notice of any claim to
hold B liable for rent   An affidavit
was sufficient which alleged an arrangement by which A, the landlord,
accepted a note and a sum of money
in full for rent due to January 13,
1874, received the keys and took possession   *Kelly* v *Donohue,* 1 W N
C 299   Tenant gave written notice
to landlord that he was going to vacate the premises   He sent word to

the agent that he had removed paid
the rent to the time of the removal,
and left the key with the agent, who
immediately took possession of the
premises, put a bill for rent up and
at length rented it   An affidavit so
averring was sufficient   *Bradley* v
Brown, 6 W N C 282   So was one
alleging that B, the tenant, complained to A, the landlord, that the
roof was leaky, that A said, ' Why
don't you move?'—that shortly
afterwards B paid the rent falling
due the next day and told A he was
about to move   that A said, "All
right," that A subsequently asked
for and got the key, and put up a notice To let "   *Sharpless* v. *Weigle*
7 W N C 376

[29] *Dos Santos* v *Hollinshead,* 4
Phila 57.

the tenant. Sometimes the landlord forms the purpose to let the premises to another, and expresses this purpose by putting a bill "to let" upon the house, or by otherwise advertising it as to let. This act is ambiguous The landlord may, believing the tenant's expression of intention not longer to occupy the premises, seek a new tenant in order to diminish the rent for which the tenant will be liable, and not for the purpose of excluding him, and a new tenant may be actually put into possession. "The landlord," says Paxson, J., "may accept the keys, take possession, put a bill on the house for rent, and at the same time apprise his tenant that he still holds him liable for the rent. All this, as was said by Mr. Justice Rogers in Marseilles v Kerr, 6 Whart. 500, is for the benefit of the tenant, and is not intended, nor can it have the effect, to put an end to the contract and discharge him from rent."[30] If the landlord may put another tenant in possession without discharging the old tenant, he may take possession himself, and keep it so long as no demand by the tenant to be allowed to re-enter is made. The withdrawal by the tenant, and the succeeding occupancy by the landlord, for nearly a year, according to his convenience or wants, would not therefore be inconsistent with a nonacceptance of the surrender.[31] After the withdrawal by the tenant from the prem-

---

[30]*Auer* v *Penn*, 99 Pa 370, 44 Am Rep 114, *Breuckmann* v *Turbill*, 89 Pa 58, *Pier* v *Carr*, 69 Pa 326, *Ker* v *Hunt*, 1 W N C 115, *Lane* v. *Nelson*, 167 Pa 602, 31 Atl. 864, *Snyder* v *Middleton*, 4 Phila 343. The landlord is not bound to find a new tenant in order to relieve the tenant If he finds a new tenant and obtains rent from him, the rent for which the original tenant is liable is *pro tanto* diminished. *Auer* v *Penn*, 99 Pa 370, 44 Am Rep. 114, *Lipper* v *Bouvé, C & Co* 6 Pa. Super Ct. 452. He may refuse to relent though an opportunity offers

LAND. & TEN. 21.

He is certainly not bound to arrange to relet in anticipation of the tenant's removal *Lipper* v *Bouvé, C & Co* 6 Pa Super Ct 452, *Reeves* v *McComeskey*, 168 Pa 571, 32 Atl 96 If the tenant tells the landlord that his lease is at an end, and that the latter may let the premises to another, and the latter acquiesces and lets to another, the tenant's rights terminate There has been a surrender and an acceptance. *Com.* v. *Conway*, 1 Brewst (Pa) 509

[31]*Ogden* v *Offerman*, 2 Miles (Pa) 40, *Philadelphia Fire Extinguisher Co* v. *Brainerd*, 2 W N. C 473.

ises and the acceptance of the key by the landlord's agent, the
putting up of a sign "For sale" and offering immediate possession are not decisive that the surrender has been accepted.[32]
The landlord may make repairs, after the tenant's departure,
e. g , he may repair the floor of a bar room over a space of 5 or
6 feet square ;[33] he may build a new bath room, and a new porch
and put in a new range, and otherwise repair generally,[34]—
without intending to accept or justifying the tenant in inferring that he has accepted the surrender, or that he precludes the
tenant from resuming the possession.

384 Right to surrender secured by lease.— The lease may
stipulate that the lessee "shall have the right at any time to surrender up this lease and be released from all moneys due and
conditions unfulfilled, then and from that time this lease and
agreement shall be null, void, and no longer binding on either
party, and the payments which shall have been made shall be
held by the party of the first part as the full stipulated damages
for the nonfulfilment of the foregoing contract." Under such
a lease, a surrender pending an action for rent or royalties, or

[32]*Reeves* v *McComiskey*, 168 Pa
571, 32 Atl 96   An affidavit saying
that the tenant delivered up quiet
possession to the landlord, who accepted the same, is sufficient *Wistar*
v *Campbell*, 10 Phila. 359   So is
one saying that the tenant "surrendered possession" to the agent of
the landlord, who accepted the pos
session   *De Morat* v *Falkenhagen*,
148 Pa 393, 23 Atl 1125

[33]*Pier* v *Carr*, 69 Pa 326; *Milling*
v *Becker*, 96 Pa 182

[34]*Breuckmann* v *Turbill*, 89 Pa
58   Making extensive repairs and
alterations is not conclusive of acceptance of surrender, when coupled
with the facts that before the end of
the term, the tenant told the landlord that he would leave the house on
a certain day, that he paid the rent.

and asked where to leave the key,
that, some days later, the landlord
designated his agent as the proper
person to receive it, and that afterwards the landlord entered and made
the repairs. *Gamble* v *O Mara*, 15
Phila. 180   The landlords assenting
to an assignment of the lease, and
receiving rent from the assignee are
not a surrender of the premises by
the lessee, and do not discharge him
from the duty to pay the rent subsequently accruing   *Ghegan* v *Young*,
23 Pa 18   Taking a note from the
sheriff's vendee of the leasehold, for
rent falling due after the sale, the
note being received as payment, if
paid, does not discharge the original
lessee upon the covenant. *Kerper* v.
Booth, 10 W N C 79.

for moneys agreed to be paid monthly until operations should begin on the premises, will not be effectual to bar a recovery in that action   To prevent such recovery, the surrender should have been made before suit was brought   Nor will the fact that the lessee had assigned the lease, and did not secure a reas signment of it until after the suit was brought, exempt him from this consequence [35]   A lease being for one year, at a monthly rental of $33, and which is to continue from year to year until three months' notice is given by the lessor or lessee, cannot be terminated within the first year by the tenant, because of the phrase added to the statement of the monthly rental, "to be paid monthly in advance on the 9th day of each month, so long as he shall occupy the said house and lot of ground."[36]

385   Lease by partnership; change of partners.— A lease by B, of the firm of A & B, signed and sealed by B alone, but professing to be made with the authority of A, will not be considered as surrendered, and a new oral lease substituted, because A ceases to be a member of the firm through a sale of his interest to C, and C unites with B in carrying on the same business, and rent is subsequently paid by the tenant to the firm of B & C. No action on covenants similar to those of the original lease can be brought against B and C on the theory that a parol lease with similar terms has been made by B and C.   "The mere receipt of the back rent by the assignee [C] of a lessor [A] is not sufficient to raise the presumption that the assignee made a parol contract, binding himself to fulfil all the covenants contained in the lease, and making him responsible in assumpsit for a future breach of such covenants."[37]

386   Consent not otherwise manifested— If the tenant takes into a portion of the premises a subtenant or assignee, the fact

---

[35]*Douthett* v *Gibson,* 11 Pa. Super Ct 543
[36]*Lane* v *Nelson,* 167 Pa 602, 31 Atl 864. This phrase was written, while most of the lease was printed It refers to the possible extension of the term from year to year
[37]*Bewley* v *Tams,* 17 Pa 485

that after the tenant retires from them within the term the landlord distrains several times for the rent due from him, upon
goods of the subtenant or assignee, is entirely consistent with the
nonacceptance of the surrender of the tenant, the landlord never
demanding the rent from the subtenant or assignee, and, in his
warrant of distress, always naming the tenant as his debtor.[38]
The tenant left the premises because of the adultery of the landlord with his wife. The wife remained until the close of the
term, the landlord proposing to her that, if she remained, she
should pay no rent. The adulterous intercourse continued
These facts do not necessarily imply an acceptance of the tenant's surrender.[39] If, the tenant going out, X enters, whether as
his assignee, sublessee, or otherwise, the receipt of the rent due
on the lease from X does not imply an acceptance of a surrender
by the tenant. The surrender would terminate the lease and the
right to rent under it.[40] The same result would follow if the
tenant, never entering under his lease, assigned it and the assignee entered.[41]

387. Destruction of premises by fire — When the lease requires the tenant to keep insurance on the property, and in case
of fire to rebuild, or pay the money obtained on the policy to
the landlord, if he prefers, if, the fire occurring, the money is
paid to the landlord, but he does not rebuild, and the tenant
abandons the possession, the jury may, and perhaps ought to,
find an acceptance of a surrender, since the landlord has the use
of the money which represents the premises [42]

388 Evidence of landlord's acceptance.— The burden of proof
of a surrender is on the party who alleges it In an action
for the rent, the tenant defending on the ground that before the

[38]*Manley* v *Dupuy,* 2 Whart 162
[39]*B——* v *H——* 3 W. N. C.
132
[40]*Frank* v *Maguire,* 42 Pa. 77.
[41]*Dewey* v *Dupuy,* 2 Watts & S
553. The giving up of possession is
not the same as the surrender of the
term The tenant may resume possession Withdrawal is therefore
not proof of surrender *Goldsmith* v
Smith, 4 Phila 31.
[42]*Boyer* v *Dickson,* 7 Phila 190.

rent accrued for which the suit was brought he had surrendered, it would be for him to prove the surrender and the acceptance of it [43] On the other hand, in an ejectment by the landlord against the tenant, presupposing a surrender of the lease, the former could not recover without proving it [44] It is not necessary that the evidence to support it should be clear, precise, and indubitable. A preponderance is enough [45] Declarations of the party can be used to prove against him the fact of a surrender; but the facts that the landlord tells X that his tenant has given up the premises, and that he offers to rent them to X, are not conclusive that he has accepted the surrender. They do not operate as an estoppel, but may be satisfactorily explained.[46]

389. Surrender to an agent.— An acceptance by an agent of the landlord, having authority to accept the tenant's surrender, will bind the landlord.[47] In *Weightman v. Harley*,[48] Arnold, J., remarks that "the powers of a real-estate agent are different

[43]*Auer* v *Penn*, 99 Pa 370, 44 Am Rep 114, *Lane* v *Nelson*, 167 Pa. 602, 31 Atl 864, *Rohbock* v *McCargo*, 6 Pa Super Ct 134 *Vide Pratt* v *Richards Jewelry Co* 69 Pa 53, where the sufficiency of evidence of a surrender is considered

[44]*Hooks* v *Forst*, 165 Pa. 238, 30 Atl 846

[45]*Rohbock* v *McCargo*, 6 Pa. Super. Ct 134 Cf *Hooks* v *Forst*, 165 Pa 238, 30 Atl 846

[46]*Kiester* v *Miller*, 25 Pa 481, *Milling* v. *Becker*, 96 Pa 182. Declarations of a landlord made before the tenant moved out, and in pursuance of which he moved out, were submitted to the jury, in *Morgan* v. *Luzerne Lodge*, 5 Kulp 512 An offer by the tenant to prove that he was told, previously to his vacating the property, that the lessor would take the property and that he might leave, was too vague, because it did not indicate who told him.

Reeves v *McComeskey*, 168 Pa 571, 32 Atl 96

[47]*Weightman* v *Harley*, 20 W N C 470, *Bradley* v *Brown*, 6 W N C 282, *Auer* v *Penn*, 99 Pa 370, 44 Am Rep 114, *Reeves* v *McComeskey*, 168 Pa 571, 32 Atl 96, *De Morat* v *Falkenhagen*, 148 Pa 393, 23 Atl 1125, *Rohbock* v *McCargo*, 6 Pa Super Ct 134.

[48] 20 W N. C 470 An affidavit of defense averring surrender to an agent, but not stating the authority of this agent, was held sufficient In *De Morat* v *Falkenhagen*, 148 Pa. 393, 23 Atl 1125, the affidavit does not seem to have set out the authority of the agent, but the court holds it sufficient, saying "But here the acceptance by an agent for the landlord is averred, and we cannot question the legal effect without denying his authority, which we certainly cannot do in the face of the affidavit"

from those of an insurance agent, broker, factor, attorney, or
special agent with limited powers   .   .   .   Agents for manag-
ing real estate, like stewards in England, are considered as having full control of the property for leasing, receiving rents, and
accepting surrenders.   .   .   .   Landed proprietors, great
and small, do not permit tenants to trouble them about such
matters.   When a landlord places his property in the hands of
an agent, the custom is for the tenant to deal with the agent, and
not with the landlord; otherwise conflicting acts may be done,
tending to confusion and litigation "   It cannot be assumed
that the solicitor of a corporation, the landlord, has authority to
accept for it a surrender from its tenant [49]   In *Murphy* v.
Losch[50] the authority of the agent was properly submitted to
the jury, with the instruction that if they found that he was
agent only to collect the rent, no act of his, in accepting a surrender of a lease, would bind the landlord unless it had been
ratified by the latter

390. Effect of surrender.— The accepted surrender of a lease
prevents the accruing of new rights under the lease from the time
of the surrender   No rent can subsequently accrue [51]   It also
destroys the right to rent which has been accruing but has not
yet become due, the right to distrain for such rent; and the
right to claim such rent for one year from the proceeds of an
execution which was levied after the surrender.[52]   Thus the
surrender occurring on January 8, and the levy in execution on
January 9, the rent for the year, payable on April 1, could not
be apportioned to the date of the levy, and paid from the proceeds
of the execution sale.   The tenant's surety in the lease becomes

[49]*Jamestown & F R Co* v *Egbert*,
152 Pa 53, 23 Atl 151
   [50] 148 Pa 171, 23 Atl 1059. Cf
Philadelphia v *Elvins*, 1 W N C 2,
where after the dissolution of a firm
one of the partners undertook to surrender the lease and accept a new
one to himself.

[51]*Kiester* v *Miller*, 25 Pa 481,
Auer v *Penn*, 92 Pa 444, *Milling* v.
Becker, 96 Pa 182; *Pratt* v *Richards
Jewelry Co* 69 Pa 53
   [52]*Greider's Appeal*, 5 Pa. 422.

exempted from liability for any rent accruing due after the surrender.[53] The surrender by the tenant destroys his right to rent accruing in the future under a sublease made by him,[54] and passes it to his landlord [55] The tenant's right to the possession of the premises is ended by his surrender of the term He cannot recover it in ejectment from the landlord or a later tenant,[56] and the landlord may, without breach of the peace, lawfully put his goods off the premises [57] The landlord recovers his right of possession and can assert it in ejectment against a third person.[58] With the surrender of the term, the right to a house erected by the tenant, under the privilege of removing it at the end, passes with the soil to the landlord. Though it has been distrained upon by a constable before the surrender, yet, if this is not known to the landlord when he accepts the surrender, the constable cannot sell and take it away [59]

391 Termination of lease by lessee's death — The lease does not determine with the death of the lessee unless its continuance to the end mentioned in it is expressly or impliedly conditioned on the continuance in life of the lessee. Some contracts are for the performance of such acts by one party that the other party must be understood to have known that the former was to be bound only in case he should continue in life This principle was applied in *Jaquette's Estate,*[60] where, the lease

[53]*Auer* v *Penn,* 99 Pa 370, 44 Am Rep 114, 92 Pa 444, *Teller* v *Boyle,* 132 Pa 56, 18 Atl 1069, *Reaney* v *Fannessy,* 14 W N C 91, *Bradley* v *Brown,* 6 W N C 282, *Kelly* v. *Donohue,* 1 W N C 299, *Pier* v *Carr,* 69 Pa 326, *Wistar* v *Campbell,* 10 Phila 359, *Frank* v *Maguire,* 42 Pa 78 The surety in a recognizance conditioned to pay costs and rents that might accrue may show, in suit upon it, that the tenant had surrendered, and so escape liability *Wistar* v. *Campbell,* 10 Phila. 359.

[54]*Pratt* v *Richards Jewelry Co* 69 Pa 53 The surrender of the lease destroys the warrant of attorney to confess judgment for the rent *Philadelphia* v *Elkins,* 1 W N C 2

[55]*Hessel* v *Johnson,* 142 Pa 8, 11 L R A 855, 21 Atl 794

[56]*Hooks* v *Forest,* 165 Pa. 238, 30 Atl 846

[57]*Com* v *Conway,* 1 Brewst (Pa) 509

[58]*Tate* v *Reynolds,* 8 Watts & S. 91

[59]*Thropp's Appeal,* 70 Pa 395

[60] 1 Chester Co Rep 197

of a farm containing provisions touching fencing, rotation of crops, and other points about the mode of farming, it was held that the lease ended with the lessee's death, and that consequently his administrator was not entitled to credit, in his account, for rent accruing after the lessee's death, which he had paid to the lessor, nor for expenses incurred by him in conducting the farm. A different view was taken in *Walker's Estate*,[61] where the court refused to see that exercise of the personal skill of the lessee in farming the premises was solely in the contemplation of the parties, and held that the administrator was entitled to the expenses incurred in working the farm after the lessee's death, although had he refrained and quickly sold the goods, making the estate liable for the nonperformance of the contract, it would have proved better for the estate The lease of a house does not end with the death of the tenant, and the administrator who pays the rent falling due subsequently is entitled to a credit in his account. Nor does he lose the right to this credit by reason of the fact that the son-in-law and daughter of the lessee, who had resided with him, continued to occupy the premises after his death, and that the lessor might have distrained on the son-in-law's goods on the premises [62]

392 Termination by merger — The relation of lessor and lessee may determine by the coalescence of the leasehold and the reversion   This might be brought about by the surrender of the leasehold , or by the release to the tenant, or by other conveyance to him, of the reversion. The lessee may acquire, during the lease, the reversion by devise or inheritance[63] or by a conveyance resulting from a contract.[64] The lessor dying, and

[61] 6 Pa Co Ct 515
[62]*Rainow's Estate*, 4 Kulp, 153 Cf *Logan's Estate* 10 Pa Co Ct. 554, *Wiley's Appeal*, 8 Watts & S 244 *Keating* v *Condon*, 68 Pa 75 , *Coppel's Estate*, 4 Phila. 378, *Re Ralston*, 2 Clark (Pa) 224, *Col-* *houn's Estate*, 8 Pa Co Ct 550, 20 Phila 46, 26 W N. C. 303
[63]*Debozear* v. *Butler*, 2 Grant, Cas 417
[64]*Dougherty* v *Jack*, 5 Watts, 457, 30 Am Dec. 335.

the reversion descending to heirs, the lessee may acquire the interests of some of these heirs. "By the purchase of the fee simple of three fifths," said Huston, J , "the term for years for
those three fifths is extinguished, for nothing is better settled
than that where a term for years, or life, exists in a person in
his own right, and he subsequently acquires the fee in his own
right, the former is lost and merged in the latter "[65]   A contract to sell the land, entered into since the lease was made, if
so formed as to be enforceable in equity, will so merge the lease
in the fee as to deprive the lessor of his remedies for rent, or for
the recovery of possession.[66]   The lease may itself provide that
the lessee may purchase the premises   When, in conformity
with its terms, the lessee signifies his exercise of the option, he
confers on the lessor the right of a vendor, and he acquires the
right of a vendee   A lease for one year with the privilege of
extending it to five grants the lessee the privilege of purchasing the lot at any time within one year.   At the end of the year
the tenant demands a conveyance   From that time the lease
is at an end, and the contract is one of sale   The lease is of
no effect; there can be no distress for rent[67] falling due after
the election to buy, or recovery of it by common-law action,[68] or
recovery under the landlord and tenant acts.[69]

   393. When merger does not occur — The merger of the leasehold will not result from the union of the ownership of it with
that of the reversion in the same person, if for any reason appealing to equity it would be detrimental to the lessee, or if the person in whom the ownership unites owns them in different
capacities, or if the term has been created for a special purpose
not yet accomplished, and this object cannot be accomplished if

[65]Kershaw v Supplee, 1 Rawle,
131 The lessee could not maintain
a suit on the covenants of the dead
lessor
[66]Debozear v. Butler, 2 Grant, Cas.
417.

[67]Newell's Appeal, 100 Pa 513.
[68]Knerr v. Bradley, 105 Pa 190
[69]Newell's Appeal, 100 Pa 513
Cf. Koons v. Steele, 19 Pa. 203

a merger occurs.[70] If the effect of the merger would be to imperil the ownership for the period of the term, whereas that ownership would have been effectual for the term had the lessee not acquired the reversion, a fusion of the leasehold in the fee will not result. If, e. g , after a lease is made to B the lessor conveys the premises to C, under such circumstances that this conveyance would prevail against a later conveyance to B, after such later conveyance to B, he will be considered as owning two estates,—the leasehold, which was originally, and continues to be, valid against C's conveyance, and the reversion, which is not valid against C's conveyance [71] A leased land to B for ten years, and subsequently conveyed the land to C in fee. Later and within the ten years, A conveyed the premises to B in fee If the deed to C gave a better right than that to B, B's leasehold would not merge in the fee conveyed to him by the second deed, so as to enable C to expel him from the premises during the term [72]

394 Termination by ejectment.— If B is in possession of land under A, an ejectment by A against him, resulting in a judgment for A, terminates the relation of landlord and tenant between them, though no *habere facias possessionem* issues, and B remains in possession It follows that A cannot claim the possession of B during the pendency of the ejectment and after its termination in judgment, in order to attach it to B's possession prior to the institution of the ejectment, so as to make a title for himself as against the true owner, by the statute of limitations.[73] If B, the tenant of C, is in possession of land, and an ejectment being brought by A against C, a judgment is obtained and a *habere facias possessionem* issued, under which

---

[70]*Kershaw* v *Supplee,* 1 Rawle, 131

[71]*Dougherty* v *Jack,* 5 Watts, 457, 30 Am Dec 335

[72]*Ibid* As the lease contained also an agreement to convey the fee, and the tenant was apparently in pos- session, it is not easy to see how the lease could prevail against the deed to C, while the agreement to convey did not

[73]*Koons* v. *Steele,* 19 Pa 203.

B attorns to A, the setting aside of the *habere facias posses-sionem* will, at the option of B, liberate him from his duties as tenant to A, and leave him free to accept a fresh lease from C, his former landlord "So long as the writ of possession and the sheriff's return remained in force, the lease taken under its influence was valid and the tenant's relation to his former landlord was legally dissolved But when that writ was set aside, the lease fell with it, without an express order of restitution, and the tenant was restored to his former condition of subordination to the vendee [C] as his landlord."[74]

[74]*Coughanour* v *Bloodgood,* 27 Pa. 285.

CHAPTER XXI.

EVICTION.

395 Covenant for quiet enjoyment.— The lease confers the right on the tenant, for the period named in it, to the possession according to its terms, and any interference with this possession by the landlord will be a breach of the contract. It is, perhaps, unnecessary to discover any additional covenant, express or implied, to support a right of the tenant to exclude the landlord from interference with his possession. There may be and often is an express covenant by the lessor for the quiet enjoyment of the lessee, as against disturbances by the lessor or anyone else. If there is no express covenant of this sort the words *concessi et demisi,* or the English let or demise,[1] or lease,[2] or "demise and lease"[3] imply one. If, said Thompson, J., of a certain agreement, it "is to be regarded as a lease of the premises, it would pass the possession of the buildings on it to the lessee It would necessarily be a covenant for quiet enjoyment "[4]

396. What is an eviction; generally.— Although it is said from time to time that an eviction is "an actual expulsion of the lessee out of all or some part of the demised premises,"[5] that it is "a dispossession or turning out of the tenant,"[6] it is also said that, in the modern sense of the word, "actual physical expulsion is not necessary, but any interference with the tenant's beneficial enjoyment of the demised premises will amount to an eviction in law,"[7] and in *Doran* v. *Chase,*[8] the court speaks of an "eviction *per minas," i. e ,* by threat of the landlord to make any subtenant pay rent to himself as well as to the subtenant's immediate landlord, whereby the tenant is prevented from subletting "Originally, an eviction," says Williams, J., "was understood to be a dispossession of the tenant by some act of his landlord, or by the failure of his title. . . . It has come

---

[1] *Hemphill* **v.** *Eckfeldt,* 5 Whart. 274, *Lanigan* v *Kille,* 97 Pa 120, 30 Am Rep 797, *Ross* v *Dysart,* 33 Pa 452, *Barns* v *Wilson,* 116 Pa 303, 9 Atl 437

[2] *Maule* v. *Ashmead,* 20 Pa 482, *Cozens* v. *Stevenson,* 5 Serg. & R. 421.

[3] *Hazlett* **v** *Powell,* 30 Pa 293.

[4] *Steel* v *Frick,* 56 Pa 172

[5] *Tilcy* v. *Moyers,* 43 Pa 404, Bennet v *Bittle,* 4 Rawle, 339

[6] *Sutton* v *Foulke,* 19 Phila 419

[7] *Hoeveler* v *Fleming,* 91 Pa 322

[8] 2 W. N. C. 609.

in later years to include any wrongful act of the landlord which may result in an interference with the tenant's possession in whole or in part. The act may be one of omission as well as of commission."[9]

397. Making repairs.— The landlord may enter and cause repairs to be made, so slight in character as not to interfere with the tenant's possession. Such repairing is not an eviction. In *Pier* v. *Carr*[10] a distress was made on the tenant's goods for taxes. Before the sale, the tenant left the premises. The constable who made the sale left the key with the landlord. On the day after the sale, a notice "to let" was affixed to the house. Four or five weeks after the sale a new tenant took possession. During the vacancy, the lessor repaired 5 or 6 feet square of one of the rooms These acts did not constitute an eviction. The tenant dying, his administrator left the key, in February, with the lessor, who made considerable repairs in March, but did not rent the house until April 1st. The administrator, knowing that the repairs were being made, made no objection. He also kept the goods of the deceased in the house until sometime in March. There was no eviction, and the monthly rent for March could be recovered.[11] In *Townsend* v. *Hendrickson*,[12] the building being partially destroyed by fire, the tenant went out, leaving his goods on the premises, and retaining the key. The lessor had the building repaired and then notified the tenant of

---

[9]*Oakford* v *Nixon*, 177 Pa 76, 34 L R A 575 35 Atl 588, *Gallagher* v *Burke*, 13 Pa Super Ct 244.

[10] 69 Pa 326 After saying that the mere receiving of the key and taking care of it, or putting up the notice "to let," or entry for repairing the floor, would not of itself, release the tenant from rent the court left it to the jury to say whether "under all the evidence" there had been "an actual adverse possession, and substantial eviction of the tenant" In *Willcox* v *Philadelphia*

Sectional Electric Underground Co. 15 W N C 367, an affidavit of defense by the tenant, sued for the rent, that the plaintiff without his consent, took possession of the premises and made certain alterations, and a supplemental affidavit alleging that he took exclusive possession and accepted the keys from the tenant, were not enough to prevent judgment

[11]*Gallagher's Estate*, 20 Pittsb L. J N S 306

[12] 5 W N C 492.

the completion of the work. The tenant did not return, and the landlord advertised the premises for rent. In these acts was no eviction, and no defense to the claim for rent. Entering after a fire, not for the purpose of rebuilding, but simply to restore the division fence, would, at most, be a trespass, and not an eviction [13]

398. Extensive repairs.—The repairs made may be so extensive as to displace the possession of the tenant, and constitute an eviction. An illustration of this is found in *Hoeveler* v. *Fleming*.[14] The building was in March so injured by fire as to become untenantable, and the lessee vacated it. The insurance company, with the assent of the lessor, and without objection from the tenant, employed a contractor to make the repairs, and the key was delivered to him. The building was not ready for reoccupancy until August, and the tenant declined to resume possession, and declined to pay rent for the quarter during which the repairs were made. The lease obliged neither the lessor nor the lessee to repair, in case of fire. The tenant was not liable for the rent.[15] The consent of the lessee to the repairs, and to his continued liability for rent, will, of course, prevent the making of them operate as a discharge from liability on the lease for rent.[16] This consent may be expressed in the lease, as when it authorizes the lessor to do any repairing,[17] or "to

---

[13]*Mannerbach* v. *Keppleman*, 2 Woodw Dec 137.

[14] 91 Pa 322

[15]Cf *Magaw* v *Lambert*, 3 Pa St 444, in which, the building being destroyed by fire, the court said "If a landlord take possession of the ruins of his premises destroyed by fire, for the purpose of rebuilding, without the consent of his tenant, it is an eviction, if with his assent, it is a rescission of the lease, and in either case, the rent is suspended." In *Garrett* v. *Cummins*, 2 Phila 207, the landlord entered on the premises and extended a wharf, which had been cut off from the river by the operations of a railroad, sufficiently far to give those who used it access to deep water. This was said to suspend the rent

[16]*Garrett* v *Cummins*, 2 Phila 207, *Magaw* v *Lambert*, 3 Pa St 444

[17]*Mayberry* v *Dudley*, 2 Pennyp 367. The barn being burnt down, the lessor could rebuild it without losing his rent.

make any changes or alterations,"[18] or requires the landlord to
make repairs,[19] or it may be given after the fire[20] or other accident has made repairs necessary, or after the need of repairing
has been discovered. If, *e. g.,* the tenant, after the building has
been condemned for insecurity, agrees to accept a reduction of
the rent as compensation for any inconvenience or damage, he
could recover no damages for inconvenience, unless the work
was done in an unreasonably tardy, or in an improper, way.[21]
If the tenant consents to the landlord's tearing down the frame
portion of a barn, on condition that he should erect a new
barn, which, however, he failed subsequently to do, he is not
guilty of an eviction, but simply of a breach of the contract to
erect [22]

399. Acts which are an eviction.— Although acts of trespass
are not an eviction, if the landlord asserts a right to use, in fact
frequently uses, and threatens to continue to use, the premises
in a way in which he has no right to use them, and to the inconvenience of the tenant, the latter may be considered evicted,
though he retains possession. A lease of a room and the front
cellar of a house did not reserve to the lessor the right to pass
through the front cellar to a back cellar. The lessor claimed
this right, however, and perservered in using it; he forfeited the
rent for the time during which he exercised it.[23] If, after leasing a store, without excluding the tenant from particular uses
of it, the landlord prevents the use of it as a flour and feed store,
by obtaining a preliminary injunction, which is afterwards dissolved, he discharges the tenant from rent for the period of the
injunction.[24] The premises being leased for a certain business,

[18]*Clark* v *Lindsay,* 7 Pa Super
Ct 43 The tenant must suffer the
inconvenience which unavoidably at-
tends the changes

[19]Cf *Hoeveler* v *Fleming,* 91 Pa
322

[20]*Heller* v. *Royal Ins Co.* 151 Pa.
101, 25 Atl 83, 177 Pa 262, 35 L R.
A 600, 35 Atl 726

[21]*Reineman* v *Blair,* 96 Pa 155

[22]*Heayn* v *Felton,* 13 W N C 28

[23]*Vaughan* v *Blanchard,* 4 Dall
124, 1 L ed 769

[24]*Pfund* v. *Herlinger,* 10 Phila 13

e. g., a boarding house, possibly if the lessor, who rooms in the house, speaks ill of the character of the lessee, or of the manner in which the business is conducted, and by so doing influences people not to patronize the business, he commits an eviction which destroys his right to rent.[25] If the tenant goes out of possession, arranging with another to enter, and the landlord locks up the barn, interdicts the subtenant from entering, and puts another person in possession, he evicts the tenant, although goods of the latter remain in the house, and his hay in the barn [26] "The lessor entered and locked the barn," says Coulter, J., "and thereby evicted the defendant from it. He interdicted the subtenant, to whom his lessee had transferred the term, from coming in, and he put another person into possession of the house and premises when the lease was a little more than half expired If all these acts do not constitute an entry of the lessor upon the lessee, such as will suspend the rent, it is difficult to imagine what kind of entry will, unless it be required that the landlord should take hold of the tenant and put him and his household out by actual force But that surely is not necessary."

400. **Lessor's acts, eviction.**— The removal of most of the tenant's goods from the premises, during the term, without notice to the landlord, does not justify the latter in removing the locks, the lessee's business signs, and his remaining goods, and in using the premises for his own purposes. A let to B two rooms in New

But, had no injunction been issued, the attempt to procure one would be no eviction *Jarden* v. *Lafferty*, 19 W N C 144

[25]*Huang* v. *Cottman*, 9 Pa Super. Ct. 444

[26]*Briggs* v *Thompson*, 9 Pa 338

If the lessor interferes with sub letting, the lease not prohibiting it, and deters persons from becoming subtenants by threatening to make them pay rent to himself, he evicts

LAND & TEN. 22.

the lessee, and suspends the rent *Doran* v *Chase*, 2 W N C 609

Whether the landlord's warning the tenant not to use certain machines which he had been using, and directing him to remove them from the building would be "such a wrong ful interference with the beneficial enjoyment of the premises" as would be an eviction, not decided, in *Megargee* v. *Longaker*, 10 Pa Super Ct 491.

York for five months   During the second month, the rent having been paid, B, without notice to A, removed his goods, *viz ,*
patent medicines, to Scranton, leaving behind some gas fixtures,
a sink, and a lot of boxes   The key he left with the janitor.   He
had no intention of again permanently occupying the rooms.
The landlord removed the locks, signs, and tenant's goods, and
used the rooms till the close of the term for the storage of trunks
This was an eviction   There could be no recovery of rent for
the residue of the term [27]   The lessor, treating A, with whom
A's son, B, lives on the premises, as his tenant, may, by landlord and tenant proceedings against A, expel B and his property from the premises   If B is in fact the tenant, and not A,
this would be an eviction of B.[28]   The tenant's departure
from the premises during the term, at the bidding of the landlord, will discharge him from any rent for the remainder of the
term.[29]

   401. Lessor's acts which are not eviction — The   distinction
is drawn between an eviction and a trespass by the landlord.
He may commit the latter without committing the former   If,
without leave, the landlord walks over the tenant's field, or enters the orchard and carries off a basket of apples or peaches, or
if, the greater part of a day, he takes manure from the barn-
yard, his acts are trespasses, but not an eviction.[30]   There is

---

[27]*Burr* v *Cattnach,* 19 W N C 22
   The tenant occupying a room on
the second story, if the landlord
takes off the roof of the building,
and, in consequence, a rain penetrates
into   the   room,   destroying   the
tenant's goods, the tenant may maintain trespass for the injury   *Herbst*
v *Hafner,* 7 Pa Super Ct   363
[The roof was not a part of the demised room]
   In *Sutton* v *Foulke,* 19 Phila 419,
it is said that if the landlord deprives the tenant of the beneficial
enjoyment of the premises, the tenant may remove and escape rent, but

if he remains he must pay the rent,
but in that case the tenant was not
deprived of any of the rooms which
he had rented   He alleged that in
consequence of an alteration made in
the other parts of the building, effluvia from the water closets per-
meated the rooms
   [28]*Dosch* v *Diem* 176 Pa 603, 35
Atl 207
   [29]*Yanko* v *Leiscrowitz* 18 Lanc L.
Rev 1
   [30]*Bennet* v *Bittle,* 4 Rawle, 339
Noble v *Warren* 38 Pa 340, *Harris*
v *Watson,* 1 Phila Leg Int May 8,
1844

nothing from which an eviction can be inferred in these facts. Distress levied on goods of the tenant for rent, and a watchman left in charge, information by the landlord before a justice that the tenant was fraudulently removing the goods distrained on, whereupon a warrant issues, the tenant is arrested and bound over to answer the charge of forcibly removing the goods with intent to defraud the lessor, and, finally, expulsion of the tenant by proceedings under the act of 1830 [31] The owner of the premises, occupying a room in them, leases them to A, agreeing to board with A. Seventeen days after commencing thus to board, he is notified by A that she will no longer board him, and that he shall give up the room He ceases to board with her, but retains the room until the close of the term. This act is not an eviction from the room. "He entered as a boarder, by their permission [i. e., that of the lessee and her husband], and in subordination to their rights He paid for his board and lodging. . . . His unwillingness to then cease [on being notified] to occupy the room, but his subsequent payment to them for the use and occupation thereof, took from the case the technical character of an eviction by a landlord "[32] The lease is of a coal mine. The lessee is to pay so much per bushel of coal mined. For the lessor to prevent any mining would be an eviction; but his entry and taking coal from a portion of the tract which the tenant was not working would not be an eviction

---

The lease forbids the use of the premises except as a store and dwelling house If, without lessor's consent, the tenant commences a manufacturing business, and introduces a steam boiler, the landlord's stopping off the water for a short time during the dispute between them will not be an eviction that will relieve from the rent *Ladomus* v *McCormick*, 5 Del Co Rep 147

[31] *Noble* v *Warren*, 38 Pa 340 "In its worst aspect, it was but a tres-

pass " Cf *Murphy* v *Marshell*, 179 Pa 516, 36 Atl 294, where making a distress, allowing the goods to remain on the premises until appraisement and sale, putting up a sign "to let," the lease expressly authorizing that act, changing the locks in order that the constable might have a more secure custody of the goods, were not an eviction destroying the right to the rent

[32] *Diehl* v *Woods*, 4 Pennyp 57.

that would suspend the rent. It would simply entitle to a deduction for damages [33] The lease being of a storeroom, a defect in the heating apparatus in another portion of the building, whereby the tenant's goods are damaged by escaping steam, is not an eviction, the tenant not vacating the premises.[34]

402. Nondelivery of possession.— The lessee has a right, as against the lessor, to take possession of the premises at the beginning of the term. If he is obstructed and prevented by the lessor, he may resort to an action of ejectment for the obtaining of possession, or to an action for the damages. In the ordinary case, however, the court will not, by bill in equity, compel the delivery of the possession. If, the premises being a hotel, the lessor, although he has covenanted to apply to the court of quarter sessions for a transfer of the liquor license to the lessee, refuses to do so, a court of equity will not ordinarily compel him to do so. The tenant can obtain damages by an appropriate action, and no other remedy is necessary [35]

403. Lessee's remedy to obtain or preserve possession.—The lessee may, when the term begins, obtain possession of the premises by an action of ejectment against the lessor or any other person who is in possession If his right is denied, the denial can be made by the defendant in the action. If the lessor who is in possession desires to procure an adjudication on the asserted right to the possession of a lessee who has not taken possession, he may proceed under the act of May 25th, 1893,[36]

---

[33]*Tiley* v *Moyers*, 43 Pa 404 Apparently, interrupting the tenant's operations by ejectments and estrepements was regarded not as an eviction, but as simply a ground for damages, to be set off against the rent

[34]*Krohn* v *Wolf*, 7 Northampton Co Rep 18 Damages can be recovered only for lessor's negligence

[35]*Effinger* v. *Hain*, 18 Lanc L. Rev 3.

The lessee attempting to take possession, or taking possession, under his lease, will not be enjoined from excluding one who claims adversely to the lessor, ejectment being a sufficient remedy *Stout* v *Williams*, 203 Pa 161, 52 Atl 169

[36] P L 131, 1 Pepper & Lewis Digest, 1697.

and of March 8th, 1889,[37] by petition for a rule to show cause
why an ejectment should not be brought within six months from
the service of the rule [38]

404 **Effect of eviction on rent.**—If, while rent is accruing,
the landlord evicts the tenant, and the eviction continues down
to the time at which that rent becomes due and payable, the
landlord has no right to collect that rent or any part of it. If
the rent is payable yearly, an eviction beginning any time within the year destroys the right to the year's rent   Rent payable
half-yearly,[39] quarterly,[40] or monthly[41] cannot be collected for
any half year, or quarter, or month if the tenant is evicted within the half year, quarter, or month and remains evicted to its
close. If the eviction occurs even on the day before the expiration of the lease, the month's rent will be forfeited, the rent
being payable monthly [42] "But where the parties apportion
rent by agreement," says Allison, J., "providing for its division
and for intermediate times of payment, during the term, it is
binding on them, and for an expulsion or eviction of the tenant,
by the landlord, from the whole or any part of the premises, the
accruing rent only is suspended   It may, therefore, be a suspension or forfeiture for a month or quarter, a half year or the
entire year, according to the terms of the contract for payment

[37] P L 10, 1 Pepper & Lewis
Digest, 1697
[38] Cf *Miller* v *Fretts,* 25 Pa Co Ct
669 In *Pickering* v *O'Brien,* 23 Pa
Super. Ct 125, B, a lessee of a lot
for the purpose of exhibiting advertising signs, filed a bill against A, a
former tenant of the same lot, to pre
vent A from obliterating the signs.
As A had been tenant from year to
year, and had received no notice to
quit, the lease to B was invalid It
was not decided whether, otherwise,
an injunction would have been the
proper remedy
[39] *Vaughan* v *Blanchard,* 4 Dall.
124, 1 L. ed. 769.

[40] *Linton* v *Hart,* 25 Pa 193, 64
Am Dec 691, *Hoeveler* v *Fleming,*
91 Pa. 322 Cf. *Hemphill* v *Eckfeldt,* 5 Whart 274, *Doran* v *Chase,*
2 W N C 609, *Murphy* v *Marshell,*
179 Pa 516, 36 Atl 294, *Heayn* v.
Felton, 13 W N C 28, *Horberg* v
May, 153 Pa 216, 25 Atl 750,
Thomas v *Schook,* 1 W N C 38
[41] *Pier* v *Carr,* 69 Pa 326, *Gallagher's Estate,* 20 Pittsb. L J. N S.
306
[42] *Kessler* v. *M'Conachy,* 1 Rawle,
435.

of rent " [43] It is needless to say that if the eviction occurs during one month, and the tenant continues excluded through the
succeeding months, he cannot be compelled to pay the rent of
the month in which he suffered the eviction or of any of the following months [44]

405. Rent due prior to eviction — The rent that has become
payable, according to the terms of the lease, prior to the eviction,
remains payable It is not suspended,[45] but damages to which
the tenant is entitled on account of an eviction can be set off
against a claim for rent that became payable before the eviction
occurred [46] Thus, damages for an eviction suffered in December, 1836, might be set off in a suit for rent that became payable
the preceding October 1st,[47] and if the damages should exceed
the rent, the jury may certify[48] the excess, in accordance with
the provisions of the act of 1705 [49] The parties agreeing, pending the term, that the landlord might enter and make extensive
repairs, in consideration of a reduction of the rent, damages
arising from an unnecessary protraction of the work of repairing could be set off in an action for the rent.[50] Possibly, if the
rent is payable in advance, an eviction during the period for
which it is payable would not destroy the right to it If, e g ,
the rent is payable monthly in advance, an eviction occurring in
March would not prevent the subsequent collection of the rent
payable on the first day of February and of March.[51] But probably if the eviction occurs on the first day of the month, the

[43]*Wolf* v *Weiner*, 7 Phila 274
[44]*Burr* v *Cattnach*, 19 W N C 22
In *Pier* v *Carr*, 69 Pa 326 Stowe,
J , suggested that if the eviction occurred in the midst of a month, the
rent for the month could be apportioned to the day of eviction, and
collected
[45]*Linton* v *Hart*, 25 Pa 193, 64
Am Dec 691, *Briggs* v *Thompson*,
9 Pa 338, *Pier* v *Carr*, 69 Pa 326
Pfund v *Herlinger*, 10 Phila 13,

Tilcy v *Moyers*, 43 Pa. 404, *Mc-
Cleary* v *Allen* 2 Penr & W 144
[46]*Tilcy* v *Moyers*, 43 Pa. 404
[47]*Hemphill* v *Eckfeldt*, 5 Whart
274
[48]*Garrett* v *Cummins*, 2 Phila 207
[49] 1 Pepper & Lewis Digest, 1613,
1 Smith's Laws, 49
[50]*Reineman* v *Blair*, 96 Pa 155
[51]*Gallagher's Estate*, 37 Pittsb L.
J 306

day on which the rent is payable, it will destroy the right to any part of the rent that month.[52]

406. Rent after termination of eviction.— Rent which begins to accrue after an eviction has terminated—after the resumption of full possession by the tenant—is not suspended Says Paxson, J. [53] "It does not suspend rent due prior to the eviction, nor rent accruing subsequent thereto, if the defendant remain in possession after the eviction is over " If, e g , there is an eviction in November, and a resumption of possession by the tenant before February, there can be a recovery of the rent for the quarter from March to May, inclusive [54]

407. Eviction from part of premises.— The tenant may be excluded from a part of the premises, while allowed to remain in the possession and enjoyment of the rest. If the partial eviction is the act of the landlord, the effect of it is precisely the same, so far as the suspension of rent is concerned (though not as respects liability for damages) as if the eviction had been total "If," says Woodward, J., "a landlord might evict his tenant from part of the demised premises, and hold him for an apportioned rent of the residue, this would be a substitution of his arbitrary will for the mutual agreement which a lease is. The law apportions rent in certain cases, but it does not allow a lessor to apportion it by means of a partial eviction "[55] Eviction from any part, e. g , from 2 acres of a tract of 400 acres,[56] from a strip used by a railroad for its way,[57] from an 11-acre field, the lease embracing besides a tavern, barn, sheds, and four

[52]*Murphy* v *Marshell*, 179 Pa 516, 36 Atl 294

[53]*Pfund* v *Herlinger*, 10 Phila 13

[54]*Noble* v *Warren*, 38 Pa 340

[55]*Tiley* v *Moyers*, 43 Pa 404, *Wolf* v *Weiner*, 7 Phila 274, *Vaughan* v *Blanchard*, 1 Yeates, 175, 4 Dall 124, 1 L ed 769, *West Ridge Coal Co* v *Von Storch*, 5 Lack Legal News 189, *Bauer* v *Broden*, 3 Phila 214; *Kessler* v.

M'Conachy, 1 Rawle, 435, *Seabrook* v *Moyer*, 88 Pa 417 Kennedy, J, intimates in *Bennet* v *Bittle*, 4 Rawle 339, that if there is a partial eviction the tenant will be liable for the part occupied by him, on a *quantum meruit*

[56]*Reed* v *Ward*, 22 Pa 144

[57]*Linton* v *Hart*, 25 Pa 193, 64 Am Dec. 691.

lots of ground;[58] from one room in the demised house,[59] from a building or a piece of land, but not from that part of the land which is not covered by the building,—will destroy the right to any rent becoming payable during the continuance of the tenant's exclusion. A surety for the rent may take the same advantage of an eviction, partial or total, as the lessee himself, as a defense to the rent.[60]

408. Failure to give possession of part of premises.—The landlord may refuse to give to the tenant possession, according to the stipulation of the lease, of a portion of the premises. The lease, e. g., being of a whole building, may provide for the delivery of possession of all of it but the fourth and fifth stories on a day named, and of these stories whenever the tenant may demand it. The refusal of the landlord, when it is demanded, to give the possession of the fourth and fifth stories, does not, says Williams, J., constitute an eviction in law   It is doubtless true that there may be an eviction without an actual physical expulsion, but there can be no eviction, actual or constructive, without an antecedent possession   "Nevertheless, the same result upon the right to collect rent follows, as if the refusal to give possession was an eviction." The lease of the building being for an entire consideration, for the part performance of the contract there can be no recovery, unless the lessee prevents or waives complete performance   Hence, there could, in the case supposed, be no recovery in a suit for the use and occupation of all the building except the fourth and fifth stories.[61] With the case last referred to may be compared *Smart* v. *Allegaert* [62] A let to B four adjacent buildings at a gross rent, which was arrived at by putting a rent on each, and adding the four rents together   The lessor had a right

[58]*Bennet* v *Bittle,* 4 Rawle 339
[59]*Diehl* v *Woods,* 4 Pennyp 57
[60]*Euing* v *Cottman,* 9 Pa Super Ct 444, *Pier* v *Carr,* 69 Pa 326, *Duff* v *Wilson,* 69 Pa 316, 72 Pa. 442.

[61]*McClung* v *Price,* 59 Pa 420, 98 Am Dec 356
[62]8 W N C 217, Affirmed in 10 W. N C 29.

to and expected the possession of all the buildings in time to give
it to the tenant immediately, but the previous tenant wrong-
fully refused to vacate one of the buildings for more than a year.
Knowing of his refusal, the lessee nevertheless took possession
of the other three buildings, and ultimately, on the expulsion of
the prior tenant, of the fourth. The landlord, at the close of the
term, brought an action for the rent of the three buildings in
whose occupancy there was no delay. It was held that the
tenant might have declined to enter into possession of the three
buildings, but, having taken and retained them, his failure to
obtain the fourth for some time would not prevent an apportionment of the rent, and the recovery of a proportional part of
it, less any proper damages arising from the disappointment
with respect to the fourth building,[63] but he may recover damages for the breach of the lessor's implied covenant that he
should have possession.[64]

409. Refusal of former tenant to vacate — A lease made February 3rd for a term beginning March 23rd, recited that the
premises were then occupied by "W. Hugg," who was tenant
under a lease about to expire before March 23rd. There was
no covenant that Hugg would go out as his lease required. He
in fact did not go out until by landlord and tenant proceedings,
instituted by the succeeding lessee in the name of the lessor, he
was ejected December 20th. As the act of Hugg was without
right, it violated no implied covenant of the lessor with the suc-

[63] In the absence of bad faith on
the part of the lessor, the damages
would be for the rent of the fourth
building, if it had been paid. As it
had not been paid, only nominal
damages could be recovered. Had
the lessor been guilty of bad faith,
the tenant could recover as damages
the loss of the bargain, i e, the difference between the rent he had
agreed to pay and the actual annual
value, for renting purposes, of the
building. Loss on goods bought in
expectation of occupying the building, which the tenant had been compelled to sell at a loss, would in no
case be relevant. The lessee failing
to obtain possession of a part of the
premises because it belonged to another than the lessor, is entitled to a
reduction from the rent. *Watson* v.
Scrieerson, 1 Del Co Rep 87.

[64] *Steel* v *Frick*, 56 Pa 172.

ceeding tenant, who therefore could not obtain damages from the lessor.[65] In *Yeager* v. *Weaver*,[66] the lessee of a hotel was kept out of possession by the preceding tenant. The lessee, prior to the commencement of the term, had bought furniture. The lessor promised him possession in ten days, but failed to give it. The lessee, it was held, could recover as damages compensation for the loss on resale of the furniture, and compensation for loss arising from his being without a house, and being compelled to board.

410. Partial eviction; royalty.— If the lease is of a coal bank or an ore bank, for a given time, the rent being so much per bushel or ton for every bushel or ton mined and taken away, and the lessor enters on a portion of the tract where the lessee is not operating, and takes away coal or ore, the act is not to be regarded as a partial eviction, which would suspend the rent, so long as it lasted, *i. e ,* which would allow the tenant to escape from the payment for the coal or ore actually taken by him. He would be liable for the payment of the stipulated royalty, less any damages he may have suffered by the removal of any of the coal or ore by the lessor, whether the estate of the lessee under the lease be regarded as a corporeal or an incorporeal hereditament. If, contesting the right of the lessee to do certain acts on the premises, the lessor institutes ejectments, and causes writs of estrepement to issue, whereby the operations of the lessee are interrupted, the damages arising from this interruption can be deducted from the royalty, collectable by the lessor, but the right to the royalty is not *in toto* destroyed [67]

411. Partial eviction by other than lessor.— If the eviction

[65]*Cozens* v *Stevenson*, 5 Serg & R 421

[66] 64 Pa 425 The plaintiff showed that he would have made, as annual profits, $500 had he obtained the possession The court refused to strike out the evidence This was not error The defendant should have requested an instruction to the jury to disregard the evidence

[67]*Riley* v *Moyers*, 43 Pa 404 As the lessor had a right to bring the ejectments to test the lessee s right, he is not liable to the lessee for his counsel fees, the cost of printing the paper books, etc.

is not by the lessor, but by another, under a title superior to that which the lessor has when he makes the lease, even if the evicting party has obtained his title from the lessor by conveyance or contract prior to the lease, the rent will be apportioned, and the eviction will bar the recovery only of so much of the rent as represents the value of the part of the premises from which the tenant has been excluded. In *Seabrook* v. *Moyer*[68] there was a demise for three years, at a monthly rent of $250, of a house having a right of way over an alley, 3 feet, 10 inches in width. Before making the lease, the lessor and X, the owner of the adjacent land, had released to each other the right of way over the alley, so that each might, if he chose, inclose his half of the alley. After the tenant had been in possession thirteen months, X began to build, and in so doing, he constructed a party wall on eleven inches of the alley, which, extending above the alley, reduced the width of the rooms in the second and third story. The tenant continuing in possession was liable for a fair rent for the part of the premises thus retained by him, in an action for use and occupation "If," says Mercur, J, "the defendant had been evicted by paramount title from the whole premises, he would have been discharged from the payment of the whole rent, after that time. But an eviction by such title from a part only of the demised premises, when the tenant continues in possession of the remaining part, using and enjoying it, does not work a suspension of all subsequent rent. He remains liable to the payment of such proportion of the rent as the value of the part retained bears to the whole. On having been evicted from a part, he might have removed from the residue, and thereby wholly relieved himself from the payment of future rent; failing to do so he became liable to a just apportionment."

412. Eviction by one who purchases reversion during the term. —A conveyance by the lessor of the reversion in a portion of the

[68] 88 Pa 417.

premises does not so far make him responsible for an eviction
by the grantee from the part granted, that such eviction will
deprive him of the right to collect the rent which, by due apportionment, belongs to the reversion which he retains[69] "The
owner of a reversion has the right," remarks Lewis, Ch. J , "to
sell the whole or any part of it Such right is incident to the
right of property, and necessary to the full enjoyment of it.
The exercise of it is not wrongful, and, therefore, in the case
of a sale of a part of the reversion, the law will apportion the
rent, and the right of apportionment attaches the moment the
sale is made No action of the purchaser, or his aiders and
abettors, in dispossessing the tenant of the part purchased, after
such severance, can have any effect upon the rent growing out
of the unsold part remaining in his undisturbed possession. It
matters not that the original reversioner, after such severance,
becomes a party to the trespass by aiding his vendee in committing it The trespass has relation only to the part sold, and
cannot be visited upon the other part of the premises."[70] A
leased to B for five years a house and piece of ground with a
ferry   Fourteen months afterwards, A sold a part of the land
embraced in the lease to a railroad company, releasing the
company from all damages by reason of the location and construction of the railroad   The company constructed their road
on the part thus sold to them. In an action for the apportioned
rent, by A, the eviction by the railroad company furnished no
defense.[71] After leasing a farm of 400 acres to B, A conveys
1 acre of it to C, and another acre to D   C and D exclude F
from the possession of their respective acres. A could, nevertheless, distrain for a due portion of the rent falling due after

---

[69] *Seabrook* v *Moyer*, 88 Pa 417
[70] *Linton* v *Hart*, 25 Pa 193, 04
Am Dec 691
[71] *Linton* v *Hart* 25 Pa 193, 64
Am Dec 691   The company had no
right, as against the tenant, to enter
without making compensation to
him   The tenant has an ample
remedy for the injury, without depriving the lessor of the just portion
of rent due for the premises enjoyed
under the lease.

this dispossession   Nor is A deprived of this right because, in addition to conveying the acres, he advises C and D to take possession of them.   Though he may be liable in trespass for this tort, his rights "issuing out of other lands are not thereby forfeited "[72]

413. Eviction by sheriff's vendee of the fee.— An eviction of the tenant by one who purchases the lessor's interest at a sheriff's sale, under a judgment earlier than the lease, suspends the rent.[73]   If, after the sale, the landlord sues for rent payable in advance, before it accrues, the election of the sheriff's vendee to disaffirm the lease, and to expel the tenant, would be a defense, as it would also support an action on the lessor's covenant for quiet enjoyment.[74]

414   Eviction under eminent domain — The state may, directly or indirectly, take land under its eminent domain, and thus deprive not only the landlord, but the tenant, of the enjoyment of it   If A sells or leases land to B, both parties know of this eminent domain, and neither, in the absence of a special stipulation, can be understood to assume any liability with respect to the other.[75]   If, after the lease is made, the state or its delegate —some corporation—takes all or some of the premises, e g , for the laying out,[76] or the widening,[77] of a street, or for a railroad,[78] or takes for a canal water from a stream, to the detriment of a riparian owner,[79] no eviction occurs which can defeat a recovery of rent, or expose the lessor to an action for damages on his covenant for quiet enjoyment.   If, however, the power of the state to expropriate has already been asserted and exercised, but the right to its exercise is disputed when the lease is made,

[72]*Reed* v *Ward*, 22 Pa 144
[73]*Sallade* v *James*, 6 Pa 144
[74]*Market Co* v *Lutz*, 4 Phila 322
[75]*Barns* v *Wilson*, 116 Pa 303, 9 Atl. 437
[76]*Workman* v *Mifflin*, 30 Pa. 362, (Ground-rent.)

[77]*Frost* v *Earnest*, 4 Whart 86. The tenant could not recover on the covenant for quiet enjoyment
[78]*Schuylkill & D Improv & R Co* v *Schroele*, 57 Pa. 271: *Rapp* v *Klair*, 5 Montg Co L Rep 16
[79]*Peters* v *Grubb*, 21 Pa 455

and the lease contains a covenant for quiet enjoyment, so expressed that it must be held to embrace all antagonistic claims, whether of the state or of private persons, the subsequent exercise of it may be a ground for abating the rent, to the extent of the damages suffered. The state, e g , erected a dam, a feeder, and gates, for the purpose of turning water from a river. They were structures evident to the senses. The right of the state thus to turn off the water was contested by A, the owner of riparian land   A leased this land to B, covenanting to protect B in the use and enjoyment of it, "against the claims or interruption or molestation of any person or persons whomsoever, so that the said lessee shall suffer no loss from any defect of title of the lessors to the premises." During the lease, the state wholly diverted the water from the mill of the tenant. The damages thence arising could be set off against a claim for rent, in replevin after a distress [80]

415. Eviction,—Uhler v. Cowen.— The city of Philadelphia had authority to increase by 100 feet the width of Delaware avenue. Before any exercise of this authority, A leased to B a pier on the east side of that avenue for a term of ten years, commencing April 1st, 1888. Under an ordinance passed March 11th, 1895, notice was given by the city, on October 28th, 1896, to the lessor, that at the expiration of three months from the date of the notice, the city would require that portion of his property that lay within the bed of the avenue. A copy of this notice was served by the lessor on his lessee on November 12th, 1896, who, in pursuance of it, vacated the premises on January 26th, 1897. The city filed its bond to secure payment of damages on January 18th, 1898, and entered on the premises March 18th, 1898 The viewers assessed the lessor's damages at $17,597, stating that that sum included any claim for rent against the lessee of the premises at the time of the taking, and that it

[80]*Peters* v *Grubb,* 21 Pa 455.

was intended to operate as a release to the tenant from any rent
It was held that the tenant had a right to obey the notice and
quit the premises, and that, doing so, he ceased to be liable for
rent for any period following the close of his occupancy, although, had he remained, his possession, as the event showed,
would not have been disturbed. Not deciding that a taking of
part of the premises would relieve altogether from the rent, it
was held that, as the portions of the pier not taken by the city
were of no value, the whole of the premises had virtually been
taken; that the damages awarded to the lessor took the place
of the land, and that the relation of landlord and tenant, and
all the covenants growing out of that relation, were necessarily
at an end.[81]

416. Eminent domain; effect of compensation.—While the
mere taking of the land or of a part of it, under the power of
eminent domain, may not relieve the tenant from rent,[82] this
relief may follow from the mode in which damages are awarded
Thus, if all or a part of the premises being taken by a railroad,
compensation for the fee of the part taken is paid to the landlord, the money takes the place of the land whose price is thus
paid, and no duty survives on the part of the tenant to pay rent
for this land to the landlord   And all parties having interests
in the land should intervene to secure the proper division among
them of this compensation. The failure of any to do so does not

---

[81] *Uhler* v *Cowen,* 199 Pa 316 49
Atl 77, 192 Pa 445, 44 Atl 42

If, when a lease is accepted, a railroad already has a bridge or viaduct
over the premises, the presence of
this viaduct is not an eviction   The
lessee must be regarded as taking the
lease subject to the railroad company's right not only to maintain,
but to repair, the viaduct   Inconvenience suffered by the repairing,
whether larger than necessary or
not, would be no ground for abating

the rent   If an unnecessary inconvenience is caused by the company,
it must compensate the tenant.
Friend v *Oil Well Supply Co* 179
Pa 290, 36 Atl 219

[82] But see *Uhler* v *Cowen* 92 Pa.
443, 44 Atl 42, where McCollum, J ,
intimates that the tenant is relieved
from rent, whether, by the exercise
of the eminent domain, he is deprived of all or a part only of the
premises   Cf *Uhler* v. *Cowen,* 199
Pa 316, 49 Atl 77.

preserve his former right. A leases a lot to B, and B sublets a part of it to C. A railroad company takes all the lot, paying as damages $10,000 for the fee, which the viewers have assessed Whether B in fact obtained a portion of this money, or not, he cannot recover any future rent from C.[83] But, only a part of the premises being taken, if compensation is made to the tenant for the reduction of the value of the leasehold, and to the landlord for the reduction of the value of the reversion, there is no reason why the tenant should not pay the stipulated rent. He must continue to pay it without reduction [84]

417. Interference by public authority.— The public may, under law, abate a building or a part of it which has become dangerous, and the landlord is not liable for its acts, even though they result in the expulsion of the tenant, and this expulsion is agreeable to the landlord, and is acquiesced in by him A leased a storeroom in a building to B. A part of the wall of this building falling and killing a child, the city inspector of buildings, on the request of two citizens, finding the building dangerous, ordered the landlord to remove it in five days The landlord not doing so, an agent of the city, after notice to the tenant, tore the building down For this act the landlord was not responsible in trespass on the case [85] If the owner of the adjacent lot, intending to build on it, causes the wall of the house occupied by A's tenant to be condemned, under the provisions of the act of May 20th, 1857,[86] and, being authorized

[83]*Dyer* v *Wightman*, 66 Pa 425
If the landlord has received the compensation which ought to have been given to the tenant, the mistake cannot be corrected in the action for the rent, nor in an action on the covenant for quiet enjoyment. *Frost* v *Earnest*, 4 Whart. 86

[84]*Rapp* v. *Klair*, 5 Montg Co L Rep 16
Under an unconstitutional law, Pittsburg opens a street, and an order is given to its officer to tear down a certain house within the lines of the street, if the owner neglects to do so. This is sufficient authority to the owner to do so, notwithstanding the invalidity of the act of assembly *Dunn* v *Mellon*, 147 Pa 11, 30 Am St Rep 706, 23 Atl 210

[85]*Hitchcock* v *Bacon*, 118 Pa 272, 12 Atl 352

[86] P. L 590.

by the proper authorities, he removes it, so leaving the rooms of the house open and exposed, to be entered at pleasure, and open to wind and rain, and cutting the pipes for water and gas, and the flues for heating the house, so as to render it uninhabitable, —in these acts, which are followed by the removal of the tenant, there is nothing to prevent the recovery of the rent for the premises, for the period in which the dispossession occurred. "Titles to real estate," said Clark, J , "are everywhere held subject to such constitutional and legal conditions affecting the enjoyment thereof, as shall, from time to time, be established; all are subject to the commonwealth's right of eminent domain, and to such statutory and other police regulations as affect the safety, health, and good order of society; one tract of land, from its mere location with respect to another, may owe it a servitude, and one man must so use his property as not unnecessarily to injure another. These are not defects in title, they are simply the legal conditions which affect the owner's enjoyment of his own property "[87]

418. Acts done on adjacent land.— Acts done by its owner on land adjacent to the premises demised are not a breach of the lessor's covenant for quiet enjoyment, whatever their results as to the tenantableness or enjoyableness of the premises The leased house has, on one side, a wall of studding, lath, and plaster, but the wall of the next house is in immediate contact with it. The exposure to the weather of this lath and plaster wall by the taking down of the neighboring house, resulting in

---

[87] *Barns* v *Wilson,* 116 Pa 303, 9 Atl 437 In *Dougherty* v *Wagner,* 2 W N C 291, next to the house occupied by A s tenant was a house belonging to X Under the direction of the building inspector, X tore down his back building He was obliged to dig under the foundation of the old party wall, making it dangerous The privies of A's premises, by the extension of the ad- joining house, were left exposed, so that they could not be used To avoid injury to them, the tenant removed his family The improvements in the next house were not completed until the end of the term, nor the back building of the tenant's house susceptible of use until then These facts, embodied in an affidavit of defense, could not prevent judgment for the rent.

LAND. & TEN 23

the injury to the tenant's goods by wet and dampness, is no cause of action against the landlord.[88] "It is too clear for argument," says Sharswood, J., "that there was here no breach of the implied obligation of the landlord that the tenant shall enjoy quiet and peaceable possession during the term."[89] A leased to B a hotel having eighteen side windows looking over the adjoining land belonging to another person, C, making no covenants or representation with respect to these windows. Subsequently C erected a party wall on his lot, thus closing up these windows This act and its results were no reason for diminishing the rent for which B was liable. They were no breach of the covenant for quiet enjoyment, implied in the words "demise and lease" There was no duty on A's part to disclose to B, before he accepted the lease, the fact, known to A, that C was intending to close the windows [90] The occupant of a house which is taller than its neighbors, leases to A the roof and so much of the wall as projects above the neighboring houses, for the exhibition of stereopticon advertisements. Subsequently the tenant of one of the neighboring houses makes a lease of his roof, for a similar purpose, to a rival, who uses a screen which intercepts the view of the advertisements thrown upon the wall. This fact furnishes to A no defense to a claim for the rent, notwithstanding that he has renounced the contract, and ceased to use the wall and roof.[91]

419. Eviction by stranger.— An eviction or disturbance of the possession by a stranger, without right, is not within the scope of the covenant, express or implied, for quiet enjoyment, and for it, therefore, the lessor is not liable [92] A lease for mining coal

---

[88] *Moore* v *Weber*, 71 Pa 429, 10 Am Rep 708

[89] There was no duty on the lessor to keep the house tenantable or to make repairs, in the absence of a contract

[90] *Hazlett* v. *Powell*, 30 Pa 293.

[91] *Oakford* v *Nixon*, 177 Pa 76, 34 L R A 575, 35 Atl 588

[92] *Pollard* v *Shaaffer*, 1 Dall 210, 1 L ed 104, 1 Am Dec 239 Cf. *Naglee* v *Ingersol*, 7 Pa 185, *Spear* v *Allison*, 20 Pa 200.

requires a certain royalty to be paid, whether coal is mined or not. A third person brings ejectment and issues an estrepement, so arresting the mining operations. This does not excuse from the payment of the royalty. If the ejectment issued in a judgment for the plaintiff therein, and an ouster of the tenant, there would be an eviction for which the tenant would have a right of recourse to the covenant for quiet enjoyment, but the mere pending of the ejectment furnishes no excuse for nonpayment of rent. Hence the lessor will not be restrained from enforcing the forfeiture of the term on account of the tenant's default.[93] If, before making an oil and gas lease, the lessor has granted all the coal under the land, reserving to himself the right to drill three oil and gas wells, an interference with the lessee, by the grantee of the coal, beyond his right, will not make the lessor liable for breach of the covenant for quiet enjoyment.[94]

420 Liability for mesne profits.— In *Bauders* v. *Fletcher*[95] an ejectment was brought by X against both the lessor, A, and the lessee, B, but it was not terminated by judgment for X until the expiration of the term for which A sought to recover rent from B   It was held that as the judgment was against A as well as B, it was conclusive as to A as well as B, of the right of X to mesne profits for the period following the inception of the ejectment, the rent for which was sued for by A.   Hence A could not recover the rent.[96]   In *McCleary* v. *Allen,*[97] however, where the lease was for three years from April 1st, 1823, and an ejectment by a stranger was brought to May term, 1824, against both lessor and lessee, resulting in a judgment for the plaintiff, and an expulsion of both defendants by the *habere facias possessionem,* these facts were held to constitute no de-

[93]*Schuylkill & D Improv & R Co v Schmoele*, 57 Pa 271
[94]*Chambers* v *Smith*, 183 Pa. 122, 38 Atl 522   Not decided whether the word "grant" implies a covenant for quiet enjoyment

[95] 11 Serg & R 419
[96] Nor was the result different when the tenant bought the title of X, to avoid being ejected
[97] 2 Penr & W. 144.

fense in an action for the rent brought after the close of the
term   Shippen, J , saying: "As the eviction by Flock was not
until after the lease, upon which suit is brought, had expired,
and McCleary, the tenant, enjoyed all the benefits of the lease,
the evidence offered, if true, would not be either a legal or an
equitable defense against the payment of the rent."

421 **Eviction by stranger under paramount title.**—An eviction
of the tenant in virtue of a title superior to that of the
lessor destroys the duty to pay rent for the period during
which the exclusion lasts   If the eviction is from a fractional
interest, *e. g.,* from three undivided tenths of the land,[98] there
will be a release from any duty of paying more than seven tenths
of the rent. If the eviction occurs after the commencement of
the month, quarter, or year for which, according to the lease, the
rent is payable, the duty of paying a part of the rent, apportioned
to the time of possession, will remain on the lessee   If, *e g ,*
eight days elapse since the last pay day before the tenant is put
out of possession, he will be liable for the rent of these eight
days [99] The eviction may be by one having a title adverse to
that of the lessor,[100] or by one who, under a lien created by the
lessor, becomes the owner of his interest by means of a sheriff's
sale thereon, during the term [101] The eviction may occur by
peaceable entry of the owner,[102] or by means of the action of
ejectment   The mere recovery of the judgment may not be an
eviction, but if a *habere facias possessionem* issues, the tenant,
though he may be,[103] need not be, actually expelled from the
possession   He may attorn to the successful plaintiff, and by that

[98]*Garrison* v *Moore*, 1 Phila 282
[99]*Ross* v *Dysart*, 33 Pa 452
[100] In *Maule* v *Ashmead*, 20 Pa
482, the widow of X leased his land,
which was afterwards sold by order
of the orphans' court for the payment
of debts   The purchaser expelled the
tenant
[101]*Hulseman* v *Griffiths*, 10 Phila

350, *Hemphill* v *Eckfeldt*, 5 Whart
274, *Duff* v *Wilson*, 69 Pa 316, 72
Pa 442

The mere existence of a lien is not
an eviction, nor a defense to suit for
rent   *Coxe* v *Williams*, 15 Phila
187
[102]*Kellam* v *Janson*, 17 Pa 467.
[103]*Duff* v *Wilson*, 69 Pa 316

act become his, and cease to be the lessor's tenant [104] Or he may contract to purchase the land from the plaintiff, and continue to hold the possession as the plaintiff's vendee, instead of as the lessor's tenant.[105] If, after possession is thus retained by the tenant, the *habere facias possessionem* is set aside, the tenant is remitted, *ipso facto,* without any writ of restitution, to his former relation to his landlord, and the lease from the plaintiff in the ejectment falls,[106] but if the judgment is reversed on appeal, and a writ of restitution issues, and is executed to the satisfaction of the plaintiff, without actual expulsion of the former tenant, who has attorned to the plaintiff in the ejectment, the tenant, having attorned to the plaintiff, cannot be considered as otherwise than evicted, during the interval from the execution of the *habere facias,* to the execution of the writ of restitution, and he will not be liable for rent during this interval The right of the lessor to recover mesne profits from the former lessee does not prevent the exemption of the tenant from liability for the rent. The lessor "cannot compel the tenant to pay him rent for the time his own covenant was in a state of breach."[107]

422. **Effect of tenant's guaranty against lien.**—The principle that the tenant is excused from rent accruing after an eviction is not rendered inapplicable by the fact that the lessor had purchased the land from X, taking from X a guaranty against

---

[104]*Hulseman* v *Griffiths*, 10 Phila 350, *Coughanour* v *Bloodgood*, 27 Pa 285 Cf *Wray* v *Lemon*, 81* Pa 273, where a lessee assigned the lease, and covenanted to indemnify the assignee for any loss One of the two lessors, a married woman, brought ejectment against the assignee, because she had not acknowledged the lease A *habere facias* issued, and in order to avoid expulsion, the assignee accepted a new lease, and agreed to pay higher rent. After this the original lease was totally gone, with all its incidents and benefits.

[105]*Ross* v *Dysart*, 33 Pa 452, *Hulseman* v *Griffiths*, 10 Phila 350
[106]*Coughanour* v *Bloodgood*, 27 Pa 285

[107]*Ross* v *Dysart*, 33 Pa 452 The former lessee bought the premises from the successful plaintiff and remained in possession during the two years and eight months of the term, and after He was liable, therefore for mesne profits But he was held not liable in an action on the lease for the rent

the enforcement of a mortgage on the premises, and had then
leased the land to X, who, in breach of his guaranty, allowed a
sheriff's sale upon the judgment on the mortgage. His liability
as guarantor cannot be confused with that as lessee. Hence,
both he and his surety will be discharged from liability for the
rent, despite the fact that his delinquency caused the eviction [108]
But if, A and B being tenants in common of land, A lets his
half to B, for whom C becomes surety, and B mortgages his
interest in the land to C, and if C buys an outstanding mortgage
on both the interests, under which he causes a sheriff's sale to
another, as trustee for him, who takes possession under a *habere
facias possessionem,* C, when sued as surety for the rent, cannot
set up the sheriff's sale and the action of the sheriff on the
habere, as an eviction. As cotenant with A, C was under a duty
to protect the property from sale under the common lien, and
having bought it in, he held it for the benefit of both, and had no
right to dispossess A or his tenant B, before giving A an opportunity to reimburse him for the purchase money.[109]

423. Tenant takes the risk of the title — The tenant may be
aware of the defect of the lessor's title and agree to take on
himself the risk of it. If he does, the loss of possession in consequence of the defect will be no defense to the demand for
rent or royalty. But if he covenants to pay at least $10,000
every three years, whether the coal mined will or will not be
sufficient, at the rate of 50 cents per ton, to yield that sum,—
unless it shall be impossible to obtain enough coal to yield it, it
is permissible for him to show that, after the loss of the possession of a part of the land by an eviction, on the part that remains there is not sufficient coal to furnish, at the rate of
50 cents per ton, so much as $10,000.[110]

[108]*Duff* v *Wilson,* 69 Pa 316.   [110]*Kemble Coal & I Co* v *Scott,*
[109]*Duff* v *Wilson,* 72 Pa 442   But   90 Pa 332, *Kemble Coal & I. Co* v.
if C's conduct was fraudulent, he   *Scott,* 15 W. N C. 220.
would not be entitled to reimburse-
ment

424. Tenant waives the eviction.— The tenant may seek and obtain compensation from the owner of the conflicting title, derived from the lessor prior to the making of the lease, and if he does so, he will not be allowed to use the interference with his possession as a defense to the lessor's action for rent. Before making a lease of a farm to B, the lessor has leased the same tract to A for "oil and gas purposes." If A pays $1,000 to B on account of damages for past interferences with B's possession, and agrees to pay B for future interferences, and thereupon B gives A full right of entry in and upon the premises, defining what his rights shall be, and remains in possession, he cannot defend against the landlord's claim for rent by alleging the acts of A as an eviction.[111]

425. Actions by tenant for disturbance.— The tenant may maintain an action (viz., assumpsit) on the covenant, express[112] or implied,[113] for quiet enjoyment, and, if the lease has been assigned, the assignee, in the name of the assignor[114] or in his own, may institute it, or, being sued for the rent, the tenant may set off the damages arising from the breach of the covenant,[115] or, a distress being made for the rent, the tenant, alleging damages which he has a right to set off, may, in his replevin, show such damages. For invasion of his right by trespassing on the premises, and wholly or partially excluding the tenant, the ac-

[111]*Horberg* v *May*, 153 Pa 216, 25 Atl. 750.

If, after an eviction from a part of the premises, the tenant continues to pay the rent, and holds over, he will be liable for the rent accruing while he holds over, despite the eviction *Ward's Estate*, 22 Pa. Co. Ct. 284

[112]*Lanigan* v *Kille*, 97 Pa. 120, 39 Am Rep 797; *Frost* v *Earnest*, 4 Whart 86, *Walter* v. *Transue*, 22 Pa Super Ct 617.

If the rights of the tenant are precisely the same under the lease as proven as they would be under the lease as alleged, and the case is tried on the merits, the difference between the *allegata* and *probata* will be no ground for reversal, the testimony having been admitted without objection, and no motion having been made to strike it out. *Walter* v. *Transue*, 22 Pa. Super Ct 617.

[113]*Maule* v *Ashmead*, 20 Pa 482, *Steel* v *Frick*, 56 Pa 172

[114]*Maule* v *Ashmead*, 20 Pa 482

[115]*Hemphill* v *Eckfeldt*, 5 Whart 274, *Garrett* v *Cummins*, 2 Phila 207, *Reintman* v *Blair*, 96 Pa 155

tion of trespass will lie,[116] and if the goods of the tenant are sold under an improper distress by the landlord, compensation for the injury to the tenant as such, and also as owner of these goods, can be recovered in the same action.[117]

426. Damages; total eviction — When the tenant is evicted from all the premises, whether by the landlord[118] or by one having a superior title,[119] for whose act the landlord is liable on his covenant for quiet enjoyment, he is entitled to recover damages from the landlord When the eviction is by the landlord himself, the damages will be measured by the market value of the lease [120] If improvements have been made by the tenant which enhance the market value of the lease, he is, of course, entitled to this enhanced value. What the lease, e g , would be worth, in view of the plowing and sowing of crops shortly before the eviction, will be allowed the tenant [121] It would be improper to allow to the tenant the cost of the improvements, or the value of the improvements remaining on the premises at the date of the eviction What he is entitled to is the value of the lease for the remainder of the term, in the actual state of the premises, with its improvements [122] In *Seyfert v. Bean*[123] the landlord evicted the tenant from a dwelling house in which the latter conducted a boarding school He also caused a dis-

---

[116] Cf *Clark* v *Lindsay*, 7 Pa Super Ct 43, *Dunn* v *Mellon*, 147 Pa 11, 30 Am St Rep 706 23 Atl 210, *Hitchcock* v *Bacon*, 118 Pa 272, 12 Atl 352, *Gallagher* v *Burke*, 13 Pa Super Ct 244, *Garrett* v *Cummins*, 2 Phila 207, *Moore* v *Weber*, 71 Pa 429, 10 Am Rep 708, *Dosch* v *Diem*, 176 Pa 603, 35 Atl 207, *Seyfert* v *Bean*, 83 Pa 450, *Bowman* v *Bradley*, 151 Pa 351, 17 L R A 213 24 Atl 1062

[117] *Seyfert* v *Bean*, 83 Pa 450

[118] *Long* v *Wood*, 22 Pittsb L J 93, *O'Neal* v *Sneeringer*, 12 York Legal Record, 141, *Walters* v *Transue*, 6 Northampton Co Rep. 406.

[119] *Lanigan* v *Kille*, 97 Pa 120, 39 Am Rep 797, *Maule* v *Ashmead*, 20 Pa 482

[120] *Long* v *Wood*, 22 Pittsb L J 93 Coal lease Cf *Burgwin* v *Bishop*, 91 Pa 336

[121] *O'Neal* v *Sneeringer*, 12 York Legal Record, 141

[122] *Walters* v *Transue*, 6 Northampton Co Rep 406 Cf *Maule* v *Ashmead* 20 Pa 482 where it is remarked that the produce of the farm for the remainder of the term would have been worth much more than in the earlier portion of the term, because of the tenant's improvements

[123] 83 Pa 450

tress to be levied on her goods, for rent, having no right to distrain. In trespass on the case by the tenant, she was, without error, permitted to show the number of pupils in the school, the number of teachers employed, the amount of money expended by her in advertising the school, and the price paid by her for the goods which had been sold in distress. Mercur, J , observed that the price of the goods was some evidence of their value, that the number of teachers and pupils indicated the facilities for instruction and the extent of the school's patronage, that many of the articles had a value when used in connection with the school, much greater than after they were removed therefrom, and that the deprivation of the house and of the goods destroyed the business, so that the tenant lost all profit on the investment made, the good will, and the entire capital

427. Damages, total eviction by stranger.— When the eviction takes place by a stranger, a different rule obtains from that which applies when it takes place by the landlord's own act [124] The measure of damages is generally the consideration paid in advance, or a proportional part of it, and such mesne profits as a tenant has paid or is liable for to the owner of the paramount title   If the lessor has been guilty of fraud or bad faith, he will be liable for the loss of the bargain   The loss to him of the improvements put on the premises by the tenant, whether at his own option, or, if they are not to become the property of the lessor, under a stipulation in the lease, requiring him to make them, though, by reason of their annexation to the freehold, they pass with it to the successful adverse claimant of the land,— is no ground for compensation from the lessor.   Hence, it is proper for the trial court, in the lessee's action on the covenant for quiet enjoyment, alleging an eviction by one having a title superior to the lessor's, to exclude evidence of the value of the improvements.   Nor is it admissible to show that, in an action

[124] *Lanigan* v *Kille,* 97 **Pa 120, 39** Am Rep 797.

by the true owner against the lessor, for mesne profits, the latter reduced the verdict that would have been recovered against him by setting off the value of these improvements. The fact that the lessor has made this use of it does not entitle the tenant to recover it [125]

428. Damages; partial eviction.— For a partial eviction of the tenant by the landlord, the measure of damages is the difference between the value to the tenant of the possession of the whole for the period of the exclusion, and that of the possession of the part which he has been allowed to retain   In *Gallagher* v. *Burke*[126] the tenants having been excluded from one room the trial court, with the approval of the appellate court, instructed the jury that, on considering the value of the premises to the tenant at the time of the eviction, they were "to take into consideration the nature, the amount, and the profits of the plaintiffs' existing grocery business as viewed at that time, and the necessities of the plaintiffs in that business for the additional room in which to conduct it, as also their inconveniences and injuries to their business in not having the use of the whole building "

429 Exemplary damages.— In the absence of wantonness or malice, the damages recoverable from the lessor for his eviction of the tenant should be compensatory only,[127] but for wanton or malicious eviction, in addition to compensatory damages, vindictive or exemplary damages may be allowed [128]

[125]*Lanigan* v. *Kille*, 97 Pa. 120, 39 Am Rep 797

[126] 13 Pa Super Ct 244   In *Irwin* v *Nolde*, 176 Pa 594, 35 L R A 415, 35 Atl. 217, a person without right, but thinking that he had right, dispossessed the tenant of two fields, parts of a large tract. One of these fields had been planted in corn by the tenant, the other had been ploughed and manured   The evictor planted the latter field, and, when the crops of both fields matured, appropriated them   It was said by

Fell, J, that the proper measure of damages was the difference between the rental value of the whole tract, and that of the part retained, not the rental value of the parts taken, and not the value of the crops raised on the part taken

[127] The same rule applies in an action against a stranger for an eviction without right   *Irwin* v *Nolde*, 176 Pa. 594, 35 L R A 415, 35 Atl 217

[128]*Gallagher* v. *Burke*, 13 Pa. Super. Ct 244

430. Function of jury.— The definition of an eviction is to be given to the jury by the court, which also declares the legal consequences of an eviction, but, as in other cases, whether the facts have occurred which constitute an eviction is for the jury to decide,[129] when there is sufficient evidence.[130] If there is not sufficient evidence, if, *e. g.,* a fire having destroyed a portion of the building and the division fence, the lessor enters in order to replace the division fence, but there is no evidence that he intends to take exclusive possession and control of the property, it would be error to allow the jury to find an intention to take such exclusive possession and control, and therefore an eviction.[131]

[129]*Bennet* v *Bittle,* 4 Rawle, 339; *Burgwin* v *Bishop,* 91 Pa 336, *Gallagher* v *Burke,* 13 Pa Super Ct 244, *Ewing* v *Cottman,* 9 Pa. Super. Ct. 444, *Pier* v. *Carr,* 69 Pa. 326.

[130]*Walters* v *Transue,* 6 Northampton Co Rep 406

[131]*Mannerbach* v *Keppleman,* 2 Woodw Dec. 137.

CHAPTER XXII.

ASSIGNMENT OF TERM.

431. Transmission at lessee's death — The interest of the lessee in the premises may be transferred from him to another. By his death it passes to his executor or administrator, who may maintain the proper action to recover the possession under the lease or damages for the dispossession,[1] and who will be liable

[1] *Keating* v *Condon*, 68 Pa 75;
Kunkle v *Philadelphia Rifle Club*,
10 Phila 52

for the value of what remains of the term, to creditors of the deceased lessee or his next of kin [2] And the right of renewal of the lease is also an asset, for which the administrator must account [3]

432 Sheriff's sale of term.— The interest of a tenant in a lease, of whatever duration, is a chattel interest. A judgment against him is not a lien upon it,[4] but it may be sold in execution, and being a chattel, and not real estate,[5] it may be sold on a fieri facias, without inquisition and condemnation,[6] and by a constable on a judgment of a justice of the peace [7] An undivided half of the leasehold may be assigned, and then the other half may be sold by the sheriff to the assignee [8] A husband's interest as lessee may be seized on a warrant for deserting his wife, under the act of June 13, 1836 [9] The purchaser at sheriff's sale, of the leasehold, becomes an assignee with all the rights and liabilities of an assignee in any other mode.[10]

433. Lessee's assignment for benefit of creditors.— The lessee may make an assignment of all his property for the benefit of his creditors. Such an assignment will pass to the assignee his leasehold interest,[11] but the assignee may refuse to accept the leasehold, if he deems it of no value above the rent to be paid.

[2] *Wiley's Appeal*, 8 Watts & S 244, *Walker's Estate*, 6 Pa Co Ct 515, *Ramow's Estate*, 4 Kulp, 153, *Buck's Estate*, 185 Pa 57, 64 Am St Rep 616, 39 Atl 821, *Emeret's Estate*, 2 Pars Sel Eq Cas 195, *Fow's Estate*, 3 Pa Dist R 316 Though only a month remains. *Coppel's Estate*, 4 Phila 378

[3] *Emeret's Estate*, 2 Pars Sel Eq Cas 195, *Fow's Estate*, 3 Pa Dist R 316, cf *Johnson's Appeal*, 115 Pa 129, 2 Am St Rep 539, 8 Atl 36

[4] *Krause's Appeal*, 2 Whart 398

[5] *Brown v Beecher*, 120 Pa 590, 15 Atl 608, *Duke v Hague*, 107 Pa 57, *Titusville Iron Novelty Works' Appeal*, 77 Pa 103

[6] *Dalzell v Lynch*, 4 Watts & S 255, *Williams v Downing*, 18 Pa 60, *Kile v Grebner*, 114 Pa 381, 7 Atl 154, *McDermott v Crippen*, 5 Law Times N S 109, *Wetherill v Curry*, 2 Phila 98, *Goss v Woodland Fire Brick Co.* 4 Pa Super Ct. 167

[7] *Lerew v Rinehart*, 3 Pa Co Ct 50, *Bismarck Bldg & L Asso v. Bolster*, 92 Pa 123

[8] *Guldin v Butz*, 2 Woodw Dec. 74

[9] *Sterling v Com* 2 Grant, Cas. 162

[10] *Simons v Van Ingen*, 86 Pa. 330

[11] *Goodwin v Sharkey*, 80 Pa 149, *Weiter v Kershner*, 109 Pa 219.

He may thus escape liability as assignee in an action for the rent by the lessor against him,[12] and protect the estate in his hands from liability for rent becoming due after the assignment,[13] since, without some action of the assignee constituting an acceptance, rent falling due after the assignment is not entitled to payment from the assigned estate.[14] The assignee's permitting some assigned goods to remain on the demised premises eleven days after the assignment is not an acceptance of the lease, which would make the estate liable for more than compensation for the occupancy for eleven days,[15] and the fact that the assignee continued for two months to carry on, in the leased stores, the assignee's business of selling retail furniture, during which time he made purchases of such articles as were necessary in order advantageously to dispose of the stock on hand, he then making a sale and vacating the premises, cannot be construed into an acceptance of the lease. "The nature and purpose of this possession," says McCollum, J, "were known to the lessor, and it negatived, rather than warranted, an inference of an intention to charge the estate with the rent which he [the lessor] now seeks to recover from the fund appropriated by the assignment to the claims of the then existing creditors of the assignor"[16] If the assignee both enters on the premises to wind up the assignor's business, and pays one instalment of the rent when it becomes due according to the terms of the lease, and receives a receipt to him as "assignee of X," the tenant, he becomes tenant to the lessor, and is personally liable for the future instalments of the rent of the term. The lease of a store being

[12]*Pratt* v *Levan,* 1 Miles (Pa) 358 Cf *Grant* v *Gill,* 2 Whart 42

[13]*Re Snyder,* 8 Phila 302, 1 Legal Gaz 302, *Weinmann's Estate,* 164 Pa 405, 30 Atl 389

[14]*Bosler* v *Kuhn,* 8 Watts & S 183, *Sweatman's Appeal,* 150 Pa 369, 24 Atl 617, *Weinmann's Estate,* 164 Pa 405, 30 Atl 389.

[15]*Morris* v *Parker,* 1 Ashm (Pa) 187

[16]*Weinmann's Estate,* 164 Pa 405, 30 Atl 389 The assignee paid the rent for the two months preceding his sale The lessor could recover no more

for one year, from January 1, 1830, the lessee held over beyond
January 1, 1832, making an assignment on March 17, 1832.
The assignees conducted the store until June 30, when they
closed the store, and on July 3 sent the key to the lessor, who refused to receive it. The assignees had previously paid the rent
for the quarter ending June 30. "This," said Sergeant, J.,
"showed an occupation by them under the assignment and made
them tenants for the year The defendants could not afterwards
terminate the lease when they pleased; it could not be apportioned at their will. .   .   .   They were bound till the end of
the year if the plaintiff insisted on it, and in legal contemplation
they used and occupied the premises from the 1st of July to
the 1st of October, even though they did not choose to keep possession all the time "[17]

434. Assignment with intention of lessee.— Whether the lease
is oral or written, the lessee may assign the term, and the effect
is the same in the former as in the latter case, when the statute of
frauds does not invalidate the lease [18] The assignment may be
in writing and under seal,[19] in writing without seal, or in parol.
If the lease was not for longer than three years, the parol assignment of it would be unquestionably valid The 1st section
of the act of March 21, 1772,[20] enacts that "no leases, estates,
or interests, either of freehold or terms of years, or any uncertain interest of, in, to, or out of any messuages, manors, lands,
tenements, or hereditaments, shall, at any time after the said
April 10, 1772, be assigned, granted, or surrendered, unless it
be by deed or note in writing signed by the party so assigning,
granting, or surrendering the same, or their agents thereto lawfully authorized by writing or by act and operation of law."
This statute requires an assignment of a lease to be in writing,

[17]*Grant* v. *Gill*, 2 Whart 42   [20] 1 Pepper & Lewis Digest, 2191;
[18]*Lloyd* v *Cozens*, 2 Ashm (Pa.) 1 Smith's Laws, 389
131
[19]*Hinkson* v. *Wagner*, 3 Pa Co. Ct.
297.

irrespective of the duration of the term [21]   But if the assignment has been fully executed by the assignee's payment of the
consideration, by the delivery to him by the assignor and by his
retention of the possession for a long time, e g , two years, the
lessor, who has recognized its validity, cannot set up the statute
as against the assignor or his surety.[22]   A term for three years
from October 1, 1864, with the privilege of renewing the lease
for two years longer, was orally assigned in 1865.   It was held
that if the lessors had consented to this assignment and acquiesced in it and accepted the assignees as their tenants under
the lease, the assignees acquired the rights of the lessee, and,
inter alia, that of renewing the lease.[23]   An assignment may
be validly made in advance of the time when, in pursuance of
its terms, the assignee will have the rights and liabilities of
the lessee   A lease, e g , being for five years from April 1,
1848, the lessee sold, September 9, 1848, all his right under
the lease for and during the period of four years from April 1,
1849 [24]   Such assignment is valid as against a sheriff's vendee
at a sale in March, 1849   One of two lessees may assign his
interest in the term to the other[25] or to a third person.

---

[21]Wiley's Estate, 6 W N C 208
[22]Wiley's Estate, 6 W N C 208
The lease had more than three years
to run when the assignment was
made   The lessor, who had recognized its validity, could not dispute
it, and hold the assignor or his
surety liable for the rent falling due
after the assignment, the assignor
having been himself, not the lessee
but an assignee
[23]Barclay   v   Steamship   Co   6
Phila 558   A written assignment
followed the oral assignment two
years afterward   The lessor had re
ceived twenty-one monthly payments
of rent from the assignee   In Benz
v Langan, 5 Northampton Co Rep
139, it is said that a parol assignment of a lease running longer than

three years, if with the lessor's con
sent, and with delivery of possession
to the assignee, is good for three
years at least   In Spencer v Darlington, 74 Pa 286 the lease having
more than three years to run, the
court refrained from saying whether
a parol assignment of it would be
valid, because it did not appear that
an assignment had been made
[24]Williams v   Downing, 18 Pa 60
The fact that the assignor retained
possession of a part of the premises
did not impair the assignee's right,
as against a subsequent purchaser at
sheriff's sale of the lessee's interest
Cf Pennsylvania   v   Kirkpatrick,
Addison (Pa) 193 , Huntingdon v
Longacre, 1 W N C 120
[25]Douty v Bird, 60 Pa 48.   The

435. Conditional assignment — The leasehold may be assigned as collateral security for a debt   The assignment will be valid though written and absolute in form, the defeasance being in parol; the act of June 8, 1881,[26] not applying to parol defeasances of transfers of chattel interests in land.   When one partner assigns his interest in the firm's assets as security for an obligation, and in doing so does not comply with the act of May 13, 1876,[27] respecting mortgages of leaseholds in collieries, mining lands, etc , he does not deprive himself of his partner's equity that the leasehold shall be applied to the payment of partnership debts as against the assignee of the other partner for the debt of the latter [28]   The lease may be assigned to B on B's undertaking to pay certain notes as they fall due, and all ground rents and taxes, and to keep up insurances, and on the stipulation that "in case any of the foregoing obligations remain unpaid" for longer than thirty days "after maturity," the amounts previously paid are to be forfeited and the lessee may enter and resume possession of the premises   The word "obligations" will be understood to refer to the notes, and the lessee cannot resume possession of the premises and annul the interest of his assignee simply because he fails to pay the ground rents, taxes, and insurance [29]

436. Consideration for the assignment —The consideration for the assignment is sometimes, when the lease is supposed to have a value, a sum of money and the assumption of the duty of paying the rent to the landlord.[30]   The assignee may agree to pay a rent to the assignor, expecting the latter to pay the rent reserved in the lease to the lessor ,[31] and, if the lease is worth more

former colessees may form a partnership and, as such, operate the leasehold, without again becoming colessees

[26] 1 Pepper & Lewis Digest, 1613; P L 84

[27] 1 Pepper & Lewis Digest, 1612; P. L 160

LAND & TEN 24,

[28] *Brown* v *Beecher*, 120 Pa 590, 15 Atl 608   A mortgage of the lease is an assignment, *Becker* v *Werner*, 98 Pa 555

[29] *McGinnis* v *Thompson*, 29 Pittsb L. J 336

[30] *Williams* v *Downing* 18 Pa 60

[31] *Reukauff* v *Aronson*, 13 Phila

than the original rent, the rent thus reserved by the lessee may exceed that which he is bound by the terms of the lease to pay the lessor. The lease, *e. g.*, reserving an annual rent of $300, the lessee may, when assigning to X, reserve a rent of $450, and X in turn may assign to Y, reserving a rent of $500. Y may then assign to Z, reserving no rent at all [32] The lessee having made improvements which he has the right to remove may assign the lease and them for the estimated value of the improvements only.[33] If the lessee agrees with the assignee, who contracts to pay rent for the remainder of the term, that, at the end of the term, he will take out a new lease in the names of both, and, in violation of the agreement, he takes out the new lease in his own name, he cannot recover from the assignee the rent stipulated for in the agreement for the two months during which the latter holds over, though he may recover, possibly, for use and occupation [34] The lessee who reserves rent from the assignee cannot distrain for it, unless he expressly stipulates for the power to distrain.[35]

437. Contract to assign conditioned.—The contract to assign the lease in consideration of the payment of $100 at the time, and certain other moneys subsequently, stipulated that the assignee should not underlet to any one in the insurance business, and that the assignee, in the event of his intention to remove,

87, *Hinkson* v *Wagner*, 3 Pa Co Ct 297 The assignor may compel the payment of the rent from the assignee

[32]*Adams* v *Beach*, 1 Phila 99

[33]*Spencer* v *Darlington*, 74 Pa 286 Cf *Barclay* v. *Steamship Co* 6 Phila 558

[34]*Hinkson* v *Wagner*, 3 Pa Co Ct 297 The lessee may assign the lease, reserving a royalty for iron ore mined The assignee may covenant to indemnify the lessee against a claim of a prior assignee, and of third persons, for damages arising from the washing of the ore If the assignee allows the lease to be forfeited and so disables himself from performing his covenants, the assignor may sue him from time to time for the royalties reserved, or, treating the contract as "rescinded," may claim damages in one action for the entire breach *Keck* v *Bieber*, 148 Pa 645, 33 Am St Rep 846, 24 Atl 170

[35]*Ege* v *Ege*, 5 Watts, 134 The power was stipulated for in *Reukauff* v. *Aronson*, 13 Phila 87.

should give the assignor notice of this intention, in order that he, the assignor, might have an opportunity to become again possessed of the premises. Before the time for the delivery of the possession, the assignee assigned his interest to a liquor dealer. The assignor might refuse to deliver the possession to the liquor dealer, and if he did so, the assignee could not recover back the $100 paid when the agreement to assign was made, and additional damages [36]

438. Assignment of leasehold in part of premises.—The lessee may assign his rights under the lease, in the whole of the premises, or in a part of them only. He may, *e. g.*, assign one part to X, and retain the rest, or he may subsequently assign the rest to Y.[37]

439. Covenants against assignment—The lessee may covenant in the lease that he will not assign, or that he will not assign without the written consent of the lessor The covenant is not, *ipso facto,* a condition; and a breach of it, while exposing the lessee, who, despite it, assigns, to damages, will not make void or, at the will of the lessor, even voidable, the assignment [38] At all events, if the lessor chooses to recognize the assignment by enforcing the liabilities arising therefrom under the lease, the assignee cannot, by alleging that the assignment was in violation of a covenant, escape these liabilities.[39] And, after the lessor has repeatedly received rent from the assignee, and thus accepted him as his tenant, he cannot refuse to permit the assignee to exercise the rights conferred by the lease on the lessee, and, *inter alia,* that of renewing the lease.[40]

---

[36] *Huntingdon* v *Longacre,* 1 W N. C. 120

[37] *Weidner* v. *Foster,* 2 Penr. & W 23

[38] *Brolaskey* v *Hood,* 6 Phila 193. The covenant against subletting or against using the property otherwise than as a sewing machine store can be enforced against the assignee.

[39] *Oil Creek & C Branch Petroleum Co* v *Stanton Oil Co* 23 Pa Co Ct. 153; *Brolaskey* v *Hood,* 6 Phila 193

[40] *Barclay* v. *Steamship Co.* 6 Phila 558.

440. Enforcing the covenants — For a violation of the covenant against assigning, the proper remedy is an action for damages against the lessee. The lessor does not forfeit the right thus to recover damages, by causing X, the assignee, to assign the premises to his, the lessor's, agent, in order that he may recover the possession before the expiration of the term, and so prevent the injury to the premises which the use of them by X would have produced.[41] Possibly, an assignment being contemplated, a court of equity would enjoin the lessee against making it. At all events, the lease containing a covenant not to assign, or to use the premises otherwise than in a certain way, if the assignment is in fact made, the court may enjoin both the lessee and the assignee against the forbidden mode of using the premises.[42]

441. Conditions against assignment — To covenant against assignment is not the same thing as to make the refraining from assignment a condition on whose breach the lease becomes void, or voidable by the lessor.[43] The lease may provide that if the lessees transfer it without the written assent of the lessors they shall forfeit it and the improvements,[44] or that, on the "transferring without the written sanction of said lessors, said lessee and his assigns shall forfeit said lease and improvements."[45] If in violation of such provisions an assignment is made, it is in the power of the lessor to avoid it.[46] The assignment is as respects the landlord a nullity, and cannot be set up against a title to improvements on the premises acquired under a landlord's distress sale, or against the title acquired by the forfeiture of the lease for another ground, e. g., the nonpayment of rent[47]

---

[41]*Hazlehurst* v *Kendrick*, 6 Serg & R 446

[42]*Brolaskey* v *Hood*, 6 Phila 193

[43]*Barclay* v *Steamship Co* 6 Phila 558

[44]*Spencer* v *Darlington*, 74 Pa. 286.

[45]*Becker* v *Werner*, 98 Pa 555

[46]*Spencer* v *Darlington*, 74 Pa. 286

[47]*Becker* v *Werner*, 98 Pa 555

A mortgage by the lessee will be a violation of the condition against assignment.[48]   The lease may by its terms make a sheriff's sale of the lease an assignment   It may stact, e. g.   "The lessee under penalty of instant forfeiture shall not . . . assign the term . . . without the written consent of the lessor indorsed hereon; an assignment within the meaning of this lease being understood to comprehend not only the voluntary action of the lessee, but also every levy or sale on execution or other legal process, ete ;" and it may authorize a judgment in ejectment on ten days' notice, for the breach of this stipulation.   Under such a provision, after a sheriff's sale of the leasehold the lessor may enter the judgment and recover possession by means of a *habere facias possessionem*[49]   But a lease of a coal mine to A and B providing that the lessees will not assign or transfer the lease without the consent of the lessor or permit the leasehold to be taken in execution; and that a violation of these agreements "shall, *ipso facto,* work a forfeiture of this lease and all the rights of the party of the second part of, in, and to the same,"—the condition is not violated when, A and B subsequently to the lease forming a partnership to work the mine, A files a bill against B, and the court decrees a sale of the premises.[50]

442 Waiver of stipulation against assigning.—The lessor may waive the right to enforce either the covenant or the condition against assigning the lease.   If, e. g., he receives the rent falling due after the assignment from the assignee, with knowledge that he is paying it as assignee, he will be considered as having waived the condition,[51] but there would be no waiver

[48]*Becker* v *Werner*, 98 Pa 555
[49]*Leon* v. *Groswith*, 2 W. N C 535
[50]*Patterson* v *Sillman*, 28 Pa 304 Two lessees form a partnership, making the leasehold firm property One of the partners filing a bill for an account and a dissolution of the firm, a sale of the leasehold under the decree of the court would not forfeit the lease, though it stipulated that it should become void on the making of a transfer of it

[51]*Barclay* v *Steamship* Co 6 Phila.

if he was ignorant of the assignment.[52] The receipt, however, of rent from the assignee, with knowledge that he was paying it as such, while it would confirm his right, would not condone the breach of the lessee's covenant in making the assignment. The lessee would continue liable for damages.[53] The receipt of the rent from the assignee, as agent for the lessee, will imply no recognition by the lessor of the assignment.[54]

443 Lessee continues liable after assignment —The lessee, having entered into the lease, is liable upon its covenants, and he cannot divest himself of this liability by assigning his interest to another.[55] Nor is he released by the further fact that the lessor recognizes the assignee as his tenant, by receiving rent from him, as due from him,[56] and also that the assignment was made before the term began and that the lessee never entered on the possession.[57] Nor is he released from intermediate rent by the fact that the assignee surrenders the term before its expiration and the surrender is accepted by the lessor,[58] or from future rent by the circumstance that earlier instalments have been distrained for, on goods of the assignee.[59] But if the lessor, in addition to receiving rent from the assignee, receives it from him in the place and stead of the lessee, and even, by parol, releases the lessee from all further liability,—the latter will be no further liable[60] If the lease is made to X, as a

558, *Hazlehurst* v *Kendrick*, 6 Serg & R 446, *Leon* v *Groswith*, 2 W N C 535

[52]*Leon* v *Groswith*, 2 W N. C 535

[53]*Hazlehurst* v *Kendrick*, 6 Serg & R 446

[54]*Hazlehurst* v *Kendrick*, 6 Serg & R 446

[55]*Thompson's Estate*, 205 Pa 555, 55 Atl 539

[56]*Ghegan* v *Young*, 23 Pa 18, *Douthett* v *Gibson*, 11 Pa Super Ct 543 Cf *Fisher* v *Milliken*, 8 Pa 111, 49 Am Rep 497, *Dewey* v *Dupuy* 2 Watts & S 553, *People's Sav*

Bank v *Alexander*, 140 Pa 22. 21 Atl 248

[57]*Dewey* v *Dupuy*, 2 Watts & S 553 The assignee holding over after the end of the term, the lessee is liable for the rent thus becoming due, the assignee never having been recognized by the lessor, and the lessee having occasionally paid rent after the assignment *Fulmer* v *Crossman*, 2 Luzerne Legal Obs. 331, 8 Del Co Rep 78

[58]*Hall* v *Bardsley*, 5 W N C 553

[59]*Manley* v *Dupuy*, 2 Whart 162

[60]*People's Bank* v *Alexander*, 140 Pa 22, 21 Atl 248 Accepting the

mere trustee for a corporation about to be formed, and the lessor knows this, not X, but the corporation to which he assigns the lease, will be treated as the lessee, and he will not be liable for the rent [61] If the assignee holds over beyond the term, the lessee will be liable for the rent for the hold-over period.[62]

444. Liability of assignee for rent.— The covenants which run with the lease fall on the assignee   Among these is a covenant to pay rent or royalties.   All such rents or royalties as become payable subsequently to the assignment, and during the ownership of the assignee, he becomes bound to pay [63] "In general terms," remarks White, P J , "it may be said that when a covenant is for the performance of some duty in connection with the possession, and relating to the land, or in the nature of rent or royalty for the use and enjoyment of the premises, it is a covenant running with the land . . .   The rent need not be money , it may be a share in the product,[64] as a share of the crops on a farm or the share of oil in an oil lease "[65] The rent being payable quarterly, March 27, June 27, September 27, and December 27, if the assignment is made on September 24, the assignee is liable for the quarter's rent falling due three days later.[66]   The goods of the assignee, whether on the premises or

assignee "as tenant, instead of the lessee," is said not to discharge the latter, in *Ghegan* v *Young*, 23 Pa 18, *Frank* v *Maguire*, 42 Pa 77

[61]*Heckman's Estate*, 172 Pa 185, 33 Atl 552   The knowledge of the fact by the agent of the lessor, through whom the lease was negotiated, will be imputed to the lessor

[62]*Fulmer* v *Crossman*, 8 Del Co Rep 78

[63]*Fennell* v *Guffey*, 139 Pa 341, 20 Atl 1048, 155 Pa 38, 25 Atl 785, *Goss* v *Woodland Fire Brick Co* 4 Pa Super Ct 167, *Lockard* v *Robbins* (Pa) 7 Cent Rep 565, 10 Atl 120, *Guldin* v *Butz*, 2 Woodw Dec 74, *Jones* v *Gundrim*, 3 Watts &

S 531, *Bender* v *George*, 92 Pa 36, cf *Landell* v *Hamilton*, 175 Pa 327, 34 L R A 227, 34 Atl 663, *Acheson* v *Kittanning Consol Natural Gas Co* 8 Pa Super Ct 477

[64] The rent being 1¼ tons of bar iron, the assignee becomes liable to deliver it   *Jones* v *Gundrim*, 3 Watts & S 531

[65]*Stone* v *Marshall Oil Co* 188 Pa 602, 41 Atl 748, 1119, citing *Fennell* v *Guffey*, 139 Pa 341, 20 Atl 1048, 155 Pa 38, 25 Atl 785, *Landell* v *Hamilton*, 175 Pa 327, 34 L R A 227 34 Atl 663

[66]*Coulter* v *Conemaugh Gas Co* 14 Pa Super Ct 553   As the assignee is liable for the rent, he has a right to tender it and prevent a

clandestinely removed therefrom, can be distrained upon, as those of the tenant might be [67] As the assignee is bound to pay the rent, his tender of it can be taken advantage of by the lessee, in replevin for distraining on the goods of the latter [68]

445. Covenants running with the land; general principle — The test for determinating of what covenants the obligations will devolve on the assignee is somewhat vague and is variously expressed. Such covenants as "may have attached to the property demised," as "are annexed to the estate," are said by Mercur, J., to run with the leasehold, whether the covenant was of the lessee and his assigns, or merely of the lessee [69] "If the covenant or condition," says Huston, J., "affect a thing *in esse,* parcel of the demise, it is immediately affixed to the estate, and binds the assignee whether named in the lease or not "[70] Remarking that "it is not very easy to determine which covenants are real and which are personal," Ludlow, J, quoted with approval the opinion of Cowen, J.,[71] "that the question depended

---

distress of his goods *Lyon* v *Houk,* 9 Watts, 193 The lessor, by requiring a surety for the rent from the assignee and by receiving payments from the assignee, does not abrogate the original lease, and make a new lease *Wiley's Estate,* 6 W. N. C 208

[67]*Jones* v *Gundrim,* 3 Watts & S 531 If the lease for ten years stipulates that if the lessee removes during the term the whole rent for the term shall become payable, and the lease is verbally assigned when more than nine years have to run, the assignment is valid for three years If the assignee removes during the three years (not having in turn assigned to another) the rent for the whole three years following the assignment to him becomes payable at once by him *Lobach* v *Breisch,* 8 Northampton Co Rep 193 The duty to pay rent in kind, e g, 20 bushels of wheat, of rye, of corn, falls on

the assignee *Herbaugh* v *Zentmyer,* 2 Rawle, 159

[68]*Lyon* v *Houk,* 9 Watts, 193 A lease being made to A and B, who, the next day, arrange to form with a third person a limited partnership to carry on business on the premises, the fact that this partnership carries on the business on the premises, paying rent directly to the lessor, will not make the partnership the lessee, or the assignee of the lessee, nor make it liable for rent accruing after it ceases to occupy the premises Its possession must be considered as that of a sublessee under A and B, the partnership never ratifying the lease nor accepting it as lessee, and the lessor never accepting the partnership as lessee *Campbell's Estate,* 21 Pa Super Ct 424

[69]*Simons* v *Van Ingen,* 86 Pa 330.
[70]*Jones* v *Gundrim,* 3 Watts & S. 531
[71]*Norman* v *Wells,* 17 Wend 136.

'in a greater degree upon judicial discretion than almost any other of equal importance,' " and, adopting from him the following expression of the test, *viz*, that, in order that a "covenant may run with the land, its performance or nonperformance must affect the nature, quality, or value of the property demised, independent of collateral circumstances, or must affect the mode of enjoyment," added that "covenants which affect the thing *in esse* parcel of the demise, and benefit the estate, run with the land."[72]

446. Particular covenants falling on the assignee.—The covenant not to use the premises otherwise than as a sewing machine store,[73] or to bore an oil well within a certain time,[74] or to pay $231 per year for every year's delay beyond a named time in completing an oil well,[75] or to continue with due diligence and without delay to prosecute the business of raising oil,[76] or to pay taxes assessed from year to year,[77] or to leave the premises in good order and repair,[78] or to construct an improvement, *e. g.*, a railroad, and at the end of the term leave it on the premises,[79] or to keep the premises insured for the benefit of the lessor,[80] run with the leasehold. For his own violation of these covenants, the assignee would be liable If, *e. g.*, the covenant requiring the prosecution of the business of developing the premises for oil with due diligence, the assignee, who became such nine months after the making of the lease, completes one well in about three months after the assignment, but drills no more

[72]*Brolaskey* v *Hood*, 6 Phila 193
[73]*Brolaskey* v *Hood*, 6 Phila 193
[74]*Washington Natural Gas Co.* v *Johnson*, 123 Pa. 576, 10 Am St Rep 553, 16 Atl. 799.
[75]*Fennell* v. *Guffey*, 139 Pa 341, 20 Atl 1048
[76]*Bradford Oil Co* v *Blair*, 113 Pa 83, 57 Am Rep 442, 4 Atl 218
[77]*Oil Creek & C Branch Petroleum Co* v *Stanton Oil Co* 23 Pa Co Ct. 153

[78]*Pollard* v *Shaaffer*, 1 Dall 210, 1 L ed 104, 1 Am Dec 239 The assignee would be bound by the covenant, although the lease did not mention "assigns "
[79]*Morgan* v *Negley*, 3 Pittsb 33 If a sublessee under the assignee sells the railroad to him, and he to another, he will be liable for its value to the lessor
[80] Cf *Simons* v. *Van Ingen*, 86 Pa. 330

during the following two years and five months of his owner-ship of the lease, he is liable to the lessor for damages [81]

447. Action on the covenant.— The action against the as-signee by the tenant is brought upon the covenants in the lease, under the statute of 32 Hen VIII. chap 34, whether the assign-ment was by contract or by sheriff's sale [82] Hence, formerly, the lease being under seal the action was in covenant[83] or debt,[84] and an action in assumpsit could not be sustained [85] Though assumpsit is now sustained, it is "in substance an action of cove-nant upon the lease."[86] Whether, the premises being in one county, the action can properly be brought in the common pleas of another county, the lessee and the assignee never having taken possession of the premises, was presented, but not decided, in *Fennell* v. *Guffey.*[87] This objection to the jurisdiction could be waived, and it was waived when it was not made until after plea pleaded. "It was at most a personal exemption, and the point should have been raised before the trial"

448 When the assignment is complete.— The assignment is so far complete as to make the assignee liable on the covenants of the lease, when he has the right to the possession, although, there being no obstacle opposed to his taking possession by others, he in fact does not take possession. "Under an absolute assignment the assignee is liable before he has taken *actual* possession; for by the assignment the title and possessory right pass and the as-signee becomes possessed in law. As to the actual possession

---

[81]*Bradford Oil Co* v *Blair*, 113 Pa 83, 57 Am Rep 442, 4 Atl 218 The lessor was to receive as royalty one eighth of the oil The court told the jury that the damages would be the value of the oil which would have been delivered to the lessor had the work been prosecuted with due diligence, less the cost of producing it

[82]*Jones* v *Gundrim*, 3 Watts & S. 531, *Guldin* v *Butz*, 2 Woodw Dec. 74

[83]*Guldin* v *Butz*, 2 Woodw Dec 74, *Blume* v. *M'Clurken*, 10 Watts, 380

[84]*Blume* v *M'Clurken*, 10 Watts, 380

[85]*Blume* v. *M'Clurken*, 10 Watts, 380

[86]*Fennell* v. *Guffey*, 155 Pa. 38, 25 Atl 785

[87] 155 Pa. 38, 25 Atl 785.

that must depend on the nature of the property, as in the case of waste, unprofitable, or vacant ground, or ground intended to be built upon."[88] Though there are subleases made before the assignment, the assignee becomes liable upon the covenants in the lease, *e. g.*, for the payment of taxes, although they are assessed prior to the expiration of the sublease.[89] If the sublessee covenanted with the lessee to pay the taxes and perform the other acts which the lessee had bound himself to perform, the assignee becomes entitled to the performance by the sublessee of his covenant. The leasehold being exposed to sale, A buys it but directs the deed to be made to B, with the understanding that B is a mere trustee for him. Though B takes possession, A will be considered the assignee and, as such, he will be liable for the rent accruing after the purchase [90]

449. Assignee's covenant runs with the lease.—If the lessee assigns the lease for a rent, and the assignee in turn assigns, the lessee may compel the ultimate assignee to pay the rent thus reserved in the first assignment. The lessee, *e g*, assigns to A at a rental of $450; A to B, at a rental of $500; and finally B to C apparently without rental. The lessee, whose rent was by the terms of the lease $300, had a right to collect from C $150, the difference between the rent reserved in the lease and that reserved in the assignment to A [91]

450. Liability of assignee ceases.—The assignee is liable upon

---

[88]*Fennell* v *Guffey*, 139 Pa 341, 20 Atl 1048, *Borland's Appeal*, 66 Pa 470, *Weidner* v *Foster*, 2 Penr & W 23 The purchaser at the sheriff's sale of land subject to a ground rent is not liable for rent falling due between the sale and the delivery of the sheriff's deed *Thomas* v *Connell*, 5 Pa 13

[89]*Oil Creek & C Branch Petroleum Co* v *Stanton Oil Co* 23 Pa Co Ct 153

[90]*Morgan* v. *Yard*, 12 W N. C. 449

[91]*Adams* v *Beach*, 1 Phila 99. The assignments to A and B are termed underleases The lessee of a mine grants to the owner of a subjacent mine the right to make an airway through the upper mine for ventilation This right attaches to the estate of the owner of the lower mine, and passes with it to his grantee *Philadelphia & R Coal & I Co* v *Taylor*, 1 Legal Chronicle, 335, 5 Legal Gaz 392

the covenants of the lease, only in virtue of the privity of estate
between him and the lessor. If he in turn assigns, he is not liable for rent or royalty falling due subsequently to that assignment.[92] If the rent or royalty becomes annually payable July
18, and the assignee, A, assigns to X August 20, 1894, X is liable for the whole year's rent falling due July 18, 1895 [93] So
if the lease requires one oil well to be completed in six months,
and, if not, that $171 be paid each year for the delay, and the
years end July 18, X will be liable for the $171 for the year
running from July 18, 1894, to July 18, 1895. Each successive
assignee is liable for the rents or royalties falling due during
his ownership, and not the preceding assignee.[94] If the assignment is made to X and Y, a subsequent assignment by Y of his
interest in the lease terminates his liability as respects future
instalments of rent, and also that of one who had become surety
for X and Y, who has a right to the continued liability to him of
both the principals [95] The second assignee is not liable for
rent which fell due before the assignment to him.[96]

451. When the assignee ceases to be owner —The assignee may
cease to be owner by a gift of the estate, in pursuance of which
he passes the possession to the donee, though he makes no deed
or conveyance of any sort,[97] and his assignee becomes owner,
and as such liable, by the acceptance of the assignment, although
he does not take possession, if there is no obstacle to his taking
possession.[98] If the assignment reserves to the assignor the

[92]*Washington Natural Gas Co* v
Johnson, 123 Pa 576 10 Am St
Rep 553, 16 Atl 799, *Watt* v *Equit-
able Gas Co* 8 Pa Super Ct 618,
Goss v *Woodland Fire Brick Co* 4
Pa Super Ct 167, *Weidner* v
Foster, 2 Penr & W 23, *McClaren*
v *Citizens' Oil & Gas Co* 14 Pa
Super Ct 167, *Wiley's Estate,* 6 W
N C 208

[93]*Watt* v *Equitable Gas Co.* 8
Pa Super Ct 618.

[94]*McClaren* v *Citizens' Oil & Gas
Co* 14 Pa Super Ct 167

[95]*Wiley's Estate,* 6 W N C 208

[96]*Acheson* v *Kittanning Consol
Natural Gas Co* 8 Pa Super Ct.
477

[97]*Wickersham* v *Irwin,* 14 Pa 108
(Ground rent) Cf *Berry* v. *M'Mul-
len,* 17 Serg & R 84

[98]*Hannen* v *Ewalt,* 18 Pa. 9
(Ground rent).

right to continue to possess the premises until a future day, he must pay the rent becoming due between the time of assigning and that future day. "Something more then," says Strong, J., "is required to terminate the privity of an assignee of premises subject to rent, and his consequent liability, than an assignment, which does not put an end to his actual or beneficial possession and his right to possession "[99]

452. Insolvency of the second assignee — There are *dicta* to the effect that the assignment to an insolvent person, for the mere purpose of escaping the burdens of the lease, will, terminating the privity of estate, terminate the liability on the covenant which springs from that privity. In *Hannen v. Ewalt*,[100] an owner of land charged with a ground rent conveyed it to A and B, who were guardians of X. Chambers, J., says that, the property being suddenly ruined by a fire, "they might have protected themselves against the accruing rents by an assignment to their wards, if there were a prospect of the property acquiring any value for them; or if no such value was reasonably to be expected, they might have assigned to any person, with or without means, who would accept of the assignment. The assignee being liable upon the covenants merely in respect of the privity of estate, and no privity of contract existing between them and the original lessor, his liability lasts only so long as he remains possessed of the estate. An assignment to a mere pauper will not be deemed fraudulent, and an assignment to a *feme covert* will discharge the assignee " "While he [the assignee] holds the estate and enjoys its benefits, he bears its burdens, but he lays down both the estate and its burdens by an assignment, even though, as is said in some of the cases, his assignment be to a beggar."[101] Hence it matters not that the assignee attempted

---

[99] *Negley* v. *Morgan*, 46 Pa. 281.
[100] 18 Pa 9. But in *American Academy of Music* v *Smith*, 54 Pa 130, it was held that a conveyance by the grantee of land subject to ground rent, for no other purpose than to avoid the payment of accruing ground rent, was void as against the covenantor and his representatives.
[101] *Washington Natural Gas Co* v

to sell the lease for $8,000, and then for $5,500, and at length sold it to an employee for $25, the employee being largely in debt and without property; and that the object of the transfer was to avoid the further payment of royalties.[102]

453. Assignee primarily liable as respects lessee.—The lessee does not emancipate himself from his liability toward the lessor, upon his covenants, by assigning the lease,[103] but the assignee is under a duty to indemnify him from the liability, so far as performance within the period of the ownership of the assignee is concerned. If the surety for the lessee becomes the purchaser at a sheriff's sale of the lease, he loses all right to securities given to him by the lessee, to indemnify him for the necessity of paying the rent, if all the rent that can accrue prior to the sheriff's sale has been paid. He has no right to these securities as an indemnity against rent falling due subsequently to the sale,[104] and if the original lessee or his sureties are compelled to pay rent falling due after the assignment of the lease, they have an action over against the assignee or his sureties.[105]

454. Covenants broken before assignment.— A covenant that is broken before the assignment ceases, so far as the act or omission with regard to which the breach has occurred is concerned, to run with the lease. The lessee or the assignee during whose possession the breach has occurred continues liable for it, and one who subsequently accepts an assignment of the lease assumes no responsibility with respect to it. The lease requires, *e. g.,* a second oil well to be commenced by a certain date. B is the owner of the lease, by assignment, when that date arrives. One who subsequently acquires the lease by assignment is not liable

Johnson, 123 Pa 576, 10 Am St Rep 553, 16 Atl 799, *Negley* v *Morgan,* 46 Pa. 281, *Borland's Appeal,* 66 Pa 470

[102]*Goss* v *Woodland Fire Brick Co.* 4 Pa Super. Ct. 167.

[103]*Washington Natural Gas Co* v. *Johnson,* 123 Pa 576, 10 Am St. Rep 553, 16 Atl 799

[104]*Borland's Appeal,* 66 Pa. 470.

[105]*Bender* v *George,* 92 Pa 36.

for the breach of this covenant [106]   The covenant to pay rent at certain dates is broken, as respects each of these dates, on its arrival and lapse without payment.   An assignment, while it would make the assignee liable for payment accruing during his ownership, would not make him liable for the payment that was overdue when he became owner.   A covenant may require not a particular act but a series of acts within a particular period.   If it requires the latter, although there has been a breach before the assignment within the period, there may also be a continuance of the breach after the assignment; and for this continuance the assignee will be liable   An oil lease provided that if the well was not completed in six months, the lessee should pay $231 within three months after the close of the six months as compensation for a year's delay.   The lease was made May 12, 1886, and it was assigned on January 24, 1887, within three months after the expiration of the six months.   The well not having been completed, the assignee was liable for the $231.[107]

455. Sublease by assignee — The assignee does not so terminate his interest in the lease by subletting, as to cease to be liable during the period of the sublease for the performance of covenants, e g , covenants to pay rent, whose performance then becomes due.   And if the assignee, though transferring all his

---

[106]*Washington Natural Gas Co* v *Johnson*, 123 Pa 576, 10 Am St Rep 553, 16 Atl 799

[107]*Fennell* v. *Guffey*, 139 Pa 341, 20 Atl 1048   In *Bradford Oil Co* v *Blair*, 113 Pa. 83, 57 Am Rep 442, 4 Atl 218, the lease was made July 17, 1875   A few days after, three undivided quarters were assigned to B and C.   On April 25, 1876, the lessee and B and C assigned the lease to X   One well was completed by December, 1875, X finished another in August, 1876.   It drilled no other wells during its ownership of the lease, which lasted until January 7, 1881   The lease required the lessee to "continue with due diligence and without delay to prosecute the business to success or abandonment, and, if successful to prosecute the same without interruption "   X was liable for the nonprosecution of the business for the period between May 13, 1876, and October, 1878   Cf *Washington Natural Gas Co* v *Johnson*, 123 Pa 576, 10 Am. St. Rep. 553, 16 Atl 799.

powers over the premises for the whole residue of the term, requires the transferee to perform acts not required by the lease itself, such as laying pipe lines and paying to him one fourth of the residuary proceeds of the leasehold, he is so far a sublessor, and not an assignor, as to remain liable for the payment to the lessor of the royalties reserved in the lease.[108]

456. Rights of assignee.—The rights given by the lease with respect to the premises pass by the assignment to the assignee. The right to renew the term, on six months' notice,[109] or to prolong the term by one year,[110] may be exercised by him. The right, on the happening of a certain contingency, to terminate the lease and escape further liabilities, passes to the assignee,[111] as does that to become a purchaser of the reversion for a price and upon terms defined in the lease [112] The lessee covenants to take out insurance and to deposit a sum of money for this purpose. This money, less 5 per cent, is to be paid back to the lessee The money having been deposited and an insurance procured, a sheriff's sale of the leasehold takes place The purchaser, and not the original lessee, becomes entitled to the money at the expiration of the term. The lessor has a right to retain it, in payment of the rent last becoming due, and the assignee may insist on its being so applied in relief of himself, who is under a duty to pay that rent.[113] The assignee probably has a right to the compensation for improvements made by the lessee, in accordance with the terms of the lease [114] If the lease gives the tenant the right to remove doors and bulk-windows put in the

[108]*McClaren* v *Citizens' Oil & Gas Co* 14 Pa. Super Ct 167

[109]*Barclay* v. *Steamship Co* 6 Phila 558

[110]*Young* v *Algeo*, 3 Watts, 223 The assignee was a purchaser at a sheriff's sale

[111]*Oil Creek & C Branch Petroleum Co* v *Stanton Oil Co* 23 Pa Co Ct. 153.

[112]*Kerr* v *Day*, 14 Pa 112, 53 Am Dec 526, *Napier* v *Darlington*, 70 Pa 64, *Young* v *Algeo*, 3 Watts, 223

[113]*Simons* v *Van Ingen*, 86 Pa. 330

[114]*Simons* v *Van Ingen*, 86 Pa. 330 But *vide Peterson* v *Haight*, 1 Miles (Pa.) 250.

premises by him, unless the lessor compensates him, this right passes to the assignee[115] The assignee may in turn assign his interest and impose on his assignee liability for the future performance of covenants with the lessor[116] The assignee (e g, by a sheriff's sale) may obtain possession by ejectment, and possibly, though the lessee holds over beyond the term, the assignee may recover the possession, but it would be permissible for the lessee to show that after the expiration of the term he had obtained a new lease, and that his present possession was under this new lease.[117]

457 Assignment subject to lessor's rights.— The rights of the lessor are, generally speaking, not diminished by the lessee's making of an assignment The lease being from year to year, if the lessee assigns within a year, reserving an annual rent payable at a different time from that at which the rent under the lease is payable, the lessor may nevertheless require the giving up of the possession, by a notice preceding by three months the close of the year, as defined in the lease.[118] If the lease provides for a forfeiture on the occurrence of certain facts, the assignee takes subject to this right; and he is bound to inquire whether the facts have occurred, and the lease has been forfeited, before he accepts the assignment. The lessor has a right to continue to treat the lessee as owner of the leasehold until he has notice of the assignment. He is not bound to regard a mere general rumor that the lease has been assigned. The information must come to him from someone who is interested in the property and must be directly communicated to him. Otherwise he can treat the lessee as still the owner of the lease. He can notify the lessee that he forfeits the lease, and he can enter

[115]*Peterson* v *Haight*, 3 Whart 150
[116]*Negley* v *Morgan*, 46 Pa 281, *Goss* v *Woodland Fire Brick Co* 4 Pa Super Ct 167; *Adams* v. *Beach*, 1 Phila 99

[117]*Young* v *Algeo*, 3 Watts 223
[118]*Lloyd* v. *Cozens*, 2 Ashm. (Pa) 131.

into a new lease with the lessee; and this new lease will be valid despite the previous assignment of the original lease.[119]   The lessor can recover possession of the premises after the assignment, in the mode in which he might have recovered before the assignment, e. g., by ejectment, or the proceedings under the various landlord and tenant acts [120]

458. Recording lease — The act of March 18, 1775,[121] does not apply to any lease not exceeding twenty-one years, where the actual possession and occupation go with the lease.   In 1851, Chambers, J., remarked that it had not been the practice in this state to record leases of lands for a term of years, or their assignments.   As the act of 1775 does not require them to be recorded, when possession accompanies the lease, unless the lease is for more than twenty-one years, there is little or no occasion to record leases in practice, as leases without possession in the lessee, and terms exceeding twenty-one years, are both of rare occurrence.   An assignment made September 9, 1848, for the period of four years to begin April 1, 1849, is valid against a purchaser at a sheriff's sale, held March 26, 1849, on a judgment recovered against the tenant, the assignor, March 6, 1849, though neither had the assignee taken possession nor had the assignment been recorded.[122]

[119]*Carnegie Natural Gas Co v Philadelphia Co* 158 Pa 317, 27 Atl 951

[120]*Lloyd v. Cozens,* 2 Ashm (Pa.) 131.

[121] 1 Pepper & Lewis Digest, 1570; 1 Smith's Laws, 422

[122]*Williams v. Downing,* 18 Pa. 60.

CHAPTER XXIII.

SUBLEASES.

459. Subletting.— A sublease or underlease is defined to be "a lease granted by one who is himself a lessee for years, for any fewer or less number of years than he himself holds If a deed passes all the estate or time of the termor, it is an assignment, if it be for a less portion of time than the whole term, it is an underlease, and leaves a reversion in the termor "[1] To transfer the whole or a part of the premises for a part of what remains of the term so that there will be a reversion in the transferrer is to make a sublease, while to transfer the premises, or a part of them, for the whole of the residue of the term, beginning at the transfer or some period subsequent to the transfer, is an assignment.[2] When the whole of the term is made over by the lessee, at a rent which is payable to him and at different times from those mentioned in the lease, and the lessee reserves the

---

[1] Longaker. P J (quoting 4 Kent Com 96) in *Noble* v *Becker*, 3 Brewst (Pa) 550 *Ege* v *Ege*, 5 Watts, 134 Shortly after a lease for ten years was made to A he transferred it for five years to B with the privilege of five additional years This was an assignment, and not a sublease *Lobach* v *Breisch* 8 Northampton Co Rep 193

[2] *Brown* v. *Butler*, 4 Phila 71.

right to annul the transfer on the transferee's breach of his covenant to pay rent, the transfer is an assignment, and not a sublease.[3] It follows that the tenant's sale of the lease together
with his goods on the demised premises is an assignment, and
not a sublease.[4] The distinction, however, between assignment
and sublease is frequently lost sight of Thus, of a term of
three years, two years and three months had run when the lessee
transferred the premises for nine months, the whole of the remainder of the term. Willson, J., terms the transaction, "tech-
nically a subletting "[5] In *Adams* v *Beach*,[6] A, having a lease
for five years at the annual rental of $300, is said to have "un-
derlet for the remainder of the term" to B, reserving to himself
a rent of $450 per annum   Lowrie, J , remarked· "It seems
equally clear that where a lessee transfers the whole term, reserving a rent to himself, such transfer is an underlease as between the parties thereto, so far as to allow the lessee to have
an action of debt for rent against the underlessee or any assignee
under him, .   .   .   but it is treated as an assignment where
the lessee claims a right of distress   .   It seems equally
clear that such an underlease for the whole unexpired term is,
as between the original lessor and the underlessee or his assigns,
an assignment so far as to allow the lessor to have an action of
debt against such underlessee or his assigns."[7]

  460. Sublease of part of premises.— The whole of the premises may be sublet, as may also only a part,[8] although it is said

[3]*Lloyd* v *Cozens*, 2 Ashm. (Pa)
131
  [4]*Troxell* v *Wheatly*, 2 Luzerne
Legal Reg 37   Such sale does not
violate a covenant against subletting
  [5]*Towt* v *Philadelphia*, 173 Pa
314, 33 Atl 1034   The distinction
was unimportant for the solution of
the problem before the court
  [6]1 Phila 99
  [7]The lessee transferred (the word

used was "underlet") the remainder
of the term to A for a rent exceeding
by $150 that which he was to pay to
the lessor   A in turn "underlet' to
B, i e , transferred the remainder
of the term for a rent $50 greater
than A's B "assigned" to C It was
held that the lessee could maintain
an action for the $150 rent against
C. on account of the privity of estate
  [8]*Hessel* v *Johnson*, 129 Pa 173,

by Longaker, J., in *Noble* v. *Becker*,[9] that "putting a person, therefore, in possession of a part of the demised premises for a less time than the whole term is not a sublease. To constitute a sublease, the lessee must part with his entire estate, and not a part of it, for a less portion of time than the whole term."

461 Restricting transferee's right.— The lessee may, in transferring the lease, restrict the power of the transferee. The lessee, *e. g*, having a right to use the premises in any way, may transfer them to X for the whole term at a certain rent, but may restrict X to the use of them as a "Chicago beef store."[10] A, the assignee of a lease of an oil tract for the purpose of drilling and operating for oil or gas, granted, assigned, and transferred to X the exclusive right and privilege of drilling on the premises, of extracting oil, and of selling the same, "during the term of" the lease. X was, at his own expense, to connect the wells with the pipe line and conduct the gas to New Castle, to sell the gas, and from the proceeds pay the royalties reserved in the original lease, and the expenses of drilling and operating, and to pay one fourth of the remainder every quarter to A. A failure by X to keep his covenants was to forfeit his interest. It was held that this transfer did not amount to an assignment of the lease, that would discharge A from further liability, as assignee to the original lessor, for the royalties, but that it was a lease by A to X. "When the assignee of a leasehold estate executes a lease of the premises, reserving a larger rent or containing covenants more advantageous to the lessor than those found in the original leasehold, he reserves to himself a benefit derived under the original lease, and his priv-

5 L R A 851, 15 Am. St Rep, 716, 18 Atl 754, *Brown* v *Butler*, 4 Phila 71, *Boteler* v *Philadelphia & R Term R Co* 164 Pa 397, 30 Atl 303, *Hey* v *McGrath*, 81* Pa 310, *Stone* v *Marshall Oil Co* 188 Pa 602 41 Atl 748, 1119

*3 Brewst (Pa) 550. But the decision was that a covenant that "the demised premises shall not be underlet or rented" was not broken by a letting of one room of the building

[10]*Hinkson* v. *Wagner*, 3 Pa Co Ct. 297.

ity of estate is thus continued   He does not convey the estate which he had accepted as assignee of the original lessee, but creates a new estate, to which he assumes the character of land-lord "[11]

462. Right to underlet.— If the lease says nothing concerning subletting, the lessee may sublet[12] however brief his term.   He may, e. g., sublet, though he is a tenant from quarter to quarter.[13]   A covenant against assigning is not broken by under-letting, and a covenant that "the demised premises shall not be underlet or rented without the lessor's written consent" is not violated by the underletting of a part of the premises [14]   An assignee of the term may make a sublease,[15] and the lessee, and his assignee of an undivided part of the lease whose term is of three years, and so long thereafter as oil and gas in paying quan-tities may be found, may jointly transfer a part of the premises for one year or so long thereafter, "less than the term of the original lease," as oil and gas in paying quantities shall be found.[16]   The lease may prescribe a penalty, e. g., of $300 for subletting, to be collected as an additional rent payable monthly   This penalty, which may be treated as liquidated damages for breach of the covenant, may be recovered in an action against the lessee [17]   For the lessee's breach of the covenant not to sub-let, he is liable to an action for damages, and, in his action against the lessor for the breach by the latter, of his covenant, the latter may set off these damages. But his affidavit of defense,

[11]*McClaren* v *Citizens' Oil & Gas Co* 14 Pa Super Ct 167

[12]*American Pig Iron Storage War-rant Co* v *Sinnemahoning Iron & Coal Co* 205 Pa 403, 54 Atl 1047

[13]*Manley* v *Dupuy,* 2 Whart 162, *Hessel* v *Johnson* 129 Pa 173 5 L. R A 851, 15 Am St Rep 716, 18 Atl 754 142 Pa 8 11 L R A 855, 21 Atl 794, *Brown* v *Butler,* 4 Phila 71

[14]*Noble* v *Becker,* 3 Brewst (Pa) 550

[15]*McClaren* v *Citizens' Oil & Gas Co* 14 Pa Super Ct 167

[16]*Stone* v. *Marshall Oil Co* 188 Pa. 602, 41 Atl 748, 1119.   The trans fer is called a sublease

[17]*Miller* v. *Rankin* (Pa) 11 Atl. 615.

which fails to allege the amount of these damages, will be insufficient to prevent judgment.[18]

463. Underletting a breach of condition.— If there is merely
a covenant in the lease against underletting without the written
consent of the landlord, an underletting without that consent
does not impair the lease, and the sublessee acquires a title which
cannot be defeated by the lessor because its origin involved a
breach of the lessee's contract.[19]   The lease may, however, not
only contain the lessee's covenant not to sublet,[20] or not to sublet for any other purpose than to carry on the dry goods business,[21] but also reserve to the lessor the right to declare the lease
forfeited and to re-enter,[22] or to enter a judgment in ejectment
on a warrant of attorney and recover possession by means of a
habere facias possessionem [23] The subtenant will have no standing to ask the court to open the judgment entered on the warrant
of attorney, and to set aside the *habere facias possessionem* unless the lessor has waived the condition against subletting   The
fact that he was in possession under former tenants, who also
were forbidden to underlet, will not prevent his dispossession.[24]
Nor will the fact that the lessor commenced proceedings under
the act of May 25, 1825, by requiring security for at least
three months' rent, and that, the subtenant tendering the security, the lessor refused to accept it, stopped the proceedings,
and entered judgment on the warrant. If the lessor re-enters,
alleging a sublease, on him will be the burden of proving it,
in an action against him by the lessee upon the covenant for
quiet enjoyment.[25]   If the lessor notifies the sublessee that he
will treat him as a trespasser, and that he will be liable to be put

[18]*Cosgrave* v *Hammill*, 173 Pa.
207, 33 Atl 1045
  [19]*Brown* v *Butler*, 4 Phila 71
  [20]*Long* v. *Wood*, 22 Pittsb L J
93
  [21]*Kister* v *Remsen*, 1 W N C 507
  [22]*Long* v *Wood*, 22 Pittsb L J
93

[23]*Shermer* v *Paciello*, 161 Pa 69,
28 Atl 995, *Kister* v *Remsen*, 1 W
N C 507
  [24]*Shermer* v *Paciello*, 161 Pa 69,
28 Atl 995
  [25]*Long* v *Wood*, 22 Pittsb L J
93.

out at any moment, the sublessee, not having known of the prohibition in the lease against subletting, may leave the premises
and escape liability within the month, whose rent he has paid,
to his immediate landlord (the lessee) for future rent.[26]   The
sublessee who is in possession of the premises will be as liable
to third persons for negligence on the premises, although the
sublease violated a condition in the lease, as if the sublease were
permitted by the lease.   The horse and cart of one using a wharf
(the subject of the lease) having been lost in the river for
want of a proper cap-log, the sublessee then in possession, though
in violation of a condition against subletting, would be liable
to their owner, if the imperfection of the cap-log began during
his occupancy[27]   A condition against subletting is not broken
because the tenant consents to proceedings on the part of X to
procure a right of way over the premises[28]

464 Sublessee's duty to pay rent.— The sublessee is under the
same duty to pay to his landlord, the lessee, the rent reserved in
the lease to him, that any lessee is under towards his lessor.
His goods can be distrained for it.[29]   If the lessee should surrender the lease to the primary lessor, this lessor could distrain
for the sublessee's rent, but not for the lessee's rent,[30] and if
the lessor should, after accepting the surrender, make a new
lease to X, X, and not the landlord, would be entitled to receive the after-accruing rent, and could distrain for it.[31]   The
primary lessor may distrain for the rent due him, on the goods

---

[26]*Kister* v. *Remsen*, 1 W. N. C.
507

[27]*Tout* v. *Philadelphia*, 173 Pa
314, 33 Atl. 1034

[28]*Long* v. *Wood*, 22 Pittsb L J
93

[29]*Ege* v *Ege*, 5 Watts, 134, *Manuel* v *Reath*, 5 Phila 11

[30]*Hessel* v *Johnson*, 129 Pa 173,
5 L R A 851, 15 Am St Rep 716,
18 Atl 754   If A and B agree to
occupy a room together, paying the
rent equally, and A procures a lease

at a rental of $900, and the lessor
remits to A a portion of the rent,
and B takes sole possession under a
later agreement to pay A $500 B
cannot claim any reduction from the
$500 because A was not obliged to
pay as much rent as it was originally
expected that he would pay *Van-
sant* v *Fishel*, 1 York Legal Record,
101

[31]*Hessel* v *Johnson*, 129 Pa 173,
5 L R A 851 15 Am St Rep 716,
18 Atl 754

of the subtenant found on the premises.[32] and as he is neither a debtor nor a tenant to the lessor, he is not entitled to the $300 exemption.[33] If the lessee, after subletting, assigns the lease, the sublessee must pay the subsequently accruing rent to the assignee [34]

465. Surrender by lessee.— A sublease which violates no condition in the lease[35] is not defeasible by the primary lessee's surrender of the lease to the lessor.[36] The sublessee, after such surrender, is not liable to have his goods distrained on for any rent accruing under a new lease made by the lessor, nor, of course, for rent accruing under the extinguished lease. A, having a lease from year to year beginning September 1, 1858, let a part of the premises April 1, 1859, to B, without any specification as to time. On September 15, 1859, without previous notice to quit, A surrendered the premises to the lessor. B, being put out of possession by the lessor's agent, could recover in trespass against

---

[32]*Hessel* v *Johnson,* 129 Pa 173, 5 L R A 851, 15 Am St Rep 716, 18 Atl 754, *Rosenberger* v *Hallo-uell,* 35 Pa 369, *Collins* v *Whilldin* 3 Phila 102

[33]*Rosenberger* v *Hallouell,* 35 Pa 369 The sublessee is not liable to the original lessor for rent (*James* v *Kurtz,* 23 Pa Super Ct 304), after he vacates the premises, adds *Campbell's Estate,* 21 Pa Super Ct 424 But he is not personally liable ever The subtenant may bind himself to perform towards the original lessor the duties of the lessee, and may make his performance a condition of the sublease *Goddard's Appeal,* 1 Walk. (Pa) 97

[34]*Morgan* v *Negley,* 3 Pittsb 33 In *Ardesco Oil Co* v *North American Oil & Min Co* 66 Pa. 375, the lessee of a coal tract mortgaged the premises and then sublet them The sublessee agreed to pay all interest due and to become due on the mortgage, all sums advanced by M for

insurance on the premises, all arrearages of taxes as well as all taxes to be assessed on the premises during the term, all rents due under the original lease and such as should become due He agreed to pay all labor claims, and to keep the premises insured The interest already due on the mortgage, and other sums already due when the sublease was made, it was the duty of the sublessee to pay at once or in a reasonable time If he did not, a suit could be brought against him before the end of the term, by the lessee, before he had paid the mortgagee, or had been sued by the latter

[35] To violate a covenant is not enough to deprive the sublessee of the immunity *Brown* v *Butler* 4 Phila 71

[36]*Hessel* v. *Johnson,* 129 Pa 173, 5 L R A 851. 15 Am St Rep 716 18 Atl 754, 142 Pa 8, 11 L R A 855, 21 Atl. 794 *Brown* v *Butler.* 4 Phila 71

him   Sharswood, P. J , held that A could not waive his right
to a three months' notice to quit, to the detriment of his sublessee.   After accepting the surrender, the landlord could have
given B notice to quit in April (the commencement of the sublease), or, being ignorant of the term of the sublease, and not
having accepted the sublessee as his immediate tenant, he could
have served the sublessee with notice in the name of A to quit
September 1, 1860.[37]

466. Sublessee's powers.— The sublessee may acquire the reversion from the primary lessor, and, as successor to the lessor, may
terminate the original term, which is from year to year, by giving the proper notice to quit, and may recover possession by ejectment.[38]   The sublessee has no right to procure from the primary
lessor a new lease for a period of time embraced within the term
of the lessee, and such new lease will be invalid   Even if the
original lease might have been forfeited for breach of condition
in it, the new lease, making no reference to the right to forfeit
and recognizing the possibility that the claimants under the former lease have a right to the premises, will not be deemed an
exercise of the right to forfeit, and will be void with respect to
the claimants under the original lease [39]   The sublessee, like the
lessee, may, in the absence of a condition against assigning, assign the sublease.   The assignee becomes liable to pay the same
royalties which fall due after his purchase as the assignor would
have been bound to pay.[40]

467. Lessee's covenants do not bind the sublessee.—The lessee's
covenants run with the leasehold, but the leasehold is not conceived to run when a sublease, and not an assignment, is made;
and the sublessee is under no duty to perform the covenant of
his immediate lessor [41]   He is not bound, e. g , to pay rent to

[37]*Brown* v *Butler*, 4 Phila 71
[38]*Hey* v *McGrath*, 81* Pa 310
[39]*Stone* v *Marshall Oil Co* 188 Pa
602, 41 Atl 748, 1119
[40]*Stone* v *Marshall Oil Co* 188 Pa

602, 41 Atl 748, 1119, *Adams* v
Beach, 1 Phila 99
"*Oil Creek & C Branch Petroleum
Co* v *Stanton Oil Co* 23 Pa Co Ct
153

the lessor,[42] but the lessee may require the sublessee to covenant to perform the covenants of the former.[43] However, since the goods of the sublessee may be distrained by the primary lessor for rent due him from his lessee, if any rent is due him, the sublessee may pay it out of the rent owed by him to his immediate landlord. Nor must he wait, before doing this, until his goods are taken in distress. Hence, if, a distress being made, though invalid, the sublessee pays the rent, he will not be compelled to pay it again to his immediate lessor (the lessee) or to the attaching creditor of the latter. "It appears, then, to be unimportant," says Sharswood, P J, "whether the particular distress upon which the subtenant made his payment was or was not rightful, either as to its manner or objects; there was a right to distrain on the subtenant's goods on the premises, whether there were any there or not; he could not bring any there without their being immediately subject to be seized and detained and his enjoyment thus interfered with; he was, moreover, liable to be ejected on ten days' notice from the original lessor."[44]

468 Subtenant liable to eviction — The lessee cannot deprive the lessor of the right to recover possession for which he stipulates in the lease, by making a sublease. If, *e g.,* the lease authorizes the lessor to eject the tenant for nonpayment of rent, on ten days' notice, the subtenant will be liable to ejection, on ten days' notice, for the nonpayment of the lessee's rent.[45] and if for nonpayment of rent a judgment is entered on the warrant of attorney in the lease, and a *habere facias possessionem* issued, the writ will not be set aside on the application of a subtenant, although he has tendered the rent since the writ issued, and remains ready to pay it He has "no standing in court."[46]

[42]*Rosenberger* v *Hallowell,* 35 Pa 369
[43]*Rosenberger* v *Hallowell,* 35 Pa 369
[44]*Collins* v *Whilldin,* 3 Phila 102
[45]*Collins* v *Whilldin,* 3 Phila 102.

Hence the subtenant may pay the rent and obtain a credit on account of his own rent to his immediate lessor
[46]*Kennedy* v *Canavan,* 2 W N. C 226

469. Eminent domain — A sublessee has a right to compensation for the taking of the property under the power of eminent domain.   If the whole premises are taken, the value of so much of the term created by the sublease as has yet to run will be the measure of damages.   If the sublease prohibited the undertenant from occupying, or permitting to be occupied. the premises "otherwise than as lodge rooms for Hall Association O. U. F ," the damages will be the value of the term for this use, and for this use only.   The fact that the original lease stipulates that should a railroad, of whose construction there was rumor, be located over the premises, the lease should end immediately and the lessees should vacate within a reasonable time, but that nothing therein contained should prevent the lessor or lessee from recovering damages for the taking by the railroad, will not prevent the sublessee's obtaining damages, the sublessee having no actual notice of its existence, and the clause in the lease preserving the rights of both parties to it to obtain damages.[47]

⁴⁷Boteler v *Philadelphia & R.
Term. R. Co.* **164** Pa. **397, 30** Atl.
303.

CHAPTER XXIV.

CONDITIONS SUBSEQUENT.

470. Denial of title — There are some implied conditions to
the continuance of the rights of a lessee under the lease.   One
of these is that the lessee shall not deny the title of the lessor   If
he attorns to some other person, or, when the rent is demanded,
says that he is no longer tenant, the lessor may treat him as tenant, or as a trespasser.[1]   A lease expiring October 10, 1886, the
landlord on December 15, 1885, gave the tenant notice to quit
at the expiration of the lease   The tenant, when he received
the notice, said. "It doesn't make any difference to me, I am
not here under him.   I am here under another man " After
this denial of the title, the landlord could, at his option, treat
the lease as ended, and on January 15, 1886, institute an action
of ejectment.[2]   But when there is no denial of the title of the
original lessor, but only of the devolution of his title by inheritance, devise, or grant upon X, who now claims to be landlord,
such denial would not, should X be entitled, forfeit the lessee's
interest.[3]   The lessee's making a contract to convey the premises
in fee, or an actual conveyance of it by deed, is not such a denial
of the lessor's title as forfeits the lease   It is only a feoffment
by the lessee that produces that result   Hence, the contract by
the assignee of a term of 999 years, to convey the land in fee,
did not entitle the lessor, or his grantee of the reversion, to recover the land in ejectment before the expiration of the term.[4]
A conveyance in fee by a lessee, by a deed of bargain and sale,
acknowledged and recorded, does not forfeit the lease [5]

471. Failure of consideration by operation of law — If the performance by the tenant of one of the considerations for the lease

[1] Cf *Newman* v *Rutter*, 8 Watts,
51   The relation of landlord and
tenant had not been discovered when
the denial of the title of the former
occurred   It did not work a forfeiture   *Hill* v *Hill*, 43 Pa 528

[2]*Willard* v *Earley*, 22 W N C
122

[3]*Newman* v. *Rutter*, 8 Watts, 51

[4]*Griffin* v *Fellows*, 81* Pa 114
  When tenant for life suffered a
common recovery, he forfeited the
life estate, and destroyed contingent
remainders, *Lyle* v *Richards*, 9
Serg & R 322

[5]*M'Kee* v *Pfout*, 3 Dall 486, 1 L.
ed 690, *Dunwoodie* v *Reed*, 3 Serg.
& R. 435.

is rendered impossible by a change in the law, the lease, at the instance of either party, will be declared rescinded "if things remain in such a position that the parties can be placed in their original situation " Hence, the lessee in a lease for eight years covenanting to erect a frame dwelling on the lot, which is to remain after the term has expired, if before the time limited for its erection an ordinance of the city where the premises are is passed, prohibiting the erection of wooden buildings, the lessor will be permitted to recover the possession by ejectment, within the eight years.[6]

472. Covenant not condition.— Covenants are not the same as conditions.[7] The remedy for breach of a covenant is an action for money compensation. A condition is a stipulation making the continuance of the estate of the lessee dependent on the happening or nonhappening of a certain event. The lease may make the covenants conditions by providing that, for a breach of any of them, the estate of the lessee shall determine either absolutely, or upon the lessor's doing something to manifest his intention to resume control of the premises, and to treat the term as having come to an end.[8] The lessor may make any conditions that he chooses, if they be not illegal, unreasonable, or repugnant to the grant itself [9] Conditions in a sublease[10] are as valid and enforceable by the lessee as those in the lease are valid and enforceable by the lessor.

473. Kinds of conditions.— A frequent condition is that the lessee punctually pay the rent.[11] Sometimes payment of the

---

[6]*Rooks* v *Seaton,* 1 Phila 106.

[7]*Marshall* v *Forest Oil Co* 198 Pa 83, 47 Atl 927, *Kreutz* v *McKnight,* 53 Pa 319

[8]*Hand* v *Suravitz,* 148 Pa 202, 23 Atl 1117, *Becker* v *Werner,* 98 Pa 555 The lease authorized a three months' notice to give up the premises at the end of each year, for a breach during the year of any of the covenants *Quinn* v *McCarty,* 81 Pa 475

[9]*Newman* v *Rutter,* 8 Watts, 51 See this case for implied conditions

[10]*Goddard's Appeal,* 1 Walk (Pa) 97

[11]*Bausman* v *Kreider,* 18 Lanc L. Rev 103, *White* v *Murray,* 7 Phila 302

water rent or of the gas bills[12] or of the taxes[13] by the tenant is
made a condition.   The stipulation that he shall pay his "own
gas and water bills" means that he shall pay them to the company
which supplies the gas or water   A prohibition against subletting[14] or assigning the lease may be enforced by making the assignment a ground of forfeiture[15] (and making a mortgage of
it on which a sale ultimately takes place, is such an assignment)[16] as may one against selling anything other than corsets
on the premises,[17] or using them for certain[18] immoral or other
purposes,[19] or one against the tenant's taking off the hay, straw,
etc.[20]   The continuance of the tenant's right may be conditioned
on his building a house within a specified time,[21] or on his making repairs or refraining from committing waste [22]   In *Muller
v. Bohringer*[23] a covenant was made to sell on the premises—a
lager-beer saloon—no beer except that furnished by the lessor
The court suggested that such a condition was in restraint of
trade, and was without mutuality, because the lessor had not
bound himself to furnish beer.   The lease may provide that
should the lessee become objectionable to the lessor for any cause,
the lessee shall give up possession on twenty days' notice [24]
The lease may provide that, on failure of the lessee to comply
with all the terms of the lease, the lease shall terminate on thirty
days' notice in writing to the lessee, who agrees to surrender possession.   One of these terms may be the payment of rent when

[12]*Hand* v *Suravitz*, 148 Pa 202. 23
Atl 1117.
  [13]*Becker* v *Werner*, 98 Pa 555
  [14]*Suartz's Appeal*, 110 Pa 208, 13
Atl 69, *Zeigler* v *Lichten*, 205 Pa
104, 54 Atl 489, *Shermer* v *Paciello*,
161 Pa 69, 28 Atl 995
  [15]*Grossman's Appeal*, 102 Pa 137,
Becker v *Werner*, 98 Pa 555, *National Pub Asso* v *Shupe* d \
Furniture Co 18 W N C 379
  [16]*Becker* v *Werner*, 98 Pa 555
  [17]*Inman* v *Vandervoode*, 1 W N.
C 40.

[18]*Hughes* v *Moody*, 10 Pa Co Ct
305
  [19]*Dikeman* v *Butterfield*, 135 Pa
236, 19 Atl 938
  [20]*Quinn* v *McCarty*, 81 Pa 475
  [21]*Newman* v *Rutter*, 8 Watts, 51
  [2] *Suartz's Appeal*, 110 Pa 208, 13
Atl 69, *Scherr* v *Seymour*, 2 W. N.
C 534
  [3] 3 Pa Co Ct 144
  [24]*Adam* v. *Clark*, 2 W. N. C. 429

due, the construction of a new railroad by the lessee, a railroad company, and payment of a share of the earnings to the lessor, in addition to the rent.[25] The lease, e g , of a stone quarry, may condition itself on the lessee's keeping the boilers in repair, keeping a sufficient strip of dirt cleaned on top of the quarry, may provide for the decision of an expert when complaint by the lessor is made of the failure, in these respects, of the lessee, and make the refusal to comply with his decision within ten days after written notice of it, a ground of forteiture. Whether there could or could not be a forfeiture until the decision of an arbitrator was procured, there could not be until specific notice of the lessee's breach had been given to him, and the lapse of ten days without remedying the defects.[26] The agreement being that the lease shall become void unless, prior to June 1, 1893, the lessee obtains a license to sell liquor, the condition is fulfilled if he obtains the license within that time. The lease will continue valid despite a subsequent revocation of the license [27] The lease providing that it shall become void if the tenant ceases for twelve months to mine iron ore, such cessation will terminate the lease, at the will of the lessor. The lessee's entry from time to time in order to clean and grease the engine erected by him on the premises is not a continuance of mining operations that will prevent the forfeiture [28] The abstaining from operation of a coal mine for one year may be declared to be "an abandonment of the lease."[29] Failure to work a quarry for the space of three successive months may be a ground of forfeiture.[30]

[25]Pittsburg, J E & E R Co v Altoona & B C R Co 196 Pa 452, 46 Atl 431; Pittsburg, J E & E R Co v Altoona & B C R Co 203 Pa 108, 52 Atl. 13

[28]East Conshohocken Quarry Co v Boyd, 18 Montg Co L Rep 58

[27]Fell v Betz 5 Pa Dist R 310

[28]Davis v Moss, 38 Pa 346

[29]Moyers v Tiley, 32 Pa 257 The nonoperation the first year of the

term was held not to be within the scope of the provision

[30]Miller v Chester Slate Co 129 Pa 81, 18 Atl 565 It is for the court to interpret a written lease If the quarry becomes filled with snow, ice, water, making the removal of rock impossible, the quarry is worked" by the removal of the water, ice, etc.

LAND & TEN 26.

474. Payment of rent a cond^tion.— The lease, *e. g.*, of coal land, may make the payment of the royalties[31] or of rent[32] a condition. The payment may be required punctually upon the day named, even though it be in advance.[33] Sometimes the provision is that, for nonpayment within five or some other number of days after the rent becomes payable, the lease may be terminated.[34] Sometimes the nonpayment of rent for a period, *e. g.*, sixty days, is made to authorize a distress, and it is provided that if there are not sufficient goods on the premises to satisfy the rent by distress, the landlord may repossess himself of the premises [35] Under such a stipulation, it is necessary that a distress should be made, and should prove ineffectual because of insufficiency of goods. Sometimes the lease may authorize, after a three[36] or five[37] or other number of days' default, a notice to the tenant that on a day to be fixed therein or on a day at a prescribed distance from the giving of the notice, the lease shall terminate. Or it may make the simple default, without respect to the period over which it has lasted, a forfeiture, *e. g.*, failure to perform any of the covenants. Under such a lease, one of whose covenants is that the tenant shall pay his own gas and water bills, the tenant's failure to pay the water bill to the company forfeited the lease, at the option of the lessor.[38]

[31]*Kreutz* v *McKnight*, 53 Pa 319, *Verdolite Co* v *Richards*, 7 Northampton Co. Rep 113, *Walnut Run Coal Co* v *Knight*, 201 Pa 23, 50 Atl 288

[32]*Hand* v *Suravitz*, 148 Pa 202, 23 Atl 1117, *Becker* v *Werner*, 98 Pa 555

[33]*Murphy* v. *Marshell*, 179 Pa 516, 36 Atl 294

The landlord's recovery of the possession during the period covered by the rent in advance may not entitle the tenant to a credit for the rent, or a proportional part of it *Evans* v *Fries*, 9 W N C 462

The right to forfeit for nonpay- ment of rent when the lease so provides is indisputable *Reams* v *Fye*, 24 Pa Co Ct. 671.

[34]*Evans* v *Fries*, 9 W. N. C 462, *Pennsylvania Co for Ins. on Lives & G A* v *Shanahan*, 10 Pa Super Ct 267, *Ellis* v *Ambler*, 11 Pa. Super Ct 406

[35]*Newman* v *Rutter*, 8 Watts, 51

[36]*Ellis* v *Ambler*, 11 Pa. Super. Ct 406

[37]*Pennsylvania Co for Ins on Lives & G A* v *Shanahan*, 10 Pa Super Ct 267

[38]*Hand* v *Suravitz*, 148 Pa. 202, 23 Atl 1117.

475 Right of forfeiture lost.— The landlord's contract right of forfeiture for nonpayment of rent by means of a judgment in ejectment is not lost by reason of his having made a distress for previously due rent upon the leasehold itself, and sold it to the use-plaintiff, and having subsequently made a written agreement for a lease of the same premises to the use-plaintiff, to whom later the reversion was conveyed   Nor is the right of forfeiture lost by the simple fact that the landlord had attempted to recover rent in arrear by means of a distress, nor by the additional fact that this attempt to collect the rent is recited in the affidavit on which the judgment is entered.[39]   Tender of the rent after a judgment in ejectment has been properly entered on the warrant of attorney, for the failure to pay it, does not revive the tenant's right to the term and to the possession.[40]

476. Waiver of forfeiture.— The landlord need not insist on the forfeiture, although the causes of it exist [41]   He may, *e g* . waive his right to dispossess the tenant for nonpayment of the rent, at the appointed time   If there are other grounds of forfeiture in addition to the nonpayment of rent, receiving payment of the rent does not preclude a subsequent forfeiture on one of these grounds   Under a lease declaring that, on the violation of any of the covenants, or on the transfer of the lease without the written sanction of the lessor, the lessor should, at his option, re-enter and repossess himself of the premises, there were three grounds of forfeiture, the rent was in arrear, the taxes were

[39]*Pennsylvania Co for Ins on Lives & G A* v *Shanahan,* 10 Pa Super Ct 267
The landlord who proceeds according to his warrant, enters judgment, and dispossesses the tenant, is not liable to him in an action for the malicious use or abuse of process *Reams* v *Pancoast,* 111 Pa. 42, 2 Atl 205
[40]*Reams* v *Fye,* 24 Pa Co Ct 671, 10 Pa Dist R 242, *Evans* v. *Fries,* 9 W N C 462, *Long* v *Wood,* 22 Pittsb L J 93
[41]*Wills* v *Manufacturers Natural Gas Co* 130 Pa 222, 5 L R A 603, 18 Atl 721, *Galey Bros* v *Kellez man,* 123 Pa 491, 16 Atl 474, *Long* v *Wood,* 22 Pittsb L J 93   The tenant cannot insist that he is not liable for rent accruing subsequently to the facts which authorize a forfeiture, if the landlord has not chosen to forfeit.

unpaid, the lessee had transferred the lease   A distress for the
rent secured money enough to pay it.   It was, nevertheless, in
the power of the lessor to forfeit the lease for the other reasons,
even for the nonpayment of taxes, which, had the lessor so
chosen, might have been included in the distress for rent.[42]
Proceedings can be simultaneously prosecuted for the recovery
of the rent due, and for the dispossession of the tenant on account of it   "The right to recover rent in arrear, and the right
to recover possession, coexist, and may be exercised at the same
time   In fact, these two rights are often exercised in one and
the same proceeding "[43]   Receiving rent falling due subsequently to the existence of facts which justify a forfeiture, with
knowledge of the facts, will estop the lessor from subsequently
forfeiting the lease on account of those facts;[44] but not receiving
rent after the knowledge of those facts, which had fallen due
before their occurrence [45]   No waiver is to be inferred from the
delay for two years in enforcing a forfeiture [46]

477 Waiver, continued.— The landlord, by suffering a breach
of the condition several times without insisting on it, may in
duce a belief in the tenant's mind that he does not intend in the
future to insist on it, and so betray the tenant into future omission of, or tardiness in, performance.   In such cases it has

---

[42] *Becker* v *Werner*, 98 Pa 555
The   court   expresses   no   opinion
whether, after a successful distress
for rent, there could be a forfeiture
for the neglect to pay the same rent
when it was due

[43] Beeber, J *Pennsylvania Co for
Ins on Lives & G A* v *Shanahan*,
10 Pa Super Ct 267

[44] *Newman* v *Rutter*, 8 Watts, 51
After default in respect to the election of a house the grantee paid
ground rent that accrued after the
default   The ground landlord could
no longer forfeit   Cf *Davis* v *Moss*,
38 Pa 346, *Elliott* v *Curry*, 1 Phila
281, *National Pub Asso* v *Shupe &*

N Furniture Co 18 W N C 379
Hughes v *Moody*, 10 Pa Co Ct 305
The lessee covenanted to quarry
nothing but soapstone   He violated
this covenant, to the knowledge of
the lessor, who, with this knowledge,
continued to receive royalties from
him   This was a waiver of the
prior breaches   *Verdolite Co* v
Richards, 7 Northampton Co Rep
113

[45] *Long* v *Wood*, 22 Pittsb L J.
93   It is said that a forfeiture for
nonpayment of rent when due, if
made after the rent has been paid, is
improper

[46] *McKnight* v *Kreutz*, 51 Pa 232.

been held that the landlord will be precluded from taking advantage of a subsequent breach of the condition, unless he has, since his last indulgence, given warning that in the future he will strictly enforce the condition "Cases are numerous," says Mitchell, J., "where rent has not been paid on the day, but has been accepted later without objection; so that the tenant has been led to believe that the strict time will not be insisted on, and equity has relieved against an attempted forfeiture "[47] For two years the monthly rent, payable in advance, had not been paid in advance, and sometimes not until the month had expired The landlord could not thereafter forfeit the lease for want of punctual payment, unless he had previously given notice of an intention to insist on punctuality [48] The lessor is in the habit of buying coal from the lessee, and deducting the rent from the purchase money, when he makes settlements with the

---

[47] *Rea* v *Eagle Transfer Co* 201 Pa 273 88 Am St Rep 809 50 Atl 764, *Haldeman* v *Sampter* 2 Del Co Rep 106, *Cogley* v *Browne* 11 W N C 224, *Humane Engine Co* v *Salvation Army*, 18 Montg Co L Rep 13 If, the tenant having a claim against the landlord for disturbance of his possession, the latter agrees that the former shall remain on the premises for two months, rent free, the latter cannot, during the first of these months eject the former by means of a judgment entered on the warrant of attorney *Humane Engine Co* v *Salvation Army* 18 Montg Co L Rep 13

In *Gregg* v *Krebs*, 5 Pa Dist R 779, out of sixteen annual payments, only two had been paid after the five days of grace allowed in the lease One of these was on the 7th, and the other on the 9th, day, and so far as appears, the tenant did not infer from these cases that punctual compliance with the lease would not be insisted on The landlord could insist on a forfeiture for the third default.

The lease provided that the lessee of oil land should pay $30 per month until drilling should commence Operations were never begun After three months the lessor brought suit for $90, and recovered Another month's rent was subsequently paid tardily The rent of several additional months fell due and was unpaid, when the lessor, exercising the right secured in the lease, of declaring it void and of re entering and disposing of the oil as if the lease had never been made, made a lease to another, who took possession It was held that the receipt of the four months' rent after it had become due did not waive the right to forfeit for subsequent defaults A tender of eleven months' rent at once could be refused by the lessor, who had previously made the second lease Equity is not unfriendly to provisions for forfeiture, when they promote justice *Brown* v *Vandergrift*, 80 Pa, 142 Cf *Axford* v *Thomas*, 160 Pa 8, 28 Atl 443

[48] *Wanamaker* v *McCaully*, 11 W N C. 450

tenant. Departing from this habit he now refuses to deduct an
instalment of the rent due, and pays the coal bill in full. A few
days thereafter, he sues the tenant for nonpayment of the rent.
He is liable in damages.[49] On the first occasion for paying rent
the lessee comes to the house of the lessor after he is in bed,
calls him up, and pays the rent; the lessor saying his coming
that day was unnecessary, that payment on the next day would
have been satisfactory. The second quarter's rent was again
paid punctually. The third quarter's became due December 12.
On December 8 or 9, the lessor being at the lessee's barn, the
lessee offered to pay the rent, and went to the house to get the
money. The lessor meantime drove away The lessee tendered
the rent on December 13, a day too late, when it was refused
Failure to pay the rental promptly was, by the terms of the
lease, made a forfeiture. It was for the jury to say whether the
lessor's conduct did not put the lessee under the impression that
payment on the day following the day of maturity would be
accepted. If they so found, the landlord could not insist on
the forfeiture.[50] When the tenant has reason to believe that
the lessor's practice of forbearance will be changed, he cannot
extenuate his want of punctuality by such practice Thus, the
lease for one year required the rent to be paid monthly, in advance, and made nonpayment a ground of forfeiture. In case
of holding over with the lessor's consent, after the expiration of
the year, it required a three months' notice from either party
previous to the expiration of any year, to terminate the tenancy.
The tenant held over for five years Of the fifth year, the
second month's rent was due January 1. It was tendered on
January 5, and was refused. Over-due rent had been frequently
accepted. But notice had been given by the lessor two and one

[49]*Long* v *Wood*, 22 Pittsb L J Atl 695, *Oliver* v. *Brophy*, 18 W. N.
93.　　　　　　　　　　　　　C. 427.
[50]*Steiner* v *Marks*, 172 Pa 400, 33

half months before the close of the fourth hold-over year, that he would terminate the tenancy at the end thereof. Seven days after the rejection of the tender of rent on January 5, the lessee told the lessoi that, as he had not received proper notice of the termination of the lease, he would not surrender any of his legal rights. "After this notice," says Ludlow, P J ,[51] "the landlord had a right to believe that the parties, no longer depending upon any course of business theretofore established, would deal at arm's length. If the tenant could thus compel an exact compliance with any covenant contained in the lease, so could the landlord, and if, in this contest, the tenant has overreached himself, he surely ought not to complain."

478. **Enforcement against assignee of term.**— The assignment of the term does not preclude the enforcement of a forfeiture for nonpayment of rent falling due subsequently; nor even of rent that was already due when the assignment was made, in the absence of a contract with the assignee, or estoppel   The lessor's statement to the assignee after the assignment had been consummated, that no rent was due, does not preclude a forfeiture for rent that in fact was due. The fact that he indicates to the person contemplating taking an assignment of the lease, the bounds of the tract, but says nothing concerning any rent then due (not being asked with respect to rent), will not estop the lessor from subsequently forfeiting the lease for nonpayment of the rent.[52]

479. **Apportionment of condition.**— The grantees of the reveision have the same right to enforce a condition subsequent that the lessor himself had   Probably if the reversion in a part of the premises is granted, the grantee acquires no right to insist on the condition, and the grantor loses the right he had, but a mere contract to convey the reversion in a part of the premises,

[51]*Times Co* v *Siebrecht*, 11 W. N C. 283   [52]*Comegys* v. *Russell*, 175 Pa. 166, 34 Atl. 657.

not executed by a conveyance, will not have this effect   The
lessor, until conveyance, retains the right to forfeit for condition broken [53]

480 Nonpayment of rent.— The landlord, whose rent is payable in money, may decline a tender of anything else than
money, *e. g.,* of a check   But a course of conduct on his part
may preclude him from forfeiting the lease because a check, instead of cash, was tendered to him on the day of payment.   The
lessor had instituted proceedings to recover possession because of
a breach of a condition as to subletting, and had failed.   While
these proceedings were pending, the tenant sent two checks for
two instalments of rent which became due   The checks were
returned for the assigned reason that the litigation was pending.
A subsequent instalment became due, and a check was sent for
it, but was refused.   There could be no forfeiture for failure
to pay this instalment   If the landlord had intended to insist
on the cash he should, in view of his having made no objection
to the former checks, as such, have informed the tenant [54]   If
the tenant sends a sum of money which is less than the rent
due by a sum which he thinks the landlord owes him, and the
landlord does not in fact owe him, the landlord may refuse to
receive it, and annul the lease for nonpayment of rent [55]   A
tender after the day on which the rent should be paid may be
refused by the landlord, and he may enforce the forfeiture [56]
But under a lease allowing forfeiture on five days' default, and
ten days' notice to the tenant to give up the possession, when
the interest of the lessee was sold by the sheriff, the court, by
injunction, at the suit of the purchaser, enjoined against the forfeiture on the tender of the rent with interest within the ten
days following the notice, on the ground that payment of the

[53]*Carnegie Natural Gas Co* v *Phil-*   [55]*Pershing* v *Feinberg,* 203 Pa.
adelphia Co 158 Pa 317, 27 Atl 144, 52 Atl 22
951   [56]*Sheriff Machinery Co* v *Singer,*
[54]*Pershing* v *Feinberg,* 203 Pa. *N. & Co* 32 Pittsb L J. N S. 90.
144, 52 Atl 22.

rent with interest was in equity compensation, and that a loss to the sheriff's vendee and, in effect, to creditors, ought to be avoided.[57] If the lessor has moneys of the tenant in his hands which the latter may equitably apply to the rent, the rent will be deemed paid, *e. g,,* if the landlord has, for three months, received double payments of the rent, the rent for the following three months will be so far paid that a forfeiture for its nonpayment will not be permissible.[58] An oil lease provided that if no well was commenced in thirty days from its date it should become null and void, but that this forfeiture might be prevented by paying in advance per quarter $52 25 at the X bank until the well should be commenced. The lessee, not having commenced the well within the thirty days, called at the X bank and was informed that the lessor (the president of the bank) had left town for a few days. Being told by the cashier that his check on the Y bank would be accepted as cash and put to the credit of the lessor in his account, the check was presented and received by the cashier, and the account of the lessor was credited with it as cash. On his return home, the lessor repudiated the payment. The court, in a bill in equity to cancel the lease, found the payment sufficient to prevent forfeiture.[59]

481 Days of grace — The lease may grant the lessee a respite of a certain number of days after the rent falls due, within which there can be no forfeiture.[60] A lease for the mining of clay and ochre required payment of a royalty per ton, on a minimum number of tons, the lessee to "pay for the same at the end of each and every year, in default of which the above lease is to be null and void." "It is further agreed that if any of the covenants above mentioned should not be complied with for the term of three months, then the above lease is to be null and void." There could be no forfeiture for nonpayment of the royalty due

---

[57]*Kemble* v *Graff,* 6 Phila 402   [59]*Sayers* v *Kent,* 201 Pa 38 50
[58]*Freeland* v *South Penn Oil Co.* Atl 296
189 Pa 54, 41 Atl 1000   [60]*Kemble* v *Graff,* 6 Phila 402

at the end of the year, until default continued three months subsequently.[61]

482. Modes of enforcing forfeiture; re-entry.— The lease may simply declare that, on the doing or omitting to do certain things, it shall become void,[62] or it may give to the landlord the right of re-entry for breach of any of the conditions,[63-5] or the right to employ a judgment in ejectment, whether obtained adversely or on a warrant of attorney and a *habere facias possessionem,* issued thereon, or the right to employ either method at his option[66] The right to re-enter may be made to follow immediately upon the default of payment on the day, or upon a notice of intention to re-enter after a certain minimum period of time, e. g,. sixty days,[67] or after an absolute period of three months or six months from the day of default[68] Demand of the rent on the premises and on the day when it becomes payable must, as in all cases of forfeiture, precede the default, otherwise entry cannot be made[69] The entry is made on the premises by the landlord or his agent,[70] with the intention to resume possession, in annulment of the lease, and this purpose should probably be declared to the tenant or other persons in possession[71] The right to re-enter for breach of condition may be exercised by the landlord himself without the aid of the court, or he may obtain that aid by the process of ejectment[72] or otherwise. Whether it can be dispensed with altogether and

[61]*Hoch* v *Bass,* 126 Pa 13, 17 Atl 512

[62]*Davis* v *Moss,* 38 Pa 346

[63-65]*Rea* v *Eagle Transfer Co* 201 Pa 273 88 Am St Rep 809, 50 Atl 764, *Smith* v *Meanor,* 16 Serg & R 375

[66]*Reams* v *Pancoast,* 111 Pa. 42, 2 Atl 205, *Reams* v *Fye,* 24 Pa Co Ct 671

[67]*Walnut Run Coal Co* v *Knight,* 201 Pa 23, 50 Atl 288

[68]*Smith* v *Meanor,* 16 Serg & R 375.

[69]*Royer* v *Ake,* 3 Penr & W 461
[70]*Becker* v *Werner,* 98 Pa 555

[71]*Becker* v *Werner,* 98 Pa 555 The agent went on the premises, took possession of the leasehold, served notice on the subtenants, and on the lessee

[72]*Rea* v *Eagle Transfer Co* 201 Pa 273 88 Am. St Rep 809, 50 Atl 764, *Walnut Run Coal Co* v *Knight,* 201 Pa 23, 50 Atl 288, *Quinn* v *McCarty,* 81 Pa 475.

the landlord or others may treat the lease as null by the mere occurrence of the breach, and deal with the land as if there were no outstanding rights in the lessee, may be questioned.[73] The right peaceably to re-enter is not lost by reason of the fact that the landlord has given the tenant notice to quit, with a view to proceeding for the recovery of possession before a justice of the peace.[74] The possession of the lessor after re-entry may be defended by showing the forfeiture in an ejectment by the lessee [75]

483 Re-entry unnecessary.— When the lease or grant is subject to a condition subsequent, but without specifying how advantage of the breach is to be taken, a re-entry is the normal manifestation of the lessor's intention to insist on the breach and treat himself as revested with his former estate. But if he is already in possession concurrent with that of the grantee or tenant, re-entry is not feasible, and is unnecessary [76] Thus, if land containing iron ore is let to one, subject to the right of the lessor to continue in possession for all uses not inconsistent with the mining operations, a re-entry is unnecessary to take advantage of the condition that mining operations should not cease for twelve consecutive months.[77] If the lessee has not gained possession, the lessor may forfeit for nonperformance of condition, without entry or declaration of forfeiture.[78]

484. Re-entry when lease becomes null and void.—When the lease provides that upon the doing or omission to do something, it shall become null and void, it becomes, *ipso facto,* void by the breach, without any re-entry.[79] The lease stipulated that if the

[73]*Joyce* v *Lynch*, 17 W. N. C. 79
[74]*Bauer* v *Harkins*, 15 Lanc L Rev 70, 6 Northampton Co Rep 103 The tenant cannot maintain trespass
[75]*Comegys* v *Russell,* 175 Pa 166, 34 Atl 657
[76]*Hamilton* v. *Elliott,* 5 Serg & R 375, *Sheaffer* v *Sheaffer*, 37 Pa 525
[77]*Davis* v *Moss*, 38 Pa 346
[78]*Carnegie Natural Gas Co* v *Philadelphia Co* 158 Pa 317, 27 Atl 951
[79]*Kenrick* v. *Smick,* 7 Watts & S. 41.

lessee should remain in default for three months, it should, after **ten** days' notice, left with the lessee, become null and void. On such default and notice, the lessor might treat the lease as extinct, and convey the premises to another, who could also treat it as extinct [80]

485 When landlord reserves power to terminate—When the lease reserves to the lessor, for nonpayment of the rent, "full power to dissolve, terminate, and annul this article of agreement or lease entirely," the lessor, under this reservation, cannot terminate or annul the lease simply by putting another tenant on the premises, without demand on the tenant to pay the rent, or notice to him of the intention to supersede him. But the lessee would lose his right to recover the possession in ejectment by gross default while in possession, and by suffering an intruder to remain in possession for two years and a half, during which time the landlord was obtaining no rents. Such acts are equivalent to an abandonment of the premises [81]

486 Ejectment, equity.—When the lease declares that, for failure of the tenant to observe his covenants, the lease shall be null and void, the appropriate remedy for the enforcement of the forfeiture is the action of ejectment [82] A bill in equity to

<hr />

[80] *Kenrick* v *Smick*, 7 Watts & S 41

[81] *Kreutz* v *McKnight*, 53 Pa 319

[82] *Miller* v *Chester Slate Co* 129 Pa 81, 18 Atl 565, *Quinn* v *McCarty*, 81 Pa 475, *Axford* v *Thomas*, 160 Pa 8, 28 Atl 443, *Hoch* v *Boss*, 133 Pa 328, 19 Atl 360, *Walnut Run Coal Co* v *Knight*, 201 Pa 23, 50 Atl. 288, *Moyers* v *Tiley*, 32 Pa 267.

The lease provided that the lessors might re enter, and that any goods, machinery, or other property of the lessees on the premises, seized or levied on for rent, after the sale of so much of it as was necessary to pay arrears, should be appraised by disinterested parties and accounted for and paid to the lessees or that they should be permitted to take it away within thirty days. This was a stipulation for the benefit of the lessors They were not bound either to appraise and take at the appraisement, or to deliver the property to the lessee, nor were they under a duty to sell the goods. They were not liable on a bill in equity for an account for the value of this property if they had simply resumed possession of the land, no demand having been made upon them for leave to take away the property, especially since twelve years had elapsed between the assumption of possession and the filing of the bill. *Gray* v. *Catawissa R Co* 18 W N. C 9.

restrain, by injunction, the tenant from entering on, occupying, or using the premises, is not the proper remedy, depriving the tenant of the right of trial by jury.[83] On the other hand, if the tenant has a defense to the claim of the landlord that he has forfeited the lease, the landlord's ejectment should not be interfered with by an injunction issued on the bill in equity of the tenant [84] While it is sometimes said that forfeitures are not favored,[85] they will be enforced when the facts exist upon which tenants have agreed that their leases shall become null and void, or forfeited.[86] Substantial performance of the covenants and conditions would prevent forfeiture,[87] but the excuses offered by the tenant being found insufficient, the court will not refrain from entering judgment in ejectment for the landlord [88] In *Muller v. Bohringer*,[89] the lease contained a condition that the tenant of a beer saloon should sell only beer furnished by the lessor The lessee alleging that he had sold other beer only because he could obtain none from the lessor, because he was unable to furnish any on account of a strike or for some other reason, the court opened the judgment entered on the warrant of attorney

487 Respite of forfeiture —The lease requiring prompt payment of rent and the construction by the lessee, a railroad company, of a connecting road, and payment to the lessor of a share of the profits of its operation, and providing that, for the lessee's failure to perform the stipulations, the lessor may terminate the

[83]*Hoch* v *Bass*, 133 Pa 328, 19 Atl 360 In *Freeland* v *South Penn Oil Co* 189 Pa 54, 41 Atl 1000, such a bill was dismissed on the merits In *Sayers* v *Kent*, 201 Pa 38, 50 Atl 296. the bill was dismissed because the tenant had made sufficient payments of money under his lease

[84]*Grassy Island Coal Co* v *Hillside Coal & I Co* 1 Lack Jur 297 But an injunction was issued to prevent proceedings under a judgment confessed on a warrant, in *Kemble* v *Graff*, 6 Phila 402

[85]*Rea* v *Eagle Transfer Co* 201 Pa 273, 88 Am St Rep 809, 50 Atl 764 , *National Pub Asso* v *Shupe & N Furniture Co* 18 W N C 379

[86]*Hand* v *Suravitz*, 148 Pa 202, 23 Atl 1117 , *McKnight* v *Kreutz*, 51 Pa 232 , *Reams* v *Fye*, 24 Pa Co Ct 671

[87]*Kreutz* v *McKnight*, 53 Pa 319

[88]*Walnut Run Coal Co* v *Knight* 201 Pa 23, 50 Atl 288

[89] 3 Pa. Co. Ct 144.

lease on thirty days' notice in writing, the court may properly, on a bill of the lessee, enjoin against the forfeiture, if circumstances exist making the forfeiture harsh and inequitable, and the court may allow a further time for the performance   The common pleas not granting the respite, the supreme court, feeling that "under all the facts developed" they "ought to mitigate" the forfeiture, allowed the lessee until July 1, 1900, to pay the rental that fell due December 8, 1899, and until January 1, 1901, to construct the road which ought to have been constructed in a reasonable time after the making of the lease, which was executed December 8, 1897.[90]

488 Prohibiting the forfeiture — If the lessor is about to evict the tenant by an entry, when the facts do not exist which warrant a forfeiture according to the terms of the lease. and the lessee will, if evicted, suffer irreparable injury, the court will prevent the eviction by a preliminary and final injunction.   The irreparableness of the injury may grow out of the fact that permanent improvements have been made in contemplation of the prosecution of business on the premises.[91]   A mining lease providing that the lessor may declare the lease void, and re-enter on failure to pay the royalties, and the lessor having given no-

---

[90]*Pittsburg, J E & E R Co v Altoona & B C R Co* 196 Pa 452, 46 Atl 431

The supreme court subsequently extended the period for the building of the railroad until January 1, 1902   The lessee not having complied with the order of the supreme court, the common pleas awarded a writ of assistance to the lessor to recover the possession of the leased railroad under the 82d equity rule of the court   The supreme court refused to reverse the allowance of the writ although the application for the writ was presented five days before January 1, 1902, there remaining 50 or 60 miles of railroad to complete, and the les-

see's covenant being clearly incapable of performance before January 1, 1902   *Pittsburg, J E & E R Co v Altoona & B C R Co* 203 Pa 108, 52 Atl 13

[91]*East Conshohocken Quarry Co v. Boyd*, 18 Montg Co L Rep 58, *Grassy Island Coal Co v Hillside Coal & I Co* 1 Lack Jur 297

The complete stoppage of mining by re-entry, without process of law, is such irreparable injury as may justify an injunction against the lessor, until his rights are determined at law, i e by ejectment   *Frisbie Coal Co v Brennan,* 1 Lack Jur. 417,

tice of a forfeiture for nonpayment of the minimum royalties, the court will enjoin the lessor if the demand for royalties was excessive, and was not made on the premises [92] The court will not restrain the lessor from re-entering unless there was fraud or mistake in entering into the stipulations concerning forfeiture, or there is something contrary to law or equity in enforcing them. A sublease requires the sublessee to pay the minimum royalty which the lease requires to be paid to the lessor. The fact that when the sublease is made four months of the year have already elapsed, does not excuse him from paying that royalty If he does not, and the lessee has to pay, and pays it, the latter may enforce the forfeiture under the clause of the sublease.[93] The bringing of an ejectment by a third person against the tenant, and the arrest of the tenant's operations on the premises, e g, mining for coal, by an estrepement, do not, *ipso facto,* excuse the tenant from paying the rent, the ejectment not being yet determined. It will not be assumed that the plaintiff in the ejectment has the better title. The landlord will not be restrained by injunction from exacting a forfeiture by re-entry, until the estrepement is withdrawn, and the ejectment ended successfully for the tenant. Should the ejectment be subsequently decided adversely to the tenant, he has his remedy on the covenant for quiet enjoyment [94]

489. Demand conditions forfeiture for nonpayment of rent.— Ordinarily, it is the duty of the debtor to seek the creditor and to tender payment to him, and without any previous demand by him.[95] There are, however, implied qualifications of the right to take advantage of a condition for the payment of rent, or of a provision for forfeiture for nonpayment. Before the right can

[92] *West Ridge Coal Co* v *Von Storch,* 5 Lack Legal News, 189
[93] *Goddard's Appeal,* 1 Walk (Pa) 97 The evidence showed that the raising in eight months of the minimum quantity of coal, i e, 40,000 tons, was not impossible
[94] *Schuylkill & D Improv & R Co* v *Schmoele,* 57 Pa 271
[95] *Royer* v *Ake,* 3 Penr & W 461

be exercised, unless the agreement of the parties dispenses with
it, the landlord must demand the rent from the tenant.   The
rent thus to be demanded is rent in any form,[96] including royalties upon a coal,[97] a stone quarry,[98] or other lease [99]   The demand must be made on the leased premises[100] unless the contract
names another place,[101] and making a distress on the premises
is probably no proper demand.[102]   "Where there is," said Duncan, J., "a condition of re-entry on nonpayment of rent, several
things are required by the common law to be previously done, to
entitle the reversioner to re-enter   There must be a demand of
the precise rent due, on the very day on which it becomes due,
on the most notorious place on the land, and a demand must in
fact be made on the land although there should be no person on
the land ready to pay it   *Duppa v. Mayo,* 1 Wms. Saund. 287,
note 16.   This part of the common law has been adopted by us;
it is our own common law "[103]   "I do not find," remarks Mitchell, J., after quoting the passage just given, "that the law thus
declared has ever before now been questioned so far as to require
a citation by this court of that case in the eighty-one years since
it was decided "[104]   The fact that the tenant has been in the
habit of bringing the rent to the lessor does not dispense the lat-

---

[96]*Royer v Ake,* 3 Penr & W 461,
Wilcox v Cartright, 1 Lack Legal
Record, 130

[97]*Kreutz v McKnight,* 53 Pa 319,
Wilcox v Cartright, 1 Lack Le
gal Record, 130, *West Ridge Coal
Co v Ton Storch,* 5 Lack Legal
News, 189

[98]*East Conshohocken Quarry Co v
Boyd,* 18 Montg Co L Rep 58

[99]*Verdolite Co v Richards,* 7
Northampton Co Rep 113

[100]*Hughs v Lillibridge,* 8 Pa Dist
R 358, *East Conshohocken Quarry
Co v Boyd,* 18 Montg Co L Rep
58, *Robert v Ristine,* 2 Phila 62
[here the rent was granted out of
the land, not reserved in a grant of
the land], *West Ridge Coal Co v.*

Von Storch, 5 Lack Legal News,
189, *Evans v Fries,* 9 W N. C
462, *Haldeman v Sampter,* 2 Del
Co Rep 106, 6 Law Times N S 139

[101]*Rea v Eagle Transfer Co* 201
Pa 273, 88 Am St Rep 809, 50
Atl 764   In *Haldeman v Sampter,*
2 Del Co Rep. 106, 6 Law Times N
S 139, it was said that the demand
could not be waived in the lease

[102]*Past Conshohocken Quarry Co
v Boyd,* 18 Montg Co L Rep 58

[103]*McCormick v Connell,* 6 Serg
& R 151   Cf *Stoever v Whitman,*
6 Binn. 419

[104]*Rea v Eagle Transfer Co* 201
Pa 273, 88 Am St Rep 809, 50 Atl
764

ter, if he wishes to insist on a forfeiture, from the making of a demand for the rent on the premises.[105] If the forfeiture is en forced by a judgment in ejectment, confessed on a warrant of attorney, the record must aver that there had been a demand on the premises[106] for the rent If it does not the judgment will, on rule, be stricken off, [107] and equity will refuse to enforce the forfeiture by injunction, when no previous demand for the rent was made.[108]

490. Demand unnecessary.—Whether, when the lease provides that for nonpayment of royalty or rent at or within a certain time, the lease "is to be null and void," a demand for the royalty or rent must precede the forfeiture, was left undecided by the supreme court in *Hoch* v *Bass*.[109] It was decided to be unnec essary by Hagenman, J , in the common pleas.[110]

491. Ejectment on warrant of attorney—A favorite method of enforcing forfeitures for breach of condition is the judgment in ejectment and the execution appropriate thereto, and it is quite usual to insert into leases warrants of attorney to appear for the defendant in any action of ejectment and to confess judgment. The authority may be variously conditioned, *e g* , upon five days' default,[111] upon ten days' notice of intention to en force forfeiture after default,[112] instantly upon default, without

[105]*Rea* v *Eagle Transfer Co* 201 Pa 273, 88 Am St Rep 809, 50 Atl 764

[106]' Or, at least, an averment," says Morrison, J , "that the plaintiff or his agent was there on the proper days, ready to receive the rent, and that the defendant then neglected and refused to pay the same" *Hughs* v *Lillibridge,* 8 Pa. Dist R 358

[107]*Hughs* v *Lillibridge,* 8 Pa Dist R 358 , *Wilcox* v *Cartright,* 1 Lack. Legal Record, 130

LAND & TEN 27.

[108]*Verdolite Co v Richards,* 7 Northampton Co Rep 113

[109] 126 Pa 13, 17 Atl 512

[110]*Hoch* v *Bass*, 126 Pa 13, 17 Atl 512   The cases cited are *Sheaffer* v *Sheaffer*, 37 Pa 525 , *Davis* v *Moss*, 38 Pa 346

[111]*Evans* v *Fries,* 9 W N C 462 , *Reams* v *Fye,* 24 Pa Co Ct 671 The lease may allow either an entry by the lessor without judgment, or a judgment, at his option

[112]*National Pub Asso* v *Shupe & N Furniture Co* 18 W N C 379

any demur.[113] The lease containing the warrant need not be under seal [114]

492. Who may act under the warrant.—It seems to be understood that though the warrant expressly states that the lessor shall be plaintiff, and that the judgment to be entered shall be in his favor, the purchaser of the reversion from the lessor, if he receives also an assignment of the lease, may cause a judgment to be entered on the warrant, in his own favor.[115] Without the assignment of the lease, the warrant has been held not to run to the grantee of the reversion, although the lease expressly declares that all its covenants shall extend to the heirs, executors, administrators, and assigns of the lessor and lessee [116] A lease contained eight covenants made by the lessee for himself, his executors, administrators, and assigns, to the lessor, his executors, administrators, and assigns. It was said by Morrison, J , that for any violation of these covenants, the lessor, and, perhaps, his grantee of the reversion, might recover possession under the power of attorney, though the warrant, though made, by its terms, binding on the lessee and his assigns, was restricted to the lessor personally.[117]   But in *Jenks v. Hendley*,[118] Sharswood, J., held under a warrant for any attorney as "attorney of the lessee," to confess judgment when the "lessor," after violation of any of the covenants, had given a notice to determine the lease on the expiration of ten days, that the grantee of the reversion could not cause the confession of judgment. "Now the warrant in this case does not authorize the confession of a judgment in

---

[113]*Hughs v Lillibridge*, 8 Pa Dist. R 358

[114]*Benz v Langan*, 5 Northampton Co Rep 139

[115]*Hand v Suravitz*, 148 Pa. 202, 23 Atl 1117   The court declined to open a judgment entered on warrant, in favor of the sheriff's vendee of the reversion in *Israel v. Clough*, 5 Pa. Dist. R 325.

[116]*Hockley v McGlinn*, 40 Phila. Leg Int 279 In *Ellis v Ambler*, 11 Pa Super Ct 406, *Evans v Fries*, 9 W N C 462, the grantee of the reversion caused a judgment in his own favor to be entered

[117]*McClintock v. Loveless*, 5 Pa. Dist R 417

[118]6 Phila. 518.

favor of the assignee of the reversion. It is strictly confined to the lessor, and not to his assigns. And though the right to the covenants of the lease does pass to the grantee of the reversion, this will not hold as to this special power, where the word assigns has not been used." The lessor need not sign the lease in order to avail himself, as plaintiff, of the warrant of attorney.[119] If the lease is made by "James G Davis for Patterson Mills" (a firm) the judgment must be in the name of Davis as plaintiff, and not of the members of the firm [120]

493 **Against whom judgment can be entered under the warrant.**— Though the lease stipulates against any sublease or assignment without the written consent of the lessor, a judgment is sometimes entered against the lessee and the subtenant for various reasons, including the making of the sublease or assignment [121] But it is held in *Stewart* v. *Jackson*[122] that only the person who signs the lease can be made defendant in the judgment entered on the warrant contained therein. The mere fact that X enters on the premises under the tenant, and that the warrant authorizes the entry of a judgment against the lessee or any subtenant, if not signed by such subtenant, will not authorize a judgment against him. But the judgment being against the tenant alone, the subtenant or any other person who has come in under the tenant may be expelled by the *habere facias possessionem* issued therein If the lessee, a firm, assigns the lease to a corporation, composed in part of the members of the firm, and the landlord contracts in writing directly with the corporation, extending the lease, and intending the new arrangements to be a continuation of the old lease, the conditions and terms of

[119]*Schultz* v *Burlock*, 6 Pa Super Ct 573

[120]*Patterson* v *Pyle*, 1 Monaghan (Pa) 351, 17 Atl 6

[121]*Swartz's Appeal*, 119 Pa 208, 13 Atl 69 The covenants do not seem to have in terms bound the assigns of the lessee In *Limbert* v *Jones*,

118 Pa 589 12 Atl 584, the judgment was entered against the tenant and his assignee, though the warrant of attorney was for an attorney to appear for the 'lessee only"

[122] 181 Pa 549, 37 Atl 518 It was reversible error not to strike off the judgment against the subtenant

thc old lease being understood to continue except where specially
changed, judgment can be entered on the warrant in the original
lease against the corporation [123] "It is true," says Arnold, J,
"that the lease to the firm of Shupe & Noble would not of itself
authorize the entry of a judgment by confession against any
other persons than themselves, unless such other persons have
subjected themselves to the terms of the lease   The furniture
company has accepted an extension of that lease, and the evidence shows that the terms and conditions of the lease, except as
changed by the renewal agreement, were to remain in force
If, therefore, there was a forfeiture of the term, we think the
judgment was rightly entered against the furniture company."
The lessee's signature to the lease being Edward M. Schoenhut,
judgment was entered on the warrant of attorney against
Michael Schoenhut.   It being clear that Michael procured the
lease, and as tenant occupied the premises, and the court of common pleas being satisfied that he, in fact, signed the lease, it
properly refused to set aside the execution and to open the judgment entered against Michael, upon the warrant.[124]   A married woman, prior to the act of June 8, 1893,[125] could not give a
warrant of attorney to confess judgment in ejectment in a
lease [126]

   494 What period of time covered by warrant — When a lease
is made for a definite time, e g , for one year, and contains no
provision for a prolongation of the term, a warrant of attorney
therein to confess judgment for the rent will, in the absence of
expressions of a contrary sense in the lease, be understood to apply simply to the rent arising during the term, and not to that
arising during a holding over   While the covenants concerning rent will be generally held to continue, in case of holding

[123] *National Pub Asso* v *Shupe & N Furniture Co* 18 W N C 379

[124] *Schoenhut's Appeal,* 43 Phila Leg Int 347

[125] 2 Pepper & L Digest, 2887, P L 344

[126] *Wilkinson* v *Nichols,* 20 W N C 350

over the warrant will not, unless its terms clearly show that it is so intended.[127]   If the lease is for one year at a rental of $450, and the lessee therein "confesses judgment for the full sum of $450, with interest, costs of suit, and attorney's fee,'' and the rent for the year is paid in full, no judgment can be entered on the warrant for $450, as rent for the next year, during which the tenant holds over[128]   When, however, the lease itself provides for a holding over (*e g ,* the lease being for seventeen months, it provides that it is to continue from month to month after the expiration of the term, until written notice, at least thirty days before the end of any month, is given to quit at the end of that month), a warrant to confess judgment in ejectment for nonpayment of rent, gas, and water bills will apply to rent and gas and water bills accruing during the month-to-month tenancy.[129]

495 Filing of warrant with prothonotary.— An attorney may undertake to accept service and to confess a judgment for a defendant, or to agree to an amicable action, and therein to confess judgment, without any warrant of attorney.   Hence, should he confess judgment against a lessee, in an amicable action, no warrant being filed, the supreme court will not reverse on a writ of error from it to the common pleas   "It has never been understood to be the law of this state," says Agnew, J , "that the authority of an attorney must be in writing to enable him to confess a judgment."[130]   If a rule of court forbids confessions by attorneys without written warrants, or forbids confession by them on written warrants without filing the warrants, the proper remedy, when a judgment is confessed without compliance with the rule, is to ask the common pleas to set aside the proceedings[131]   In *Tanner v. Hopkins,*[132] Biddle, J., held that the

[127]*Hughs* v *Lillibridge,* 8 Pa Dist. R 358

[128]*Smith* v *Pringle,* 100 Pa 275

[129]*Hand* v *Suravitz,* 148 Pa 202, 23 Atl 1117.

[130]*Flanigen* v *Philadelphia,* 51 Pa 491

[131]*Flanigen* v *Philadelphia,* 51 Pa 491

[132] 12 W N C 238.

warrant in a lease need not be filed unless called for in behalf of those whom the attorney claims to represent, and upon order of the court, and that the court must recognize a judgment confessed by an attorney until it appears that he had no warrant to do so. He refused to set aside the judgment because the warrant was not, while a copy of it was, filed with the amicable action, and in *Betz* v. *Valer*,[133] Briggs, J , declined to strike off a judgment confessed by an attorney on a lease, even when neither the warrant nor a copy had been filed; but in order to comply with a rule of court, gave leave to the plaintiff to file a copy of the lease In *Maloney* v. *White*,[134] however, where the prothonotary entered judgment on a copy of a lease, whose warrant was in these words: "And the party of the second part hereby confesses judgment for the above-mentioned rent, or for as much thereof as may at any time hereafter be due and remain unpaid," the rule to strike off the judgment was made absolute because the prothonotary had only the alleged copy of the lease, and not the lease itself, before him when he entered the judgment

496. Filing an averment of breach.— The law will not presume that the lessee has broken the conditions of his lease, but will presume the contrary, until an averment is filed of such breach. A judgment confessed on a warrant filed, which authorizes the confession only when the tenant has broken the conditions of the lease, will properly be stricken off by the common pleas if there is no averment of breach.[135] The warrant itself often stipulates that an affidavit shall be made of the facts constituting

---

[133] 15 Phila 324 "The lease," said the judge, "is an important original paper, and there is no reason which requires the plaintiff to part with its possession"

[134] 24 Pa Co Ct 23 The opinion was expressed that even when an attorney confessed judgment on an instrument with warrant, he should file the warrant A *fortiori* should it be filed when the prothonotary enters the judgment without the mediation of an attorney

[135] *Patterson* v *Pyle*, 1 Monaghan (Pa) 351, 17 Atl 6 Averment of breach filed in *Reams* v *Fye*, 24 Pa Co Ct 671 Cf *Goddard's Appeal*, 1 Walk. (Pa.) 97.

the breach   On the affidavit's being made, the judgment may be properly entered [136]   A judgment confessed by an attorney, on such a warrant, without the affidavit, will be stricken off even after the delivery of possession to the plaintiff under a *habere facias possessionem*.[137]

497. Description of the premises.— The premises must be adequately described in the record   If they are described as "a certain messuage or tenement, with the appurtenances, situate in the borough of S., county of N , and commonwealth of Pennsylvania," the judgment will, on motion, be stricken off,[138] but the description was sufficient which stated that the object of the ejectment was the "premises situated No. 136 South Third street in the city of Philadelphia," that city "having a known system of notation, regulated by municipal laws, recognized in the transactions of general business, and acted upon by everyone."[139]

498 Signing by attorney.— If the warrant of attorney in the lease says that "any attorney" may, as attorney for the lessee, at the sole request of the lessor, sign an agreement for entering an amicable action and judgment, and the record does not

---

[136]*Pennsylvania Co for Ins on Lives & G A v Shanahan*, 10 Pa Super. Ct 267, *Limbert v Jones*, 118 Pa. 589, 12 Atl 584, *Tanner v Hopkins*, 12 W. N C 238, *Hughes v Moody*, 10 Pa Co Ct 305, *Grossman's Appeal*, 102 Pa 137, *Stout Coal Co v O'Donnell*, 4 Kulp, 495

[137]*Miller v Neidzielska*, 176 Pa 409, 35 Atl 225 Cf *Dikeman v Butterfield*, 135 Pa 236, 19 Atl 938, *Pennsylvania Co for Ins on Lives & G A.* v *Shanahan*, 10 Pa Super Ct. 267.

The lease authorizing a judgment "upon breach of any condition," by confession of an attorney, the prothonotary cannot enter the judgment without the intervention of an attorney   Neither he nor the land-lord can determine that there has been a breach   He cannot hear evidence   *Secor v Shippey*, 7 Pa Co Ct. 555

A judgment confessed by an attorney for breach of a condition against keeping a disorderly house, which breach was stated upon the record, was stricken off because there had been no determination of the fact of breach, no one having been constituted a judge, and the lessee not having waived his right to be heard upon the question   *Benz v Langan*, 5 Northampton Co Rep 139

[138]*Benz v Langan*, 5 Northampton Co Rep 139

[139]*Flanigen v Philadelphia*, 51 Pa. 491

show that any such agreement was signed by any attorney for the lessee, the judgment will be stricken off [140]

499. Forms of warrant — The lessee may in the lease "agree to the entering of an amicable action in ejectment," and may "hereby confess judgment in said amicable action in favor" of the lessor, and against himself   This does not authorize an acceptance of service of a summons for him by the attorney of the lessor in an action begun by the latter by the filing of a præcipe and the issue of a summons, and the confession of a judgment. An action of ejectment begun by issuing a summons to the defendant is, in no possible sense, an amicable action, and therefore the judgment confessed will be stricken off and the *habere facias possessionem* issued upon it will be set aside [141]   The lease providing that, if certain covenants were broken, any attorney might appear for the lessee in an action of ejectment to be brought against him by the lessor, and confess judgment therein, the attorney of the lessor may frame and enter an amicable action and enter judgment therein.   It is not necessary to begin the action by præcipe and summons.[142]   Of two leases of adjacent buildings between the same parties, each provided for the confession of a judgment.   One action of ejectment was filed for the recovery of possession of both buildings, and judgment was entered   The court declined to strike off, despite the defendant's contention that, the leases being of different dates, and for different lots, and the warrants of attorney being separate, they could not be joined in one action [143]

---

[140]*Weaver* v *McDevitt*, 21 Pa Super Ct 597

[141]*Stout Coal Co.* v *O'Donnell*, 4 Kulp, 495   The agreement was for an amicable action in *Dikeman v Butterfield*, 135 Pa 236, 19 Atl 938

A provision that on default the lessor may "re-enter" "or, at his option, enter judgment in an action of ejectment to be brought" does not contemplate the commencement of an action by writ, but the entry of an amicable action   *Reams* v *Fye*, 24 Pa Co Ct 671

[142]*Van Beil* v *Shure*, 17 Phila 104   The court refused to open the judgment and set aside the *habere facias possessionem*

[143]*Dikeman* v *Butterfield*, 135 Pa 236, 19 Atl 938   The supreme court remarked that no application was made to open it

500. Judgment for land and for rent.— The warrant may authorize a judgment both for the land and for rent which may be due.[144] "The right to recover rent in arrear, and the right to recover possession," are often exercised in one and the same proceeding,[145] but if the warrant is to confess a judgment in an amicable ejectment, and to issue a *habere facias possessionem* thereon, it is no authority for the confession of a judgment for the land and also for the rent due   The judgment for the land will on rule be allowed to stand, while that for the money will be set aside.[146]

501. Striking off and opening judgment.— When the judgment is regular on its face, but the tenant alleges that the facts did not exist which justify the entry of it, an application should be made to the court of common pleas to open it, but not to strike it off [147]   The application should be supported by the defendant's affidavit.[148]   The application to open may accordingly be made when the cause of entering the judgment is alleged default in paying the rent punctually, and the previous demand for it is denied,[149] or its payment is averred by the lessee,[150] or when nonpayment of the water bill for whose nonpayment the judgment has been entered is not, by the terms of the lease, a ground of forfeiture;[151] or when the default has not lasted for

[144]*Murphy* v *Marshell*, 179 Pa 516, 36 Atl 294, *Dikeman* v *Butterfield*, 135 Pa 236, 19 Atl 938

[145]*Pennsylvania Co for Ins on Lives & G A* v *Shanahan*, 10 Pa Super Ct 267

A judgment both for the land and for the rent due being entered the judgment for the rent may be opened, while that for the land is allowed to stand   *Murphy* v *Marshell*, 179 Pa 516, 36 Atl 294

[146]*Ellis* v *Ambler*, 11 Pa Super Ct 406

[147]*Dikeman* v *Butterfield*, 135 Pa 236, 19 Atl 938

[148]As in *Dikeman* v *Butterfield*, 135 Pa 236, 19 Atl 938.

[149]*Evans* v *Fries*, 9 W N C 462. Though after the judgment was entered, on the same day, a tender of the rent was refused, the court declined to open the judgment   Cf. *Wilcox* v *Cartright*, 1 Lack Legal Record, 130

[150]*Bausman* v *Kreider*, 18 Lanc L Rev 103   The judgment will not be opened if the uncorroborated testimony of the defendant that he has paid all the rent is contradicted by the plaintiff

[151]*Hand* v *Suravitz*, 148 Pa 202, 23 Atl 1117.

the period named in the lease, *e. g.,* five days;[152] or when the
lessor, by a course of dealing, has betrayed the lessee into the
unpunctuality in paying the rent for which the judgment was
entered,[153] or when the default in paying rent, alleged by the
landlord, is denied by the tenant;[154] or when the cause of forfeiture alleged is the tenant's carrying on of any business which
is unlawful[155] or prohibited by the lease,[156] and his having done
so is denied; or when the cause of forfeiture is a subletting, and
an oral simultaneous agreement that the tenant might sublet is
sufficiently proven;[157] or an assignment of the lease, and the con
dition against forfeiture has been eliminated by the lessor's
waiver,[158] or the fact of assignment is denied,[159] or when the
judgment has been entered on account of the cessation of the
term, and the giving of the notice to quit, on which that cessation depends, is denied by the tenant,[160] or he alleges a second
lease, prolonging the period of possession;[161] or when the cause
of forfeiture is allowing water to run over a floor, and thus
to destroy the fresco in the room below, and the tenant denies.[162]
The conclusiveness of the judgment as to third parties is not
affected by its being opened.   Thus, in an ejectment by one who
has bought the leasehold under a mechanic's lien, against the

[152]*Gregg* v *Krebs,* 5 Pa Dist R
779   The lease authorized a judgment on a default of five days   The
last of the five days was Sunday
The tenant had therefore the whole
of Monday on which to pay   A judgment entered on Monday was too
soon

[153]*Cogley* v *Browne,* 11 W N C.
224, *Wanamaker* v *McCaully,* 11
W N C 450, *Times Co* v. *Sie-
brecht,* 11 W N C 283, *Humane
Engine Co* v *Salvation Army,* 18
Montg. Co L Rep 13

[154]*Schultz* v *Burlock,* 6 Pa. Super.
Ct 573

[155]*Hughes* v. *Moody,* 10 Pa. Co. Ct.
305

[156]*Inman* v. *Vandervoode,* 1 W. N
C 40

[157]*Zeigler* v *Lichten,* 205 Pa 104,
54 Atl 489   The oral agreement
was not satisfactorily proven.

[158]*National Pub Asso* v *Shupe &
N Furniture Co* 18 W N. C 379

[159]*Huber* v *Grossman,* 14 W N C
157

[160]*Byrne* v *Funk,* 13 W N C 503,
Williams v *McAnany,* 1 Pa Dist R.
128; *Gill* v. *Ogborn,* 1 W. N C 28

[161]*Gibson* v. *Vetter,* 162 Pa 26, 29
Atl 292

[162]*Scherr* v. *Seymour,* 2 W. N. C.
534.

landlord, who has been put in possession by a *habere facias pos-sessionem,* the latter could defend by means of the judgment, so long as it had not been set aside.[163]

502. Rule to strike off —To justify the striking off of a judgment it should appear that its entry was unauthorized, and that the plaintiff had no right to place it on record as an adjudication;[164] that it was irregular upon its face.[165] This rule is properly resorted to when the judgment has, despite the requirement of the warrant, been entered without the lessor's affidavit as to the facts.[166] A judgment for rent due will be stricken off when the warrant is for a judgment for the land only.[167] A judgment for the land will be stricken off if the prothonotary has entered it without the intervention of an attorney, and the ascertainment of the fact of breach has not been provided for in the lease.[168] The lease providing that on default any attorney, as attorney for the lessee, at the sole request of the lessor, may sign an agreement for entering an amicable action and judgment in ejectment, a judgment will be stricken off if the record does not show that such agreement was signed by an attorney for the lessee [169]

503. Who may ask for the rule.—Only the lessee, or one who is in privity with him, may obtain the rule to open or strike off

[163]*Seltzer* v *Robbins,* 181 Pa 451, 37 Atl 567

[164]*Miller* v *Neidzielska,* 176 Pa 409 35 Atl 225

[165]*Dileman* v *Butterfield,* 135 Pa 230, 19 Atl 938 The court has no power to strike off a judgment "except for a fatal irregularity apparent on the face of the record " *Pennsylvania Co for Ins on Lives & G S* v *Shanahan,* 10 Pa Super Ct 267

[166]*Miller* v *Neidzielska,* 176 Pa 409, 35 Atl 225

[167]*Ellis* v. *Ambler,* 11 Pa. Super Ct 406.

[168]*Secor* v *Shippey,* 7 Pa Co Ct 555 In *Pottsville Bank* v *Cake,* 12 Pa Super Ct 61, the tenant, as cause for striking off the judgment, alleged duress and fraud in inducing him to accept the lease The appellate court found no such evidence as would justify the opening, much less the striking of it off The lessor had bought the land on an execution against the defendant, and had forced him either to vacate the premises or to accept the lease

[169]*Weaver* v *McDevitt,* 21 Pa Super Ct 597.

the judgment Thus, the tenant of A, having attorned to B, a claimant of the premises, and having accepted from B a new lease containing the warrant of attorney, on which judgment for B has been entered, A cannot support a rule to strike it off.[170] A's tenant having vacated the premises without paying rent, Q, claiming adversely to the lessor to own the land, enters and leases to T T cannot support the rule to open the judgment entered on the warrant in A's lease [171] As a competing claimant of the land cannot take the rule, neither can the tenant allege as cause for opening or setting aside the judgment, that the land belongs to another than the lessor, on notice from whom, after paying the rent for some time to the lessor, he has ceased to pay it, and yielded the possession to a tenant of the lessor's competitor. These facts will be no justification for setting aside the *habere facias possessionem* and opening the judgment.[172] The tenant cannot allege, as cause for opening the judgment, that he had gone into possession one month prior to his lease from the plaintiff. under another, X, who claimed the land adversely to the plaintiff, that he always recognized X as his landlord, paying him rent, and that he had accepted a lease from the plaintiff because of threats of ouster, and intimidation.[173] In *Kelly* v *Northrop*,[174] after the *habere facias* was in the sheriff's hands, L, not a party to the proceedings, but found in possession, induced him to desist from executing the writ, by averring that the lessee had never been in possession, that before and at the entry of the judgment, she was in possession, in her own right,

---

[170]*Smith* v *Harley*, 1 W N C 132 The rule to strike off was discharged A *habere facias possessionem* had been executed

[171]*Weeks* v *Clause*, 19 W N C 108

[172]*Nehr* v *Krewsberg*, 187 Pa 53, 40 Atl 810

[173]*McLaughlin* v *Zeidler*, 13 Pa Co Ct 47 The lessor had brought ejectment against X and obtained a

judgment and X had then brought an ejectment against him, but he again obtained the judgment Then X had begun a third ejectment which was pending when the judgment against the tenant was entered on the warrant of attorney

[174]159 Pa 537, 28 Atl 364 Vide remarks in *Nehr* v *Krewsberg*, 187 Pa 53, 40 Atl 810.

not holding nor claiming to hold under the tenant. Other parties, however, were in possession of parts of the premises, under a lease from the tenant. The court properly made absolute a rule on the sheriff to proceed with the execution of the writ. In a case in which the lease was accepted by a mortgagor from his mortgagee, as a means of putting the latter into possession, the mortgagor agreeing to pay rent to the mortgagee as lessor, who should apply it to prior liens and his own debt, creditors who levied on the personalty upon the premises obtained a rule to show cause why the judgment, entered after their execution, upon the warrant in the lease, should not be opened, and the *habere facias possessionem* set aside, they having tendered the mortgage debt and interest to the mortgagee, who was the lessor, and who refused to receive the money. The rule was made absolute.[175] When the lease contains a condition against subletting, and a sublease is made, without waiver of the condition by the lessor, the subtenant has no standing to petition the court for the opening of the judgment entered on the warrant of attorney. That he went into possession under earlier tenants, whose leases also covenanted against subletting, will give him no standing.[176]

504. Setting aside habere facias possessionem.—If, before the application to the court to open a judgment, a *habere facias possessionem* has been issued and executed by the dispossession of the tenant, the court, in opening the judgment, need not set aside the execution until the decision upon the hearing as to whether the judgment should be stricken off;[177] but in *Smith v. Hailey*[178] the court found an additional difficulty in setting aside the judgment in the fact that the *habere facias* had been executed.

505. Appeal.— The 1st section of the act of May 20, 1891,[179]

[175]*Entenman v Keebler,* 13 Phila 56
[176]*Shermer v Paciello,* 161 Pa 69, 28 Atl 995.
[177]*Grossman's Appeal,* 102 Pa 137
[178]1 W N C 132
[179]1 Pepper & Lewis Digest, 135, P L. 101, *Pottsville Bank* v. *Calc,* 12

authorizes an appeal to the supreme court in all cases of application for the opening, vacating, and striking off of judgments of
any kind, whether entered by amicable confession, upon warrant of attorney, or otherwise, and whether the appellant com-
plains of the opening, vacating, and striking off by the lower
court, or of refusal to open, vacate, and strike off. Before this
act it had been held that no appeal lay from the refusal of the
lower court to open a judgment [180]   The appellate court will
reverse the decision of the court below, refusing to vacate a judgment, only for an abuse of discretion.[181]   An appeal to the
higher court from the judgment entered on the warrant of attorney, as distinguished from the decision of the lower court on
a rule to open or set aside, will be quashed.[182]

506 Lessee takes advantage of condition — There may be conditions in leases for the benefit of the lessee, — who may renounce
the lease and all his future obligations under it, upon the breach
of them. But when the condition is intended for the benefit of
the lessor, the lessee cannot disengage himself from his liabilities
by pleading that, by a default of his own, the lease has become
void, the lessor not having elected to treat it as void for that reason. Being for the benefit of the lessor, it may be enforced or
waived at his option. The violated condition may be for the
punctual payment of rent,[183] or the commencement of mining

Pa. Super Ct 61   As to the force
of a clause in the lease, releasing all
errors and defects in entering the
judgment, vide Jenks v Hendley, 6
Phila 518, Ankermiller v O'Byrne,
2 Monaghan (Pa.) 766. Groll v
Gegenheimer, 147 Pa. 162, 23 Atl
440

[180]Dikeman v. Butterfield, 135 Pa
236, 19 Atl 938, Limbert v Jones,
118 Pa 589, 12 Atl. 584, Swartz's
Appeal 119 Pa 208, 13 Atl 69 But
the discharge of the rule to open was
reversed in Grossman's Appeal, 102
Pa 137

[181]Pennsylvania Co for Ins on

Lives & G. A v Shanahan, 10 Pa.
Super Ct 267

[182]Bonniwell v Hopson, 3 W N C.
492   The judgment was affirmed in
Flanigen v. Philadelphia, 51 Pa 491
In Kelly v Philadelphia Riding
Club, 2 W N C 584, pending an appeal from the judgment, the court
dissolved an injunction to prevent
the sheriff from proceeding with the
habere facias possessionem, saving
relief should have been sought by an
application to the court to open the
judgment

[183]English v. Yates, 205 Pa 106, 54
Atl 503.

operations under a gas lease, within a specified time,[184] or any other In the exaction of a covenant from the lessee not to occupy the premises otherwise than as a saloon and dwelling. without the lessor's consent, there is no implied condition to the lessee's obligation as such, that he shall be able to obtain a license to sell liquor, in order to maintain a saloon He continues liable for the rent though the court refuses him a license.[185]

507. Right of lessee after forfeiture —The forfeiture of the interest of the lessee under the lease does not impair his ownership of any personal property on the premises, or his right to access to it, in order to take it away If he has mined coal which still lies in the mine, he may reasonably use the railway and other instrumentalities for its removal.[186]

[184] *Wills* v *Manufacturers Natural Gas Co* 130 Pa. 222, 5 L. R. A. 603, 18 Atl 721, *Westmoreland & C Natural Gas Co* v *DeWitt*, 130 Pa 235, 5 L R A 731, 25 W N C 103 18 Atl 724 *Bartley* v *Phillips*, 179 Pa 175, 36 Atl 217 *Fennell* v *Guffey*, 139 Pa 341, 20 Atl 1048, *Galey Bros* v *Kellerman*, 123 Pa 491, 16 Atl 474.

[185] *Teller* v *Boyle*, 132 Pa 56, 18 Atl 1069 If the lessor was endeavoring to forfeit the lease because of the lessee's not selling liquors the failure to get the license would be a good defense

[186] *Lykens Valley Coal Co* v *Dock*, 62 Pa. 232.

CHAPTER XXV.

STATUTORY FORFEITURE FOR NONPAYMENT OF RENT.

508. Act of April 3rd, 1830 —That rent is in arrear does not, in the absence of a stipulation in the lease making that fact a termination of the lease, or a ground upon which the landlord, by re-entry or otherwise, may terminate it, avoid the lease or forfeit the tenant's rights under it. The act of April 3rd, 1830,[1] however, gives to the landlord in certain cases where the method prescribed therein is pursued, the power to end the term before its contractural termination, rent being in arrear. He gives the tenant notice to quit within fifteen or thirty days. If the tenant neglects to remove within that term or afterwards, and also neglects to pay the rent in arrear, he makes complaint before a justice, who, certain facts being alleged, issues a precept to a constable to summon the tenant to appear. The justice hears the evidence, and, if satisfied of the truth of the averment of the landlord, enters a judgment for him and issues a writ of possession, and the interest of the tenant in the lease comes to an end

509 The lease.—The applicability of the method of the act of 1830 depends on there being "a lessee for a term of years or at will or otherwise of a messuage, lands, or tenements, upon the demise whereof any rents are or shall be reserved." Comprehensive as this language is, the act furnishes no remedy when the tenancy is for life, or subject to a ground rent in fee.[2] The demise must be for a definite period, from year to year[3] (which includes from quarter to quarter, from month to month, etc.), or strictly at will.

510. Continuance of relation of landlord and tenant to inception of the proceedings.—Possibly the term must not have elapsed when the proceedings are resorted to. If it has, the landlord has the remedy of ejectment, or that furnished by the act of March 21st, 1772, and December 14th, 1863, and would not

---

[1] 1 Pepper & Lewis Digest, 2655   76 Pa 277, *McDermott* v *McIlwain*, P L 187   For reasons for this 75 Pa 341, *McCarthy* v *Sykes*, 7 statute, see *Clark* v *Everly*, 8 Pa Dist R 243 Watts & S 226   [3]*Palethorp* v *Schmidt*, 12 Pa Su- [2]*Leinbach* v *Kaufman*, 2 Walk per Ct. 214. (Pa) 515; *Trimbath* v *Patterson*,

need that furnished by the act of April 3rd, 1830. So, if by the
tenant's denial of the landlord's title, the latter has, at common
law, the right to treat the lease as forfeited, and instantly resort
to an ejectment, the act of 1830 is not applicable. "Why, then,"
asks Gibson, Ch. J., "should the provisions of our statute be extended to a refusal to pay under a claim of right to the reversion,
which, being a denial of the landlord's title, gives him an immediate right of entry and action at the common law? The statute
remedy is founded on a continuance of the tenure till the moment of notice to quit, which is required not only to warn the
tenant, but to dissolve the tenancy, but a previous repudiation
of the lease, which equally puts an end to it, renders notice unnecessary and gives the landlord a right to recover at the common
law, unless the tenant disprove the lease   When that is done a
conflict of adverse paramount title arises which the legislature
has never confided to the determination of a summary tribunal "
X, having leased to B, dies, leaving a daughter, the wife of A.
The wife dying, A became owner of the land for life by the
curtesy. B, denying A's right to the rent, insists that X had
made a will devising the land to him, and that A and his wife
had suppressed it   There is litigation concerning this will in
another court. The assertion by B that the title was not in A,
but in himself, before the institution of the proceedings, put the
case beyond the jurisdiction of the justices   The assertion of the
title "previous to the commencement of the proceeding may be
set up as an insuperable objection to the jurisdiction "[4]   A
claims as landlord under the lessor, X. The tenant alleges that
X had died before the rent accrued for which the demand is
made by A, and that he has recognized the remainderman as
entitled to the rent, and has paid it to him. Such a controversy
cannot be decided by the justices.[5]

[4]*Clark* v. *Everly,* 8 Watts & S.   [5]*Allen* v *Ash,* 6 Phila. 313

511. Supersedure of relation by that of vendor and vendee.— Though there has once been the relation of landlord and tenant, it may have been superseded by a contract of sale; and if the former tenant continues in possession under the new contract, making payments which are not intended to be of rent, but of purchase money, the former landlord denying the enforceableness of the contract of sale, because in parol, and because the facts which exempt it from the operation of the statute of frauds do not exist, cannot recover the possession under the act of April 3rd, 1830, though in fact a chancellor would not award specific performance.[6]

512. Who may institute the proceedings—"It shall be lawful for the lessor," says the act of 1830, "to make complaint." But not only the lessor, but any person claiming the reversion under him may make it;[7] e g., the heir of the lessor,[8] or the husband of the heir, claiming as tenant by the curtesy,[9] the grantee of the lessor,[10] the sheriff's vendee of the reversion,[11] the executor of the lessor, who is directed by his will to sell the premises and divide the proceeds.[12]   A lessee of a term may in turn make a sublease and institute the proceedings against the sublessee.[13]

513. Conditions for inaugurating proceedings.—There must be a lease reserving rents, and the lessee must neglect or refuse to pay the rent. This is the indispensable prerequisite to the institution of the procedure   It is the fact which justifies the expulsion of the tenant from the premises prior to the normal close of his term.

---

[6]*Mohan* v. *Butler,* 112 Pa 590, 4 Atl 47

[7]*Trimbath* v. *Patterson,* 76 Pa 277. In *Smith* v *Crosland,* 106 Pa 413, the proceedings were begun by "A R agent." After appeal to the common pleas the name of the principal was by amendment, substituted as plaintiff

[8]*Clark* v. *Everly,* 8 Watts & S 226

[9]*Clark* v. *Everly,* 8 Watts & S. 226

[10]*Bergman* v *Roberts,* 61 Pa 497.

[11]*McKeon* v *King,* 9 Pa. 213

[12]*Marsteller* v *Marsteller,* 132 Pa 517, 19 Am St Rep 604, 19 Atl 344

[13]*Smith* v *Crosland,* 106 Pa 413, *Palethorp* v *Schmidt,* 12 Pa Super Ct 214.

514. Conditions; absence of goods — One of the conditions for resorting to the procedure of the act of 1830 is expressed by the words: "Where there are no goods on the premises adequate to pay the said rent so in arrear, except such articles as are exempt from levy and sale by the laws of the commonwealth." If two or more premises are included in the lease, there must be on neither of them sufficient goods to satisfy the rent in arrear.[14] This fact must be averred in the complaint[15] and must be found to be a fact by the justices,[16] for if the rent can be made by a distress, it is not the policy of the law to deprive the tenant of his interest in the land.

515 Notice to quit. — Where there is a lease for years or at will, or otherwise, reserving rent, and there is rent in arrear, and not sufficient goods upon the premises to make a distress for the rent successful, it shall and may be lawful for the lessor to give the lessee notice to quit the premises within fifteen days from the date of the notice, if such notice is given on or after the first of April and before the first of September, and within thirty days from the date thereof, if given on or after the first of September and before the first of April The notice is by the lessor or by him who is the owner of the reversion when the notice is given Notice given in the name of the "heirs of A. J Reid" is sufficient, though in the complaint following their full names are given as plaintiffs.[17] Possibly the notice is sufficient if signed "William J Bell, agent for Charles B. Roberts"[18] If there is a sublessee of the land, or an assignee of the lease in possession, notice must be given to him. "He [the landlord] was bound," says Parsons, J , "to serve the notice of the nonpayment of rent upon the tenant in the actual possession at the time,

---

[14]*Clark* v *Everly,* 8 Watts & S 226, *Bergman* v *Roberts,* 61 Pa 226   497; *Thomas* v *Flamer,* 1 Phila
[15]*McKeon* v *King,* 9 Pa 213, *Reid* 518
v *Christy,* 2 Phila 144   [17]*Reid* v *Christy,* 2 Phila 144
    [16]*Clark* v *Everly,* 8 Watts & S   [18]*Bergman* v *Roberts,* 61 Pa 497

in order to deprive him of his estate. If he was a sublessee he cannot be turned out of his possession without notice, for he may be willing to pay the rent demanded rather than to be turned out with his family into the street."[19] In *Hartnack* v *James*,[20] X being in possession under some connection—that of assignee or sublessee—with the lessee, notice was served on the lessee and also upon X personally, on the premises, a copy of the notice being left with him.

516. Notice to quit; demand of rent.—The notice to quit must be accompanied with a statement of the rent claimed to be due by the landlord The proceeding is "only another means," says Parsons, J., "of enforcing the payment of the rent, and that too in a way quite [*sic*] more summary than by the warrant of distress." On the payment of the sum thus claimed, and costs, the tenant may avoid dispossession. He should, therefore, know how much rent the landlord demands when payment is the condition of his retaining the possession.[21]

517. Period of notice.—The notice to the tenant is to quit the premises "within fifteen days," or, "within thirty days" from the date of the notice. according as the notice is given between April 1st and the following September 1st, or between September 1st and following April 1st. "Within" seems to be understood to mean "at the expiration of.", Proceedings before the justice

---

[19]*Clark* v *Everly*, 8 Watts & S 226

[20] 8 Phila. 317

[21]*Clark* v *Everly*, 8 Watts & S 226 In *McCarthy* v *Sykes*, 7 Pa Dist R 243, $6 00 was demanded in the notice as the rent in arrear In *O'Neill* v *Cahill*, 2 Brewst (Pa) 357, the notice reads thus "James Cahill and all whom it may concern You are hereby notified to quit the premises situate in Fourth above Master street, which I have leased to you, reserving rent, or pay and satisfy the rent due and in arrear, being six dollars, which amount was due on the 15th day of May, 1852, and is hereby demanded (you having neglected or refused to pay the amount so reserved as often as the same has grown due, according to the terms of our contract, and there being no goods on the premises adequate to pay the rent so reserved, except such articles as are exempt from levy and sale by the laws of this commonwealth) within fifteen days from the date hereof, or I shall proceed against you as the law directs Ann T. O'Neill."

begun only ten days after the notice given between April 1st and September 1st,[22] or only twenty-six days after the notice given between September 1st and April 1st,[23] are void, the act of 1830 saying. "If the lessee shall not, within the period aforesaid, remove from, and deliver up, the premises to the said lessor, or pay and satisfy the rent so due and in arrear, it shall be lawful for the lessor to make complaint;" nor can the time be reduced by "the fraction of a day, or a full day, or more " The courts will not enforce an agreement in the lease for a shorter term of notice. The tenant in the lease agreeing that, if the rent becomes in arrear the landlord may dispossess him on five days' notice to quit, no authority is thereby given to the landlord to commence the proceedings under the act of 1830, unless the fifteen days' or the thirty days' notice is given.[24]

518. The complaint —If the tenant pays the rent mentioned in his notice within or after the period, the right of the lessor to terminate his possession ends so far as that rent is concerned. If other rent has become due, or should subsequently become due, a new notice must be given Or, if not paying the rent the arrear of which has occasioned the notice, the tenant retires from the possession,[25] no necessity exists for making an information before the justice. If the tenant neither pays the rent nor removes from and delivers up the possession, the lessor is authorized to "make complaint on oath or affirmation," to any alderman or justice of the peace of the county [26] It is the "lessor or his authorized agent" who makes the complaint. By "lessor" is to be understood not merely the maker of the lease, but anyone

---

[22]*Hopkins* v *McClelland*, 8 Phila 302

[23]*Goodwin* v *Shoemaker*, 5 Kulp, 321

[24]*McCloud* v *Jaggers*, 3 Phila 304

[25] If he retires, the relation of landlord and tenant is at an end *Donnon* v *Moore*, 1 Chester Co. Rep.

[26] The 1st section of the act of March 22nd, 1861; 1 Pepper & Lewis Digest, 2658, P. L 181, repeals so much of the act of April 3rd, 1830, as requires the complaint to be made before two aldermen or justices of the peace, and authorizes it to be made before one.

who, having succeeded to the reversion, is entitled to the rent [27] A complaint made by a "stranger to the lease and in his own behalf" will not support the proceedings.[28] It must doubtless be in writing.[29] It "shall be lawful for any such lessor or his authorized agent," say the acts of 1830 and 1861, "to make such complaint on oath or affirmation."[30] Where, under the former law, a party could not be a witness for himself, he could make this oath or affirmation.[31] Indeed, the oath or affirmation by him or his agent is indispensable. The oath of the agent or attorney of the landlord is sufficient if he has personal knowledge of the facts,[32] but the oath of a stranger in his own behalf is insufficient.[33] If the landlords are named in full, the fact that the notice to quit did not name them, but described them as heirs of the lessor, is immaterial.[34]

519. Constituents of complaint — The complaint is the basis of the proceedings, and it must set out all the facts essential to the jurisdiction of the magistrate under the act.[35] Hence, it must contain an averment as to when the term commenced and when it is to end, and show that the lease is not for life nor in fee.[36] It must aver the reservation of a rent, what the rent is, and how much is in arrear.[37] It must state that there are on the premises no goods not exempt from distress, adequate to satisfy the rent in arrear.[38] The issue of the notice, and the failure of the tenant to pay the rent or to vacate the premises, must also be averred.

---

[27] The heirs of the lessor *Reid* v *Christy*, 2 Phila 144

[28] *Hopkins* v *McClelland*, 8 Phila 302.

[29] Though Archibald, J, refrained from saying that it must be written, he said it ought always to be written, in *Mogg* v. *Stone*, 4 Del Co Rep 170

[30] *Clark* v *Everly*, 8 Watts & S 226; *Fisher* v *Bailey*, 1 Ashm (Pa) 209, *Maxwell* v *Perkins*, 93 Pa 255

[31] *Fisher* v *Bailey*, 1 Ashm (Pa) 209

[32] *Reid* v *Christy*, 2 Phila 144

[33] *Hopkins* v *McClelland*, 8 Phila 302

[34] *Reid* v *Christy*, 2 Phila 144

[35] *Leinbach* v *Kaufman*, 2 Walk. (Pa) 515

[36] *McDermott* v *McIlwain*, 75 Pa. 341, *Leinbach* v *Kaufman*, 2 Walk. (Pa.) 515, *Trimbath* v *Patterson*, 76 Pa 277 *Mogg* v *Stone*, 4 Del Co Rep. 170, *Tyrell Bldg & L. Asso* v *Daughen*, 7 W N C 244

[37] *Clark* v *Everly*, 8 Watts & S 226, *McKeon* v *King*, 9 Pa 213

[38] *McKeon* v *King*, 9 Pa 213 In

520. Action of the justice on the complaint.—The justice, "on its appearing to them [him] that the lessor has demised the premises for a term of years or otherwise, whereof any rent or rents have been reserved, that the said rent is in arrear and unpaid, that there is not sufficient goods and chattels on the premises to pay and satisfy the said rent, except such as are by law exempted from levy and sale, and that the lessee has, after being notified in manner aforesaid, refused to remove and deliver up possession of the premises, shall then and in that case issue their [his] precept, reciting substantially the complaint and allegation of the lessor, directed to any constable of the proper city or county," commanding him to summon the lessee [39] Subsequently the justice is to "proceed to hear the case" The justice is therefore to issue the precept to the constable only when the above recited facts "appear" to him. He, however, does not hear any evidence at this stage. The complaint, averring these facts and verified by the oath or affirmation of the lessor or his agent, is his only means of information

521. The precept or warrant.—The complaint averring the necessary facts, and being sworn to or affirmed, the justice issues a precept to the constable commanding him to summon the said lessee to appear before the said alderman or justice at a day and time to be therein fixed, not less than three nor more than

---

Leinbach v *Kaufman*, 2 Walk (Pa) 515, this complaint was condemned City of Reading, Berks county, ss On the sixth day of March, A D 1884, personally appeared hefore Isaac R Fisher, an alderman of the city of Reading, said county, David K Kaufman, of Reading, who, being sworn according to law, saith that the premises situated at the corner of Centre Avenue and Amity Street, in the city of Reading, he leased to Elias Leinbach reserving rent, that the said rent is in arrear and unpaid, that there are not sufficient goods and chattels on the premises to pay and satisfy the said rent, except such as are by law exempted from levy and sale and that the said lessee has (after being notified to quit the said premises within thirty days from date of said notice) refused to surrender and deliver up possession of the said premises   David K Kaufman

Sworn and subscribed befoie me, Isaac R Fisher, Alderman

[39] Act April 3rd, 1830, § 1, 1 Pepper & Lewis Digest, 2655, P. L 187.

eight days thereafter, to answer the said complaint. If the summons is in the ordinary form when a debt is to be recovered, it is no notice to the tenant that a dispossession proceeding is in contemplation, and if the tenant does not appear, the judgment of dispossession ultimately entered will be void [40]   The summons should be served on the lessee, or upon the person in possession who has acquired his right by sublease or by assignment. In *Hartnach* v. *James*,[41] the lessee's interest being sold by the sheriff, and the sheriff's vendee transferring his interest to X, the summons was served both on the lessee, "and personally, on the premises," on X.   The service, if on the lessee personally, need not be made on the premises.[42]   A copy of the writ must be delivered to the lessee, or, when personal service is not made, to some member of his family   A nonpersonal service made by "delivering a true copy on the premises, in the presence of Malinda Nash, an adult neighbor," is not sufficient.[43]   The defendant in the writ being one person, the constable's return, "Served the within by reading the same to them," would leave too uncertain the inference that the defendant was intended.[44]   The constable's return must show that a valid service has been made by him; otherwise, in the absence of an appearance by the defendant, the judgment rendered by the justice for the lessor will be voidable on certiorari.

522. The hearing and judgment.—On the day appointed in the summons served on the lessee "or on some other day then to be appointed" by the justice, he is directed by the act to "proceed to hear the case," and he is to ascertain whether the complaint is "in all particulars just and true." If the complaint is found to be thus just and true, then the justice "shall enter judgment

[40]*Cassel* v *Seibert*, 1 Dauphin Co. Rep 16   The tenant can attack it collaterally by suing in trespass the landlord and the justice for evicting him under the judgment.
[41] 8 Phila 317

[42]*Reid* v *Christy*, 2 Phila 144
[43]*McCarthy* v *Sykes*, 7 Pa Dist. R 243
[44]*Mogg* v *Stone*, 4 Del Co Rep 170

against such lessee that the premises shall be delivered up to the lessor." He is also required to ascertain and determine, on due and legal proof, the rent actually due and in arrear, and the costs of the proceeding, and to indorse this rent and these costs on the writ which he may issue at the request of the lessor for the delivery of the possession. If the justice finds the complaint vexatious and unfounded, he dismisses it with costs, to be paid by the lessor.

523. Finding the rent due.— The object of ascertaining the rent due and of indorsing it upon the writ of possession is, "that the tenant may, if he sees fit, supersede the writ by paying to the constable, for the use of the lessor, the amount of the rent, together with the costs of the proceeding."[45] The rent thus to be ascertained is the rent which was due when the notice was sent to the tenant, and not that in addition which subsequently accrues. Thus, the notice specifying $6 00 as in arrear, a finding by the justice of $12.00, the additional six being the rent of another month fallen due since the notice, would vitiate the proceedings.[46] The notice specifying as rent due, the rent due on January 1st, 1860, the ascertainment of rent due to February 1st, 1860, is erroneous.[47] The object of the statement of the rent is to enable the tenant to retain the possession, on paying it,[48] and he has a right to retain the possession on paying the rent of default as to which he was notified in the notice, and default as to which was alleged against him in the complaint. No judgment, however, is entered for the rent due,[49] and therefore no execution can issue for the collection of it[50] A judgment for $146.67, the rent claimed, "or the possession of the house and premises," was

[45]*Trimbath* v *Patterson*, 76 Pa 277, *McCarthy* v *Sykes*, 7 Pa Dist R 243

[46]*McCarthy* v *Sykes*, 7 Pa Dist R 243

[47]*Stoever* v *Miller*, 4 Phila 149

[48]*Hazen* v. *Culbertson*, 10 Watts, 393

[49]*Hazen* v *Culbertson*, 10 Watts, 393

[50]*Castle* v. *Weber*, 2 Pearson (Pa) 79, *Rubicum* v *Williams*, 1 Ashm (Pa) 230 Cf. *Philadelphia & R R. Co.* v *Thornton*, 3 Phila 257.

held to be erroneous because there can be no judgment for rent, because if there could, a judgment for more than $100 exceeded the justice's jurisdiction; and because a judgment in the alternative is not certain, and is not sanctioned by the act of 1830 [51] However, if a judgment for the delivery of the possession of the premises to the lessor, and also for the payment of the rent to him, be entered, the latter will be treated probably as surplusage on certiorari,[52] but an execution issued on it for the rent would be reversed.[53]

524. The execution.— The justice must, after judgment, "at the request of the lessor, issue a writ of possession directed to the said constable, commanding him forthwith to deliver actual possession of the premises to the lessor, and also to levy the costs on the defendant in the same manner that costs are now by law levied and collected on other writs of execution." The rent found due is to be indorsed on this writ of possession. If it is not, the writ, doubtless, and all proceedings upon it, will be set aside on certiorari.[54]

525. When execution may issue.—"No writ of possession shall be issued . . . for five days after the rendition of judgment, and if, within the said five days, the tenant shall give good, sufficient, and absolute security, by recognizance, for all costs that may have and may accrue, in case the judgment shall be affirmed, and also for all rent that has accrued or may accrue up to the time of final judgment, then the tenant shall be entitled to an appeal to the next court of common pleas, which appeal shall be then tried in the same manner that other suits are tried: and *Provided further,* That nothing herein contained shall prevent the issuing of a certiorari, with the usual form and

[51]*Evans v. Radford,* 2 Phila 370 The judgment was set aside on certiorari

[52]*Castle v Weber,* 2 Pearson (Pa) 79, *Hazen v Culbertson,* 10 Watts, 393

[53]*Castle v Weber,* 2 Pearson (Pa) 79

[54]*Trimbath v Patterson,* 76 Pa 277, *McCarthy v Sykes,* 7 Pa Dist. R 243 See form of writ in *Trimbath v. Patterson,* 76 Pa 277.

effect."[55] It is "flagrant error" to issue the writ of possession on
the day on which,[56] or before the lapse of five days after the day
on which, the judgment has been entered. The writ of possession, if issued, is superseded if, at any time before it is actually
executed, the tenant pays to the constable the rent found by the
justice to have been actually due and in arrear, and the costs [57]
It cannot issue if, within the five days following the entry of the
judgment, the tenant gives the recognizance for an appeal, and
appeals.[58] A court of equity will not arrest the execution of the
writ by injunction when the tenant, denying that he was tenant
of the plaintiff, but asserting that he was tenant of a third person, X, made no effort in the proceedings before the justice, or
by appeal, to maintain his alleged rights, and when he does not
in his bill show how X claims [59] A certiorari is not a supersedeas. The proviso that nothing in the act of 1830 should prevent the issue of certiorari "with the usual form and effect" does
not make it such.[60]

526 Certiorari.— The provision for appeal in the act of 1830
expressly saves the right to issue a certiorari, and this writ has
frequently been employed by the court of common pleas to review the regularity of the proceedings before the justice. Either
party, doubtless, may sue out the writ, though the landlord sel-
dom has occasion to do so. Either party, his agent or attorney,
may obtain it. When the judgment is in favor of the lessor, as
it almost invariably is, it is not the tenant alone who can obtain
the writ. A claimant of the reversion by a sheriff's sale of the
plaintiff's title since the making of the lease, who alleges that the

[55] Act April 3rd, 1830, 1 Pepper &
Lewis Digest, 2657, P L 187, § 1
   [56]*Trimbath* v *Patterson*, 76 Pa
277
   [57]*Stoever* v *Miller*, 4 Phila 149,
Hartnack v *James*, 8 Phila 317
   [58]*Rubicum* v *Williams*, 1 Ashm
(Pa) 230
   [59]*Hartnack* v *James*, 8 Phila 317.

The court says also that the tenant,
not having paid rent admitted by
him to be due to X, had not done
equity Paying the plaintiff after
judgment would have been paying
under compulsion
   [60]*Duddy* v. *Hill*, 3 Leg. & Ins Rep.
59.

tenant has attorned to him, having obtained the judgment of the justice, the lessor, denying that his title passed by the sheriff sale, may procure the writ [61]   The 21st section of the act of March 20th, 1810,[62] concerning the jurisdiction of the justices, which requires an oath and recognizance in order to obtain a certiorari, does not apply to a certiorari of the proceedings under the act of 1830,[63] though the affidavit is not infrequent.[64] It may issue beyond twenty days after the judgment if no jurisdiction of the person of the tenant was obtained because of defective service of the summons and of his nonappearance [65]

527. Certiorari, the record.— The facts necessary to justify a judgment of dispossession against the defendant must have been found to exist by the justice, and that he has thus found them must appear in his record.   If the complaint is a part of the record, and if it avers all the necessary facts, as it must, a general averment by the justice, in the language of the act of 1830, that the complaint is found by him "in all particulars just and true," will make unnecessary the statement by the justice of the particular facts, *e. g.*, that the tenant was in possession under the plaintiff, that rent was in arrear, that there were not sufficient unprivileged goods on the premises to satisfy the rent.[66] If there is no such general averment in the record of the justice, specific averments by him that he has found the facts, severally, which must exist to justify the expulsion of the tenant, are necessary.   They must state what the demise was, so that it may appear that it was for years or at will,[67] that the plaintiff or

[61]*Tyrell Bldg & L Asso v Daughen,* 7 W N C 244   The court refused to quash the certiorari at the instance of the plaintiff

[62] 1 Pepper & Lewis Digest, 2612, 5 Smith's Laws, 161

[63]*Rubicum v Williams,* 1 Ashm (Pa) 230   Cf *Allen* v. *Ash,* 6 Phila 312

[64]*Thomas* v. *Flamer,* 1 Phila 518,

Tyrell Bldg & L. Asso v *Daughen,* 7 W N C 244

[65] *Mogg* v *Stone,* 4 Del Co. Rep 170

[66]*Maxwell* v *Perkins,* 93 Pa 255 *Reid* v *Christy,* 2 Phila 144, *Thomas* v *Flamer,* 1 Phila 518, *McKeon* v *King,* 9 Pa 213

[67]*Trimbath* v *Patterson,* 76 Pa 277, *McDermott* v. *McIlwain,* 75 Pa

one under whom he claims made the lease,[68] that there were not on the premises sufficient goods liable to distress to satisfy the rent,[69] that the fifteen or thirty days' notice was given;[70] what the rent is which is reserved in the lease, and what rent is in arrear.[71] If the complaint alleges the rent to be monthly, $45.84, and that the rent due July 1st, $45 84, is in arrear, and the justice mistakenly states that the complaint alleges an annual rent of $540 00, but the justice finds all the averments of the complaint to be true, and also ascertains that the rent due by the tenant is $45.84, there is, in the discrepancy between the complaint and the justice's statement about it, no cause for reversal on certiorari.[72]

528. Errors affirmatively shown by the record.—For errors explicitly appearing in the record, the common pleas will reverse on certiorari; *e. g ,* when an inadequate service of the summons is manifested by the constable's return,[73] or it appears that the complaint was made less than the prescribed time after the service of the notice to quit,[74] or the record shows that the only witness who proved the amount of rent due the plaintiff was as the law then was, incompetent; *viz ,* the plaintiff himself,[75] or the record shows that the defendant offered to prove that the lessor claimed under a life tenant, that the life tenant was dead, and that the tenant had attorned to the grantee of the remain-

341, *Leinbach* v *Kaufman,* 2 Walk. (Pa) 515, *McCarthy* v *Sykes,* 7 Pa Dist R 243, *Tyrell Bldg & L Asso* v *Daughen,* 7 W N C 244

[68]*Trimbath* v *Patterson,* 76 Pa 277, *McDermott* v *McIlwain,* 75 Pa 341

[69]*Thomas* v *Flamer,* 1 Phila 518

[70]*Long* v *Swavely,* 1 Just 75 The statement in the summons, which is a part of the record, that the tenant, after being notified according to law failed to pay the rent, is not a sufficient averment *Mogg* v *Stone,* 4 Del Co Rep 170.

[71]*Tyrell Bldg & L Asso* v *Daughen,* 7 W N C 244, *Long* v *Swavely,* 1 Just 75

[72]*Maxwell* v *Perkins,* 93 Pa 255

[73]*Mogg* v *Stone,* 4 Del Co Rep. 170

[74]*Goodwin* v *Shoemaker,* 5 Kulp, 321

[75]*Fisher* v *Bailey,* 1 Ashm (Pa) 209 In *Reid* v *Christy,* 2 Phila 144, one exception was that the testimony was by the plaintiff In fact, the testimony was by the plaintiff's agent, who was competent

derman, paying him the rent, and that the justice refused to hear this evidence.[76]   Though the record shows that the tenant objected to the jurisdiction of the justice, and filed an affidavit that the title to the land would come in question, and that he did not hold by lease or otherwise under the plaintiff, but claimed himself to own the land, this was no cause for reversal, because, though a disputed ownership might preclude the jurisdiction of the justices, the affidavit of the defendant was not the way to prove that the ownership would be disputed.[77]   In the absence of fraud, evidence not in the record will not be considered in order to impeach it,[78] not even evidence of a prior proceeding before another justice for the same defaults, in which the justice had entered judgment for the defendant[79]   The sufficiency of the evidence to support the justice's findings of facts will be presumed[80]   In case of a certiorari to the judgment of a magistrate, the statute requires him to certify the whole proceeding had before him, by sending the original precepts as well as a copy of the judgment and execution, if any   The lessor's complaint is, therefore, made a part of the record[81]

529. Review of decision of common pleas.—The judgment of the common pleas in reversing or affirming the justice might be

---

[76]*Allen* v *Ash*, 6 Phila 312   It was not necessary to file an affidavit of the tenant with the justice averring that the title of the lessor was in question.

[77]*Fssler* v *Johnson*, 25 Pa 350 Unless the fact that the ownership would be disputed appeared affirmatively by the plaintiff's showing it had to be proved by the defendant, like any other fact in the cause The affidavit of a third person that he claims the reversion, filed with the justice. does not oust his jurisdiction   If he refuses to proceed, the common pleas will remit the record to him, for further action. *Daly* v *Barrett*, 4 Phila 350.

[78]*Maxwell* v *Perkins* 93 Pa 255

[79]*Castle* v *Weber*, 2 Pearson (Pa) 79   The earlier record ought to have been offered in evidence in the second proceeding before the justice

[80]*Reid* v *Christy*, 2 Phila 144, *Scott* v *Lohyer*, 3 Luzerne Legal Obs 393

No bill of exceptions to evidence can be taken before the justice so as to secure a review of the evidence, or the admission of the witnesses *McKeon* v *King*, 9 Pa 213

[81]*Maxwell* v *Perkins*, 93 Pa 255. See *Marsteller* v *Marsteller*, 132 Pa 517, 19 Am St Rep 604, 19 Atl. 344, for a form of record

reviewed formerly by writ of error; now by appeal, in the appellate courts. The common pleas affirming, its judgment may be reversed[82] or affirmed;[83] and its judgment reversing may be reversed[84] or affirmed.

530 Execution from the common pleas.— On affirming the judgment of the justice, the court of common pleas issues, as the writ of execution, a *habere facias possessionem*, the judgment becoming a judgment of that court,[85] and this writ cannot be superseded by the payment of the rent found due by the justice, and of the costs[86] So, after a judgment for the plaintiff on an appeal to the common pleas, that court issues the *habere facias possessionem*,[87] but if on that appeal there is a reference to arbitrators, whose judgment, instead of being that the landlord recover the land, is simply "We do award in favor of plaintiff the sum of $450.00," and the award becomes a judgment by reason of the omission to appeal from it, the *habere facias possessionem* cannot issue on it. If it is issued, it will, on a rule, be quashed[88]

531 Appeal to the common pleas — No execution is to issue after the giving of judgment by the justice, for five days. Within that time[89] the tenant may appeal to the court of common

[82]*Leinbach* v *Kaufman*, 2 Walk (Pa) 515, *Trimbath* v *Patterson*, 76 Pa 277, *McDermott* v *McIlwain*, 75 Pa 341

[83]*Essler* v *Johnson*, 25 Pa 350, *McKeon* v *King*, 9 Pa 213

[84]*Maxwell* v *Perkins*, 93 Pa 255

[85]*Essler* v *Johnson*, 25 Pa 350, *Trimbath* v *Patterson*, 76 Pa 277

[86]*Duncan* v *Brady*, 1 W N C 314 A rule to set aside the *habere facias possessionem* on which were indorsed the rent found due by the justice, and the costs, was, on the tender of these amounts, discharged

[87]*Philadelphia & R R Co* v *Thornton*, 3 Phila 257

[88]*Philadelphia & R R Co* v *Thornton*, 3 Phila 257. There is no right to the $300 00 exemption in proceedings under the act of 1830 *Williams* v *Sheridan*, 7 Luzerne Legal Reg 14 If the judgment is reversed on certiorari, even for a mere irregularity, the landlord will be liable in trespass if, before the reversal he has evicted the tenant by a writ of possession, the constable setting the tenant's goods out into the road *Hickey* v *Conley*, 18 Montg Co L Rep 124

[89] If the justice misleads the defendant by telling him that he can appeal in ten days, and on the seventh day after the entry of the judgment the tenant applies to offer security for the appeal, which the justice refuses, because it is too late

pleas on giving a recognizance   If the appeal is taken one day too late it will be dismissed by the common pleas,[90] nor does the fact that the defendant did not appear before the justice deprive him of the right to appeal [91]   The tenant, after the judgment of the justice, may give up the possession without losing the right to appeal within the five days.[92]

532. The recognizance.— In order to take the appeal, the defendant must "give good, sufficient, and absolute security by recognizance for all costs that may have accrued, or may accrue in case the judgment shall be affirmed, and also for all rent that has accrued or may accrue up to the time of final judgment " The dismissal of the appeal because it was taken one day too late is a final judgment, and the surety in the recognizance becomes liable,[93] but a judgment by confession for the rent and costs, and not for the premises, is not the judgment stipulated for in the recognizance,[94] while a judgment both for the rent and also for the land, will be sufficient to give an action on the recognizance, and will be conclusive as to the rent which may be recovered upon it [95]   The recognizance may be given by a surety alone,[96] or, more regularly, by the tenant and a surety.[97] Nor is it necessary that any penal sum should be named in it   A recognizance in these words: "I become bail absolute in this case, conditioned for the payment of all costs that have accrued, and all the costs that may accrue in case that the said judgment be affirmed , and also for all rent that has accrued, and may accrue up to the time of final judgment. Signed, A A Hardy,"—

the court, on rule to show cause why an appeal *nunc pro tunc* should not be allowed, will order the justice to allow the appeal   *Kelly* v *Gilmore,* 1 W N C 73   Cf *Eagen* v *Wilkins,* 7 W N C 486

[90]*Mair's Estate,* 12 Phila 2

[91]*Eagen* v *Wilkins,* 7 W N C 486

[92]*Stewart* v *Hasson,* 4 Legal Gaz 85

[93]*Mair's Estate,* 12 Phila 2

[94]*Hazen* v *Culbertson,* 10 Watts, 303

[95]*Hackett* v *Carnell,* 106 Pa 291 That the name of the plaintiff has, during the appeal, been changed by amendment, does not discharge the recognizors

[96]*Hackett* v *Carnell* 106 Pa 291, *Hardy* v *Watts,* 22 Pa 33

[97]*Hazen* v *Culbertson* 10 Watts,

is sufficient.[98] The surety to whom a claim against the landlord,
belonging to the tenant, has been assigned by the latter, may set
it off when sued on the recognizance, notwithstanding the decision in favor of the landlord by the magistrate, and on appeal,
despite the effort to use the set-off. Such decision is not an adjudication as to the amount of rent owed by the tenant, nor consequently that there is no set-off. It ascertains simply that some
rent, not how much rent, is in arrear in excess of the set-off [99]

533. The statement or declaration.— The plaintiff may make
the transcript of the justice answer for a declaration[100] unless a
rule of court requires a declaration or statement to be filed, and
even when the transcript may be used as a substitute for a declaration, in most courts the plaintiff, if he chooses, may file a
statement.   If the plaintiff files a statement he must incorporate into it all the facts whose existence is necessary for a recovery.   He cannot aver some of these, and for the rest resort to
the transcript.   At all events, if he files a statement and there is
a demurrer to it, and it is in fact inadequate, judgment cannot be
entered upon the demurrer, for the plaintiff, however adequate
the transcript would be, standing alone as the declaration.[101]

534. The pleading.— The declaration or the transcript must
show all the essential facts.   The demise, the reservation of rent,
the tenant's failure to pay it, the insufficiency of the goods on
the premises, not exempt from distress, to satisfy the debt, the
service of the proper notice to quit, and the tenant's failure to
pay the rent in arrear or to remove from the premises before the
inception of the proceedings.   A declaration alleging simply
the tenancy, the rent reserved, the rent in arrear, and the tenant's failure to pay after demand, is demurrable [102]   If judg-

393, *McMichael* v *McFalls,* 23 Pa
Super Ct 256
    [98]*Hardy* v *Watts,* 22 Pa 33
    [99]*McMichael* v *McFalls,* 23 Pa.
Super Ct 256
    [101]*Mohan* v *Butler,* 112 Pa. 590, 4
Atl 47

[101]*Palethorp* v *Schmidt,* 12 Pa Super Ct 214 Possibly, says Rice, P
J , the plaintiff could amend the
statement or withdraw it, and demand a plea to the transcript
    [102]*Palethorp* v *Schmidt,* 12 Pa.
Super Ct 214, *McMichael* v *Me-*

ment has been entered in the common pleas in favor of the plaintiff, on a defective statement, the court may open it and give him leave to withdraw it and treat the transcript as a statement.[103] The tenant may plead *non demisit* (the plaintiff has not demised the premises to him); that there was no rent in arrear, that there were sufficient goods on the premises, and that no notice to quit had been served on him.[104] The proceeding before the justice having been prosecuted by Joseph Hackett and Mary Jane Hackett, in right of the latter, the court may, on the appeal, allow an amendment eliminating the name of Mary Jane Hackett, and such amendment will not discharge the surety in the recognizance on which the appeal in the name of Joseph Hackett and Mary Jane Hackett was allowed[105]

535. Facts to be proven.— The appeal is not simply to try a collateral fact, as under the act of March 21st, 1772, but to try all the facts necessary to a recovery before the justice; *viz*, those which must be averred in the transcript or declaration, and all the facts which would defeat a recovery before him,[106] *e g*, that the plaintiff holds the relation of lessor, or of successor to the reversion towards the defendant;[107] that the notice to quit had been given, embracing a demand for the rent claimed, and specifying for what part of the term the rent was claimed;[108] that there were not sufficient goods on the premises not exempt from distress to pay the rent;[109] that the notice to quit was served not merely on

---

Falls, 17 Lanc L Rev 279, 7 Northampton Co Rep. 66.

[100]*McMichael* v *McFalls*, 17 Lanc L Rev 279, 7 Northampton Co Rep. 66 The 5th section, act May 21st 1806, 4 Smith's Laws, 326, respecting statements, and the 3rd section. act May 25th, 1897, P L 271, concerning statements in assumpsit and trespass, do not apply to proceedings by landlords against tenants

[104]*Bergman* v *Roberts*, 61 Pa 497

[106]*Hackett* v. *Carnell*, 106 Pa 291.

[106]*Clark* v *Everly*, 8 Watts & S. 226, *Palethorp* v *Schmidt*, 12 Pa. Super Ct 214

[107]*Clark* v *Everly*, 8 Watts & S. 226

[108]*Clark* v *Everly*, 8 Watts & S. 226

[109]*Clark* v *Everly*, 8 Watts & S 226, *Bergman* v *Roberts*, 61 Pa. 497 Whether it is necessary to show that every part of the house was examined, see this case.

the lessee, but upon any subtenant or assignee who is in possession of the premises [110]   Unless these facts are admitted by the
pleading, they must be proven   The plea of *non demisit* makes
it necessary for the plaintiff to prove that he is landlord   If he
does not undertake to do this otherwise than by showing payments of rent to him by the wife of the defendant while he was
in the army, the court must allow the defendant to show that he
entered as tenant of another person, S, that his wife had no
authority from him to pay rent to the plaintiff, that he repu-
diated her act, informing the plaintiff or his agent that she had
no authority, and that she had been deceived into making the
payments   It may also be shown that the payments of the wife
were not made to the plaintiff, but to B, whose agency for the
plaintiff has not been established [111]

536 Defensive facts; lapse of landlord's title.— The right of
the plaintiff depends on his being, at the commencement of the
proceeding, the landlord of the defendant.   He might once have
been, he might have let the premises to the defendant, who took
and retained possession in virtue of the lease, and yet, he would
have no right to recover the possession if he had ceased to be the
owner of the reversion.   The tenant may, therefore, show that
the reversion has passed from the plaintiff to a third person by
a sheriff's sale on a judgment against him, or on a lien existing
on the land when he became the owner [112]   The tenant, *e. g.*
may show that the lease being made September 6th, 1882, a
sheriff's sale of the premises took place on September 23rd, 1882,

---

[110]*Clark* v *Everly*, 8 Watts & S
226   Service of notice signed ' W
J B, agent for C R R," was proved
in *Bergman* v *Roberts*, 61 Pa 497

[111]*Bergman* v *Roberts*, 61 Pa 497

[112]*Heritage* v *Wilfong*, 58 Pa 137,
Smith v *Crosland*, 106 Pa 413, *Con
tra, Tannery* v *Schoch*, 1 Phila 428
In *Stewart* v *Hasson*, 4 Legal Gaz
85, after judgment by the justice
against the tenant, he appealed   At

the trial the defendant offered to
prove by X that X had appeared before the justice, exhibited a sheriff's
deed to him for the premises, and
been sworn as to his ownership   X
had at his own instance thus intervened   Evidence of these facts was
properly excluded at the trial on the
appeal   It was not proof that the
title would come in question

on two executions which were liens on the premises (a leasehold) when the plaintiff became the owner of them   The landlord's title having been devested, Green, J., remarks: "This being so, the case is brought within the line of decisions which hold that the tenant, in a proceeding by his landlord to recover possession, may show in defense that the title of the plaintiff has come to an end by expiration, by his own act, or been devested by act of the law "

537 Defensive facts, generally.— While the lapse of the title of the lessor since the making of the lease may be shown by the tenant to defeat the recovery, such fact being within the competence of the justice to decide, if, before the institution of the proceedings before him, the tenant (alleging bona fide that since the making of the lease, and the taking of possession under it, the lessor has conveyed to him, or has contracted to sell to him) has ceased to recognize the lessor as landlord and to pay rent to him, the development of that fact ousts the jurisdiction of the justice, and also of the common pleas, on the appeal   Pending the lease the lessor orally contracts to sell the land to the lessee   From the time of the agreement, through several years, the tenant continues in possession, treating the lease as at an end, and making many payments, intended by him to be on account of the purchase money, but not on account of rent   Whether the facts would or would not be sufficient to justify a chancellor in awarding specific performance, the relation of landlord and tenant is at an end so far, at least, that the former landlord must resort to ejectment rather than to the remedy furnished by the act of 1830 [113]   Indeed, Clark, J., says that if it appeared from the

[113]*Mohan* v. *Butler*, 112 Pa 590, 4 Atl 47   Judgment for defendant *non obstante veredicto*   "By the agreement of sale the tenancy came to an end," said the court below, "and the tenant acquired a different estate.   This estate, so far as its duration was concerned, was only an estate at will, but, having acquired such an estate, it is evident that the mere disavowal of the vendor cannot have the effect of altering the nature of the estate, and of changing it into a tenancy under the original lease "

evidence that this claim of the defendant was bona fide and that
the payment of the rent was resisted on that ground, the jurisdiction of the magistrate and of the court of common pleas on
appeal was at an end. In *Clark* v. *Everly*,[114] M had made a lease
to E in 1826. M died in 1828, leaving a daughter, wife of C.
The daughter died in 1832, leaving issue, C becoming tenant
by the curtesy   No rent was demanded by C until October 21st,
1841, when a notice to quit was served on E, the alleged tenant
E, after the death of M, alleged that M had devised the premises
to him, that C destroyed this will. The existence of this will
was the subject of a suit pending in 1841, when the notice to
quit was served.   It was held that the fact that the tenant had
claimed the land adversely to the plaintiff before the commencement of the proceedings might be set up as an insuperable
obstacle to the jurisdiction of the justice, and of the common
pleas, on appeal. "Where the fact of assertion is sustained by
evidence, it is fatal to the proceeding, without regard to the
validity of the title "[115]   A denial by the tenant that he has ever
been the tenant of the plaintiff, and an assertion by him that he
has been the tenant of another rival claimant of the land, though

---

[114] 8 Watts & S 226   The defendant can deny before the justice that
there ever was a tenancy, and may
show that the contract was one of
sale, and not of lease   Hence, he
does not need to resort to a bill in
equity to restrain the alleged landlord from proceeding against him
before the justice   *Vanarsdalen* v
Whitaker, 2 Legal Chronicle, 190

[115] In *Essler* v *Johnson*, 25 Pa 350,
it is said that the mere affidavit of
the tenant that he claimed title did
not oust the jurisdiction   Cf *Bergman* v *Roberts*, 61 Pa   497   In
Marsteller v *Marsteller*, 132 Pa 517,
19 Am St. Rep 604, 19 Atl 344, one
heir of A was in possession   A's
executor alleged that he was in
under a lease from him, and instituted proceedings under the act of
1830 to dispossess him   The justice
giving judgment against the tenant,
who appealed, he alleged that he was
in under a contract with A, and that
the lease had never been made, and
gave evidence to support that alle
gation   The court below instructed
the jury that if the defendant
had title, or there was evidence
of a claim of title, the justice
could not proceed, but that there
was merely the assertion of the tenant here that he owned the land, no
evidence of a sale by the heirs or
executor to him, nor of a sale by A
in her lifetime   Hence the jury
were told they must disregard his
title.

the denial and assertion preceded the notice to quit, will, if made out, prevent judgment for the plaintiff, but they do not arrest the inquiry by the justice, or the common pleas on appeal.[116] The principle is general that on the appeal no defenses are allowable that would not have been allowable before the justice. The scope of his jurisdiction is the scope of that of the court of common pleas, on appeal [117]

538. Former recovery.— On the appeal, as well as before the justice, it is competent to show, as a bar to the proceeding, that in a former proceeding before another justice, by the same plaintiff, alleging the same demise and default in payment of rent, the justice's judgment for the defendant remained unreversed. The justice in the former proceeding having found that there was no demise, that the relation of landlord and tenant did not exist, and having therefore dismissed the complaint, his judgment "is final and conclusive on both parties until legally set aside or reversed."[118]

539 Set-off — Before the justice, and also on the appeal, the defendant may show that his rent has been paid, and also that he has a set-off to it. He may show, e g., that the plaintiff covenanted in the lease that the premises should be in good repair and that the stable accommodation should be such as to enable the tenant conveniently to carry on the hotel business, and stable the horses of his customers; that this covenant has not been kept, and that in consequence the defendant has suffered damages exceeding the rent.[119]

[116] *Bergman v. Roberts*, 61 Pa 497 , In *Mohan v Butler*, 112 Pa 590, 4 Atl 47, Clark, J , states that the principle which excludes the jurisdiction of the justice where a question of title arises between the plaintiff and defendant is peculiar to the act of April 3rd, 1830 It does not apply to the act of December 14th, 1863 or to that of March 21st, 1772

[117] *Bergman v Roberts*, 61 Pa 497 , *Essler v Johnson*, 25 Pa 350, *Clark*

v *Everly*, 8 Watts & S 226, *Tennery v Schoch*, 1 Phila 428, *Marsteller v Marsteller*, 132 Pa 517, 19 Am St Rep 604, 19 Atl 344

[118] *Marsteller v Marsteller*, 132 Pa 517, 19 Am St Rep 604, 19 Atl 344

On certiorari a former recovery not offered in evidence before the justice cannot be considered *Castle v Weber*, 2 Pearson (Pa) 79

[119] *Broad v Winsborough* 1 Northampton Co Rep 330 Though the

540 Trial, verdict, and judgment — The case, on appeal, can be referred to arbitrators, whose award, unappealed from, will become the judgment of the court.[120] The defendant may waive a trial by confessing judgment.[121] A verdict generally "for the plaintiff" is not erroneous. It is not necessary that the jury find the amount of rent in arrear,[122] and the judgment should be for the land, and not for the rent. If it is for the rent, and not for the land, and is unappealed from, it will not support an execution for the delivery of possession of the land,[123] nor, if the confession of a judgment for rent and costs is accepted by the plaintiff, the tenant retaining the premises, can any action on the recognizance for appeal be sustained for the rent.[124] If the judgment entered after the trial is for the plaintiff for possession of the demised premises, and also for $200 00 rent in arrear, and is not appealed from, it becomes conclusive, and both parts of it may be carried into execution by appropriate writs. In an action on the recognizance, the judgment for the rent due will be conclusive as to the amount of rent due, upon the surety.[125]

set-off was not attempted in the proceeding before the justice, the surety in the recognizance for appeal was allowed to avail himself of it when sued thereon Cf *Hackett* v *Carnell*, 106 Pa 291

[120]*Philadelphia & R R Co* v *Thornton*, 3 Phila 257 The parties may agree to a case stated

O'Neill v. *Cahill*, 2 Brewst (Pa.) 357.

[121]*Hazen* v *Culbertson*, 10 Watts, 393

[122]*Bergman* v *Roberts*, 61 Pa 497.
[123]*Philadelphia & R R Co* v. *Thornton*, 3 Phila 257
[124]*Hazen* v *Culbertson*, 10 Watts, 393
[125]*Hackett* v *Carnell*, 106 Pa 291

CHAPTER XXVI.

REPETITION AND PROTRACTION OF TERM.

541. Commencement of term—The term may commence simultaneously with the execution of the lease. There may be an interval more or less considerable between the making of the lease and the inception of the term. A lease for eighteen years of coal land, to run from the commencement of the taking of

coal from it, is not void because no year is specified for the commencement of the taking of coal.   The coal must begin to be
taken within a reasonable time, and the court will not say, as
matter of law, that the delay of three and one half years is unreasonable.   The jury must decide, in view of the circumstances,
the price of coal, the nearness of a railroad, the obstacles presented by the lessor [1]   There may be an oral agreement for a
lease, and possession taken under it, and the lease may be subsequently executed and bear the date of its execution [2]

542. When the term ends — When a lease entitles the lessee
to take immediate possession,[3] or when, made in advance of the
intended term, it designates the day on which the term is to
begin, if it is for a year or any multiple of a year, it closes on
the midnight of the day before that day of the following year
or multiple of year which corresponds in month and number
with the day on which the lease was made, or the term began
Thus, a lease being made on February 24, 1848, "from the
1st day of April next ensuing the date hereof, for and during
the term of one year, thence next ensuing," the term begins
on April 1.   The tenant has a right on that day to take possession, and the term ends at midnight on March 31st, 1849. "The
1st day of April, 1849," says Knox, J, "was the commencement of another year, and on the morning of that day, at any
moment after 12 o'clock of the preceding night, the rent was
due and payable, for the term had then expired."[4]   An oil lease
made on June 12, 1890, authorized the tenant to hold the prem-

---

[1] *Grotz* v *Lehigh & W B Coal Co.*
1 Kulp, 53

[2] *Com ex rel Irwin* v *Contner*, 2I
Pa 266

[3] The term begins on the day on
which the lease is made unless the
lease or agreements and understand-
ings shown by circumstances indicate a later date for the commencement   *Donaldson* v *Smith*, 1 Ashm.
(Pa) 197.

[4] *Marys* v *Anderson*, 24 Pa 272
Hence, one who, during the term,
bought the land at an administra-
trator's sale, the condition of sale
being that the deed should be delivered April 1, 1849, was not entitled, as successor to the reversion,
to any of the rent. Cf. *Duffy* v
Ogden, 64 Pa 240.

ises during the full term of twenty-one years "next ensuing the day and year above written, and so long thereafter as oil or gas shall continue to be found thereon, in paying quantities." It also empowered the lessee to declare the lease null and void, and to be immediately released from any responsibilities, if he should find that it would not pay him "to continue this lease " On June 12, 1891, the lessee gave notice to the landlord that he elected to terminate the lease As he had entered on the second year, it was held that he could not avoid paying the rent for that year A present interest in the land commenced from the day of the date "In such a case the day of the date is included "[5] A lease made November 4, 1886, for three years from that date, ended at the last moment of November 3, 1889.[6] A lease of a field "for the raising of two successive crops" covers the interval between the first and second crops, and during this interval the tenant may put his cattle into the field to eat the damaged portion of the first crop still there.[7]

543. End of term, continued.— A lease between Fraley and Glassey, wherein the former says that he "doth lease unto the said Jane Glassey, her heirs and assigns, a strip of ground whereon is erected a brick dwelling house . . . for the term of five years, . . . for the yearly rent of three dollars," is not a grant in fee, subject to a rent, but for the period of five years, notwithstanding the use of the words "her heirs and assigns."[8] A had a log house, and, within 20 feet from it, a frame building, making use of both, but for the most part occupying,

[5]*Nesbit* v *Godfrey*, 155 Pa 251, 25 Atl 621

[6]*Cairns* v *Llewellyn*, 2 Pa Super Ct 599

[7]*Irwin* v *Mattox*, 138 Pa 466, 21 Atl 209.

If, during the occupancy of the tenant, the lessor sells the land to X, and in order to be able to deliver the possession the lessor notifies the tenant to leave on a certain day, stating in the notice that the term closed on that day, in an action by the tenant against the purchaser for disturbing his possession, the purchaser is precluded from asserting that the lease ended a year before the time indicated in the notice *Biggs* v *Brown*, 2 Serg & R 14

[8]*Berridge* v *Glassey*, 112 Pa 442, 56 Am Rep 322, 3 Atl 583

for sleeping and eating, the log house. B, desiring to procure
the vacation of the road on which the houses stood, induced him
to petition the court of quarter sessions to vacate it, by agreeing,
under seal, to lease to A "the right of way across the land,
. . . the said right of way to be occupied by said" A "and
all others for the uses and purposes of a public highway, to
travel upon at all times, without let or hindrance from the said"
B "so long as the said" A "shall reside in his now dwelling-
house, and no longer." Years after making the agreement A
used the frame building more, and the log house less, than previously, but the two continued to be used in the household's
economy. The supreme court found that he had not so ceased to
"reside in his now dwelling house" as the agreement contemplated [9] A railroad company, desiring to enlarge its depot,
leased a strip of land from A at the annual rental of $12 "so long
as the same shall be used for railroad purposes." After a use of
it for the railroad for thirty years the company conveyed all
their interest in the buildings and land to an individual, P, who
used it as a private siding. The lessor could recover possession
in ejectment against P, since the strip was no longer used "for
railroad purposes" in the sense in which these words must be
understood.[10]

544. Provision for renewal.— The lease, while naming a termination of the term, may also provide for the prolongation of
the term. While a covenant for a term might be void for indefiniteness, the expression "the lease [which was for seven
years] to be renewable at the pleasure of the lessees," it was
held, "implies not only the right of renewal, but also upon the
terms and for the time specified in the instrument, at the will
and pleasure of the lessee, for at least another term." It was
therefore not too vague to be enforced [11] A similar result was

[9] *Webster* v *Ross*, 42 Pa 418.   [11] *Creighton* v *McKee*, 7 Phila. 324.
[10] *Augel* v *Painter*, 166 Pa 592,
31 Atl 338.

reached when the words of a lease for three years were "tho said lessees shall have the privilege and option of renting the said premises for a further term of three years from the expiration of this lease." If, said Wickham, J., this phrase stood alone it would be void for indefiniteness; "but taken in connection with the context and the situation, circumstances, and evident intention of the parties, it must be regarded as a covenant to renew,—that is, to give another lease containing the same terms and stipulations as the original lease, except the renewal agreement "[12]

545. Mode of expressing right to renew.— Various words are employed to express the right given to the tenant to remain on the premises beyond the term. Sometimes "renew" or "renewal" is used "Rerent," "rent again," "privilege of another term," "refusal of the premises," and like expressions, without more, are sufficient, provided that the length of the new term is specified [13] Sometimes words implying that a new lease is to be made are employed, e. g, the option of "renting for a further term,"[14] "with leave of renewal for five years,"[15] "the privilege of four years' additional lease,"[16] "this lease (for seven years) to be renewable." etc [17] It does not seem, however, to be understood that the right of the tenant to hold over depends on his obtaining a second lease, and that for the refusal, on his application, of the lessor to make such lease, his only remedy could be an action for damages The court would treat the case as if the lease had been made, and would protect the tenant in the possession without it, should the lessor endeavor to eject him.[18] On the other hand, if the lessee simply remains in pos-

---

[12]*Cairns* v *Llewellyn*, 2 Pa Super Ct 599 Cf *Betz* v *Delbert*, 16 W N C 360

[13]*Cairns* v *Llewellyn*, 2 Pa. Super Ct 599

[14]*Cairns* v *Llewellyn*, 2 Pa. Super Ct 599.

[15]*Pittsburgh & A Drove Yard Co's Appeal*, 123 Pa 250, 16 Atl 625

[16]*Harding* v *Seeley*, 148 Pa 20, 23 Atl 1118

[17]*Creighton* v *McKee*, 7 Phila 324

[18]*Pittsburgh & A Drove Yard Co's Appeal*, 123 Pa 250, 16 Atl 625

session, after the expiration of the lease, he will be considered as
having elected to take the renewal lease, and will be liable to the
landlord for rent, etc , as he would be had the second lease been
in fact executed and accepted by the tenant.[19]   The word
"lease" is said by a sort of metonymy to mean the "term" or
'estate" created by a lease, and may be understood as equivalent to "term," unless the parties show that it is used in its
strict sense.[20]

546 The right to renew implied — The right of the tenant to
repeat the term may be simply implied , as, *e g.,* when the lease
is for six months, at the end of which period the lessee covenants
to give up the possession ; but it is added, "the rent for the following six months is to be paid in advance, on or before" the last
day of the first six months, "and in default of such payment the
lessor may take possession thereof and let the same to any other
tenant "[21]

547. Frequency of renewal; length of renewed term — The
lease, in giving the right to renew the lease, or to renew the term,
may indicate the length of the additional term. Thus a lease for
one year with "the privilege of four years' additional lease[22]
from the first day of January, 1888," gives a privilege to hold

---

The court refused jurisdiction in
equity to compel the making of a renewal lease In *Juergen* v *Allegheny
County*, 204 Pa 501, 54 Atl 281, the
lease was for five years, at the rental
of $3 000 per annum, with "the
privilege of re-leasing at an increased annual rental " The tenant
having been evicted by proceedings
under the act of March 21, 1772,
brought trespass for damages, alleging that the actual agreement was
that the renewal should be for ten
years at $3,500 annual rent The
justice's adjudication was conclusive
that there had been no "re-leasing "
That the action was not for damages

for the lessor's refusal to re lease is
adverted to

[19]*Harding* v *Seeley*, 148 Pa 20,
23 Atl 1118

[20]*Harding* v *Seeley*, 148 Pa 20 23
Atl 1118 The word "lease" in the
phrase "with the privilege of a four
years' additional lease" was found
equivalent to "term "

[21]*Com* v *M'Neile*, 8 Phila. 438

[22] A lease for five years "with the
privilege of having said lease re
newed for the term of five years from
and after the 1st day of January,
1887," contemplates one second term
of five years *McBrier* v *Marshall,*
126 Pa. 390, 17 Atl. 647.

over for one term, which is of four years' duration, and not to
hold over for one year, and if the tenant choose, no longer; or, if
the tenant choose, to remain for a second year and no longer, unless he desires to remain longer, or, if he choose, for a third year,
etc.[23] The additional term is often of the same length as the
primary term, e. g., three years,[24] five years.[25] Sometimes more
than one renewal is intended, but the number is defined   A lease
to B for the term of one year, with the privilege of three years
from the 1st day of April, 1885, was interpreted to be a lease for
one year, with the privilege of holding over during a second, and,
at the option of B, during a third   It contemplated two holdings
over, each of a year, at the option of the tenant.[26] A lease of
premises from the 1st day of December, 1878, at the rent of
$600 per annum, payable monthly, contained the stipulation
that if the tenant "should continue on the above-described premises after the termination of the above contract, then he shall
have the privilege of staying there for another five years at the
above-fixed rent per annum." Prior to the last stipulation was
a sentence to the effect that if the tenant should continue on the
premises the contract was to continue in full force for another
year, and so on from year to year, until legal notice should be
given for a removal. The lease was interpreted to mean that

[23]Harding v Seeley, 148 Pa 20, 23
Atl 1118 The lease contained a
provision that if the tenant continued on the premises after the
termination of the above contract,
the contract should continue in full
force for another year, and so on
from year to year until legal notice
for a removal might be given This
provision was held to apply only
when the second term of four years
had ended   In Burgwin v Bishop,
91 Pa 336, the lease was for two
years and three months, with the
privilege of three additional years.

[24]Cairns v Llewellyn, 2 Pa Super
Ct 599

[25]Pittsburgh & A Drove Yard Co's
Appeal, 123 Pa. 250, 16 Atl 625
McBrier v Marshall, 126 Pa 390, 17
Atl 647, McClelland v Rush, 150
Pa 57, 24 Atl 354

[26]Gillion v Finley, 22 W N C
124 Hence, having held over the
second year, the tenant was not
bound to pay rent for the third year
if he chose to vacate the premises,
giving three months' notice at the
end of the second Cf Lipper v
Bouve, C & Co 6 Pa Super Ct 452

the tenant might remain from year to year, for five years after the first year, and no longer [27]

548. Frequency of renewal, continued.— A lease for one year at a certain rental, with the words, "with privilege of rerenting and remaining on said premises at same rental and conditions for any number of years that second party may desire," does not give the privilege of two or more elections to continue in possession for terms indicated, but of one option only to continue in possession for any period that the tenant may indicate. If he once elects for one or more years, he has no further elections. He might once elect for one, or ten, or one hundred, or one thousand years, or possibly forever, but he cannot repeat the election The word "rerent," it was said, implied that the tenant must indicate by some more expressive act than simply remaining in possession that his will was to remain, and for what period it was his will to remain Having once made this indication, his right in the premises ended with the expiration of the period indicated Hence, the tenant, three months after the expiration of the second year since the making of the lease, having notified the landlord "I intend to remain in possession of the premises . . . during the year beginning April 1st, 1899, at same rental and conditions contained in the original lease," he could not again elect to remain after March 31st, 1900 [28]

549. Indefiniteness of protraction of right of possession—A lease may be made for twenty years,[29] or for a hundred years,[30] or any other definite period, and it may provide that the lessee may hold the premises after the definite term, as long as he and his heirs and assigns shall think proper, they paying the rent,[31]

---

[27] *Jones* v *Kroll*, 116 Pa 85 8 Atl 857

[28] *Swigert* v *Hartzell*, 20 Pa Super Ct 56 Nothing is said of the effect of simply holding over during the year following the first term of one year

[29] *Myers* v *Kingston Coal Co* 126 Pa 582, 17 Atl 891.

[30] *Lewis* v *Effinger*, 30 Pa 281, 32 Pa 367

[31] *Lewis* v *Effinger*, 30 Pa 281, 32 Pa 367.

or "for such other and longer times as the parties of the second
part and their legal representatives shall continue to pay the
rent."[32] Such a lease is valid not only for the definite term, but
for the additional term, whose limit, if it ever has any, is to be
fixed by the will of the tenant, expressed merely by his ceasing
to pay the rent. A lease for seven years, concluding with the
words, "This lease to be renewable at the pleasure of the lessees,"
it was held that the lease was renewable "for at least another
term."[33]

550. Renewal conditioned on notice.—The lease may confer
the privilege of renewal or of continuing in possession for a prescribed time beyond the term, upon giving previous notice to the
landlord of the intention to claim it. Giving the notice in such
a case is requisite.[34] The burden is upon the tenant if he claims
any rights upon the renewal clause, to prove the giving of the
notice. Apparently the notice must be actual. Leaving a written notice at the dwelling of the lessor, with an adult member of
his family, is useful only as it tends to prove that he obtained
actual notice of the lessee's intention to remain on the premises [35]
The lease may require the notice to be in writing, at least three
months before the expiration of the primary term. The requirement that it be written may be waived, and it is waived, if, before the beginning of the three months, oral notice is given to
the lessor, and, upon receiving it, he expressly assents to the renewal, making no objection to the notice; *a fortiori* if he states
that the lessee need do nothing further to secure the renewal.[36]

551. Oral notice and statute of frauds.— When the lease provides for an additional term upon notice, and the notice is given,
the right of the lessee is derived from the lease. The lease

[32]*Myers* v *Kingston Coal Co.* 126
Pa 582, 17 Atl. 891
[33]*Creighton* v *McKee,* 7 Phila 324
[34] If the notice is not given, the
lease is not extended *Pollman* v.
Morgester, 99 Pa 611.
LAND & TEN. 30.

[35]*Burgwin* v *Bishop,* 91 Pa 336
Cf *Pollman* v *Morgester,* 99 Pa 611
[36]*McClelland* v *Rush,* 150 Pa. 57,
24 Atl 354 Cf *Pittsburgh & A
Drove Yard Co's Appeal,* 123 Pa.
250, 16 Atl 625.

creates and defines the second term as well as the first. It subjects the second to a condition to be performed after the making of the lease, but none the less is the second its creature. Hence, the statute of frauds has no application to the notice. Though only an oral notice is required by the lease,[37] or if, written notice being required, the landlord is, by facts which are orally proved, estopped from insisting on more than oral notice, the notice is valid, and the new term conditioned by it, so far as the statute of frauds is concerned, indefeasible.[38]

552 Renewal conditioned on lessee's notice.—The lease, e. g., for five years, may stipulate for an extension at an increased rental, the lessee's acceptance of the extension to be manifested by his giving written notice thereof to the lessor nine months (or some other time) before the end of the term If it also provides that, should the extension not be accepted, the lessee shall pay an additional rent, the mere continuance in possession, without the notice, by the tenant, who does not tender the additional rent, will make him liable for rent as if he had accepted the extension. The continuance of the possession may be by sublessees or assignees of the tenant, or by persons whom he has allowed to take possession.[39]

553. Renewal conditioned on fixing the rent.—The lease being for a term, e. g., of seven months,[40] or of five years,[41] may give to the lessee the right to continue the existing lease from year to year,[42] or for two and one half years,[43] or other period, at a rental to be fixed prior to the close of the term, and not at the

---

[37]*Cairns* v *Llewellyn*, 2 Pa Super Ct 599

[38]*McClelland* v *Rush*, 150 Pa 57, 24 Atl 354 The lease being for three years, with right to renew for two years more, a parol assignment of the lease before the expiration of the three years does not pass the right of renewal to the assignee If he is recognized as tenant by the landlord, he becomes a tenant from year to year. *Muller's Estate*, 16 Phila 321

[39]*Thompson's Estate*, 205 Pa 555, 55 Atl 539

[40]*Arnsthal* v *Patterson*, 3 Pennyp. 25

[41]*Abbot* v *Shepherd*, 4 Phila 90

[42]*Arnsthal* v *Patterson*, 3 Pennyp

[43]*Abbot* v. *Shepherd*, 4 Phila 90.

rent payable during the term, but at a rent to be fixed by appraisers, to be selected, some by the lessor and some by the lessee. Under such a provision, it is not enough for the tenant to notify the landlord prior to the close of the term, that he intends to continue the occupancy of the premises for the additional term, unless the tenant's duty of causing the appointment of appraisers is waived by the landlord [44] The requirement may be waived; e. g., by the landlord's refusal, on the request of the lessee, to give him a copy of the lease in order that he may know how to proceed in order to have the appraisement made,[45] or by his uniting with the tenant, who has remained in possession after the close of the term, in the selection of appraisers After each party has, six weeks after the end of the term, the lessee holding over, united with the other in the selection of appraisers, who have chosen a fifth, the lessor cannot effectively withdraw his participation in the appraisement. If he revokes the reference, and the appraisers thereupon refuse to proceed, he cannot maintain an action for the use and occupation of the premises. He must cause the appraisers to proceed, and rely on their award as the measure of the compensation he is entitled to for the continued occupancy of the premises [46]

554 Renewal conditioned on prepayment of rent.—The lease may be for a certain time, e. g , six months, with a provision that the rent of the following six months shall be paid in advance, on or before the end of the first six months, and that, in default of such payment, the lessor may take possession. If the landlord, before the expiration of the first period, informs the tenant that he will not be allowed to remain beyond its close, he excuses the tenant from tendering the rent in advance. The latter may continue in and defend his possession though he does

[44] *Arnsthal* v *Patterson,* 3 Pennyp   [46]*Abbot* v. *Shepherd.* 4 Phila 90.
25
[45]*Arnsthal* v *Patterson,* 3 Pennyp.
25

not make the tender till the first or later day of the second period, and when it is made, it is rejected by the lessor.[47]

555. **Notice by tenant of nonrenewal** —The lease for a term of five years, giving a "privilege of having said lease renewed for the term of five years," but prescribing no condition to the exercise of this privilege, it may be exercised simply by holding over. If the tenant gives notice to the lessor, the lessor may doubtless insist that the tenant shall withdraw from the premises in accordance with it; but if he does not, and the lessee remains in possession after the term has closed, for however short a period, he becomes bound, at the option of the landlord, for the rent of the whole secondary term. If, *e. g ,* the lease being for five years, with the privilege of renewal for a second five years, the lessee, before the close of the first term, notifies the lessor that he will not remain, if in fact he does remain for one year, he cannot escape from the duty of paying rent for the remaining four years by withdrawing at the end of that year.[48]

556. **Lessee's option to remain, unless notified by lessor.**—Not only may the lease give to the tenant the right, despite the changing will of the lessor, to remain beyond the term, either unconditionally or in compliance with certain defined conditions; it may also give him the right to remain unless the landlord does some act,—usually, a notification, a certain period in advance, to withdraw at the end of the term. The lease, after creating a definite term, may provide, *e. g.,* that either party hereto may determine this lease at the end of said term by giving the other notice thereof in writing at least three months prior thereto; but, in default of such notice, this lease shall continue upon the same terms and conditions as are herein contained, for a further period of one year, and so on from year to year unless, or until, terminated by either party thereto giving to the other three

[47] *Com* v *M'Neile,* 8 Phila 438
[48] *McBrier* v *Marshall,* 126 Pa 390, 17 Atl 647. To remain one year with the permission of the lessor is not equivalent to making a new lease for one year.

months' notice in writing for removal previous to the expiration
of the then current term [49]   Such language is so explicit that
controversy as to its significance is scarcely to be expected.   If
the lease is for the term of one year, with privilege of two additional years, and provides that at the expiration of said term the
lessee shall deliver up the premises; and further, that either
party may determine the lease by giving the other notice three
months prior to the end of the term, but, in default of such
notice, the lease shall continue from year to year unless and until
three months' notice is given,—the term does not expire at the
end of the first year unless the tenant withdraws from the possession   If he holds over, the term continues two years more.
The provision for three months' notice has no application until
after the expiration of the third year.   Hence, when the lessee
held over beyond the first year, he could not, by giving notice
three months before the end of the second year, of his intention
to leave, and by leaving, discharge himself from liability for the
rent of the third year.[50]

557. Second leases.— It is elsewhere seen that a term may be
surrendered by the making of a new lease covering a portion of
it and extending beyond its termination.   When such a lease
is made, the lessee acquires a right under it to continue in possession of the premises beyond the termination of the original term
A lease being made for three years, with the privilege of renewing it for a period of years, it may be shown that, prior to the
expiration of the three years, a fire occurred on the premises,
when it was agreed that thereafter the tenant should occupy the
premises without paying any rent, if he would repair the brewhouse on them, and that later it was agreed that he should pay
the taxes and the ground rent and nothing more.[51]   The lease

---

[49] Cf. *Megargee* v *Longaker*, 10 Pa.   [51] *Betz* v *Delbert*, 16 W N C 360
Super Ct. 491   The agreement was found in fact not
   [50] *Lipper* v *Bouvé*, *C. & Co.* 6 Pa.   to have been made.
Super Ct 452.

requiring three months' notice before the end of the year of the lessee's intention to retire, after the notice is given, the parties may, before the year expires, agree that the tenant may continue in possession as tenant from month to month   Under such an agreement, the lessee could, after the original lease had expired, leave at the end of a month without liability for rent for the future [52]   A lease for years being about to end, the parties may agree that the tenant shall remain in possession with leave to retire at any time, paying rent for so long a time only as he shall occupy the premises   The tenant might, under such an agreement, hold over from April 5th to September 4th, paying the rent for this period [53]

558. Second lease made during a hold-over period —The lease for a term of years expiring, and the tenant holding over from year to year, a change may be made in the terms of the lease, or a new lease may be made.   Thus, a lease for five years being made to B and C, which expired August 1st, 1881, they hold over for a series of years, and in October, 1885, with the consent of A, the lessor, the property is divided by B and C between them, each taking one half, and A agrees to receive one half the former rent, for the whole of which they had been jointly liable, from each.   Says Mitchell, J . "The term under the lease had admittedly expired, but appellant had continued in possession, and the presumption, therefore, was that he was a tenant from year to year under all the terms of the lease that were applicable.   But it was entirely competent for the parties to make a different agreement at any time, and, of course, for either to prove such new agreement by any proper evidence."

---

[52] *Smith* v *Snyder*, 168 Pa 541, 32 Atl 64   Before the end of the year, the lessee told the landlord's agent that he would be willing to remain as tenant from month to month   The agent said he would communicate with the lessor   and let the lessee know the decision in time   The lessee remained over, hearing nothing further from the agent   He had no right to infer from the circumstance that he had the lessor's consent to his proposal

[53] *Harvey* v *Gunzberg*, 148 Pa 294, 23 Atl 1005   The agreement was not in fact made.

Even if the agreement whereby each former colessee was released from liability for more than half the rent would not be binding on the lessor without some new consideration so far as the year in the midst of which it was made was concerned, it would be valid for the following years The continuance of the tenant in possession, paying the agreed rent, would be sufficient consideration [54] A lease for ten years being about to expire, the tenant applies for a renewal None being made before the end of the term, the lessee nevertheless holds over, and a month or two after the close of the term an offer of a new lease with a new period of commencement is made, providing for vacating the premises at any time on a year's notice If made, such an agreement would regulate the right of the tenant to continue in possession [55]

559 Agreement for renewal — Though the original lease contains no provision for its continuance, the lessor and lessee may, during the term, agree for a repetition of it on the same conditions, and the breach of the new agreement by the eviction of the tenant at the close of the original lease will give him a right to recover damages,[56] or the agreement for renewal may be set up to defeat the proceedings of the lessor to oust the tenant at the expiration of the original term.[57] The original lease having, by a posterior agreement, been renewed once, may be renewed for a second time. If it is, the tenant cannot be dis-

[54]*Walker* v *Githens*, 156 Pa 178, 27 Atl 36 Even if the agreement was not binding, nevertheless, being understood by the parties to be binding, it constitutes the agreement on which the succeeding years were entered upon The subsequent payment by B of one half the rent, and receipt of it by A, would be evidence of the understanding

[55]*Phœnixville* v *Walters*, 147 Pa 501, 23 Atl 776, 184 Pa. 615, 39 Atl 490

[56]*Kelley* v *Bogue*, 1 Phila 91

When sued for arrears of rent in the first lease, the tenant can set off these damages

[57]*O'Neal* v *Sneeringer*, 12 York Legal Record 141 In order to show the agreement for renewal it may be shown that about the time of the alleged renewal the lessor ordered the tenant to sow clover seed on another tract let to the latter by the former at the same time as the farm in question, and farmed in connection therewith.

possessed until the expiration of the period of the second renewal. And, the original term being for a year, the renewal of
it might be oral; or, the first renewal being written, the second
might be oral. The burden of proving the agreement is upon the
tenant,[58] and if, in proceedings to eject him, he succeeds in defeating the landlord by setting up a second lease for the year
following the original term, he will be estopped from denying
the making of the lease in a replevin by him for goods distrained
on by the landlord, for rent of the second term.[59]

560. Tenant's right to renew not expressly conditioned —If
the lease gives to the tenant a right to renew it for a definite
time, but prescribes no conditions, the only kind of notice of the
intention to exercise this right which the tenant needs to give
to the landlord is by simply remaining in possession at the end
of the first term; and when he thus remains in possession he
must be understood to avow to the landlord that he has elected to
exercise the contractual privilege for an additional term. He
becomes bound to pay the rent for the whole of this term. The
lease being for one year ending January 1st, 1888, "with the
privilege of four years' additional lease" at the same rental, the
tenant remained on the premises until sometime before January 1st, 1890 He was liable for the rent of the subsequent
years until January 1st, 1892.[60] And it matters not with what
intention the tenant holds over, nor even that he has notified
the landlord that he will not avail himself of the right to another term.[61] A lease for eight months provided that "a lawful
continuance of the tenancy beyond said term shall be deemed a

[58]*Lutz* v *Wainwright*, 193 Pa 541,
44 Atl 565, *Kelly* v *Lochr*, 1
Brewst (Pa) 303
    The landlord's accepting two
months' rent, supposing it to be of
the first year, when in fact the rent
of that year had been fully paid, will
not justify the inference that he has
agreed to a continuance of the pos-

session. *Sizer* v *Russett*, 11 Pa.
Super Ct 108.
    [59]*Hostetter* v. *Hykas*, 3 Brewst
(Pa) 162
    [60]*Harding* v *Seeley*, 148 Pa 20, 23
Atl. 1118, *Lipper* v *Bouric, C & Co*
6 Pa Super Ct 452
    [61]*Cairns* v *Llewellyn*, 2 Pa Super
Ct 599.

renewal thereof for the further term of one year " The tenant,
continuing in possession after the eight months, became liable
for the rent of the full succeeding year.[62]

561. Tenant's right to renew with consent of lessor.—The lease
for a term of years may contain the agreement that should the
tenant "continue to occupy" the premises after the end of the
term, "by consent of" the lessor, "without entering into any further or other agreement," the rent, the terms of payment. and
other covenants shall be continued.   The continuance in possession by the tenant, without an expression of dissent from the
landlord, so far continues the relation of landlord and tenant
that third parties, e. g., creditors of the tenant, cannot dispute
it; cannot, e g., deny the lessor's right to receive rent for the
period following the original term from the proceeds of an execution sale of chattels on the premises.[63] "Simon," says Gordon.
J., "continued to occupy the premises, and as Reineman did
not dissent to such occupancy, his assent must be presumed
Certainly that was a matter for themselves to settle, and if
they were satisfied with the arrangement, no third party can be
heard to complain."

562. Lease to continue until notice from tenant.—The lease for
a definite time may provide that it shall continue from year to
year unless either party shall give notice to the other of his intention to terminate it. The notice may,[64] or may not, be required to be written. It may be a notice for sixty days[65] or for
three months[66] prior to the end of the original term, or of any

[62]*Hoban* v *Lavall,* 3 Lack Jur. 38
The defective condition of the cellar,
known before the close of the eight
months, was no excuse for going out
in the midst of the year following
the eight months, no fraud, accident,
or mistake in the making of the lease
being shown

[63]*Vetter's Appeal,* 99 Pa. 52

[64]*Graham* v *Dempsey,* 169 Pa 460,
32 Atl 408.

[65]*Wilcox* v *Montour Iron & Steel
Co* 147 Pa. 540, 23 Atl 840.   The
tenant's paying the first month's
rent of the hold-over period is not
ipso facto an affirmance by him of
his liability for a year, but it is evidence thereof

[66]*Megargee* v *Longaker,* 10 Pa
Super Ct 491, *Gardner* v *Barr,* 10
Pa Super Ct 74.

added year If the tenant fails to give the notice, he becomes bound for the rent for the additional year [67] Nor can he escape this liability by showing defects on the premises, and notices from the landlord to refrain from using the premises as he desires and needs to use them, if these defects and notices were known to him prior to the time when he should have given the notice to quit.[68] The giving of the notice must be followed up by an actual withdrawal from the premises. If the tenant, despite it, remains in possession, he will be liable for the rent for the year, precisely as if he had given no notice.[69] If the lease is for one year, "or so long as it shall be the will and pleasure" of the lessor, and no longer, and if it contains an agreement by the tenant, on sixty days' notice from the lessor, to surrender possession at any time, the tenant, holding over, does not acquire a right to remain for a year, and so on from year to year, but notice can be given at any time, and in sixty days thereafter his right of possession will end.[70] If the lease for a year provides that if the tenant remains on the premises after the termination of a year, the lease shall remain in force for another year, and so on from year to year, until legal notice for a removal, the lease does not end at the expiration of the first year, despite a notice from the landlord to quit, if the tenant, nevertheless, holds over, and for the rent of the second year the surety in the lease will be liable.[71] After allowing the tenant to remain in possession for eleven years under a lease for one year, which provided that either party might terminate it at the end

[67]*Megargee* v *Longaker*, 10 Pa Super Ct 491

[68]*Megargee* v *Longaker* 10 Pa Super Ct 491 Cf *Hoban* v *Lavall*, 3 Lack Jur 38

[69]*Graham* v *Dempsey*, 169 Pa 460 32 Atl 408, *Dauphin County* v *Bridenhart*, 16 Pa 458 Cf *McBrier* v *Marshall*, 126 Pa 390, 17 Atl 647

[70]*Potter* v *Bower*, 2 W N C

408 Hence, judgment in ejectment, entered on the warrant of attorney in the lease, will not be stricken off because the notice required the tenant to leave in the midst of a year

[71]*McNamee* v *Cresson*, 3 W N C 450 The trial court said that a landlord's notice three months before the end of the first year would end the lease Cf *McBrier* v *Marshall*, 126 Pa 390, 17 Atl 647.

of the year by giving the other notice thereof at least thirty days prior thereto, the landlord gave him three months' notice to leave at the end of the eleventh year. After giving this notice the landlord may revoke it, and no consideration for the revocation is necessary if the tenant, in pursuance of it, remains on the premises. "The notice being withdrawn, both parties were remitted again," says Mitchell, J., "to the lease, whose mutual covenants were sufficient consideration." The tenant could not be ejected during the year to whose beginning the notice to quit had reference.[72] The notice to quit, however, is not revoked simply because the tenant holds over and the landlord refrains from expelling him for more than an entire year He can be ejected at any time.[73] The acceptance of rent after the period at which, according to the notice, the tenant must vacate the premises, does not, *ipso facto,* prove, while it is evidence of, a withdrawal of the notice. It may have occurred under a mistake.[74]

563 Holding over after definite term.— If the lease is for a definite term, the tenant is bound to leave the premises at the expiration of that term, without notice from the lessor. If, however, he remains, and the definite term is a year or more, he may be treated as a tenant from year to year by the landlord, and at his option will be liable as such Thus, the lease being for one

[72]*Supplee* v *Timothy*, 124 Pa 375, 23 W N C 386, 16 Atl 864   The previous request of the tenant for leave to continue in possession, and the withdrawal of the notice, made a contract. The landlord's statement to the tenant that the tenant might remain, followed by the tenant's promise to remain, would make a contract

[73]*Boggs* v *Black* 1 Binn 333
[74]*Fitzpatrick* v *Childs*, 2 Brewst (Pa) 365   If A, allowing B to oc cupy four rooms under an agreement that B is to pay for board, and not for the rooms, at length gives notice to B to give up the rooms, which, however, B does not do, but continues for eighteen months to occupy them as before, receiving and paying for his board as before, B will be regarded as occupying the rooms under the former terms He can not be compelled to pay for the use of them *Shoemaker* v. *Beaver*, 42 Phila. Leg Int 511.

year,[75] two years,[76] three years,[77] for five years,[78] for ten years,[79] for fifteen years,[80] if the tenant does not give up the possession before or at the expiration of the period, the landlord can, if he chooses, treat him as a tenant, holding him responsible for the rent of a full year   If the lease was for a month, the tenant, on holding over, may be treated as a tenant from month to month; but, even if he holds over for more than twelve months, he cannot be treated as a tenant from year to year, and, as such, bound to pay rent for a whole year, if he has been in possession for any month of it [81]   If the tenant remains in possession after the expiration of the first year subsequent to the lease, he is considered as still a tenant from year to year; e g., if he remains into the 28th year after the close of the contract term, he is liable for the rent for the whole of that year [82]

564 Repetition of same terms and conditions — Though, as we have seen, one who holds over after a lease for more than a year cannot be treated, when the lease does not make provision for holding over, as continuing tenant for more than one year, and so on, from year to year, the stipulation as to rent, the periods of payment, the covenants, so far as they are reasonably applicable to the holding over, are understood to attend the possession after the expiration of the lease, if the landlord chooses to recognize

[75]Hollis v Burns, 100 Pa 206, 45 Am Rep 379, Diller v Roberts, 13 Serg & R 60, 15 Am . Dec 578, Phillips v Monges, 4 Whart 226, Hemphill v Flynn, 2 Pa St 144, Hughs v Lillibridge, 8 Pa Dist R 358, Dauphin County v. Bridenhart, 16 Pa 458

[76]Muller's Estate, 16 Phila 321

[77]Bauders v Fletcher, 11 Serg & R. 419, Wagle v. Bartley (Pa) 9 Cent Rep 551, 11 Atl 223   The tenant remained in possession for thirty-one years, and was liable for rent, though it exceeded the amount of a penalty in the lease

[78]Harvey v. Gunzberg, 148 Pa 294,

23 Atl 1005, Walker v Githens, 156 Pa 178, 27 Atl 36

[79]Phœnixville v Walters, 147 Pa 501, 23 Atl 776

[80]Williams v Ladew, 171 Pa 369 33 Atl 329

[81]Hollis v Burns, 100 Pa 206, 45 Am Rep 379

The tenant under a lease for six months, rent payable monthly, held over one month. The landlord was held entitled to recover rent only for the one month   Harris v Watson 1 Phila Leg Int May 8, 1844

[82]Wagle v. Bartley (Pa) 9 Cent Rep 551, 11 Atl. 223.

the lessee as still his tenant. "When a landlord suffers his tenant," says Rogers, J., "to remain in possession after the expiration of the tenancy, and receives rent from him, a new tenancy from year to year is established. And if no new agreement be entered into, the law will presume, in the silence of the parties, that the tenant holds the premises, subject to all such covenants contained in the original lease as apply to his present situation "[83]   If the rent was, by the original contract, payable monthly, it continues to be payable monthly.[84]   And the same rent continues to be payable.[85]   But a warrant of attorney to confess judgment in ejectment, for default in paying rent, unless the lease stipulated that it should apply to holding over, is not available after the expiration of the term.[86] The stipulations in the lease may be of such a nature as indicates that they were intended to apply only during the term. When such is the case, there can be no inference, when a tenant holds over, that he believes the landlord will expect him to observe these stipulations, and he cannot be compelled to observe them. A lease of a tavern was made for one year at a rent of £47, payable in advance. The tenant held over, and at the end of a month, distress was made on his goods for £47 rent in advance for the hold-over year. The court held that the law did not imply an agreement by the tenant to pay £47 for the second or later years should he hold over, because the lease contained several collateral matters to be done by each party, which could be performed in the first year only. The tenant, e g , was to finish a certain room, and was to be repaid by the landlord,

[83]*Phillips* v *Monges,* 4 Whart 226, *Hemphill* v *Flynn,* 2 Pa St 144, *Diller* v *Roberts,* 13 Serg & R 60, 15 Am Dec 578, *Graham* v *Dempsey,* 169 Pa 460, 32 Atl 408

[84]*Laguerenne* v *Dougherty,* 35 Pa 45, *Carter* v *Collar,* 1 Phila 339

[85]*Bedford* v *M'Elherron,* 2 Serg & R. 48. In *Wagle* v *Bartley* (Pa) 9 Cent Rep 551, 11 Atl 223, the lease contained a penalty of $200 00 to secure the payment of the rent The penalty was tacitly assumed to apply to the rent of the last of a series of twenty-eight years after the expiration of the original term

[86]*Hughs* v *Lillibridge,* 8 Pa Dist R 358.

within the year, the money advanced by him. The landlord was to have a right to keep a horse in the stable for four months of the term , he was to have the roof of the stable repaired within the first two months. "As some of the things which were to be done the first year could not be done the second year," says Tilghman, Ch J., "I do not see on what ground the law would imply a contract that the same money [as rent] should be paid the second year and on the first day of the year "[87] A repetition of an agreement in the lease by the lessee, to erect a building during the term, for which he is to have credit of $100.00 on the rent, will not be implied when he holds over, not having erected it. The agreement is applicable only to the original term [88] If the lessor is owner for life, and he dies during the term, it comes to an end; but the remainderman may consent to the continuance of the tenant in possession for the rest of the term. If he does so, he tacitly consents to the stipulation in the lease that the tenant may remove or sell the building which he has erected. He does not consent, however, to be bound by agreements which are collateral and subsequent to the lease, of which he had no knowledge. If, *e. g.,* the agreement that the tenant might remove the building was made after the lease, the remainderman, having no knowledge of it, does not, by assenting to the continuance in possession of the lessee, also consent to the removal of the building.[89] But a lease for one year, containing the lessee's covenant to deliver up possession at the expiration of the lease, without further notice, and agreeing that the lessor may re-enter and repossess himself of the premises at the end of the term, or at any time thereafter, the lessor may

[87]*Diller* v *Roberts,* 13 Serg & R 60, 15 Am Dec 578

[88]*Pollman* v *Morgester,* 99 Pa 611 The reversion having been sold during the hold over year, the right of action for the breach of the contract to erect the building did not pass to the purchaser, but remained in the original lessor

[89]*White* v. *Arndt,* 1 Whart 91.

recover possession in the midst of the eleventh year after the expiration of the term, without notice [90]

565 Express provision that same terms shall continue —The lease may stipulate that if the tenant remains in possession after the term has expired, the amount of rent, terms of payment, and other covenants shall be continued This would continue a provision in the lease that all repairs are to be made by the tenant Hence, if the tenant held over, he would be liable for the rent, and could not have it reduced by reason of the lessor's omitting to make needed repairs [91]

566. The landlord's option.— The landlord must do something indicative of an intention to recognize the hold-over tenant as still a tenant. The tenant does not avoid becoming a trespasser except by an implied or express contract, wherein a different status is imputed to him The ordinary way in which the landlord shows his acceptance of the tenant as such for another period is his acceptance of rent for a period of possession that is later than the expiration of the term. If the tenant pays rent for a part of the[92] hold-over year, the act is evidence of an affirmance by him of the lease for the entire year, and acceptance by the landlord of this rent would be evidence of a concession by him of the lessee's right to remain for the year Having held over, the tenant, paying rent for a part of the year, which is received by the landlord, acquires a right to remain for the rest of the year,[93] and falls under a duty to pay the rent for the remainder of the year [94] In *Bedford* v. *M'Elherron,*[95] the lease was for four years, at an annual rent of a turkey, and the tenant was each year to clear four acres of ground, pay all

[90]*McCanna* v *Johnston,* 19 Pa 434
[91]*Patterson* v *Park,* 166 Pa 25, 30 Atl 1041
[92]*Wilcox* v *Montour Iron & Steel Co* 147 Pa 540, 23 Atl 840
[93]*Harvey* v *Gunzberg,* 148 Pa 294, 23 Atl 1005, *Muller's Estate,* 16 Phila 321.

[94]*Fahnestock* v *Faustenauer,* 5 Serg & R 174, *Phœnixville* v *Walters,* 147 Pa. 501, 23 Atl 776, *Muller's Estate,* 16 Phila 321.
[95]2 Serg & R 48.

taxes, and inclose with a fence He remained in possession after the close of the term, seventeen years. The lessor was not permitted to eject him during the seventeen years, or at the end of it, without having given him three months' notice to quit. From the continuance for seventeen years in possession, "it may be fairly presumed," said Tilghman, Ch J., "that the defendant retained the possession with the consent of the plaintiff, and if so, he was tenant at will, at least; or perhaps it might be more easily inferred that he remained tenant from year to year at the same rent which was reserved by the written lease for four years. But whether he was tenant at will or from year to year is immaterial, because, in both cases, notice to quit was necessary"

567. Landlord's option, continued—The landlord need not recognize the former tenant as tenant any longer, unless he wishes. He may treat him as a trespasser, or as a tenant from year to year.[96] Hence, the tenant remaining in possession after the close of the term, the lessor may, almost immediately, re-enter and repossess himself of the premises, setting out on the highway the goods of the tenant.[97] The lessor may wait for several months, and then, having received no rent, or otherwise recognized the former lessee as present tenant, may oust him by an ejectment[98] Giving a notice to quit is evidence that the landlord has resolved to treat the tenant, if he holds over, as a trespasser. The fact that the tenant remains in possession afterwards, longer than a year, does not make him anything else than a trespasser, the landlord receiving no rent for the possession, nor otherwise recognizing him as a tenant,[99] though, after giving

---

[96]*Hemphill* v *Flynn*, 2 Pa St 144, *Pittfield* v *Ewing*, 6 Phila 455, *Williams* v *Ladew*, 171 Pa 369, 33 Atl 329

[97]*Overdeer* v *Lewis*, 1 Watts & S 90, 37 Am Dec 440

[98]*Bush* v *National Oil Ref Co* 5 W N C 143, cf *National Oil Ref Co* v *Bush*, 88 Pa 335. But, after

ejecting the former tenant, assumpsit for use and occupation may be maintained for the period of possession prior to the ejectment

[99]*Boggs* v *Black*, 1 Binn 333 The lease for eight months provided that it should continue from year to year until either party gave legal notice to the other. Three months before

such notice, the landlord may so far acquiesce in the continuance of possession as to entitle him to maintain assumpsit for use and occupation, while not so far as to entitle the tenant to retain possession for the whole of a year [100]

568. Option as to use and occupation — The landlord, if he declines to recognize the former tenant as still tenant, may, either after the tenant has voluntarily given up the possession,[101] or before he has gone out under compulsion of the landlord's ejectment, bring an action, not for the former rent, but for use and occupation. The rent reserved in the lease will not be the measure of the sum to be recovered. It may be less[102] or greater than that sum. The lease having been of water, the plaintiff is entitled to a sum representing, not what it would have cost the defendant to procure the water elsewhere, or what loss he would have suffered if he had failed to get a supply, but what the plaintiff could probably have got for the use of the water from

the expiration of the eight months, the lessor gave the notice to quit He had a right to take possession and make changes in the premises, of which equity would not deprive him by injunction *Fitzpatrick* v *Childs,* 2 Brewst (Pa) 365 If A makes title against B by adverse possession, and shows this possession through that of a tenant, under a lease from him, the holding over of the tenant does not interrupt the possession It will be treated as in subordination to A, the landlord *Schuylkill & D Improv Co* v. *Mc-Creary,* 58 Pa 304 The tenant, remaining after his lease has expired, is not entitled to compensation for the taking of any portion of the premises for a street under the power of eminent domain *Shaaber* v *Reading,* 150 Pa 402, 24 Atl 692

[100]*National Oil Ref Co* v *Bush,* 88 Pa 335, *Bush* v *National Oil Ref Co* 5 W N C 143 In *Com.* v *Knarr,* 135 Pa 35, 19 Atl 805, a LAND & TEN 31.

lease expiring in two months was assigned by A to B B continued in possession after the expiration of the term, the landlord in no way recognizing him as tenant On the con trary, a new lease was made to A, who endeavored to take possession in pursuance of it B was not guilty of forcible entry or detainer, in putting A off the premises with force He was said to be in no sense a trespasser, and to have a right to a notice to quit

[101]*Williams* v *Ladew,* 171 Pa 369, 33 Atl 329 The rent reserved in the lease may be a guide to the value of the use Hence the plaintiff can show that the rent was not the whole consideration, but he cannot show an incidental advantage to himself arising from the lessee's business, when such advantage was not a part of the consideration for the lease

[102]*National Oil Ref Co* v *Bush,* 88 Pa. 335, *Bush* v *National Oil Ref Co* 5 W N C 143

other parties [103] If the stipulation in the lease for rent cannot
be regarded as repeated by the fact of holding over, the landlord will have to resort for compensation to an action for use
and occupation,[104] or in trespass. A was in possession of land
under a lease for three years from X. A railroad being expected to be built across this land, he refused to enter into a
renewal lease for three years, for which he had offered $275.00
per annum, but he continued in possession not only for one
year, which ended March 1st, 1887, but until August, 1889.
The railroad was laid across the lot in February, 1886. When
A retired from the premises in August, 1889, he paid rent at
the rate of $275.00 per year to March 1st, 1888. It was held
that by continuing in possession after the actual taking of a part
of the premises by the railroad, A impliedly agreed to pay at
the same rate for the use and occupation of so much of the
demised property as was not affected by the building of the
railroad, and it was not error to find that $275.00 per year was
a fair compensation for the use and occupation, since the part
retained by A after the construction of the railroad was by far
the more valuable, and since A had paid $275.00 per year for
one year at least since its construction.[105]

569. Holding over makes a new contract.—The tenant, by
holding over, and the landlord, by assenting thereto, do not prolong the life of the old lease. It expires according to its own
terms   These acts of the tenant and landlord make a new
contract by implication.[106] Hence, though the original lease
being under seal, the action on it under the former law was
covenant or debt, and not assumpsit, the action by the landlord

[103]*Williams* v *Ladew,* 171 Pa 369,
33 Atl 329

[104]*Miller* v *Roberts,* 13 Serg & R
60, 15 Am Dec 578

To show the value of the occu
pancy, the defendant may show an
interference by the plaintiff with his
privileges as occupant. *Harris* v.

Watson, 1 Phila Leg Int May 8,
1844

[105]*Ward's Estate,* 22 Pa Co Ct.
284, 8 Pa Dist R 153   Rehearing
denied in 22 Pa Co Ct 516, 8 Pa.
Dist R 369

[106]*Hughs* v *Lillibridge,* 8 Pa Dist.
R 359.

for rent against the holding-over tenant was assumpsit.[107] So, the original lease being under seal, the implied contract arising from holding over is parol, and the statute of limitations applies to rent for the hold-over period [108]

570 What constitutes a holding over.—The retention of the premises by the tenant for however brief a period, *e. g*, a week,[109] a month,[110] after the termination of the lease, is a holding over to which the consequences of such will attach   If the tenant, after the last day of his term, keeps his property on the premises under such circumstances, or to such an extent, as induces and justifies in his landlord a reasonable belief that he intends to remain, and he thus prevents the landlord from regaining practically full possession, he holds over, in the eye of the law   Merely leaving some rubbish on the premises, which, at the subsequent request of the lessor, is removed, or, indeed, the mere leaving of something valuable on the premises, is not equivalent to a retention of the possession, and the exclusion of the landlord. On the other hand, the fact that the lessee has stopped before the close of the term the business that he had prosecuted, and does not pursue it afterwards, and that such occupancy of the premises as he retains is simply to remove his property, is not inconsistent with his so holding over as to make him liable as a hold-over tenant. "If," says the court, "the appellees [the tenants] actually withheld possession, it mattered

---

[107]*Carter* v. *Collar*, 1 Phila 339

[108]*Davis's Estate*, 1 Phila 360   Cf *Bauders* v *Fletcher*, 11 Serg & R Pa 155

[109]*McCarroll* v *Clements*, 2 W. N C. 305

[110]*Cairns* v *Llewellyn*, 2 Pa Super Ct 599

If B allows heavy machinery to remain on the premises after they have become the property of A, he will be liable to A for the compensa-tion for the use and occupation of his premises   *Grove* v *Barclay*, 106 Pa 155

If the county takes a lease of a house for one year for the sheriff, and before the close of the year notifies the tenant that it will not take the house for the next year, it will be nevertheless liable if the sheriff does not vacate at the end of the first year   *Dauphin County* v. *Bridenhart*, 16 Pa. 458,

not what use they put the premises to. They might choose to keep the building locked up and unused for business purposes, or as a dwelling. If they kept their property on the premises in such a way or to such an extent as to deprive the appellants of possession, they would, as hereinbefore explained, be liable for the rent."[111] The tenant may hold over by the occupancy of a subtenant or assignee [112] He does not need to seek out the landlord in order to make a surrender [113]

[111]*Cairns* v *Llewellyn*, 2 Pa Super Ct 599 The lease for one year being made January 1st, 1887, it was error to refuse to say to the jury that, it appearing that the tenant "remained in possession under the lease after January 1st, 1888," he became liable for the rent of a new term of four years. *Harding* v *Seeley*, 148 Pa 20, 23 Atl. 1118.

[112]*Pitfield* v *Ewing*, 6 Phila. 455.

[113]*Cairns* v *Llewellyn*, 2 Pa. Super. Ct. 599.

CHAPTER XXVII.

FIXTURES.

571. Fixtures, what are — The tenant may introduce upon the premises property of various sorts, without making it the lessor's either absolutely or qualifiedly. He may bring chairs, tables, or other furniture into a house or store, and they will remain his as fully as they were before, so that he can remove them freely, whether within or after the expiration of the term.[1]

[1]*Straight* v. *Mahoney*, 16 Pa Super Ct 155 Cf *Ritchie* v *McAllister*. 14 Pa Co. Ct 267   A lessee of a stone quarry cuts stones on it, and leaves them there for two years after he gives up the

He may introduce gas fixtures, lamps, awnings, signs, and they will not become even qualifiedly a part of the realty.[2] A steam boiler, steam engine, worm, worm tub, and tank may be brought, by the lessee of a distillery, into it, and remain as fully personalty as they ever were [3] On the other hand, personalty may be so annexed to the leased premises as to cease to be personalty, becoming a part of the premises, or, while remaining for some purposes personalty, as to become subject to conversion into realty unless it is severed from the latter within a certain time. It is not easy to discover in the cases a criterion by which are to be distinguished chattels which, though brought on the leased premises, always remain chattels, and chattels which become in danger of losing their chattel quality if they shall not be withdrawn from the premises on a certain time. Some difference in the degree of physical connection distinguishes the classes, but how to define this difference is impracticable.

572. Annexation not decisive — Among things which are rather intimately annexed, there is the distinction between such as are unconditionally merged in the realty, and such as remain personalty *sub modo* ready to become realty by the inaction of the tenant. The difference between these was formerly one of degree of closeness of physical annexation. It is said no longer to be such, but to be the difference of the intention of the tenant, when he introduces the thing into, and physically unites it with, the premises. The tenant intends to do what he does do. If he physically connects the thing with the land, he intends to do so But the intention to connect may be accompanied by an intention no longer to regard the thing as a separate object of ownership, to regard it, rather, as become a part of the house, building, or land, and, as such, the property of their owner, and not his

possession   He also leaves tools
there   The property in the stones
and tools does not cease to be in him,
unless he abandons them   Whether
he has abandoned them is for the

juiy   *Russell* v *Stratton*, 201 Pa
277, 50 Atl 975
[9]*Wilson* v *Freeman*, 7 W N C.
33
[8]*Campbell* v *O'Neill*, 64 Pa. 290

own   When this intention exists at the time of the connection, or possibly at any later time, the thing is no longer a separable thing, subject to an ownership different from that to which the premises are subject.   It is the landlord's [4]

573   Evidence of intention — When the relation of landlord and tenant exists, there is an improbability that the latter will intend, in excess of his contract obligations, to benefit the landlord by increasing the value of the premises, to his own detriment.   Hence, when an improvement or addition is made which is physically removable without destroying the substantial identity of state of the premises after its removal with their state before the making of the improvement or addition, the presumption is that the tenant, in making it, intended to remain its owner [5]   The law more readily for him, and against the landlord, than for an executor or administrator, and against the heir, convinces itself of the continued separate existence of the fixture as a subject of ownership [6]   Acts and declarations of the tenant, while in possession of the premises, and after the introduction of the fixtures, showing that he regarded them as his own, are admissible in evidence to prove his intention [7]   A *fortiori*, his admissions, while occupying the premises, that he intended the fixtures to be irremovable, would be receivable against him.[8] The intention of the parties is spoken of as declared by them, or as flowing from the nature and character of the acts, the clear purpose to be served,[9] the manifest relation which the thing

---

[4]*Carver* v *Gough*, 153 Pa 225, 25 Atl 1124, *Albert* v *Uhrich*, 180 Pa 283, 36 Atl 745   *Wick* v *Bredin*, 189 Pa. 83, 42 Atl 17, *Hill* v *Sewald*, 53 Pa 271, 91 Am Dec 209, *Seeger* v *Pettit*, 77 Pa 437, 18 Am Rep 452, *Gulick* v *Heermans*, 6 Luzerne Legal Reg 227, *Pratt* v *Keith*, 4 Del Co Rep 69

[5]*Hill* v *Sewald*, 53 Pa 271, 91 Am Dec 209, *Albert* v *Uhrich*, 180 Pa 283 36 Atl 745, *Watts* v *Lehman*, 107 Pa 108   *Hey* v. *Bruner*, 61

Pa 87   Cf *Kile* v *Grebner*, 114 Pa 381, 7 Atl 154, *Lemar* v *Miles*, 4 Watts. 330, *Church* v *Griffith*, 9 Pa. 118, 49 Am Dec 548, *White's Appeal*, 10 Pa 252

[6]*White* v *Arndt*, 1 Whart 91; *Wilson* v *Freeman*, 7 W N C 33

[7]*Seeger* v *Pettit*, 77 Pa 437, 18 Am Rep 452

[8]*Carrer* v *Gough*, 153 Pa 225, 25 Atl 1124

[9]A tenant fitting up the premises as an opera house is inferred, when

bears to the realty, and the visible consequence, upon its severance, upon the proper and obvious use of it.[10] The fact that the
lessor contributes to the expense of constructing a tramroad over
a timber tract, whose timber is to be cut off by the lessee, and
that its construction was part of the expressed consideration for
the grant of the timber leave, is evidence that it was built by the
tenant without an intention that it should be his [11] It is not the
undisclosed purpose of the lessee, but the intention implied and
manifested by his acts, that decides [12]

574. Other criteria — There is occasionally a reference to
other tests of the removable character of fixtures than the intention of the lessee   The question of fixtures or not is said by
Agnew, J , to depend "on the nature and character of the act
by which the structure is put in place, the policy of the law connected with its purpose, and the intentions of those concerned in
the act "[13]   But it does not clearly appear whether what is meant
by the nature and quality of the act is its physical nature and
quality, or the mental states, projects, purposes, with which it is
done. The severability of the thing without injury to its in-
tegrity is alluded to. "Fixtures," said the court in *Furbush* v
Chappell,[14] "which the tenant has no right to remove from the
freehold, are not distrainable, but fixtures slightly attached,
which the tenant may remove at his pleasure   .   .   .   without
destroying their character or injuring them, may be distrained.

introducing chairs, which he fastens
to the floor, to intend to remain their
owner   *Pratt* v *Keith,* 4 Del Co
Rep 69

[10]*Silliman* v *Whitmer*, 11 Pa
Super Ct 243, affirmed in 196 Pa
363, 46 Atl 489   The lease forbidding the lessee's sale of his interest
in the lease, except with the consent
of the lessor, if the lessee sells his
interest,   specifying   the   tramroad
and the fixtures as part of the
property sold, and the lessor gives
his written consent to the sale, this

will be a species of admission by
him that the property in the tramroad is in the lessee, but is not decisive

[11]*Silliman* v *Whitmer,* 11 Pa.
Super. Ct 243, affirmed in 196 Pa.
363, 46 Atl 489.

[1] *Straight* v. *Mahoney,* 16 Pa.
Super Ct 155

[13]*Meigs's Appeal,* 62 Pa 28, 1 Am.
Rep 372, *Justice* v. *Nesquehoning
Valley R Co* 87 Pa 28, *Silliman* v.
Whitmer. 11 Pa Super. Ct 243.

[14]105 Pa 187.

They can be restored in the same plight." Although the fact that the removal of the fixtures will injure the freehold is said not to be decisive that it is not a legally removable fixture,[15] the intention that fixtures should not be removed was inferred from the fact that to remove them would do serious injury, and also from their character and the manner in which they were made. The court, in *Kenny's Appeal*,[16] restrained the tenant of a hotel from tearing down and taking away an ash and walnut floor laid by him in the front and side halls, a frame addition used for a summer dining room, a coat or store room, a second-story dining room elevation, comprising three bed chambers, the carving room, and cupboard therein, hitching posts and rails on one of the fronts of the property, fences on the drove lot, the material used in the alteration of the ends of the shedding on the stableyard into carriage houses, registers and slabs around them, in the dining room and the hall above, gas pipes in the summer dining room, and other rooms, a sheet-iron sink in the kitchen, an iron sink in the washhouse, and tin spouting on the stableyard shed.

575. Question of fact and law — "What are fixtures is always a mixed question of law and fact "[17] When they are capable of a separate existence, as useful chattels, it cannot be assumed by the court that they are not chattels, but are a part of the realty. The facts additional to the qualities implied in their names, which are necessary to make them irremovable fixtures, or, indeed, fixtures at all, *viz.*, the kind of annexation and the intention of it, must be, in a jury trial, submitted to the jury. If, *e g.*, it simply appears that the tenant had, in a distillery leased by him, a steam boiler, a steam engine, a still, a worm, a

---

[15]*Seeger* v *Pettit*, 77 Pa 437, 18 Am Rep 452 A stairway fastened to the floor and wall, despite a hole cut through the joists and floor of the second story to admit access to it from the stairway, shelves and closets built on the wall and permanently fastened, so that they could not be removed without injury to the freeholder, were the property of the tenant He could remove them For the resulting injury he would be liable in damages

[16] 22 W N C 89, 12 Atl 589

[17]*Campbell* v *O'Neill*, 64 Pa 290; *Furbush* v *Chappell*, 105 Pa 187

worm tub, a tank—since these may be ordinary chattels, in no
way incorporated into the building, the court could not decide,
simply from the designation of these articles and their utility
in a distillery, that they had become parts of the distillery.[18]
It is not enough to submit to the jury the mode of the physical
connection of the things with the realty; the tenant's intention
must also be determined by them [19] Sometimes, it is said, it
may be declared, as matter of law, that a fixture is removable
or not removable. But when facts are in dispute, or different
inferences can be legitimately drawn from them, as to the tenant's intention in connecting them with the realty, the jury
should decide.[20]

576. Usage.— When under the facts the fixture would be irremovable by the tenant, and belong to the landlord, it is not permissible to show a usage of trade that the fixture should belong
to the tenant   Standing timber being sold, and a right given to
the vendee to lay a tramroad over the land to facilitate ingress
and egress, a custom of that business to regard and treat the
tramroad as the lessee's cannot be invoked to show that it belongs
to the tenant.[21]

577. Contractual modification of right.— The lease may provide that improvements introduced by the tenant shall unconditionally be the lessor's.[22] The lease may provide for the erection of certain improvements by the tenant, and for his retention of the rent until he shall be reimbursed.[23] The lease stip-

---

[18]*Campbell v O'Neill*, 64 Pa 290
The additional facts necessary to
make   these   articles   annexations
would have to be found by the jury

Whether shelves, a counter, a pre-
scription case were part of the realty
or mere chattels, not even fixtures,
must be decided by the jury, on evidence of other facts   *Straight v
Mahoney*, 16 Pa Super. Ct 155

[19]*Seeger v Pettit*, 77 Pa 437, 18
Am Rep 452

[20]*Silliman v. Whitmer*, 11 Pa

Super Ct 243   The tenant, having
asked the court to submit the question, cannot complain because the
court did not decide it

[21]*Silliman v. Whitmer*, 11 Pa.
Super. Ct. 243. *Christian v Dripps*,
28 Pa. 271.

[22]*Hey v Bruner*, 61 Pa 87, *Whitney v Shippen*, 89 Pa. 22, *Folsom v
Cook*, 115 Pa 539, 9 Atl 93

[23]*Collender Co v. Speer*, 29 Pittsb.
L J 125.

ulating that "all improvements erected or placed in said building shall be and remain, at the expiration of this lease, the
property of the lessor," except certain described things, a floor,
costing between $4,000 and $5,000, laid down on joists which
rested on blocks placed on the brick floor of the building, and
which was not otherwise connected with the building than by
resting on its brick floor, became the lessor's.[24] The lessee agreeing to leave, at the expiration of the term, the farm in as good
condition as it is or may be made by improvements to be, he
would be precluded from removing a kitchen, erected by him,
costing several hundred dollars, and a frame house for curing
tobacco, costing $1,200[25] A stipulation that the lessee would,
at the end of the term, give up the premises and "all and every
the improvements and additions" which he may have made,
would not embrace machinery, when the lease distinguishes
between the former and the latter[26]

578. Agreement that fixtures shall be lessor's.— The right reserved to the lessor, by the lease, to such improvements as might
be made to the premises, may be qualified; and unless the circumstances exist upon which it is to become absolute, the fixtures will remain the property of the tenant, if, without the

---

A steam heater and fixtures may
be put in by the tenant under an
agreement by the landlord that he
shall do so, so as to make the latter
liable for the costs Such improvements would not be personalty that
could be levied on and sold for the
tenant's debt, but in the distribution
of the proceeds of the sale in execution of property of the tenant, the
landlord's claim for rent could be
reduced by the cost or the value of
the fixtures for which he had not
paid the tenant *Wilkinson* v. *Kugler*, 153 Pa 238, 25 Atl 1133

A had contracted to furnish coal
to a railroad company He leased
his coal mine to B who was to put
in a pump, which A had contracted

for, and would pay for, no right was
reserved to B to take the pump at
the end of the term   B was to
furnish all the coal necessary to
satisfy A's contract with the rail
road company The court found that
the parties intended that the pump
should be the lessor's   *Jermyn* v
Dickson, 3 Luzerne Legal Reg 100

[24]*Harris* v. *Kelley* (Pa) 12 Cent
Rep 394, 13 Atl 523 The court
should say that the floor was includ
ed in the "improvements" mentioned
by the lease

[25]*Carter* v *Gough*, 153 Pa 225, 25
Atl 1124 Cf *Justice* v *Vesquehon-
ing Valley R Co* 87 Pa 28.

[26]*Hey* v *Bruner*, 61 Pa 87.

stipulation, they would remain his. A lease for eight years, of land on which were salt wells, provided that, should the wells fail at any time, the lessee might renounce the lease on paying up all rent then due, and should such failure occur within three years, the lessee should be "at liberty to take away all the metal and improvements of the works, or be paid the value thereof, at the choice of the lessor." This implied that if no failure occurred within three years, but afterwards, and the lessee gave up the lease, the metal and improvements should be the lessor's. But unless, after the three years, there was a failure of the wells, and a giving up of the lease, the provision would not apply [27] A stipulation that machinery put by the tenant on an iron ore bank "is to remain on said premises if said lease is forfeited from any cause whatever, unless all royalties and certificates of weight are paid and furnished within thirty days from notice of forfeiture," makes the machinery the lessor's only on the happening of the conditioning events [28]

579 **Improvements to be lessor's on paying price** —The lease may stipulate that the fixtures put up by the tenant shall become the lessor's, and that the lessor shall pay the sum at which

---

[27]*Lemar* v *Miles*, 4 Watts, 330 Hence, a sheriff's sale of an engine, put in by the tenant, passed the title to the purchaser The court also thought that an engine would not be covered by the words "metal and improvements," and hence would be a removable fixture under the general law In *Cook* v *Folsom*, 2 Lanc L. Rev. 185, the lease of a building for the manufacture of sugar stipulated that repairs, additions, and improvements made to the building and machinery should remain at the expiration of the lease If the lessor desired, the property was to be restored to its original state, but, in any event, "these additions, repairs, and improvements shall be the property of the lessor." By these words

were meant additions to existing machinery, e. g, tubing for the boiler, pipes put in place of pipes torn out, but wholly new machinery, which did not supply the place of other pre-existing machinery, in the building when the tenant took possession, was not included It would not be supposed that the tenant, who spent $10,000 on new machinery, intended to give it to the lessor Cf *Folsom* v *Cook*, 115 Pa 539, 9 Atl 93

[28]*Watts* v *Lehman*, 107 Pa 108

A boiler put in a brewery by the tenant was an "alteration or improvement," within the sense of the contract *Agnew* v *Whitney*, 10 Phila 77 Cf *Beech Grove Coal & C Co* v *Mitchell*, 193 Pa 112, 44 Atl 245

they shall be valued, not exceeding $1,000   If the valuation is made two days after the expiration of the term, by persons chosen by the parties, the landlord is bound to pay the value, not exceeding $1,000, and if he refuses, the tenant, though he in consequence refuses to vacate the premises until he is put off by proceedings under the landlord and tenant act, may recover the value [29]   The lease may not compel the lessor to take the improvements, at a valuation, but may give him the option to take or refuse.   Unless otherwise indicated, the landlord may require the appraisement to be made before he determines whether to accept the fixtures or not;[30] and this privilege may be explicitly secured to him by the terms of the lease.[31]   The lessor, under such a stipulation, must take all the improvements or none   He cannot select from them, taking some and rejecting the rest.[32]   Until appraisement and the landlord's election to take, he acquires no property in them,[33] and should he take them without paying for them, the lessee would have the remedy arising from the invasion of a property right,—trespass (or formerly trover).   He cannot set off the value of the cost of the improvements against the rent, when distress is made for it, and when he replevies the goods distrained.[34]

580 **Agreements extraneous to lease.**—Subsequent to the lease, agreements may be made between landlord and tenant, regulat-

---

[29]*Taylor* v *Maule*, 2 Walk (Pa) 539   The lessor sold the fixtures to the succeeding tenant

[30]*East Sugar Loaf Coal Co* v *Wilbur*, 5 Pa. Dist R 202

[31]*Seitzinger* v *Marsden*, 2 Pennyp 463

[32]*East Sugar Loaf Coal Co* v *Wilbur*, 5 Pa Dist R 202

[33]*Seitzinger* v *Marsden*, 2 Pennyp 463

[34]*Peterson* v *Haight*, 3 Whart 150 Bulk windows and doors, to be put in by the tenant, were provided for by the lease   The lessor was to contribute $50 to the expense, and at the end of the term was to receive this sum back, the lessee taking the windows and doors, unless the lessor took them at a valuation, when, they becoming his, he was to pay the valuation, less the $50   The tenant should, in a reasonable time, have required the lessor to join in the selection of appraisers, and if the latter refused should have taken the doors and windows away   If he allowed them to remain for several weeks, and the landlord then took control of them, set off in replevin was not permissible.

ing their rights respecting fixtures. Though the lease stipulates
that alterations or improvements made by the tenant shall not
be removed by him, but shall be surrendered to the lessor, the
lessor may, later, orally agree that the lessee or one to whom he is
about to assign the lease,[35] shall be their owner The lessee may
surrender his term and the improvements upon it. The lessor
will then become the owner of the latter, despite a levy on them
already made by a constable,—of which, when the surrender was
accepted, the lessor had no knowledge,—and a subsequent sale [36]

581. Instances of removable fixtures.— A great variety of fixtures have been adjudged to belong to the tenant, and to be
removable by him, in the absence of a negativing stipulation;
e. g., an engine and boiler put on a foundation built for the
boiler, not being removable except by cutting it apart or tearing
down the building in which it was,[37] machinery used in an ore
mine,[38] a stationary sawmill and its appurtenances,[39] a coal bin.
gas fixtures, walnut railing, walnut stairs firmly fastened to wall
and floor, and banister, closet, shelves, platform scales,[40] chairs
secured to the floor, the building being used as an opera house,[41]
a frame barber shop and stable,[42] a boiler built into a stone wall,
and an engine connected with screws and pipes;[43] rails laid in
a tunnel, for use in mining coal,[44] a building used as a shovel
factory, furnaces, chimneys, machinery, and tools;[45] an engine

[35]*Whitney* v *Shippen*, 89 Pa 22

The court would enjoin the tenant
or assignee from removing a fixture,
until proper proof of the subsequent
agreement was made in an action at
law *Agnew* v *Whitney*, 10 Phila.
77

[36]*Thropp's Appeal*, 70 Pa 395

A parol agreement inducing the acceptance of the lease, that the tenant
should have the right to remove improvements and additions, unless the
lessor should compensate him for
them, might be shown *Kenney's
Appeal*, 22 W. N C. 89, 12 Atl 589

[37]*Hey* v *Bruner*, 61 Pa 87

[38]*Watts* v *Lehman*, 107 Pa 108

[39]*Kile* v *Giebner*, 114 Pa 381, 7
Atl 154

[40]*Seeger* v *Pettit*, 77 Pa. 437, 18
Am Rep 452

[41]*Pratt* v *Keith*, 4 Del Co. Rep 69

[42]*White* v *Arndt*, 1 Whart 91

[43]*Lemar* v *Miles*, 4 Watts 330
Cf *Albert* v *Uhrich*, 180 Pa 283, 36
Atl 745

[44]*Heffner* v *Lewis*, 73 Pa 302

[45]*Church* v *Griffith*, 9 Pa 117, 49
Am Dec 548.

with necessary gearing for working a mine, boilers, buckets, wheel-barrows,[46] machinery and a railroad switch;[47] a frame building and machinery;[48] a steam sawmill and machinery, used to saw lumber for the lessor,[49] a spinning mule 90 feet long, occupying 11 feet of space in width, having over four hundred spindles, and being fastened to the floor by screws.[50] a range used in a restaurant,[51] coal breakers, engines, rollers, rails, and ties,[52] machinery introduced by the tenant, a newspaper publisher,[53] a derrick to raise coal from a shaft.[54]

582. Kinds of premises.— The premises onto which fixtures removable by the tenant may be introduced are of all sorts, dwelling houses, a woolen mill,[55] an iron ore mine,[56] a drug store,[57] salt wells,[58] coal mines,[59] a shovel factory,[60] lead and copper mine,[61] box and keg factory,[62] mining and grinding flint,[63] a restaurant,[64] an opera house [65] In *White* v. *Arndt*[66] Rogers, J., says: "I cannot believe that the nature of the business, whether agricultural or mercantile, can make any difference" with respect to the right of the tenant to remove fixtures In *Carver* v. *Gough*[67] Paxson, Ch. J., observes that "the question whether the tenant for years of farm lands comes within the same exception to the common-law rule [i. e, the exception in favor of tenants in trades, the rule being that fixtures are, when once made, inseparable from the freehold], has not been much dis-

[46]*Davis* v *Moss*, 38 Pa. 346

[47]*Darrah* v *Baird*, 101 Pa 265.

[48]*Thropp's Appeal*, 70 Pa 395

[49]*Overton* v *Williston*, 31 Pa 155

[50]*Furbush* v *Chappell*, 105 Pa 187

[51]*Townsend* v *Underhill*, 6 Pa Co. Ct 544

[52]*Gulick* v *Heermans*, 6 Luzerne Legal Reg 227

[53]*Wilkes-Barre Times* v *Wilkes-Barre*, 10 Pa Dist R 691 The machinery is not taxable as realty

[54]*Timlin* v *Brown*, 158 Pa 606, 28 Atl 236

[55]*Hey* v *Bruner*, 61 Pa 87.

[56]*Watts* v *Lehman*, 107 Pa 108

[57]*Seeger* v *Pettit*, 77 Pa 437, 18 Am Rep 452

[58]*Lemar* v *Miles*, 4 Watts, 330

[59]*Heffner* v *Lewis*, 73 Pa 302

[60]*Church* v *Griffith*, 9 Pa 117, 49 Am Dec 548

[61]*Davis* v *Moss*, 38 Pa 346

[62]*Darrah* v *Baird*, 101 Pa 265

[63]*Thropp's Appeal*, 70 Pa 395

[64]*Townsend* v *Underhill*, 6 Pa Co Ct 544.

[65]*Pratt* v *Keith*, 4 Del Co Rep 69.

[66]1 Whart 91

[67]153 Pa 225, 25 Atl 1124.

cussed in this state," stating that *McCullough* v. *Irvine*,[68] which denies to a tenant for life, against a remainderman, the right to remove a barn, "cannot be said to be authority upon the subject"

583. Sublessee's right.— A right similar to that of a lessee to remove fixtures put on the premises seems to inhere in a sub lessee, against both his immediate lessor and the primary lessor A rented to B, who sublet a portion of the premises to C C erected a range, but, before the expiration of his lease, he sold it to D.   E followed C in the possession of the premises, and with the consent both of E and of B, D removed the range D had a right, says Finletter, P. J, to remove it at any time before the expiration of the tenancy of B and E.[69]

584. Right of lessee as lessor's vendee.— Fixtures, *e. g,* a steam boiler and engine, a still, a worm, a worm tub, a tank, used in a distillery, may be sold by the landlord to the lessee of the distillery at the time of making the lease.   If at that time, however, there was a mortgage on the premises which would bind the fixtures as a part of the realty, the lessee's title would be defeated by a subsequent sheriff's sale of the premises, on the judgment on the mortgage, or on any judgment, the sale on which would discharge the mortgage.[70]

585. Removal of fixtures during the term— The tenant may, unless restrained by his agreement with the lessor, remove any removable fixtures, at any time during the term, and if he does, the lessor will have no right of ownership in them [71]   Hence during the term, there may be a levy and sale of them by a constable[72] or the sheriff,[73] or by the landlord in distress for rent.[74]

---

[68] 13 Pa 438.

[69] *Townsend* v *Underhill,* 6 Pa Co Ct 544

[70] *Campbell* v *O'Neill,* 64 Pa 290 But, if the articles were not so connected with the realty as to be a part of it, they would not be bound by the mortgage, and the sale to the tenant would convey an indefeasible title

[71] *Townsend* v. *Underhill,* 6 Pa. Co Ct 544.

[72] *Thropp's Appeal,* 70 Pa 395

[73] *Lemar* v *Miles,* 4 Watts, 330, *Heffner* v *Lewis,* 73 Pa 302, *Hey* v *Bruner,* 61 Pa. 87; *Wick* v *Bredin,* 189 Pa 83, 42 Atl 17

[74] *Furbush* v. *Chappell,* 105 Pa 187, *Gulick* v *Heermans,* 6 Luzerne Legal Reg 227.

The levy and sale in execution may, at the same time, be on and of the leasehold and the fixtures[75] as well as on and of the fixtures alone. A lessor's option to purchase them at the end of the term does not preclude a sheriff's sale of them during the term.[76]

586 When removal must be made.— The tenant has a right to sever the fixtures so long as he is in possession, in pursuance of the terms of the lease, but, generally, not afterwards He must remove them during the term. Allowed to remain beyond the term, they are deemed given to the lessor.[77] "Certainly a tenant," says Strong, J , "can make accessions to the freehold of his landlord He does when he makes additions not for the purpose of trade Fixtures for such purposes the law permits him to take away, if he exercises his right during the term. If he does not, he waives his right to remove at all, and dedicates them as permanent accessions to the freehold Were it not so, the rights of a tenant upon a property leased would continue longer than the term to which they were limited by the contract which created it Yet the tenant is but a purchaser of the enjoyment for a defined period, the rent being but a mode of paying the purchase money." [78] If the tenant for a definite term holds over, and the lessor, not treating him as a trespasser, as he might, recognizes him as still a tenant, his right to remove the fixtures continues until the close of the hold-over period,[79] but if the lessor dissents from the holding over, the right of removal of

[75]*Seitzinger* v *Marsden,* 2 Pennyp 463, *Kile* v *Giebner,* 114 Pa 381, 7 Atl 154, *Church* v *Griffith,* 9 Pa. 117, 49 Am Dec 548

[76]*Seitzinger* v *Marsden,* 2 Pennyp 463

[77]*White* v *Arndt,* 1 Whart 91; *Justice* v. *Nesquehoning Valley R Co* 87 Pa 28, *Heffner* v *Lewis,* 73 Pa 302. *Dariah* v *Baird,* 101 Pa

LAND & TEN 32,

265; *Davis* v *Moss,* 38 Pa 346, *Overton* v *Williston,* 31 Pa 155, *Straight* v *Mahoney,* 16 Pa Super Ct 155, *Albert* v *Uhrich,* 180 Pa 283, 36 Atl 745, *Schock* v *Vogle,* 18 Lanc L Rev 257

[78]*Overton* v *Williston,* 31 Pa 155
[79]*Davis* v *Moss,* 38 Pa. 346, *Darrah* v *Baird,* 101 Pa 265

the fixtures is lost [80]   Negotiations begun during the term for a new lease, resulting in an agreement, two days before the close of the term, that the lessee should continue to operate the collieries during the next month, until a new arrangement should be made, the lessee, two weeks afterwards, the parties having failed to make a new arrangement, announced to the lessor that he would surrender at the end of the month, and would remove the improvements if the lessor did not exercise his option to take them at an appraisement. He was entitled to a reasonable time to remove the engine, building, pumps, and railroad which he had put upon the premises [81]

587. Life-tenant lessor —If, the lessor being a life tenant, the term is cut short by his death before its close, the tenant loses the right to remove fixtures on the premises at the lessor's death, even though the lessor had agreed that the lessee might remove them at or after the expiration of the term, unless he. the lessor, bought them, since this agreement is not binding on the remainderman.[82]   "If the tenant for life, or the person with whom he contracts," says Rogers, J., "wishes to avoid the consequences, the improvements must be removed during the continuance of the first estate, or the assent of the remainderman or reversioner must be obtained."   The fact that the remainderman consented to the continuance in possession of the lessee, receiving rent from him, but without knowledge of the agreement of the lessor with the lessee, could not preclude his denying the lessee's right of removal of the fixtures.

[80]*Taylor* v *Maule*, 2 Walk (Pa) 539 *Dictum* of Stroud, J   In *Charlotte Furnace Co* v *Stouffer*, 127 Pa 336, 17 Atl 994, Green. J, remarks that the necessity of removing fixtures before the end of the term is subject to an exception in favor of trade fixtures   If the principle is invoked by any one that the ownership of a thing has been lost by reason of its owner's being a tenant and having allowed it to remain on the premises, at the expiration of the term, the burden is upon him to show the lease and the expiration of the term

[81]*East Sugar-Loaf Coal Co* v *Wilbur*, 5 Pa Dist R 202

[82]*White* v. *Arndt*, 1 Whart. 91.

588. Lease ending at no certain time.— If the lease is to end at no certain time, if, *e g.,* being an oil lease for ten years, it is provided that, if oil is found in paying quantities, the term shall last until it shall cease to be found in such quantities, and, the condition being realized, the tenant continues in possession beyond the ten years, but on the exhaustion of the oil, suspends operations, and the lessor terminates the lease and re-enters, a reasonable time after this termination must be allowed to the lessee for the removal of the fixtures [83] Should the lessor bring an ejectment because of the cessation of the production of oil in paying quantities, and recover a judgment, it would not be too late for the lessee to take away his personalty, and should the lessor refuse to allow him, he would be liable in trespass for the conversion.[84]

589. Forfeiture.— The lease may be subject to forfeiture. Being for ninety-nine years, it may provide that if mining operations should cease for one year, it shall become void. After the cessation of the operation for one year, the fixtures were allowed to remain on the premises three years longer. They could not then be taken by the tenant, nor levied on and sold by the sheriff under executions against him [85] The lessee becomes a bankrupt, and in a contest between the assignee and the landlord, who takes possession under a provision of the lease that on thirty days' notice, for failure to pay rent, he may repossess himself of the premises, the court decides that the possession be given up to the landlord, the right of the fixtures to be determined subsequently. From the time of the decision, if not before, the landlord has legal possession of the premises, and the right of the lessee or one claiming under him, to take the fixtures, is lost.[86] The lease may stipulate that the fixtures

[83]*Cassell* v. *Crothers,* 193 Pa 359, 44 Atl 446

[84]*Sattler* v *Opperman,* 14 Pa Super Ct 32

[85]*Davis* v *Moss,* 38 Pa 346

[86]*Dariah* v *Baird,* 101 Pa 265 The fact that the right of property in the fixtures was to be determined

may be removed after a forfeiture, within thirty days of notice thereof, and such a stipulation will regulate the right of removal.[87] An agreement which was virtually a sale of coal in place in consideration of the payment of royalties, gave to the lessee the right to abandon the mining at any time and to remove his buildings and fixtures. It was subsequently modified by a provision that it should remain in force until all the merchantable coal had been mined and removed, and by a provision that on a failure to pay any of the semiannual royalties for six months, the lease should become null and void at the election of the lessor. For a failure for six months to pay a royalty, the lease was declared forfeited. A bill in equity was filed by the lessor to prevent the removal of the fixtures It was held that the original lease preserved the personalty character of the fixtures, not only when the lessee abandoned the work, but also when, under the later agreement, the lessor declared the "lease and contract" null and void. "By that contract "[the original lease], says Dean, J , "the mining fixtures and machinery were the personal property of the lessee, and so continued ; destroying, forfeiting, or making void his contract affected not that which was excluded from the operation of it; the intention of both in the beginning to distinguish it as personalty from realty could not be defeated by the act of one of them." [88] The coal lease providing that on a sale of the term in execution, the lease should be forfeited, and also providing that the fixtures put on the premises by the tenant should, at the lessor's option, become his on his paying the value, as ascertained by appraisers, the only effect of a sheriff's sale of the lease and the fixtures, as the property of the lessee, would be to make the former forfeitable If, the lease not being forfeited by the lessor, on account of the sheriff's sale, the purchasers at that sale of the lease and fixtures

later did not affect the unconditional character of the surrender of the premises.

[87] *Watts* v *Lehman*, 107 Pa 108
[88] *Wick* v *Bredin*, 189 Pa 83, 42 Atl. 17.

take possession of the premises, and after some weeks, give notice to the lessor that they desire an appraisement of the fixtures, and the lessor refuses to recognize their right, and, a few days afterwards, serves notice on them and the lessee that he forfeits the lease for nonpayment of rent, for suspension of work at the colliery, and for taking up some of the fixtures, and if thereupon the lessor takes possession of the premises and the fixtures, he will be liable for a conversion of the latter [89]

590. Remedies of the lessee.— If the lessee is prevented from removing the fixtures at a time when, under the law and his contract, he has a right to remove them, he may maintain trover[90] for them, although they remain fixed to the land, which was in the possession of the lessor before the attempt to remove the fixtures [91]   If the lessor takes possession of the fixtures, and agrees to be accountable for them, assumpsit can be sustained to recover their value [92]   Trespass was employed in *Straight* v. *Mahoney* [93]   In replevin to recover goods distrained on for rent, whether they be the tenant's[94] or a stranger's,[95] the plaintiff cannot set off the value of the fixtures improperly appropriated by the landlord, or show in defense an agreement of the landlord that the cost of a building erected on the premises by the tenant, and at his expense, should be applied to the payment of the rent, and that if thus applied, no rent would be due [96]   The tenant, whose right of possession of the premises has ended, cannot

[89]*Seitzinger* v. *Marsden,* 2 Pennyp 463

[90] In 1884.

[91]*Watts* v *Lehman,* 107 Pa 106 Tacitly disparaging a portion of the opinion in *Darrah* v *Baird,* 101 Pa 265, and in *Overton* v *Williston,* 31 Pa 155   Cf *Campbell* v *O'Neill,* 64 Pa 290

[92]*Seitzinger* v *Marsden,* 2 Pennyp 463   In *Charlotte Furnace Co* v *Stouffer,* 127 Pa 336, 17 Atl. 994, replevin for an inclined plane was allowed to one who was alleged to have been a tenant, and to have lost the right to it because he had permitted it to remain after the expiration of the term   His relation as tenant was not shown in the evidence

[93] 16 Pa Super Ct 155   Cf *Albert* v *Uhrich,* 180 Pa 283, 36 Atl. 745

[94]*Peterson* v *Haight,* 3 Whart 150 Cf *White* v *Arndt,* 1 Whart 91

[95]*Collender Co* v *Speer,* 29 Pittsb L J 125

[96]*Collender Co* v *Speer,* 29 Pittsb. L J 125.

maintain ejectment for them, even though the lessor, on taking possession, intended to deprive, and continues to intend to deprive, the lessor of the fixtures, and though the lessee's object in bringing the ejectment is to regain possession long enough only to secure and remove the fixtures [97]

591. Remedies of lessor — For fixtures which, at the making of the lease, are already the lessor's or which, by the terms of the lease, if erected by the lessee, are to be the property of the lessor, and which, during the term, the lessee removes and sells, the lessor may maintain trover. Previous demand for the article is not necessary, if the vendee knew, before the purchase, the facts on which the lessor's right rests The right to the use of the fixtures during the rest of the term is lost to the tenant by his unlawful act.[98] If the fixture is a tramroad, and the lessee continues to use it after his right to be on the premises has ended, trespass q c f. will lie [99] An estrepement[100] or an injunction[101] may be employed by the landlord, to prevent the removal of a boiler from a brewery[102] or various fixtures from a hotel.[103] If a covenant obliges the tenant to leave the fixtures, for the removal of them in violation of it, an action on it will lie,[104] and a case stated may be resorted to, to obtain the judgment of the court upon the rights of the lessor and lessee [105]

---

[97]*Cassell* v *Crothers*, 193 Pa 359, 44 Atl 446

[98]*Morgan* v *Negley*, 3 Pittsb 33 But in *Townsend* v *Underhill*, 6 Pa Co Ct 544, it was held that when the lessor had no right to the fixtures until the expiration of the lease, he could maintain no action until then Apparently, he would have had no action even then

[99]*Stillman* v *Whitmer*, 11 Pa. Super Ct 243 Cf *Townsend* v *Underhill*, 6 Pa Co Ct 544, where trespass q c f was brought for the removal of a range

[100]*Cook* v *Folsom*, 2 Lanc L Rev 185, *Folsom* v *Cook*, 115 Pa. 539, 9 Atl 93.

[101]*Agnew* v *Whitney*, 10 Phila 77
[102]*Agnew* v *Whitney*, 10 Phila 77.
[103]*Kenney's Appeal*, 22 W N C. 89, 12 Atl 589

Trespass on the case was employed by the lessor for injury to his freehold by removing the fixtures, in *Seeger* v. *Pettit*, 77 Pa. 437, 18 Am Rep 452

[104]*Whitney* v *Shippen*, 89 Pa 22

[105]*Harris* v *Kelley* (Pa) 12 Cent. Rep 394 13 Atl 523, *Jermyn* v *Dickson*, 3 Luzerne Legal Reg 100 In *Farmakis* v *Boyle*, 8 Pa Dist R 696, A leased to B the pavement for a fruit stand With A's consent, three or four months later, B erected a galvanized awning, supported by

592. Manure.— Whether manure made upon the demised premises belongs to the tenant or to the landlord is occasionally a matter of dispute. The principle recognized is, that when the land has been let for agricultural purposes, the manure made on it during the term is the tenant's in the sense that he may use it for the ends of good husbandry upon the premises, but in no other. All manure made on the land, and remaining on it at the close of the term, is to be deemed a part of the land, and belongs to him to whom the land belongs, in reversion or remainder. Nor is this principle to be accepted only where, on an investigation in the particular case, it appears to be the custom in this state to respect it. It is established by the court as a matter of law; but a stipulation in the lease, regulating the respective rights of landlord and tenant, will be respected.[106]

593. Land let for agriculture — "The doctrine," says Lewis, J., "that the manure goes with the land is, of course, confined to farms which are let for agricultural purposes "[107] Though the land is used in a subordinate degree to support dairy cows,[108] nay, though it is used solely as a grazing farm,[109] it is to be deemed devoted, in the sense of the principle in question, to agricultural purposes The farm being let as a "milk farm," that is, to raise therefrom food for cows, in order that the tenant might sell the milk produced by them, Thompson, P. J., remarked:[110] "That a grazing farm is not in use strictly for agricultural purposes, I should not like to be the first to de-

posts, and a framework covering the whole width of the pavement Subsequently A tore off the top of the awning His tearing down the posts and frame was enjoined

[106]*Barrington* v *Justice*, 2 Clark (Pa) 501

[107]*Lewis* v *Jones*, 17 Pa 262, 55 Am Dec 550, *Barrington* v *Justice*, 2 Clark (Pa) 501

[108]*Lewis* v *Jones*, 17 Pa. 262, 55 Am Dec. 550.

[106]*Waln* v *O'Connor*, 1 Phila 353 In *Rinehart* v *Olwine*, 5 Watts & S. 157, the court abstained from deciding whether ' when a farm is taken by a tenant for agricultural purposes, the manure made upon it belongs to the farm and not to the tenant " A compromise between landlord and tenant, regarding it, was binding

[110] In 1852, *Waln v. O'Connor*, 1 Phila. 353.

termine   I can see no difference, in an agricultural sense, between the cultivation of grass or turnips as food for cattle, and of wheat, rye or any other grain, for human consumption. . . . Every farm which is let for the purpose of obtaining the product of the soil by tillage is let for 'agricultural purposes' whether those products are consumed upon it or disposed of in any other manner." A tract containing zinc ore was let for his life to X "for agricultural or farming use, and none other;" but the lessor reserved the right to mine upon it, under the limit that the mining should be so conducted as to cause as little injury as possible to X, in his farming operations   The premises were within the rule, with respect to manure formed on them [111]

594. Manure; kind of term.— Ordinarily, the term in respect to which the rule under consideration is invoked and applied, is a tenancy at will, for years,[112] or from year to year, but the rule applies as well to a grant for the life of the tenant [113]

595. Source and place of manure.— It is not necessary that all the manure made on the premises should be made by the cattle or horses, out of grass, hay, fodder produced on the premises.   In a case in which the tenant kept a dairy farm, and bought considerable quantities of hay, brewhouse grain, and other articles as food for his cattle, Thompson, Ch J., concluded that all the manure made on the farm belonged to it, being influenced by reflection on the difficulty of separating the part of the manure attributable to the cattle food procured beyond the farm, from the other part, on the fact that the manure is a part of the soil, no more separable from it than a fixture, and on the detriment to the farm, as property, and to the agricultural interests of the community considered in their generality, which would be occasioned by the abstraction, by each tenant, of the manure made

[111] *Pearson* v. *Friedensville Zinc Co* 1 Pa Co Ct 660
[112] For one year, *Barrington* v *Justice*, 2 Clark (Pa) 501.

[113] *Pearson* v *Friedensville Zinc Co.* 1 Pa. Co. Ct. 660.

on the land during his term "There are few farmers at the present day who do not expend their money in purchasing manure to improve then crops; and where is the difference whether the manure itself is purchased, or the food from which it is made? It should equally belong to the soil."[114] In *Lewis v. Jones*,[115] the tenant kept dairy cows, and eight or nine horses He purchased "some" grain, and "some" hay, but how much was not shown. The court refused to sanction the principle that the tenant owned so much of the manure as exceeded that amount which was produced from the produce of the farm itself, because the jury had no test, in the evidence, for determining what this excess was; because, by his own act, the tenant had confused his manure with that of the landlord. The tenant, remarked Lewis, J., cannot justify taking away any part of the manure, by showing that he has occasionally employed his teams in business not connected with the cultivation of the soil, and that he has supplied them in part with hay and grain purchased elsewhere, so long as the manure thus made is commingled with that made from the produce of the farm The manure which is scattered over the farm would rather easily be conceded to be intermingled with the soil, and to be irremovable by the tenant, but it has likewise been held that manure in heaps, in the barnyard, or other depository, is no less exempt from a tenant's right to take it away. "True it is," said Parsons, J., in the leading case in Pennsylvania,[116] "often large heaps are collected in the farmyard, yet the quantity in which it is collected cannot in any way change its character, or the species of prop-

[114]*Waln v O'Connor*, 1 Phila 353
[115]17 Pa 262, 55 Am Dec 550
[116]*Barrington v Justice*, 2 Clark (Pa) 501 Cf *Pearson v Friedensville Zinc Co* 1 Pa Co Ct 660

The lessee covenanting to leave, at the end of the term, as much hay as he finds on the premises when he takes possession an affidavit of defense to the lessor's action on this covenant, to the effect that six tons of hay were found on the farm when possession was taken, and that six tons, either as hay or manure were left on the farm, not distinguishing how much of each, will not prevent judgment *Harnish v Musser*, 19 Lanc L Rev 283.

erty by which it must be known on legal principles. If we once admit the principle that a tenant can remove that which is collected in a large quantity in a yard, what is there to prevent' him from going over the farm, and gathering all which is deposited in less quantities by accident in the pastures, or by design for future use, on any part of the premises, even when in a state of decomposition, and about to be commingled with the soil? What would prevent the tenant from scraping the deposits around every stackyard, or gleaning all which had been formed in a sheepfold during the year, just as his lease was about to terminate?" The manure, he argues, though in the yard, is connected and identified with the earth, it can be taken off with no more propriety than could rails from the fences. The maintenance of the fertility of the farm, the interests of agriculture, require that the manure, even in heaps, shall be irremovable by the tenant at the close of the term.

596. Remedies as respects manure.— The 1st section of the act of March 29th, 1822,[117] authorizes a landlord who has let his land for years, or at will, at any time during the continuance or after the expiration of the term, and due notice to the tenant to leave the premises, to apply by petition and affidavit to the common pleas for a writ of estrepement against the commission of waste of the freehold; and the tenant's removal, at the end of the term, of the manure made during it, on the premises, may, as such waste, be prevented by this writ.[118] The landlord may also maintain trespass for the conversion,[119] or his right may be adjudicated upon a case stated.[120]

---

[117] 2 Pepper & Lewis Digest, 4806, 7 Sm. L 520
[118] *Barrington* v *Justice*, 2 Clark (Pa) 501, *Waln* v. *O'Connor*, 1 Phila. 353.
[119] *Lewis* v *Jones*, 17 Pa 262, 55 Am Dec 550
[120] *Pearson* v *Friedensville Zinc Co* 1 Pa. Co. Ct 660.

CHAPTER XXVIII.

THE WAY-GOING CROP AND EMBLEMENTS.

597. The way-going crop.—Additional to the right secured by the common law with respect to emblements, there prevails in Pennsylvania what is known as the right to way-going crops. The tenant, after the close of the term, continues to own the crop then in the ground, unripe and uncut, and may assert this ownership in appropriate ways.

598. Kind of lease.—The law of emblements is applicable only in cases of tenures of uncertain duration, whose time of termination can therefore not be foreseen when a crop is sown The law of way-going crops operates in regard to tenancies of a different class · to leases for a term of years, or from year to year It has been applied when the lease was for one,[1] for two,[2] for

---

[1] *Miller v Clement,* 40 Pa 404   *Bittinger v Baker,* 29 Pa 66, 70 Am
The lease may expressly give the   Dec 154
tenant the way going crop   *Yeager*   [2] *Forsythe v Price,* 8 Watts, 282,
v. *Cassidy,* 12 Pa Super Ct. 232,

five,[3] or other period,[4] and also from year to year[5] The lease may originally be for a definite term, and, by the tenant's holding over, become a lease from year to year.[6] The leases in respect to which the right has been recognized have probably all begun in the spring time, generally on April 1st.[7]

599 The kind of crop — The only crops the right to which under the denomination of "way-going" has been recognized are such as are sown in the fall or winter preceding the expiration of the term, e. g., rye,[8] wheat.[9] Hare, P. J, in *Hunter v. Jones,*[10] and Tilghman, Ch J., in *Stultz v. Dickey,*[11] speak of the crop as "winter grain." In *Biggs v Brown,*[12] though termed generally, "corn," "grain," it had been sown in 1810, and had ripened in 1811. In *Demi v. Bossler,*[13] Huston, J , remarks that the "way-going crop" "heretofore has been confined to grain sown in the autumn, to be reaped the next harvest." In that case, the tenant for one year received notice December 28th to leave on the 1st of April following. He sowed oats in March following the notice Holding that he had no right to this crop, on its maturing, after the expiration of the lease, Huston, J , suggested that, were his right recognized, "the tenant who rents a farm for the ensuing year will not know whether he can put in a spring crop until he knows

34 Am Dec 465, *Shaw* v *Bowman,* 91 Pa 414.

[3]*Stultz* v *Dickey,* 5 Binn 285, 6 Am Dec 411.

[4]*Bittinger* v *Baker,* 29 Pa 66, 70 Am Dec 154

[5]*Biggs* v. *Brown,* 2 Serg & R 14

[6]*Clark* v *Harvey,* 54 Pa. 142 , *Borrell* v *Dewart,* 37 Pa 134, *Whorley* v *Karper,* 20 Pa Super. Ct 347

[7]*Demi* v. *Bossler,* 1 Penr & W. 224, *Stultz* v *Dickey,* 5 Binn 285, 287, 6 Am Dec 411

[8]*Clark* v *Harvey,* 54 Pa 142 , *McKeeby* v *Webster,* 170 Pa 624, 32 Atl 1096, *Stultz* v *Dickey,* 5 Binn. 285, 6 Am Dec. 411.

[9]*Stultz* v *Dickey,* 5 Binn 285, 6 Am Dec 411, *Forsythe* v *Price,* 8 Watts 282, 34 Am. Dec 465, *Hunt* v *Scott,* 3 Pa Co Ct 411, *Bittinger* v *Baker,* 29 Pa 66, 70 Am Dec 154, *Shaw* v *Bowman,* 91 Pa. 414, *McKay* v *Pearson,* 6 Pa. Super Ct 529, *Waugh* v *Waugh,* 84 Pa 350, 24 Am Rep 191, *Whorley* v *Karper,* 20 Pa Super. Ct 347

[10]7 Phila 233

[11]5 Binn 285, 6 Am Dec 411.

[12]2 Serg & R 14

[13]1 Penr. & W. 224.

whether the month of March will be clement or inclement, or whether the previous tenant was regardful of the rights and interests of others, and the general laws and usages of the country."[14] The tenant has the right to sow fall crops, and to reap them, despite the warning of the landlord not to sow them.[15]

600 Straw included — The straw of the wheat or rye is a constituent part of the way-going crop, and as such the tenant has a right to it, despite the termination of the lease prior to the maturation of the crop   Why should landlords, asks Kennedy, J , receive the rents from the tenants "and make profit beside out of the product of their labor by taking from them the straw, and selling it ? Distributive justice in such case would seem to give the straw as well as the grain to the tenant, as part of the way-going crop, to be taken and disposed of by him as he pleases, seeing it is the product of his own labor , from the land of his lessor, to be sure, but, then, he has paid the lessor a full compensation for the use of the land "[16] If the lease requires the tenant to deliver one half of the grain to the landlord, he is to deliver one half of the grain and the straw, and retain the other half.[17] If the tenant is to deliver one third of the wheat "in the bushel," the tenant has a right to all the straw; if the former is to deliver to the latter one third of the wheat in the "sheaf," the landlord is to have one third of the straw also.[18] A lease giving one half of the crops to the tenant, but stipulating that he is to take away no manure, hay, or straw, he is not entitled to any straw.[19]

---

[14] Huston, J , also observes that, if the tenant can sow the land "with oats, flax or other grain, in March, before his lease expires, which is always about the first of April, he in fact gets the benefit of the farm for two years, although he pays the rent of but one "

[15] Stultz v Dickey, 5 Binn 285, 6 Am Dec 411.

[16] Craig v Dale, 1 Watts & S 509. 37 Am Dec 477

With the close of the term, the relation of landlord and tenant ends, notwithstanding the tenant's right to the still growing, way-going crop. Shaw v Bowman, 91 Pa 414

[17] Rank v Rank, 5 Pa 211

[18] Iddings v Nagle, 2 Watts & S 22

[19] Hunt v Scott, 3 Pa Co Ct 411

601 Who entitled.— The tenant has the right to sow the fall crops and to reap them despite the intervening termination of the lease His assignee of the lease has the right,[20] as also has the subtenant. Indeed, if there is a sublease, and the sublessee puts in the crop, he alone has the right to take it, not the lessee; and he alone can maintain the action for the denial of the right by anybody.[21] The tenant may sell the crop, or, he dying. it may pass to his administrator. The vendee or administrator will then have, and be able to enforce, the right,[22] and if the lessor is aware of the sale, he cannot destroy the vendee's right by accepting a surrender of the term prior to its expiration [23] The crop may be sold as personalty, as in execution, or in distress for taxes, and the purchaser, though he be the tenant, the former owner, himself may buy it in [24] After the expiration of the lease the way-going crop may be sold for taxes due by the tenant. The landlord could not recover in replevin, from the purchaser.[25]

602. Effect of sheriff's sale of the reversion.— A sale in execution, after making the lease, of the lessor's reversion, does not impair the lessee's right, but simply substitutes the sheriff's vendee, as landlord. Though the lien on which the sale afterwards takes place exists before the lease is made, if the crop is sown before the issue of the execution and sheriff's sale, the tenant's right to the way-going crop is not destroyed by a sheriff's sale before or after the termination of the lease. Thus, after a judgment recovered against X, he made, in the spring, a lease of the land. In the following fall the tenant put rye into the

---

[20]*Stultz* v. *Dickey*, 5 Binn 285, 6 Am Dec 411, *Miller* v. *Clement*, 40 Pa. 484

[21]*Stultz* v *Dickey*, 5 Binn 285, 6 Am Dec 411; *Biggs* v. *Brown*, 2 Serg & R 14.

[22]*Shaw* v *Bowman*, 91 Pa 414.

[23]*Shaw* v *Bowman*, 91 Pa 414 The crop may, of course, remain on the premises till ripe After the end of the term, and after a sale of it by the tenant, who planted it, it cannot be taken in distress for his rent *Wardlaw* v *Sharpless*, 13 Lanc Bar, 124, 1 Del. Co Rep 155.

[24]*Miller* v *Clement*, 40 Pa 484

[25]*Hazlett* v *McCutcheon*, 158 Pa. 539, 27 Atl. 1086.

ground   A sheriff's sale followed, but before the close of the term.   The purchaser gave notice to the tenant to give up possession, and he did so, at the expiration of the term.   He was entitled to the way-going crop [26]   The lease was made April 1, 1851, of land on which was already a lien.   A crop was sown in the fall. Later, a fi. fa. issued, and a sheriff's sale of the land took place April 13th, 1852.   The fall crop belonged to the tenant.[27]   A bought at an administrator's sale, what had been X's land, but did not complete the payment of the purchase money, nor receive a deed.   Taking possession, however, he mortgaged the land.   Subsequently to the mortgage, he leased it.   After the expiration of this lease, and while the fall crops were still in the ground, occurred a sheriff's sale upon the judgment on the mortgage.   The grantee of the purchaser, in taking the way-going crop, was a trespasser.[28]   It has been held, however, that if a levy in execution preceded the making of the lease, and a sheriff's sale took place after the planting of a crop, *e. g.*, corn, the purchaser became the owner of the crop [29]   The effect of the sheriff's sale on the right to the crop is the same whether the lease is oral or written.[30]

[26]*McKeeby* v *Webster*, 170 Pa 624, 32 Atl 1096

[27]*Bittinger* v *Baker*, 29 Pa 66, 70 Am Dec 154   In *Adams* v *McKesson*, 53 Pa 81, 91 Am Dec 183, Strong, J., remarked that it made no difference at what time, prior to the sheriff's sale, the lease was made or the grain sown   The tenant's right to the crop would not be affected The contract was made after a *vend ex* had issued

[28]*Miller* v. *Clement*, 40 Pa 484. The sale was made to B, to whom, having been a creditor of the decedent, X, C, the administrator, had confessed a judgment   B subsequently conveyed to C. This did not affect the principle

[29]*McIlvaine* v *Souders*, 15 Lanc L.

Rev 371.   But in *Yeager* v *Cassidy*, 16 Lanc L Rev 305, when a lease for a money rent ran from April 1st, 1896, to April 1st, 1897, and the lease stipulated that the fall crops should be the tenant's, it was held that though the fall crops were sown after a sheriff's sale of the reversion, the tenant had a right to the crops, as against the transferee of the sheriff's vendee

[30]*Adams* v *McKesson*, 53 Pa 81, 91 Am Dec 183   In *Hewitt* v *McIlvain*, 10 Pa Co Ct 562, McClean, J , held that, the judgment on which the sheriff's sale occurred being prior to the lease and notice to quit in three months being given to the tenant by the purchaser after he obtained the sheriff's deed, the tenant

603. **Inconsistent with right to crop.**—The custom as to the tenant's right to the way-going crop is reported by Yeates, J.,[31] to have been proven by witnesses in such terms as to make the right depend on the fact that there was no fall crop in the ground at the commencement of the lease, which became the tenant's. "Several witnesses, including two of the jurors," he remarks, "were examined," *i. e.,* in an earlier case,[32] as to the custom of the country, that tenants for years who did not receive crops at the commencement of their leases were entitled to take off the crops which had been sown during the continuance of their leases." That this is a correct condition to the right is intimated by Pettit, J., in *Comfort* v. *Duncan.*[33] In *Loose* v. *Scharff*[34] a custom in Berks county is recognized as valid, that the incoming tenant has the benefit of the winter crop in the ground at the commencement of his term, and that he must leave his last winter crop in the ground for the benefit of his landlord. A sheriff's sale of the lessor's title occurring after the expiration of the term, but while the winter crops are in the ground, the tenant did not estop himself from claiming the crops, as against the sheriff's purchaser, by giving notice that he had put in the crop, and that he had also bought it at a sale of it, under distress for taxes. The notice did not mislead. No notice, indeed, was needed to save the tenant's crop. The purchaser was bound to know it was there and to respect it. The notice was no disavowal of the late tenancy.[34½] The instrument which creates the tenant's estate may virtually stipulate that crops in the ground at its close shall belong to another. Effect will be given to the stipulation.[34¾]

---

had no right, during these three months, to cut and make hay. The purchaser at the sheriff's sale was allowed to recover it in replevin

[31]*Stultz* v *Dickey*, 5 Binn 285, 6 Am Dec 411

[32]*Diffedorffer* v *Jones*, 5 Binn 289, 6 Am Dec 413

[33]1 Miles (Pa.) 229.

[34]6 Pa Super. Ct 153.

[34½]*Miller* v *Clement*, 40 Pa 484 The crops could be levied on as personalty, and be sold for taxes, and the tenant, already the owner, could buy them in

[34¾]*Waugh* v *Waugh*, 84 Pa 350, 24 Am Rep 191.

604. Remedies for denial of tenant's right — The tenant has, as incident to his ownership of the crop, the right to its being permitted to grow in the fields until it matures, to its being exempt from injury occasioned by the wilfulness or the negligence of the succeeding occupant of the premises, or of another, and the right of access to it, probably to cultivate it; certainly, when it is ripe, to reap it and take it away. The tenant has a possessory right to so much of the land as is covered by the crop If the landlord, after the expiration of the lease, wilfully or negligently allows his horses to get into the tenant's way-going wheat, he is liable in trespass q. c f,[35] and the succeeding tenant, who harrows down the winter grain planted by his predecessor, and plants corn for himself, will be similarly liable.[36] If the landlord enters the field, and takes the crop, he is also a breaker of the close.[37] Formerly the action of trover and conversion lay,[38] now trespass lies,[39] for depriving the tenant of his crop, considered as personalty. If, when the crop is ripe, the former tenant goes to the land with a man and machinery for the purpose of cutting it, and the present occupant of the premises positively denies access to him,[40] or, the crop being cut and put in the landlord's barn, if the landlord locks his barn, and forbids the tenant to take it,[41] a conversion is committed The fact that, nine days later, the succeeding tenant changes his mind and advises his predecessor that he may cut the crop, does not expunge the previous conversion. The owner is not

[35]*Forsythe* v. *Price*, 8 Watts, 282, 34 Am Dec 465

[36]*Clark* v *Harvey*, 54 Pa 142 The landlord was held jointly liable

The tenant may be held solely liable   *McKay* v *Pearson*, 6 Pa Super Ct 529

[37]*Stultz* v *Dickey*, 5 Binn 289, 6 Am Dec 411, *Biggs* v *Brown*, 2 Serg & R 14.

[38]*Shaw* v *Bowman*, 91 Pa 414, *Demi* v *Bossler*, 1 Pen: & W. 224.

[39]*McKay* v. *Pearson*, 6 Pa Super Ct 529

The tenant took the straw of the crop, when, in the opinion of the landlord, he should not, the landlord brought trover   *Craig* v *Dale*, 1 Watts & S 509, 37 Am Dec 477, *Iddings* v *Nagle*, 2 Watts & S 22

[40]*McKay* v *Pearson*, 6 Pa. Super. Ct 529

[41]*Rank* v. *Rank*, 5 Pa. 211

bound to accept the permission. If he does, and the crop has
been damaged by the delay, he will be entitled to recover the
difference between what would have been the value of the crop if
cut when application to cut it was denied, and its lesser value,
cut now.[42] Besides the remedies mentioned, the tenant may replevy the crop, in the hands of the landlord or succeeding tenant, or the purchaser of the reversion at a judicial sale,[43] or, as
the tenant has the right to the possession of the field so far as
is necessary to enable him to harvest the crop and remove it, he
can maintain trespass against one who enters, cuts, and takes
away the crop.[44]

605. Origin of tenant's right — In the earliest cases, the right
of the tenant, when not expressed in the lease, was held to be
founded on a custom which, as a fact, had to be proved by witnesses. In *Stultz* v. *Dickey*,[45] in 1812, "many witnesses" swore
to such a custom, as existing in the year 1804, and reference is
there made to a case[46] arising in 1780, in which the custom was
proved by several witnesses. "When the custom of a country,"
said Tilghman, Ch J.,[47] "or of a particular place, is established, it may enter into the body of a contract without being
inserted. . . . In the nature of the thing, it is reasonable

[42]*McKay* v *Pearson,* 6 Pa Super
Ct 529   The refusal to allow the
tenant to take the crop is none the
less a conversion because the refuser
gains nothing by it

[43]*Whorley* v *Karper,* 20 Pa Super
Ct 347, *Yeager* v *Cassidy,* 16 Lanc
L Rev 305, affirmed in 12 Pa Super
Ct 232, 13 York Legal Record, 141
The landlord may replevy straw,
taken by the tenant in contravention
of the stipulation of the lease (*Hunt*
v *Scott,* 3 Pa Co Ct 411), and the
purchaser of the reversion at a sheriff's sale may bring replevin for the
crop   *McIlvaine* v *Souders,* 15 Lanc
L Rev 371   Futhey, J, said, in
Hunt v *Scott,* 3 Pa. Co Ct. 411, that,

the lease forbidding the tenant's tak
ing away the straw, the landlord
could obtain an injunction to pre
vent its removal   In an action of
trespass by the tenant, it is no de
fense that he was guilty of bad husbandry in planting the crop   He may
be compelled to pay damages for bad
husbandry, but does not forfeit the
crop   *Clark* v *Harvey,* 54 Pa 142
   "*Dutton* v *Wetmore,* 10 Pa Super
Ct 530
   [45]5 Binn 285, 6 Am Dec 411
   [46]*Diffedorffer* v *Jones,* 5 Binn 289,
6 Am Dec 413
   [47]*Stultz* v *Dickey,* 5 Binn 285, 6
Am Dec 411.

that where a lease commences in the spring of one year, and ends in the spring of another, the tenant should have the crop of winter grain sown by him the autumn before the lease expired; otherwise he pays for the land one whole year without having the benefit of a winter crop If the parties intend otherwise, it is easy to control the custom by an express provision in the lease " In the later cases, the courts recognized the tenant's right without any proof of a custom,[48] saying that it was a part of the common law of the state,[49] and, the trial judge having mentioned the right as being according to the custom of Pennsylvania, Kennedy, J., remarked, "according to the custom thereof, or law thereof, they ought rather to have said,"[50] and denied the right of a landlord to show a custom that though to the tenant belonged the way-going crop, the straw of it was excepted, and belonged to the landlord. The lease may, it is scarcely necessary to state, expressly confer upon the tenant the privilege of taking the way-going crop,[51] and it may likewise deny that right.[52] A let land to B at $400 per year, ending April 1st, 1893. On December 16th, 1892, a lease for the next year was made at a rent of $400, providing that B should have what crops the farm might produce, and "is to get all of the crops now sown and growing, but is to put out another crop of wheat in the fall of 1893 at his own cost, to equal the crop now sown." B continued from year to year in possession until April 1st, 1900 He was entitled to the way-going crop, the evidence not clearly showing a contrary intention of the parties [53]

606. Emblements.— To the way-going crop the tenant for a

[48]*Forsythe* v *Price*, 8 Watts, 282, 34 Am Dec 465, *Biggs* v *Brown*, 2 Serg & R 14

[49]*Shaw* v *Bowman*, 91 Pa 414, *McKay* v. *Pearson*, 6 Pa Super Ct 529.

[50]*Craig* v *Dale*, 1 Watts & S 509, 37 Am Dec 477

[51]*Miller* v. *Clement*, 40 Pa 484;

Yeager v *Cassidy*, 16 Lanc L Rev 305, *McKay* v *Pearson*, 6 Pa Super Ct 529.

[52]*Stultz* v *Dickey*, 5 Binn 285, 6 Am Dec 411, *Clark* v *Harvey*, 54 Pa 142, *Whorley* v *Karper*, 20 Pa Super Ct 347

[53]*Whorley* v *Karper*, 20 Pa Super Ct 347.

definite term had no right, by the English common law, "For
the tenant knew," says Blackstone,[54] "the expiration of his
term, and therefore it was his own folly to sow what he could
never reap the profits of." But, "If a tenant for his own life
sows the lands and dies before harvest, his executors shall have
the emblements or profits of the crop, for the estate was determined by the act of God, and it is a maxim in the law that,
Actus Dei nemini facit injuriam."[55] "Where the lease for
years depends upon an uncertainty, as upon the death of a lessor,
being himself only tenant for life, or being a husband seised in
right of his wife; or, if the term of years be determinable upon
a life or lives,—in all these cases, the estate for years not being
certainly to expire at a time foreknown, but merely by the act
of God, the tenant or his executors shall have the emblements in
the same manner that a tenant for life or his executors shall be
entitled thereto."[56]

607. The nature of the lease.— The lease may be made to run
until the death of the tenant or of some other person, or until
the lessor's will determines it. It may be made to last until
the occurrence of some other event, equally uncertain. It may
be for a definite time, but, because of the defeasibleness of the
lessor's interest at any time, be liable to termination before the
expiration of that time. It may be subject to conditions subsequent. It may be stated generally, that if a lease, the time of
whose termination cannot be foreseen when a crop is put into
the ground, comes to an end before the crop matures, the tenant,
his assignee, or his executor, or administrator, will be entitled
to the crop at its maturity, and, incidentally, to its being permitted to grow in the soil until it becomes ripe. Thus, a life
tenant's executor will own the crop planted by him before his
death, but still in the ground when he dies. So, if the life tenant lets the land to another for a definite term of years, he can

[54] 2 Bl Com 145   [56] 2 Bl Com 145
[55] 2 Bl Com 122.

safely plant, not only the crop which will mature within that term, but that also which, planted in the fall, will not ripen until after its end To whatever crops his lessor's executors would have been entitled, the tenant will be entitled [57] If the landlord's interest is sold in execution, after crops of the tenant have been sown, whether the execution has been issued before the sowing of the crop[38] or not, the tenant may, nevertheless, take the crop, though his lease has determined by the will of the sheriff's vendee. The tenant at will owns crops sown before the lessor's will to terminate the tenure was made known.[39] If the lease for five years provides for its earlier termination in case of sale of the reversion and three months' notice to quit, and in the fall of the third year the reversion is sold and the tenant surrenders, whether with or without notice, at a time when there is a crop in the ground, the tenant will own this crop, though but little of it had been sown when he became aware of the sale. Knowledge of the sale is not equivalent to the notice.[60]

608 Lease terminable by act of party.—The lease may be terminable by the act of the tenant. It may last until marriage, and he may marry.[61] It may be subject to a condition subsequent, the tenant may violate the condition, and the landlord may re-enter, or, under a warrant in the lease, obtain a judgment in ejectment, and recover possession by a *habere facias possessionem*.[62] The lease may be surrendered by the tenant, or he may forfeit it.[63] In all such cases, the loss of the estate in the land involves the loss of the ownership of the crops. Distinction must be made between the emblements of a life tenant, and the rent, though payable in kind, to the life tenant. His share, as

[57]*Reiff* v *Reiff*, 64 Pa. 134. Cf. *Borie* v *Crissman*, 82 Pa. 125

[58]*Adams* v *McKesson*, 53 Pa 81, 91 Am Dec 183

[59]*Bittinger* v *Baker*, 29 Pa 66, 70 Am Dec 154

[60]*Comfort* v. *Duncan*, 1 Miles (Pa) 229.

[61]*Bittinger* v *Baker*, 29 Pa 66, 70 Am Dec 154, *Waugh* v *Waugh*, 84 Pa 350, 24 Am Rep 191.

[62]*Hunter* v *Jones*, 7 Phila 233

[63]*Waugh* v *Waugh*, 84 Pa. 350, 24 Am. Rep. 191.

landlord, of the crops is rent, and on his death, as rent, passes, if it be not then due, to the reversioner or remainderman, as well as to the life tenant's executor or administrator, subject to apportionment.[63½]

609. Nature of the crops.—"The vegetable chattels called emblements," says Read, J., "are the corn and other growth of the earth which are produced annually; not spontaneously, but by labor and industry, and thence are called, *fructus industriales."* In this class, Chapman, J , admitted that corn, wheat, rye, oats, buckwheat, potatoes, hemp, Hungarian grass, flax, and millet belong. He denied, however, that clover, timothy, and meadow grass are of it The former are annual products; when they are cut the root dies. But clover does not mature until the second summer, timothy not until the third. The meadow grass is perennial. The suggestion that the representative of the life tenant, or a tenant under him might, two or three years after the end of the term by the life tenant's death, enter and cut these grasses, or turn cattle into the fields where they are grown, in order to graze upon them, would seem abhorrent. "But it would be arbitrary to say that these grasses could be taken the first year after the close of the term, but not in later years." If the tenant is entitled to the first yield of grass, why not to the second, third, and fourth, or until the root is exhausted ?" A life tenant having made three leases of the land to A for three successive years, the last of which ended on April 1st, 1869, died June 15th, 1868. There was then standing uncut on the premises mixed timothy and clover grass, timothy, and grass part meadow and part timothy It was held that the life tenant's executor, had she been in possession of the land at her death, would not have been entitled to these grasses as emblements; and therefore that her tenant was not entitled to them. They were properly cut and hauled away by the remainderman.[64] Manure made by

[63½]Cf *Bone* v *Crissman,* 82 Pa 125, *Waugh* v *Waugh,* 84 Pa. 350, 24 Am Rep 191   [64]*Reiff* v. *Reiff,* 64 Pa 134 "The growing crop of grass, even if grown

cattle that have been fed on the premises with the grain and straw raised on them is not an emblement.[65]

610. Crop in the ground at commencement of term.—Crops in the ground when the lease is made do not become the property of the lessee unless the lease so stipulates. Nor is it usual for the lease so to stipulate   The lease made in November may, however, provide that the tenant shall have one half of all the farm may produce from its date to the expiration of the term, and this would probably entitle the lessee to one half of the crop of wheat in the ground when the lease was made, and belonging to the lessor   It would, however, give no right to any portion of it if the landlord had previously sold it to another, who did not estop himself from asserting his ownership. If the prior purchaser of the crop knows of the making of the lease, and of its containing a sale of half of the crop to the lessee, and is present at the negotiation, it will be his duty to give notice to the lessee of his title; but knowledge simply that a lease was being made would impose on him no duty to suspect that it would undertake to sell a portion of his crop to the lessee   The owner of the crop could maintain trespass against the lessee and any other, though an attorney at law, who, having a joint interest in it, counselled him to take and appropriate it.[66]

611 Hay and fodder on the premises.—Hay and fodder on the premises at the time the lessee enters into possession do not become his unless the lease so stipulates. Perhaps a custom that they should, at his option, become his, provided that he compensated the lessor on removing from the premises, either in money

---

from seed, and though ready to be cut for hay," says Read, J , "cannot be taken as emblements, because, as it is said, the improvement is not distinguishable from what is natural product, although it may be increased by cultivation "
  Corn and potatoes are emblements.
Hunter v *Jones*, 7 Phila 233

[65]*Pearson* v *Friedensville Zinc Co* 1 Pa Co Ct 660   Emblements are here stated to be "products of the earth that grow yearly and are raised by annual expense and labor "
  [66]*Dutton* v *Wetmore*, 10 Pa Super. Ct 530

or in an equivalent amount of hay and fodder, would be valid, and if proven would be assumed to enter into the contract between the parties   But a custom that they should become the lessee's absolutely would be "so wholly unreasonable that it could not be set up as a defense " It would be "a custom that the tenant may use the property of his landlord without making compensation. The tenant might, with equal propriety, have set up a custom that his landlord should pay his debts or give him his share of the crops." Hence, if, in the absence of any agreement, the tenant feeds to his cattle hay and cornstalks which were on the land when he entered, he will be compelled to pay their value in an appropriate action.[67]

612. Timber.— The right of the lessee with respect to timber growing on the premises may be regulated by the lease   The lease, *e. g ,* may give to the tenant the privilege of "selling posts and rails from fallen or burnt timber, the removal of which may benefit the growing timber." This would give the right, when an extensive fire swept over the land,—a furnace property,— killing a large number of trees, to make posts and rails from these trees, and to sell them   If, by arrangement with the lessor, he sells this ruined timber, the lessee will be entitled to what he would have made, had he exercised his privilege of converting it into posts and rails [68]

613. Hay, straw, fodder — The lessee's covenant may limit his right with respect to the crops raised by him. He may stipulate, *e g.,* that he will "not remove any hay .   .   or anything that can be converted into manure,"[69] or that all hay, straw, and corn fodder which may be raised from the premises are "to be consumed thereon" except an amount equal to what the tenant buys or brings upon the premises and uses there,[70] or that he will

[67] *Inewalt* v *Hummel,* 109 Pa 271. The custom was insufficiently proved, also
[68] *Stevens's Estate,* 11 Lanc. L Rev. Rep 22.
[69] *Donnon* v *Moore,* 1 Chester Co. Rep 65
[70] *Sharpless* v. *Murphy,* 7 Del Co.

not sell any straw, hay, or fodder, but feed the same in the barn-yard, nor keep on the place more than fifteen cattle or four horses, he having the privilege of feeding a sufficient quantity of hay in the barn when the lease is made, to keep the stock until grass grows in the pasture, on condition that he leave an equal amount of hay in quantity and quality when he vacates the premises.[71] If, being notified by the lessor to quit, on account of nonpayment of the rent, the tenant vacates the prem-ises and takes off a quantity of the hay and corn fodder, in violation of his covenant, the lessor may recover it in replevin,[72] or he may recover damages in assumpsit for the breach of the lessee's covenant. The measure of damages would, according to Waddell, J., be the value of the hay at the time of its removal. If, *e. g.,* despite the lessee's covenant not to sell any hay, but to feed it in the barnyard, he removes some at the end of his term, the sum recoverable from him would not be the value of the manure, merely, that would have been made from the hay if fed on the farm, but the market value of the hay itself.[73] On the other hand, Clayton, P J., held, under a lease forbidding the sale or removal of any hay, straw, or corn fodder, that for a breach of this covenant, the lessee would have to pay the land-lord the value of manure only which the hay removed would have made,—that is, instead of $14 or $15 per ton, the value of the hay, $2 or $3 per ton of hay, the value of the manure that would have been made from it [74]

[71]*Young* v. *Watters,* 5 Pa Co. Ct 127.

[72]*Donnon* v. *Moore,* 1 Chester Co. Rep 65

[73]*Young* v. *Watters,* 5 Pa Co Ct 127

[74]*Sharpless* v *Murphy,* 7 Del Co. Rep 22 The lease stipulated that for the violation of his agreement, the tenant should forfeit and pay $15 for every ton of hay, straw, or corn-fodder, as liquidated damages This was held to be a penalty, and not enforceable There was no diffi-culty in ascertaining the actual dam-ages In *Plumstead* v *Conway,* 2 Del Co Rep 43, the lessor, A, orally promised the tenant, B, that all the straw and hay not consumed by the outgoing tenant should be left for B's

use, the former to be converted into manure and used on the farm, the latter to be fed on the farm, and B to pay for it at $10 per ton A, for $46, allowed the outgoing tenant to sell all the hay and straw B purchased 10 tons at $20 per ton B's damages must be not less than $46 and as much more as the jury should find B had actually lost; but the measure of this damage was not the difference between $10 and $20 per ton, since B was not to get for $10 an absolute property in the hay, and since the outgoing tenant's leaving any was contingent He might have fed it all to his stock.

CHAPTER XXIX.

TRANSFER OF REVERSION DURING THE TERM.

614. Lease no obstacle — The existence of a lease is no legal obstacle to the transfer by the lessor, pending it, of the reversion The grantee will acquire the reversion, subject to the existing lease, if the lease is on record, or there is possession of the premises under it The lessee may assert all the rights conferred on him, or insist on the performance by the grantee of all the grantor's covenants that run with the land. If, *e. g.*, the lease gives the lessee the option to buy the premises in fee, and possession is held under it when the lessor grants the reversion, the lessee or his assignee may enforce his equity against the lessor's alienee.[1]

[1] *Kerr* v *Day*, 14 Pa 112, 53 Am Dec 526. After A and B, tenants in
523

615. Effect of transfer on rent.— When the landlord conveys his reversion during the term of a lease, the grantee acquires the land, subject, usually, to the lease; but while he has no right as grantee to rent which has already become payable, though in fact not paid,[2] he becomes entitled to all the rent which, by the terms of the lease, becomes payable after his ownership begins. If the rent, e. g , is payable monthly, to the grantee becomes payable the first rent falling due after his acquisition, and all subsequent instalments.[3] If the rent is payable quarterly, or semiannually, or annually, to him becomes payable the first quarter's or half year's or year's rent falling due after he becomes owner   If quarterly rent is payable in advance, and being due, an instalment for the next three months is paid on April 1st, one who obtains a conveyance of the reversion on the following May 1st will be entitled to no rent for the quarter ending June 30th   He will not be allowed to withhold from the purchase money two thirds of the rent paid to his grantor on April 1st [4]

616 Action for rent by assignee.— Whether, at common law, the alienee of the reversion could maintain, in his own name, an action on the covenant in the lease for rent, or not, this right was secured by the statute, 32 Hen. VIII., chap 34, which is in force in Pennsylvania. Under this statute the assignee of the reversion may, for rent becoming due after his acquisition, bring covenant against the lessee upon such express covenants as run with the estate in the land demised, and the covenant for

common, have made a lease to C, with option to purchase, B transfers his interest in the land to A   A subsequently transfers the reversion to X   C transfers his lessee's interests to B   B can defend his possession in ejectment by X by means of his right to become a purchaser
[2]*Neubold* v   *Comfort,* 2   Clark (Pa) 331. The grantor may also assign his right to the already due rent, to the grantee, who then, as assignee, may recover such rent
[3]*Neubold* v   *Comfort,* 2   *Clark* (Pa) 331, No 2 *Assistance Bldg & L Asso* v   *Wampole,* 6 Pa Super. Ct 238
[4]*Singer* v *Solomon,* 8 Pa. Dist. R. 402

payment of rent is one of these [5]   Indeed, for nonpayment of rent, or for other breaches of covenants, which occur after the transfer of the reversion, only the transferee, in his own name, can maintain the action.   An action to his use, but in the name of the lessor, must fail [6] For rent which has fallen due before the transfer of the reversion, even though it has been assigned to the transferee of the reversion, the action must be in the name of the lessor, to the use of the assignee, unless the assignment has been made, as the act of May 28th, 1715,[7] dictates, for the passing of the legal title to a chose in action.[8]

617 Transfer by death.— On the death of the lessor during the term, the right to receive the rents falling due subsequently passes to his heirs,[9] or devisees,[10] and not to the administrator or executor.   It matters not whether the rent is payable in money or in kind   Thus, at the death of the landlord September 23d, 1861, there was a crop of corn in the ground which was not severed from the ground until October 15th   This crop passed altogether to the heirs [11]   "It was a growing crop at the death of the intestate," says Woodward, J , "and was harvested and divided afterward, the tenant taking his part, and delivering to the heir the landlord's share.   As a rent payable in kind it

[5]*Newbold* v. *Comfort,* 2 Clark (Pa) 331, *Hemphill* v *Eckfeldt,* 5 Whart 274.

[6]*Stoddard* v *Emery,* 128 Pa 436, 18 Atl 339

[7] 1 Pepper & Lewis Digest, 350, 1 Smith's Laws, 90

[8]*Newbold* v. *Comfort,* 2 Clark (Pa.) 331

The lessor may convey to X, to whom also the lease may be assigned by the lessee   The rent will be merged   By agreement the lessor may be entitled to a part of the rent accruing, but not due, when he makes his conveyance.   *Lyon* v *Houk,* 9 Watts, 193.

[9]*Merkel's Estate,* 131 Pa 584, 18 Atl 931, *M'Coy* v *Scott,* 2 Rawle, 222, 19 Am Dec 640, *Bakes* v *Reese,* 150 Pa 44, 24 Atl 634, *Haslage* v *Krugh,* 25 Pa 97, *Heges' Estate,* 12 Lane L Rev 105, *Johnston* v *Smith,* 3 Penr & W 496, 24 Am Dec 339

The tenant cannot renounce the existing lease and take another from the administrator, and discharge himself from the rent in respect to the heirs, by paying the administrator   *Haslage* v *Krugh,* 25 Pa 97

[10]*Cobel* v *Cobel,* 8 Pa 342, *Schwartz's Estate,* 14 Pa 42

[11]*McDowell* v *Addams,* 45 Pa. 430

passed with the inheritance and belonged to the heir rather than the administrator."

618. Transfer by death of life owner.—At common law, when a life owner, having made a lease, died before the rent under it had become payable, no right to the rent, or any portion of the rent, passed to his administrators or executor. It passed, instead to the remainderman or reversioner. The 7th section of the act of February 24th, 1834,[12] enacts that the rent accruing to any tenant for life who has demised the land for a term of time not fully expired at his decease, shall go to his executor or administrator, "and the due proportion of such accruing rent, to be computed according to the time elapsed at the decease of such tenant, shall be included in the inventory of personal assets;" and the 30th section of the same act secures to the executor or administrator of a life owner an apportionment of rent accruing for the "last year or quarter of a year, or other current period of payment" Application of this rule was made in *Borie* v. *Crissman*.[13] A life tenant made a lease for one year, commencing April 1st, 1874, reserving a share of the crops Spring and fall crops were put in by the lessee, the former before June 1st, and the latter before September 12th. The lessor died September 18th, 1874. The fall crop was not harvested until July, 1875 "The combined value of these products," says Gordon, J., "would be the rent for the current period, and it ought to be apportioned according to the theory above stated So that part of said rent now in the hands of the administrator [*viz*, the spring crops], and which is the subject-matter of the case stated, should be divided between the parties [the administrator of the lessor and the remainderman] in the same proportion that the time from the beginning of the lease to the death of Mrs. Crissman bears to the whole year "[14]

---

[12] 1 Pepper & Lewis Digest, 1474; P L 70
[13] 82 Pa 125.

[14] The parties asked the court to indicate the proportion of the full crop that would be payable to Mr.

619. Transfer by sheriff's sale.— The 119th section of the act of June 16th, 1836,[15] enacts that, on a sale of land in execution, which, at the time of such sale or afterwards, shall be held by a tenant or lessee under the defendant in the execution, the purchaser of such land "shall, upon receiving the deed for the same, be deemed the landlord of such tenant, lessee, . . . and shall have the like remedies to recover any rents or sums accruing subsequently to the acknowledgment of a deed to him as aforesaid, whether such accruing rent may have been paid in advance or not, if paid after the rendition of the judgment on which sale was made, as such defendant might have had, if no such sale had been made." If the sheriff's sale has taken place on a lien arising later than the making of the lease, the purchaser takes subject to the lease [16] If, however, it was on a lien, e. g., a mortgage[17] or judgment,[18] a mechanic's lien,[19] which already existed when the lease was made, the right of the purchaser at the sheriff's sale is superior to that of the tenant. The 105th section of the act of June 16th, 1836,[20] authorizes the purchaser to give notice to the persons in possession, whether it be the defendant in the execution, or any who are in possession "under him, by title derived from him subsequently to the judg-

Crissman's administrator, but the supreme court does not explicitly refer to this point

[15] 1 Pepper & Lewis Digest, 1993

This act does not apply to the case of a cropper, e g, to one who is hired by the landowner to work the land and receive as compensation a portion of the crop *Adams* v *McKesson*, 53 Pa 81, 91 Am Dec 183 Cf *Fry* v *Jones*, 2 Rawle, 11

If B is in possession of A's land under an agreement to pay rent, the amount of rent not being defined, from March 3d, 1863, to April 1st, 1864, and the compensation becomes due on the latter date, a sheriff's vendee at a sale July 15th, 1863, is entitled to the compensation for the thirteen months *Hayden* v *Patterson*, 51 Pa 261

[16]*Halo* v *Schick*, 57 Pa 319

[17]*Garrett* v *Deuart*, 43 Pa 342, 82 Am Dec 570, *Hemphill* v *Tevis*, 4 Watts & S. 535, *Stockton's Appeal*, 64 Pa 58, *No 2 Assistance Bldg & L Asso* v *Wampole*, 6 Pa Super Ct 238 *Duff* v *Wilson*, 69 Pa 316

[18]*Menough's Appeal*, 5 Watts & S. 432, *Farmers' & M Bank* v *Ege*, 9 Watts, 436, 36 Am Dec 130, *Bittinger* v *Baker*, 29 Pa 66, 70 Am Dec 154, *Hoover* v. *Hoover* 10 Pa Co Ct 563, *Wilson* v *Hubbell*, 1 Pennyp 413

[19]*Walbridge's Appeal*, 95 Pa 466

[20] 1 Pepper & Lewis Digest, 1987

ment under which the same [the lands or tenements] were sold, and require him or them to surrender the possession thereof to him within three months from the date of such notice."[21]   The vendee's title is not so far perfected that he may give this notice, until the delivery of the sheriff's deed.[22]

620. Election of sheriff's vendee to disaffirm.— The purchaser at the sheriff's sale has the option to affirm or disaffirm the lease. If he chooses to affirm, the tenant will remain bound by the terms and provisions of the lease.   If he chooses to disaffirm, he loses all rights under the lease and, *inter alia,* the right to rent,[23] and, as incident thereto, the right to be paid it from the proceeds of an execution sale of the tenant's goods on the premises.[24]   The sheriff's vendee of the reversion elects to disaffirm the lease when he gives notice to the tenant to remove in three months [25] He elects, on the other hand, to affirm the lease, when he demands rent or receives payment of rent from the lessee,[26] as, *e. g ,* when he gives notice to the tenant that he claims the landlord's share of the grain, the lease providing for rent in kind ,[27] or when he enters a judgment for the rent on a warrant of attorney in the lease.[28]   In a suit by the landlord for an instalment of rent payable in advance for a period of time within which the sheriff's sale has taken place, before the suit was begun, the absence of an election by the sheriff's vendee to affirm, whereby the tenant is in peril of losing, in part, the consideration for

---

[21] A sheriff's sale on a judgment entered after the lease, upon a bond accompanying a mortgage executed before the lease, will discharge the mortgage, and the sheriff's vendee may eject the lessee   *M'Call* v *Lenox,* 9 Serg & R 302

[22] *Hawk* v *Stouch,* 5 Serg & R 157

[23] *Garrett* v *Deuart,* 43 Pa 342, 82 Am Dec 570

[24] *Farmers' & M Bank* v *Ege,* 9 Watts, 436, 36 Am Dec 130.

[25] *Farmers' & M Bank* v *Ege,* 9 Watts, 436, 36 Am Dec 130 , *Hemphill* v *Tevis,* 4 Watts & S 535

[26] *No 2 Assistance Bldg & L Asso* v *Wampole,* 6 Pa Super Ct 238

[27] *Garrett* v *Deuart,* 43 Pa 342, 82 Am Dec. 570

[28] *Israel* v *Clough,* 5 Pa. Dist R 325   Prior notice to the tenant of the election is unnecessary if the tenant in fact knows of the purchase.

the rent sued for, will be a defense.   The burden is on the plaintiff to prove the affirmance.[29]   If, after notice to quit by the sheriff's vendee, the lessee continues in possession, he is not liable for the rent mentioned in the lease for the period of his occupancy, though he will be liable for the actual value of the possession in an assumpsit for use and occupation [30] If the sheriff's vendee chooses to eject the tenant by the action of ejectment, he does not need to give three months' notice to quit.[31]

621. Rent paid in advance — The sheriff's vendee is entitled to the rent accruing after his purchase, "whether such accruing rent may have been paid in advance or not, if paid after the rendition of the judgment on which sale was made."   It is understood, however, that the provision of the statute does not preclude the making, after a lien is on the premises, of a lease which shall stipulate for payment in advance.   Such lease, with such stipulation, being made, the lessee may safely pay the rent in advance, according to its terms.   The lease, e g , for a term beginning April 1st, requiring the year's rent to be paid in advance, the rent belongs to the lessor, and not to one who purchased at a sheriff's sale the title of the lessor, and obtained the sheriff's deed on August 24th [32]   If the lease authorizes the tenant to apply the rent payable in grain to a debt of the lessor for which the tenant is surety, one who becomes the sheriff's

[29]*Market Co.* v. *Lutz,* 4 Phila 322 Sharswood, J , suggests that until there has been an affirmance, the purchaser may disaffirm at any time, and, therefore, he might disaffirm after the former landlord had compelled the tenant to pay the rent sued for   In *Murphy* v *Cawley,* 7 Kulp, 128, Rice, P J., assumes that until it is shown that the purchaser has disaffirmed, he must be taken to have affirmed   The proceeding was a rule to open the judgment for the rent

[30]*Hemphill* v *Tevis,* 4 Watts & S. LAND. & TEN. 34.

535   The former tenant would not be estopped from denying his liability for the rent of the lease, because, in a suit for a recovery of rent for a period following the notice to quit, but preceding that for which the present action is brought, there had been a recovery.

[31]*M'Call* v. *Lenox,* 9 Serg & R 302

[32]*"Farmers' & M Bank* v *Ege,* 9 Watts, 436, 36 Am Dec 130, *Market Co* v *Lutz,* 4 Phila 322. *Menough's Appeal,* 5 Watts & S. 432.

vendee, during the term, cannot require the rent to be paid to him [33]   If the landlord induces the tenant to accept a renewal lease, by agreeing that he may make improvements and apply the cost of them to the rent, he has a right to make these improvements and to be credited with their cost upon the rent, even though such credit extinguishes rent beginning to accrue, as well as falling due and payable after the sheriff's sale of the reversion.[34]   A judgment note being given for rent at the making of the lease, on which judgment was not entered until after the sale of the lessor's reversion, the court will not, after the judgment has been paid, open it, in the absence of evidence that the sheriff's vendee has elected to disaffirm the lease (or to require the tenant to pay the rent over again).[35]

622. Rent assigned before sheriff's sale — If, after the recovery of the judgment on which the reversion is subsequently sold, the lessor assigns the rent, the assignee gets no title, as against the subsequent sheriff's vendee.   The term commencing April 2d, 1839, the lessor, notwithstanding that a judgment had been recovered March 13th against him, assigned the rent on August 12th, 1839.   The sheriff's deed was made November 9th, 1839. A sale of the whole crop was effected on an execution against the tenant   The sheriff's vendee, and not the lessor's assignee, was entitled to the landlord's share   "The accruing rent," says Sergeant, J , "runs with the land, and cannot be separated from it by the act of the debtor before it is due, as against the purchaser under the judgment.   The right to the current rent is a mere contingency, made indefeasibly subject to the will of the subsequent purchaser at sheriff's sale, by the act of 1836.   The act prohibits the payment of the rent in advance, where such

---

[33]*Fullerton* v *Shauffer,* 12 Pa 220 But in *Bittinger* v *Baker,* 29 Pa 66, 70 Am Dec 154, Lowrie, J , says of this case that it is "so defectively reported that we cannot regard it as an authority for anything "

[34]*Kost* v *Theis,* 20 W N C 545 Other advance payments in excess of any legal liability resting on the tenant would not be good against the sheriff's vendee
[35]*Murphy* v *Cauley,* 7 Kulp 128

has not been the express stipulation, and the right to sell and assign the rent in advance would produce the same effect as payment of it in advance." [36]   An order from the lessor on the tenant to let X have the lessor's share of the grain, and an acceptance of the order, April 16th, 1842, will not entitle X to it, as against one to whom the sheriff conveyed the lessor's reversion December 13th, 1842, under a judgment recovered before the lease was made [37]   An assignment by the lessor for the benefit of his creditors made during the term, and after the lien on which the sheriff's sale of his reversion is subsequently made, will not confer on the assignee a right to the landlord's share, if the sheriff's vendee becomes such before the crops are payable [38]   In *King* v *Bosserman*,[39] there was a term ending April 1st, 1897.   On the preceding September 6th the lessor made an assignment for the benefit of creditors   The farm was sold by the sheriff on October 15th, 1896.   Previous to the sale, some of the corn planted that year had been severed, husked, garnered, and the landlord's share had been set apart in his crib   The rest of the corn was in the shock in the field, and none of it had been set apart for the landlord   It was held that the assignee was not entitled to the landlord's share of the corn which had not been set apart to him before the sheriff's deed was made, though it had been harvested

623. Sheriff's sale of the landlord's share.— A purchaser of the landlord's interest under a lease commencing April 1st, 1879, in the winter crop, under a fi fa. against him, cannot claim that interest as against one to whom the reversion is subsequently conveyed by the sheriff on January 19th, 1880 [40]   If, under the

---

[36]*Menough's Appeal,* 5 Watts & S. 432. The grain was possibly winter grain, sown in 1839

[37]*Boyd* v *McCombs,* 4 Pa 146 The rent was assumed not to be due until the end of the term, April 1st, 1843. A similar assumption was made in *Menough's Appeal,* 5 Watts & S 432   Cf *King* v *Bosserman,* 13 Pa Super Ct 480

[38]*Holtsman* v *Loudensleyer,* 1 Pearson (Pa) 241

[39] 13 Pa Super Ct 480

[40]*Long* v *Seavers,* 103 Pa 517.

custom of the county, the winter crop put in by the tenant is wholly the landlord's, a sheriff's sale in December, 1894, of his interest in this crop, will not pass it as against one who becomes the sheriff's grantee February 16th, 1895, the crop being in the ground.[41]

624. Attaching the rent.— The rent cannot be effectively attached in execution attachment so as to entitle the creditor of the landlord or his grantee to it, as against one who, in proceedings in bankruptcy, begun later, against the landlord or his grantee, is appointed assignee or trustee before the coming due of the rent.[42]

625 Money-rent; effect of sheriff's sale on right to crop.—If the tenant is to pay a money rent, the whole crop belongs to him. Should, therefore, there be, during the term, a sheriff's sale of the lessor's reversion, even on a lien prior to the making of the lease, the tenant will, nevertheless, retain the right to the entire crop. The lease being made for one year from April 1st, 1851, at a money rent, the sheriff's deed delivered April 22d, 1852, after the term had expired, on a sale upon a judgment entered May 23d, 1848, did not pass to the vendee a right to the crop which was put in the ground in the fall of 1851, but not cut till the summer of 1852.[43]

626 Other judicial sales.— The 119th section of the act of June 16, 1836, is concerned with sheriffs' sales in execution. The lessor's interest may be destroyed by other judicial sales, e. g , by a sale in partition proceedings,[44] or by an administrator's sale under the order of the orphans' court for the payment of debts.[45] The effect of such sales is similar to that of non-

[41]*Loose* v. *Scharff*, 6 Pa Super. Ct. 153

[42]*Evans* v *Hamrick*, 61 Pa 19, 100 Am Dec 595 The rent was money

[43]*Bullinger* v *Baker*, 29 Pa 66, 70 Am Dec 154 *Sallade* v *James*, 6 Pa 144, and *Groff* v *Levan*, 16 Pa. 179, are overruled.

[44]*Burns* v *Cooper*, 31 Pa 426

[45]*Strange* v *Austin*, 134 Pa 96, 19 Atl 492, *Lau's Estate* 20 Phila. 10, *Marys* v *Anderson*, 24 Pa 272, 2 Grant Cas 446.

judicial sales.   The guardian of the heirs making a lease, a sale
in partition takes place on November 7th, shortly after the
tenant has sown a crop of wheat.   The purchaser becomes the
owner of the landlord's share.[46]   A lease being made March
30th, 1887, by the widow and heirs, an administrator's sale took
place on the 25th of June following   The rent was payable in
two semiannual instalments on October 1st, 1887, and February
1st, 1888.   The deed was delivered to the purchaser on March
1st, 1888.   As all the rent had become payable before the delivery of the deed, none of it belonged to the purchaser [47]   When
the rent fell due on the last moment of March 31st, 1849, and
the deed was, by the terms of sale, not to be delivered to the purchaser at the administrator's sale until April 1st, the rent was
payable before the right to receive the deed.   None of it was
payable to the purchaser, although April 1st being Sunday, the
administrator in fact delivered the deed on March 31st.[48]

627. No apportionment of rent between lessor and grantee.—
If, when a conveyance is made by the lessor, no reservation with
respect to rent is made, the grantee becomes entitled to the rent
that becomes payable after the conveyance, however much of the
period for possession during which the rent is the consideration,
precedes, and however little of it follows, the conveyance.   The
parties may, however, agree upon an apportionment of the rent
by the ratio of the part of the rent period which precedes the
conveyance to the part which follows it,[49] or in any other way.
When they do not, a year's, a quarter's, a month's, rent would be
payable to the grantee, where purchase was made at any time
during the year, quarter, or month , no portion of it would belong
to the grantor.   Hence, if the purchaser is the lessee himself,

[46]*Burns* v *Cooper*, 31 Pa 426
[47]*Strange* v *Austin*, 134 Pa 96, 19
Atl 492 , *Law's Estate*, 20 Phila 10
[48]*Marys* v *Anderson*, 24 Pa 272, 2
Grant Cas 440
[49]*Lamberton* v. *Stouffer*, 55 Pa.
284 , *Johnston* v *Smith*, 3 Penr. &
W 496, 24 Am Dec 339
    An agreement for apportionment
may be made.   *Lyon* v. *Houk*, 9
Watts, 193

he will not be liable for any portion of the rent which did not
become payable prior to the purchase [50]   The same principle
applies when the title of the lessor is sold in execution.   The
rent, *e. g.,* being payable every six months, if the sheriff's deed is
delivered only thirteen days before the close of one of the semi-
annual periods, the purchaser will be entitled to the whole six
months' rent.[51]   If the rent is payable yearly, and the sale
occurs between the termini of a year, the purchaser may distrain for a full year's rent.   He is not bound to accept a tender
of an apportioned part of it [52]   A lease for four years, reserving
rent payable at the end of each year, ending April 1st, 1838,
and the sheriff's deed being delivered January 5th, 1838, the
purchaser was entitled to a full year's rent; and not merely to
one quarter of it.[53]   An assignee for the benefit of creditors
leased, in July, 1869, the premises until April 1st, 1870, for the
rent of $275.00   Prior to April 1st, 1870, a sheriff's sale
occurred on a judgment against the assignor.   As the vendee
had a right to receive all the rent, the assignee was not liable to
account for any of it [54]

628. When the alienee's title begins — When conveyances are
the subject of a prior contract, the parties will prescribe a time
when the deed is to be delivered and the tenant in possession is
to recognize the vendee as his landlord [55]   The 119th section of

---

[50]*Young* v *Jones*, 1 Lehigh Valley
Law Rep 175

If a quarter's rent is payable in
advance, a sale within the quarter
entitles the purchaser to none of that
quarter's rent   *Singer* v. *Solomon*,
8 Pa Dist R 402

[51]*Bank of Pennsylvania* v *Wise*,
3 Watts, 394

[52]*Hart* v *Israel*, 2 Browne (Pa)
22

[53]*Braddee* v *Wiley*, 10 Watts, 362,
Hayden v *Patterson*, 51 Pa 261,
Heir v *Binkley*, 1 Del Co Rep 391
8 Lanc L Rev 234

[54]*Sharpless's Estate*, 8 Lanc. Bar,
125

A letting to B a right of way over
his farm at an annual rent one who
bought at a sheriff's sale within the
year had a right to the year's rent
West v *Herrod* (Pa) 1 Cent Rep
924 2 Atl 871

[55] The contract being made June
24th, and the deed delivered July
14th, it was held that the grantee
had a right to the wheat crop cut on
July 10th, but an arrangement apportioning the landlord's share between lessor and grantee was carried

the act of June 16th, 1836, makes the acknowledgment and delivery of the deed to the purchaser the point from which he acquires the rights of a lessor   The rent being payable quarterly on the 20th of February, of May, of August, and of November, if the sale takes place on June 23d, but the deed is not acknowledged until September 6th, the vendee is not entitled to the quarter's rent falling due on August 20th [56]   The sale occurring in February, and the deed being delivered in June, the rent falling due between these dates belongs to the landlord, and not to the sheriff's vendee,[57] nor is the right of the vendee varied because, being required by the terms of sale to pay at the sale only one third of the price bid, the rest being payable on the delivery of the deed, he in fact pays the whole price when the land is knocked down to him [58]   The same principle is applicable to orphans' court sales [59]

629 When rent matures — There is no difficulty in determining when rent in money becomes payable   The lease usually states whether it is to be paid at intervals, and how long these intervals shall be,—years, quarters, months. If rent is to be paid in advance, the lease so specifies   Where no time for the payment is named, the rent is payable at the end, not at the beginning, or in the midst of the period for which it is payable   If the lease is for a year, at an unapportioned rent, the rent will be payable at the end of the year.[60] The year beginning on April 1st, it closes at the last minute of the following March 31st,[61] and the rent is payable the next day   If March 31st is Sat-

---

out   *Lamberton* v *Stouffer*, 55 Pa 284

[56]*Scheerer* v *Stanley*, 2 Rawle, 276 This was under the act of April 6th, 1802, 3 Smith's Laws, 535, which is re-enacted and supplied by that of 1836   *Bank of Pennsylvania* v *Wise*, 3 Watts, 394.

[57]*Third Nat Bank* v *Hanson*, 1 W N C 613, *Garrett* v *Dewart* 43 Pa 342 82 Am Dec. 570

[58]*Garrett* v *Dewart*, 43 Pa 342, 82 Am Dec 570   The fact that the lien on which the sheriff's sale took place preceded the making of the lease does not affect the question

[59]*Strange* v *Austin*, 134 Pa 96, 19 Atl 492, *Law's Estate*, 20 Phila 10

[60]*Menough's Appeal*, 5 Watts & S 432

[61]*Marys* v *Anderson*, 24 Pa 275

urday, the rent will be payable on the following Monday.[62] If
the transfer of the reversion occurs on the same day on which
the rent becomes payable, the alienee is not entitled to any portion of it,[63] and the terms of sale fixing the time when the deed
is to be delivered, an anticipation of the delivery of the deed by
the act of the officer who makes the sale, e. g , the administrator,
the sale being for the debts of the deceased owner, will not give
the vendee a right to the rent to which, had the terms been carried out, he would have had no right.[64]

630. **Rent in kind, when payable** — Rent payable in a portion of the crops is not payable, in the absence of a stipulation,
before the crops have been harvested. If the sale or devolution,
by death, of the reversion, is completed while any crop, spring[65]
or fall,[66] is in the ground, the landlord's share of that crop
passes to the alienee, whether the sale or devolution occurs within the year of the term in which the crop was sown,[67] or after
the close of that year, but before the winter crop, sown within

[62]*Marys* v. *Anderson,* 24 Pa 275,
Gregg v *Krebs,* 5 Pa Dist R 779

[63]*Marys* v *Anderson,* 24 Pa 272
On a demise for one year beginning
May 1st, the rent is said to be due
on the following May 1st, in *Prentiss*
v *Kingsley,* 10 Pa 120

[64]*Marys* v *Anderson,* 24 Pa 272
The deed was to have been delivered
on April 1st, 1849 That day being
Sunday, the administrator delivered
it on March 31st on which day the
year of the term closed The vendee
was not entitled to the year's rent

[65]*Lamberton* v *Stouffer,* 55 Pa
284, *Borie* v *Crissman,* 82 Pa 125,
Kauffman v *Schaeffer,* 2 Walk
(Pa) 331

[66]*Long* v *Seavers,* 103 Pa 517,
Johnston v *Smith,* 3 Penr & W
496, 24 Am Dec 339, *Lamberton* v
Stouffer, 55 Pa 284, *Loose* v
Scharf, 6 Pa Super Ct 153,
Adams v *McKesson,* 53 Pa 81, 91
Am Dec 183

[67] The lessor's share of wheat sown
in the fall of 1860, and ripening in
the summer of 1861, passed to one
who became purchaser at sheriff's
sale on Nov 2d, 1860, after the
wheat was sown. *Adams* v *McKesson,* 53 Pa 81, 91 Am Dec 183 Or
to one who bought from the lessor in
March, 1861 *Johnston* v *Smith,* 3
Penr. & W 496, 24 Am Dec 339
Cf *Lamberton* v *Stouffer,* 55 Pa
284, *Burns* v *Cooper,* 31 Pa 426
In *Borie* v *Crissman,* 82 Pa 125, the
lessor a life tenant who had leased
the land on shares, died September
18th 1874, a few days after the
wheat was sown The question was
presented to the court below, but
apparently not decided, as to whether
the administrator of the lessor or the
remainderman was entitled to the
landlord's share of the wheat when
it was cut in July, 1875.

it, has matured.[68] If the winter crop has been harvested before the conveyance of the reversion, it belongs to the lessor, and not to the alienee. Wheat and rye were sown in the fall of 1858, under a lease from year to year beginning on April 1st This grain was harvested the following summer, and subsequently, on November 19th, 1859, a sheriff's deed for the land was delivered to X. X had no right to the lessor's share of the wheat and rye[69] "At the utmost we cannot suppose," says Lowrie, Ch. J., "the term of 1858 to extend for this crop beyond harvest, 1859, and that cannot avail the defendant [the sheriff's vendee], for the sale was after that. It was therefore a sale after the expiration of the term out of which the rent accrued, and the purchaser has no right to that rent." If spring crops are harvested within the term in which they are sown, the landlord's share in them, apparently, belongs to one who becomes, within the term, though after their harvesting, a purchaser of the reversion The sheriff's deed being delivered November 19th, 1859, the vendee was entitled to the spring crops, though they had been harvested and garnered in the barn before that time.[70] A term beginning April 1st, 1882, a sheriff's deed for the reversion was delivered October 17th, 1882. Of the corn planted by the tenant, six sevenths had been cut before that

---

[68] The lease expiring April 1st 1847, the tenant had, the preceding winter, sown a wheat crop. The succeeding tenant sowed spring crops The landlord died in May, 1847 The heirs were entitled to his share of all the crops. *Cobel* v *Cobel*, 8 Pa 342 In *Lamberton* v *Stouffer*, 55 Pa 284, wheat sown in 1863 was cut on July 10th, 1864 The lessor contracted on June 24th, 1864, to sell the land to X, and on July 14th, 1864, the deed was delivered It was assumed that, in the absence of an agreement to the contrary, the crop belonged to the grantee, X The parties, however, agreed that the vendor should have a portion of the rent up to July 1st The term began April 1st It was held that the lessor had a right to one quarter of the landlord's share of the crop, and the vendee, X, three quarters

Sheriff's sale Nov 2d, 1860 The landlord's share in grain then in the ground, which is cut the following summer, passes to the purchaser *Adams* v *McKesson*, 53 Pa 81, 91 Am. Dec 183, *Burns* v. *Cooper*, 31 Pa 426

[69] *Borrell* v *Dewart*, 37 Pa 134, *Garrett* v *Dewart*, 43 Pa 342, 82 Am Dec 570

[70] *Borrell* v. *Dewart*, 37 Pa 134.

date, but none of it had been husked or divided. The purchaser
was entitled to the lessor's share in all of it.[71] In *Boyd* v. *Mc-
Combs*[72] the term is assumed to have begun April 1st, 1842. On
December 13th, 1842, a sheriff's deed for the reversion was delivered. It was held that though the tenant might deliver the
landlord's share of the crop before, he was, in the absence of
stipulation in the lease, not bound to deliver it before the end
of the year. It was then payable, and hence, even if it had in
fact been delivered before the sheriff's sale, or even if the tenant had obligated himself sixteen days after the term began, to
deliver the landlord's share to a third person, the sheriff's vendee
was entitled to it. "The rent, therefore," says Coulter, J.,
"which fell due on the 1st of April, 1843, although the same
might have been actually paid or an order accepted by the tenant for the payment of it before the acknowledgment of the
deed, followed the reversion, and was payable to the purchaser
at sheriff's sale." The lease may, however, fix a time when
the lessor's share shall be delivered, or may make it the tenant's
duty to deliver after the harvest, at a time to be designated by
the lessor, and, in accordance with the power thus reserved,
the lessor may have designated the time. In such a case, the
lessor's share is to be deemed payable when the time arrives
which is named in the lease, or on the designation of the lessor.
A sheriff's conveyance of the reversion after that time would
pass to the grantee no right to the crop, whether fall or spring.
A lease for three years began April 1st, 1859. It required the
lessee to deliver one half of all the grain to the lessor "in the
mow or crib" upon the premises. A crop of wheat was sown in

[71] *Hoover* v *Hoover*, 10 Pa Co Ct
563, *Holtsman* v *Loudensleyer*, 1
Pearson (Pa.) 241. In *King* v *Bosserman*, 13 Pa Super Ct 480, it is
apparently held that not the harvesting, but the subsequent setting apart
of the landlord's share, makes that
share his, as against the subsequent
sheriff's vendee. Hence, so much of
the crop as was divided and set apart
to the landlord, belonged to him, but
so much of it as, though harvested,
was as yet undivided, passed to the
subsequent sheriff's vendee.

[72] 4 Pa. 146.

September, 1859, and of oats in April, 1860. These crops were harvested and put in the mow in July, 1860 On August 1st, 1860, the lessor notified the tenant in writing to thresh and deliver his share of the crop by the 1st day of September. A sheriff's sale of the premises was consummated by the delivery of the deed on the 27th day of September. The crops were in fact not delivered to the lessor. They nevertheless belonged to him, and not to the sheriff's vendee [73] "We are of opinion," says Strong, J., "that the rent which is in controversy in this case had accrued before the acknowledgment and delivery of the deed to the purchasers at sheriff's sale.   .   .   . Now, if it be conceded that the time of delivery in the mow was not the time fixed for the payment of the rent, it is not to be questioned that the rent was payable when the landlord directed the grain to be threshed and delivered. It matters not what the custom of the country is in regard to the time of threshing The parties did not leave the time to be determined by custom. *They defined it by their contract.*"[74] Nor has it anything to do with the case that the grain may not in fact have been so delivered as to vest the ownership in "the landlord so as to enable him to maintain replevin."

631 Conveying part of reversion.—If the lessor conveys a part of the leased premises during the term, his grantee becomes *ipso facto* entitled to a share of the rent [75] If he dies, and several persons inherit the land, there is an apportionment between them of the rent [76] If two cotenants make a lease, and one of them assigns his interest in the rent or royalty, he does not apportion the rent in such sense that the tenant cannot safely pay the whole rent to the assignee until he receives notice from the

[73] *Garrett* v *Dewart*, 43 Pa 342, 82 Am Dec 570

[74] Italics not used in the opinion

[75] *Reed* v *Ward*, 22 Pa 144, *Linton* v *Hart*, 25 Pa. 193, 64 Am. Dec. 691.

[76] *Swint* v. *McCalmont Oil Co* 184 Pa 202, 63 Am St Rep. 791, 38 Atl. 1021.

other cotenant to pay his half of the rent to him.[77] When part
of the land embraced within the lease is sold, the apportionment
of the rent between the lessor and his grantee will be in
the ratio of the rental value of the part retained to that of the
part sold, and not in the ratio of the area of the former to the
area of the latter [78] The lease may contain the agreement of the
parties that if the landlord sells parts of the premises the tenants
will release the parts so sold from the operation of the lease "on
a corresponding reduction being made in the rent, and on payment to them of the value of whatever crop may be in the
ground so sold." This, in the absence of indications in the
lease of a different intention, must be understood to mean not
that, the farm embracing forty (40) acres, for every acre sold
one fortieth of the rent should be taken off, but that only such
fraction of it should be taken off as represents the ratio of the
value of the acre sold, to the value of the 40 acres.[79] The
value of the part sold relative to that retained may be determined by an agreement after the sale, between the parties.
There being two colessees, if one of them, X, pays the rent stipulated in the lease, less $50 00, for the years 1888, 1889, 1890,
under an agreement between him and the lessor that the rental
of the part sold by the latter would fairly be $50 00, the money
paid being partly X's, and partly his cotenant Y's, in the absence of fraud or collusion between the lessor and X, Y should
not be permitted to allege that the abatement of $50 00 was too
small, and against the rent for the following years claim to set
off the difference between $50 00 and the higher sum alleged

[77]*Swint* v *McCalmont Oil Co* 184
Pa 202, 63 Am St Rep 791, 38 Atl
1021
[78]*Reed* v *Ward*, 22 Pa 144, *Linton*
v *Hart*, 25 Pa 193, 64 Am Dec
691, *Doyle* v *Longstreth*, 6 Pa
Super. Ct. 475. Cf *Martin's Appeal*,
2 Pa. Super Ct 67, *Lee* v *Dean*, 3
Whart 316, *Seabrook* v *Moyer*, 88
Pa 417, *Beaupland* v *McKeen*, 28
Pa. 124, 70 Am Dec 115, *Carpenter*
v *Koons*, 20 Pa 222
[79]*Doyle* v. *Longstreth*, 6 Pa **Super.**
Ct. 475.

now by him to have been the proper abatement for the years 1888, 1889, 1890.[80]

632. Effect of alienation of part on right of possession.—The alienation by the lessor of an undivided part of the land does not prevent his recovery of the entire possession at the end of the lease, unless the tenant has attorned to the grantee, or has accepted a new lease from the grantee, or unless the grantee defends the action for the lessee. And if A, owning one undivided seventh, but as agent for the owner of the other six sevenths, makes a lease in which, not designating any principals, he styles himself "Andrew M. Martin, agent," and he subsequently conveys his own undivided seventh, he may, as if he had been sole owner, recover the whole possession at the end of the lease, when, had he been sole owner, he might recover it.[81] A contract to convey a physical portion of the premises will not deprive the lessor of the right to insist on a condition for forfeiting the lessee's interest, if the tenant has never taken possession.[82] If four cotenants make a lease for twenty years of oil land, upon the share of one of whom there is a lien, the lease is not valid as against the purchaser under this lien of the one fourth. But, if this purchaser makes, with the owner of the other three shares, an amicable partition, under which a physical part of the premises is allotted to him in severalty, the partition is not valid as against the lessee, unless he was a party to it. He has a right, notwithstanding it, to the possession of three undivided fourths.[83]

---

[80]*Doyle* v *Longstreth,* 6 **Pa.** Super Ct 475. But the mere fact that an abatement of $50 only was made for three years, and acquiesced in by the tenants, does not preclude them from asserting for the future years that the abatement should be larger.

[81]*Holt* v *Martin,* 51 Pa 499

[82]*Carnegie Natural Gas Co* v *Philadelphia Co* 158 Pa 317, 27 Atl. 951

[83]*Duke* v *Hague,* 107 Pa. 57.

CHAPTER XXX.

RECOVERY OF POSSESSION AT END OF TERM. ACT OF MARCH 21st, 1772

633. Recovery of possession without legal process.— It is the duty of the tenant to give up the possession, at the end of the term, whether he expressly covenants to do so or not   He does not need to seek the lessor, and notify him that he intends to, or is going to, leave the premises, or that he is leaving or has left them, but he must withdraw his property and all obstructions to the assumption of control by the landlord.[1] The landlord would have a right to enter and remove the tenant's goods at the end of the lease, and if, in doing so, he set them on other premises belonging to himself, because they would there be less inconvenient to him, he would not be liable as for a conversion of them.[2] The landlord may forcibly dispossess the tenant as soon as the lease expires if he refuses to leave   This he may do, by night or day, but he must use no more force than is necessary, and do no wanton damage   The tenant is bound to remove his property on request, without regard to his convenience, and to find a place for it as he may.   If, on his failure to do so, the landlord removes the goods, he will not be liable in trespass, except for the consequence of excessive force or wanton injury.[3] Finding the door locked, the lessor may enter through a window and then open the door and put the goods out [4]

[1] *Cairns* v. *Llewellyn,* 2 Pa Super Ct 599
[2] *Wheelock* v *Fuellhart,* 158 Pa 359 27 Atl 997   The tenant could take the goods from the place where the lessor put them, without becoming a trespasser
[3] *Overdeer* v *Lewis,* 1 Watts & S. 90, 37 Am Dec 440
[4] *Kellam* v *Janson,* 17 Pa 467 Cf. *Leidy* v *Proctor,* 97 Pa 490, *Frick* v *Fiscus,* 164 Pa 623, 30 Atl 515.

634 Recovery by ejectment.—At the expiration of the period during which, according to the terms of the lease, the tenant has a right to the possession, the lessor may resort to the action of ejectment.[5] If the tenant's right is not terminable except by notice, the proper notice must, of course, have been given before resort can be successfully had to the ejectment,[6] but if it does terminate without notice, the notice does not need to have been given, in order to maintain ejectment.[7] During the term the lessor cannot recover the possession by ejectment, unless there has been a forfeiture.[8]

635. Act 21st March, 1772.—The 12th section of the act of March 21st, 1772,[9] furnishes a remedy to the landlord for the relatively prompt recovery of the possession after the expiration of the term of the lease. He may complain before two justices, who, with the aid of a jury of twelve men, ascertain the truth of his statements, and if they find them sufficient, award a writ by means of which he is put into possession of the premises. Nor is this remedy superseded by that of the act of December 14th, 1863 [10]

636 The justices.—It shall be lawful, says the act, for the lessor to complain "to any two justices of the city, town, or county where the demised premises are situate" The city recorder and an alderman of the city of Chester are justices in the sense of this act, since, by virtue of their offices, they are justices of the peace [11] The 12th section of the act of February

---

[5]*Evans* v *Hastings*, 9 Pa 273, *Bedford* v *M'Elherron*, 2 Serg & R 48, *Alden* v *Lee*, 1 Yeates, 160

[6]*Evans* v *Hastings*, 9 Pa 273, *Logan* v *Quigley* (Pa) 10 Cent Rep 403, 11 Atl 92

[7]*McCanna* v *Johnston*, 19 Pa 434; *MacGregor* v *Rawle*, 57 Pa 184

[8]*Penn* v. *Divellin*, 2 Yeates, 309 *Bartley* v *Phillips*, 165 Pa 325, 30 Atl 842

[9] 1 Pepper & L Digest, 2645, 1 Sm L 370 The justices are never sworn in such cases *Stroup* v *M'Clure*, 4 Yeates 523 For the object of this act, *vide* De *Coursey* v *Guarantee Trust & S D Co* 81 Pa 217; *Logan* v *Herron*, 8 Serg & R 459

The lessor may pursue ejectment, if he prefers *Newell* v. *Gibbs*, 1 Watts & S 496

[10]*Duff* v *Fitzwater*, 54 Pa 224; *Buchanan* v *Baxter*, 67 Pa 348

[11]*Wilmington S S Co* v *Haas*, 151 Pa. 113, 25 Atl 85. But in *Com.*

5th, 1875,[12] enacts that the jurisdiction of each magistrate in
the city of Philadelphia shall extend throughout the city and
county, and "where, by law, two aldermen are now required to
hear and determine any matter brought before them, the same
jurisdiction shall be exercised by one magistrate" This act
does not violate that provision of the Constitution which declares
that the jurisdiction of magistrates in Philadelphia shall not
exceed $100, since it is not the justice of the peace or magistrate,
but it is the jurors, who, under the act of March 21st, 1772,
ascertain the damages recoverable by the landlord; nor in other
respects does the act of 1875 conflict with the Constitution
Hence, one magistrate in Philadelphia may entertain the landlord's complaint, and restore to him possession, under the act
of 1772 [13]

637. The complaint.— The lessor may "complain" to the justices of the refusal of the tenant to surrender the possession at
the expiration of the lease, and upon due proof made before the
said justices, that the lessor had been quietly and peaceably possessed of the lands or tenements demanded, that he demised the
same, under certain rents, to the tenant now in possession or to
some person under whom the tenant is now in possession, and
that the term is fully ended, they are required to issue a warrant
to the sheriff of the county The complaint doubtless should be
in writing, and should be supported by an affidavit.[14] If it is
signed "Nelson Gavit, per A. F. Blair, agent," and below the
signature is the jurat "Sworn before us, this sixth day of

---

v *Denworth,* 145 Pa 172 22 Atl
820, the act of March 24th, 1877, P
L 47, which authorizes cities of not
less than 8,000, nor more than 20,-
000, population to elect a city recorder, was, in quo warranto proceedings held unconstitutional Aldermen in Philadelphia, prior to the
present Constitution, acted as justices. *Gavit* v *Hall,* 75 Pa 363.
LAND & TEN 35.

[12] 2 Pepper & Lewis Digest, 2854,
P L 56
[13] *Gallagher* v *Maclean,* 193 Pa
583, 45 Atl 76, Affirming 7 Pa
Super Ct 408
[14] *Gavit* v *Hall,* 75 Pa 363, *Cunningham* v *Gardner,* 4 Watts & S
120   A form is found in *Gavit* v
Hall, 75 Pa. 363.

August, A. D. 1872," signed by the two justices, it sufficiently appears that the affidavit was made by the person who signed the complaint; *viz ,* by Blair, as agent for Gavit. "I see not," said Mercur, J , "how that fact could have been averred in more unequivocal language."[15] The complaint should aver the facts which, by the terms of the statute, confer the jurisdiction on the justices to award restitution of the premises

638. Preliminary proof.— It is not the duty of the justices, on the mere exhibition of a complaint of due form and content to issue the warrant. They are to issue the warrant "upon due proof made before" them, that, at the making of the lease, the lessor was quietly and peaceably possessed of the land; that he demised it, on certain rent, to the present occupant, or to one under whom the present occupant claims, and that the term is fully ended. The proof might be made by the landlord's affidavit, even when the general law disqualified him as a witness in his own behalf; at least, that it had been so made was no reason for reversing the decision of the justices on certiorari.[16] "It was not material," said Huston, J., "on what testimony the precept issued.   .   .   .   The inquest and justices, so far as the latter are concerned, are to decide on evidence given before them, and on nothing but what is proved before them,   .   .   . for myself I would say, showing the [written] lease, if there is one, or swearing to a parol demise by the landlord, if the lease was by parol, would be due proof, as the plaintiff's oath of debt will hold a defendant to bail " The proof might be made by the affidavit of the agent[17] of the landlord, or, since the removal of disqualifications on the ground of interest, by the landlord himself, or by his successor in the ownership of the reversion.

639. The warrant; return day.— On the making of proof of the truth of the complaint, it is the duty of the justices.

[15]*Gavit* v *Hall,* 75 Pa 363   [17]*Gavit* v *Hall,* 75 Pa. 363.
[16]*Cunningham* v *Gardner,* 4 Watts & S. 120

"forthwith to issue their warrant, in nature of a summons, directed to the sheriff of the county, thereby commanding the sheriff to summon twelve substantial freeholders to appear before the said justices within four days next after issuing the said summons, and also to summon the lessee or tenant " The warrant is to be made returnable within four days. But though a longer time for its return is prescribed in it, the proceedings will probably not, on that account, be vitiated, certainly not, if the defendant appears and makes a defense Thus, the warrant issuing October 15th, and made returnable October 20th,[18] or issuing June 7th, returnable June 13th,[19] or issuing September 30th, returnable October 6th,[20] the irregularity was cured by the defendant's appearance The act allows to the justices a discretion as to the time for the return of the warrant, provided that it do not exceed four days. The error, if there be any, of allowing too short a time for the return, is condoned by the defendant's appearance and defense on the merits, *e. g.* when the summons issued April 3rd, and was returnable April 5th,[21] or issued August 28th, and was returnable August 31st [22] If it appeared that witnesses material to the tenant could not be procured on the return day, the justices would be able to adjourn the hearing.

640. Warrant, service.— The justices, by their warrant, summons, or precept, direct the sheriff to summon not only the twelve jurors, but also the lessee, or tenant, or other person claiming or coming into possession under the said lessee or tenant, at the same time (that is, at the time at which the jurors are to appear) to appear before them It is the object of the law that the service shall be made in such a manner that the person in

[18]*Stroup* v *M'Clure,* 4 Yeates, 523
[19]*Blashford* v *Duncan,* 2 Serg & R 480
[20]*Gallagher* v *Maclean,* 7 Pa Super Ct 408, Affirmed in 193 Pa. 583 45 Atl. 76.
[21]*Hower* v *Krider,* 15 Serg & R.
[22]*Horner* v *Wetherill,* 19 W. N C. 197.

actual possession of the premises shall have notice of the summons. Service on the demised premises upon the person in possession seems to be contemplated. The premises being a theatre, not the tenant, Fox, but his agent, Gilmore, occupied it. The sheriff returned that he summoned Fox "by leaving a true and attested copy of the within writ on the premises within described, with William J. Gilmore, his agent, and making known to him the contents thereof." The service was sufficient, and Fox was bound by the decision of the justices, though he did not appear before them.[23] A frequent return of service is served by leaving a true and attested copy of the writ at the dwelling house of which the demised premises consist, with an adult member of the tenant's family.[24]

641 The jurors — The persons to be summoned as jurors are described in the act as "twelve substantial freeholders." It is for the sheriff to ascertain whether the men whom he selects are freeholders or not. He should, in his return, state whether they are freeholders. If he does not so state, if, e. g., he states, "I have summoned twelve good and lawful men of my bailiwick," it will be assumed, on certiorari, that they were freeholders, if the "record of the magistrate" avers that they were. It will be presumed that the omission in the sheriff's return was corrected by sufficient evidence *dehors,* to justify the averment of record.[25] Indeed, it is held, on writ of error to the affirmance by the common pleas, on certiorari, of the judgment of the justices, that, as no bill of exception lies in the proceeding before the justices, the appellate court cannot know whether all the jurors were freeholders.[26] The sheriff should, possibly, name in his return

---

[23] *Watts* v *Fox* 64 Pa 336

[24] *Mullin's Appeal* (Pa) 2 Cent Rep 843, 5 Atl 738

[25] *Mullin's Appeal* (Pa) 2 Cent Rep 843, 5 Atl 738 This was so though the tenant objected, at the hearing before the justices, that the sheriff had not returned the jurors to be freeholders, and though his demand that the jurors be sworn to their competency was disallowed by the justices

[26] *McMillan* v *Graham* 4 Pa 140 In the common pleas on the cer-

the jurors selected by him.   If he does not, but contents himself with saying that he has summoned "twelve substantial freeholders," and the inquisition, which is a part of the record, names twelve jurors, on certiorari it will be assumed that they are the persons whom the sheriff selected and meant by his return.   If the defendant at the trial was not satisfied of their identity, he should have challenged the array, or have made some objection before the jury was sworn   "The maxim, 'Omnia præsumuntur rite esse acta,' applies with full force to these official acts."[27]

642. Jurors, by whom selected — The selection of jurors is a judicial act, and it is the duty of the sheriff not simply to summon, but to select, the twelve freeholders   Although the summoning might, after selection, be done by deputy, the selection itself cannot be done by deputy,[28] not even by the sworn permanent deputy sheriff[29]   Hence, the return to the writ being made by the deputy sheriff, "so answers Charles P Maguire, deputy sheriff, Peter Lyle, sheriff,"— the court of common pleas, on certiorari, reversed the judgment of the justices. Allison, J , remarking: "The return to the whole proceeding is that the deputy performed the entire duty, which the supreme court say can only be performed by the sheriff himself, and the sheriff has appended his name to the return below that of Maguire, as if by way of indorsement of what the deputy had done.   If a deputy cannot aid the sheriff to the extent of selecting and making out a list of names for his principal, from which the sheriff

tiorari, depositions showed that one of the jurors was not a freeholder Yet, in *Rhoads* v *Wesner*, 1 Woodw Dec 79, on certiorari, the judgment was reversed because several jurors were not landowners

[27]*Gavit* v. *Hall*, 75 Pa 363   How trustworthy the jurors are may be seen in *DeCoursey* v *Guarantee Trust & S. D. Co* 81 Pa 217, *Juer-*

gen v *Allegheny County*, 204 Pa 501 54 Atl 281

[28]*Ayres* v *Novinger*, 8 Pa 412

[29]*Pennsylvania R Co* v *Heister*, 8 Pa 445   In *Ayres* v *Novinger*, 8 Pa. 412, the same judge had expressed the opinion that the sworn deputy sheriff could select the jurors.

may summon the requisite number of freeholders, much less can he alone select, summon, and make return, or join with the sheriff in the performance of that duty "[30] But, the record not showing a selection or summoning of jurors by an improper person, the court of common pleas on certiorari cannot, in the absence of an allegation of fraud, hear depositions for the purpose of discovering the agency therein of an improper person. It was erroneous, *e. g.,* for the court to hear evidence that the sheriff deputized X, selected as one of the jurors, to select three others.[31] Besides the rule excluding evidence extraneous to the record, on certiorari, the principle of waiver precludes taking advantage of irregularity in the selection of jurors The tenant having been personally served, and having attended at the hearing, and gone on to trial on the merits, will be held to have waived all errors and irregularities in the selection and summoning of jurors.[32]

643 Failure of the summoned to appear and serve.—If any of the jurors fail to attend at the place and time indicated in the summons, or if, after being sworn, they fail to appear at the hearing, their places can be supplied without a new warrant, possibly, by a selection by the sheriff of substitutes In one case, after being sworn, two failed to appear Two others were selected by the sheriff, and sworn.[33] In another, the jurors being

---

[30] *McMullen* v *Orr*, 8 Phila 342

[31] *Wistar* v *Ollis*, 77 Pa 291 In *Ayres* v *Novinger*, 8 Pa 412, the record showed that one juror was deputed to select the rest, and a deposition showed that this was a special deputation at the request of the landlord's attorney It was held error for the common pleas on certiorari not to have reversed This was a "clear case of fraud on the part of the landlord," says Mercur, J, in *Wistar* v *Ollis*, 77 Pa 291

[32] *Wistar* v *Ollis*, 77 Pa 291 In *Mullin's Appeal* (Pa.) 2 Cent Rep

843, 5 Atl 738, one of the jurors who had been summoned not appearing, the deputy sheriff asked a bystander to serve The tenant then and there objected to this juror, but, on certiorari, the judgment was affirmed, because of the inadmissibility of parol evidence, possibly It does not appear whether the record showed the facts

[33] *White* v *Arthurs*, 24 Pa 96. But subsequently the whole jury was discharged, and a new jury summoned Cf *Pennell* v *Percival*, 13 Pa 197.

called, at the meeting on the return day one of them did not answer and the deputy sheriff selected a bystander in his stead [34] The irregularity of the proceeding could not be set up, on a certiorari.

644. Second jury.— For various causes, a new jury may become necessary   It will be regular, after the jury are sworn, if one or more absent themselves at any stage of the proceedings, and refuse to go further, to discharge all the jurors, and summon a new jury [35]   If, after hearing the evidence, one of the jurors refuses to sign the inquisition, they may be discharged, and, without a new complaint, a new venire may issue, and another jury be convened [36]   A formal discharge of the jurors seems to be unnecessary.   After a jury had heard the evidence and had begun their deliberations they adjourned, to meet at the same place five days later.   Two days after the adjournment, one of the justices discharged them and entered in his docket the fact that "not agreeing," they had been discharged.   He communicated this discharge to but four of them   On the day to which they had adjourned, eight of the jurors met to make up the verdict, when the justice told them that he had discharged them.   Two days before this, that is, the day following that on which the justice entered in his docket his discharge of the jurors, a new precept issued to the sheriff, without any new complaint, and the new jury met and decided in favor of the plaintiff   Says Lewis, J ·   "And where the two justices unite in issuing a new precept for another jury, and the new jury is sworn, and the parties appear, and the cause is finally tried before the last jury, this is an effectual discharge of the jurors previously sworn in the case."[37]

645 Continuance of proceedings — For   various causes,   the

[34]*Mullin's Appeal* (Pa) 2 Cent Rep 843, 5 Atl 738
[35]*White* v *Arthurs*, 24 Pa 96, *Pennell* v *Percival*, 13 Pa 197

[36]*Cunningham* v *Gardner*, 4 Watts & S 120, *White* v *Arthurs*, 24 Pa 96
[37]*White* v *Arthurs*, 24 Pa 96

justices may continue the hearing   The fact that the tenant is
not represented by counsel will not make it error to deny such
continuance,[38] but the sickness of the attorney on whom the tenant has been depending is a cause for which the justices should
continue   "When, by no fault of their own, parties are found
to be unrepresented, a due regard for the rights of suitors would
require that an honest application for continuance for this reason should be respected."   Nor is it right to condition the continuance on the tenant's prepaying costs.   By so doing the jury
and justices would exact pay for their own services before the
termination of the cause [39]   The absence of a juror, or of one of
the justices, would justify and require a continuance [40]   Time
enough for the procurement of distant witnesses should be allowed, on the application of the party, supported by his affidavit.   If it is not, on certiorari proof of the refusal may be made
by affidavit, and the court may reverse.[41]

   646. Finality of proceedings — If the inquisition finds in favor of the tenant, no judgment is given for him,[42] and the decision is no bar to a subsequent proceeding at any time by the landlord for the recovery of the premises,[43] nor indeed is it evidence
in favor of the tenant.[44]   Landlords, says Rogers, J , "may renew the complaint before other justices, until a more subservient
jury can be empaneled."[44a]   As the tenant can make no use of
the decision in his favor, in any subsequent litigation between

[38]*Boyer* v *Strickler*, 1 Docket, 35
[39]*McMullen* v *Orr*, 8 Phila 342
On proof by affidavit of the refusal of
a continuance except on such condition, the court of common pleas will,
on certiorari, reverse the judgment
against the tenant
   [40]*McMullen* v *Orr*, 8 Phila 342
   [41]*Steuart* v *Martin*, 1 Yeates 49
   [ ] *Galbraith* v *Black*, 4 Serg & R
207, *White* v *Arthurs*, 24 Pa 96
The justices, in the latter case did
not sign the report for the defendant
But in *Neumoyer* v *Andreas*, 57 Pa

446, the justices gave what reads like
a judgment
   [43]*Neumoyer* v *Andreas*, 57 Pa
446, *White* v *Arthurs*, 24 Pa 96,
Galbraith v *Black*, 4 Serg & R 207,
Ayres v *Novinger*, 8 Pa 412
   [44]*Neumoyer* v *Andreas*, 57 Pa
446, *Galbraith* v *Black*, 4 Serg & R.
212
   [44a]*Ayres* v *Novinger*, 8 Pa 412
But see *Marsteller* v *Marsteller*, 132
Pa 517, 19 Am St. Rep 604, 19 Atl
344.

the landlord and himself, involving the same questions, the decision in favor of the landlord, while evidence in subsequent litigation of the facts in favor of the landlord, is not a bar to a subsequent denial of them by the tenant.[45]   In the trial in the common pleas, after the transfer of the cause from the justices, under the 13th section of the act of March 21, 1772, evidence that there had been a previous proceeding before justices, in which the decision had been for the tenant, is not admissible.[46] The decision of the justices and jurors that the term had fully ended is conclusive, so that, after the sheriff has put the tenant out of possession, he cannot maintain trespass against the landlord for an eviction, on the ground that the lease, as actually made, provided for a renewal of the term, which provision, omitted by mistake from the written lease, the jurors refused or failed to recognize.[47]

647. **Conditions under which proceedings are permissible** — "Where any person or persons in this province," says the 12th section of the act of March 21, 1772,[48] "having leased or demised any lands or tenements to any person or persons for a term of one or more years or at will, paying certain rents," shall be desirous of repossessing himself of his estate, shall the remedy furnished be available. There must, then, be a lease or demise. And the demise must be of the ordinary sort   The act must be restrained to tenancies whose termination is independent of a contingency   If the tenant has, by the terms of the contract, a right to acquire the land, and whether he has acquired it involves the adjustment of a complicated account and a considera-

---

[45]*Galbraith v. Black,* 4 Serg & R 212

[46]*Neumoyer v Andreas,* 57 Pa 446

[47]*Juergen v Allegheny County,* 204 Pa 501, 54 Atl 281

The tenant averring in a bill in equity that he failed to notify the landlord of his election to hold over, under the lease, in consequence of a fraudulent conspiracy of the land lord, the preliminary injunction against proceeding under the act of 1772, to eject the tenant, was continued until final hearing   *Denny v. Kress,* 2 Blair 345

[48]1 Pepper & L. Digest, 2615

tion of the whole law of tender as equivalent to actual performance, the case does not fall under the jurisdiction of the justices.[49]

648 Lease from mortgagee to mortgagor.—A, having an equitable interest in land, conditioned to become perfect on his maintaining for life a certain person, and paying to another $60 per year, during the life of the payee, transferred the land to B, as a security for B's undertaking for the performance of these duties by A, and B, as mortgagee in possession, leased the land to A for two years, A to deliver to B one half of the hay, to pay the taxes, to make two fences, to save the grass.   The right of B was to determine at any time on A's repaying him whatever he might have paid out on account of A's liability, and if, at the end of the two years, A repaid B in full, B was to reconvey the premises.   The relation between A and B was not such that B could, on A's failure to surrender the possession, after the two years, resort to the proceeding furnished by the act of 1772, to regain possession

649. Kind of premises — Any sort of premises may be the subject of the lease: a theatre,[50] ore land,[51] a store and dwelling house,[52] a house.[53]

650. Duration of the lease.— The duration of the lease is described by the words "for a term of one or more years, or at will "   These words include a term for less than one year, e g , for the period between August 10, 1803, and April 1, 1804,[54] for twelve days [55]   A lease for one year[56] is within the very

---

[49]*Steel* v *Thompson*, 3 Penr & W 34 The case was "appealed" to the common pleas, and there it was decided that A had entitled himself to a reconveyance

[50]*Watts* v *Fox*, 64 Pa 336.

[51]*Neumoyer* v *Andreas*, 57 Pa 446

[52]*Newell* v *Gibbs*, 1 Watts & S 496, *Buchanan* v. *Baxter*, 67 Pa 348

[53]*White* v *Arthurs*, 24 Pa 96

[54]*Shaffer* v *Sutton*, 5 Binn 229

[55]*Scott* v *Fuller*, 3 Penr & W 55 The application of the remedy was denied because the proper rent had not been reserved

[56]*Gavit* v *Hall*, 75 Pa 363 , *Wilmington S S Co* v *Haas*, 151 Pa 113, 25 Atl 85, *White* v *Arthurs*, 24 Pa 96, *Logan* v *Herron*, 8 Serg & R 459.

words of the act, as is one for a longer period [57]   A lease "at will" is within the act.   A strict tenancy at will is rare   It exists in a majority of cases "only nominally, and is, in fact, a tenancy from year to year,"[58] and tenancies from year to year are within the remedy of the act of 1772 [59]   Though it is said by Gibson, J , that the term must be one "whose termination is independent of a contingency," the act of 1772 was tacitly assumed, in *Lloyd* v *Cozens,*[60] to be applicable to a lease from year to year which was subject to become null and void if any quarter's rent should remain due for ten days.   While, in *Wilmington S. S Co* v. *Haas,*[61] the court, finding, on consulting the lease, which was not set out in the record, that, though for one year, it was liable, by its terms, to be terminated at any time, on three months' notice, if the property should be sold, or if it, along with adjacent property of the landlord, should be leased, reversed the judgment of the justices.   The supreme court reversed the reversal because the lease was not a part of the record, and because the abstract from the lease, given in the inquisition, did not "indicate that it in any manner depended on a contingency."   Indeed, it is difficult to see why the jurors might not as readily ascertain whether this contingent event had happened, as the lapse of the term, the giving of three months' notice, etc.   The lease may be oral[62] as well as written, and the term, though the lease be oral, may exceed three years.[63]

[57]*Brown* v *Vanhorn,* 1 Binn 334, note , *Neumoyer* v *Andreas,* 57 Pa 446, *Wistar* v *Ollis,* 77 Pa 291, *Juergen* v *Allegheny County,* 204 Pa 501, 54 Atl 281

[58]*Logan* v *Herron,* 8 Serg & R 473, *Clark* v *Smith,* 25 Pa 137

[59]*Fahnestock* v *Faustenauer,* 5 Serg & R 174, *Brown* v *Vanhorn,* 1 Binn 334, note, *Logan* v *Herron,* 8 Serg & R 473

[60]2 Ashm (Pa) 131

[61]151 Pa 113, 25 Atl 85   In *Mc-Gee* v *Fessler,* 1 Pa St 126, the demise was at will, authorizing the tenant to make improvements, and remain in possession until he was reimbursed for his outlay   The proceedings were set aside because no rent was reserved

[62]*Brown* v *Vanhorn,* 1 Binn 334, note, *Logan* v *Herron,* 8 Serg & R 459

[63]*Neumoyer* v. *Andreas,* 57 Pa. 446.

651. The term must have ended.— If the lease gives the tenant the "privilege of re-leasing" sufficiently definite to be enforceable, the lessee may probably avail himself of it, for the
purpose of preventing eviction, until the end of the additional
term.[64]

652. The plaintiff.—"Any person or persons in this province,"
having demised lands, or "his or their heirs or assigns," are
those to whom the remedy of the act of 1772 is furnished. The
lessor may be a natural person, or a corporation: e. g., a
church,[65] a steamship company,[66] or a county.[67] The lessor may
himself be a tenant for years, and may have sublet the premises.[67a] Since the making of the lease, the reversion may have
passed to another than the lessor, by grant,[68] devise,[69] inheritance.[70] The grantee may be for life; e g., A, leasing land to
C for a year, at about the same time leases it to B for B's life,
subject to the lease to C. B may, at the expiration of the lease,
institute the proceedings for recovery of possession,[71] as may
executors appointed by the lessor, with power to sell and convey
and dispose of the premises,[72] or, they being superseded, the administrator *de bonis non*,[73] and the guardian of a minor heir
of the deceased lessor[74] The conveyance of the reversion may

[64]*Juergen* v *Allegheny County*,
204 Pa 501, 54 Atl 281 Not decided whether, before the justice, the
tenant could show that, by mistake,
the written lease represented the
privilege of re-leasing to be "at an
increased annual rent," not specifying the rent, whereas the terms including the rent of the renewal, were
agreed upon The decision of the
justice in favor of the landlord was
conclusive that there was no right of
renewal

[65]*Hohly* v *German Reformed Soc*
2 Pa St 293

[66]*Wilmington S S Co* v *Haas*,
151 Pa 113, 25 Atl 85

[67]*Juergen* v *Allegheny County*, 204
Pa. 501, 54 Atl 281.

[67a]*Newell* v *Gibbs*, 1 Watts & S
496

[68]*Debozear* v *Butler*, 2 Grant, Cas
417, *Thamm* v *Hamburg*, 7 Phila
266

[69]*Mullin's Appeal* (Pa) 2 Cent.
Rep 843, 5 Atl 738, *Watts* v *Fox*,
64 Pa 336, *May* v *Kendall*, 8 Phila
244

[70]*Cunningham* v *Gardner*, 4 Watts
& S 120

[71]*White* v *Arthurs*, 24 Pa 96
Watts v *Fox*, 64 Pa 336

[72]*Mullins Appeal* (Pa) 2 Cent
Rep 843 5 Atl 738

[73]*Cunningham* v. *Gardner*, 4 Watts
& S 120

not take place until after the giving of the notice to quit, and the grantee may avail himself of the notice [75]   A part of the premises may be conveyed, since the making of the lease; e g , the front of a lot to a depth, from the building line, of 11 feet. The grantee of that part may begin the proceedings under the act of 1772 to recover the possession of it,[76] but a landlord could not recover a part of the premises and compel the tenant to remain liable, as such, for rent for the residue   A remainderman to a life tenant is not an "assign" of the life tenant   Hence, if a life tenant leases the land for three years, with the privilege of remaining two years longer, and dies pending the term, the remainderman cannot proceed under the act of 1772.[77]

653. The defendant — The 12th section of the act of March 21, 1772, on the complaint of the lessor, heir, or assign, that he has demised his land 'to the then tenant in possession or some person or persons under whom such tenant claims or came into possession," directs the justices to issue a warrant to the sheriff, commanding him, inter alia, to summon "the lessee, or tenant, or other person claiming or coming into possession under the said lessee or tenant," to appear before the justices.   The assignee of the lease may, therefore, be made defendant, and this is so, though the tenant, after making the assignment, surrenders the lease to the lessor [78]   It is unnecessary to say that, there being two[79] or more tenants, or assignees of the term, they all may be made defendants

654 Kind of rent.—In order to qualify the lessor to resort to the remedy under consideration, the demise must have been to some person or persons, "paying certain rents."   In his complaint to the justices, he must aver that he demised the premises

[75]*Stroup* v *M'Clure*, 4 Yeates, 523, *DeCoursey* v *Guarantee Trust & S D. Co* 81 Pa 217
[76]*DeCoursey* v *Guarantee Trust & S D Co* 81 Pa 217
[77]*May* v *Kendall*, 8 Phila 244.

[78]*Lloyd* v *Cozens*, 2 Ashm (Pa.) 131
[79]*Wilmington S S Co* v *Haas*, 151 Pa 113, 25 Atl 85, *Gallagher* v *Maclean*, 7 Pa Super Ct 408, *Newell* v *Gibbs*, 1 Watts & S 496

"under certain rents," and the justices, before they may award
the restoration of the possession of the premises to the complainant, must find, *inter alia,* that he demised them to the person in
possession, or one under whom he claims, "at certain yearly or
other rent." Some rent must be reserved. If none is, the justices have no jurisdiction;[80] but it need not be considerable The
reservation of $1 per year would be enough [81] The rent must
also be certain. It may be certain, though not reserved in words
which define its quantity and quality, as, *e. g.,* when it is susceptible of certainty from extrinsic matters, so as to enable the
landlord to recover it.[82] Thus, when the tenant was, as rent, to
pay the taxes of the last preceding year, and to daub and chink
the house, whose dimensions were certain, "There was," said
Tilghman, Ch. J., "certainty in the rent, the taxes could be exactly ascertained [by a reference to the books of assessment] and
the work to be done on the house was accurately described "[83]
Rent reserved in kind, *e. g.,* one third of the grain, hay, etc.,
though its amount cannot be foreseen, would be esteemed certain,
because a criterion by which it can be ascertained is furnished.
A royalty, *e g.,* 25 cents per ton of iron ore, would doubtless be
"certain."[84] The demise, on the other hand, being for the term
of twelve days, "under the rent of taking care of the grain of Fuller [the lessor], on the place, and keeping out the cattle," the rent
was regarded as too uncertain to sustain a resort to the remedy of
the act of 1772. "What grain and what cattle?" asks Gibson,
Ch. J. "The grain on the farm, doubtless. But that leaves the
kind uncertain,—whether wheat, rye, buckwheat and oats, or
pulse, barley, millet, spelt and Indian corn, whether growing in
the fields, or put up in shocks, or stowed away in barns, or deposited in garners, and whether it were to be protected from cattle

[80]*Blashford* v. *Duncan,* 2 Serg &
R 480, *DeCoursey* v   *Guarantee
Trust & S D Co* 81 Pa 217, *McGee*
v *Foster,* 1 Pa St 126
   [81]*Blashford* v. *Duncan,* 2 Serg. &
P 480

[82]*Scott* v *Fuller,* 3 Penr & W 55.
[83]*Shaffer* v *Sutton* 5 Binn 228
[84]*Neumoyer* v. *Andreas,* 57 Pa 446

only, or from vermin. The enclosures or places, too, out of which the cattle were to be kept, are altogether uncertain,— whether the stables, the meadows, the fields lying fallow or with grain in them, or the open grounds   .   .   .   It seems, therefore, there was no reservation of anything that could be recovered by action, or enforced by a distress; and that the landlord was not entitled to the summary remedy provided by the legislature."[85] The tenant holding in consideration of his services to the lessor, a church, as organist, foresinger, and sexton, this rent was too uncertain, because it could not be reduced to certainty by reference to a subject in existence at the time of the contract. The services were contingent, their quantity being ascertainable only "after actual performance."[86]   In *McGee* v *Fessler*,[87] A authorized B to build, at his own expense, a house of such material and dimensions as he pleased, on A's land, and after the house was finished, they were to determine how long B should remain in possession, as compensation for his outlays   There was no agreement as to the yearly value of the land   "The rent," said Rogers, J , "if rent it may be called, was altogether uncertain, nor was there anything by which it could be rendered certain, except by the intervention of a jury   It would seem, therefore, to be a case in which the legislature did not intend to give a summary jurisdiction."

655 Peaceable possession.— One of the averments of the complaint to be preferred to the justices is that "the said lessor or lessors had been quietly and peaceably possessed of the lands or tenements" demanded, and one of the facts to be found by the justices before requiring the tenant to restore the premises to the

---

[85]*Scott* v *Fuller*, 3 Penr & W 55 In *Steel* v *Thompson*, 3 Penr & W 34, the tenant was to give one half of the hay raised on the place, to pay all the taxes, to make two fences No remarks on the nature of the rent are made

[86]*Hohly* v *German Reformed Soc.* 2 Pa St 293.

[87] 1 Pa St 126 In *Boggs* v *Black*, 1 Binn 333, the tenant was to cut off the timber so as to clear the land, put up fences, and pay the taxes No discussion of the question.

lessor is "that the lessor or lessors had been possessed of the lands or tenements in question, that he or they had demised the same " Peaceable possession by the landlord at the time of his making the lease seems, therefore, to be a prerequisite. Hence, when B was the owner, under articles of sale from A, and likewise in possession when he accepted a lease from X, whom he regarded as mortgagee of the land, to secure X from liabilities assumed for him, and X later obtained the legal title, at a sheriff's sale on the judgment, X was "destitute of that quiet and peaceable possession which the law requires, at the date of the lease "[88]

656. Notice to quit — When any person or persons, having leased land, "shall demand and require his or their lessee or tenant to remove from and leave the same, if the lessee or tenant shall refuse to comply therewith, in three months after such request to him made,"[89] the proceedings to recover the possession may be commenced The justices are to award restoration of possession to the landlord when, *inter alia*, they find "that demand had been made of the lessee or other person in possession as aforesaid, to leave the premises three months before such application to the said justices." The notice must be given by the landlord or his successor in the ownership of the reversion It may, of course, be given by his agent, but a notice in the agent's own name, and not indicating for whom, and that he is giving it with the authority of the principal, will be insufficient.[90] The reversion having passed to two executors, a notice signed with the names of both, but by one of them, will be sufficient.[91] When the notice comes from the assignee of the reversion, the tenant, if not already informed, should be advised of the fact

---

[88]*Steel* v *Thompson,* 3 Penr & W 34 It was said also that X was "without even the color or pretense of right" to the land

[89] Section 12, act March 21st 1772

[90]*Donaldson* v. *Likens,* 7 Phila 257.

The agent who signs the notice to quit, being a justice, cannot act as one of the two justices in the proceedings for recovery of the possession *Wistar* v *Conroy,* 1 Troubat & H Pr § 201 1869

[91]*Watts* v *Fox,* 64 Pa 336

that he is the owner of the reversion   If, the lease having been made by Ely, the notice to quit from Donaldson does not state why he gives the notice, the tenant, not shown to have known of a transfer of the reversion to Donaldson, may safely ignore the notice;[92] but when the record of the justices' proceedings avers that "Thamm, assignee, gave the notice to quit," the notice itself not being embodied in the record, "the legal inference is that he gave the notice as assignee," that is, apparently, that he professed in the notice to be assignee, and as such he gave the notice [93]   The notice need not be written [94]   It should be absolute; not propose the alternative of paying an increased rent or quitting [95]   The notice is given to the person in possession, when it is the purpose of the plaintiff to dispossess, hence, to the assignee of the term.[96]   It must be to quit the whole premises.   Neither the lessor nor his grantee of a portion of the premises can, by giving notice to quit this portion, entitle himself to the possession of this portion [97]

657. Waiver of notice — The right of the tenant to insist on the notice, as a precondition to his being expelled on a judgment of the justices, he may waive, and he does this if, in the lease for a year, he covenants at the end of the term to give up quiet and peaceable possession "without further notice."[98]   But, in *Gault*

[92]*Donaldson* v *Likens*, 7 Phila 257   The decision of the justices being for the plaintiff, and the defendant not having appeared before them, it was reversed on certiorari

[93]*Thamm* v *Hamburg*, 7 Phila 266   If evidence *dehors* the record could be heard, then it appeared that though the written notice did not inform the tenant that Thamm was the assignee of the lessor, he had independent knowledge of that fact If. on certiorari, the record is conclusive, there was no error   If evidence *dehors* is admissible, there was also no error

LAND. & TEN. 36.

[94]*Thamm* v. *Hamburg*, 7 Phila. 266

[95]*O'Neill* v *Cahill*, 2 Brewst (Pa) 357

[96]*Lloyd* v *Cozens*, 2 Ashm (Pa) 131

[97]*DeCoursey* v *Guarantee Trust & S D Co* 81 Pa 217

[98]*Hutchinson* v *Potter*, 11 Pa 472 The notice to quit, though given but six days before the commencement of the proceedings, would have been sufficient   But, as the record showed neither the three months' notice, nor the fact of waiver, the judgment was reversed.

v. *Neal,*[99] Allison, J., refused to find in the stipulation of a
lease from month to month, that it was to continue until one
party should give notice to the other, thirty days before the end
of any month, of his intention to terminate the lease, an intention to waive the three months' notice, as a prerequisite to a justices' judgment of ouster

658. Length of notice.— The notice must precede, by three
months, the inception of the proceedings before the justices,
whatever the length of the term, whether it be for a definite
time, or strictly at will, or from year to year, or even from
quarter to quarter, or month to month [100] Thus, the monthly
term beginning September 21, 1885, a notice given on October 6,
1885, to quit on November 21st was not sufficient to support proceedings begun November 25th.[101]

659. Notice, when term is for a definite time.— When the lease
is for one year, or two years, or any definite time, notice is unnecessary in order to terminate the lessee's estate in the land,
unless the lease requires the notice. In such cases, therefore,
the function of the notice to quit is not to end the lease, but
simply to bestow upon the lessor, after three months, the right
to the summary procedure for the recovery of the possession.
The landlord may give notice three months before the lapse of
the term, and so entitle himself instantly upon its expiration to
this remedy [102] He may give notice more than three months
before the close of the term, and entitle himself to the proceedings immediately upon its close Thus, the term ending May
31st, a notice given the preceding January 25th would entitle
the lessor to proceed on June 1st [103] The landlord may be more

[99] 6 Phila 61   The same view was
taken by Gordon, J , in *Veditz* v
Levy, 18 Phila 328
　[100]*Veditz* v *Levy,* 18 Phila 328,
Gault v *Neal,* 6 Phila 61   Cf
Lentz v *Schaffer,* 3 Hazard Penn
Reg 410
　[101]*Veditz* v *Levy,* 18 Phila 328

[102]*White* v *Arthurs,* 24 Pa 96 *Logan* v *Herron,* 8 Serg & R 459
　[103]*Lloyd* v *Cozens,* 2 Ashm (Pa)
131
　Lease ending July 31st, 1872, notice was given April 16th, 1872.
Gault v *Hall,* 75 Pa 363

forbearing or less provident, and defer giving the notice until the term has fully expired. The term ending, *e. g.*, on March 31st, the notice may be given on that day;[104] or, the term ending March 31st, the notice may not be given until April 14th [105]

660. Notice; tenancy from year to year.— When the tenancy is from year to year, a three months' notice to quit at the end of the year is necessary in order to conclude it. The notice which effects this object may also serve the other purpose of enabling the lessor to resort to a proceeding before the justices The precedence of the notice by three months, to the inception of the proceedings, will not be sufficient, unless it also precedes by the same interval the end of the year, for the tenant will have a right to hold over for another year [106] The year, *e. g ,* ending April 9, 1814, notice on April 22d to quit in three months will be ineffectual [107] The tenancy from year to year commencing on March 29, 1782, in February, 1800, notice was given to the tenant that he must surrender possession on March 29, 1801. This would probably have been sufficient. But the landlord refrained from disturbing the tenant's possession, and he gave him notice again on January 25, 1802. Application to the justices was made April 26, 1802. The notice was sufficient to support a recovery.[108]

661. How soon proceedings may begin.—The proceedings before the justices cannot begin until the expiration both of the term and of three months from the giving of the notice But they can begin immediately thereafter The lease from year to year being made June 1, 1827, on January 25, 1830, notice was given to quit at the end of the year Proceedings could properly commence on June 1, 1830, before the justices.[109] They could,

[104]*Watts* v *Fox,* 64 Pa 336

[105]*Logan* v *Herron* 8 Serg & R 459, *Rich* v *Keyser,* 54 Pa 86

[106]*Brown* v *Vanhorn,* 1 Binn 334, note

[107]*Fahnestock* v *Faustenauer,* 5 Serg & R 174

[108]*Boggs* v *Black,* 1 Binn 333

[109]*Lloyd* v *Cozens,* 2 Ashm (Pa) 131, *Donaldson* v *Smith,* 1 Ashm (Pa) 197

The notice ending July 14th, the proceedings began July 15th *Logan* v *Herron,* 8 Serg & R 459

of course, begin at any later time. The lease, *e. g*, expiring
March 31st, the proceedings began April 3d.[110] The year ending
March 31st, and notice being given the preceding January 1st,
proceedings began October 15th.[111]

662 **Certiorari** — "The act of 1772 makes no mention of a
certiorari. Such writ is not allowed by its terms Yet it has
been repeatedly held that the common-law writ of certiorari
might issue under that act "[112] Indeed, the cases are numerous
in which the common pleas has issued this writ.[113] The writ
may issue without an affidavit of the person seeking it, that he
does not seek it for the purpose of delay, the 21st section of the
act of March 20, 1810,[114] not being applicable to the common-
law certiorari.[115] The writ of certiorari is not a supersedeas,
and, pending it, the writ for the delivery of possession to the
lessor may be carried into execution by the sheriff [116] If the
court of common pleas reverses the judgment of the justices,
and, the premises having been delivered to the landlord, award
a writ of restitution, a writ of error from the supreme court
to the judgment of the common pleas, it was held in an early
case,[117] would not supersede this writ of restitution, so as to
prevent the restoration of the possession to the tenant. But
since the passage of the act of June 16, 1836, it has been held
that a writ of error from the supreme court is a supersedeas.
The common pleas having affirmed the judgment of the justices,
a *habere facias possessionem* was sued out by the landlord, and
the next day a writ of error was issued. This writ was a super-

---

[110]*White* v *Arthurs*, 24 Pa. 96

[111]*Stroup* v *M'Clure*, 4 Yeates, 523

[112]*DeCoursey* v *Guarantee Trust &
S D Co* 81 Pa 217

[113]*Grubb* v *Fox*, 6 Binn 460,
Blashford v *Duncan*, 2 Serg & R
480

The 13th section of the act of 1772
does not prevent the use of a certio
rari *McClure* v *White*, Addison
(Pa) 192.

[114] 1 Peppei & L Digest, 2612, 5
Smith's Laws, 161

[115]*Veditz* v *Levy*, 18 Phila 328
No bond for the costs is necessary

[116]*Grubb* v *Fox*, 6 Binn 460, *Stew-
art* v *Martin*, 1 Yeates, 49, *De
Coursey* v *Guarantee Trust & S D
Co* 81 Pa 217

[11] *Grubb* v *Fox*, 6 Binn 460.

sedeas of the execution, and the sheriff properly refused to execute the *habere*.[118]

663. Review on certiorari.— So far as the existence of the facts is concerned, which, under the law, are necessary to support the judgment of the justices, the record of the finding of the inquisition is the sole evidence in the common pleas. What it fails to show that the inquest have found must be assumed to be nonexistent. What it shows that they have found must be taken to be facts. It is repeatedly said that the certiorari brings up the record only.[119] The inquisition must, therefore, contain a finding that the three months' notice was given or had been waived.[120] The court of common pleas will not hear evidence or even inspect the lease, the inquisition omitting the averment that the notice was given or had been waived, and not quoting the lease. It must appear in the record that the term was fully ended.[121] It is not enough that the court might infer that it had, from the date of the notice and that of the entry of the complaint, as mentioned in the record.[122] The court cannot know that the lease is terminable on a contingency, if the inquisition does not say that it is, and does not quote it. The court cannot read a lease, or any part of it, which has not been made a portion of the record.[123] It must appear in the record that the lease was for a certain rent, and possibly, what the rent was must be stated. Otherwise the judgment will not be sustained.[124] The averment in the inquisition that the demise was "for one year and from year to year at the rent of $200 for the first year"

[118] *Wright* v *Clendenning,* 6 Phila 320   The court discharged a rule to compel the sheriff to proceed

[119] *Wilmington S S Co* v *Haas,* 151 Pa 113, 25 Atl 85, *Gallagher* v *Maclean,* 7 Pa Super Ct 408, Affirmed in 193 Pa 583, 45 Atl 76, *Buchanan* v *Baxter,* 67 Pa 348, *Cummings* v *Young,* 6 Montg. Co L Rep 161: *Boyer* v. *Strickler,* 1 Docket, 35.

[120] *Hutchinson* v *Potter,* 11 Pa. 472, *Feditz* v *Levy,* 18 Phila 328

[121] *Fahnestock* v *Faustenauer,* 5 Serg & R 174, *Blashford* v *Duncan,* 2 Serg & R 480

[122] *Hohly* v *German Reformed Soc.* 2 Pa St 293, *May* v *Kendall,* 8 Phila 244

[123] *Wilmington S S Co* v *Haas,* 151 Pa 113, 25 Atl 85

[124] *McGee* v *Fessler,* 1 Pa St 126

was deemed susceptible of the interpretation, with reasonable
confidence that it corresponded with the thought of the inquest,
—that the rent for all the years succeeding the first was the same
as for the first.[125] The record of the justices is said, in *Wilmington S S Co.* v. *Haas*,[126] to consist of the complaint, the warrant
to the sheriff, his return thereto, the inquisition, the judgment,
the writ of restitution, etc   The evidence on which the jurors
found the facts forms no part of the record, and cannot be considered on certiorari.

664. The record.— The 12th section of the act of 1772 directs
that if certain facts shall appear to the justices and freeholders,
"it shall and may be lawful for the said two justices to make a
record of such finding by them, the said justices and freeholders." It is usual to frame an "inquisition," *viz ,* a finding of
the facts by the justices and jurors, and also for the justices to
make a "record" which, besides embodying the inquisition,[127]
may find all or some of the same facts, or additional facts, or
facts inconsistent with those in the inquisition.   When the
inquisition and the record are inconsistent, the truth of the inquisition is assumed by the common pleas and the supreme
court on certiorari.   Thus, the inquisition saying that no rent
was reserved by the lease, its averment will be accepted as true
despite the averment in the "record" that rent of $1 per year
was reserved [128]   When the inquisition omits a material averment, *e. g.,* that the term is fully ended, the nonexistence of the
omitted fact will be assumed, despite the assertion in the
"record" that the justices and freeholders find that fact [129]

---

[125] *McMillan* v *Graham*, 4 Pa 140
[126] 151 Pa 113, 25 Atl 85
[127] In *Blashford* v *Duncan*, 2 Serg
& R 480 the judges leave it doubtful whether the justices are bound to
annex the inquisition to their "record," but it is said by Gibson, J ,
that if they did not the court would
compel them to send it up by a certiorari.

[128] *Blashford* v *Duncan*, 2 Serg &
R 480   In *McMillan* v *Graham*, 4
Pa 140, the court found no substantial discrepancy with respect to rent,
between the inquisition and the "record "

[129] *May* v *Kendall*, 8 Phila 244.

Sometimes the inquisition is followed immediately by the judgment of the justices, without any averment of facts.[130]

665. Form of the inquisition — In *Fahnestock* v. *Fausteneauer*[131] the inquisition instead of reciting the facts found, stated that the freeholders say "that the facts stated in the within venire facias [the warrant to the sheriff] are true " Tilghman, Ch J., said he had never known an inquisition of that kind, "and it would be difficult to support it, even if reference were made with greater precision" than was observed in that. The necessary facts should be clearly and positively found.[132-3] Some so-called inquisitions embrace not simply the facts found and the damages assessed, but, in addition, the judgment of the justices,[134] and occasionally, after an inquisition of which the judgment is a part, there follow a statement of the complaint, the warrant, the return, the swearing of the freeholders, the names of witnesses, the offers of evidence, the inquisition repeated, the repetition of the assessment of damages, and the repetition of the judgment of the justices[135] The lease may be made, but need not be, a part of the record[136] The inquisition stating it was taken 'this —— day of May," the date recited

---

[130]*Fahnestock* v *Faustenauer,* 5 Serg & R 174, *Stroup* v *M'Clure,* 4 Yeates, 523

[131] 5 Serg & R 174 One objection was, that the inquest might have meant that they found that the preliminary proof had been made before the justices before the issue of the warrant to the sheriff, rather than that they found the facts which were the subject of this preliminary truth. Another was that the inquisition did not say whether it found all the averments in the venire facias to be true, or some only, and if some it did not distinguish those found from those not found The venire facias reciting a lease made April 10th, 1810, for one year, states that the tenant still holds (*viz,*

July 27th, 1814) the same, to the damage of the lessor It does not state whether he had held over any of the intervening years with the consent of the landlord or as a trespasser for the whole time

[132,133] In *Buchanan* v *Baxter,* 67 Pa 348, is a form said to be long followed. *Vide Gavit* v *Hall,* 75 Pa 363

[134]*Buchanan* v *Baxter* 67 Pa 348, *Gavit* v *Hall,* 75 Pa 363

[135]*Gavit* v *Hall,* 75 Pa 363   For some reason, the court said that the record was correct in form

[136] *Wilmington S S Co* v *Haas,* 151 Pa 113, 25 Atl 85, *Shoup* v *M'Clure,* 4 Yeates, 523 The justices may incorporate the lease in the record, or give its substance

in the record may supply the omission of the number of the day.[136] The warrant of the justices to the sheriff is tested August 12th. It is no reversible error that the "record" states that it was tested September 12th.[138] The complaint, inquisition, warrant, and record stating that the lease was dated August 1, 1871, the lease, bearing date August 1, 1870, cannot be used to impeach the finding.[139]

666 Evidence extraneous to record.—As a rule, evidence of facts not exhibited in the record cannot be taken for use in the court of common pleas, on the hearing of exceptions to the judgment of the justices, on the certiorari. The court should not allow depositions to be taken, and, with papers and documents, filed.[140] "There is no warrant," says Sterrett, J., "for any such practice. It is dangerous, and should be discouraged."[141] But when there is an averment of fraud, partiality, or oppression, which, if established, would justify the reversal of the judgment, its truth may be shown by depositions or other evidence.[142] It may, *e. g.*, be shown that sufficient time was not allowed to the tenant to produce his witnesses,[143] or that, his counsel falling sick, a continuance was refused except on the condition that he prepay costs;[144] or, possibly, that the jurors summoned were not freeholders,—if, the tenant duly excepting on this ground, the justices and inquest nevertheless proceed to hear

---

[137]*Cunningham v Gardner*, 4 Watts & S. 120

[138]*Gault v Hall*, 75 Pa 363

[139]*Gault v Hall*, 75 Pa 363

[140] In *Stroup v M'Clure*, 4 Yeates, 523, the common pleas refused to grant a rule on the justices to return the lease and a deed by which the lessor's interest had been conveyed to the plaintiff

[141]*Wilmington S S Co v Haas*, 151 Pa 113, 25 Atl 85 In *McMullan v Graham*, 4 Pa 140, a deposition showed that the plaintiff was the only witness to prove the demand of possession The judgment was affirmed No discussion of the admissibility of the deposition

[142]*Wistar v Ollis*, 77 Pa 291 In *Buchanan v Baxter*, 67 Pa 348, Thompson, Ch J, says that the common pleas may hear affidavits, but it would be unsafe practice, is a rule. Even if that court should hear affidavits, they could not be considered in the supreme court

[143]*Stewart v Martin*, 1 Yeates, 49.

[144]*McMullen v. Orr*, 8 Phila 342

and determine the cause;[145] or it may be shown that one of the justices was the agent of the plaintiff in delivering his notice to the tenant to quit.[146]

667. Damages.— "The said freeholders," says the act of 1772, "shall assess such damages as they think right against the tenant or other person in possession as aforesaid, for the unjust detention of the demised premises " The decision of these damages is, by the letter of the act, with the "freeholders." The decisions indicate no rule by which the damages shall be ascertained Varying according to the value of the premises, and the length of the detention, and, possibly, the presence or absence of waste, the following sums have been awarded $100,[147] $3,[148] $500;[149] $21.33,[150] $50,[151] $100;[152] $120,[153] $360 [154] In *Watts* v. *Fox*[155] the rent reserved was $3,000 per annum, and the tenant was, in addition, to pay all taxes, assessments, water rents, and gas charges. The inquest awarded $916.66 damages, $600 for taxes, $101 09 for gas consumed, $26 35 for water rent, making in all $1,644.10. One of the exceptions to the judgment was that the damages were excessive and given for other objects than the unjust detention of the premises The common pleas reversed because no proper service of the summons had been made on the defendant, who had not appeared before the justices. The supreme court reversed this reversal except with respect to the damages, finding substance in the exception to the damages.

668 Costs — For the damages "and reasonable costs," says the act of 1772, "judgment shall be entered." These costs are taxed

[145] Cf *Rhoads* v *Wesner*, 1 Woodw Dec 79, with *Wistar* v. *Ollis*, 77 Pa 291

[146] *Wistar* v *Conroy*, 1 Troubat & H Pr § 201   1869

[147] *Buchanan* v *Baxter*, 67 Pa 348

[148] *Stroup* v *M'Clure*, 4 Yeates, 523

[149] *Wilmington S. S Co.* v. *Haas*, 151 Pa. 113, 25 Atl 85.

[150] *Fahnestock* v *Faustenauer*, 5 Serg & R 174

[151] *May* v *Kendall*, 8 Phila 244

[152] *Gavit* v *Hall*, 75 Pa 363

[153] *Gallagher* v *Maclean*, 7 Pa. Super Ct 408

[154] *Wistar* v *Ollis*, 77 Pa 291.

[155] 64 Pa. 336.

by the justices   On the same complaint, two or more juries may
be summoned and they may have several meetings before the final
decision in favor of the landlord is reached.   This complaint may
have been preceded by one which ended in a decision for the tenant   Whether, in the last proceeding, the costs of all the proceedings may be imposed on the tenant, is not clear.   In a case in
which they were thus imposed on him, the supreme court remarked, being unable to say what items of costs had been charged .
"But, as the complainant was not in fault, and the defendant has
been found guilty of unjustly withholding the possession, we see
no reason why he should not be charged with all the costs of the
proceedings necessary to regain it "[156]   If no agreement is
reached by the jury, each party must pay his own costs.   The
landlord, having improvidently paid the tenant's costs to the justice, may withdraw them without becoming liable to the tenant [157]
Costs of $65,[158] of $20.72,[159] of $45,[160] are specimens of as-
sessments under this head.

669 The judgment — The finding of facts is to be made by the
justices and freeholders.[161]   The damages are to be assessed by
the freeholders   Of the finding of the facts a record is to be made
by the justices.   For the damages and costs, judgment is to be entered by the justices.   Upon the entering of this judgment, *i. e.*,
for damages and costs, the justices are required to issue their warrant, commanding the sheriff forthwith to deliver to the lessor,
his heir or assign, full possession of the demised premises, and
to levy the costs and damages of the goods and chattels of the defendant.   A form of judgment that has been approved is:

[156]*White* v *Arthurs* 24 Pa. 96.
[157]*Rhoad* v *Cain*, 2 Chester Co
Rep 49b
The costs are not payable till the
conclusion of the proceedings and
prepayment cannot be exacted as a
condition of continuance of the hear
ing   *McMullen* v. *Orr*, 8 Phila 342

[158]*Gallagher* v *Maclean* 7 Pa Super Ct 408
[159]*Stroup* v *M'Clure*, 4 Yeates, 523
[160]*Buchanan* v *Baxter*, 67 Pa 348
[161] To an exception that both the
justices and jurors acted as triers,
the court said nothing, in *McMillan*
v. *Graham*, 4 Pa. 140.

"Therefore, it is considered and adjudged by us, the said aldermen [or justices], that the said Nelson Gavit shall and do recover and have of the said Mary Hall as well, the said sum of $100 for his damages aforesaid, as $45 for his reasonable costs, by him expended in and about this suit in this behalf, concerning which the premises aforesaid we do make this our record." This was preceded by what was termed the inquisition, which concluded with the words. "Whereupon, it is considered by the said aldermen that restitution of the said demised premises be made to the said Nelson Gavit, and that he recover of the said Mary Hall $100 damages aforesaid, together with the costs of suit, amounting to $45."[162] "That form," said Thompson, Ch. J,[163] "has been in use for more than a third of a century, and is copied from Graydon, which is much older   Hundreds of records have been made in accordance therewith, and, so far as I know, it has never been condemned by any court " In the form just quoted, the restitution of the premises is not awarded in the "record" but in the "inquisition." In *McMillan* v *Graham*,[164] the exception was that the inquest had assessed damages, but had not adjudicated on the right of the landlord to have the premises. The court said that "the place to award a writ of possession is in the record, not in the inquisition."

670 Warrant to deliver possession.— The justices, on giving judgment, are required by the act of 1772 to issue their warrant to the sheriff, commanding him forthwith to deliver possession of the premises to the landlord.   This writ, known often as the writ of restitution,[165] may issue on the same day on which the judgment is entered.[166]   If on certiorari the common pleas should reverse the judgment, after possession has been given to

[162]*Gavit* v *Hall,* 75 Pa 363, *Buchanan* v *Baxter,* 67 Pa 348

[163]*Buchanan* v *Baxter,* 67 Pa 348

[164] 4 Pa 140   The same thing was done in *Wilmington S S Co* v *Haas,* 151 Pa 113, 25 Atl 85

[165]*Wilmington S S Co* v *Haas,* 151 Pa 113, 25 Atl 85

[166]*DeCoursey* v *Guarantee Trust & S D Co* 81 Pa 217.

the landlord, it may not, as of course, award a writ that it be re-
delivered to the tenant, likewise called, sometimes, a writ of restitution, and sometimes of re-restitution, but may wait until that
writ is moved for by the tenant [167]   It will, ordinarily, then
award it,[168] but the reversal of the judgment does not always
make it proper to award a re-restitution to the tenant,[169] as when,
since the judgment, the landlord has acquired the right to the
possession, or where the reversal is for a fact which, since the
judgment, has ceased to exist [170]   If the common pleas affirms
the judgment of the justices, and the supreme court reverses, it
may award the re-restitution of the premises to the tenant[171] and
also of the damages paid [172]   For reasons that would properly
move the common pleas, while reversing, to refuse a re-restitution to the tenant, the supreme court may refuse such re-restitution.[173]   If the common pleas has, in reversing, awarded re-restitution to the tenant, the supreme court, in reversing the reversal, may award a writ for the redelivery of the possession to
the landlord.[174]

671. Review in appellate court.— The right to procure a review in the supreme court by writ of error, of the adjudication
of the court of common pleas upon the certiorari, was early recognized.[175]   That court may affirm or reverse a reversal or an
affirmance of the common pleas, or it may reverse so much of the
judgment of the common pleas as reverses the award of posses-

[167]*Freytag* v *Anderson,* 1 Ashm
(Pa) 98.
[168]*McGee* v *Fessler,* 1 Pa St 126
[169]*Fitzalden* v *Lee,* 2 Dall 205, 1
L ed 350   The court said the party
was in possession under the agreement of the other party, and it
would be fraudulent for the latter to
overthrow his agreement
[170]*McGee* v *Fessler,* 1 Pa St 126
[171]*Ayres* v *Novinger,* 8 Pa 412,
Stewart v *Martin,* 1 Yeates, 49
[172]*Stewart* v *Martin,* 1 Yeates, 49

[173]*Hokly* v *German Reformed Soc*
2 Pa St. 293   The rent was uncertain, and the inquisition did not find
the lease ended, but the tenant had,
plainly, no right to retain posses
sion   Cf also *Hutchinson* v *Potter,*
11 Pa 472
[174]*Boggs* v *Black,* 1 Binn 333
[175]*Clarke* v *Patterson* 6 Binn
128, *Boggs* v *Black,* 1 Binn 333,
Clark v *Yeat,* 4 Binn 185, *Wilmington S S Co* v *Haas,* 151 Pa.
113, 25 Atl 85.

sion to the landlord, while affirming so much of that judgment as reverses the award of damages to him [176]

672. Arresting the proceedings before the justices.—The 13th section of the act of March 21, 1772,[177] provides for the arrest of the proceedings before the justice, when the right to the land is claimed by some person other than the lessor, in consequence of some title accrued or happening since the commencement of the lease. On the proper presentation of this fact to the justices, they are directed to forbear to give judgment.

673. How this arrest is effected.— The justices are directed to forbear to give judgment, if the tenant shall allege that the land is claimed by another than the landlord, "and if thereupon the person so claiming shall forthwith, or upon a summons, immediately to be issued by the said justices, returnable in six days next following, before them appear, and on oath or affirmation, to be by the said justices administered, declare that he verily believes that he is entitled to the premises in dispute, and shall, with one or more sufficient sureties, become bound by recognizance in the sum of one hundred pounds to the lessor or lessors, his or their heirs or assigns, to prosecute his claim at the next court of common pleas" of the county where the land lies. The notice by the tenant of the claims of another may be given at any time; at the return day,[178] at a later hearing before the justices and jurors,[179] or even after hearing, but before the judgment. As the justices are directed, on the making of the allegation, etc , to "forbear to give the said judgment," it is likely that the interposition of the title of the third person must be

---

[176] *Watts* v *Fox*, 64 Pa 336

[177] 1 Pepper & L Digest, 2648, 1 Sm L 370

[178] *Steel* v *Thompson*, 3 Penr & W 34

[179] *Neumoyer* v *Andreas*, 57 Pa. 446, *Hoffman* v *Hoeckly*, 7 Phila 267, *Cunningham* v *Gardner*, 4 Watts & S 120 The complaint was made before the justices February 23d, 1864 The defendant filed an affidavit at the hearing on June 8th, 1864 In *Newell* v *Gibbs*, 1 Watts & S 496, it seems implied that judgment had been rendered by the justices before the tenant made his allegation of claim of a third person

made before judgment is given. It is the tenant who makes
the allegation that the title is in another His wife, it not appearing that she interposes with his authority, cannot make
it.[180] After the "allegation" of the tenant, the claimant of the
title, after notice, must make the affidavit and give the recognizance.[181] If the tenant is also the claimant of the title, he,
of course, makes the allegation and the affidavit, and enters into
the recognizance.[182] Otherwise, he cannot make the affidavit or
enter into the recognizance "If this were allowed," says Huston, J., "there would be found many a tenant who would swear,
and could give security, too, and the object of the law would be
defeated, the tenant would hold until the cause might be reached
in the course of the court some years after. . . . I will not
say that a tenant who has purchased from his lessor, or to whom
the title has descended or been devised, can be turned out under
this law, but only in such case can a tenant withdraw the
cause "[183] The tenant's wife, as claimant of the land, may, of
course, make the affidavit and enter into the recognizance.[184]
The making of the affidavit in the proper form, alleging the
proper facts, and by the proper person, *ipso facto* suspends the
right of the justices to proceed. They cannot decide on the credibility of the affiant, or the truth of the affidavit, even when the
affidavit is contradicted by a previous affidavit of the same
party [185]

674. Cause for arresting.— The existence of a claim to the
land in some other person than the lessor, in virtue of a title
acquired since the commencement of a lease, by descent, by

---

[180]*Hoffman* v *Hoeckly*, 7 Phila 267

[181]*Heritage* v *Wilfong*, 58 Pa 137. If he refuses, the jurisdiction of the justices is not superseded *Cunningham* v *Gardner*, 4 Watts & S 120

It is not necessary to summon him if he is present at the hearing *Ibid.*

[182]*Neumoyer* v *Andreas*, 57 Pa. 446, *Steel* v *Thompson*, 3 Penr & W 34, *Debozear* v *Butler*, 2 Giant Cas 417

[183]*Cunningham* v *Gardner*, 4 Watts & S 120

[184]*Alexander* v *Jones*, 13 Lanc. Bar, 43

[185]*McMullen* v *Orr*, 8 Phila 342.

deed, or under the last will of the lessor, may be averred.[186] The
deed, will, etc., must be that of the lessor, or of one claiming by
deed, will, etc, executed by him since the making of the demise.
The fact that the claimant claims by a deed made since the lease,
from X, who is not the lessor, it not appearing in the affidavit
how X became entitled, will not supersede the jurisdiction of the
justices.[187]   If the claimant asserts, not a deed from the lessor,
but a contract in writing for a conveyance, he must show such an
equitable right to a conveyance "as would sustain a bill for a
specific performance in a court of chancery."[188]   An affidavit
that, since the making of the lease, the landlord has, by a writing, sold the premises to the deponent, with an "understanding"
that the deed should be made "upon a performance of certain
matters," and that the deponent has 'kept his agreement," and
"offered to complete the transaction," but that the lessor has
fraudulently refused to execute the deed, and has conveyed the
premises to another, on a pretended consideration, with the purpose of defrauding the deponent, is insufficient, inasmuch as it
does not set forth the terms of the contract, and the manner in
which the affiant has performed it, or that there was a consideration, or whether the writing was of such a character as to satisfy the statute of frauds [189] In *Neumoyer* v. *Andreas*,[190] the
tenant alleged that after the lease for ten years of iron ore land,
on which the proceedings were begun, had been made, the lessor
contracted with the lessee that if the latter would sink a well,
plank it, put in an iron pump, put up an engine to pump out
the water, he should be entitled to dig out all the ore that could
be found on the premises, paying 25 cents per ton, so dug, to the

---

[186]If the claimant's affidavit does
not allege that he claims in virtue of
a title happening since the commencement of the lease, it is insufficient   *Hoffman* v *Hoeckly*, 7 Phila
267

[187]*Cummings* v *Young*, 6 Montg.
Co L Rep 161

[188]*Debozear* v *Butler*, 2 Grant Cas.
417

[189]*Debozear* v *Butler*, 2 Grant Cas.
417

[190] 57 Pa 446

lessor, and that, in pursuance of the contract, he remained in possession of the premises, did the acts stipulated for, paying the royalty of 25 cents per ton   This did not show such a title as ousted the jurisdiction of the justices   If the contract was a title to the ore in place, it was no reason why the landlord should not recover the possession of the surface, and the use of the timber, all the other minerals than iron ore, etc.   Besides, it was in parol, there was no possession taken in pursuance of it, and for the labor and materials expended in the improvements, compensation could easily be made.   If the contract was a mere license to dig ore,—and this view the court approves,—it conferred no right to the possession of the land, but a mere right to enter and dig for ore, with such a qualified possession as would enable the defendants to dig and take away the ore.   It was no barrier, therefore, to the landlord's recovery of the possession [191]

675. Cause, continued.— The allegation of the tenant, not that there has been an agreement, later than the lease, which entitles him to the continued possession, but that the lease itself is different from that described by the plaintiff, and that, as it actually is, it entitles to a continuance of the possession, is not a cause for ousting the jurisdiction of the justices   The landlord, *e. g ,* averred that the lease was for three years, at an annual rental of $12.   The tenant deposed that the lease was for his natural life; that he was to erect buildings, clear and improve the premises, and, at the expiration of the first three years, was to pay $12 annually during his life, that he has put up buildings, cleared and improved the land, and paid all rent falling due since the expiration of the three years.   This case, said

---

[101] The tenant may show, in a proceeding by Y against him, that since the lease was made, the lessor transferred the reversion to X, but subsequently, in fraud of X, assigned the lease to Y, and induced him to attorn to Y   This fact. properly averred, would oust the jurisdiction of the justices. *Goldsmith* v *Smith,* 3 Phila 360.

Huston, J., "presents a simple question of fact." The twelve jurors summoned to attend the justices could as well determine it as any twelve summoned for a session of the court of common pleas.[192] The allegation of the tenant that, under his lease, he still had a right to the possession,—e g., the lease, as alleged by the landlord, being for two years, the tenant avers that it gives him the privilege of three additional years,—does not oust the jurisdiction of the justices [193]

676. Expiration of lessor's title.— The lessor may own the land for life, or for a period of years, there being a reversioner or remainderman. The tenant may, if the title of the reversioner is sold since the lease was made, set up the title of the grantee of it, and the expiration of the estate of his lessor, as a cause for terminating the proceedings before the justices   In *Newell* v. *Gibbs,* [194] E. G., on September 10th, 1832, executed a lease to X, to last until May 1st, 1836.   On February 15th, 1837, the sheriff conveyed the fee belonging to E. G to W. G X had made a sublease of the premises to Y, whose terms do not appear in the report, and, some time after the sheriff's conveyance to W. G., began proceedings before two justices to recover the possession.   His tenants, by suggesting these facts, on the affidavit of W. G. superseded the jurisdiction of the justices "Although," says Rogers, J , "it must be confessed the words

---

[192]*Cunningham* v *Gardner*, 4 Watts & S 120   The court also calls attention to the fact that the derivation of title from the lessor must have been since the date of the lease, to oust the justices' jurisdiction   Yet in *Steel* v *Thompson*, 3 Penr & W 34, where the defendant alleged that the lease was made to him by his mortgagee, and that, since the making of the lease, he had, by tender of the debt, determined the lessor's (mortgagee's) right to the possession of the land, Gibson, Ch. LAND & TEN 37.

J , remarked that however consonant with the spirit of the provision in the act of 1772 for superseding the jurisdiction of justices, "it was certainly not warranted by the letter," but he declined to say that the suspending of the jurisdiction ought not to have been sustained

[193]*DeCoursey* v *Guarantee Trust & S D Co* 81 Pa 217

[194]1 Watts & S 496   Cf *DeCoursey* v *Guarantee Trust & S D Co.* 81 Pa. 217.

of the act do not embrace the case in terms, yet it comes within
the equity of the statute "

677. Proceedings after affidavit and recognizance —The exhibition of a title superseding that of the lessor, and derived from
him by will, deed, or descent, subsequently to the making of the
lease, and the filing of the affidavit and recognizance, make it
the duty of the justices to forbear to give judgment.   The claim
is prosecuted to the next term of the quarter sessions.   Though
this process of transferring the litigation to the latter court is
sometimes called an appeal to it,[195] it is not in fact an appeal [196]
It simply suspends the proceedings before the justices, and, if
the adverse claim is not prosecuted according to the true intent
and meaning of the recognizance, the jurisdiction is resumed by
the justices, and they then "proceed to give judgment" and cause
the lands and tenements to be delivered to the lessor [197]   The
single question before the common pleas is the devolution of the
title of the lessor.   Says Agnew, J.: "As remarked by Gibson,
Ch J , in *Steel* v. *Thompson,* 3 Penr. & W. 37, this is a suspension of the proceedings before the justices and freeholders,
in order to have the judgment of the court of common pleas on
the question whether the landlord has not parted with his reversionary right since the demise.   It is evident, therefore, that
when the case came into the common pleas, it was not to try the
questions committed by the act to the decision of the justices and
freeholders, but that of title to the reversion acquired after the
demise."[198]   In the common pleas, the burden of showing the

---

[195]*Newell* v. *Gibbs,* 1 Watts & S
496; *Ayres* v *Novinger,* 8 Pa 412 ,
Neumoyer v *Andreas,* 57 Pa 446

If, the claimant's attorney request
ing the prothonotary to enter his
appearance, the latter fails to do so
till judgment for want of an appearance is entered for the plaintiff, and
execution issued and possession delivered, the rule to open the judgment and set aside the execution

will be discharged   *Alexander* v.
Jones, 13 Lanc Bar, 33

[196]*Neumoyer* v. *Andreas,* 57 Pa.
446

[197] Sect 13, act March 21st, 1772

[198]*Neumoyer* v   *Andreas,* 57 Pa.
446

The transfer is for the trial of a
"collateral fact"   *Clark* v. *Everly,*
8 Watts & S 226.

devolution of title is upon the tenant,[199] but facts pertaining to the investigation of the justices are not examinable in the common pleas, *e. g.,* a former decision in favor of the tenant by justices and freeholders; an alleged agreement between the landlord and tenant for the prolongation of the term, and an acceptance by the landlord, since the alleged close of the term, as alleged by him, of rent from the defendant.[200]   If the common pleas is of opinion that the case should not have been withdrawn from the justices, because of the defectiveness of the affidavit[201] or of the recognizance, it quashes the "appeal" or transfer from the justices, and the case remains for decision by the justices. If, passing the preliminary matters affecting the right to transfer, it decides that there has been a derivation of title since the lease was made, it enters judgment for the plaintiff or defendant[202] and if for the plaintiff, it awards possession of the premises,[203] for, says Rogers, J.,[204] all the facts justifying a recovery by the plaintiff are "either found by the jury [in the common pleas], or are admitted by the tenant when he alleges the title to be in some third person."   Should the common pleas find that there had been no loss of title by the lessor, it would therefore have all the facts, either proved or admitted, on which the jus-

---

[199]*Newell* v *Gibbs,* 1 Watts & S. 500, *Neumoyer* v. *Andreas,* 57 Pa 446

[200]*Neumoyer* v *Andreas,* 57 Pa 446   Yet, in *Steel* v *Thompson,* 3 Penr & W 34 the court heard evidence as to the nature of the contract alleged to be a lease, on which the proceeding was founded, and as to payment by the tenant of the debt as security for which he had, by way of mortgage, conferred title on the lessor, and accepted the lease from him

[201]*Ayres* v *Novinger,* 8 Pa 412 The affidavit alleged simply that the affiant verily believed that he was entitled to the premises, instead of alleging that the right was disputed in virtue of a title accruing since the commencement of the lease

[202]*Steel* v *Thompson,* 3 Penr & W. 34   (Judgment for defendant)   It was suggested that there might have been a motion to remit the proceedings to the justices, had the court found that the title was derived from the lessor since the lease was made

[203]*Alexander* v *Jones* 13 Lanc. Bar 43   Judgment for want of an appearance of the claimant was entered for the plaintiff

[204]*Newell* v. *Gibbs,* 1 Watts & S 496.

tices could act.   Remission of the cause would involve delay and
expense for nothing   If the justices retain jurisdiction when
they should desist from exercising it, on the presentation of the
proper affidavit and recognizance, the remedy is a certiorari.[205]

[205]*McMullen* v *Orr*, 8 Phila. 342,
DeCoursey v *Guarantee Trust & S
D Co* 81 Pa 217, *Debozear* v *But-
ler*, 2 Grant Cas 417, *Cummings* v
Young, 6 Montg Co. L. Rep 161,
Hoffman v *Hoeckly*, 7 Phila 267
The decision of the common pleas,
on the so-called "appeal" to it, is re-
viewable in the appellate court
Steel v *Thompson*, 3 Penr & W 34,
Neumoyer v *Andreas*, 57 Pa 446,
Newell v *Gibbs*, 1 Watts & S 496,
The common pleas may award a new
trial for improper exclusion of evi-
dence   *Goldsmith* v. *Smith*, 3 Phila
360.

CHAPTER XXXI.

RECOVERY OF POSSESSION ACT OF DECEMBER 14, 1863.

678 The act of December 14, 1863.— The act of December 14, 1863,[1] furnishes a mode by which at the expiration of the term the landlord may regain the possession. He applies to a justice of the peace, alleging certain facts Thereupon the tenant is

[1] 1 Pepper & L Digest, 2650

581

summoned to appear at a place and time indicated   The justice hears the evidence and determines whether the necessary facts exist   If he finds that they do, he enters judgment against the tenant both for the premises and for damages   A writ for the recovery of possession and for the damages and costs may issue.   This act is additional to, and not a substitute for, the act of March 21, 1772,[2] under which therefore, if he chooses, the landlord may still proceed   The act of 1863 is not unconstitutional in not providing a jury to sit with the justice.   It allows an appeal; and it is immaterial from the constitutional standpoint that the appeal is not made a supersedeas, since it provides for the restoration of possession, and for the payment of damages for the dispossession, should the judgment on the appeal be for the defendant.[3]   Since all proper defenses are available in the proceeding under the act of 1863, equity will not restrain the landlord from resorting to it [4]

679. The lease or demise.— The remedy is furnished where any person or persons in this state, having leased or demised any lands or tenements to any person or persons for a term of one or more years or at will, shall be desirous, upon the determination of said lease, to have again and repossess such demised premises   The lease may be oral[5] or written.   A paper executed and sealed by the tenant alone, under which he entered upon the premises and has enjoyed them, paying the rent stipulated therein, being assented to by the owner of the land, is to be treated as a lease [6]   A written agreement to rent, signed by the owner, if assented to by X, who is in possession under a former

[2]*Rich* v *Keyser,* 54 Pa   86, *Duff* v *Fitzwater,* 54 Pa   224

[3]*Haines* v *Levin,* 51 Pa   412   The wisdom of the act is vaguely questioned, in *Brown's Appeal,* 66 Pa 155

[4]*Pittsburgh & A Drove Yard Co s Appeal* 123 Pa   250, 16 Atl   625   As to subsequent recovery of damages for wrongful ejection, see *Lambert* v. *Jones,* 136 Pa   31, 19 Atl   956

[5]*Koontz* v *Hammond* 62 Pa   177.

[6]*Kaier* v *Leahy,* 15 Pa   Co   Ct 243   Cf   *Duffee* v. *Mansfield,* 141 Pa. 507, 21 Atl   675.

lease, becomes a lease, on which the statutory proceedings may be begun.[7]

680. The term.— The lease is for a term of one or more years or at will. A lease for two months and a half,[8] it was tacitly assumed, is included in this description, as, it is needless to state, is one for a year[9] or longer term   The lease may likewise be at will, *e g ,* the tenant stipulating to leave the premises on five days'[10] or ten days' notice.[11]   It may be from year to year.[12] It may have been a lease for years, but become one from year to year by reason of the tenant's holding over with the consent of the landlord[13]   The lease may be subject to conditions on breach of which the landlord may at once determine the lease, by instituting the proceeding before the justice;[14] or he may determine the lease at the end of any year, on a previous three months' notice[15]   An alienation by the lessor and the tenant's attornment to the grantee do not make a new lease between the alienee and lessee and a new termination of the term,[16] but there may be an agreement between the grantee and the tenant

[7]*Bergner* v *Palethorp,* 2 W. N. C. 297

[8]*Wilke* v *Campbell,* 5 Pa Super Ct 618   The lessee had agreed to leave on thirty days' notice   In *Spidle* v *Hess,* 20 Lanc L Rev 385, it was denied that a lease from month to month was within the act of December 14, 1863   Though the lease was for one month from March 10, 1902, and contained an acceptance of notice to quit on the 10th day of each succeeding month without further notice, proceedings could be had under the act of 1863   *Con yngham* v. *Everett,* 11 Kulp, 179 A lease for one month is not within the act of 1863   *Vogel* v *Trumberg,* 26 Pa Co Ct 464, 12 Pa Dist R. 106.

[9]*Haines* v *Levin,* 51 Pa 412, *Rich* v *Keyser,* 54 Pa 86, *Koontz* v. *Hammond,* 62 Pa 177.

[10]*Killen* v *Haddock,* 4 Kulp, 408

[11]*Mill Creek Coal Co* v. *Androkus,* 2 Pa Dist R 764

[12]*Tilford* v *Fleming,* 64 Pa 300, *Glenn* v *Thompson,* 75 Pa 389   If the owner agrees with X that X shall work for him on his farm, and shall live in a house on the farm so long as he works it, and shall remove as soon as he ceases to work, the owner cannot eject him when he ceases to work, by the machinery of the act of 1863   *Deisinger* v *Shaud,* 12 Pa Dist R 698

[13]*Sterling* v *Richardson,* 24 Phila Leg Int 140   A lease for one year with the privilege of five years more is within the act   *Jones* v *Kroll,* 116 Pa 85, 8 Atl 857

[14]*Arnsthal* v *Patterson,* 3 Pennyp 25

[15]*Quinn* v *McCarty,* 81 Pa 475

[16]*Tilford* v *Fleming,* 64 Pa 300

whereby the former lease is displaced by a new one, having the date of the alienation for its commencement.[17]

681. Rent reserved — The 1st section of the act of March 6, 1872,[18] enacts that it shall not be lawful to prosecute proceedings under the act of December 14, 1863, "unless such proceedings shall be founded upon a written lease or contract in writing, or on a parol agreement, in and by which the relation of landlord and tenant is established between the parties, and a certain rent is therein reserved" The act of 1863 had not required that a rent should be reserved in the lease.[19] The lease being "during the will and pleasure" of the lessor, and without rent, the justice has no jurisdiction,[20] nor has he, if the lease is "at the yearly rent of the interest and taxes accruing thereon," because the rent is not certain. The interest is on what sum? and at what rate? "Is it interest," asks Sterrett, J., "on the value of the demised premises, or on the amount paid therefor by the landlord, or on the encumbrances that were then or might thereafter be charged on the property; or is it interest on debts owing by the landlord, or interest on something else? While the contract relation of landlord and tenant is perhaps set forth with sufficient certainty, the *quantum* of rent reserved is conspicuously indefinite and uncertain As to that there is not the slightest approach to precision or certainty; nor is there anything on the record that would even assist a jury if the question was before them, in endeavoring to ascertain the amount of rent reserved. Such certainty, or rather uncertainty as this, was never contemplated by the framers of the statute "[21] The rent must be so distinctly reserved that the intervention of a jury is not necessary to render it certain [22]

[17]*Rothermel* v *Dumn,* 119 Pa 632, 13 Atl 509

[18] 1 Pepper & L Digest, 2654; P L 22

[19]*Koontz* v *Hammond,* 62 Pa 177

[20]*Graver* v *Fehr,* 89 Pa 460

[21]*Davis* v *Davis,* 115 Pa 261, 7 Atl 746

[22] The record must show a rent reserved *Weber* v *Porr,* 1 Legal Rec-

682 Who may institute the proceedings.— Any person or persons having leased or demised lands, "it shall be lawful for such lessor, his agent or attorney, to complain," says the act of 1863. The lessor is usually an owner of the land in fee, but he may own it for life only.[23] He may be a lessee for a term of years and make a sublease; or he may even be a sublessee and may make a sublease   The lessee for eighty-two years, e g , made a sublease to B and C for twenty-two years, who sublet to X one room of the building from April 1, 1880, to April 1, 1881. On June 30, B sold his interest to R, who also obtained the ownership of one half of the leasehold.   Subsequently C acquired the other half of the leasehold, so that C and R owned each an undivided half of the lease and of the sublease.   R served a notice to quit on X, on December 31, 1880, but C renewed what had been the sublease to X for another year. Since the subsublease to X had been made by B and C, R, who owned only the share of B, could not, without the co-operation of C, terminate the lease [24] There may be two or more lessors, who may begin the proceedings [25] The lease being made by "William G Bedford, Agent," he as "agent" may complain to the justice. It is not necessary that the owner of the premises should. It will not be assumed that there is an owner different from William G. Bedford; but if it were assumed, the defendant would be estopped from setting up his title for the purpose of preventing a recovery of the possession by Bedford, from whom he obtained it.[26] Apparently, even when the lease was not made by A as

ord Rep 131, *Hiester* v *Broun*, 11 Lanc Bar, 159, *Reynolds* v *Robinson*, 3 C P Rep 20

[23]*Koontz* v *Hammond*, 62 Pa 177, *Bergner* v. *Palethorp*, 2 W N C. 207

[24]*Wenger* v *Raymond*, 104 Pa 33

[25] Cf. *Wenger* v *Raymond*, 104 Pa 33

[26]*Bedford* v. *Kelly*, 61 Pa 491.

The lease being by A G Stone "agent of the estate of Daniel Stone," A G Stone can institute the proceedings whether he was or not the agent of the heirs of Daniel Stone, and whether he could be the agent of an "estate" or not *Stone* v *Wimmill*, 24 Phila Leg Int 212, 6 Phila 311.

agent for B, but by B himself, A, the agent, may, styling himself such, begin the proceedings before the justice,[27] and even on the appeal the name of the owner may, by amendment, be substituted for that of the agent.[28]

683. Successors to lessor — The use of the words "lessor, his agent, or attorney," in the act of 1863, induced some courts to think that the grantee of the reversion could not begin the proceedings,[29] but in *Glenn* v. *Thompson*,[30] Sharswood, J., held that the lessor's heir, and his grantee,—the purchaser at a sheriff's sale of his interest,—could resort to the remedy. The act of February 20, 1867,[31] directs that the act of 1863 shall be so "construed as to apply to cases in which the owner or owners of the demised premises have acquired title thereto by descent or purchase from the original lessor or lessors" One who receives a conveyance from the lessor pending the lease may therefore apply to the justice for the recovery of possession at the end of the term and without any attornment to him by the tenant.[32] The devisee of the lessor, and his executors when the control of the land is given to them, may employ the remedy of the act of 1863,[33] but in *Holder* v *Hill*,[34] the complaint in 1868 by the administrator *d. b. n.* of George Focht, whose will was proved in 1829, alleging that the demise was made by Abraham Focht, was not adequate to support the judgment of the justice, because nothing in the record showed the connection between George

[27]*Heritage* v *Wilfong*, 58 Pa 137, *Supplee* v *Timothy*, 23 W N C 386, *McGregor* v *Haines*, 6 Phila 62, *Sterling* v *Richardson*, 24 Phila Leg Int 140, *McClelland* v *Patterson* (Pa.) 5 Cent Rep 734, 10 Atl. 475

[29]*Lutz* v *Wainwright*, 193 Pa 541, 44 Atl 565

[30]*Cook* v *McDevitt*, 6 Phila 131, *Dubasse* v *Martin*, 24 Phila Leg Int 92, *Dickenshcets* v. *Hotchkiss*, 6 Phila 156

[30]75 Pa 389

[31]1 Pepper & L Digest, 2653, P L. 30

[32]*Keating* v *Condon*, 68 Pa 75, *Dumn* v *Rothermel*, 112 Pa 272 3 Atl 800, *Tilford* v *Fleming*, 64 Pa 300, *Mortimer* v *O'Reagan*, 10 Phila 500, 1 Legal Chronicle, 129, *Rouan* v *Gates*, 9 Pa Dist R 564

[33] Cf *Brown's Appeal*, 66 Pa 155

[34]1 Woodw Dec 451 It would be singular, says the court if after the lapse of forty years, the administrator *d b n* still had anything to do with the land.

Focht or his administrator and Abraham Focht. If a lease is made by A as trustee, A may, especially if he does not name the *cestui que trust,* begin the proceedings [35] A receiver of the lessor probably cannot institute the proceedings, without leave of the court, or without attornment of the tenant to him [36] Possibly if there are two lessors, or two grantees of the lessor, either can begin the procedure[37] unless one of them dissents from the proceedings and desires the tenant to continue in possession.[38] Natural persons or corporations—both nonmunicipal and municipal, *e. g ,* boroughs,[39]—may commence the proceedings.

684. The defendant.— The person against whom the proceedings are had is styled in the act of 1863 the "lessee or tenant " The tenant may be a married woman, and she may therefore, despite coverture, be defendant [40] A sublessee was the defendant at the suit of the lessor, in *Chambers* v. *Shivery,*[41] and both the tenant and subtenant were defendants, in *McClelland* v. *Patterson.*[42]

685. When the proceedings may begin.—The proceedings may begin at any interval of time, however long or short, after the close of the term The term closing on April 1, proceedings were begun July 26 ;[43] the term closing March 31 at midnight, the complaint was made April 2 following,[44] the term closing December 1, the proceedings commenced December 2 [45]

686 Three months' notice.— The act of December 14, 1863,[46] gives to any person who has demised land, for years or at will,

[35]*Synder* v *Carfrey,* 54 Pa 90
[36]*Chase* v *Goodale,* 2 Law Times N S 107
[37]*Phelps* v *Cornog* (Pa) 2 Cent Rep 844, 4 Atl 922
[38]*Wenger* v *Raymond,* 104 Pa 33
[39]*Phœnixville* v *Walters,* 147 Pa 501, 23 Atl 776
[40]*Weber* v *Porr,* 1 Leg Rec Rep 131 Cf *Trimble's Appeal,* 5 W N C 396
[41] 6 Pa Dist R 101.

[42](Pa) 5 Cent Rep 734, 10 Atl 475
[43]*Wenger* v *Raymond,* 104 Pa 33.
[44]*Supplee* v. *Timothy,* 23 W N C. 386
[45]*Carter* v *Hess,* 3 W N C 325 Term ending May 23, the complaint was made May 28 *Sterling* v *Richardson,* 24 Phila Leg Int 140
[46] 1 Pepper & L Digest, 2650, P. L of 1864, 1125.

who desires, at the determination of the lease, to have the prem·
ises again, having given three months' notice of such intention
to his lessee or tenant, the right to complain to a justice, who on
proof, *inter alia*, of the fact that the term is fully ended, and
that three months' previous notice has been given of the lessor's
desire to repossess the premises, may enter judgment for the lessor and restore to him the possession

687. Notice precedes the expiration of the term.—The notice,
and three months following it, must precede the expiration of the
term   If the notice itself is not given until the lease has expired, if *e g.*, the lease for one year ends on March 5, 1866,
and the notice to quit is not given until March 8, 1866, no recovery of possession, under the act of 1863, can ever be effected.[47]   A notice given before, but not three months before,
the expiration of the term, would be ineffectual.   Proceedings
could not be begun on it after the lapse of three months from
the giving of the notice [48]

688 How compute the months.— The months are calendar
months   If the term for a year begins March 25, 1868, it closes
at midnight on March 24, 1869.   Notice to quit given on December 25, 1868, is a three months' notice [49]   "The proof to be
made by the landlord, *inter alia*, is," says Agnew, J., " 'that the
term for which the premises were demised is fully ended, and
that three months' previous notice had been given ' Previous
to what?   The act answers—previous to the determination of
the lease   But when does the lease fully end and determine?
Certainly not until the last moment of the last day of the term,
which, in this case, was the 24th day of March   The landlord's
right of re-entry did not begin therefore until the first moment
of the 25th day of March had arrived.   This corresponds with
the general custom and understanding   Leases beginning on the

[47]*Rich* v *Keyser*, 54 Pa 86   [49]*Duffy* v *Ogden*, 64 Pa 240.
[48]*Speigle* v *McFarland*, 25 Phila.
Leg Int. 165.

1st day of April expire on the 31st day of March in the following year; the old tenant giving up and the new tenant coming in on the 1st day of April, without a gap in the possession. It is obvious, therefore, that the 24th day of March counted a whole day when its last moment had arrived   Counting the 25th day of December on which the notice was given, and the 24th day of March when the lease had expired, the three months were fully ended and expired before the landlord's right of re-entry had accrued. The only defect of time which could be alleged is on the 25th of December, the day on which notice was given. But that is also to be regarded as a whole day, for the law takes no account of fractions of a day in the computation of time. Service on that day was one day's notice, and therefore the three months' notice previous to the termination of the lease was complete and fully ended. The next day, March 25th, was the beginning of a new period." Notice April 1st to quit on July 1st, the day following the close of the term, is in time.[50] There can be no question, therefore, that a notice served on February 12th, the term expiring on May 12th,[51] or a notice served December 31st, the lease expiring the following March 31st,[52] is early enough.

689 Notice longer than necessary — It is not necessary that the notice should precede, by exactly three months, the termination of the lease   It may precede such termination by any greater interval and be effectual   The lease ending February 24, 1867, notice given on November 20, 1866;[53] or the lease ending December 22d, notice given September 20th,[54] or the lease ending June 23d, notice given the preceding December

---

[50]*Currier* v *Grebe*, 142 Pa. 48, 21 Atl 755   *Contra, Parsons* v *Roumfort*, 2 Pearson (Pa) 81
[51]*McGowen* v *Sennett*, 1 Brewst (Pa) 397
[52]*Wenger* v *Raymond*, 104 Pa 33, 3 Atl 800, 110 Pa. 632, 13 Atl 592

Koontz v *Hammond*, 62 Pa 177; *Quinn* v *McCarty*, 81 Pa 475
[53]*Stone* v *Wimmell*, 24 Phila, Leg Int 212.
[54]*Dumn* v *Rothermel*, 112 Pa 272,

3d,[55] or the lease ending February 15, 1867, notice given October 22, 1866,[56] or the lease ending March 19, 1893, notice given on November 15, 1892,[57] were early enough. In *Snyder* v. *Carfrey*,[58] the demise was for one year from May 15, 1865. The notice was given on January 10, 1866 "Here," says Woodward, Ch. J., holding the notice sufficient, "was more than three months' notice to quit at the end of the term, a date that was as well known to the tenant as to the landlord." A lease was for five years with the proviso that the tenant should leave at any time, on receiving one year's notice. A notice given July 29, 1887, to leave on August 1, 1888, was sufficient, both to end the term and also to authorize the proceedings under the act of 1863.[59]

690 Notice necessary under whatever kind of lease —Though the notice is unnecessary, to end the term, as, *e. g.*, when the term is for one year[60] or other definite period, it is necessary to authorize the institution of proceedings before the justice, under the act of 1863. When the lease is at will or from year to year, notice is necessary in order to end the lease, as well as in order to validate proceedings before the justice,[61] and though, because the tenancy is from month to month, or because the lease stipulates for it[62] a shorter notice than of three months is sufficient to terminate the lease, the three months' notice will be necessary to qualify the lessor to recover the possession by the statutory proceeding.

691. Who gives the notice — The notice to quit must emanate

[55]*Tilford* v *Fleming*, 64 Pa 300

[56]*Kraft* v *Wolf*, 6 Phila. 310, 24 Phila Leg Int 212

[57]*Jalass* v *Young*, 3 Pa Super Ct 422

[58] 54 Pa 90 Lease ends May 23, notice given January 2 *Sterling* v *Richardson*, 24 Phila Leg Int 140

[59]*Phoenixville* v *Walters*, 147 Pa 501 23 Atl 776, 184 Pa 615

[60]*Ruch* v *Keyser*, 54 Pa 86, *Greenleaf* v *Haberacker*, 1 Woodw Dec. 436, *Chambers* v *Shivery*, 6 Pa Dist R 101, *Wilke* v *Campbell*, 5 Pa Super. Ct 618

[61]*Dumn* v *Rothermel*, 112 Pa 272, 3 Atl 860, 119 Pa 632, 13 Atl 509; *Phoenixville* v *Walters*, 147 Pa 501, 23 Atl 776

[62]*Killeen* v *Haddock*, 4 Kulp. 408 The lease prescribed a five days' notice.

from one having authority to demand the possession   A notice signed by the lessor and also by his grantee would sustain a proceeding by the latter to recover the possession.[63]   A notice by the lessee to his subtenant cannot, it seems, be taken advantage of by the lessor, in a proceeding to dispossess the subtenant [64]   The lease being made April 1, 1872, the lessor, A, conveyed the reversion to B, September 24, 1872.   A notice to quit served December 31, 1872, by A, stating that he desired to repossess himself of the premises on April 1, 1873, was sufficient to support proceedings by B for the recovery of the possession.   "If," said Sharswood, J , "as the inquisition expressly finds, the notice was given with the desire of delivering the possession to the alienee, and the proceeding [before the justice] is in the name and for the benefit of the alienee, the lessor was no such stranger   Every presumption is in favor of the regularity of the proceeding; and, applying this principle, we agree with the court below that the record sufficiently shows that the lessor still retained an interest in the property after the date of her deed of conveyance, to entitle her to give the necessary notice to quit."[65]

692 Notice to whom —If there are joint lessees, a service of the notice directed to both or one of them is a good notice   The lease being to James Glenn and Charles A Glenn (who is a son of James), a notice directed to James Glenn & Son was good. A "verbal mistake in the recital of names of the lessees was immaterial."[66]

693 Form of the notice.— A mistake in the date assigned in the notice for the expiration of the lease will be unimportant if

---

[63]*Jalass* v *Young,* 3 Pa Super Ct 422
[64]*Chambers* v *Shivery,* 6 Pa Dist. R 101   The lease was to P for one year from April 1, 1895   P sublet to S for the month of April 1895, but continued in possession until April 30, 1896, when the proceedings were begun   P demanded possession July 8, 1895   The lessor, not shown to have given three months' notice to quit, could not avail himself of P's notice
[65]*Glenn* v *Thompson,* 75 Pa 389
[66]*Glenn* v *Thompson,* 75 Pa 389

it must appear to the tenant that it is a mistake. A notice dated December 30, 1880, and served the next day, stated that the lease would expire on March 31, "1880," instead of 1881. The mistake was manifest and innocuous "It was explicit and clear, however, in this, that possession was demanded at the expiration of the lease."[67] A notice reciting a demise from the lessor of described premises "for a certain term which will terminate and expire on the 19th day of April, 1893," and expressing the desire of the notifier to have again and repossess the premises, and requiring the lessee "to leave the same upon the expiration of the hereinbefore-mentioned term," is not void because the lease really expired March 19th, instead of April 19th "The misstatement as to the end of the term," remarks Smith J., "could not mislead the tenant, who, of course, knew when the current year expired."[68] It is not necessary that the notice should state that possession is required at the expiration of the term It is enough if it requires the tenant to "remove from and leave the premises."[69] The notice may be given by an agent It may, e g, be signed "B. M. Miller for E. A. Miller"[70]

694 Service of notice — The written notice may be dated one day and served on a later day It is effective, of course, only upon its actual service[71] The notice may be served personally, or on some adult person on the premises If the tenant takes himself and all his family from the premises on the last hours of the period in which notice must be given, in order to make service impossible, the slipping of a notice under the front door of the house, or of a shop forming, with the house, the premises, will, if the next day the lessor verbally informs the tenant

[67] *Wenger* v *Raymond,* 104 Pa 33
[68] *Jalass* v *Young,* 3 Pa Super Ct 422 See *Dumn* v *Rothermel,* 112 Pa 272, 3 Atl 800 for a form of notice
[69] *Stone* v *Wimmill,* 24 Phila Leg Int 212 As to a discrepancy between the end of the term in the lease, and that mentioned in the notice *vide Kaier* v *Leahy,* 15 Pa Co Ct 243
[70] *Glenn* v *Thompson,* 75 Pa 389
[71] *Wenger* v *Raymond,* 104 Pa 33, *Dumn* v *Rothermel,* 112 Pa 272 3 Atl 800.

of this act,[72] or the tenant the next day finds the notice, be a good service.

695. Waiver of notice.— There may be an explicit waiver in the lease of the notice required by the act of 1863, and when there is, the notice will be unnecessary. The words: "The notice to quit required by an act of assembly previous to proceedings to recover possession of the demised premises, and the benefits of the laws granting stay of execution . . . are hereby waived by the said party of the second part,"—dispense with notice, as a preliminary to the commencement of proceedings under the act,[73] as do the words, "And the lessee hereby waives the notice to quit required by the act of assembly "[74] A provision in the lease for a shorter than three months' notice, in order to end the term, cannot be understood to intend to substitute this notice for that which is prescribed in the act of assembly. Thus, the lease being at will, the tenant engaging to leave at five days' notice;[75] or the lease being for a definite term, with a proviso to quit the possession upon thirty days' notice after a sale of the reversion,[76]—the stipulation concerning notice will be understood to refer solely to the termination of the tenant's right of possession, and not to the condition for instituting the statutory proceedings to recover the premises. But if the lease is for a definite term, e g , two and a half months, and it contains a stipulation to surrender possession on thirty days' notice, it is inferred that the purpose of the stipulation is to substitute the thirty days for the period mentioned in the

[72]*Currier* v *Grebe*, 142 Pa 48, 21 Atl 755

[73]*Sizer* v *Russett*, 11 Pa. Super Ct 103, *Wilke* v. *Campbell*, 5 Pa Super Ct 618

[74]*Kaier* v. *Leahy*, 15 Pa Co Ct. 243

[75]*Killeen* v *Haddock*, 4 Kulp. 408

[76]*Lapsley* v *Fifth Avenue Nat Bank*, 30 Pittsb L J N S 271 Cf *Matthews* v *Rising*, 31 Pittsb. L J. LAND & TEN 38.

N S 163 In *Mill Creek Coal Co* v *Androkus*, 2 Pa Dist R 764, the court thought that a provision in a lease at will, for the surrender of the possession on ten days' notice, was a waiver of the three months' notice But the waiver was not explicitly found by the justice, as it should have been in order to dispense with the statutory notice.

acts of assembly. "A waiver," says the court, "arises by necessary implication, when the lease contains a stipulation for a
notice to quit, which could have been introduced for no other
purpose but as a substitute for the statutory provision. This is
such a case. The notice stipulated for was not intended as a
condition precedent to the termination of the tenancy, as possibly it might be construed if the tenancy were at will. It was
manifestly intended to take the place of the statutory notice to
remove, and the record shows with sufficient clearness that it was
given in accordance with the terms of the agreement "[77]

696. The complaint — It shall be lawful, says the act of 1863,
for the lessor, his agent, or attorney to complain of the refusal
of the tenant to leave and surrender up the premises at the expiration of the term, to any justice of the peace in the city,
borough, or county wherein the demised premises lie. The complaint should, when presented to the justice, be in writing or at
least reduced to writing, and sworn to or affirmed before he
takes action on it.[78] This complaint is the foundation of the
action.[79] It must, according to some cases, set forth all the
facts necessary to give jurisdiction to the justice,[80] though there
is an occasional intimation that the findings of the justice of
facts not stated in the complaint might cure the error of the
omission.[81] Possibly an amended complaint may be filed after
the issue of the summons and in the presence of the parties at
the hearing. If such amended complaint professes to be complete, it cannot be supplemented by the averments of the original
complaint.[82] The complaint, it may probably be said, must state

[77] *Wilke* v. *Campbell*, 5 Pa Super.
Ct 619

[78] In *McGinnis* v *Vernon*, 67 Pa
149, no complaint in writing as the
ground of the summons was filed

[79] *Rowan* v *Gates*, 9 Pa Dist R
564, *Wenger* v *Raymond*, 104 Pa
33, *Leinbach* v *Kaufman*, 2 Walk
(Pa.) 515.

[80] *McDermott* v. *McIlwain*, 75 Pa.
341, *Leinbach* v *Kaufman*, 2 Walk.
(Pa) 515, *Rowan* v *Gates*, 9 Pa.
Dist R 564, *Spotts* v. *Farling*, 2
Pearson (Pa) 295

[81] *McDermott* v *McIlwain*, 75 Pa
341

[82] *Spotts* v *Farling*, 2 Pearson
(Pa) 295.

that the lessor was quietly and peaceably possessed of the premises when he made the lease,[83] that he demised the same to the
tenant in possession or to some other person under whom such
person claims,[84] that a rent certain was reserved;[85] that the
term is fully ended,[86] that three months' notice to quit the possession, prior to the ending of the term, was given,[87] that the
defendant nevertheless retains and refuses to give up the possession.[88] It must state whether the lease is for years or at will.
To describe it in the alternative as "for a year or at will," is at
least an irregularity, though, possibly, it would not, alone, destroy the jurisdiction of the justice.[89] The premises which are
the subject of the lease and of the action must be adequately described. The complaint describing them by adjoiners and adding the words "containing —— acres, more or less," was mildly
censured by Thompson, Ch J., who remarked: "The premises
are not sufficiently described. There are boundaries given of
the land, but the acres are in blank, with the addition of 'more
or less' By right, the number of acres should have been set out
if in the case "[90] Describing the premises merely by the township in which they lie is insufficient,[91] but describing them as
"situated on the north side of Third street, at the northeast corner of Elm and Third streets, in the borough of South Bethlehem, Pa.," is enough.[92] A complaint alleging that the lessor

[83]Rowan v Gates, 9 Pa Dist R
564, Spotts v Furling, 2 Pearson
(Pa) 295, Steigelman v Klugh, 9
Lanc L Rev 321
[84]Rowan v Gates, 9 Pa Dist R
564, Steigelman v Klugh, 9 Lanc
L Rev 321
[85]Steigelman v Klugh, 9 Lanc L
Rev 321
[86]Rowan v Gates, 9 Pa Dist R
564, Steigelman v Klugh, 9 Lanc
L Rev 321
[87]Rowan v Gates, 9 Pa Dist R
564, Steigelman v Klugh, 9 Lanc L
Rev 321
[88]Steigelman v Klugh, 9 Lanc L
Rev 321

[89]Givens v Miller, 62 Pa 133.
Thompson, Ch J, said "If everything else had been right, we might
not be disposed to disturb the judgment "
[90]Givens v Miller, 62 Pa 133
That setting out the number of
acres is unnecessary is intimated in
Spotts v Farling, 2 Pearson (Pa)
295, Quigney v Quigney, 1 Northampton Co Rep 20
[91]Spotts v Furlong, 2 Pearson
(Pa) 295, Steigelman v Klugh, 9
Lanc L Rev 321
[92]Quigney v Quigney, 1 Northamp
ton Co Rep 20.

was in quiet possession, and that he demised the same, may give a copy of the lease, to indicate the nature of it, and its period of ending If in addition it avers a notice to quit of the necessary period, giving a copy of it, and of the return of its service, and alleges that the tenant refuses to deliver up the premises, it is sufficient [93] The complaint must be filed with the magistrate in order to give him jurisdiction.[94]

697. Before whom complaint made — The justice before whom the complaint is made alone has jurisdiction to proceed upon it to an investigation and judgment It was thought in *Rowan* v *Gates*[95] that a complaint could not be made before a justice unless it was first presented to him and was sworn to before him; and that, if a complaint was sworn to before one justice without intending that the proceeding should be begun before him, it could not be carried before another justice with a view to beginning proceedings before the latter. This view is not accepted in *Chambers* v. *Shivery*,[96] where it is held that the lessor may swear to his complaint before any officer empowered to administer oaths, *e. g.*, before a notary public, and may then carry it thus authenticated to a justice, who may act upon it without requiring a fresh oath.

698. The summons.— On the presentation of a complaint containing the proper averments, it becomes the duty of the justice "to summon the defendant to appear at a day fixed, as in other civil actions," giving the defendant notice of the time and place of hearing. The return day must not be more than eight nor less than five days after the date of the summons [97] It is error

[92]*Kaier* v *Leahy*, 15 Pa Co Ct 243

[94]*Long* v *Swavely*, 1 Just 75

[95]9 Pa Dist R 564 The complaint should be written and sworn to, as in *Speigle* v *McFarland*, 25 Phila Leg Int 165, *Dumn* v *Rothermel*, 112 Pa 272, 3 Atl 800, *Wence* v *Raymond*, 104 Pa 33

[96]6 Pa Dist R 101 In *Brad*field v *Rehm*, 6 Phila. 135, judgment was rendered on an unsworn complaint, December 23, 1865 The complaint was sworn to March 8, 1866 On certiorari, several exceptions being alleged, the judgment was reversed

[97]Act March 10, 1810, § 2, 1 Pepper & L Digest, 2555, 5 Smith's Laws, 161

to make a writ issued August 28 returnable August 31 [98] But one served four days before the time of hearing was held proper though there was no appearance [99] The summons should always contain a brief statement of the grounds of its issuance,[100] and if it is misleading in this respect, if, *e g ,* the writ commands the constable to summon the defendant to appear and answer the plaintiff "of a plea of debt or demand not exceeding $100," the proceedings founded on it will be invalid, unless the defendant waives the error by appearing [101] It should designate the time and place of the hearing [102] Errors of form and contents of summons are waived by the defendant, if he appears [103] But if the error is one concerning the nature of the proceeding,—if, *e g.,* the summons has notified him of an action for a debt not exceeding $100, and not of a proceeding designed to dispossess him,—the defendant does not waive the error by coming to the justice's office at the time of hearing, if he does not remain to hear the testimony. "He appeared," says Thompson, Ch. J., "to meet a claim of debt, as commanded by the summons. This surely would not fix him as appearing in another cause in which he was not summoned "[104]

699. Service of the summons — A service "personally on the defendant at his dwelling-house, by leaving a copy of the original summons and making known the contents thereof," is said to be a sufficient service of any summons, and consequently of the

[98]*Horner* v *Wethcrell,* 19 W N C 197

[99]*Phelps* v *Cornog* (Pa) 2 Cent Rep 844, 4 Atl 922 A summons issued June 2 to appear on June 8 and served on June 2, was good *Snyder* v *Carfrey,* 54 Pa 90

[100]*McGinnis* v *Vernon,* 67 Pa 149, *Kaier* v *Leahy,* 15 Pa Co Ct 243

[101]*Givens* v *Miller,* 62 Pa 133

[102]*Phelps* v *Cornog* (Pa.) 2 Cent Rep 844, 4 Atl 922 The summons required the defendant to be and appear on the 3d day of February 1885, between the hours of 11 30 and 12 o'clock in the noon, before the magistrate at his court, 146 S Sixth street, in Philadelphia The description of the time was held sufficiently intelligible

[103]*Spotts* v *Farling,* 2 Pearson (Pa) 295, *Kaier* v *Leahy,* 15 Pa Co Ct 243 *Quigney* v *Quigney,* 1 Northampton Co Rep 20

[104]*Givens* v *Miller,* 62 Pa 133.

summons in this proceeding before the justice,[105] though it is elsewhere held that unless the original summons is shown to have been produced it is not enough to leave a correct copy on the premises, viz., the leased dwelling-house, with the defendant personally [106] It is not enough to prove, by the constable's return or otherwise, that the writ was "served personally by leaving a copy with defendant at his residence and informing him of the contents thereof," for it would not appear of what the copy left was a copy.[107] A statement by the justice in his record that A B. V , constable, returned on oath a service, giving what purports to be the language of the constable's return, is sufficient evidence on certiorari of the making of the service by A B V. and that A. B. V. was a proper constable [108]

700. What must be proved before the justice.—All the facts whose existence is by the act of 1863 made the condition upon which the lessor may recover in the proceeding furnished by it must be established before the justice, and found by him The defendant may of course furnish evidence of their nonexistence, in rebuttal of that tendered by the plaintiff.

701 Defenses allowable.— The tenant cannot deny the existence of a right in the lessor to the land at the time of making the lease. He cannot, e. g., show that prior to the alleged leasing he had acquired an interest in the premises, which entitled him to possess them independently and in defiance of the terms of the lease. The taking of the lease estops him from alleging this title, until the possession is surrendered.[109] He may, however, show the devolution of that right on another, since the lease was made, by the death of the lessor, by his conveyance, by a sheriff's

---

[105]*Snyder* v *Carfrey*, 54 Pa 90

[106]*Shourds* v *Way*, 8 Phila 301

[107]*Berrill* v *Flynn*, 8 Phila 239 In *Phelps* v *Cornog* (Pa) 2 Cent Rep 844, 4 Atl 922, a return "served on defendant by leaving a copy of the within original at the dwelling-house with an adult member of the family" was not condemned

[108]*Phelps* v *Cornog* (Pa) 2 Cent. Rep 844, 4 Atl 922

[109]*Koontz* v *Hammond*, 62 Pa 177 Cf *Fisher* v *McCauley*, 2 Dauphin Co. Rep 180.

sale of his title, etc.[110] This he does not do by asserting and proving that since the lease was made there has been a sheriff's sale of the premises to S, without also asserting and proving that the sale was of the interest of the lessor. Without proof that the interest sold was the lessor's, the justice properly gives judgment for the plaintiff, no other defense appearing[111] The tenant may show that he was induced by fraud or misrepresentation to accept the demise, and so avoid the estoppel against asserting a title superior to the landlord's.[112] The defendant may show that, although wife of X, to whom a lease had been made, she had been in earlier possession of the premises under another than her husband's lessor, and had never known of the lease to him, nor recognized it[113] He may show a new lease prolonging the period of his possession,[114] or, in short, may make any defense that would be available in an action of ejectment,[115] in addition to such as consists in the absence of any of the facts postulated by the act of 1863, as the basis of a recovery by the plaintiff.

702. The judgment.— If, after hearing, "it shall appear right and proper to the said justice, he shall enter judgment against the said tenant, that he forthwith give up the possession of the

---

[110]*Heritage* v *Wilfong*, 58 Pa 137, *Koontz* v *Hammond*, 62 Pa 177 If, between the notice to quit and the end of the term, a new arrangement is made between the lessor and lessee, extending his right of possession, the proceeding to eject him will fail *Conley* v *Hickey*, 1 Just 4

[111]*Heritage* v *Wilfong*, 58 Pa 137 The purchaser at the sheriff's sale filed an affidavit that she had purchased, and the defendant pleaded to the jurisdiction, the fact of the sheriff's sale An assertion by the defendant that he had an agreement with the plaintiff for the purchase of the premises, with which agreement he had failed to comply, does not oust the jurisdiction of the justice *Strohm* v *Carrol*, 11 Lanc Bar, 62 The wife of the defendant cannot prevent his dispossession, by asserting an interest in the land as cotenant or otherwise She must resort to ejectment *Heister* v *Brown*, 11 Lanc Bar, 159

[112]*Koontz* v *Hammond*, 62 Pa 177, *Lowenstein* v *Keller*, 3 Kulp, 361

[113]*Diefenderfer* v *Caffrey* (Pa) 9 Atl 182

[114]*Supplee* v *Timothy*, 23 W N C. 386, *McClelland* v *Patterson* (Pa) 5 Cent Rep 734, 10 Atl 475, *Kelly* v *Loehr*, 1 Brewst (Pa) 303

[115]*Livingood* v *Moyer*, 2 Woodw Dec 65, *Lowenstein* v *Keller*, 3 Kulp, 361.

said premises to the said lessor, and the said justice shall also
give judgment in favor of the lessor and against the lessee or
tenant, for such damages as, in his opinion, the said lessor may
have sustained, and for all the costs of the proceeding." If the
justice finds that the landlord has extended the term[116] or that
the lease has not terminated, by breach of conditions[117] or any
other fact inconsistent with the right to recover the possession,
he dismisses the complaint   Such judgment is no bar to a later
action of ejectment by the lessor[118]   The judgment for the
plaintiff unreversed is conclusive of the right of the plaintiff to
recover the possession by means of the appropriate writ, and he
cannot be made liable in trespass for the proper execution of
the writ of possession or for any improper conduct of the constable in executing this writ, which he does not direct or countenance[119]   A judgment in favor of the "agent" of an estate
will be valid, the words following his name being mere description and immaterial,[120] and a judgment for possession in favor
of the lessor's agent, and for damages in favor of the lessor, is
regular.[121]

   703 Damages.— The damages for which judgment is to be
given are such as, in the justice's "opinion," the lessor has sustained.[122]   The opinion is to be formed upon evidence.   If the
lessee remains in possession after the expiration of the lease,
the proof of this fact and of the rent which he had agreed to pay
will assist in forming this "opinion"   The plaintiff, besides,
may give evidence of his damages.[123]   The damages are not

---

[116]*McLaughlin* v *McGee*   79 Pa.
217   The dismissal is said to be "no
judgment"

[117]*Irnsthal* v *Patterson* 3 Pennyp
25   The justice is said to have
entered judgment for the defendant,
and it was reversed on certiorari

[118]*McLaughlin* v *McGee*, 79 Pa
217

[119]*McClelland* v *Patterson* (Pa)
5 Cent Rep 734, 10 Atl 475

[120]*Stone* v *Wimmill*, 6 Phila 311,
24 Phila Leg Int 212

[121]*Sterling* v *Richardson*, 24 Phila
Leg Int 140

[122]"Damages, of course " says Agnew, J , "from all legitimate sources
Haines v *Levin*, 51 Pa 412.

[123]*McGregor* v *Haines*, 6 Phila 62.
The act is not unconstitutional, as
allowing the justice to give judgment
for damages on an opinion not

rent, but are like the damages which a plaintiff recovers in ejectment or in an action of trespass for mesne profits. They arise
out of a wrongful act, not out of a contract They are not necessarily gauged by the rental mentioned in the expired lease [124]
In rare cases no damages are given [125] Where they have been
allowed, they have varied, according to the value of the premises,
the length of the tenant's detention of them beyond the close of
the term, etc. Specimens are $5;[126] $6,[127] $50,[128] $60,[129]
$75.75,[130] $140.80;[131] and $2,442.[132]

704. Judgment for damages — The act of 1863 directs the justice, in the proper case, to enter a judgment for the damages in
favor of the lessor and against the lessee or tenant Allison, P.
J., in *Dickensheets* v. *Hotchkiss*,[133] refused on certiorari to treat
what the record called an "assessment" of $75 75 as damages
against the defendant, as a "judgment," saying it was not a
judgment. but a mere assessment of damages But, after "as-
sessing" the damages, the justice may enter a formal judgment
for the amount, and his record then is unassailable [134] If the
record of the justice states that he "doth assess the sum of ——
dollars for the damage," etc , and then adds a formal judgment
for $5 as damages, omission of the amount in the assessment
is unimportant [135] The record stating, after alleging that dam-

founded on evidence The lease
showing the rental value and the
evidence the length of the holding
over, from these elements the justice
"could readily determine the damages" *Kaser* v *Leahy*, 15 Pa Co
Ct 243

[124]*Smith* v *Carter*, 17 Phila 344
Hence, the defendant has no claim
of exemption from levy and sale in
execution, with respect to them

[125]*Carter* v *Hess*, 3 W N C 325

[126]*Phelps* v *Cornog* (Pa) 2 Cent
Rep 844, 4 Atl. 922.

[127]*Quinn* v *McCarty*, 81 Pa 475

[128]*Dunmire* v *Price*, 12 W N C
179.

[129]*Bedford* v *Kelly*, 61 Pa 491

[130]*Dickensheets* v *Hotchkiss*, 6
Phila 156

[131]*Conner* v *Grebe*, 142 Pa 48, 21
Atl 755

[132]*Bergner* v *Palethorp*, 2 W N C
297 The court will conclusively
presume, on certiorari, the justice
having allowed damages, that the
plaintiff claimed damages *Bedford*
v *Kelly*, 61 Pa 491

[133] 6 Phila 156

[134]*Schulte* v *McCormick* 6 Phila.
313 *Bedford* v *Kelly*, 61 Pa 491

[135] *Phelps* v *Cornog* (Pa) 2 Cent
Rep 844, 4 Atl 922

ages have been assessed at $60: "Therefore it is considered and
adjudged by the said alderman that the said William G. Bedford shall and do recover and have of the said premises, as well
the said sum of $60 for his damages aforesaid, as also the sum of
$8.10 for his reasonable costs by him expended," etc, it was
held, apparently, on certiorari, that the word "premises" was
a clerical error for the word "defendant," and that the judgment was therefore valid.[136]

705 Delivery of possession to lessor.— After the entry of judgment for the plaintiff, the act of 1863 directs that the justice
"shall forthwith issue his warrant to any constable in the county, commanding him immediately to deliver to the lessor, his
agent, or attorney, full possession of the said demised premises,
and to levy the damages and costs, awarded and taxed by the said
justice, of the goods and chattels of the lessee or tenant, or other
person in possession, any law, custom, or usage to the contrary
notwithstanding." The writ of possession issues as soon as the
plaintiff desires it,—on the very day on which the judgment is
rendered,[137] or later;[138] and if it should be quashed, an alias writ
may issue;[139] but in Philadelphia, in consequence of the act of
March 24, 1865,[140] allowing a certiorari within ten days and
making it a supersedeas if the proper recognizance is given, a
writ of possession should not issue until the ten days expire, nor

[136]*Bedford* v *Kelly,* 61 Pa 491
See *Bedford* v *Kelly,* 61 Pa 491,
and *Phelps* v *Cornog* (Pa) 2 Cent
Rep 844, 4 Atl 922, for forms of judgment   That the judgment has been
publicly given is to be presumed from
the public character of the officer An
alderman pronounces his judgments
in his office and they are public   He
need not proclaim them upon the
housetop, or advertise them in the
papers   *Snyder* v *Carfrey,* 54 Pa
90   Judgment in landlord and tenant
proceedings cannot be certified into

the common pleas under § 10 of the
act of March 20, 1810, 1 Pepper & L
Digest 2585, 5 Smith s Laws, 161
Kern v *Coyle,* 12 Phila 227

[137]*Quinn* v *McCarty,* 81 Pa 475,
McGinnis v *Vernon,* 67 Pa 149,
Graver v *Fehr,* 89 Pa 460   See
form, in *McGinnis* v *Vernon,* 67 Pa
149

[138]*McClelland* v *Patterson* (Pa)
5 Cent Rep 734, 10 Atl 475

[139]*Graver* v *Fehr,* 89 Pa 460
[140]1 Pepper & L Digest, 2659, P
L 750.

after, if the proper recognizance is given, until the final disposition of the case   If the writ of possession issues and is executed before the expiration of the ten days, the court will award a writ of restitution, on rule.[141]   The plaintiff is not liable in trespass for the eviction under the writ of the tenant, his wife and children, nor for any improper acts of the constable and his assistants in effecting their removal from the premises, which he does not sanction.[142]

[141]*Connelly* v   *Arundel*, 6 Phila   [142]*McClelland* v   *Patterson*   (Pa.)
38.   Cf. *Conley* v. *Hickey*, 1 Just. 4. 5 Cent. Rep 734, 10 Atl. 475.

CHAPTER XXXII.

ACT DEC 14, 1863   REVIEW ON CERTIORARI AND APPEAL.

706. Remedies for error of justice.—The law has conferred on the landlord the right to proceed in the mode defined by the act of 1863, and has furnished the tenant two means of redress, should error be committed by the justice,—appeal and certiorari All available defenses can be made before the justice, or before the common pleas   Hence, equity should not enjoin the prosecution by the plaintiffs of the claim before the justice.   "The court," said Thompson, Ch. J., in a case in which the court below had issued a perpetual injunction against the prosecution of the case before the justice, "had no jurisdiction in equity of the proceedings   They were not contrary to law, and if they had been, an injunction was not a correctional process.   That was to be done by the process provided in the act, *viz ,* by appeal or certiorari.   These were the legal matters [*sic*] provided in the act, and a court of equity could not supplement them.   Courts may restrain acts contrary to law, but not where they are according to positive law   That would be to put the courts above the legislature.   Where a positive statutory remedy exists and may be pursued, equity cannot interfere on the ground of irreparable mischief."[1]   Notwithstanding a reversal of the judgment on certiorari, the tenant cannot maintain an action of trespass for the eviction under the judgment   The reversal of the judgment because of irregularity in making up the record does not make the landlord a trespasser in evicting the tenant by means of a writ of possession.[2]

---

[1]*Brown's Appeal,* 66   Pa 155, *Reynolds* v *Davis,* 1 Kulp, 342   A motion for a preliminary injunction was refused in *Krueger* v *Rutledge,* 2 Kulp, 371   In *Louenstein* v *Keller,* 3 Kulp 361, the court, while refusing to enjoin from proceeding before the justice, allowed the injunction to stand so far as preventing the issue of a writ of execution on the judgment was concerned, until further order   In *Chase* v *Goodale,* 2 Law Times N. S.

107, Handley, P J , continued a preliminary injunction to prevent the plaintiff in the proceeding, who had obtained judgment, from issuing execution, on the ground that he had begun the proceeding as receiver of the lessor bank, without right to do so, having no authority from the court, and no attornment from the tenant

[2]*Leese* v *Horne,* 30 Pittsb. L   J.   N S 316.

707. Review in appellate courts.— The judgment on the appeal can be reviewed in the superior and the supreme courts, as judgments in other cases.[3] Should the defendant appeal to the supreme court, and suffer a *non pros*, with an order that the penalties under the act of May 25th, 1874, relating to appeals for delay, should be enforced against him, the plaintiff may not have a writ of inquiry to assess damages for the unlawful retention of the premises by the tenant since the judgment of the justice, which assessed damages, under 16 and 17 Car II. chap 8; §§ 3 and 4 Roberts' Dig. *51. The writ of inquiry, on rule, will be set aside.[4]

708 Certiorari.— The act of December 14th, 1863,[5] enacts, as a third proviso, "that the tenant may have a writ of certiorari to remove the proceedings of the justice, as in other cases." But, the justice dismissing the proceedings, the landlord may likewise sue out a certiorari.[6] The 21st section of the act of March 20th, 1810,[7] providing that the certiorari must be sued out in twenty days from the rendition of the judgment, does not apply to the summary process for obtaining possession of leased property under the landlord and tenant acts,[8] nor, if it did, would the limitation be applicable, if, on the face of the record, the justice's want of jurisdiction is apparent. The certiorari does not supersede the execution of the justice's judgment,[9] and even after it has been issued, the justice may award a writ of possession [10]

709. Certiorari in Philadelphia—The act of March 24th,

[3]*Phœnixville* v *Walters*, 147 Pa 501, 23 Atl 776, *Bergner* v *Palethorp*, 2 W N C 297

[4]*O'Kie* v *Depuy*, 3 Pa Co Ct 140

[5]1 Pepper & L Digest 2650 Sect 8 of art V of the Constitution preceding that of 1874 did not make an allowance of writs of certiorari by the judges of the common pleas necessary. *McGinnis* v. *Vernon*, 67 Pa. 149.

[6]*Arnsthal* v *Patterson*, 3 Pennyp 25

[7]1 Pepper & L Digest, 2612, 5 Smith's Laws, 161

[8]*Graver* v *Fehr*, 89 Pa 461, *Rubicum* v *Williams*, 1 Ashm. (Pa) 230.

[9]*Graver* v *Fehr*, 89 Pa 460

[10]*McGinnis* v. *Vernon*, 67 Pa. 149.

1865,[11] applicable to Philadelphia, and to the acts of April 3d, 1830, and of December 14th, 1863,[12] declares that the certiorari shall be a supersedeas until its final determination, "provided that the said certiorari shall be issued within ten days[13] from the date of the judgment rendered in said proceedings, and upon oath of the party applying for the same, to be administered by the prothonotary of the court of common pleas, that it is not for the purpose of delay, but that the proceedings proposed to be removed are, to the best of his knowledge and belief, unjust and illegal, and will oblige him to pay more money than is justly due, a copy of which affidavit shall be filed in the prothonotary's office.   And provided, further, that the party applying for the same shall give security for the payment of all costs that have accrued or may accrue, and of the rent which has already or may become due, up to the time of the final determination of said certiorari, in the event of the same being determined against him."   If the recognizance, upon which the certiorari issues, is for the payment of debt, interest, and costs, and not in the form prescribed, the certiorari will, on motion, be quashed.[14]   No amount of bail needs to be fixed in the recognizance, and no *allocatur* is necessary.[15]   The "final determination" of the certiorari is the determination which ends the controversy between the landlord and the tenant.   If, the common pleas affirming the judgment, there is an appeal to the supreme court, there is no "final determination" until its decision.   If it affirms the judgments of the justice and of the common pleas, the surety

[11] 1 Pepper & L Digest, 2659, P L 750

[12] *Hutchinson* v *Vanscriver* 6 Phila 39, *DeCoursey* v *Guarantee Trust & S D Co* 81 Pa. 217   But not to the act of March 21st, 1772 *DeCoursey* v *Guarantee Trust & S D Co* 81 Pa 217   Or to the act of June 16th, 1836   *Jackson* v *Gleason*, 6 Phila 307.

[13] The writ may issue after the ten days, when the party applies within twenty days after he learns of the entry of the justices judgment *Campbell* v *Penn*, C P Phila

[14] *Hutchinson* v *Vanscriver*, 6 Phila 39

[15] *Hutchinson* v. *Vanscriver*, 6 Phila. 39.

in the recognizance on which the certiorari issued will be liable for all rents and costs, down to the restoration of possession to the landlord. On paying the rent and costs accruing after the appeal to the supreme court, he would be entitled to subrogation to the recognizance for the appeal [16]

710. What the record must show — The judgment of the justice can be supported only by the existence of the facts which the act of 1863 requires in order to justify the dispossession of the tenant. The finding of these facts must be averred in the record.[17] There is no other evidence of them of which the common pleas, on certiorari, can take notice These facts need not be severally and articulately stated by the justice as found by him. If they are contained in the complaint, and he avers in the record, generally, that he has found that the complaint is, in all respects, just and true, they are sufficiently found to support the judgment,[18] though Thompson, Ch. J., has expressed the opinion that it would be better for the justice to set them out distinctly as found by him.[19] Of course, if the complaint does not aver all necessary facts, a general reference to it by the justice will be insufficient, e g , if the complaint does not aver that a three months' notice was given;[20] or if the complaint describes the premises by adjoiners "containing —— acres, more or less," and no other description is contained in the record.[21] There must be a description of the premises sufficient to

[16]*Clapp* v *Senneff*, 7 Phila 214
[17]*Givens* v *Miller*, 62 Pa 133, *Rowan* v. *Gates*, 9 Pa Dist R 564, *Wilke* v *Campbell*, 5 Pa Super Ct 618

[18]*Speigle* v *McFarland*, 25 Phila. Leg Int 165, *Killeen* v *Haddock*, 4 Kulp, 408, *Givens* v *Miller*, 62 Pa 133, *Mill Creek Coal Co* v *Androkus*, 2 Pa Dist R 764, *Wilke* v *Campbell*, 5 Pa Super Ct 618, *McGrath* v *Donally*, 6 Phila 43, *Connelly* v *Trundel*, 6 Phila 49, *McGinnis* v *Vernon*, 67 Pa 149;

Livingood v *Moyer*, 2 Woodw Dec 65, *Xander* v *Weiss*, 28 Pa Co Ct 80, 12 Pa Dist R 724
[19]*McGinnis* v *Vernon*, 67 Pa 149
[20]*Mill Creek Coal Co* v *Androkus*, 2 Pa Dist R 764
[21]*Givens* v *Miller*, 62 Pa 133 But the court is not quite sure that setting out the number of acres is necessary. Pearson, J , in *Spotts* v *Farling*, 2 Pearson (Pa) 205, thinks it unnecessary Cf *Quigney* v *Quigney*, 1 Northampton Co Rep 20.

guide the constable to them [22] A description "certain premises with the appurtenances, situate on the north side of Third street, at the northeast corner of Elm and Third streets, in the borough of South Bethlehem, Pa," is sufficient [23] If the record simply states that the justice has examined witnesses and heard allegations and proofs, but finds no facts, it is inadequate [24] The court will not infer the facts from the recital in the complaint, or in the precept of the justice [25] The act of December 14, 1863, need not be recited in the record [26]

711 Peaceable and quiet possession.— That the lessor was, when he made the lease, quietly and peaceably possessed of the land, must be found by the justice, and the record must show that he has found it, either by reference to the complaint or otherwise,[27] and it is said in *Spotts* v *Farling*,[28] that if the alleged landlord was a mortgagee out of possession, who induced the mortgagor, already in possession, to take a lease, it could not truthfully be alleged that the lessor was in quiet possession The complaint alleging that the lessor was in "peaceable" possession, the record finding the complaint in all particulars just and true, sufficiently finds a peaceable and quiet possession.[29]

712. The term.— The term must be defined positively as one for years, or at will To state it as a term either for years or at will would be inadequate [30] The record should describe the term, so that it may appear that it was ended when the proceed-

[22]*Xander* v *Weiss*, 28 Pa Co Ct 80, 12 Pa Dist R 724, *Livingood* v *Moyer*, 2 Woodw Dec 65

[23]*Quigney* v *Quigney*, 1 Northampton Co Rep 20 Cf *Flanigen* v *Philadelphia*, 51 Pa 491

[24]*McGrath* v *Donally*, 6 Phila 43, *Skelton* v *Mason*, 23 Phila Leg Int 126, *Bradfield* v *Rehm*, 6 Phila 135

[25]*Miller* v *Frees*, 1 Woodw Dec 409

[26]*Sterling* v *Richardson*, 24 Phila Leg Int 140

LAND & TEN. 39.

[27]*Steigelman* v *Klugh*, 9 Lanc L Rev 321, *Xander* v *Weiss*, 28 Pa Co Ct 80, 12 Pa Dist R 724, *Rouan* v *Gates*, 9 Pa Dist R 564, *Greenleaf* v *Haberacker*, 1 Woodw Dec 436, *Spidle* v *Hess*, 20 Lanc L Rev 385, *Weber* v *Porr*, 1 Leg Rec Rep 131

[28]2 Pearson (Pa) 295 Cf *Fisher* v *McCauley*, 2 Dauphin Co Rep 180

[29]*Quigney* v *Quigney*, 1 Northampton Co Rep 20

[30]*Givens* v *Miller*, 62 Pa 133.

ings began.[31] The time when the lease began [32] and when it expired should also be stated [33] The justice may find that the term was not fully ended, and dismiss the complaint.[34]

713 Notice.— It is not enough to state that there was a three months' notice without saying that it was three months before the expiration of the term,[35] nor even that it was three months before the expiration of the lease, unless it is also stated when the lease expired,[36] but when the time of expiration of the lease is stated, it is enough to say that the lessor demanded possession three months or more than three months before, without giving the date of the service of the notice.[37] The complaint saying simply that notice to quit was given, but not showing whether three months intervened between the giving of the notice and the close of the term, so as to leave it doubtful whether a portion of the three months followed the expiration of the term, a general finding that the complaint is just and true will be inadequate.[38] If no three months' notice is averred, but reliance is put on a waiver of it by the tenant, the justice must find the waiver to have been made [39] The fact that the lease contains a waiver is of no avail unless the lease is made a part of the record.[40] Stating that ten days' notice was served according

---

[31]*Horner* v *Wetherell*, 19 W. N C 197, *McGinnis* v *Vernon*, 67 Pa 149, *Xander* v *Weiss*, 28 Pa Co Ct 80, 12 Pa Dist. R 724, *Spidle* v *Hess*, 20 Lanc L Rev 385 In *Kraft* v *Wolf*, 6 Phila 310, 24 Phila Leg Int. 212, it is said that the date of the demise or of the expiration of the term need not be stated in the record, and that it is enough to find that the term is ended, and that it was for one year or other time
[32]*Rowan* v *Gates*, 9 Pa Dist R 564
[33]*Horner* v. *Wetherell*, 19 W N. C 197
[34]*Arnsthal* v *Patterson*, 3 Pennyp. 25
[35]*Chambers* v *Shivery*, 6 Pa. Dist

R 101, *Rowan* v *Gates*, 9 Pa. Dist. 197, *McGinnis* v *Vernon*, 67 Pa 149, R 564, *Weber* v *Porr*, 1 Leg Rec. Rep 131
[36]*Horner* v *Wetherell*, 19 W N C. 197, *Xander* v *Weiss*, 28 Pa Co Ct. 80, 12 Pa Dist R 724, *Spidle* v. *Hess*, 20 Lanc L Rev 385
[37]*Bedford* v *Kelly*, 61 Pa 491, *Kraft* v *Wolf*, 6 Phila 310, 24 Phila. Leg Int 212
[38]*Speigle* v *McFarland*, 25 Phila Leg Int 165, Cf *McGinnis* v *Vernon*, 67 Pa 149
[39]*Kaier* v *Leahy*, 15 Pa Co Ct. 243
[40]*Killeen* v *Haddock*, 4 Kulp, 408; *Mill Creek Coal Co.* v. *Androkus*, 2 Pa Dist R 764

to the tenor of the lease, if the lease is not given, does not justify the inference by the common pleas on certiorari, that the three months' notice was waived,[41] but, when the lease as found by the justice is for a definite time, and it contains a provision that the tenant shall leave at the expiration of thirty days, the thirty days' notice will be understood to be a substitute for the three months' notice [42] The notice need not be attached to, or copied into, the record.[43]

714. Tenant still in possession.— The record must contain the finding that the tenant, at the date of the judgment, still occupies the premises [44] This it does if it states that the tenant is still possessed of the premises, and that he has hitherto refused, and still does refuse, to comply with the demand that he remove from and leave the same [45]

715. Rent reserved.— The record must show a finding by the justice that the lease reserved a certain rent [46] It is not enough that, being in writing, it in fact does reserve such a rent [47] The record showing the finding that the rent is "the interest and taxes accruing thereon," is inadequate, because what interest, and on what, is meant does not appear [48] The record must show that demand was made for the rent, the terms of the lease, the amount of rent reserved, the amount in arrears.[49]

716. The lessor.— The record must contain a finding of who made the lease This it will sufficiently do if it states a finding

[41]*Mill Creek Coal Co* v *Androkus,* 2 Pa Dist R 764

[42]*Wilke* v *Campbell,* 5 Pa Super Ct 618

[43]*Stone* v *Wimmill,* 24 Phila Leg Int 212

[44]*Horner* v *Wetherell,* 19 W N C 197

[45]*Bedford* v *Kelly,* 61 Pa 491, *Kaier* v *Leahy,* 15 Pa Co Ct 243 Cf *Deisinger* v *Shaud,* 20 Lanc L Rev 257, where it is said to be immaterial whether the defendant moved away from the premises at the end of the three months or not, so far as reversing on certiorari for defect of the record is concerned

[46]*Weber* v *Porr,* 1 Leg Rec Rep. 131

[47]*Graver* v *Fehr,* 89 Pa 460; *Hiester* v *Brown,* 11 Lanc Bar 159; *Reynolds* v *Robinson,* 3 C P Rep. 20

[48]*Davis* v *Davis,* 115 Pa 261, 7 Atl 746

[49]*Long* v *Snavely,* 1 Just 75 The costs, as indorsed on the writ of possession, must appear.

that the plaintiff demised the premises to the defendant.[50]　The
making of the lease to the defendant or one under whom he
claims must be found.[51]

　717　**The evidence.**— When the necessary facts are found by
the justice, the common pleas, on certiorari, will conclusively assume, unless the record shows there was no evidence to support
any of them, that they were found on sufficient evidence, or
rather, it is not the function of the certiorari to effect a recon-
sideration by the appellate court, upon the merits.[52]　The justice
finding damages, the court will presume that a claim of damages was made before him [53]　The finding that the tenure was
fully ended will be assumed to rest on sufficient evidence that
there had been no agreement to prolong the term [54]　The finding
that there was no forfeiture of the lease will be conclusive
against the landlord whose proceeding predicates such forfeiture,
notwithstanding that no evidence is exhibited in the record [55]
And the omission of the justice to find a second lease, under
which the tenant would be entitled to a continuance of the possession of the premises, cannot be shown to be erroneous [56]　It
is not necessary that the evidence heard by the justice should be
incorporated into his record,[57] and if it is not, the common pleas
cannot know what it was.　Even the lease, or other documents
used before the justice, cannot be considered by the court, unless they have been made a part of the record,[58] and the fact that

---

[50]*Stone* v　*Wimmill*, 24 Phila Leg
Int 212

[51]*Weber* v　*Porr*, 1 Leg Rec Rep
131

[52]*Bedford* v　*Kelly* 61 Pa　491,
Greenleaf v *Haberacker*, 1 Woodw
Dec 436, *Sterling* v *Richardson*, 24
Phila Leg Int 140, *Livingood* v
Mouer, 2 Woodw Dec 65

[53]*Bedford* v　*Kelly*, 61 Pa 491

[54]*Bedford* v　*Kelly*, 61 Pa 491

[55]*Ainsthal* v　*Patterson*, 3 Pennyp
25

It the justice states that, "after

hearing the proofs and allegations"
of the plaintiff, he finds certain facts,
it will not be necessary in any other
way to aver that due proof was
made after notice to the tenant of
the time and place of hearing
Phelps v　*Cosnog* (Pa) 2 Cent Rep
844　4 Atl 922

[56]*Wilke* v　*Campbell* 5 Pa Super
Ct 618

[57]*Ainsthal* v　*Patterson*, 3 Pennyp
25

[58]*Killeen* v　*Haddock*, 4 Kulp, 408,
3 Montg Co L Rep 176, *Mill Creek*

the record states that they were offered in evidence does not make them a part of it, but when the lease is set out by the justice as a part of his findings, the court, on certiorari, may take notice of its provisions [59] The lease, thus set out, providing that the tenant might continue in possession from year to year for five years, on his taking steps to have appraisers appointed, at the end of each year, to fix the fair rent for the coming year, if the justice finds that the lease was continued, and gives the facts from which he infers that it was continued, *viz*, a mere notice by the tenant to the landlord that he would continue in possession, but no attempt to cause an appraisement, and no excuse for omitting to cause it, the court of common pleas will reverse [60]

718. Record shows absence of evidence.— The justice need give no evidence He may, however, give it If, giving some, he states that it is all that was received by him, and it does not furnish any support for some of the essential facts found by him, the judgment will be reversed [61] When the record states that the plaintiff produced his lease, his deed, and the notice to quit, but does not state that any of them were offered or admitted in evidence, and adds that the constable was sworn and proved the service of the summons and notice, the court may properly infer that no other evidence than that specified was heard or received, and will reverse the judgment for the plaintiff.[62] The omission to set out the evidence is not error,[63] and though an exception alleges error in receiving testimony of an incompetent witness, the court will not inquire into the truth of the exception[64] nor will the court, on an exception to the justice's

Coal Co v *Androkus*, 2 Pa Dist R 764

[59] *Arnsthal* v *Patterson*, 3 Pennyp 25

[60] *Arnsthal* v *Patterson*, 3 Pennyp 25.

[61] *Bradfield* v *Rehm*, 6 Phila 135 There was no finding of facts in this case

[62] *Connelly* v *Arundel*, 6 Phila 49 If the documents submitted would support the finding, the hearing of further evidence would be unnecessary *Snyder* v *Carfrey*, 54 Pa 90

[63] *Bedford* v *Kelly* 61 Pa 491

[64] *Sterling* v *Richardson*, 24 Phila Leg Int 140 For errors in the admission or rejection of evidence, the remedy is appeal, and not certiorari

return of his record, alleging diminution of record because it omits the testimony, require him to return the testimony [63] Probably parol evidence would be received, on certiorari, that the justice refused to hear evidence, or that he did anything else that indicated partiality or corruption.[66]

719. Substantial conformity with statute sufficient.—Substantial conformity with the statute, in the proceedings before the justice, is all that is requisite. The act of 1863 was designed to give landlords a more convenient remedy to dispossess tenants than they had under the old act of 1772. Proceedings under these statutes, though summary, are not to be criticised with the extreme strictness that is applied to summary convictions under penal statutes, for the relation of landlord and tenant rests in contract, and involves mere rights of property, and the remedies are purely civil, and not in the slightest degree penal. Very few aldermen and justices of the peace can make up records upon penal statutes which can withstand the criticisms of a certiorari, but in committing the rights of landlords and tenants to the unaided judgment of such a magistracy, the legislature meant that superior courts should exact no unattainable precision of procedure, but only such substantial compliance with the letter and spirit of the statute as would generally be within the competence of the magistrates.[67] If the justice's record seems incomplete, the party suing out the certiorari may, by affidavit or otherwise, suggest the diminution, and ask for an order of the court to the justice, to certify the whole record, and this order may be enforced by attachment. If the exceptant fails to do

Quigney v *Quigney*, 1 Northampton Co Rep 20

[65]*Hiester* v *Brown*, 11 Lanc Bar, 159

[66]*Wilke* v *Campbell*, 5 Pa Super Ct 618. Cf *Fisher* v. *Nyce*, 60 Pa. 107.

[67]*Snyder* v *Carfrey*, 54 Pa 90, *Kaier* v *Leahy*, 15 Pa Co Ct 243, *Buchanan* v *Baxter*, 67 Pa 348, *Phelps* v *Cornog* (Pa) 2 Cent Rep 844 4 Atl 922, *Strohm* v *Carrol*, 11 Lanc Bar, 62

this, an exception that the record is incomplete will not be considered [68]

720. Review of decision on certiorari.— Appeal from the decision of the common pleas upon the certiorari can be had in the superior and supreme courts. The common pleas affirming the justice, the appellate court may affirm[69] or reverse,[70] and the common pleas reversing the justice, the appellate court may affirm, or it may reverse[71] the reversal.

721. Execution from the common pleas — If the tenant remains in possession of the premises until the decision of the common pleas on the appeal, that court may, after affirming the judgment of the justice in favor of the plaintiff, award a writ of possession.[72] Prior to the act of May 10, 1897,[73] it was held that bail having been given, a writ of error being filed in the prothonotary's office two days after the issue of a writ of possession, it suspended the writ, and the court discharged a rule on the sheriff to show cause why he should not proceed to execute the habere facias and fi. fa.;[74] and a writ of possession awarded on rule to show cause, by the common pleas after a writ of error had been sued out and a recognizance had been given, to secure a supersedeas, under the act of June 16, 1836, was, on certiorari from the supreme court, quashed by that court[75]

722 Restoring the tenant to the possession.— If the common pleas reverses the judgment of the justice, under which the tenant has been dispossessed, it is within its sound discretion whether to order a restitution of the possession to him. For

[68]*Hiester* v *Brown*, 11 Lanc Bar, 159

[69]*Tilford* v *Fleming*, 64 Pa 300, *Haines* v *Levin*, 51 Pa 412

[70]*Givens* v *Miller*, 62 Pa 133, *Horner* v *Wetherell*, 19 W N C 197, *Speigle* v *McFarland*, 25 Phila Leg Int 165

[71]*Bedford* v *Kelly*, 61 Pa 491, *Snyder* v *Carfrey*, 54 Pa 90, *Heritage* v *Wilfong*, 58 Pa 137.

[72]*Haines* v *Levin*, 51 Pa 412

[73]P L 67 See § 10

[74]*Cornog* v *Phelps*, 16 W N C 115

[75]*Haines* v *Levin*, 51 Pa 412 The recognizance was not in proper form, but had been required by the landlord Ct *Connelly* v *Arundel*, 6 Phila 59, *McDonald* v. *Gifford*, 6 Phila 315

reasons satisfactory to it, it may refuse to award this restoration;[76] *e. g.,* when the tenant has vacated the premises without waiting to be put out by execution, or when the term has ended, so that the landlord would have a common-law right to re-enter, and is now rightfully in possession [77]

723 Liability of landlord in damages — If the justice's judgment in favor of the landlord is reversed on certiorari, even for mere irregularities, the landlord will be liable in damages, if he has evicted the tenant by means of the writ of possession, *e. g ,* by the constable setting the tenant's goods into the street. He will not be liable, if the tenant peaceably retires, without compulsion [78]

724. Appeal.— The 1st section of the act of December 14, 1863,[79] directs that "the defendant may, at any time within ten days after the rendition of judgment, appeal to the court of common pleas, in the manner provided in the first section of an act relative to landlords and tenants, approved April 3, 1830." It also enacts "that such appeal shall not be a supersedeas to the warrant of possession aforesaid, but shall be tried in the same manner as actions of ejectment, and if the jury shall find in favor of the tenant, they shall also assess the damages which he shall have sustained by reason of his removal from the premises, and, for the amount found by the jury, judgment shall be rendered in his favor, with costs of suit, and that he recover possession of the premises, and he shall have the necessary writ or writs of execution to enforce said judgment "

725. Time and mode of appealing.—The appeal may be taken "at any time within ten days" after the judgment of the justice is rendered. The judgment being rendered November 20th, an appeal taken November 27th,[80] or the judgment being ren-

[76]*Leffingwell* v *Willes-Barre.* 4 Kulp, 404

[77]*Killeen* v *Haddock,* 4 Kulp, 408

[78]*Hickey* v *Conley,* 18 Montg Co L Rep 124

[79]1 Pepper & L Digest, 2650, P L of 1864, 1125

[80]*Tripp* v *Barnes,* 1 Law Times 73.

dered December 8th, an appeal taken December 18th,[81] or judgment being entered November 3rd, an appeal taken November 11th,[82] are early enough The appeal is taken when the recognizance is given The filing of the transcript in the common pleas is not a part of the act of appealing "The appeal itself is taken," says Metzger, P. J.,[83] "as soon as the recognizance is given, and the filing of the transcript is only necessary to make the appeal effectual " Hence, the recognizance being given within the ten days, the transcript may be filed on the 11th,[84] the 26th,[85] or other later day, if on or before the first day of the term of common pleas succeeding the expiration of ten days after the rendition of the judgment

726 The recognizance — The act of April 3, 1830,[86] which, *mutatis mutandis,* is adopted in this respect by the act of 1863, requires, for the appeal, that the tenant "shall give good, sufficient, and absolute security, by recognizance, for all costs that may have and may accrue, in case the judgment shall be affirmed, and also for all rent that has accrued or may accrue up to the time of final judgment " The act of 1830 provides for the dispossession of the tenant during the term, and therefore rent is running upon the lease after the institution of the proceeding. To require a recognizance to secure the payment of this rent, as a condition for appealing, is quite reasonable. The act of 1863, however, is applicable only when the lease has ended, and when the lessor is treating the former tenant as a trespasser. Rent is no longer running. Hence, it has been held[87] that the word "damages" should be substituted for the word "rent" in the recognizance for appeal, under the act of 1863

[81] *Carter* v *Hess.* 3 V. N C 325
[82] *Willard* v *Martin,* 23 Pa Co Ct 285
[83] *Willard* v *Martin,* 23 Pa Co Ct 285 The contention was rejected that the appeal must be taken in five days and the transcript filed within ten days.

[84] *Willard* v *Martin,* 23 Pa Co Ct 285
[85] *Tripp* v *Barnes,* 1 Law Times, 73
[86] 1 Pepper & L Digest, 2657
[87] *Tripp* v *Barnes,* 1 Law Times 73, Ward, Recorder Leave was given to amend the recognizance.

In *Koenig* v. *Bauer*,[88] however, the recognizance given was for "damages and costs" until final judgment On the lessor's moving to strike off the appeal because of this form, alleged to be a defect, the tenant asked and obtained leave to file a recognizance to secure payment of "rent" instead of damages. If the recognizance is defective, the court will not unconditionally quash the appeal The lessor should obtain a rule on the tenant to perfect it, and the appeal should not be dismissed, except as a penalty of his neglect or refusal to perfect it. "The right of appeal and of trial by jury," says Agnew, J , "is too precious to be frustrated by the ignorance, incompetency, or malice of inferior magistrates and officers."[89]

727 The affidavit — The act of March 27, 1865,[90] requires, in all cases of appeals from the judgments of aldermen in the city of Philadelphia, that the defendant or some person acting in his behalf, having knowledge of the facts in the case, shall file with the alderman an affidavit, setting forth that the appeal taken is not for the purpose of delay, but that, if the proceedings appealed from are not removed, he or the defendant will be required to pay more money, or receive less, than is justly due, which affidavit shall be attached to the transcript by the alderman, to be filed in the court to which the appeal is taken. If such affidavit is not made, the court to which the appeal is taken will, on motion, strike it off "[1] A similar statute operates in Lancaster[92] and other counties. An affidavit to the effect that the

---

[88] 57 Pa 168   The allowance of an amendment is approved, but nothing is said as to the propriety of the form of the recognizance The recognizance in *Carter* v *Hess*, 3 W N C 325, was conditioned for payment of rent and costs to final judgment

[89]*Koenig* v *Bauer*, 57 Pa 168, *Shenk* v *Shaeffer*, 8 Lanc L Rev 49 In *Dunmire* v *Price*, 12 W N C 179, it is said that when the tenant appealed his surety became, by the terms of the recognizance, liable "for all rent that has accrued or may accrue up to the time of final judgment "

[90] 1 Pepper & L Digest, 2610, P L 794

[91]*Carter* v *Hess*, 3 W N C 325

[92] The act of March 2d 1868 P L 256, *Shenk* v. *Shaeffer*, 8 Lanc. L Rev 49.

appeal is not for the purpose of delay, but because the defendant firmly believes injustice has been done him, sufficiently conforms to it to support the appeal.

728. Procedure — The appeal is to be "tried in the same manner as actions of ejectment." In the absence of a rule of court regulating the practice, the plaintiff may treat the transcript as a declaration,[93] and may require the defendant to plead to it.[94] The plaintiff may, if he chooses, also file a declaration.[95] To a rule to plead after the filing of the transcript, the defendant demurred on the ground that the transcript was defective in not setting out the term of the demise. The court gave leave to the plaintiff to file a declaration[96] The plea of "not guilty"[97] may be accompanied by a special plea, denying the justice's jurisdiction[98] or setting up an agreement, subsequent to the notice to quit, that the tenant might remain on the premises.[99] A case stated may be filed[100]

729. Procedure; amendment — The court may allow an amendment of the name of the plaintiff. The proceedings before the justice having been in the name of "J. H. Thompson, Agent," the name of his principal, Anton Lutz, may be substituted in the common pleas[101] But, two executors, A and B, having made the lease, and A only having given the notice to quit, and begun, in his own name, individually, proceedings before the justice, after the appeal, the court refused to allow, at the instance of A, an amendment substituting the names of A and B as executors, because the tenant was now an actor, seek-

[93]*Wenger* v *Raymond,* 104 Pa 33, *Gibbons* v *McGuigan,* 6 Phila 108

[94]*Gibbons* v *McGuigan,* 6 Phila 108

[95]*Gibbons* v *McGuigan,* 6 Phila 108, *Koenig* v *Bauer,* 57 Pa 168, *Koontz* v *Hammond,* 62 Pa 177

[96]*Steinmetz* v *Hamilton,* 1 W N C 286

[97]*Koontz* v *Hammond,* 62 Pa 177,

Rothermel v *Dumn,* 119 Pa 632, 13 Atl 509

[98]*Koontz* v. *Hammond,* 62 Pa 177

[99]*Supplee* v *Timothy,* 23 W N C. 386

[100]*Dunmire* v *Price,* 12 W N C 179

[101]*Lutz* v *Wainwright,* 193 Pa 541, 44 Atl 565

ing damages for his dispossession, and as he could have no remedy against the executors as such, the amendment would deprive him of redress from A as an individual.[102]

730. Nonsuit.— For insufficient evidence to support the plaintiff's cause, the court may enter a compulsory nonsuit,[103] but, after all the evidence on both sides is in, and the court has charged the jury, the plaintiff is not entitled to a voluntary nonsuit. The defendant then has a right to the verdict, in order "both to be restored to possession and to recover his damages for removal."[104]

731. The trial.— All the facts necessary, under the act of 1863, to recover the possession in the proceeding before the justice, must be established by the plaintiff in the appeal,[105] and the jury are "to decide the case precisely as if no prior decision in favor of the plaintiff had taken place."[106] Evidence to establish these necessary facts may be introduced by either party, which was not used before the justice. E. g., whether the original lease was in evidence before the justice or not, it can be offered by the tenant, when his object is to show that under it he was entitled to the possession beyond the time at which the proceedings began.[107] The plaintiff must show, as one of the facts which condition his right to proceed before the justice, that he was in quiet and peaceable possession of the premises when the lease was made, but the acceptance of the lease by the defendant is prima facie evidence of that possession, and until it is rebutted, no more is necessary.[108] The giving of three months' notice to quit, before the close of the term, is one of the facts to be proved by the plaintiff.[109] Indeed, this may be the

[102]*Hay* v *Parks*, 7 Northampton Co Rep 391

[103]*Jalass* v *Young*, 3 Pa Super Ct 422

[104]*Koenig* v *Bauer*, 57 Pa 168

[105]*Lutz* v *Wainwright*, 193 Pa 541, 44 Atl 565.

[106]*Koenig* v *Bauer*, 57 Pa 168

[107]*Keating* v *Condon* 68 Pa 75

[108]*Fisher* v *McCauley*, 2 Dauphin Co Rep 180

[109]*Koenig* v *Bauer* 57 Pa 168. The frequency with which a witness to this or other facts may be re-

only subject of controversy between the parties.[110] If the notice to quit required the defendant to quit on a certain day, and the sufficiency of it depends on whether the tenant is holding over under a former lease, and is therefore a tenant from year to year, or whether he has accepted a new lease which provides for a different time of ending, the jury must determine whether the new lease, offered by the lessor, was in fact accepted by the lessee.[111] Whether the notice was sufficient may depend on the term having begun on December 4th rather than December 22d, the notice having been given on September 20th. The jury must determine, aided by the evidence [112] If the waiver of the notice is relied upon, it will need to be proven [113]

732. **The trial; proving tenancy.**— One of the facts postulated by the act of 1863 is that the plaintiff, or one under whom he claims, shall have made a lease to the defendant or one under whom he has the possession This tenancy must be proven It is not enough to show that the plaintiff owns and has a right to the immediate possession of the land, and could recover, were the action an ejectment [114] The lease must have been made by the plaintiff, or a predecessor in the ownership. If it is clear that it was not, it would be error to submit the question to the jury. If the evidence, e g., shows clearly, and without contradiction, that the lease was made by two owners, A and B, and one of them, A, sells his interest to X, who gives the notice to the tenant to vacate, while B renews the lease to the tenant, C, it is error to allow the jury to find that the lease was made by B, for himself alone and in his own name.[115]

called is for the trial court to determine

[110]*Currier* v *Grebe*, 142 Pa 48, 21 Atl 755

[111]*Phœnixville* v *Walters*, 147 Pa 501, 23 Atl 776 It would be error for the court to decide, the evidence justifying either conclusion by the jury

[112]*Rothermel* v *Dumn*, 119 Pa 632, 13 Atl 509

[113]*Sizer* v *Russett*, 11 Pa Super Ct 108

If the notice were not shown, the court might nonsuit *Jalass* v. *Young*, 3 Pa Super Ct 422

[114]*Koontz* v *Hammond*, 62 Pa 177.

[115]*Wenger* v. *Raymond*, 104 Pa 33

733. The trial; proving end of term — The close of the term must be made to appear by the evidence. It might close by a surrender and the acceptance of a new lease with an earlier ending. The burden would be on the plaintiff to prove the surrender and making of the new lease.[116] The lessee, in a lease for five years, dying at the end of one year and a half after the making of the lease, his widow, not yet become the administratrix (but subsequently becoming such), could not validly agree to a surrender of the lease, and accept a new one less beneficial to the lessee, and therefore could defend, the proceedings having begun before the termination of the original lease, on the ground that that lease continued.[117] The lease for one year may stipulate that the "lawful continuance of the tenancy shall be deemed a renewal thereof" for the further term of one year. If the tenant shows that he continued in possession beyond the year, and that the lessor received from him money equal to the rent for the first two months following the close of the year, the lessor may show that he demanded this money as due, and mistakenly believing it due, for the last two months of the term, and that on discovering that he had already been paid for these months, he tendered back the money. These facts would not create the right of the tenant to a renewal of the lease.[118] The lease, e. g., for five years, may provide for its own premature termination, for breach of a covenant not to remove hay from the premises, or not to do or to do other things. If proceedings to recover possession are begun before the normal ending of the term, the burden is on the lessor to show the breach of the covenants. Of course the tenant has a right to furnish counter-evidence.[119]

This case implies that if two tenants in common lease the land, one of them, against the dissent of the other, cannot require the lessee to vacate and sustain the proceedings before the justice

[116]*Keating* v. *Condon*, 68 Pa 75.

[117]*Keating* v *Condon*, 68 Pa 75

[118]*Sizer* v *Russett*, 11 Pa Super Ct 108

[119]*Quinn* v *McCarty*, 81 Pa 475
The tenant cannot deny the title of the lessor at the time of accepting the lease. He cannot, e g, prove

734. The trial; tenant's defenses.— Whatever would properly prevent a dispossession, under the conditions of the act of 1863, can be proved by the tenant, and he can, of course, furnish evidence to rebut or contradict that by which the plaintiff has undertaken to prove the facts which must be established to justify his recovery of the possession. The defendant, sued as an individual, may show that he is in possession as an administrator, for the purpose of avoiding the effect of any alleged rescission of the lease made by him after the death of the lessee, and before he became administrator, and for this purpose he may put in evidence the letters of administration [120] He may prove the loss of the plaintiff's title by its own expiration, or by a sheriff's sale of it,[121] or by a sale of it by himself.[122] He may show that he was induced to accept the lease by a fraud on him or a misrepresentation as to facts on which his right to the land prior to the lease depends.[123] He may prove that, being a tenant in possession under X, he was induced by Y, the plaintiff, ignoring his duty towards X, to accept a lease from him, Y.[124] He may show, though the original lease had expired, an oral agreement that he might continue in possession another year, and that this year had not expired when the proceedings began.[125] He may show that there was an earlier lease than that alleged by the plaintiff, and that he is holding over under it, for the purpose

that he was the owner, and mortgaged it simply to the lessor, and accepted a lease from the mortgagee *Fisher* v *McCauley*, 2 Dauphin Co Rep 180

[120]*Keating* v *Condon*, 68 Pa 75

[121]*Heritage* v *Wilfong*, 58 Pa 137

[122]*Koontz* v *Hammond*, 62 Pa 177 *Quinn* v *McCorty*, 81 Pa 475 Tenant may show that before the end of the term he acquired the rights of a vendee *Krueger* v *Rutledge*, 2 Kulp 371

[123]*Koontz* v *Hammond*, 62 Pa 177 Cf *Baskin* v *Seechrist*, 6 Pa 154,

Hockenbury v *Snyder*, 2 Watts & S. 249, *Brown* v *Dysinger*, 1 Rawle, 408, *Boyer* v *Smith*, 5 Watts, 55

[124]*Lowenstein* v *Keller*, 3 Kulp, 361

[125]*Lutz* v *Wainwright*, 193 Pa. 541, 44 Atl 565   The burden is upon him

After the notice to quit, the tenant may show that it was withdrawn and that a new lease was made by the parties   An abortive negotiation for a new lease would be insufficient   *Brown* v *Montgomery*, 21 Pa Super Ct 262

of establishing that the notice to quit did not precede, by three months, the close of the hold-over period,[126] or for the purpose of proving that his right to the possession had not expired.[127] The plaintiff may, in turn, contend that the earlier lease, being in parol and for ten years, became, after one year's possession of the premises by the tenant, and his paying one year's rent, a tenancy from year to year merely, and he may offer evidence that, on a sale of the reversion, there was an agreement for a change of the beginning of the year, and that the year, according to this agreement, had come to an end after a three months' notice to quit.[128]

735. Tenant's defenses, continued — The tenant on the appeal has all the defenses that would have availed him had the action been ejectment,[129] and those additional ones peculiar to the justice's proceeding   He may show a former adjudication.[130]   In *Diefenderfer* v. *Caffrey*,[131] the proceedings were against the administratrix of Caffrey   She, his widow, set up a right to the possession in herself, alleging that her stepson had a contract for the purchase of the premises from X before the plaintiff bought them from X, that she had gone into possession, under the stepson, as his tenant, that, though her husband had, while they were both in possession, accepted a lease from the plaintiff, she had had no knowledge of this lease, and had never recognized the plaintiff as landlord   The court instructed the jury that if the stepson claimed the land bona fide, though his title was in fact not good, and if the defendant went into and continued in the possession under the stepson, in good faith, she was not, as administratrix, the tenant of the plaintiff, but, in her own

[126]*Bergner* v *Palethorp* 2 W N C 297

[127]*Dumn* v *Rothermel*, 112 Pa 272 3 Atl 800, 119 Pa 632, 13 Atl 509

[128]*Dumn* v *Rothermel*, 112 Pa 272, 3 Atl 800, 119 Pa 632, 13 Atl. 509   Ct *Jones* v *Kroll*, 116 Pa 85, 8 Atl 857.

[129]*Quinn* v *McCarty*, 81 Pa 475

[130]*Lowenstein* v *Keller*, 3 Kulp, 361

[131] (Pa) 9 Atl 182   Affirmed by an equally divided supreme court.

right, was the tenant of the stepson The tenant may show that the notice to quit the possession was withdrawn; that, *e. g ,* after the notice, the landlord assented to his continuing in possession for another year.[132]

736 Prohibited defenses.— The acceptance of a lease so far admits the then present right of the lessor to the possession, and to a restoration of the possession, at the expiration of the lease, as to preclude the tenant's justifying the refusal to give up the possession by a denial of that right. Though the tenant has, when he accepts the lease, a better right to the land than the lessor, he cannot set it up [133] He cannot show, *e. g.,* that he was the owner of the land, and that he conveyed it by way of mortgage to the lessor, in order to preclude the recovery of the possession by the lessor [134]

737 Appeal not a supersedeas — The appeal, the act of 1863 expressly declares, "shall not be a supersedeas to the warrant of possession" issued by the justice after rendering judgment [135] The possession may be delivered to the lessor before the appeal is taken,[136] or it may be delivered pending the appeal. The provision for an appeal presupposes the possibility that the justice mistakenly awarded the land to the lessor, and put him in possession. Hence it provides, not merely for the restoration of the possession at the conclusion of the proceedings on the appeal, but also for an indemnification in money.

738. Damages of tenant — "If the jury shall find in favor of

---

[132]*Supplee* v *Timothy,* 23 W N C 386   The fact that the tenant agreed to remain would be a consideration But without such agreement there would be a sufficient consideration The evidence of the agreement of the landlord to a continuance of the possession must be clear and convincing, and satisfy the jury, not merely that the tenant understood it so, but that the landlord fully assented   *Kelly* v. *Loehi,* 1 Brewst (Pa) 303.
LAND & TEN 40.

[133]*Koontz* v *Hammond,* 62 Pa 177; *Heritage* v. *Wilfong,* 58 Pa 137

[134]*Fisher* v *McCauley,* 2 Dauphin Co Rep 180

[135]*Koontz* v *Hammond,* 62 Pa 177; *Willard* v *Martin,* 23 Pa Co Ct 285 , *Keating* v *Condon,* 68 Pa 75; The contrary was assumed in *O'Kie* v *Depuy,* 3 Pa Co Ct 140

[136]*Quinn* v. *McCarty,* 81 Pa 475.

the tenant, they shall also assess the damages which he shall have sustained by reason of his removal from the premises; and for the amount found by the jury, judgment shall be rendered in his favor, with costs of suit, and that he recover possession of the premises; and he shall have the necessary writ or writs of execution to enforce said judgment" If the decision on the appeal is in favor of the plaintiff, there will, of course, be no damages for the defendant.[137] The defendant's damages must be those which he has sustained by reason of his removal. If, the premises being a tavern, he has, by being dispossessed, been deprived of the use of the license to sell liquors, which he has procured, the cost of the license should be allowed him, as also the value of the good will, whose use has been made impossible, and the expense occasioned by the removal.[138] If the lease provides for the making of improvements by the lessee at his expense, and that they are not to be removed at the expiration of the term, not their cost, but the value of that part of the term of which the tenant has been improperly deprived, as enhanced by them, would be the proper measure of damages.[139] In *Quinn* v. *McCarty*,[140] the defendant was allowed to show that he had spent $600 in improvements, of the enjoyment of which he had been deprived by his dispossession under the justice's judgment, as well as that the farm was worth $200 per year when he was put off, aside from what the hotel was paying, that the hotel

---

[137]*Lutz* v *Wainwright,* 193 Pa 541, 44 Atl 565 In *Brown* v *Montgomery,* 21 Pa Super Ct 262, the jury were told that the tenant could recover for the loss of possession between the ouster and the verdict on appeal, but no later, since he was entitled to repossession He could also recover the cost of removing his goods If, not being able to get another suitable house, he had to board at a hotel, he was, said the court, entitled to the cost of his board He should be compensated also for damage to his goods If the verdict is for the landlord, the tenant, on appeal to the supreme court, cannot take advantage of error in the instructions as to his own damages.

[138]*Keating* v *Condon,* 68 Pa 75

[139] Cf *Dumn* v *Rothermel,* 112 Pa 272, 3 Atl. 800, 119 Pa 632, 13 Atl 509 The court told the jury, in the language of the act of 1863, to give such damages as the defendant had sustained by reason of his removal from the premises.

[140] 81 Pa 475.

was paying $2,000 a year profits. The offer of the cost of the improvements was to establish "one basis on which the jury may assess damages." Pronouncing this error, Woodward, J., remarks that, if the defendant had been entitled to a verdict on the main question in the cause, the effect of that would have been to restore to him the possession of the premises in their improved condition. If he was not entitled to a verdict, he could not assert a claim to damages. "Peculiar and exceptional circumstances might be conceived in which such facts as these would be relevant." For the purpose for which it was offered, it was not relevant The defendant had been deprived of nearly four years of the term, on account of a breach of condition which he denied. He would have been entitled, doubtless, to the value of the term for these four years, in excess of the rent, but not to the cost of the improvements.[141] Among the damages recoverable by the tenant is the loss to him upon the sale of cows, horses, agricultural implements, etc., made unavoidable by his dispossession. He must do the best he can with the property. If he desires to hold the lessor responsible for the difference between what they may sell for and their real value, he should give him notice of this intention before the sale. An estimate by witnesses, not of the value of the property but of the loss, is not admissible [142] No damages may be allowed for "annoyance," if that is intended to express "personal chagrin and mental vexation and anxiety; and for such results of a law suit, any attempt to apportion money damages could result only in conjecture and caprice" Pecuniary loss, caused by the eviction, is the measure of damages.[143] When there is no evidence of malice or oppression in expelling the tenant, he is entitled to compensatory dam-

[141]In *Koenig* v *Bauer*, 57 Pa 168, the court allowed the defendant to show "wnat his damage was by the removal, and the value of the place to him at the time of the removal." What the evidence was is not stated.

[142]*Supplee* v *Timothy*, 23 W N C 386   The evidence on which the jury acted is pronounced sufficient

[143]*Quinn* v. *McCarty*, 81 Pa. 475.

ages only.[144] In the absence of a rule of court requiring it, previous notice to the landlord of the lessee's intention to claim damages is unnecessary.[145] If the decision is in favor of the plaintiff, and the tenant has retained the possession, the former will be entitled to damages; *viz*, to rent for the detention of the premises, down to the final judgment.[146]

739. Damages of landlord.— The verdict being for the landlord, he is entitled to damages; *e. g*, compensation for the detention of the possession between the expiration of the lease and the ouster of the tenant [147]

740. Judgment of restitution.— If the jury find for the defendant, and he has been, as he usually is, put out of possession, the judgment is "that he recover possession of the premises." He may recover this possession even if a succeeding tenant has gone into possession,[148] and he may have the necessary writ of possession.[149]

---

[144]*Koenig* v *Bauer*, 57 Pa 168

[145]*Koenig* v *Bauer*, 57 Pa 168

[146]*Dunmire* v *Price*, 12 W N C 179, *O'Kie* v. *Depuy*, 3 Pa Co Ct 140

[147]*Brown* v. *Montgomery*, 21 Pa Super. Ct. 262 The court told the jury that the landlord would properly recover, also, $30 that he had to pay to Mr Lahm No explanation was given

[148]*Hoines* v *Levin*, 51 Pa 412

[149]*Quinn* v. *McCarty*, 81 Pa 475.

CHAPTER XXXIII.

RECOVERING POSSESSION ACT MARCH 25, 1825.

741. The act of March 25, 1825.— The 2d section of the act of March 25, 1825,[1] furnishes a method by which the lessor of a term of years, on the removal of the tenant from the premises without leaving thereon goods sufficient to pay at least three months' rent and without allowing the landlord to resume possession, may recover the possession.

742 The conditions under which the remedy is given — There must be a lease for a term of years and this must be found by the aldermen, in order to secure their judgment for the plaintiff from reversal on certiorari.[2] This lessee must have removed from the demised premises without leaving sufficient property thereon to secure the payment of at least three months' rent, and he must have refused, in five days after demand for security, to give security for the payment of at least three months' rent, and he must refuse to deliver up the possession. If the tenant has not removed from the premises it is not neces-

---

[1] 1 Pepper & L Digest, 2659, P L 114 The act of 1825 is not designed to furnish a substitute for an action of ejectment between rival claimants   of the land   *Powell* v. *Campbell*, 2 Phila 42   [2]*Geisenberger* v *Cerf*, 1 Phila 17; *Mund* v *Vanfleet*, 2 Phila 41.

sary that he should have sufficient goods on them to satisfy the
rent of three months, or that he should give security. By "removal" seems to be understood the tenant's removing his "family
or goods with a fraudulent intent," or "himself" and "goods."
The fact that nearly all the tenant's goods have been removed,
so that those remaining are not sufficient to secure payment of
three months' rent, the tenant and family remaining, does not
authorize recourse to the remedy of the act.[3] Previous to the
passage of the act, says King, P. J.,[4] "insolvent and malicious
tenants would frequently remove their property from leased
premises and refuse to give their landlords possession, until
coerced by ejectment or the comparatively procrastinated remedy
given by the landlord and tenant act   To keep a dwelling-house
locked up till the end of a term, and until the end of a notice
to quit, was not an uncommon thing in hostile tenants, and landlords, rather than hazard an action of trespass, would submit "[5]
The object of the act was therefore to secure restitution of the
possession of the landlord within the term, when the tenant has
removed, not simply when he has taken away some or many of
his goods, himself continuing to occupy the premises.

743. Necessity of insufficiency of goods or refusal of security —
Even when the tenant has removed from the premises during
the term, it is further necessary, in order to entitle the lessor to
the remedy of the act of 1825, both that there shall not remain
on the premises property sufficient to secure the payment of at
least three months' rent, and that there shall have been a demand upon him to furnish security for that amount of rent,
followed by a refusal for five days to give such security. The

[3]*Freytag* v *Anderson*, 1 Rawle, 73,
Black v *Alberson*, 1 Ashm (Pa)
127
[4]*Freytag* v *Anderson*, 1 Ashm
(Pa) 98
[5] Ludlow, J , states the object of
the act to be to give the landlord the
right to dispossess a stubborn tenant,
who, before its passage, could remove
his property and himself from the
premises, refuse to pay the rent, and
turn his landlord over to his common
law remedies, under the peril of an
action for trespass *Grider* v. *Mc-
Intyre*, 6 Phila 112.

tenant has the option, in order to retain the right to the premises, notwithstanding his own removal, to allow sufficient goods to remain, or, withdrawing the goods, to give security within five days after demand.[6] If the tenant has sublet the premises without violating any condition in the lease, the subtenant has the right, the tenant surrendering the term to the lessor, to tender the security, and so save his right to continue in control. The tenant cannot surrender his term to the prejudice of a subtenant, and if the subtenant chooses to give up the term rather than give security for the rent, or keep sufficient property on the premises to secure its payment, he must be allowed to do so.[7] The demand for the security should possibly be in writing, and it must be made by the landlord, by his agent, or attorney, or by the grantee or devisee of the reversion or claimant of it, through a sale in execution or otherwise   A demand by X, who is neither the lessor nor related to him in any of these modes, is ineffectual [8] The security demanded must be that prescribed in the act of 1825. If, instead of security for at least three months' rent, security for the prompt payment of the rent (all the rent, apparently) of premises No. 39 Leonard street be demanded, the demand may be ignored, and a failure to furnish it within five days will not entitle the lessor to the remedy.[9] Upon proper demand for the security, it must be tendered within five days. If it is not tendered within that time nor until after the proceedings have begun, though before judgment, the tender will not then arrest the proceedings or save the right of the tenant to continue in control of the term. "The five days," says Coulter, J., "within which security is to be given,

[6]*Freytag* v *Anderson*, 1 Ashm (Pa) 98, Affirmed in 1 Rawle, 73

[7]*Grider* v *McIntyre*, 6 Phila 112 The subtenant was in possession, and also had sufficient goods on the premises   Must he, like the tenant, remove? Cf *Shermer* v. *Paciello*, 161 Pa. 69, 28 Atl. 995.

[8]*Powell* v *Campbell*, 2 Phila 42. The proceeding itself was also in the name of X, who apparently was agent for one claiming not under the landlord, but adversely to his title.

[9]*Powell* v. *Campbell*, 2 Phila. 42.

is an essential fact or circumstance for the protection of the lessor. For, if the tenant is not then concluded, when will he be? If it depends on his convenience or pleasure, the remedy is rendered valueless to the lessor. A time must be fixed, and the time fixed for [sic] the statute must prevail."[10]

744. Application to two aldermen.— When the conditions previously described exist, the landlord or lessor may apply to any two aldermen or justices of the peace within the city or county of Philadelphia, and make an affidavit or affirmation of the fact, and thereupon the said aldermen or justices of the peace shall forthwith issue their precepts to a constable, commanding him to summon the lessee before them The lessor accordingly makes a complaint to the two magistrates, under oath or affirmation.[11] This complaint must aver all the facts needful to authorize a judgment for the plaintiff The aldermen are authorized to issue their precept only when the facts necessary to give them jurisdiction have been sworn or affirmed to[12] But possibly the averments in the complaint of the necessary facts may be general, and if they are, it would then be necessary that they should be more specifically found by the aldermen.[13] If the complaint omits all statements that the plaintiff, or the person whose reversion he had bought at sheriff's sale, had leased the premises to the defendant,[14] or that the lease was for a term of years,[15] the judgment for the plaintiff cannot be sustained on certiorari. The complaint should, doubtless, also state that the tenant has refused to deliver up the possession.[16]

---

[10] *Ward* v *Wandell*, 10 Pa 98

[11] *Uber* v *Hickson*, 6 Phila 132, *Erety* v *Wiltbank*, 8 Phila 300 Having given notice to the tenant to furnish security, the landlord may go no further with the statutory proceedings and enter a judgment on the warrant of attorney in the lease for condition broken *Shermer* v *Pacuello*, 161 Pa. 69, 28 Atl 995.

[12] *Mund* v *Vanfleet*, 2 Phila 41, *Erety* v *Wiltbank* 8 Phila 300

[13] *Uber* v *Hickson*, 6 Phila 132, *Erety* v *Wiltbank*, 8 Phila 300

[14] *Mund* v *Vanfleet*, 2 Phila 41

[15] *Geisenberger* v *Cerf*, 1 Phila 17, *Mund* v *Vanfleet*, 2 Phila 41

[16] *Caldwell* v *Koehler*, 1 Phila 375. The necessary averments are here said to be that the plaintiff or his

745. The summons and later proceedings — The proper complaint being presented to the two aldermen, they must issue their precept to a constable of Philadelphia, commanding him to summon the lessee before them on a day certain, not exceeding eight nor less than five days thereafter, to answer the complaint. On the day appointed the aldermen are to hear the case, and if it shall appear that the lessee has removed from the premises without leaving sufficient goods and chattels, or giving security for the payment of a quarter's rent, and has refused to deliver up possession of the demised premises, they shall enter judgment against the lessee, that the premises shall be delivered up to the lessor or landlord forthwith, and shall, at the request of the lessor or landlord, issue a writ of possession directed to said constable, commanding him forthwith to deliver possession of the premises to the landlord or lessor, and also to levy the costs on the defendant, in the same manner that executions issued by justices of the peace are directed by law.

746. Evidence — The aldermen must receive evidence, the testimony of witnesses who have been sworn or affirmed, or written instruments. The facts proved, as means of proving the jurisdictional facts, do not need to appear in the record. Any attempt to there state them, it is suggested by Finletter, J., "might be fatal inasmuch as it would be presumed that the judgment had been entered alone on the facts set out "[17] It is needless to say that the defense which the tenant desires to make must be heard [18]

747 Facts established and judgment — If, says the act of 1825, it shall appear that the lessee has removed from the premises without leaving sufficient goods and chattels, or giving security for the payment of the rent as aforesaid, and has refused

predecessor demised the premises to the defendant for a term of years reserving rent, that he had removed without leaving sufficient property, that he had refused to give security within five days after demand, and that he had refused to give up the premises

[17]*Erety* v *Wiltbank,* 8 Phila 300.
[18]*Geisenberger* v *Cerf,* 1 Phila 17

to deliver up possession of the demised premises, they shall enter judgment against such lessee, that said premises shall be delivered up to the lessor or landlord forthwith. This enumeration of the things to be found is by no means exhaustive. The justice must find a relation between the plaintiff and the defendant of landlord and tenant, in virtue of a lease for years. The conditions of the demise both as to length of time and amount of rent to be paid,[19] and the time when the tenant removed from the premises;[20] that he did not leave property enough to secure payment of three months' rent, and also, after demand, refused to give other security therefor, and that he refused to give up possession after demand,—must be found.[21]

748. Certiorari.— The judgment of the aldermen may be reviewed on certiorari.[22] In this review, the principle ordinarily observed is applicable, that only the jurisdiction of the justice and the regularity of his proceeding can be considered The soundness of his deductions from the evidence cannot be examined. Though he has no right to enter the judgment for the plaintiff unless he has found the statutory facts, the courts are not so complaisant as to infer that he found these facts simply because he has entered the judgment. And the only admissible evidence that he has found the facts is his averment in the record that he has done so He does not adequately aver the finding of any fact by saying simply, "three months' rent or security for the same found to be in arrears as claimed, notice to be correct and judgment for rendition,"[23] or by saying, "considering all the circumstances they enter judgment against the tenant."[24]

---

[19]*Mund* v *Vanfleet*, 2 Phila 41, *Geisenberger* v *Cerf*, 1 Phila 17, *Erety* v *Wiltbank*, 8 Phila 300

[20]*Freytag* v *Anderson*, 1 Rawle 73, *Black* v *Alberson*, 1 Ashm (Pa) 127, *Erety* v. *Wiltbank*, 8 Phila 300

[21]*Erety* v *Wiltbank*, 8 Phila 300

[22]In *Grider* v *McIntyre*, 6 Phila 112, a rule to show cause why the certiorari should not be allowed was made absolute although, before the decision upon the rule, a longer time had elapsed than is allowed for the taking of the writ, the rule having been taken within that time

[23]*Gault* v *Lowry*, 1 Phila 394

[24]*Geisenberger* v *Cerf*, 1 Phila 17.

When the complaint has stated the facts with particularity, if the aldermen find its statements correct, they sufficiently express this finding in their record by saying that they "find the above complaint is in all respects just and true;"[25] but that expression will be inadequate, when the complaint does not recite all the necessary facts or does not recite them with sufficient particularity.[26] The record must be selfconsistent with respect to essentials The precept of the aldermen recited that the premises were rented to Vanfleet, reserving rent, but not saying who rented them and to whom the rent was payable, the transcript affirmed that Hagaman was the lessor, while the writ of possession alleged that Mund (who claimed as vendee of Allen) rented the premises to Vanfleet. Said Allison, J.: "The variance between the different portions of the record is so material as of itself to render it impossible to sustain these proceedings"[27] Not the tenant only, but a subtenant who would be injured by the execution of the judgment, may sue out a certiorari.[28] The omission of the record to find any necessary fact,—e. g.,

Saying "that, after hearing, etc , they do adjudge that the premises shall be delivered up to Gilbert Alberson, the lessor or landlord forthwith,' is insufficient   Black v Alberson, 1 Ashm (Pa) 127

[25]Caldwell v Koehler, 1 Phila 375 Finletter, J, remarks, in Erety v Wiltbank, 8 Phila 300, that in proceedings before aldermen "it must appear [on certiorari] that the judgment is founded upon properly received testimony or evidence, that is, that witnesses were sworn and gave evidence on behalf of either party, or that written testimony was duly offered and read " An exception to the judgment of the magistrate, to the effect that that officer refused to allow him to prove that he had bought the premises with his own money, but caused the deed to be made to the lessor, his mother, on her promising that she would devise the premises to him, that she had not done so, that he accepted the lease for three years from her seven years after the purchase, under a threat that, if he did not, his goods would be seized by the sheriff and his business broken up; that he had paid the rent regularly until the last quarter, when he removed from the premises, and that he had begun an ejectment, was dismissed   Reith v Reith, 13 W N C. 435

[26]Uber v Hickson, 6 Phila 132, Erety v Wiltbank, 8 Phila 300

[27]Mund v. Vanfleet, 2 Phila 41. Whether the writ of possession could be resorted to, to supplement defects in the findings of record, not decided in Black v Alberson, 1 Ashm (Pa) 127

[28]Grider v. McIntyre, 6 Phila. 112.

the removal of the tenant,[29] the lease being for a term of years;[30] who was the lessor,[31] that notice to give security was given by the lessor or his alienee or agent,[32]—will cause a reversal on certiorari.

749. The writ of possession.— The act of 1825 directs that after entering judgment the aldermen "shall, at the request of the said lessor or landlord, issue to the constable a writ of possession commanding him forthwith to deliver possession. The writ may issue on the day on which judgment is entered, or the next[33] or any later day It may be made returnable immediately, or in four[34] or other number of days. Should the judgment of the justices be reversed on certiorari after the writ of possession has been executed it is in the sound discretion of the court whether to award restitution of the tenant;[35] and it will allow the landlord to lay before it any circumstances that should prevent the award of restitution [36]

[29] *Freytag* v. *Anderson,* 1 Rawle, 73, *Black* v. *Alberson,* 1 Ashm (Pa) 127

[30] *Mund* v *Vanfleet,* 2 Phila 41, *Geisenberger* v *Cerf,* 1 Phila 17

[31] *Mund* v *Vanfleet,* 2 Phila 41

[32] *Powell* v *Campbell,* 2 Phila 42 From the judgment of the court of common pleas on the certiorari there may be an appeal to the superior or supreme court. *Freytag* v. *Ander-* son, 1 Rawle, 73, *Ward* v *Wandell,* 10 Pa 98

[33] *Freytag* v. *Anderson,* 1 Rawle, 73

[34] *Freytag* v *Anderson,* 1 Rawle, 73

[35] *Freytag* v. *Anderson,* 1 Ashm (Pa) 98

[36] *Black* v. *Alberson,* 1 Ashm. (Pa) 127.

CHAPTER XXXIV.

PROCEEDINGS IN PHILADELPHIA ON LOST LEASE.

750. Act of February 28, 1865.— The act of February 28, 1865,[1] furnishes a method by which, when the lease is lost, and the time of its ending is not known to the landlord, he may compel the tenant to disclose the time of its ending or suffer an eviction within a specified time

751. Conditions under which the remedy exists— The premises, the subject of the letting, must be in the city of Philadelphia There must be a "lease or verbal letting of property for a term of years or from year to year." When all that appears is that, when the plaintiff became the owner, the defendant was "and is yet tenant of said premises," the alderman has no jurisdiction. Such fact neither is nor implies a lease or verbal letting. One in possession is a tenant, whether he holds as owner, or intruder, or under a lease "The act applies only to a tenancy created by a lease which fixes a term and a rent And to give it any broader application would make it equivalent to ejectment for the recovery of land, however in the possession of another."[2] The present landlord must have lost the lease, or evidence of the beginning and conclusion of the term, and must be unable to produce proof thereof. One who has purchased the re-

[1] 1 Pepper & L Digest, 2654; P L 253.   [2] *McMullin* v *McCreary*, 54 Pa 230

version from the lessor,[3] as well as the lessor, when he retains the reversion, may institute the proceedings. The first year, if the lease is from year to year, or the term, if the lease is for years, must be ended,[4] although, as Finletter, J., remarks, in considering the exception on certiorari that the alderman's record did not find that the term had ended: "And when it is considered that the whole proceeding and the act itself is founded upon the fact that all knowledge of the commencement and ending of the term is lost, it is scarcely to be expected that any statement of the commencement, duration, or ending of the term should appear. Indeed, if it did, it would vitiate the whole proceedings, because it would contradict the initial fact [the loss of the evidence of the ending of the term] without which the jurisdiction would not attach "[5]

752. Conditions; demand of information from tenant.—When the preceding conditions exist, "it shall be lawful, at any time after the first year or after the term of years, as the case may be, for the landlord [whether the lessor or his successor], desiring to recover possession of the demised premises, to give notice in writing to the tenant that he has lost such lease, or is unable to make such proof, and requiring the tenant, within thirty days from the time of service of such notice, to furnish him in writing with the date at which his term of tenancy commenced, and such notice, if supported by affidavit, shall be evidence of what it sets forth " The landlord's notice does not need to be supported by an affidavit.[6] On receiving the notice the tenant may comply with or disregard it. If he "shall furnish, in writing, the date as required, such writing shall be evidence of the facts contained in it," and the landlord, assuming the term to end when the tenant says it does, may doubtless recover possession,

[3]Dubasse v Martin, 24 Phila Leg Int. 92, McMullin v McCreary, 54 Pa 230

[4]McMullin v McCreary, 54 Pa 230.

[5]Mooney v Rogers, 8 Phila 297

[6]Gifford v McDonald, 24 Phila. Leg Int. 92.

under the act of 1772, or of 1863, or by the action of ejectment. "If the tenant shall fail or refuse within thirty days to
comply with the said requirement, the landlord may, at the expiration of that period, give to the tenant three months' notice
to quit the premises occupied by him, and shall proceed thereafter in the same manner as is now provided in cases of the
usual notice to quit at the end of the term " Though the tenant
fails to give the information, if, within the thirty days of the
notice, he shall make affidavit "that he is unable to comply with
the requirement of the landlord, stating the causes of such inability," the landlord must give six months' notice to the tenant
to remove, "upon which he shall proceed as provided in the
cases of the three months' notice as aforesaid."

753. Proceedings before justice.— If the tenant fails to give
the information required, the proceeding before an alderman,
in the mode indicated by the act of December 14, 1863, is resorted to.[7] His jurisdiction is not ousted by the filing of an
affidavit of the tenant that he claims the land by virtue of a purchase of it from X, who owned it before it came into his possession, and before the plaintiff ever claimed to own it. The tenant
cannot defeat a recovery by alleging a title rival of that of the
plaintiff, whether that title be in a stranger or in himself.[8] The
justice's record must show all the facts which must exist in order
to justify his proceeding under the act of February 28, 1863,
e. g., the fact of a lease or letting to the defendant, by the plaintiff or one from whom he has acquired the reversion, and if it
does not, his judgment will be reversed on certiorari.[9]

[7]*Dubasse* v *Martin*, 24 Phila Leg
Int 92
[8]*Mooney* v *Rogers*, 8 Phila 297
[9]*McMullin* v. *McCreary*, 54 Pa.
230 Cf *Mooney* v *Rogers*, 8 Phila.
297, where the record was found to
be "singularly perfect."

CHAPTER XXXV.

ESTOPPEL AGAINST DENYING LESSOR'S TITLE.

754. The estoppel.— Within certain restrictions, there arises an estoppel against denying the lessor's ownership of the land, by accepting the lease from him and taking possession in pursuance of it But there is no general estoppel against denying that ownership Accepting a lease is a species of admission of the lessor's rights to the land, and as an admission can be proved in all cases in which an admission by the lessee would be pertinent as evidence. But, as an admission to anyone that he has a right does not preclude the subsequent denial by the admitting party of that right and the exhibition of evidence to support that denial, so the tenant is not precluded to deny the right of the lessor, because he has in a way admitted it by accepting the lease   He may prove that, despite his admission, the right was not in the lessor, if the object of the proof is not to prevent the lessor's recovery of the possession at the close of the term, or of rent which accrues during the term   When the former tenant has lost the possession, he may sustain an ejectment to recover the land even when the grounds on which recovery is sought imply the nonexistence of a right in the lessor to the land at the time when the lease from him was accepted by the lessee.   Hence if B, being the owner, accepts a lease from A, and after the death of B all his interests in the land are sold for the payment of his debts, one of which is a lien attaching to the land prior to the lease, the purchaser out of possession may recover in eject-ment by showing the defects of the title of the former lessor, who is now in possession.[1]

755. Scope of the ordinary estoppel.— The ordinary estoppel of the tenant results simply in an incapacity to defeat the recov-ery of the possession of the premises, by opposing to the actions of the lessor begun for that purpose, the defects of his title.   In possessory actions of the lessor, whether ejectment,[2] or proceed-ings under the various landlord and tenant acts[3] or under the act of June 16, 1836, for the recovery of possession by a pur-chaser at a sheriff's sale, the lessee cannot attack the title of the

[1]*Kennedy* v *Whalen,* 5 Kulp 35, *Anderson* v *Brinser,* 129 Pa 376, 6 L R A 205, 11 Atl 809, 18 Atl 520, *Brown* v. *Dysinger,* 1 Rawle, 408, *Hockenbury* v *Snyder,* 2 Watts & S 240

[2]*Boyer* v *Smith,* 5 Watts, 55, *Gal-loway* v *Ogle,* 2 Br & 468, *Jones* v *Tatham,* 20 Pa 398, *Logan* v *Quig-ley* (Pa) 10 Cent Rep 403, 11 Atl 92; *Lebanon School Dist* v *Lebanon*
LAND & TEN 41

Female Seminary, 22 W N C 65, *Eister* v *Paul* 54 Pa 196, *Kline* v *Johnston,* 24 Pa 72, *Wolf* v *God-dard,* 9 Watts, 544

[3]*Mohan* v *Butler,* 112 Pa 590, 4 Atl 47 *Heritage* v *Wilfong,* 58 Pa 137, *Koontz* v *Hammond,* 62 Pa 177, *Newell* v *Gibbs,* 1 Watts & S 496, *Goldsmith* v *Smith,* 3 Phila. 360.

lessor[4] If, under a warrant of attorney in the lease, the lessor
causes judgment in ejectment to be entered, the tenant cannot,
as cause for opening it or setting it aside, set up a title in a
stranger, nor may the stranger himself intervene in order to
procure it to be set aside[5] After the lessor has recovered the
possession, the tenant, if he has a title superior to that of the
lessor, may enforce it by himself becoming plaintiff. The object
of the estoppel is simply, so far as possessory procedure is concerned, to compel the tenant to yield the possession, and to incur
the inconveniences of a plaintiff.

756. Proceedings for rent.— By accepting a lease and the possession of the premises in pursuance of it, the tenant precludes
himself from effectively refusing to pay the rent on account of
the defects of the title of the lessor. He may be compelled to
pay the rent, despite such defects, if any, and therefore proof
of such defects is irrelevant and inadmissible, in actions of assumpsit for the rent,[6] or for use and occupation, no rent having
been specified by the parties.[7] If, after accepting a lease from
A, the tenant accepts another for the same time from B, he is
bound to pay rent to both. He must pay B, and, when sued for
the rent by B, cannot show that A's title is the better.[8] The
lessor may waive the right to insist on the estoppel, and, the
rent being overdue, may agree that if the lessor "holds the land
by law" against a rival the rent shall be paid, otherwise not.
On this contract the lessor may recover, on showing that all risk
of the tenant's having to pay mesne profits to the rival has

[4]*Wilson* v *Hubbell*, 1 Pennyp 413
[5]*Nehr* v *Krewsberg*, 187 Pa 53,
40 Atl 810
[6]*Long* v *Fitzimmons*, 1 Watts & S
530, *School District* v *Long* (Pa)
9 Cent Rep. 350, 10 Atl 769, *Ewing*
v *Cottman*, 9 Pa Super Ct 444,
Wagle v *Bartley* (Pa) 9 Cent Rep
551, 11 Atl 223, *Ward* v *Philadelphia*, 4 Cent. Rep 662, 6 Atl 263
The power of the lessor, a married
woman, to make the lease, cannot be
questioned by the tenant who has enjoyed the possession and is sued for
the rent   *Ewing* v. *Cottman*, 9 Pa.
Super Ct 444

[7]*Glenn* v *Rise*, 6 Watts, 44, *Stokes*
v *McKibbin*, 13 Pa 267, *Bauders* v.
Fletcher, 11 Serg & R 419

[8]*Hamilton* v. *Pittock*, 158 Pa. 457,
27 Atl 1079.

passed, by the lapse of more than six years since the close of the tenant's possession and of more than twenty-one years since the lessor's adverse possession began [9]   The omission of the tenant to take possession when he might have taken it and the lessor was ready to deliver it does not exempt him from the estoppel against denying the title of the lessor when sued for the rent [10]

757. Kind of lease.—The lease, out of the acceptance of which the estoppel of the lessee springs, may be oral[11] as well as written [12]   An agreement to make a lease was followed by the writing of it   The writing shown to X, the person expected to become lessee, was assented to by him, and he in consequence took possession of the land, but the writing was never signed by anybody.   The estoppel of a tenant, however, affected X [13]

758. No estoppel against denying the lease.—The estoppel arises

[9]*Sassaman* v *Feagly*, 4 Watts, 268
[10]*Howard* v *Murphy*, 23 Pa 173

In *Kunkle* v *People's Natural Gas Co* 165 Pa 133, 33 L R A 847, 30 Atl 719, the lessee of a gas and oil tract covenanted to commence operations within six months, and complete one well, or to pay to the lessor $500 and a rental of $130 until its completion   The lessee took possession and retained it for one year and nine months, but did not commence the well nor pay anything   On the lessor's demanding $630 shortly after the close of the first six months, it was disclosed to the lessee that the wife of the lessor, who had not united in the lease, had an interest in the premises   The lessor offered to procure the execution of the lease by his wife, but the lessee declined except on conditions he had no right to insist on   As the lessee had had the possession for the six months, and as the wife concurred in the contract, the former could not defeat a recovery of the $630 by showing the title of the wife   It is suggested that if the lessee had commenced operations within the first six months, and taken gas or oil, equity would probably have decreed that the wife join in the lease before payment of royalty or rent, and that if the lessee had been deterred from taking possession by fear of the wife's adverse claim, or if he had been induced to accept the lease by fraud or trick of the lessor, he would not be compelled to pay the rent   In *Rhoades* v *Patrick*, 27 Pa 323, it was held that if A, in possession, sold stones from the land to B, B must pay the price, because he could not be compelled to pay it again to the true owner   The owner could not maintain trespass, because he was not in possession, nor could he maintain assumpsit

[11]*Long* v *Fitzimmons*, 1 Watts & S. 530, *Wilhelm* v *Shoop*, 6 Pa 21 *Moderwell* v. *Mullison*, 21 Pa 257.

[12]*Swint* v *McCalmont Oil Co* 184 Pa 202, 63 Am. St Rep 791, 38 Atl 1021, *Moderwell* v *Mullison*, 21 Pa 257, *Wagle* v *Bartley* (Pa) 9 Cent Rep 551, 11 Atl 223

[13]*Jones* v. *Tatham*, 20 Pa 398

out of the relation of landlord and tenant; and in an ejectment by A against B, for the land, or in assumpsit by A against
B, for the rent, or in assumpsit by B against A, for improperly
distraining on B's goods and compelling him to pay rent, when B
was not a tenant of A,[14] the existence of the tenancy will not
be assumed simply because A avers it. His averment must be
allowed to be contradicted It would be a *petitio principii* for
the court to fail to submit to the jury the alleged tenant's dis-
proof of the tenancy [15] The acceptance of a lease from the alleged lessor must be clearly shown [16] The tenant can deny his
acceptance of A's lease, and his entry upon the land under it,
and offer proof that he entered under a lease from B [17] Against
A, who claims to be lessor of X, X may show that he accepted
no lease from A, but that he accepted one from A and B, a partnership; the land being partnership land.[18] B may show that he
had a contract with X to buy the land from X, and that as vendee
he took and retained possession until, X conveying to Y, he accepted a lease from Y, and that the purpose of this arrangement
was to secure Y's consent to his continuance in possession without otherwise paying the unpaid purchase money than by periodical instalments, like rent [19] The widow of A, and also his
administratrix, who is in possession of land of which A had
taken a lease, may show that she was not in possession as his
widow or administratrix but that she had entered into possession
prior to the making of this lease, under another lease from another person, and that she had continued in possession ever since,

[14]*Moderwell* v *Mullison*, 21 Pa
257, *Emery* v *Harrison*, 13 Pa 317
[15]*Moderwell* v *Mullison*, 21 Pa
257, *Emery* v *Harrison*, 13 Pa 317
[16]*Reigart* v *Ehler*, 1 Whart 18
[17]*Reigart* v *Ehler*, 1 Whart 18,
Long v *Fitzsimmons*, 1 Watts & S
530
[18]*Moderwell* v *Mullison*, 21 Pa.
257.

[19]*Anderson* v *Brinser*, 129 Pa 376,
20 W N C 505, 6 L. R A 205, 11
Atl 809, 18 Atl 520 But the question here was whether the contract
had been given up, and the relation
of lessor and lessee substituted Cf
Berridge v. *Glassey*, 20 W. N. C. 50

under this earlier lease.[20]   B was already in possession of land,
when A obtained an agreement from him that he would occupy
it until April 1, 1816, and then give peaceable possession of it
to A. Subsequently A asked B when he intended to leave the
place, and B replied that, if he would give him nine or ten days,
he would be ready to leave   Gibson, J , professed to be unable
to "discover in this agreement a single feature of a lease," remarking that "it contains neither words of demise, nor reservation of rent, nor any other part of a regular lease   These ingred-
ients, no doubt, are not essential, it being sufficient if it appear
to have been the intention of the lessor to dispossess himself of
the premises, and of the lessee to enter pursuant to the agreement   In our case, however, the agreement was nothing more
than that a person already in possession under a claim of title
should abandon the premises at a day certain   For a breach of
this an action would lie, but it created nothing like tenure; nor
could it operate as an estoppel "[21]

   759 No relation of tenure.— If A is in possession of land as
a tenant of X, and on the death of X there is a dispute as to
who is the succeeding owner, A does not become a tenant of B,
one of the rival claimants, by admitting, when called on by B to
pay the rent, that B is entitled to it, and by A's promising to
continue on the premises at the old rent, if the promise is re-
tracted before a bargain is struck on account of a disagreement,
and subsequently no rent is paid to B [22]   If the lease is made in
the name of Boileau & Sankey, who sign it, adding to their
names the words "agents" but not indicating any one whom

---

[20]*Diefenderfer* v. *Caffrey* (Pa) 9
Atl 182
   [21]*Miller* v *M'Brier*, 14 Serg & R
382 A owns land which is intersected by a canal the fee of which belongs to the state   If A makes a
lease to B of coal in his land, but
the lease does not define the premises
leased so as to embrace what lies under the canal, B, when sued for royalty on the coal taken as well from
under the canal as from the land of
A is not estopped from denying the
title of A to the coal under the canal
Wyoming Coal & Transp Co v
Price, 81 Pa 156
   [22]*Stokes* v *McKibbin*, 13 Pa 267.

they represent, no tenure arises between their principal and the lessee that will sustain a distress by the principal for the rent. The tenant "leased the house of Boileau & Sankey They let the premises to her. By the terms of the lease the relation of landlord and tenant was exclusively between them. In the body of the lease Boileau & Sankey are described as the sole lessors. It is true, at the foot they sign it as 'agents' Agents for whom? The lease is silent As is clearly shown in *Holt* v *Martin,* 51 Pa. 499, in regard to a lease executed in a similar manner, the defendant did not thereby become the tenant of an unknown landlord."[23] But the lease being orally made in his own name by A, of land which belongs to and is used by a firm composed of A and B, the lease is to be considered as the lease of the firm, and not of A, and the lessee may safely recognize the firm as his lessors Having paid the rent to it, A would have no right to compel the lessee by distress to pay it again to him, and if A does compel him to pay it again, he may recover it back from A.[24] If on a part of land belonging to A and B as tenants in common, C, a daughter of B, and her husband, son of A, reside, and, after the death of B, of whom the daughter is heir, A brings an ejectment against her, alleging a partition by which the land occupied by her was allotted in severalty to him, C will not be estopped from denying the validity of the partition by which what had been her undivided half had been transferred to A. She will not be deemed to have gone into possession as tenant of A, of more than A's undivided half; but will be regarded as having been tenant of her father, B, as respects B's undivided half.[25] If a lease is signed by A and his son, of land which belongs to A, the tenant may resist paying rent to the son, and may show that the son signed the lease as a subscribing witness, or in order

[23]*Seyfert* v *Bean,* 83 Pa 450 Cf *Bandel* v *Erickson,* 3 Pa Super Ct 389, *Barrett* v *Bemelmans,* 163 Pa 122, 29 Atl 756.

[24]*Modernell* v *Mullason,* 21 Pa 257

[25]*Feather* v *Strohoecker,* 3 Penr. & W 505, 24 Am. Dec 342.

to attest that his father was not being imposed upon, or for some purpose other than to become landlord towards the tenant.[26]

760 **Duration of the estoppel.**—The tenant during the term is estopped from denying the rights of the landlord to the rent, on account of a defect of title to the land, and, within the original term, should the lessee's right to continue in possession be forfeited or otherwise terminated, he cannot resist the lessor's recovery of the possession by setting up any defects of title. But this inability to exhibit any defects of the lessor's title continues after the original term. The tenant may hold over, however long, and with or without the consent of the lessor. Until he gives up the possession he cannot challenge the title of the lessor. Thus, a lease for three years being made in 1854, but the possession of the lessee continuing until 1885, his disability to take advantage of any defects of the lessor's title, in the action of the latter to obtain the possession[27] or to compel payment of rent, continued.[28] If in 1829 at the instance of A, claiming land under a former survey, B entered to clear and cultivate it and to pay the taxes on it for the use of it, B could not, having continued in possession until 1846, successfully resist an ejectment then brought by A, by showing that the survey under which A claimed, made in 1775, had not been returned to the land office when B took possession or since[29] Under a lease for five years made in 1870, the lessee continued in possession until 1886, when an ejectment was brought against him by the lessor. He could not be heard to deny the lessor's title.[30]

761. **Eviction under superior title** — The lessee cannot procure

[26]*Swint* v *McCalmont Oil Co* 184 Pa 202, 63 Am St. Rep 791, 38 Atl. 1021

[27]*Wagle* v *Bartley* (Pa) 9 Cent Rep 551, 11 Atl 223 The possession of the tenant however long continued will not make a title for him by the statute of limitations *Crail* v *Crail*, 6 Pa 480

[28]*Bauders* v *Fletcher*, 11 Serg & R 419

[29]*Wilhelm* v *Shoop*, 6 Pa 21

[30]*Lebanon School Dist* v *Lebanon Female Seminary*, 22 W N C. 65

a reduction of the rent by showing that the lessor's title to a
portion of the premises is bad, if the lessee agreed to take the
risk of the title. After an eviction from a part of the premises,
by the owner of the superior title, the lessee may have a proportional reduction of the rent or royalty. If he is by the lease
to pay royalty upon so many tons of ore, whether mined or not,
he can show that the loss of the possession of a part of the premises has reduced the amount of ore accessible to him, and obtain
a corresponding reduction of the rent [31] If a successful ejectment is brought against the tenant, by one claiming a superior
title to that of the landlord, the tenant, being liable for the
mesne profits, is discharged from rent for his occupancy since
the commencement of the ejectment [32]

762. To what the estoppel applies.—The estoppel is provision-
al and is against the denial of the right of the lessor to the land,
in an action or proceeding by him either to obtain the possession
or the rent The tenant cannot assert the badness of the title
of the lessor, by showing that someone else had a good title at
the time when the lease was made,[33] if the lessor was then in
actual possession and delivered it to the lessee.[34] The tenant has
no right voluntarily to attorn to the claimant of a rival title to
that which the lessor had when he made the lease, and if he does
he cannot resist the claim of his landlord by means of the title
of the person to whom he has attorned.[35] The tenant, accepting
a lease from his lessor's rival, cannot defend against his primary
lessor by means of the rival's title [36] B accepts a lease from the

---

[31]*Kemble Coal & I Co* v *Scott*, 15
W N C 220, *Kemble Coal & I Co*
v *Scott*, 90 Pa 332

[32]*Banders* v *Fletcher*, 11 Serg &
R 419   But the court intimates
that, if the claim for rent had been
for the time covered by the written
and sealed lease, and not for a hold-
over period, the tenant would be
liable on his express covenant

[33]*Long* v *Fitzsimmons*, 1 Watts & S.

533, *Cooper* v *Smith*, 8 Watts 536,
Ewing v *Cottman*, 9 Pa Super Ct.
444, *Willard* v *Earley*, 22 W N C
122

[34]*Ewing* v *Cottman*, 9 Pa. Super
Ct 444

[35]*Mohan* v *Butler*, 112 Pa 590, 4
Atl 47

[36]*Wolf* v *Goddard*, 9 Watts, 544;
Boyer v *Smith*, 5 Watts, 55, *Jones*
v *Tatham*, 20 Pa 398, cf *Bostwick*

agent of seven persons   He subsequently takes a lease from six of these persons, who claim that they own the whole land   B cannot resist the recovery of possession of one undivided seventh by the seventh principal to his lease [37]   To accept a lease from a rival is to acquire in part his ownership   As the tenant cannot acquire the ownership of the rival of his lessor for a period of years, and avail himself of it until he gives up the possession, so he cannot, acquiring during the term the entire interest of the rival, defend under it the action of his lessor for rent or for possession [38]   The tenant cannot defeat the landlord's recovery of possession in ejectment, because the latter does not show that the title has ever passed from the commonwealth or because he himself shows that it has not.[39]

763. Misrepresentation or fraud — B, who is already in possession of land when he accepts a lease from A, under the influence of A's representations that he is the owner, which representations are untrue, is not estopped from defeating A's action for rent[40] by showing that he is not the owner. "The distinction," says Huston, J., ' is between a case where a lessor was in possession and a lessee obtained possession under him, and a case where the person in possession did not obtain it from him who, under some false pretence, obtained the position of a lessor   In the first case the lessee cannot object to the title of him who put him into possession , in the latter, he will be admitted to prove

v *Ormsby Coal Co* 129 Pa 592, 18 Atl 538

[37]*Thompson* v *Graham*, 9 Phila 53
[38]*Galloway* v *Ogle*, 2 Binn 468, *Russell* v *Titus*, 3 Grant Cas 295, *Eister* v *Paul*, 54 Pa 196, *Prutz-man* v *Ferree*, 10 Watts, 143, *Wilson* v *Hubbell*, 1 Pennyp 413; *Wolf* v *Goddard*, 9 Watts, 544

[39]*Kline* v *Johnston*, 24 Pa 72, *Thompson* v *Graham*, 9 Phila 53, *Prutzman* v *Ferree*, 10 Watts, 143

[40]*Gleim* v *Rise*, 6 Watts, 44   On a lease by A after he has assigned the land for the benefit of creditors and the assignees have sold the land to X, the lessee will not be liable on showing that A asserted that he was the owner and had a right to make the lease   So if the lessor exhibits to X a forged conveyance to him as proof of his title, X, who already in possession accepts the lease, will not be estopped   *Miller* v. *M'Brier*, 14 Serg & R 382

the imposition; if he does prove it, he is not bound to give up possession nor is he liable for use and occupation " If, after A has sold the land to X, he induces B, who has been his tenant, to attorn to C, he commits fraud which will authorize B to deny C's right to recover the possession from him.[41] A, having no good title, induces B, who is in possession, to accept a lease, by representing that he has a good title and will make a lease on favorable terms, but that if B will not accept he will turn B off by process of law. B is not estopped from showing, in A's ejectment, that A's title is bad, whether A knew that his representations were untrue or not.[42]

764. Violence.—The tenant or one claiming under him may show in Y's ejectment that the tenant was in possession under a lease from X, when Y, with two companions armed with guns, visited him and threatened to turn him off unless he took a lease from Y, and that he thereupon did so The tenant or his successor in the possession would not be estopped from denying Y's title [43]

765 Fraud on the commonwealth.— It is said that the lessee can escape the estoppel of the lease by showing that it was made in fraud of the commonwealth.[44] If B, already in possession, is induced to accept a lease from A, by A's exhibiting to him a patent to himself from the state which recites a conveyance from the warrantee to him, and this conveyance is a forgery, B can defend the ejectment of A by showing this fact.[45]

766. Lessee already owner when he accepts lease — If the lessee has not been in possession of the premises, but obtains possession from the lessor, and in consequence of the lease, the mere fact that the lessee already owned the land, and that the lessor

[41]*Goldsmith* v *Smith*, 3 Phila 360
[42]*Baskin* v *Seechrist*, 6 Pa 154 A claimed by a sheriff's sale but it did not appear that a deed had ever been made to him.

[43]*Hamilton* v *Marsden*, 6 Binn 45; *Rankin* v *Tenbrook*, 5 Watts, 386
[44]*Boyer* v *Smith*, 5 Watts, 55
[45]*Miller* v. *M'Brier*, 14 Serg & R. 382.

did not own it, will not authorize the lessee to refuse to surrender possession. He cannot defeat the lessor's ejectment by
showing his own superior title [46]   "Justice," says Black, Ch J.,
"requires that the parties should assume their original position
before any dispute about the title can be tolerated," and the
tenant, if sued for the rent, cannot defend by showing that he
was already the owner of the land when the lease was made.[47]
If the tenant was induced by the lessor to accept the lease by
fraud or misrepresentation, he would probably escape the estoppel ordinarily arising from the acceptance of a lease.[48]   But
the fraud that will effect this result is a fraud on the lessee him
self, or on the commonwealth, not a fraud on another.   The
tenant, *e g ,* is not permitted to show that on the death of X, an
owner of land, two brothers of X took out letters of administration on his estate, and combined with their father fraudulently
to dispossess the widow and children, and, in pursuance of this
scheme, got the father to make the lease.   The father, as lessor,
can recover from the tenant, despite his want of title.[49]   If B,
having a lien on A's land, takes a lease of it, he cannot during
the term cause a sheriff's sale of it and become the purchaser,
except subject to the right of A to compel a reconveyance on a
tender of the purchase money.[50]

767 Lessee owner and already in possession.—One already the
owner by a legal or an equitable title, and already in possession,
may nevertheless accept a lease of the premises from another.

[46]*Thayer* v *Society of United
Brethren,* 20 Pa 60, *Kennedy* v
Whalen, 5 Kulp, 35; *Gleim* v *Rise,*
6 Watts, 44   A parol vendee of land
lost the right of setting up his title
by subsequently accepting a lease
from the vendor.   *Turner* v. *Reynolds,* 23 Pa 199

[47]*Wagle* v *Bartley* (Pa) 9 Cent
Rep 551, 11 Atl 223, *Ward* v *Phila-
delphia* (Pa) 4 Cent Rep 662, **6**
Atl 263.

[48]*Boyer* v *Smith,* 5 Watts, 55,
Rankin v *Tenbrook,* 5 Watts, 386,
Cramer v *Carlisle Bank,* 2 Grant
Cas 267, *Koontz* v *Hammond,* 62
Pa 177, *Wagle* v *Bartley* (Pa) 9
Cent Rep 551, 11 Atl 223, *Ward* v
Philadelphia (Pa) 4 Cent Rep 662,
6 Atl 263

[49]*Boyer* v *Smith,* 5 Watts, 55
[50]*Matthews's Appeal,* 104 Pa 444

If he does so, he cannot refuse to surrender possession to the lessor, unless he was induced to accept the lease through fraud, misrepresentation,[51] or force[52] It is said, also, that accepting the lease in mistake will prevent the estoppel, but that the mere fact that the tenant has a better title than his landlord does not of itself raise the presumption that the lease was a fraud or was accepted by mistake.[53] But if a person in possession and having a good title accepts a lease in consequence of fraud or misrepresentation of the lessor,[54] or on account of a mutual mistake of the facts by both parties, he is not estopped from alleging his title as a defense against the lessor's action to recover possession[55] If A is in possession of land so long as to have made a title by limitation, there is a probability, if he accepts from X, who has no title, not even that against which the adverse possession has prevailed, a lease of the land, there was some misrepresentation of fact or law, or both, and it will require little

[51]*School District* v *Long* (Pa) 9 Cent Rep 350, 10 Atl 789, *Thayer* v *Society of United Brethren*, 20 Pa 60, *Lebanon School Dist* v *Lebanon Female Seminary*, 22 W N C 65, *Kennedy* v *Whalen*, 5 Kulp, 35 If A accepts a lease of land from B, he cannot refuse to pay the rent under it, although he already had a lease for the same land from X, and X was the owner and B not *Hamilton* v *Pittock*, 158 Pa 457, 27 Atl 1079

[52]*Hamilton* v *Varsden*, 6 Binn 45, *Rankin* v *Tenbrook*, 5 Watts, 386

[53]*Thayer* v *Society of United Brethren*, 20 Pa 60, *School District* v *Long* (Pa) 9 Cent Rep 350, 10 Atl 769, *Lebanon School Dist* v *Lebanon Female Seminary*, 22 W N C 65, *Hamilton* v *Pittock*, 158 Pa 457, 27 Atl 1079

[54]*Berridge* v *Glassey*, 20 W N C 50, *Brown* v *Dysinger*, 1 Rawle 408

[55]*Berridge* v *Glassey*, 20 W N C 50 A and B owned adjoining lands The result of a survey showed that B's buildings encroached some inches on A's land, and B not wishing to tear down the buildings agreed in writing to pay A a yearly rental of $2 A new survey showed that B's buildings did not encroach on A's land, but were wholly within B's boundaries When sued by A in ejectment, B could defend by showing this fact In *Brown* v *Dysinger*, 1 Rawle, 408, at a sheriff's sale A bought land under an agreement with B to buy it for him, which made A a trustee for B, who was poor and ill of consumption Instead of recognizing his trusteeship A threatened to put B off of the premises (he had been on before the sale) unless B accepted a lease from him. B accepted the lease. This, it was held, did not constitute an abandonment of his equity But B had given up the possession and his heir was endeavoring by ejectment to recover it.

proof of fraud or threats or undue influence or of A's imbecility to exonerate him from the effect of accepting a lease; indeed, Huston, J , remarks if one whose right to land had become perfect under the statute of limitations "was induced to take a lease from, and become a tenant to, those who had no title [they had never had a good title] this must have occurred from misrepresentation. fraud, or mistake, and slight evidence of imbecility, or weakness, or of poverty, worked on by threats, would be sufficient to avoid it."[56]   After B had been in possession for fourteen years claiming adversely to everybody, A, asserting that he was owner, induced B to accept a lease for the land   B continued in possession for thirty years longer, paying no rent   This lease did not preclude B, when sued in ejectment at the end of the forty-four years' possession, from showing that A had in fact no title, and that A had induced him by trick or artifice, by fraud practised on him under the garb of friendship, to accept the lease [57]

768 Who may avail himself of the estoppel — The lessor himself may insist on the estoppel arising from the acceptance of a lease from him   So may his executor, when, the land being devised to him, he sues for the rent, or to recover the possession,[58]

---

[56]*Hockenbury* v *Snyder,* 2 Watts & S 240   In *Reith* v *Reith,* 13 W N C 435, the tenant asserted that the landlord had a life estate, and was to devise the land to him, and that having made a devise she the lessor, had subsequently destroyed the will This was no defense to the lessor's recovery of possession under the landlord and tenant acts

[57]*Evans* v *Bidwell,* 76 Pa 497 B's land was sold to A by the sheriff on a levari facias sur mortgage   Four months before the deed was delivered A induced B to accept a lease, which covered not only the land sold, but an additional piece, to which A had no right at all   B was not es-topped from setting up his title in A's ejectment, because the lease was obtained unfairly   A had stated falsely that he had a right to possession, when he would not have it until he obtained the sheriff's deed   Even had he received the deed, he could not remove B in less than three months after receiving it When B proposed to consult his counsel, before accepting the lease, A refused him time   B was artfully inveigled and hurried into the acceptance of the lease   *Hall* v *Benner,* 1 Penr & W 402, 21 Am Dec 394

[58]*Boyer* v *Smith,* 3 Watts, 449, 5 Watts, 55.

or the heir,[59] or his grantee;[60] or the sheriff's vendee of his re
version.[61]   It has been said that the lessee from the agent of X
is estopped from denying X's title when X brings an ejectment
to recover the possession;[62] but it has been held that the lessee
can successfully resist a distress for rent, authorized by the principal of the lessor, who, though calling himself "agent" in the
lease, has not therein named any principal, and for injury
caused by such distress may recover damages [63] The agent of the
owner of land having made the lease in his own name, mention-
ing no principal, the tenant cannot deny his title to the land or
his right to recover the possession [64]   A mere intruder on X's
land may make a lease and deliver possession to the lessee.   The
latter cannot by voluntarily attorning to X deprive the lessor
of the right to claim the tenant's possession as his own, and to
maintain that it is as adverse as his own would have been [65]
But if an intruder does not make a lease to X, but a contract to
sell the land to him, and X, as vendee, enters and makes improvements, X cannot effectively orally surrender the contract
so as to become a lessee.   Hence if, after such abortive oral surrender, X continues in possession and admits the owner, the
owner's entry upon the land will prevent the completion of the
intruder's title under the statute of limitations, by the possession
of the owner.[66]   A, who with a view to its pre-emption puts X
in possession in order to begin and continue the settlement, has
a right to consider Y, to whom X delivers the possession and who
continues it, in possession under himself, A, and A can claim
the title as made by the settlement, as against Y [67]

   769. To what the estoppel does not relate.— The estoppel is a

[59]*Cooper* v *Smith*, 8 Watts, 536.
[60]*Weaver* v. *Craighead*, 104 Pa. 386,
288
[61]*Wilson* v *Hubbell*, 1 Pennyp 413
[62]*Thompson* v *Graham*, 9 Phila 53
[63]*Seyfert* v *Bean*, 83 Pa 450.
[64]*Holt* v *Martin*, 51 Pa 499.

[65]*Rankin* v *Tenbrook*, 5 Watts,
Cravener v *Bouser*, 4 Pa 259,
56 Pa 132
[66]*Cravener* v *Bowser*, 4 Pa. 259, 56
Pa 132
[67]*Cooper* v *Smith*, 8 Watts, 536.

prohibition against denying that the landlord had a title at the time of making the lease. This title may have since passed from him, and with it the rights of a landlord. The tenant may accordingly show, when sued by the lessor for the possession or for the rent, that before the action was brought in the former case, or before the rent accrued in the latter, the reversion had, since the making of the lease, passed from the plaintiff. He may show, *e. g*, that it has passed to himself, by a contract of sale[68] or by a parol sale, if the facts exist which, under the statute of frauds, make such a sale valid,[69] or by an estoppel. He may show that his lessor claimed through her husband, that the latter, becoming insolvent, made an assignment for the benefit of creditors; that his assignees undertook to sell the premises in the lessee's possession; that the widow advised him to buy them and agreed to the sale, and that he bought them. This would terminate the lessor's rights.[70] The lessee may set up in the lessor's action, a sheriff's sale during the term of the title of the latter, and its purchase by himself.[71] The tenant of a devisee may purchase at a sheriff's sale on a judgment against the devisor, and thus defeat the lessor's recovery.[72] The tenant of two cotenants (who is daughter of one of them, B), the land occupied by whom has, by partition, been allotted to one of them, A, may, on A's attempt to recover possession in ejectment, defeat his recovery as to one undivided half by showing that the partition has become void, and her title as heir of B has revested.[73]

770. **Tenant may show transfer of lessor's title.**—The tenant may defeat a recovery of the possession by the lessor by proving that he has, by a legal or an equitable transfer,[74] conveyed the

[68]*Mohan* v *Butler,* 112 Pa 590, 4 Atl 47.

[69]*Aurand* v *Wilt,* 9 Pa 54. The lessee may show that since the lease was made he has bought the land at a sale under a lien that preceded the lease. *Kennedy* v. *Whalen,* 5 Kulp, 35.

[70]*Hill* v *Miller,* 5 Serg & R 355

[71]*Elliott* v *Smith,* 23 Pa 131

[72]*Elliott* v *Ackla,* 9 Pa 42

[73]*Feather* v *Strohoecker,* 3 Penr & W 505, 24 Am Dec 342

[74]*Sparks* v *Walton,* 4 Phila 72.

reversion to another since making the lease,[75] or that a sheriff's sale of the reversion has occurred,[76] and it is immaterial that the lien on which the sheriff's sale took place existed prior to the acquisition by the lessor of the title[77]   After the lessor has conveyed the reversion to X, the tenant may attorn to X   If the lessor in fraud of X induces the tenant to attorn to Y, the tenant may, nevertheless, deny Y's title, in a proceeding by Y to eject him.[78]   If A, who is cotenant with six others, makes a lease in his own name styling himself as "agent," A's proceeding to recover possession of the whole premises cannot be defeated by the lessee, by showing that A had conveyed his own interest in the land, and that the other cotenants had revoked his agency and notified the tenant that they desired him to continue in possession.   With respect to A's conveyance of his seventh, the court remarks that no attornment or acceptance of a new lease by the tenant to or from A's grantee had been shown, nor that the tenant was defending the possession for the grantee A's "very purpose," says Agnew, J., "in proceeding upon the covenant [to surrender possession] in the lease may have been to comply with his sale to Harper, and invest him with the possession by determining the lease"   As respects the supersedure of A's authority as agent, the court notes that the relation of landlord and tenant was between A and the tenant, and not between A's principals and the tenant, and a supersedure of authority as agent would not affect the relation, and that the covenant in the lease to surrender possession was indivisible. The conclusion is that to allow the defense would be to allow a denial of the lessor's title at the time of the creation of the lease.[79]

771. Extinction of lessor's interest.— The   lessor's   interest

[75]*Koontz* v *Hammond*, 62 Pa 177
[76]*Smith* v *Crosland*, 106 Pa 413, *Heritage* v *Wilfong*, 58 Pa 137
[77]*Smith* v *Crosland*, 106 Pa 413.

[78]*Goldsmith* v *Smith*, 3 Phila 300
[79]*Holt* v *Martin*, 51 Pa 499   Cf *Bedford* v *Kelly*, 61 Pa 491.

may expire rather than be transferred, and the tenant may resist a recovery of rent accruing subsequently, or of the possession, by showing this expiration.[80] The tenant, e g, may prove that the lessor claimed under a life tenant, and that the life tenant having died prior to the bringing of the ejectment, the reversioner has the right to the possession [81] The lessor being tenant *pur autre vie*, the tenant may resist his ejectment by showing the death of the *cestui que vie*.[82] If a lessee sublets and the lease expires, the sublessee is under no duty to surrender the possession to the lessee A leases to B, e. g , and B sublets to C. A sheriff's sale of A's interest is made Prior to this sale, the term having ended, A gave notice to B to quit and the sheriff's vendee repeated the notice. As B's estate was thus at an end, he could not recover possession from C. A devise of a mill being made to trustees in order that they may let the premises until the rents shall have yielded $2,000, and thereafter to X, the lessee of the trustees may probably show, when sued for the rent, that the $2,000 have been obtained since the making of the lease and that X therefore has become entitled to the rent, provided that he has been required to attorn and has attorned to X, or has accepted a lease from X. Unless he proves such attornment or acceptance of a lease, he cannot defeat the recovery of the rent by the trustees, simply by producing receipts for rent purporting to be X's. Such receipts might have been antedated, and not actually made until after the commencement of the action. They ought to be proved, since they are used to affect another than X.[83] If an estate is given to a trustee for the sole and separate use of a married woman for life, and if she survives her husband in trust to convey to her and her heirs,

[80]*Thompson* v *Clark*, 7 Pa 62
[81]*Heckart* v *M'Kee*, 5 Watts, 385
[82]*Newell* v *Gibbs*, 1 Watts & S 496, *Young* v *Algeo*, 3 Watts, 223 [Citing *England ex dem Syburn* v. *Slade*, 4 T R 682]
[83]*Newlin* v *Palmer*, 11 Serg & R 98 On a retrial the actual payment of the money would be better evidence than the receipts.

and during her life she and her husband convey the premises, and she survives her husband, her grantee gets a fee.[84]   Hence a lease being made by him, he continues the owner, notwithstanding the married woman's death   He may therefore recover the possession at the end of his lease.[85]   If A, recovering judgment in ejectment against B, issues a *habere facias possessionem*, under the pressure of which C, a tenant of B, accepts a lease from A, the subsequent setting aside of the *habere facias* dissolves the relation of landlord and tenant between A and C, by destroying A's right of possession, and restores the former relation between B and C or, at least, makes it impossible for C to accept a new lease from B, so that his possession shall be B's and not A's.[86]

772. Loss of agency.— Despite the authority of *Holt* v. *Martin,* 51 Pa. 499, if a lease is made by A, styling himself as "agent" but not naming his principal, the lessee may show who the principal was, that he has died, devising the land to X; and that he has paid the rent to X; and thus justify a replevin of the goods seized in distress by A.[87]   Six cotenants of land authorized A, one of their number, as agent to make leases and collect the rents.   A made a lease, calling himself agent but not naming the principals.   Subsequently B, one of the principals, notified the tenant to pay one sixth of the rent to him, and also notified A that his agency for B was revoked.   Notwithstanding this the tenant continued to pay all the rent to A   The tenant could be compelled to pay one sixth of it again to B.[88] The following propositions were affirmed by Williams, J.: "(1) Mrs. Bennett had a right to revoke the agency of Barrett

---

[84] Why a conveyance by a married woman, whose estate was clogged with a sole and separate use was valid, does not appear.

[85] *Thompson* v *Graham,* 9 Phila 53

[86] *Coughanour* v *Bloodgood,* 27 Pa 285. This effect is wrought without

the award of a writ of restitution

[87] *Bandel* v *Erickson,* 3 Pa Super. Ct 389.

[88] *Barrett* v *Bemelmans,* 163 Pa. 122, 29 Atl 756, 155 Pa. 204, 26 Atl. 307.

whenever she pleased; (2) Barrett acquired, under the terms of his agency, no interest in the rent due to his principals other than that necessarily acquired by one authorized to collect money for another, and he had no right to object to the revocation of his authority at the will of his principals, (3) when this revocation was duly made and notice thereof given to the tenant, the tenant was bound to take notice of the fact. No equitable or other right existed in the tenant to object to the revocation except as to acts done or rent paid before the notice was received."

773. Denial that claimant is transferee of lessor.—The tenant is not estopped from denying that the claimant of rent or of the possession is the heir, devisee, or alienee of the lessor. He may show that another is transferee from the lessor, and justify his refusal to pay rent or to give up the possession to the claimant;[89] or that another is an earlier grantee and hence clothed with a better right.[90] He may show that a partition under which the claimant claims to own the premises in severalty was void, so that no title to an undivided half, additional to that which the claimant already had, passed to him.[91]

774. Declarations of tenant.—As a tenant cannot while in possession effectively deny the landlord's title, he cannot by declarations while in possession give to another the means of denying that title. His assertions which are restrictive of the area of the land of which he is in possession as tenant cannot be taken advantage of by one who adversely claims a portion of the land which, according to the landlord's contention, had been embraced within that which he demised to the tenant. "No landlord would be safe," says Thompson, J., "if his tenant might affect his title by declarations about his boundaries."[92] "It

[89]*Newman* v *Rutter*, 8 Watts, 51.   [92]*Oakman* v *Sheaffer*, 48 Pa 176,
[90]Cf *Goldsmith* v *Smith*, 3 Phila. *Sheaffer* v *Oakman*, 56 Pa 144
360
[91]*Feather* v *Strohoecker*, 3 Penr. &
W 505, 24 Am Dec 342

would certainly be very extraordinary," remarks Strong, J., "if a tenant put into possession of land and owing fealty to his landlord, bound to protect his landlord's possession, could be allowed to confess away that landlord's title. Had he [the tenant] surrendered the possession to Shaffer [the adverse claimant of a portion of the demised premises] Shaffer could have gained nothing by it How then can he profit by such a declaration, which is much less than a surrender ?"[93]

775. **Who are estopped.**— Besides the tenant, any who acquire the possession from him are estopped from asserting a title superior to the lessor's as a ground for refusing to give up the possession, or to be responsible for rent, for use and occupation, or for profits. Thus if the tenant dying, his heir,[94] his widow,[95] his devisee, continues in possession, his successor is estopped precisely as he was If the tenant is induced to accept a later lease from a hostile claimant, in an ejectment against the tenant by the original landlord, the second lessor, defending the action, has no better position than the tenant himself [96] Though the adverse claimant brings ejectment against the tenant and induces him to confess judgment, to be put off by a *habere facias possessionem,* and then to accept a lease, the lessee does not escape the estoppel, nor the adverse claimant. The lessee should call on his landlord to defend him. If, thus called on, the landlord refuses to make him safe by defending the action, he may probably make terms with the adversary.[97] The lessee's assignee of the leasehold is under the assignor's disability[98] whether the assignment is voluntary or effected by a judicial sale.[99] If the

[93]*Sheaffer* v *Eakman,* 56 Pa 144 *Galloway* v *Ogle,* 2 Binn 468 [95]*Bannon* v *Brandon,* 34 Pa 263, 75 Am Dec 655, 38 Pa 63, *Diefenderfer* v *Caffrey* (Pa) 9 Atl 182 [96]*Jones* v *Tatham,* 20 Pa 398, *Wolf* v *Goddard,* 9 Watts, 544, *Dikeman* v *Parrish,* 6 Pa 210, 47 Am Dec 455

[97]*Stewart* v *Roderick,* 4 Watts & S. 188, 39 Am Dec 71 Cf *Dikeman* v. *Parrish,* 6 Pa 210, 47 Am Dec 455; *Sheaffer* v *Eakman,* 56 Pa 144 [98]*Hamilton* v *Pittock,* 158 Pa 457, 27 Atl 1079, *Thompson* v. *Graham,* 9 Phila 53 [99] Cf *Kennedy* v *Whalen,* 5 Kulp, 35

tenant, obtaining an adverse title during the term, conveys it to X and puts X in possession, X must surrender the possession before taking advantage of his title,[100] but if X simply abortively bargains with the tenant for the tenant's adverse title, never in fact acquiring it, X, who subsequently and without collusion with the tenant, obtains the possession, may defend it by means of any title superior to the lessor's.[101] If A, intending to claim land by settlement, puts X in possession in order to maintain the settlement, and Y, intending to deny A's right and make a settlement for himself, bribes X to give to him the possession, Y is precluded, as X would be, from denying the incipient possessory right of A and from denying that his own possession inures to the benefit of A.[102] All persons, who, however numerous, succeed to the possession by derivation from the tenant, are affected by his incapacity to challenge the lessor's title.[103] If the tenant dies, leaving his widow on the premises, and she remarries and the second husband comes to reside on the premises, his possession is not to be deemed adverse so as, under the statute of limitations, to destroy the lessor's title, until he disowns privity between himself and the lessor by some unequivocal act [104] If after A contracts to sell land to B, B leases it to C, and if subsequently, the contract not being fulfilled, A resumes his former right, in an ejectment by A against C the latter is probably precluded from proving a defect in A's title [105] A municipal corporation, e g , a school district, is affected, like any other tenant, by the estoppel.[106]

776. Others affected by estoppel.—If, after A has made a lease

[100]*Prutzman* v *Ferree*, 10 Watts, 143 , *Thompson* v *Clark*, 7 Pa 62.

[101]*Prutzman* v. *Ferree*, 10 Watts, 143

[102]*Cooper* v *Smith*, 8 Watts, 536

[103]*Thompson* v *Clark*, 7 Pa. 62, *Dikeman* v. *Parrish*, 6 Pa. 210, 47 Am. Dec. 455.

[104]*Brandon* v. *Bannon*, 38 Pa 63.

[105]*Galloway* v. *Ogle*, 2 Binn 468, Tilghman, Ch J , refrains from a decision, Yeates, J., thinks the tenant estopped

[106]*Lebanon School Dist* v *Lebanon Female Seminary*, 22 W N C 65, *School District* v *Long* (Pa) 9 Cent. Rep 350, 10 Atl 769.

to B of a certain tract, B assigns the lease to C, but subsequently surrenders the lease to A, who has no notice of the assignment and has never given possession to B, and B accepts a new
lease for the same tract except 5 acres, and as agent of C, his assignee of the first lease, B enters on the land outside of the 5
acres (A supposing, however, that he was entering as lessee under
the second lease) C is estopped, by taking possession through
B, from denying A's right to make the second lease, under
which A delivered the possession to B, the agent of C, and from
asserting, therefore, that the first lease was still operative, although C had no notice of the surrender of the first lease, and on
entering into possession by B, his agent, supposed that he was
entering into possession as assignee of the first lease, not in pursuance of the second lease.[107] A contracts to sell land to B, but
remains in possession as B's tenant at a monthly rental which
was to be credited on the purchase money. A, while in possession, conveys the land to C. B's right to recover in ejectment
against A does not depend on B's having tendered the purchase
money to A, for to allow A to retain possession and allege the
nonpayment of the money, would be to allow him to question
his lessor's title　C's being affected with the same incapacity
would depend on his having had knowledge of the prior sale and
lease [108]

777. When successor to tenant not estopped —If　the　tenant
acquires a title hostile to that of his landlord, and while in possession conveys the land to one who has no knowledge of the
mode in which the tenant's possession began, the grantee will be
justified in presuming that that possession began in virtue of the

---

[107]*Carnegie Natural Gas Co* v
Philadelphia Co 158 Pa 317, 27 Atl
951　An injunction at C's instance
to restrain operations on the 5 acres,
by a lessee of that part, under a lease
made subsequently to the surrender
of the lease to B, was denied. In

asking it C was denying the right of
the landlord, A, to make the second
lease under which he had in fact,
though not knowingly, taken possession of the rest of the tract
[108]*Weaver* v *Craighead,* 104 Pa.
288.

title which the tenant now has, and he will not be affected by the tenant's estoppel   He may defend the possession, when sued by the lessor, by setting up the hostile title.[109]   A demised land to B in 1822.   C obtained the possession from B.   There had been a tax sale of the land in 1816, the title under which was conveyed to C in 1819.   C conveyed the land, as owner, in 1841 to D.   In an ejectment by A's alienee, against the alienee of D, the defendant could set up not only the tax sale, but if that was void, any title superior to A's, if D purchased from C without any knowledge or means of acquiring knowledge of the tenancy [of B], and for a valuable consideration.[110]   The tenant dying leaving his widow on the premises, she may defend against the lessor by showing that she had taken possession under a lease to herself from another owner, and that she had uninterruptedly continued in possession under the lease, and had neither by paying rent nor otherwise recognized the lease made to her husband.[111]   Though A and his son are in possession of B's land and after A's death the son continues in possession, declarations of A that he is in possession as tenant of B will not estop the son from denying that his father or himself was tenant of B, from claiming upon his naked possession, and denying the title of B.[112]

778. When there is no estoppel — If the plaintiff in ejectment does not repose solely on the fact that the defendant is his tenant, but also exhibits his title, the defendant may deny both the tenancy and also the goodness of the title, and the court must allow him to support his denial by appropriate evidence[113]   But after the evidence is before the jury, the court may and should tell them that if they find that the tenancy exists, they need not

[109]*Thompson* v *Clark*, 7 Pa 62,   [111]*Diefenderfer* v *Caffrey* (Pa) 9
Weaver v *Craighead*, 104 Pa 288,   Atl 182
Dikeman v *Parrish*, 6 Pa 210, 47   [112]*Emery* v *Harrison*, 13 Pa 317
Am Dec 455   [113]*Miller* v *M'Brier*, 14 Serg & R.
  [110]*Thompson* v *Clark*, 7 Pa 62   382

consider the goodness of the plaintiff's title. If at the trial of
the lessor's ejectment the parties agree that the title to the lot
shall be investigated, evidence of the tenant's superior title will
be admissible [114] A lessor who claimed under a Connecticut
title when he made the lease was denied the benefit of the principle of estoppel, and the lessee was permitted to show that he
so claimed and that a Pennsylvania title obtained by him since
making the lease was invalid.[115]

779. **When tenant renounces and afterwards resumes possession.**
—A tenant may give up the possession to the landlord and notify
him of the act, and if, after clearly sufficient time has elapsed
for the landlord to resume, he does not resume possession, the
former tenant, or an adverse claimant to whom he attorns, may
re-enter under another title or without title, and they will not be
subject to the estoppel which precludes a tenant, or one who induces him to attorn, from preventing the lessor's recovery in
ejectment except by means of proof of a good title.[116] Giving
notice to the landlord that the tenant intends to give up the possession will be useless, if it is not followed by an actual withdrawal from possession [117] The tenant's removal might precede his notice to the lessor, but the removal must be complete
and sufficiently long before the resumption of possession by the
tenant, or by a hostile claimant, to allow the lessor to regain the
possession The lease terminating on March 31, 1825, A, the
tenant, on that day moved his goods from the house, depositing
some in a near neighbor's house and some on the roadside, 4 or
5 perches from the house, and immediately in front of the
neighboring house Here they were on the morning of the next
day. In the evening of March 31 the tenant went to the lessor's,

---

[114] *Philadelphia* v *Schuylkill Bridge,*
4 Binn 283

[115] *Satterlee* v. *Matthewson,* 13 Serg
& R 133

[116] *Wolf* v *Goddard,* 9 Watts, 544,
Graham v *Moore,* 4 Serg & R 467

[117] *Graham* v *Moore,* 4 Serg & R.
467 The tenant simply moved the
fence so as to throw the house out
of the inclosure, but he continued to
dwell in the house, which was on the
demised land.

5 miles distant, and notified him that he had vacated the house. He was back to the neighborhood of the house about 8 o'clock on the morning of April 1, and remarked to X that he had no place to go to. X, who claimed adversely, immediately said that he would lease the land to him, and the goods and family of the tenant were at once carried back to the house. The court, inferring that the tenant did not expect to part with the possession, and that there had been an understanding between him and X, looking to the putting of X into possession, that there was no intention to give the lessor time, and that, in fact, sufficient time was not given to him to arrive and take possession before the tenant should reoccupy the house under X,—decided that the tenant, on a subsequent ejectment by his landlord, remained estopped from disputing the title of the latter. "It is not only evident," says Kennedy, J., "from the testimony of the defendant himself, that no reasonable time was allowed for such purpose, but that he had resolved with himself not to allow it, lest Boyer should improve it by taking the possession. In short, it is plain from his own showing, that he had determined to prevent Boyer from retaking it, by seizing it himself and withholding it from Boyer."[118]

[118]*Boyer* v *Smith*, 3 Watts, 449 Cf. *Bannon* v *Brandon*, 34 Pa. 263, 75 Am. Dec 655, 38 Pa. 63.

CHAPTER XXXVI.

LANDLORD'S AND TENANT'S LIABILITY AS TO OTHERS.

780. Sidewalks.— It is the duty of the tenant, or other persons in possession of premises facing upon the street, towards persons using the street, to keep the sidewalks in safe condition. If the cover in the sidewalk to a cellar vault falls out of repair, the tenant will be liable to a passenger for an injury arising from its nonrepair,[1] and if the cellar extends under the pavement, the excavation must be covered by planks or other material, so as to avoid the falling in of pedestrians, or of a horse and wagon, in case, from fright or other cause, the horse should run from the cartway to the sidewalk.[2] When the different rooms of a building are let to different tenants none of them have exclusive control of the hallways and of the pavement. The landlord will have general control of them, and not they, but he, will, as being in possession, be responsible for the condition of the pavement.[3] If the sidewalk is in good repair when the lessee takes possession, he only, and not the lessor, it is held, will be liable to a passer who is injured by a defect consisting of the loosening of bricks and the digging by children, which arises during his pos-

[1] *Bears* v *Ambler,* 9 Pa 193
[2] *Guier* v. *Sampson,* 27 Pa. 183.
[3] *Brown* v *Weaver,* 17 W. N. C. 230

606

session ;[4] although in *Mintzer* v. *Greenough*[5] the supreme court approved the refusal of the trial judge to say: "An owner out of possession, whose house is in the actual occupation of a tenant, is not required to keep a constant supervision of such house and of the highway in front of it, and if a defect occurs in the sidewalk during such occupation by a tenant, by reason of which a person walking on the street is injured, the landlord is not liable to the person injured, unless knowledge or notice of such defect is traced to him " In an action to recover for personal injuries sustained by a fall upon the ice on the landlord's sidewalk, he will not be heard to allege that his tenant, and not he, is liable for the condition of the sidewalk, where the evidence shows that the landlord constructed the pipe which carried the water off the pavement, and the use of the pipe by the tenant was in conformity with the defendant's intention when he leased the premises [6] So the owner of the leased premises, though not in possession, will be liable for injuries resulting from a cellar door, the hinges of which were broken off, and a board removed, and which was so unsafe as to cause a policeman to notify the tenant of it, who in turn notified the agents of the landlord and the landlord himself as to its condition.[7]

781 Area-ways.— Probably it is the duty of the tenant of property in front of which there is an area way, to put guard rails about it, or to cover it with a hurdle or other device, so as to avoid injury to foot-passengers But whether he is liable or not, the lessor will be liable if the area-way at the time of letting of the premises is without guard rail, loose slat door, hurdle,

---

[4] *Early* v *Ashworth*, 17 Phila 248
[5] 192 Pa 137, 43 Atl 465 When the house was let, there were some loose bricks in the pavement The tenant's sweeping and cleaning had enlarged the hole, which at the time of the accident to the pedestrian was 2 feet long by more than 1½ feet wide, and nearly 1 foot deep
[6] *Brown* v *White*, 202 Pa 297, 58 L R A 321, 51 Atl 962, 206 Pa 106, 55 Atl 848
[7] *Carson* v. *Mackin*, 23 Pa Super Ct. 50.

etc , and continues in the same condition when an injury occurs
to a pedestrian,[8] and though there was a strong movable cover
for the area-way which the tenant had neglected to pull over it
at night, it would still be a question for the jury whether it was
not negligence on the lessor's part not to place a permanent
guard around it. If the furnishing of a movable cover, instead
of such permanent guard, was negligence, the lessor would be
liable despite the fact that the negligence of the tenant in not
placing the cover over the area was the immediate cause of the
accident[9] The lessee's covenant to repair would not apply to
the furnishing of a guard rail, hurdle, etc., nor confine to him
the liability for injury to others[10]

782. Injury to adjacent property.— For nuisances to adjacent
property arising during the tenant's possession, he is responsible, and the nuisances may arise from the use of the premises
in a mode contemplated by the lessor. If, *e. g.,* a cess pool is so
defectively made, or is so near to the boundary line, that by its
continued use by the tenant, its contents invade the cellar of a
neighboring house, he will be liable for the nuisance. He is
bound to desist from such a use of the premises as will constitute
a nuisance.[11] A privy well is built so close to the cellar wall of
a neighbor that, when its contents reach the level of the cellar
floor, they percolate through the cellar wall into it. The tenant
would be liable for such use of it as would produce this result.[12]
But on the other hand, the landlord will be liable for a nuisance
arising during the tenancy, and by the tenant's use of the premises, "if the premises are so constructed or in such a condition
[when the lease is made] that the continuance of their use by the

[8]*Reading* v. *Reiner,* 167 Pa 41, 31 Atl 357.

[9]*Simons* v. *Thompson,* 2 W N C 209

[10]*Reading* v *Reiner,* 167 Pa 41, 31 Atl 357, *Simons* v. *Thompson,* 2 W N C 209. Cf *Eisenbrey* v *Pennsyl-*

vania Co for Insurance, 141 Pa 566, 21 Atl 635

[11]*Knauss* v *Brua,* 107 Pa 85

[12]*Fow* v *Roberts,* 108 Pa 489, *Wunder* v *McLean,* 134 Pa 334, 19 Am St Rep. 702, 19 Atl 749.

tenant must result in a nuisance to a third person, and a nuisance does so result." If, *e. g.*, a privy and sewer connection are in so defective a state when the lease is made, that the use of the former causes a nuisance to the occupant of the adjacent house, the landlord will be liable [13] If, however, the cesspool is properly built, and in good condition when the lease is made, the lessor is not liable for a leakage from it into the neighboring cellar during the term, arising from the want of repairs. The tenant would be liable [14]

783 **Length of landlord's ownership; trustee** — If A becomes owner of the premises during a term, so that he has no right to enter for the purpose of making changes, he will not be liable to third persons for injuries springing from the actual state of the premises, *e. g*, from an area-way, so long as the tenant's right interferes with his resumption of possession or control.[15] An executor who is required by the will to allow X to occupy the premises until a sale, and who has no power with respect to them except to sell them, is not responsible as a landlord for an accident occasioned by the manner in which X uses the premises, *e. g.*, by the sudden opening outwardly, upon the sidewalk, of a gate in front of the door steps, whereby a passer-by is injured [16] A trustee, having the legal title and power to manage the land, will be liable for injuries caused by it, as any other proprietor [17]

784. **Liability of landlord, continued.** — If the property is in a safe condition when the lease is made, and the tenant takes possession, the lessor is under no liability to one who is injured by the condition into which it is permitted to fall by the tenant

[13]*Knauss v Brua,* 107 Pa 85, *Fow v Roberts,* 108 Pa 489 Cf *Palmore v Morris,* 182 Pa 82 61 Am St Rep 693, 37 Atl 995
[14]*Wunder v McLean,* 134 Pa 334, 19 Am St Rep 702, 19 Atl 749
[1]*Broun v Weaver,* 17 W N C 230   Cf *Palmore v Morris,* 182 Pa 82, 61 Am St Rep 693, 37 Atl 995
[16]*Eisenbrey v Pennsylvania Co for Insurance,* 141 Pa 566, 21 Atl 635.
[17]*Mintzer v Greenough,* 192 Pa 137, 43 Atl 465.

A wharf having, when leased, a cap-log or other appliance to prevent horses and carts from falling into the dock, if, owing to the removing or covering up of this log while the tenant is in possession, a horse slips over into the river, the landlord is not liable. If the lessee sublets while the wharf is in proper condition, he will not be liable for an accident arising from the removal or covering up of the cap-log during the sublessee's occupancy[18] A hole 6 feet deep being dug 58 feet from the steps at the rear of the dwelling by the lessor, at the request of the lessee, he is not liable to the parent of a child less than three years old, who, while visiting the lessee, falls into the hole, which has been uncovered for a month, and drowns[19] But if the lessor allows the wall of a privy which is on an alley to which the occupants of the houses on both sides of the alley and others have proper access in order to reach a factory, to become dangerous before making the lease, and during the term it falls into the alley injuring a son of the tenant of one of the other houses while walking there at the time, he will be liable.[20]

785. Liability of lessee to third persons — A paper ware-house which, prior to the lease, had been used as such for twenty years, collapsed during the term, and a laborer in the tenant's employ was killed The lessee would not be answerable in the absence of any reason on his part to suspect the soundness of the building, and of any proof of overloading[21] Where a third party is injured, the action is to be brought against the one committing the tort, and the fact that there was an agreement to indemnify is immaterial So, where an employee was injured on a date prior to that of the execution of a lease by his employer, the

[18]*Toivt* v *Philadelphia,* 173 Pa 314, 33 Atl 1034

[19]*Moore* v *Logan Iron & Steel Co* (Pa) 4 Cent Rep 505, 7 Atl 198 The hole was known to all the tenant's family and to the person having charge of the child, and the lot was inclosed by a fence.

[20]*Schilling* v *Abernethy,* 112 Pa 437, 56 Am Rep 320, 3 Atl 792

[21]*McKenna* v *Martin & Wm H Nixon Paper Co* 176 Pa 306, 35 Atl 131

employer is liable, though it had been agreed that the lease should be effective as of a date prior to the accident.[22] If the public have access to an alley, whether for business, curiosity, or pleasure, and the presence of children may be readily anticipated as probable, a tenant of property will be liable for injury to young children by the fall upon them of a heavy platform fastened at its under edge by hinges to the wall of a building along the alley, and which being slightly tilted against the wall is not held fast to it by any other force than its own weight.[23] So the lessee is liable to the occupant of a floor below by water escaping from a spigot, which he had failed to turn off, or which one, using it by his permission, had failed to close [24]

786. Lessor's liability to third persons for condition of premises.— Although the lessor does not generally tacitly covenant that the premises are tenantable and fit for the uses to which with his knowledge, the tenant is going to apply them, nevertheless, the owner who superintends the erection of the building, deciding on the plan, selecting the materials, but who causes it to be built loosely, carelessly, unskilfully, and negligently, and with insufficient and improper materials, and lets it to a tenant who has indicated the uses to which it is to be put, will be liable to a person who, being on the building as a workman, is injured by its collapse,[25] or to the owner of goods which are also injured by the same cause.[26] A built on his ground a building, expecting the collector of the port of Philadelphia to take a lease of

[22]*Wieder* v. *Bethlehem Steel Co* 205 Pa. 186, 54 Atl 778

[23]*Hydraulic Works Co* v *Orr*, 83 Pa 332 Cf *Schilling* v *Abernethy*, 112 Pa 437, 56 Am Rep 320, 3 Atl 792, which approves, and *Gramlich* v *Wurst*, 86 Pa 74, 27 Am Rep 684, *Gillespie* v *McGowan*, 100 Pa. 144, 45 Am. Rep 365; *Rodgers* v *Lees*, 140 Pa 475 12 L R A 216, 23 Am St. Rep 250, 21 Atl. 399;

Feehan v *Dobson*, 10 Pa Super Ct 6.

[24]*Killion* v *Power*, 51 Pa 429, 91 Am Dec 127

[25]*Godley* v *Hagerty*, 20 Pa 387, 59 Am Dec 731 The action was trespass on the case Cf *Curtin* v *Somerset*, 140 Pa 70, 12 L R A 322, 23 Am St Rep 220, 21 Atl 244

[26]*Carson* v *Godley*, 26 Pa 111, 67 Am Dec 404.

it as a public storehouse, and attempting to construct it so as to meet the requirements of such a storehouse. Not being an architect or builder, he nevertheless superintended the construction of the building, formed the plans, and gave the directions. After it was finished, the expected lease was made to the collector. A laborer employed in the building was injured by its collapse under the weight of the articles stored in it. The fall of the building being due to its having been built of insufficient material, and in a careless and unskilful manner, the owner was liable to the laborer, because he knew that the building would be used for heavy storage and he took no stipulations against such use. It would follow that if the injury had been to the tenant himself, or to his property, the lessor would be liable to him. A lessor, in the absence of a covenant to repair, is not responsible to his tenant or to a lodger with his tenant, for the falling down of the ceiling of a room and the infliction of personal injuries thereby,[27] nor for the breaking through of a well floor[28] The front steps extending before the doors of two contiguous houses, occupied respectively by A and B, tenants of X, their common owner, X is not liable to A for injuries from falling on that portion of the steps in front of B's house, when leaving it at the close of a visit, A knowing of the condition of the steps before using them[29]

[27]*Tennery* v. *Drinkhouse*, 2 W N C 210

[28]*Lutz* v. *Haley*, 10 Montg Co L Rep 18. There was contributory negligence in using the floor after knowledge of its dangerous state

[29]*Sheridan* v *Krupp*, 141 Pa. 564, 21 Atl 670.

CHAPTER XXXVII.

MINES AND MINERAL LEASES.

787. Mines and minerals.—By the term "mine" is generally meant a worked vein, or a tunnel made for the purpose of secur ing underlying minerals.[1]

The term "mineral" embraces everything not of the mere sur face, which is used for agricultural purposes, the granite of

[1] *Westmoreland Coal Co's Appeal,* 85 Pa 344

the mountain, as well as metallic ores and fossils, are comprehended within it [2] It includes not only metallic substances, but coal,[3] soapstone,[4] clay,[5] salt,[6] limestone,[7] sand,[8] and oil and gas [9] Leases for the production of oil and gas will be considered separately.

788. Options to lease.— Where an option to lease has been given, in case certain things are done, but the lease has never been asked for or accepted, though the conditions entitling the grantee to it have been complied with, no liability thereunder attaches. So, where the agreement provided that, upon the completion by the defendant of a certain railroad within a certain time, the plaintiff would lease to the defendant certain iron ore interests at certain royalties, a mere option was given, and no rent could be claimed under it, the defendant not having mined any ore, or called for or accepted a lease, although the railroad was completed within the time fixed [10]

789. Contracts to lease.— Where the lessee receives in settlement of disputes a new lease, which he agrees to accept and operate, provided the lessor secures possession of the land, upon tender thereafter to him he becomes liable for a failure to take the lease if the tender be made in a reasonable time But where it is offered after the lapse of a reasonable period (in this case four years), during which time the property has deteriorated, he is not liable for his refusal to accept.[11] Though it is a general rule of law that, in all contracts where the time within which an act is to be performed is not named in the contract, the time does not begin to run until the party for whose benefit

[2]*Griffin* v *Fellows,* 81* Pa. 114, 124

[3]*Caldwell* v *Fulton,* 31 Pa 475, 72 Am Dec 760

[4]*Verdolite Co* v *Richards,* 7 Northampton Co Rep 113

[5]*Sheets* v *Allen,* 89 Pa 47

[6]*Kerr* v *Peterson,* 41 Pa 357.

[7]*Clement* v *Youngman,* 40 Pa 341

[8]*Com* v *Hipple,* 7 Pa Dist R 399

[9]*Gill* v *Weston,* 110 Pa 312, 1 Atl 921

[10]*Proctor* v *Benson,* 149 Pa 254, 24 Atl 279

[11]*Kille* v *Reading Iron Works,* 141 Pa 440, 21 Atl 666.

the contract is to be performed has notified the other to perform it within a fixed time, yet, where the tender of performance by one party is necessary to fix the liability, and no time is fixed by the contract, the tender must be made within a reasonable time.[12] So, a lessor who has contracted to lease, but fails to comply with his agreement after work has been done by the lessee is liable in damages to the value of the work done[13] Where a bill is filed to compel the specific performance of a contract to lease the defendant will not, in aid thereof, be restrained from boring, where the right is not clear, and it does not appear that plaintiff has been prevented from doing so.[14]

790. Execution of lease — Whatever words are sufficient to show the intent of the parties to be that the one should devest himself of the property and the other come into it for a determinate time, whether they run in the form of a license, covenant, or agreement, will, in construction of law, amount to a lease as effectually as if the most proper and technical words were made use of for that purpose.[15] In estimating the language which constitutes a lease, the form of words used is of no consequence ; it is not necessary that the term "lease" should be used. Whatever is equivalent will be equally available, if the words assume the form of a license, covenant, or agreement, and the other requisites of a lease are present[16] Being a lease, the privilege may be granted by parol, provided the term is not longer than three years.[17] So, the entry may be by virtue of a parol license, which is revocable at the will of the licensor, unless followed by expenditure on the faith of it, in which case it becomes irrevocable.[18] Though the parol lease be for a period greater than three years, and, as such, ineffective by virtue of

[12]*Kille* v *Reading Iron Works*, 141 Pa 440, 21 Atl 666

[13]*Heilman* v *Weinman*, 139 Pa 143, 21 Atl 29

[14]*Davies* v *Maxwell*, 5 Kulp, 351

[15]*Watson* v *O'Kern*, 6 Watts, 362

[16]*Moore* v *Miller*, 8 Pa 272

[17]*Moore* v *Miller*, 8 Pa 272, *Sheets* v *Allen*, 89 Pa 47

[18]*Huff* v *McCauley*, 53 Pa 206, 91 Am. Dec 203

the statute of frauds, yet a recovery may be had by the lessee for the work done and the expense incurred by him.[19] Though the agreement be signed and sealed by but one party, yet, if accepted by the one not signing, he is bound to the same extent as if he had done so[20] And the same is true where the lease is signed by one pretending to act as agent for the lessee, who had no such authority, the lessee having subsequently accepted the grant.[21] Though a guardian has exceeded his powers in executing a lease, his acts may be ratified by the minor after attaining majority.[22] As administrators have no control of the land of the decedent, they have no power to lease the same, or to receive the rents and profits accruing after the death of the intestate.[23] Though a consideration is necessary to the validity of the contract, yet the same is not void because the amount agreed to be paid is small[24]

791. Successive conveyances.— The same principle governs mining leases, that actual possession of the tenant carrying on the mining operations is notice of his interest to a third person, as fully as in the tenancy of a dwelling house The right of a tenant in possession, under such a lease is not extinguished in favor of a purchaser who knew the fact.[25] So, where coal was conveyed, but the deed was unrecorded before the land was purchased and paid for by another who had no notice of such conveyance, but the first deed was first recorded, the title acquired by it will have precedence. A subsequent purchaser, to be first in right against a prior purchaser, must be first on record.[26]

[19]*Heilman* v *Weinman,* 139 Pa 143, 21 Atl 29

[20]*Grove* v *Hodges,* 55 Pa 504, *Carnegie Natural Gas Co* v *Philadelphia Co* 158 Pa 317, 27 Atl 951

[21]*Grove* v *Hodges,* 55 Pa 504

[22]*Myers* v *Kingston Coal Co* 126 Pa 582, 17 Atl 891

[23]*Merkel's Estate,* 131 Pa. 584, 18 Atl 931.

[24]*Grotz* v *Wilkes Barre Coal Co* 1 Kulp, 53

[25]*Sheets* v *Allen,* 89 Pa 47 See *Delaware & H Canal Co* v *Hughes,* 183 Pa 66, 38 L R A 826, 63 Am. St Rep 743, 38 Atl 568

[26]*Pennsylvania Salt Mfg Co* v. *Neel,* 54 Pa 9.

792. Fraud.— As in other cases, a contract may be set aside for fraud, accident, or mistake, but such relief must be sought in an action to rescind.[27] The fact that the vendee was aware of the presence of minerals, of which the vendor was ignorant, is not ground for impugning the validity of the conveyance, where there has been no wilful misstatement of a material fact by which the vendor was misled.[28] Nor can a lessee be relieved of his obligation because there is no coal upon the land, there being no implied warranty that such exists,[29] nor because he was mistaken as to the amount of ore,[30] nor because the contract was made upon the belief that a branch railroad was to be constructed.[31]

793. Construction of lease — Each instrument is to be construed, like any other contract, by its own terms.[32] [33] Where a modification of a written lease by parol is alleged, the same principles apply as in the case of alteration of any writing. But if a written lease provides for the development of land upon one side of a road, and by parol the right is given to develop on the other side, the second agreement is independent, and no change of the written contract by parol is involved [34]

Where the lease gives the right to mine certain minerals only, such deposits, and others which are absolutely incident, can be taken   Such pass as an appurtenant, but not such as are merely important, useful, or convenient. So, where the right was given to mine soapstone only, other rocks could not be taken [35]   Or where land is leased for oil purposes, gas cannot be taken.[36] But where the additional mineral is incident, it may be used.

[27]*Harlan* v *Lehigh Coal & Nav Co.* 35 Pa 287

[28]*Harris* v *Tyson*, 24 Pa. 347, 64 Am Dec 661

[29]*Harlan* v *Lehigh Coal & Nav Co* 35 Pa 287

[30]*Kemble Coal & I Co* v *Scott*, 90 Pa 332

[31]*Kemble Coal & I. Co* v *Scott*, 90 Pa 332

[32] [33]*Denniston* v *Haddock*, 200 Pa. 426, 50 Atl 197

[34]*Heilman* v *Weinman*, 139 Pa. 143, 21 Atl 29

[35]*Verdolite Co* v *Richards*, 7 Northampton Co Rep 113

[36]*Polmer* v *Truby*, 136 Pa 556, 20 Atl 516, *Kitchen* v. *Smith*, 101 Pa 452.

So, where iron ore was leased and a furnace, sufficient limestone to operate the furnace could be taken by the lessee [37] But where the right has been given, for a nominal consideration, to take iron ore and limestone, the evident motive being to secure the erection of an iron furnace, no such right passes to the limestone as will enable purchasers from the vendee to maintain ejectment for the limestone quarry [38] So, where the lease is of salt wells, no right exists to take petroleum. And if such rises with the salt, and is sold by the lessee, he must account therefor to the lessor, though trover cannot be maintained, since the right to possession is in the lessee [39]

The lease of two veins of coal, followed by a second lease of two other veins to a lessee who has acquired the rights of the first lessee, will not be construed as a merger of all of the veins, so as to relieve from the covenants in the first lease [40]

794. Certainty.— Certainty as to the commencement and duration of the term is an essential quality of a lease But if the commencement is capable of being reduced to a certainty by an event to occur after the date of the lease, the contract itself is not void simply for want of certainty. So, where the lease was for a definite term, a certain royalty to be paid for all coal mined, the lease was not invalid for uncertainty, because no date was fixed for the beginning of the operation. Whether work was commenced within a reasonable time is a question for the jury.[41] Nor is a lease uncertain which provides for a fixed term, and gives to the lessee the right to continue operation as much longer as rent shall be paid. In such case the right to continue is at the will of the lessee.[42]

[37] Watterson v Reynolds, 95 Pa 474, 40 Am. Rep 672

[38] Clement v Youngman, 40 Pa 341

[39] Kier v Peterson, 41 Pa 357

[40] Lehigh Coal & Nav Co v Harlan, 27 Pa 429.

[41] Grotz v Wilkes Barre Coal Co 1 Kulp, 53

[42] Myers v Kingston Coal Co 126 Pa 582, 17 Atl 891, Effinger v. Lewis, 32 Pa 367.

795. Option to purchase —Where the lessee has been given the option to purchase the land, such privilege runs with the land, and is not a mere right of election which must be exercised in the lifetime of the parties [43] But the right accrues only to the holder of the lease, or to the person to whom it has been assigned with the consent of the lessor. The privilege cannot be reserved by the lessee, when he assigns the lease to another, so as to enforce the right against the lessor or his executors [44] So, the lessee may give an option to purchase the lease, and if the conditions are complied with and the option accepted, the rights of the grantees will be protected. They cannot be ousted for nonpayment of royalties, where the lessor has stated to them that none are due, and time and money have been spent on the faith of such declaration [45]

796. Assignments and subleases.—Where a lease has been assigned, the assignees take the same subject to the covenants of the lease, of which they are bound to take notice [46] The sublessee acquires the rights of his assignor. Thus, an assignee of a subjacent mine secures the privilege to put air shafts through superjacent mines, the assignor having had this right, since the easement attaches to the estate, and not to the owner.[47] So, the assignee for the benefit of the creditors of the lessee may use a railroad, constructed for the purpose of moving coal, belonging to the lessee.[48] But the sublessee is not liable upon covenants contained in the original lease, except for breaches committed while the right of possession is vested in him.[49] Where liability exists, the assignee may be sued directly.[50] But if the sub-

[43]*Strickhouser* v *York County Iron Co* 1 York Legal Record, 46

[44]*Winton's Appeal*, 111 Pa 387, 5 Atl 240

[45]*Comegys* v. *Russell*, 185 Pa. 283, 39 Atl 956

[46]*Comegys* v *Russell*, 175 Pa 166, 34 Atl 657

[47]*Philadelphia & R Coal & I Co* v *Taylor*, 1 Legal Chronicle, 335

[48]*Lykens Valley Coal Co* v *Dock*, 62 Pa 232

[49]*Oil Creek & C Branch Petroleum Co* v *Stanton Oil Co* 23 Pa Co Ct 153

[50]*Watt* v *Diminny*, 141 Pa 22, 21 Atl 519.

lessee has agreed to assume all of the covenants in the original lease, he will be bound So, liability accrues where the covenant provided for the mining of a minimum number of tons per year, although possession was not taken until after the beginning of the year.[51] If the sublessee has covenanted to pay certain coal royalties due and in arrear, he is bound to do so, and cannot set off debts due to him by the assignor, in an action on the covenant.[52] The original lessee remains liable to the lessor upon the covenants in the original lease.[53]

If the original lease prohibits its assignment, the lessor may forfeit the same and bring suit for the damages sustained, and need not wait and sue for the royalties as they become due[54] A stipulation that the lease shall be forfeited if assigned, transferred, or taken on execution is not violated by reason of the sale of a leasehold held by partners, by order of court, in order to settle the partnership affairs.[55] The fact that an assignment of the lease is in violation of the covenant therein does not prevent the passing of the title. It does not lie in the mouth of an assignee to set up such an irregularity while holding under an assignment which the assignor has ratified by suit or in any other way[56]

797. Interest conveyed.—*Sale.*—What is termed a "mineral lease" is frequently found to be an actual sale of a portion of the land. "It differs from an ordinary lease in this, that, although both convey an interest in land, the latter merely conveys the right to its temporary use and occupation, whilst the former conveys absolutely a portion of the land itself. It is one of the essential properties of a lease that its duration shall

[51]*Goddard's Appeal*, 1 Walk (Pa) 97

[52]*Ardesco Oil Co* v. *North American Oil & Min Co* 66 Pa 375

[53]*Oil Creek & C Branch Petroleum Co* v *Stanton Oil Co* 23 Pa. Co Ct 153, *Fisher* v *Milliken*, 8 Pa 111, 49 Am Rep 497.

[54]*Keck* v *Bieber*, 148 Pa 645, 33 Am St Rep 846, 24 Atl 170

[55]*Patterson* v *Silliman*, 28 Pa 304

[56]*Oil Creek & C Branch Petroleum Co* v *Stanton Oil Co*. 23 Pa Co Ct 153.

be for a determinate period, shorter than the duration of the es
tate of the lessor; hence the estate demised is called a 'term,' and
necessarily implies a reversion   If the entire interest of the
lessor is conveyed, in the whole or a portion of his land, the con
veyance cannot, therefore, be properly regarded as a demise,
but as an assignment."[57]   The extent of the interest transferred
is first discussed in *Caldwell* v. *Fulton*[58]   In that case a deed
was made, in consideration of the payment of a lump sum, by
which the grantee was given the full right, title, and privilege
of digging and taking away stone coal to any extent that he
might think proper to do or cause to be done   This grant was
held to be more than a license,—an estate in the land itself,—
and more than an incorporeal hereditament, since the grantor
reserved no interest in himself, but gave to the grantee the right
to remove or cause to be removed every available foot of the coal,
subject only to the duty to make the opening upon a particular
tract.   So, in *Harlan* v *Lehigh Coal & Nav. Co.*[59] the lease of
the right to mine coal in the land of the lessor was held to grant
an interest in the land, and not a mere license to take the mineral   The agreement in this case provided for a lease, for a
definite term, of the right to take such coal as was desired, paying a certain sum per ton, and in any case to pay a minimum
royalty.   The same determination is found in *Scranton* v.
Phillips,[60] in which the court says: "Although called a lease, it
was virtually a sale of all the coal, with unlimited time to remove
it, with the right at their election to yield it up after the expiration of ten years."   The question was next considered in *Sanderson* v. *Scranton*,[61] in which the liability of the grantee under
such a conveyance, for taxes, was determined.   The contract in
this case was called a lease, by which the grantee was given the
right to mine coal and to pay a certain royalty.   The maximum

[57] *Sanderson* v *Scranton*, 105 Pa.
469
[58] 31 Pa. 475, 72 Am. Dec 760.

[59] 35 Pa 287.
[60] 94 Pa 15
[61] 105 Pa 469.

quantity was unlimited, but the lessee was required to mine a minimum quantity, or pay for the same if he did not do so. It was further provided that the lease should be perpetual until all the coal under the tract of land was mined   It was held by the court that the entire interest in the coal in place was transferred. There was such a severance of the surface from the underlying strata as created a divided ownership in the distinct portions of the land   This decision was followed in construing the same lease in *Delaware, L & W. R. Co.* v. *Sanderson* [62]   So a severance is worked where the grant gives the right to mine until exhaustion.[63]

Where the words "grant, bargain, and sell" are used in connection with coal, and words of inheritance are added, it is to be presumed, unless a contrary intent clearly and affirmatively appears, that the parties intended them to have their ordinary legal effect, which is to vest in the grantee the entire ownership of the coal in the land described. But these technical words are not necessary to the creation of a separate estate in the coal, provided the intention to sell it is manifest, and it is now well settled that an instrument which is in terms a demise of all the coal in, under, and upon a tract of land, with the unqualified right to mine and remove the same, is a sale of the coal in place. And this, too, whether the purchase money stipulated for is a lump sum or a certain price for each ton mined, and is called rent or royalty; and, also, notwithstanding a term is created within which the coal is to be taken out.[64] But if the intention appears that no sale shall be worked, the contrary is true.[65] If the agreement is to grant the privilege of mining all of the ore upon the payment of a certain consideration, the contract will be treated in equity as a conveyance of the title to

[62] 109 Pa 583, 1 Atl 394   [64]*Hosack* v *Crill*, 18 Pa Super Ct
[63]*Sillibridge* v *Lackauanna Coal*   90, *Hosack* v *Crill*, 204 Pa 97, 53
Co 143 Pa 293, 13 L R A 627, 24 Atl 040
Am. St Rep 544, 22 Atl 1035.   [65]*Clement* v. *Youngman*, 40 Pa 341.

the ore in fee, the price agreed upon having been paid [66] Though called a lease and providing for a fixed price, an agreement naming a liquidated gross sum, payable in instalments, but giving a long period for the removal of the coal, is a sale, and the money due is payable to the executors of the deceased lessor as personal estate.[66 1-2] So a lease for a term of years, with the right to remove all of the coal is a sale.[67] It is a sale conditioned upon removal of the coal within a specified time; and the royalties are to be treated as purchase money in the distribution of the lessor's estate;[68] or in determining whether the same will pass by devise of the lessor [69] So, a sale and conveyance of mine buildings, and the coal under a tract of land, with the privilege of mining and removing the same during seven years, is to be treated as an absolute conveyance of the coal plant and coal which should be mined, and the vendee has the right to remove the buildings and other appliances necessarily connected with the mining and the transportation of the coal [70] Likewise it is to be treated as a sale in determining whether title has been acquired by adverse possession,[71] and in determining the liability of the lessee for a minimum rental which he has agreed to pay.[72]

Though such conveyances are to be treated as sales of the coal in place, yet not all of the incidents of sale are to be applied to such instruments   In discussing the earlier decisions, the

[66]*Fairchild v Dunbar Furnace Co* 128 Pa 485, 38 Atl 443, 444

[66½]*Hope's Appeal*, 29 W N C. 365

[67]*Kingsley v Hillside Coal & I Co* 144 Pa 613, 23 Atl 250, *Plummer v Hillside Coal & I Co* 160 Pa 483, 28 Atl 853, *Lehigh Valley Coal Co v Wilkes Barre & E R Co* 8 Kulp, 540, *Weakland v Cunningham*, 7 Atl. 148

[68]*Lazarus's Estate*, 145 Pa 1, 23 Atl 372, *Gardner's Estate*, 199 Pa 524, 49 Atl 346, *Fairchild v Fairchild* (Pa) 9 Atl. 255, *Hancock's Estate*, 7 Kulp, 36, *Maffet's Estate*, 3 Kulp, 184.

[69]*Hosack v Crill*, 18 Pa Super Ct 90, *Hosack v Crill*, 204 Pa 97 53 Atl 640

[70]*Montooth v Gamble*, 123 Pa 240, 16 Atl 594

[71]*Finnegan v Pennsylvania Trust Co* 5 Pa Super Ct 124, *Armstrong v Caldwell*, 53 Pa 284

[72]*Timlin v Brown*, 158 Pa 606, 28 Atl 236, *Lehigh & W B Coal Co v Wright*, 177 Pa 387, 35 Atl 919, *Kemble Coal & I Co v Scott*, 90 Pa 332.

court said in *Denniston* v. *Haddock:*[73] "With the decisions in
these cases no fault can be found, but the expression that a conveyance of coal in place, even by a lease for a limited term, is a
sale, is inaccurate as a general proposition of law, and unfortu-
nate from its tendency to mislead, which is apparent in some of
the subsequent cases. Whether it would be better to call such
an instrument accurately, what it certainly was at common law,
a lease without impeachment of waste, or to endeavor to recon-
cile all the decisions by calling it a conditional sale, is not necessary at present to discuss The point to be noted is that the rules
applicable to sales are not to be applied indiscriminately to
such instruments, but each is to be construed, like any other
contract, by its own terms." So it was held in this case that the
lessee of coal for a term of twenty years, required by his contract to pay minimum royalties, which had been done,—and a
greater sum in all having been paid than the value of the coal
mined, because of strikes and other circumstances, which prevented mining to the full extent,—cannot, after the lease has
expired by limitation and a new lease has been taken, defalk
the overpayment under the old lease from the royalties due
under the new one.[74]

Licenses and incorporeal hereditaments—A license is defined to be a power or authority given to a man to do some lawful
act, and is a personal liberty to the party to whom given, which
cannot be transferred over, but it may be made to a man or his
assigns. But where an estate or interest is evidently intended
to be conveyed, it must be either a corporeal or an incorporeal
hereditament[75] So, the grant of the privilege to dig ore at a
fixed price per ton, there being no covenant compelling the licensee to dig any quantity or to mine within any given time is a
mere license.[76] A license to take coal is revocable, but, if fol-

[73] 200 Pa 426, 50 Atl 197   [75] *Caldwell* v *Fulton*, 31 Pa 475,
[74] *Denniston* v *Haddock*, 200 Pa 72 Am Dec 760
426, 50 Atl 197.   [76] *Neumoyer* v *Andreas*, 57 Pa 446

lowed by expenditure on the faith of it, the license becomes irrevocable, and equity will treat the license thus executed as a contract giving absolute rights.[77]   If the owner grant to another the right or privilege to take minerals from his land, this grant, if not an exclusive one, is not a grant of an interest in land, but of an easement or incorporeal right, which leaves the title to the minerals in place remaining in the grantor.[78]

But the grant of the privilege of raising ore at a specified price per ton, to the grantees and their assigns, the privilege to be given to no one else, is more than a mere license revocable at the will of the licensor.   It is a valid grant of an incorporeal hereditament, the right, however, not being exclusive in the grantee, but to be enjoyed in common with the grantor, his heirs and assigns[79]   So, where the grant was to one, his heirs and assigns, with the right of ingress and egress, no exclusive right being granted, the interest is an incorporeal hereditament, and the joint right of the grantor to take the minerals exists[80]   And where land was devised to three sons, each of whom was to have the privilege of taking coal from an opening then made, the grant was held to be of a privilege in the coal bank,—not a share or portion of the coal,—and an easement in the adjacent land necessary to its enjoyment.   Since the devise was of a mere privilege, an easement and incorporeal hereditament, a right in, or issuing out of, the land, ejectment was not the proper remedy for a deprivation or interruption of such right or privilege[81]   So, the conveyance of land, with the right to take ore from an adjoining tract so long as the furnace upon the land was carried on by charcoal, gave a limited privilege to take ore, and did not

[77]*Huff* v *McCauley*, 53 Pa 206, 91 Am Dec 203

[78]*Delaware & H Canal Co* v *Hughes*, 183 Pa 66, 38 L R A 826, 63 Am St Rep 743, 38 Atl 568

[79]*Johnstoun Iron Co* v *Cambria Iron Co* 32 Pa 241, 72 Am Dec 783;

Grove v *Hodges*, 55 Pa 504, *Harlan* v *Lehigh Coal & Nav Co* 35 Pa 287

[80]*Gloninger* v *Franklin Coal Co.* 55 Pa 9 93 Am Dec 720

[81]*Carnahan* v. *Brown*, 60 Pa 23

convey the corporeal estate in the mine hill [82]   Where a portion
of a tract has been conveyed, with a collateral covenant granting
the right to take ore upon the remaining portion of the tract,
and the land conveyed is sold at sheriff's sale, the easement will
not pass to the purchaser, it not appearing that such was appurtenant to the tract conveyed [83]   And where a devise of land is
made with the privilege of taking coal from another tract, the
privilege is personal, and does not pass to devisees.[84]

As has been seen, the granting of all of the coal, though the
instrument is called a lease, and a term is fixed, and royalty is
reserved, will be treated as a sale.   Yet this rule does not apply
where a contrary intention appears from the agreement [85]   And
though the exclusive right has been given to take all gas, and in
addition coal, the word "all" not being used, and a royalty being
reserved, an incorporeal hereditament alone will pass, such facts
showing that it was not the intention of the parties to convey
the coal absolutely, or to exclude the grantor from mining [86]

798. Interest of lessee.— The interest of the lessee in the lease
for minerals is a chattel real, and as such is a partnership
asset [87]   It is a grant of a leasehold, and subject to the mechanics' lien law.[88]   And the instrument, being one for the payment
of money, is within the meaning of the early acts of assembly
requiring an affidavit of defense to actions thereon.[89]   But the
estate acquired thereby was held in *Elk Twp* v. *Beaver Twp.*[90]
not to give such a settlement for a poor person as is contemplated
by the act of June 13, 1836   (The theory on which this case was
decided is that the contract between the parties constituted a sale

[82]*Grubb* v *Grubb*, 74 Pa 25

[83]*Grubb* v *Guilford*, 4 Watts, 223,
28 Am Dec 700

[84]*Youghiogheny River Coal Co.* v
Pcairs, 2 Pa Dist R 134

[85]*Clement* v. *Youngman*, 4C Pa
341

[86]*Jennings Bros.* v *Beale*, 158 Pa.
283, 27 Atl. 948.

[87]*Patterson* v. *Silliman*, 28 Pa.
304, *Brown* v *Beecher*, 120 Pa 590,
15 Atl 608

[88]*McElwaine* v *Brown* (Pa) 9
Cent Rep 789, 11 Atl 453   See act
June 4, 1901, P L 431

[89]*Johnston* v *Cowan*, 59 Pa 275.

[90]6 Pa. Co Ct 562.

of the coal in place. The agreement is not set forth). Where
the agreement constitutes a lease, the rent due is entitled to
priority as against execution creditors, as in the case of ordinary
leases,[91] and possession of the premises may be obtained by
virtue of the provisions of the landlord and tenant act.[92] So the
lessee is within the act of assembly providing a special remedy
when land is taken under the power of eminent domain [93]

799. Right to work open mines.—The lessee of lands is entitled to work open mines upon the premises, unless restricted
by the terms of his lease. As the same privilege exists on the
part of the tenant for life,[94] so he may lease this right, and his
lessee will acquire the same privilege [95]

800 Right to open new mines—The right to open new mines
does not exist unless the demise includes this privilege.[96] The
habendum determines what estate is granted, and may lessen,
enlarge, explain, or qualify the estate in the premises, and,
unless totally repugnant to it, is to be construed as if contained
in the first part of the deed. When anything is granted, all the
means to obtain it, and all the fruits and effects of it, are also
granted. Therefore, when the lessee is given the privilege of
mines and minerals, he is given the right to them, and the right
to dig for them.[97] If the right has been granted to take all of
the coal, the lessee has the privilege of making all necessary
openings.[98] So, the tenant for years of the superjacent mine
has authority to permit an opening to a subjacent mine for the
purposes of ventilation.[99]

[91]*Oram's Estate*, 5 Kulp, 423;
Greenough's Appeal, 9 Pa 18

[92]*O'Donnell* v *Luskin*, 12 Montg.
Co L Rep 109

[93]*Mine Hill & S H R Co* v *Zerbe*,
2 Walker (Pa.) 409.

[94]*Neel* v *Neel*, 19 Pa 323, *Lynn's
Appeal*, 31 Pa 44. 72 Am Dec 721;
Shoemaker's Appeal, 106 Pa 392

[95]*Sayers* v *Hoskinson*, 110 Pa.
473, 1 Atl 308

[96]*Griffin* v *Fellows*, 81* Pa 114

[97]*Griffin* v *Fellows*, 81* Pa 114,
School Board's Appeal, 2 Walk
(Pa) 37, *Tiley* v *Moyers*, 25 Pa.

[98]*Trout* v *McDonald* 83 Pa 144.

[99]*Philadelphia & R Coal & I Co.*
v. *Taylor*, 1 Legal Chronicle, 361.

In case the lessee acts to the injury of the reversion, a writ of estrepement may be granted to stay the waste, but such will not be allowed where it does not clearly appear that the acts complained of are unwarranted by the lease and injurious to the land [100]

801. Right of lessor to mine.—Where the conveyance does not constitute a sale of the coal in place, and no exclusive right is given to the lessee, the grantor, his heirs or assigns, may also mine [101] If the grant is coextensive with the coal vein of the whole tract, and the lessor enters and takes coal, he is guilty of a breach of the implied covenant for quiet possession, and the lessee can set off the damages resulting therefrom against the claim for rent accrued under the lease The rent would be suspended in case of an actual expulsion of the lessee out of all or some part of the demised premises But that already accrued and overdue is not forfeited, though the tenant may defalk the damages caused by.[102]

802 Interest of the lessee when severed.— After the mineral has been severed from the ground it becomes personal property, and passes to the assignee for the benefit of creditors,[103] and may be sold on execution against the lessee,[104] or may be recovered in an action of replevin.[105] So, culm mined from its original place, and piled on the ground, is personal property, and when taken by a railroad company under the right of eminent domain, the owner is entitled to recover its value.[106]

803 Right to surface — Where the exclusive right to mine coal has been given, the grantee may take possession of the sur-

[100]*Heil* v *Strong*, 44 Pa 264.

[101]*Johnstown Iron Co* v *Cambria Iron Co* 32 Pa 241, 72 Am Dec 783, *Neumoyer* v *Andreas*, 57 Pa 446, *Jennings Bros* v *Beale*, 158 Pa 283, 27 Atl 948, *Gloninger* v *Frank lin Coal Co*. 55 Pa 9, 93 Am Dec. 720

[102]*Tiley* v *Moyers*, 43 Pa 404.

[103]*Lykens Valley Coal Co* v *Dock*, 62 Pa 232

[104]*Watts* v *Tibbals*, 6 Pa 447

[105]*Green* v *Ashland Iron Co* 62 Pa. 97

[106]*Lehigh Coal Co* v *Wilkes Barre d E R Co* 187 Pa 145, 41 Atl 37, 720

face necessary to carry on the operations, even as against the owner of the soil, and may recover in ejectment the land itself against an intruder. Where it does not appear what portion of the land is necessary, it will be presumed that the entire tract is required.[107] So, the lessee of coal who has never gone into possession may maintain ejectment against the lessor, provided his rights have not been forfeited.[108] If the lease has designated the sites which may be taken, the lessee is limited to them.[109] And when the parties have agreed upon the mode of access to the coal conveyed, no implication can be allowed of any other way, however convenient.[110] An agreement regulating the manner of removing the coal is a covenant which runs with the land.[111] A grant of a surface right, with a stipulation that it shall be used only for the purpose of a coal breaker and dirt room for the deposit of coal and dirt, is the grant of an easement only.[112] Where the lease provides that the lessee shall have sufficient surface room for the erection of a breaker and the deposit of culm, he may exercise the privilege, but is not compelled to erect a breaker or to deposit culm.[113] Though the lessee is granted surface rights for the purpose of preparing coal and dumping refuse from the land leased, such privilege cannot be exercised for the purpose of preparing coal from other land. If this privilege has been expressly granted, to be paid for, it is a covenant running with the land, and a purchaser of part of the tract can recover from the lessee for such use of the surface. No privilege exists to use the right of way granted, for removing coal from an adjoining tract, though both tracts were at one time owned by one person, who used the right of way.[114]

[107]*Turner* v. *Reynolds*, 23 Pa 119
[108]*Grotz* v *Lehigh & W B Coal Co* 1 Kulp, 53
[109]*Duffield* v *Hue*, 129 Pa 94, 18 Atl 566
[110]*Bascom* v. *Cannon*, 158 Pa 225, 27 Atl 968
[111]*Electric City Land & Improv Co* v *West Ridge Coal Co* 187 Pa 500, 41 Atl 458
[112]*Big Mountain Improv Co's Appeal* 54 Pa 361
[113]*Lance* v *Lehigh & W B Coal Co* 163 Pa 84, 29 Atl 755
[114]*Webber* v. *Vogel*, 159 Pa, 235, 28 Atl 226

LAND & TEN. 44

804. Subterranean rights.— Where land is sold with a reservation of minerals and subterranean passages, the lessee who takes the same has the right to pass through the land over the soil lying under the coal vein [115] Subterranean passages may be used for removing coal from other lands, unless the lease restricts the inside workings to the mining and preparing coal upon the land leased.[116] A lessor who has reserved the rights to oil and gas may drill through the coal for that purpose, but an injunction will be granted in case the lessee is interfered with or injured by leakage.[117] In the absence of a reservation, the grantor has the right of access to the strata underlying the coal [118]

805 Lessee's rights when mineral removed.— An estate in coal is determinable upon removal of the coal, and when all the coal is removed, the space it occupied reverts to the grantor by operation of law.[119] The estate terminates with the exhaustion of the mineral, and the owner of the land above and below has a right to a reversion of the space occupied, within the time contemplated by the parties [120]

806 Lessee's right to refuse.— Where the lessor is to receive a certain sum per ton for all coal passing over a screen of a certain mesh, and to have all the culm or refuse coal from the mines, he is entitled to only such culm or refuse coal as the lessee rejects and places upon the refuse pile, and not to such smaller coal as would pass through the mesh, but which the lessee chooses to sell [121] Where the lease was granted for the

[115]*Park Coal Co v Cummings*, 2 Law Times, O S 121

[116]*Rockafellow* v *Hanover Coal Co* 2 Pa Dist R 108, 12 Pa Co Ct 241

[117]*Chartiers Block Coal Co* v *Mellon*, 152 Pa 286, 18 L R A 702, 34 Am St Rep 645, 25 Atl 597

[118]*Chartiers Block Coal Co* v *Mellon*, 152 Pa 286, 18 L R A 702, 34 Am St Rep 645 25 Atl 597.

[119]*Chartiers Block Coal Co* v. *Mellon*, 152 Pa 286, 18 L R A 702, 34 Am St Rep 645, 25 Atl 597

[120] *Webber* v *Vogel*, 189 Pa 156, 42 Atl 4, *Lillibridge* v *Lackawanna Coal Co* 143 Pa 293, 13 L R A. 627, 24 Am St Rep 544, 22 Atl. 1035

[121]*Lance* v *Lehigh & W B Coal Co* 163 Pa 84, 29 Atl 755.

purpose of searching for mineral and fossil substances, the grantees to pay for all zinc and iron ores, the refuse material must be regarded as a substance other than ores, and for its conversion by the grantees the grantor is entitled to recover the value thereof as damages, and to an injunction restraining the grantees from its further sale and removal from the land demised.[122] The intent of the parties at the time the contract is entered into should govern its enforcement, and where the right was given to take iron ore, and the lessee subsequently attempted to use the refuse for paint purposes, an injunction was granted, it being clear that the crude ochre in the refuse dam was not intended to pass under the terms of the lease.[123]

807. Duty of the lessee to furnish surface support —If minerals are demised, and the surface is retained by the lessor, there arises a prima facie inference, upon every such demise, that the lessor is leasing them in such a manner as is consistent with the retention by himself of his own right of support.[124] The lessee is bound to leave enough of the mineral in place to answer the purposes of support for the surface, unless the right has been expressly released[125] The lessee cannot remove the minerals in such a way as to injure the surface[126] This right to support extends to the portion of the highway belonging to the surface owner[127] It is no defense to an action for injury sustained, that the greatest of care was taken by the lessee, since an absolute right to the support exists[128] And a custom to deprive the surface of proper support is not reasonable, and cannot be set up in defense.[129]

[122]*Doster* v *Friedensville Zinc Co* 140 Pa 147, 21 Atl 251

[123]*Irwin's Appeal,* 20 W N C 278

[124]*Jones* v *Wagner,* 66 Pa 429, 5 Am Rep 385.

[125]*Allshouse's Estate,* 23 Pa Super Ct 146, *Horner* v *Watson,* 79 Pa 242, 21 Am Rep 55, *Nelson* v *Hoch,* 14 Phila 655, *Nelson* v. *Miller,* 1 Legal Record Rep 187

[126]*Lowry* v *Hay,* 2 Walk (Pa) 239

[127]*Barnes* v *Berwind,* 3 Pennyp. 140

[128]*Robertson* v *Youghiogheny River Coal Co* 172 Pa 566, 33 Atl 706, *Gumbert* v *Kilgore* (Pa) 6 Cent Rep 406

[129]*Jones* v *Wagner,* 66 Pa 429, 5

The owner of the mineral rights is liable to the surface owner, though he has subsequently leased his rights to another, where the injury has occurred prior to the lease. But where it has occurred subsequently, the lessor is prima facie not liable In case the action is based upon a covenant of the first lessee, the second lessee woud not be a proper party to the action [130] The lessor, who merely reserves the right to examine the mine, is not liable for the deprivation of surface support.[131] But the contrary is true if the work is done under his direction.[132]

808 Release of right.— The owner of the surface may release the lessee from his obligation to furnish surface support Such right is not to be taken away, however, by a mere implication from language not necessarily importing such result. So, the reservation that the lessee "shall do as little damage to the surface as possible will not relieve from liability."[133] Nor will a release be effective which provides for freedom from obligation in case "all ordinary precautions" are taken.[134] Where an exception has been made, the lessee or those who claim through him may mine all the coal, even though by said mining the surface should fall in [135] If a covenant appears by which the occupier of the surface agrees to remove his railroad upon demand so that all the coal may be taken, and he fails to do so, damages may be recovered for the breach.[136] Where the agreement of the parties has been put in writing, the lessee cannot show a parol alteration of the lease, allowing him to withdraw the surface support.[137] In case the right has been released, it will be

Am Rep 385, *Horner* v *Watson*, 79 Pa 242, 21 Am Rep 55

[130]*Hill* v *Pardee*, 143 Pa. 98, 22 Atl 815,

[131]*Offerman* v *Starr*, 2 Pa St 394, 44 Am Dec 211 See *Little Schuyl lill Nav R & Coal Co v Richards*, 57 Pa 142, 98 Am Dec 209

[132]*Histler* v *Thompson*, 158 Pa 139, 27 Atl 874

[133]*Williams* v. *Hay*, 120 Pa. 485, 6 Am St Rep 719, 14 Atl 379

[134]*Youghiogheny River Coal Co* v *Hopkins*, 198 Pa 343, 48 Atl 19

[135]*Scranton* v *Phillips*, 94 Pa 15

[136]*Mine Hill & S H R Co* v *Lippincott*, 86 Pa 468

[137]*Heckscher* v *Sheaffer* (Pa) 14 Atl 53, *Lowry* v *Hay*, 2 Walk. (Pa.) 239.

effective, provided the grantor of the right possesses power to
so do, but executors authorized by a will to sell coal underlying
certain lands, with "the usual mining privileges," are not authorized to sell the coal and release the right of surface or
lateral support.[138]

809. **Remedy for failure to furnish support** — Where the lessee
has deprived the owner of the surface support, the right not having been released, an action may be maintained to recover the
damage suffered.   The statute of limitations in such case runs
from the time when the coal was removed without leaving sufficient support, although the owner of the surface may have been
ignorant of the violation of his right.[139]   Where the injury has
occurred by reason of an error of judgment, only compensatory,
and not vindictive, damages are to be awarded.[140]   And the
plaintiff is not entitled to interest on his damages from the time
they accrued.[141]   The rights of the surface owner may likewise
be protected by injunction.[142]

810. **Duty of lessee to adjacent owners** —Where adjacent mines
are held by different owners, the lessee must ascertain the divid-
ing line at his peril   And the lessor who directs the lessee to mine
beyond the line is liable to the adjoining owner [143]   But this rule
does not apply where the plaintiff is the lessor of both of the adjoining mines, and he has not protected himself by covenant.   If
he not only gives his tenant the power, but makes it his duty, to
explore, and marks a theoretical line upon his own premises, the
tenant cannot be treated as a trespasser, if in an honest attempt

[138]*Allshouse's Estate*, 23 Pa Super
Ct 146

[139]*Noonan* v *Pardee*, 200 Pa 474,
55 L R A. 410, 86 Am St Rep 722,
50 Atl 255, *Pantall* v *Rochester &
P Coal & I Co* 204 Pa 158, 52 Atl
751

[140]*Thompson* v *Pennsylvania Coal
Co* 1 Luzerne legal Obs 25, 4 Luzerne Legal Reg 86

[141]*Emerson* v *Schoonmaker*, 135
Pa 437, 19 Atl 1025

[142]*Nelson* v *Hoch*, 14 Phila 655.
Heckscher v *Sheaffer* (Pa) 14 Atl
53   *Ganley* v *Kirst*, 7 Lack Legal
News, 172, *Wier's Appeal*, 81* Pa.
203

[143]*Dundas* v. *Muhlenberg*, 35 Pa
351.

to ascertain the line he should chance to pass over it. In such case the lessor can recover damages only for improper mining or criminal negligence.[144] By the act of May 8, 1876, treble damages may be recovered for the taking of minerals known to be upon the lands of others. Act May 8, 1876 (Pamph. Law, 142). Such act applies to the taking of building stone from an open quarry on the surface of the ground.[145] So, the lessee must refrain from injuring the adjoiner by the depositing of coal dirt,[146] and from polluting the streams in the operation of his mine.[147] And he owes the duty to the adjoining owner to refrain from wilfully injuring his shaft with water. If this duty is violated, the damage sustained may be recovered.[148]

An injunction to restrain from mining upon adjoining lands will not be granted, unless the rights of the parties are clear,[149] or where the adjoining owner has permitted such conduct, and the expenditure of large sums has taken place as the result.[150] But an answer to a bill for an injunction will be insufficient where it sets up an anterior lease, but fails to set forth a copy of it, or the extent of the interest granted by it.[151] Though an injunction is refused, an accounting may be ordered.[152] The action in such case is to be brought in the county in which the mine lies.[153] If the lease is held by a partnership, though standing in the name of one of the members who owns the fixtures, a joint action of trespass by both for such injury is maintainable.[154]

[144]*Freck* v *Locust Mountain Coal & I Co* 86 Pa 318

[145]*Rattledge* v *Kress,* 17 Pa Super Ct 490

[146]*Hoffman* v *Mill Creek Coal Co* 16 Pa Super Ct 631

[147]*Stevenson* v *Ebervale Coal Co* 201 Pa 112, 88 Am St Rep 805, 50 Atl 818, *Stevenson* v *Ebervale Coal Co* 203 Pa 316, 52 Atl 201, *Keppel* v *Lehigh Coal & Nav Co* 200 Pa 649, 50 Atl 302.

[148]*McKnight* v *Ratcliff,* 44 Pa 156

[149]*Alter* v. *Bowman,* 2 Legal Chronicle, 324

[150]*Mammoth Vein Consol Coal Co's Appeal,* 54 Pa 183

[151]*Hurley* v *Delaware & H Canal Co* 6 Pa Dist R 257

[152]*Wilkes Barre & S L Coal Co* v. *Elliott,* 4 Lanc Bar, 43

[153]*Provost* v *Gorrell,* 11 Phila 263

[154]*Douty* v *Bird,* 60 Pa 48.

CHAPTER XXXVIII.

MINES AND MINERAL LEASES—CONTINUED.

811 Covenants.— The dependency or independency of a covenant is to be determined, not alone from any particular words or phrases, but also from the nature of the transaction and the object of the parties as evidenced by the contract After the agreement has been made, the subsequent independent action of either party cannot change the right, under the contract of the nonassenting party.[1] A covenant to pay rent for coal mined is

[1] *Potter* v *Gilbert*, 177 Pa 159, 35
L R A 580, 35 Atl 597.

distinct from a covenant to mine a certain quantity.[2] So, a covenant to mine is distinct from a covenant to pay rent for houses, and the one is not dependent upon the other.[3] The conveyance of a coal plant, with the coal under a tract of land, is distinct from the lease of houses for miners, though included in the same agreement.[4]

A breach of the covenant by the lessee does not in itself give to the lessor the right to re-enter. Conditions that work a forfeiture are not favorites of the law, and it must clearly appear that what is alleged to be such, was intended to be such [5]

812. Duty to mine — Where the terms of the lease show that the parties contemplated that the mine should be worked, there is an implied covenant to do so with reasonable diligence. Upon the failure of the lessee to perform this duty, damages are recoverable by the lessor,[6] and may be had for such amount as the lessee could reasonably have mined. The measure of damages is the difference between the stipulated rate of compensation and the value of the coal left unmined.[7] The lessor is not bound to show the amount which could have been mined. If the defendant fails to do so, the jury must assess the damage [8] This implied obligation will not be enforced in a court of equity, as an adequate remedy is afforded by an action at law for damages, unless there are special reasons for equitable interference.[9] If the contract has fixed the amount to be removed, the lessee is not required to mine more. And where the agreement is in writing, the lessee cannot show an oral stipulation made at the same time, that he was to be required to remove only so much as he could dispose of.[10] Where no provision appears in the lease, fixing the amount of minerals to be removed, the intention

[2]*Powell* v *Burroughs*, 54 Pa 329
[3]*Big Black Creek Improv Co* v *Kemmerer*, 162 Pa 422, 29 Atl 739
[4]*Montooth* v *Gamble*, 123 Pa 240, 16 Atl 594
[5]*McKnight* v *Kreutz*, 51 Pa 232

[6]*Watson* v *O'Hern*, 6 Watts, 362.
[7]*Lyon* v *Miller*, 24 Pa 392
[8]*Watson* v *O'Hern*, 6 Watts, 362.
[9]*Koch's Approl*, 93 Pa 434
[10]*Lyon* v *Miller*, 24 Pa 392.

of the parties must be taken to be that the mine should be worked with such reasonable diligence as circumstances will permit.[11] If a bond is given, conditioned upon the boring into coal land within a specified time under an option to lease, the sum provided for is ordinarily to be treated as a penalty, and not as liquidated damages[12]

813. Manner of working — Where no stipulation is made in the contract as to the time of the commencement of the work, the lessee may begin within a reasonable time; and what constitutes such is a question of fact for the jury.[13] In conducting the operations, the lessee is bound to act according to accepted methods. But he cannot be compelled to accept the plans of the lessor,—especially where the right has been given to the lessee to carry on the operations with reference to an adjoining tract held, to which the plan proposed could not apply.[14] Changing the method of mining from compressed air to electricity is a trade improvement which the lessee may take advantage of in accordance with the usage in mining, as well as by the terms of a deed of mining right[15] Though the improvements are not justified, yet the plaintiff may be estopped, where the same have been permitted for a long time without objection.[16]

814 Rent and royalties.—As has been noticed, a conveyance of all the coal in place, though called a lease and providing for a term of years, is a sale, and the amount paid by the grantee is to be treated as purchase money. Though there has been a grant of the coal until exhaustion, yet if a new agreement is made by which defendants are to enter and mine coal and pay a

[11]*Guth's Appeal* (Pa) 5 Atl 728; *Lyon* v *Miller*, 24 Pa 392, *Anspach* v *Bast* 53 Pa 356

[12]*Siedel* v *Shelly*, 7 Lack Legal News, 286

[13]*Grotz* v *Lehigh & W B. Coal Co.* 1 Kulp 53.

[14]*West Ridge Coal Co* v *Von Storch*, 5 Lack Legal News, 189

[15]*Potter* v *Rend*, 31 Pittsb L J.

[16]*Potter* v *Rend*, 31 Pittsb L J N S 223.

royalty, the lessors may recover the amount agreed upon.[17]   The
amount of rent or royalty due is to be determined by the terms of
the lease   So, a royalty for each bushel of coal will be held to
mean coal in the mercantile sense, and the lessee will be chargeable only with lump coal, and not nut or slack, where such seems
to be the intention of the parties[18]   The term "miners' weight"
signifies that which is employed in paying the miner by the
ton.[19]   Where the royalty provided was 10 cents for each ton
of merchantable screened coal of 2,240 pounds, and 10 cents for
each ton of merchantable screened bituminous coal, a ton of
2,240 pounds of the second class of coal was also contemplated[20]
Where the royalty is proportioned to the selling price at the
breaker, the actual selling price, less the cost of selling, including the commissions of selling agent and freight, is meant, such
being the custom[21]   Where the royalty is payable for screened
coal, such is meant as will pass over the customary screen in
general use in the section where the mine is located, whether the
coal be lump or nut[22]   And the grantee who screens and removes both the lump and nut coal is estopped from alleging that
the nut coal so screened and sold is not within the meaning of
the contract.[23]   Where the payment is to be for all coal passing
through a screen of certain dimensions, it is immaterial if the
lessee passes it a second time over a smaller mesh, and thus obtains a nut coal which he can sell on the market.[24]   If the lease
provides that the lessor shall have the culm or refuse coal passing through the screen, the lessee may, nevertheless, take such
as passes through the screen, which he does not reject as value-

[17]*Watt* v *Dininny*, 141 Pa 22, 21 Atl 519

[18]*Long* v. *Wood*, 22 Pittsb L J 93

[19]*Drake* v *Lacoe*, 157 Pa 17, 27 Atl 538

[20]*Johnston* v *Filer*, 201 Pa 60, 50 Atl 940.

[21]*Shoemaker* v *Mount Lookout Coal Co* 177 Pa 405, 35 Atl 731

[22]*Dunham* v *Haggerty*, 110 Pa. 560 1 Atl 667

[23]*Mercer Min & Mfg Co* v *McKee*, 77 Pa 170

[24]*Johnston* v *Filer*, 201 Pa 60, 50 Atl 940

less [25]   Where the lessee is to pay a royalty for coal mined, the same being measured by bushels, and to pay, at the end of the term fixed, by computing the balance remaining unmined in bushels, the solid coal remaining is to be computed in bushels each containing in solid coal the equivalent of a bushel of mined or broken coal.[26]   Where the lease provides for different royalties for different grades of coal, and at the time of the making of the lease the smaller sizes constituted 15 per cent of the output, which amount was subsequently increased by the breaking up of the larger sizes, the lessor is entitled to full royalties upon all of the smaller sizes in excess of 15 per cent of the product of the mine.[27]   Though the lease provides for the payment of a royalty upon all bushels mined, the number to be ascertained from the pay roll, the lessor is entitled to recover for the amount of coal removed in making entrances, though not noted upon the pay roll by bushels, but by yards.[28]

The lessor is entitled to royalties upon the coal mined upon the leased land by virtue of the lease, but he cannot recover under his lease for coal taken from another part of his land, though an action in trespass could be maintained against the lessee for such acts [29]   Under the custom which prevails in the anthracite coal region, coal used by the lessee in the operation of the furnaces of the mine is not subject to royalties, unless provision is made therefor in the lease [30]

815 Preference of rent due — The claim of the lessor for rent is entitled to preference.[31]   But a claim for money advanced by the lessor for the purpose of making improvements, to be repaid by the lessee by an additional royalty of 10 cents per ton,

[25]*Lauee* v *Lehigh & W B Coal Co* 163 Pa 84, 29 Atl 755
[26]*Reiner* v *Cambria Steel Co* 28 Pa Co Ct 13
[27]*Wright* v *Warrior Run Coal Co* 182 Pa 514, 38 Atl 491
[28]*Jack* v *Forsyth*, 194 Pa 227, 45 Atl 50

[29]*Lyon* v *Miller*, 24 Pa 392
[30]*Wright* v *Warrior Run Coal Co* 182 Pa 514, 38 Atl 491
[31]*Wood's Appeal*, 30 Pa 274, *Spangler's Appeal*, 30 Pa 277, note, *Greenough's Appeal*, 9 Pa 18 See *Com* v. *Dunn*, 17 Pa Super Ct 90

is merely a loan, and not rent.[32]   Where the lessor has a first
lien for rent on the proceeds of personalty, and upon the proceeds of the leasehold estate and fixtures, against the former of
which there are labor claims, he will, for the benefit of the laborers, be thrown on the latter fund, though the amount remaining
is insufficient to pay the mortgagee of the lease.[33] The restriction
in the local act of March 30, 1859, of the lien for rent to that
due for one month and any fraction, applies only to such property as is liable to distress.   All of the rent due may be taken
from the proceeds of the sale of the leasehold.[34]   Though rent
is to be preferred, yet it is not a prior lien, under the act of April
6, 1830, relating to mortgages, so that a mortgage of the leasehold will be discharged by sheriff's sale of the term under an
execution against the lessee.[35]

816. Eviction.— An eviction of the lessee will suspend the
payment of royalties subsequently accruing.[36]   To suspend the
rent, there must be an actual expulsion of the lessee out of all or
some part of the demised premises.[37]   The rent already accrued
and overdue is not forfeited by eviction, but in an action for it
the tenant may defalk the damages caused by the eviction.[38]
Where the eviction is by the holder of the paramount title, without fraud on the part of the lessor, the lessee can only recover
as damages the consideration paid, and where the royalties contracted for during his possession have alone been paid, the damages are merely nominal.[39]   To recover damages for breach of
a covenant for quiet enjoyment, it must appear that some act
was done by the lessor, his heirs or assigns, prejudicial to the
lessee.[40]

[32]*Miners' Bank* v *Heilner*, 47 Pa
452
[33]*Farmers Bank's Appeal*, 1 Walk
(Pa) 33
[34]*Farmers Bank's Appeal*, 1 Walk
(Pa) 33
[35]*Miners' Bank* v *Heilner* 47 Pa
452

[36]*West Ridge Coal Co* v *Von
Storch*, 5 Lack Legal News, 189
[37]*Tiley* v *Moyers*, 43 Pa 404
[38]*Tiley* v *Moyers* 43 Pa 404
[39]*Lanigan* v *Kille*, 97 Pa 120, 39
Am Rep 797
[40]*Chambers* v *Smith*, 183 Pa 122,
38 Atl 522

817 Denial of lessor's title — The lessee is estopped in an action for rent from denying the title of the lessor under whom he holds.[41] And if he takes a second lease from one claiming adversely, he cannot refuse to pay on the ground that the first lessor had a better title.[42] Nor can he refuse to pay because of the failure of the proper parties to sign the lease, where possession was kept, and the willingness to sign upon demand appeared.[43] The lessee of land upon two sides of a canal owned in fee will not thereby become a tenant as to the land beneath the canal, so as to prevent him from denying the title of the canal owners to coal removed from the land beneath the canal.[44]

But where a son has entered upon land by virtue of a parol agreement with his father that he should have a smaller vein, if he should open it, but subsequently accepts a lease from his father for another vein, he will hold as a tenant, and not as an owner.[45]

818 Minimum royalty — The ordinary provision contained in mining leases, where a certain minimum amount is agreed upon to be taken out each year, and, if not taken out, the lessee agrees to pay the royalty notwithstanding, is based upon the theory that the ore or coal is in place, and can be taken out if proper efforts are made, and is intended as an incentive to compliance with the duty of adequate performance and prompt payments.[46] Where a lessee holds under two leases from the same lessor, agreeing to remove a specified amount under each lease, but not more than a railroad could take, the leases are distinct, and he has no right to refuse to work one of the mines because of insufficient cars. Nor is it any defense in such case that as much coal was taken from one mine as if both had been worked.[47] If

[41] *Rhoades v Patrick*, 27 Pa 323
[42] *Hamilton v Pittock*, 158 Pa 457, 27 Atl 1079
[43] *Kunkle v People's Natural Gas Co* 165 Pa 133, 33 L R A 847, 30 Atl 719.
[44] *Wyoming Coal & Transp Co v Price*, 81 Pa 156
[45] *Turner v Reynolds*, 23 Pa 199
[46] *Boyer v Fulmer*, 176 Pa 282, 35 Atl 235
[47] *Powell v Burroughs*, 54 Pa 329

the royalty differs according to the size of the coal, and the lease
provides for the mining of a minimum number of tons, the damage for failure to remove that number will be measured by the
royalty upon the number of tons agreed upon, to be made up of
different sizes, proportioned to the ordinary production, when
carefully mined and prepared, in accordance with the terms of
the agreement [48] Where the lessee was bound to mine a certain number of tons of coal, and it is agreed that, had such been
done, a certain proportion would have been nut coal, which
was to be paid for in case it was shipped from the mine, but not
if sold at that place, no recovery can be had for royalties upon
it.[49]

819. Defenses.—Where the lease provides for the payment of
a minimum royalty, and there is no stipulation that the covenants may be avoided by abandonment or surrender of the contract by the lessee, the same may be recovered, though operations
by the lessee cease [50] The fact that there is no merchantable ore
is no defense, provided there is workable ore suitable for use in a
furnace.[51] The lessee is bound to continue the payment of the
stipulated minimum royalty as long as any coal remains, although he may pay an amount in excess of the sum fixed per
ton for all the coal under the land, both mined and unmined.[52]
The question of profitable mining is immaterial where all of the
merchantable mineral has not been exhausted. Nor can the
lessee refuse to pay on the ground that a sum already paid in
royalties is greater than the value of all of the merchantable coal,
where more remains, though it cannot be sold at a profit.[53] Nor
will the lease be canceled as inequitable where ore remains,

[48]*Schooley* v *Butler Mine Co* 175
P.a 261, 34 Atl 639

[49]*Lostwick* v *Ormsby Coal Co* 129
Pa 592 18 Atl 538

[50]*Kemble Coal & I Co* v *Scott*, 90
Pa 332.

[51]*Kemble Coal & I Co* v *Scott*, 15
W N C 220

[52]*Lehigh Valley Coal Co* v *Everhart*, 206 Pa 118, 55 Atl 864

[53]*Acme Coal Co* v *Stroud*, 5 Lack.
Legal News, 169.

though it is of too poor a quality to work profitably [54] Nor will the lessee be relieved where one of the bores made shows the presence of good ore, though faults appear in the vein, until a more complete test is made to ascertain the quality [55] But the lessee may show the nonexistence of ore in the land, or that it was in a seam too small for mining, or affected by such irregularities as to prevent the taking out of the minimum quantity.[56] And if no ore is present at the beginning of the lease, or it becomes exhausted, so that it cannot be mined in a stipulated quantity, the lessee will not be liable for the minimum royalty [57] But this rule does not apply where the contract between the parties constitutes a sale of the coal in place.[58]

Where the lease gives the right to abandon, responsibility continues until there has been an abandonment by the lessee or his assigns [59] And in such case the granting of a release and a surrender of all of the coal conveyed will not relieve the grantees, who afterward remained in possession and continued their operations [60] So, if the lessee is given the right to abandon the contract, he may do so, the burden being upon him to show that the coal was unmerchantable, or not to be found upon the premises, this question to be passed upon by the jury;[61] and the lessor in such case is not bound to show that the coal was merchantable.[62] A failure to surrender the lease is evidence that sufficient mineral is present, but a failure to do so is not conclusive upon him.[63] But where a minimum royalty is to be paid in case the minerals can be advantageously mined, the lessee is not

[54] *Kraber's Appeal*, 2 York Legal Record, 55

[55] *West Ridge Coal Co v Von Storch*, 5 Lack Legal News, 189

[56] *Kemble Coal & I Co v Scott*, 90 Pa 332

[57] *Boyer v Fulmer*, 176 Pa 282, 35 Atl 235; *Muhlenberg v Henning*, 116 Pa 138, 9 Atl 144

[58] *Timlin v Brown*, 158 Pa. 606, 28 Atl 236

[59] *Buhl v. Thompson*, 3 Pennyp 267

[60] *Bestwick v Ormsby Coal Co* 129 Pa 592, 18 Atl 538

[61] *Wilson v Beech Creek Cannel Coal Co* 7 Pa Super Ct 241

[62] *Wilson v Beech Creek Cannel Coal Co* 161 Pa 499, 29 Atl 95

[63] *McCahan v Wharton*, 121 Pa 424, 6 Am St Rep 799, 15 Atl 575

bound to continue where the expense of removing the same is greater than its value [64] So, where a certain quantity is to be taken unless the lessee is prevented by unavoidable accidents or circumstances beyond his control, it is a valid defense to an action for the royalties that the mineral has become exhausted [65]

It is no defense to an action for the minimum royalty that the coal in place is more valuable than if it had been taken out,[66] nor is a surrender of the lease, where the lessee continues in possession;[67] nor that the right was given to elect to pay an annual sum in lieu of the minimum royalty, where such election was not made at the time fixed [68] The assignees of the lessee are bound by the covenant to make the annual payments.[69] But the lessee is not relieved from his liability because the lessor has permitted the assignee to mine a less quantity.[70] An eviction of the tenant will relieve from liability for rent or royalties.[71] But where the lessee has taken possession of several tracts, knowing that the title to one is doubtful, from which he is subsequently evicted, he cannot defend an action for rent due upon the other tract, because of such ouster.[72]

Where the lease contains an absolute and unqualified covenant to operate, upon default of which a minimum royalty is to be paid, and the right is given to put an additional switch on the leased premises, the defendant cannot defend an action for the royalty on the ground that the railroad company refused to put in the new switch Nor can he set up that the operation would not be as profitable to him as he expected it would be, when he made his contract, having obligated himself to pay.[73]

---

[64] *Garman* v *Potts*, 135 Pa 506, 19 Atl 1071

[65] *Bannan* v *Graeff*, 186 Pa 648, 40 Atl 805

[66] *Powell* v *Burroughs*, 54 Pa 329

[67] *Bestwick* v *Ormsby Coal Co* 129 Pa 592 18 Atl 556

[68] *Fisher* v *Milliken*, 8 Pa 111, 49 Am Rep 497

[69] *Buhl* v *Thompson*, 3 Pennyp 267

[70] *Fisher* v *Milliken*, 8 Pa. 111, 49 Am Rep 497

[71] *Tiley* v *Moyers*, 43 Pa 404

[72] *Kemble Coal & I Co* v *Scott*, 15 W N C 220

[73] *Skullen* v *Logan*, 21 Pa Super. Ct. 106

820 Release from liability.— The lessee may be released from liability for the minimum royalty by the lessor. A provision relieving the lessee from liability for the minimum sum during such time as is necessary to overcome a fault relieves him upon the happening of such event, only *pro tanto.* If possible he must mine the minerals, and, if he does not, the burden is upon him to show that it was impossible.[74] In an action on a contract for the sale of a colliery, to be paid for at a certain rate per ton, on each ton of coal mined therefrom, parol evidence is admissible to prove that, at the time of the execution of the contract, it was agreed between the parties that the vendee should not be bound to mine the necessary amount of coal, and that the vendor should take the risk of his doing so, since such testimony does not contradict the written instrument [75]

821. Where more than minimum mined.— If a lease provides for the payment of royalty on all coal mined, and also for the mining of a certain number of tons, upon default in which the same are to be paid for as if mined, the covenants are distinct; and a settlement for the coal actually mined in any year is not, as a matter of law, a discharge from the liability upon the covenant to mine the specified number of tons, or to pay the royalty on the same as if mined [76] Where a minimum number of bushels is to be mined in one year, and a specified number of bushels within a longer term, the lessee may make up the deficiency of any year during the next year, except the deficiency during the last one [77] And where the lessee is to pay if the coal can be advantageously mined, and he has paid the royalty for the minimum number of tons required by the lease, which is in excess of the number of tons actually mined by him, he will be entitled to a credit on the royalty for such excess [78] Where he

---

[74] *West Ridge Coal Co* v *Von Storch,* 5 Lack Legal News, 180

[75] *Chalfant* v *Williams,* 35 Pa 212

[76] *Powell* v *Burroughs* 54 Pa 329.

[77] *Hodgson's Estate,* 158 Pa 151, 27 Atl 878

[78] *Garman* v *Potts,* 135 Pa 506, 19 Atl 1071

LAND & TEN 45

is given the right to abandon, and fails to do so, the lessee is liable for the minimum, although he has already made payment exceeding the value of all the coal originally in place.[79] And he is liable, though he has mined more in past years than the minimum requirement [80] If the contract constitutes a sale of the coal in place, the lessee remains liable as long as he holds possession, though he has already paid in previous years sums amounting in the aggregate to more than the value of all the coal at the rate fixed.[81] Where a lease of coal for a term of twenty years provided for the payment of minimum royalties, and the lessee was prevented by strikes and other circumstances from mining coal to the full extent of the minimum which he has paid, he cannot, after the lease has expired by limitation and he has taken a new lease, defalk the overpayment under the old lease from the royalties due under the new one though the conveyance was a sale of the coal in place, since the rules ordinarily applicable to sales will not be applied indiscriminately to instruments which are leases, though in fact sales in form [82]

822. Accounts.—The statement of the lessee of the amount of coal mined and the sum due is not an ordinary case of mutual settlement of accounts, but of a party making a statement of what he has done, and paying accordingly. If it be shown that the statements were false, that coal ought to have been screened and weighed which was not, the burden is on the party who did the wrong to show that the other knew the real facts when he received the statements and gave the receipts   Unless there was an actual settlement, there is no ground for the application of the rule that a statement is conclusive unless fraud or mistake be shown by clear and satisfactory evidence.[83]   So, if the state-

[79]*Buhl* v. *Thompson,* 3 Pennyp. 207

[80]*Stark* v *Scott,* 4 Luzerne Legal Reg 49.

[81]*Lehigh & W B Coal Co* v. *Wright,* 177 Pa 387, 35 Atl. 919.

[82]*Denniston* v *Haddock,* 200 Pa. 426, 50 Atl 186

[83]*Dunham* v *Haggerty,* 110 Pa. 560, 1 Atl 667.

ments are received without objection, and payments made in accordance therewith, they are not conclusive where the returns are false and fraudulent, but this the lessor must show by clear and indubitable evidence.[84] And the lessor is not estopped by his receipt of the accounts and the accepting of payments from claiming royalties for a different kind of coal, where he has objected to the accounts on the ground that such was not included.[85] If the lessor, with knowledge of all the facts, accepts the accounts and receipts in full, he can assert no further claim; but this waiver of rights by the lessor will not bind his representatives from claiming a greater sum, after his death, for coal mined after the last settlement.[86] A presumption arises in favor of the accuracy of the account, where no objection is made and the return is acquiesced in for a long period [87]

The lessee is entitled to credits for an excess paid in previous years, where he was required to pay only in case the mineral could be advantageously mined.[88] Credits cannot be allowed to a lessee who has paid for all the coal taken to a person whom he believed to be the owner of the land from which it was removed, though in fact it belonged to the grantors.[89] Ordinarily, interest is chargeable from the date at which the payment becomes due. But where the lessor frequently accepted the payments thereafter without charging interest, and finally gave a receipt in full, no recovery could be had for interest and royalties due prior to the date of the receipt [90]

823. To whom payable.— The rent or royalty is payable to the lessor or to his assignee.[91] It is no defense to an action by the lessor, that the royalty was paid to another party through

[84]*Shillingford* v *Good*, 95 Pa. 25
[85]*Lance* v *Lehigh & W B Coal Co* 163 Pa 84, 93, 25 Atl 755
[86]*Wright* v *Warrior Run Coal Co* 182 Pa 514, 38 Atl 491
[87]*Wyoming Coal & Transp Co* v. *Price*, 81 Pa. 156

[88]*Garman* v *Potts*, 135 Pa 506, 19 Atl 1071
[89]*Bestwick* v *Ormsby Coal Co* 129 Pa 592, 18 Atl 538
[90]*Waller* v *Kingston Coal Co* 191 Pa 193, 43 Atl 235
[91]*Re Hancock*, 7 Kulp, 36.

the mistake of the lessee, who believed the coal taken to be on the other's land.[92]

Where the conveyance is of all the minerals in place, thus constituting a sale, the royalty is to be treated as purchase money, and is distributable as such[93] It will pass to the executors as personalty, and not to the husband as tenant by the curtesy;[94] or to the administrator, and not to the heirs[95] But when not a sale, the rents and profits accruing after the death of the intestate belong to the heirs, and the administrators have no right, by virtue of their office, to occupy and lease the land, or receive the rents and profits accruing thereafter.[95a] Where there is a devise of the land to a tenant for life, and it appears to be the intention of the testator that the rentals shall be invested as principal, the life tenant will be entitled only to the income from such sum,[96] or if the testator has expressly declared that it shall be treated as principal[97] If no intention appears to give to the life tenant the interest alone from the rents, which is shown by the failure to provide for the investment of the sum received, he will be entitled to the entire rent, although the lessee has the right to mine until exhaustion[98] So, a devise to a wife of the testator's interest in coal, with the remainder to another, subject to the life use of the wife, entitles her to receive the royalty directly.[99] The same is true where the devise is in trust[100]

[92]*Bestwick* v *Ormsby Coal Co* 129 Pa 592, 18 Atl 538

[93]*Re Brown*, 27 Pittsb L J N S 228, *Re Hancock*, 7 Kulp, 36

[94]*Hope's Appeal*, 29 W N C 365, 33 Pittsb L J 370

[95]*Lazarus's Estate*, 145 Pa 1, 23 Atl 372, *Gardner's Estate*, 199 Pa 524, 49 Atl 346, *Re Hancock*, 7 Kulp, 36, *Maffet's Estate*, 8 Kulp, 184

[95a]*Merkel's Estate*, 131 Pa 584, 18 Atl 931

[96]*Jones* v *Strong*, 5 Kulp, 7.

[97]*Sharp's Estate*, 6 Kulp, 467

[98]*Eley's Appeal*, 103 Pa 300, *Woodburn's Estate*, 138 Pa 606, 21 Am St Rep 932, 21 Atl 16

[99]*Duffy's Estate*, 17 Pa. Super Ct 244

[100]*Shoemaker's Appeal*, 106 Pa. 392, *Smith* v *Raule*, 19 Phila 378, *Bedford's Appeal*, 126 Pa 117, 17 Atl 538, *McClintock* v *Dana*, 106 Pa 386, *Wentz's Appeal*, 106 Pa. 301.

But where the contract constitutes a sale, the income of the sum received is alone payable to the life tenant or *cestui que trust*.[101]

Where the royalties are paid to a trustee, he is entitled to commissions thereon, treating the same as corpus of the estate [102] Compensation of 1 per cent was held proper where the only duty consisted of collecting the royalties and at once distributing them,—especially where this was the custom in the mining region.[103] Though a devise of the royalties is for the use of a wife, and a trust is created by implication by the terms of the will, no trustee being nominated, the royalties will be directly payable to the life tenant without having them pass through the hands of the executor as trustee [104] If the trustee has received royalty, and is cited to file an account, he must do so, and it is no answer to the same to say that the money has been divided among the proper parties.[105]

824. Actions to recover royalties.— The county in which the land lies has jurisdiction of an action to recover the royalties due.[106] And a justice of the peace will have jurisdiction of the action, provided that such claim is within the jurisdictional amount.[107] The legal plaintiff should be the lessor.[108] And a trustee of the lessor may sue for and recover the royalty which has accrued before, as well as after, the testator's death [109] If a joint lease has been made by different owners of contiguous lots, by which the lessee agrees to pay each a proportionate share, an action may be maintained by either of the owners for his share of the rent, without a joinder of the others [110] An

[101]*Re Brown*, 27 Pittsb L J N S 228, *Blakley* v *Marshall*, 174 Pa 425, 34 Atl 564, *Marshall* v *Mellon*, 179 Pa 371, 35 L R A 816, 57 Am St Rep 601, 36 Atl 201
[102]*Thomas's Estate*, 1 Dauphin Co Rep 381
[103]*Re Dorrance*, 186 Pa 64 40 Atl 149.
[104]*Duffy's Estate*, 17 Pa Super. Ct. 244

[105]*Myers* v *Loveland*, 10 Kulp, 289
[106]*Fennell* v *Guffey*, 155 Pa 38, 25 Atl 785
[107]*Rhoades* v *Patrick*, 27 Pa 323
[108]*Bannan* v *Miller*, 6 Pa Dist R. 719
[109]*Shillingford* v *Good*, 95 Pa 25
[110]*Stark* v *Scott*, 4 Luzerne Legal Reg. 49

agreement giving the right to mine clay for a certain term, with the provision for a minimum money rate, was held to be an instrument in writing and requiring an affidavit of defense [111] (This was prior to the act of 1887). But an action on a covenant, assigning for breaches the failure of the lessee to take away any coal or to pay the lessor, was held not to be an instrument of writing for the payment of money, it not being for a sum of money for a certain amount of coal dug and taken.[112] After evidence has been heard by a master, the defendant cannot assert a new defense upon the oral argument, based on the fact that the privity of estate with the plaintiff had terminated by an assignment of the lease.[113]

825. Termination by lessee — Where the lease provides that the lessee may abandon the premises, his liability extends to the time at which the abandonment is made.[114] But a surrender of the lease, and a release of all the rights thereunder, do not terminate his liability in case possession of the premises is retained by him.[115] Where the lessee is given the right to abandon before the expiration of any year during a term, it is too late for him to terminate the same on the first day of any subsequent year. In such case his liability for the ensuing year continues.[116] The death of the lessor did not entitle the lessee to cancel his agreement, where the covenants bound his executors, administrators, and assigns, it appearing that the representatives and heirs of the lessor executed an instrument in writing to protect the lessee against dispossession until the end of the term.[117] Where the interest of the lessor under a lease which provided that he shall have coal for domestic use is sold at sher-

[111]*Johnston* v *Cowan,* 59 Pa 275
[112]*Eshelman* v *Thompson,* 62 Pa 495
[113]*Drake* v *Lacoe,* 157 Pa 17, 27 Atl 538
[114]*Buhl* v. *Thompson,* 3 Pennyp 267.
[115]*Bestwick* v *Ormsby Coal Co* 129 Pa 592, 18 Atl 538
[116]*Nesbit* v *Godfrey,* 155 Pa 251, 25 Atl 621
[117]*Lake Erie Gas Coal & C Co* v *Patterson,* 184 Pa 364, 39 Atl 68

iff's sale, the lessor will have no right of action against the lessee for such coal, whether the right be considered personal to the lessor, or as a portion of the rent which he was to receive [118] An eviction amounting to an actual expulsion of the lessee out of all or some part of the demised premises will suspend liability under the covenants of the lease [119]

826. Forfeiture.— Conditions that work forfeitures are not favorites of the law, and to make stipulations conditions, there must be a clear expression of intention. If the causes of forfeiture are specified, it is not to be inferred that there are any grounds for forfeiture not so declared; and if the lessor re-enters the premises for breach of condition, the burden is upon him, in an action of ejectment, to prove the forfeiture.[120] So, a provision for the carrying on of mining so as to do no injury to the surface, and giving the lessor the right to examine the manner in which the business is carried on, is not a condition for breach of which the lessor may enter, but a covenant, for breach of which the lessee is liable in damages [121] Where a covenant provides for forfeiture upon default, it may be enforced against the assignee of the lessee, and the lessor is under no obligation to disclose to the assignee before he purchases, that the conditions warranting a forfeiture exist.[122] So, the right to forfeit is not affected by an assignment of the lessee for the benefit of his creditors [123]

827. Time for forfeiture.— The forfeiture must be asserted within a reasonable time. Such a decree will not be entered for the lessor, after a delay of twelve years, for the nonpayment of rent.[124] But a mere delay of two years in asserting the right to

[118] *Hull* v *Delaware & H Canal Co* (Pa) 2 Cent Rep 786, 4 Atl 471.
[119] *Tiley* v *Moyers*, 43 Pa 404
[120] *McKnight* v *Kreutz*, 51 Pa. 232.
[121] *McKnight* v *Kreutz*, 51 Pa 232.
[122] *Comegys* v *Russell*, 175 Pa. 166, 34 Atl. 657.

[123] *Potter* v *Gilbert*, 177 Pa 159, 35 L R A 580, 35 Atl 597
[124] *Drake* v. *Lacoe*, 157 Pa 17, 27 Atl. 538.

forfeit for nonpayment of rent cannot be considered a waiver of the lessor's rights [125]   A stipulation giving the right to terminate the lease for nonpayment of royalty at the end of any year is to be read with a second stipulation giving the right of forfeiture if any covenant is not complied with for three months; and in such case, although rent is due at the end of the year, no forfeiture can be declared for three months thereafter.[126]   If a forfeiture can be declared in case of failure to work a mine for one year, but the lessee is given it rent free for one year in consideration of putting the same in good working order, the forfeiture cannot be enforced during the first year [127]   If the lessee or his assignee rely upon a statement of the lessor that no royalties are due, and afterwards expend time and money on the faith of such statement, the lessor will be estopped from denying its truth [128]

828. Forfeiture for failure to work.—Where the covenant provides for forfeiture for failure to operate the mine fairly or equitably, a working in good faith is all that is required [129]   If such may be done in case the mine is left idle for one year, such provision cannot be applied if coal be taken from the bank by any means of access leading to the coal.[130] Nor can there be a forfeiture where the failure to work the mine is due to the fact that the lessee is engaged in removing water, snow, and ice, so as to make it possible to reach the mineral [131]   A failure to comply with the condition to work forfeits without a re-entry by the lessor, and this is not waived by the lessee's going on the premises from time to time to clean and grease an engine.[132] Where a lessee has agreed to sell all the coal mined to another, who is to pay the expense of mining, reserving the right to forfeit for failure

[125]McKnight v Kreutz, 51 Pa 232
[126]Hoch's Appeal, 126 Pa 13, 17
Atl 512
[127]Moyers v Tiley, 32 Pa 267
[1-8]Comegys v Russell, 185 Pa 283,
39 Atl 956, 175 Pa. 166, 34 Atl 657.

[129]West Ridge Coal Co v Von
Storch, 5 Lack Legal News, 189
[130]Tiley v Moyers, 25 Pa 397
[131]Miller v Chester Slate Co 129
Pa 81, 18 Atl 565
[132]Davis v Moss, 38 Pa. 346.

to pay this expense, upon default he may so forfeit, and no action can be maintained upon a mortgage which the purchaser has given to secure the performance of his engagement [133]

829. Notice of forfeiture — Ordinarily, the lessor is bound to give notice to his lessee of an intention to forfeit because of his default. The putting of a tenant in possession upon default, without demand or notice, is not the way to enforce a forfeiture.[134] So, a demand of the amount due is a prerequisite to the enforcement of the forfeiture [135] Where the forfeiture may be for any one of several causes, the lessor should give notice of the one relied upon; and if more is demanded than is proper, the notice is ineffective [136] Where the only occasion for terminating the lease is the nonpayment of rent, the notice will be sufficient, though not explicit in stating the reasons for forfeiture,— particularly where the evidence shows no excuse for the default of the lessee.[137] Even though no notice has been given, if the premises have been abandoned by the lessee, and there has been an utter failure on his part to perform, or to offer to perform, his covenant, he cannot recover in ejectment.[138] Where the agreement is one of sale, the rights acquired thereunder to be forfeited upon failure to pay instalments on certain dates, time is of the essence of the contract, and a failure to pay any instalment will in itself work a forfeiture of the agreement [139] The effect of a notice is to disaffirm the lease, and amounts to an eviction, which will suspend the minimum royalty subsequently accruing.[140]

830. Actions to enforce. — If such provision is made in the lease, judgment may be entered by amicable confession, and such

[133]*Columbia Coal Co* v *Miller*, 78 Pa 246

[134]*Kreutz* v *McKnight*, 53 Pa 319

[135]*Wilcox* v. *Cartright*, 1 Lack Legal Record, 130

[136]*West Ridge Coal Co* v *Von Storch*, 5 Lack Legal News, 189.

[137]*Walnut Run Coal Co* v *Knight*, 201 Pa 23, 50 Atl 288

[138]*Kreutz* v *McKnight*, 53 Pa 319

[139]*Axford* v *Thomas*, 160 Pa. 8, 28 Atl 443

[140]*West Ridge Coal Co* v *Von Storch*, 5 Lack Legal News, 189

will not be opened where default appears [141] Nor will such
judgment be stricken off because of a failure to aver the cause of
the forfeiture, at the time of the entry of the judgment.[142]
Nor is it material that the lease provided for the submission of
questions in dispute to arbitrators to be chosen mutually, the
lessee having notified the lessor of his readiness to so act [143]

A court of equity will not enforce a forfeiture for a failure
to pay royalties, where the lessee is in possession, since the lessor
has an adequate remedy at law [144] But a re-entry after forfeiture will ordinarily not be restrained, where the lease provides for such by the lessor, yet if it appears that irreparable
injury will be done, the injunction may be continued until the
rights of the parties have been determined at law [145] If neither
party is free from blame, the costs of the proceeding may be divided.[146]

831. Improvements.— In determining whether personal property has become a fixture and part of the land, it is not the character of the physical connection with the realty which constitutes
the criterion of annexation, but it is the intention to annex and
identity the property with the realty.[147] Where the agreement
provides that the lessee shall have the right to abandon the land
at any time, and remove the buildings and fixtures, it is the clear
intention of the parties that the buildings and fixtures shall not
become a part of the realty, either before or after abandonment;
and this intention is not defeated by a subsequent agreement
providing for a forfeiture of the contract for nonpayment of

[141]*Beedle* v *Hilldale Min Co* 204
Pa 184, 53 Atl 764

[142]*Stroud* v *Acme Coal Co* 3 Lack
Legal News, 57

[143]*Acme Coal Co* v *Stroud*, 5 Lack
Legal News, 169

[144]*Hoch* v *Bass*, 133 Pa 328, 19
Atl 360

[145]*Grassy Island Coal Co* v *Hillside Coal & I Co* 1 Lack Jur 297,

Frisby Coal Co v *Brennan*, 1 Lack
Jur 417, *West Ridge Coal Co* v
Von Storch, 5 Lack Legal News, 189
In this case the court passed upon
all of the equities

[146]*West Ridge Coal Co* v *Von
Storch* 5 Lack Legal News, 189

[147]*Wook* v *Bredin*, 189 Pa. 83, 42
Atl. 17.

rentals, and a declaration of such forfeiture.[148] And where there is an express covenant giving the right to remove the fixtures, it is independent, and may be enforced without reference to the other parts of the agreement. For any default under the contract the lessee must be pursued through appropriate legal action, and his property cannot be taken or arbitrarily held.[149] So, where it is agreed that the improvements shall remain the property of the lessor, but the agreement excludes "mules, mine or coal cars, powder, mine rails, and tools," such may be taken at the expiration of the term, and will include a haulage system introduced by the lessee to take the place of the mules, where it appears that such a system was not in general use when the lease was made, and that its introduction was not contemplated by either party, and was such an appliance as could be removed without injury to the land, and used in another mine [150] Where the lessee is given the right to remove a colliery, evidence of those familiar with the use of the term may be given to show that it embraces all the movable property at the mines, or placed there to be used in the working of them, and that such has been the general understanding in the particular community.[151] And if the covenant provides for the giving up of the mine in a workmanlike condition, the lessee may remove a derrick used to raise coal, and which had been abandoned upon the substitution of another system. But he must preserve a shaft for ventilation, necessary for the use of the mine [152]

832. Where no covenant allowing removal.— In the absence of a special agreement as to the fixtures, a tenant may remove from demised premises fixtures erected by him thereon for the benefit of his trade or business, if the removal be made during

[148]*Wick* v *Bredin,* 189 Pa. 83, 42 Atl 17
[149]*Patterson* v *Hausbeck,* 8 Pa Atl. 236. Super. Ct 36
[150]*Beech Grove Coal & C Co* v. *Mitchell,* 193 Pa 112, 44 Atl 245
[151]*Carey* v *Bright,* 58 Pa 70
[152]*Timlin* v. *Brown,* 158 Pa 606, 28

the term,[153] or, at least, within a reasonable time thereafter.[154] Ordinarily, articles placed upon the land for the purpose of mining, whether fast or loose, and which are necessary to constitute the mine such, and without which it would not be equipped and ready for use, are a part of the freehold, and pass with the realty.[155] And where the agreement constitutes a sale of the coal in place, as well as the plant, the grantee may remove the chutes, tipple, siding, cars, and other appliances necessarily connected with the mining and transportation of the coal.[156] If the lessee has been improperly prevented from removing improvements, he may maintain an action against the lessor.[157]

833. Set-off of value — Where the lease provides for the set-off of the value of improvements made, against rent, the lessee is limited in so doing to rents accruing upon the vein leased, and cannot charge his expenditure against rent arising from the operation of other veins leased from the same lessor.[158] If the improvements are permitted to be set off, with interest, against rent, interest upon the sum expended will run from the time of making them.[159]

834. Appraisement. — Where the lease gives to the lessors the option of taking all improvements made by the lessees, at an appraisement, the lessees may remove the same in default of the exercise of this option. If they do elect to take, they must receive all or none, and are entitled to an appraisement before exercising their option to take.[160] Such a stipulation is for the

[153]*Davis* v *Moss*, 38 Pa 346
[154]*Shellar* v. *Shivers*, 171 Pa 569, 33 Atl 95, *Sattler* v *Opperman*, 14 Pa Super Ct 32, *East Shuga Loaf Coal Co* v *Wilbur*, 5 Pa Dist R 202
[155]*Ege* v *Kille*, 84 Pa 333, *Ritchie* v *McAllister*, 14 Pa Co Ct 267, *Williams's Appeal*, 1 Monaghan (Pa) 274, 16 Atl 810 See *Advance Coal Co* v *Miller*, 7 Kulp, 541.

[156]*Montooth* v. *Gamble*, 123 Pa 240 16 Atl 504
[157]*Watts* v *Lehman*, 107 Pa 106, *Patterson* v *Hausbeck*, 8 Pa Super Ct 36
[158]*Lehigh Coal & Nav Co* v *Harlan*, 27 Pa 429
[159]*Union Improv Co* v *Markle*, 191 Pa 329, 43 Atl 1103
[160]*East Shugar Loaf Coal Co* v. *Wilbur*, 5 Pa Dist R 202

benefit of the lessor, and he is under no duty to take the same at the appraisement [161] Where the lease gives the right, upon re-entry by the lessor, to sell so much of the improvements as will pay the rent, the balance to be apprai-ed and its value paid to the lessees, the lessor is not bound to so act. A bill for accounting cannot be maintained when filed a long time after, where it does not appear that the property was ever taken,—particularly when there was an adequate remedy at law.[162]

835. Improvements where the lessee is evicted.— Where one was a bona fide occupant of land, holding under a claim of title, but possession has been taken from him by an action in eject-ment, he may set off the value of such improvements of a perma-nent character as increase the value of the land, in an action for mesne profits.[163] So, if the owner permits others to lease the coal, and allows the lessee to mine the same for many years with out objection, he cannot, in an action of trespass, refuse credit for the improvements.[164] It the lessee has been evicted with-out fraud on the part of the lessor, he cannot recover from him the value of such improvements, where he had the right to re-move them, and the fact that the lessor has set off their value in an action brought by the holder of the paramount title is imma terial.[165]

[161] *Potter* v *Gilbert*, 177 Pa. 159, 35 L R A 580, 35 Atl 597

[162] *Gray* v *Catawissa R Co* 18 W. N C 9.

[163] *Lge* v. *Kille*, 84 Pa. 333.

[164] *McGowan* v *Bailey*, 179 Pa 470, 36 Atl 325

[165] *Lanigan* v *Kille*, 97 Pa 120, 39 Am. Rep. 797.

CHAPTER XXXIX.

OIL AND GAS LEASES.

836 Execution of lease.—The usual mode of creating the relationship of landlord and tenant is by an express agreement which fixes the rights and duties of the respective parties.

Since oil is a mineral, it is to be considered a part of the realty, and the guardian therefore cannot lease the land of his ward for the purpose of its development, as it would in effect be a grant of a part of the corpus of the estate. In such case the approval of the orphan's court must be obtained.[1] The lessee

[1]*Stoughton's Appeal*, 88 Pa 198

will be bound by the covenants provided for in the agreement, though the writing has never been signed and sealed by him, when he accepts the same and acts thereunder Particularly is this true where the lease is subsequently signed by him.[2] Nor can a lessee defend to an action upon the agreement on the ground that the same was not acknowledged by a married woman, as required by law, where she has in all respects complied with her contract, and has not sought to avoid the instrument, nor interfered with the defendant, or in any way or manner prevented him from operating thereunder.[3] Likewise, the objection is futile where based on the failure of the wife to join with her husband in the lease, where it was agreed that she should do so upon the presentation of the writing to her by the lessee's agent, who was never sent, and where it appeared that she was present at the negotiation, which led to the execution of the lease, and that she did not then, or afterward, object thereto[4] If the agreement has been entered into by an agent of the lessor, acting by virtue of a letter of attorney, the powers conferred must be strictly interpreted, and the authority is never to be extended beyond that which is given in terms, or that which is necessary and proper for carrying the authority so given into full effect. Whoever deals with an agent constituted for a special purpose deals at his peril, when the agent passes the precise limits of his power[5]

In proceedings arising from the agreement, the lease is ordinarily to be proved by the subscribing witness But if not directly in issue, it may be proved by the lessor without calling such witness[6] If the writing has been destroyed by the defendant's agent, in whose possession it was, it is not permissible

[2]*Carnegie Natural Gas Co v Philadelphia Co* 158 Pa 317, 27 Atl 951

[3]*Agerter v Vandergrift,* 138 Pa 593, 21 Atl 202

[4]*Kunkle v People's Natural Gas Co* 165 Pa 133, 33 L R A 847 30 Atl 719

MacDonald v O'Neil, 21 Pa. Super Ct 364

[6]*Kitchen v Smith,* 101 Pa 452

for the defendant to prove the form of a lease usually taken by him in that community, and so frequently taken that a book was prepared by the recorder of deeds with the form offered printed therein.[7]

The contract to drill a well may properly be proved by parol, the statute of frauds having no bearing [8]

837. Fraud — Where the agreement has been induced by the fraudulent representations of the lessor, the agreement may be set aside, or a defense made to an action upon the covenants therein, or to actions upon promissory notes given as a result thereof.[9] Or a judgment given as collateral security therefor may be opened [10] Or in an action of ejectment [11] And this defense for fraudulent misrepresentation may be made to subsequent notes given, though some have been paid without objection.[12] Where the lessee has been imposed upon by the fraud of the lessor, he may rescind the lease and recover the purchase price, or he may elect to retain the lease and recover the damage which he has sustained.[13] Or an action will lie for damages in falsely representing that a well transferred had not been torpedoed [14] Though it was held admissible in such case for the defendant to show that one torpedo had been used, though it was not effective.[15]

So the vendor may ask for the cancelation of the transfer where fraudulently secured But it is not ground to so order where there was a mere failure to inform the vendor that oil had been found on adjoining land.[16]

[7]*Morris* v *Guffey,* 188 Pa 534, 11 Atl 731

[8]*Haight* v *Conners,* 149 Pa 297, 24 Atl 302

[9]*Weirel* v *Lennox,* 179 Pa 457 36 Atl 229

[10]*Weixel* v *Lennox,* 179 Pa 459, 36 Atl 248

[11]*Christie* v *Blakeley,* 2 Monaghan (Pa) 118, 15 Atl 874.

[12]*Smolley* v *Morris,* 157 Pa 340, 27 Atl 734

[13]*Guffey* v *Clever,* 146 Pa 548, 23 Atl 161

[14]*Verboch* v *Davis,* 3 Walk (Pa) 176

[15]*Verbach* v *Davis,* 3 Walk (Pa) 176

[16]*Neill* v *Shamburg,* 158 Pa 263, 27 Atl 992

Or an action for damages may be maintained for breach of a contract to purchase an interest in an oil lease; but if there is no evidence of fraud or bad faith, or of actual damage incurred, and no resale of the lease or tender of deed by the vendors, no more than nominal damage can be recovered, for the vendors cannot retain the property and recover part or all of the price [17]

838. Description of premises.— The description of the premises as set forth in the lease must control Where a clause appears, providing that no well shall be drilled within a limited area, this constitutes neither an exception nor a reservation. but simply a limitation upon the privilege of drilling granted to the lessee, confining his drilling within the area specified [18] Where such a limitation appears in the deed, no right to drill for oil within such boundaries exists Thus where land "surrounding farm buildings and marked by stakes" was reserved [19] Or all land within a township was leased, excepting a specified strip.[20] Or reserving a protection 8 rods on the north and 10 rods on the east, by which was meant the land included within the lines where they intersected [21] Or where no wells were to be drilled within 300 yards of the brick or stone building belonging to the lessor [22] Or where the lease restricted the operations to certain specified sites [23] Or where a town lot was conveyed by deed, it being provided in the habendum that the vendee should have no right to drill or mine for oil thereon [24]

When the grantor retains a part of a thing, and does not create a new right or interest, it is an exception, and not a reservation, and can only refer to the part which was the property of

[17]*Carner* v *Johnston,* 9 Pa Super Ct. 29

[18]*Westmoreland & C Natural Gas Co* v *DeWitt,* 130 Pa 235, 5 L R A. 731, 25 W N C 103, 18 Atl 724

[19]*Lynch* v *Burford,* 201 Pa 52, 50 Atl 228

[20]*Funk* v *Haldeman,* 53 Pa 229.

[21]*Allison's Appeal,* 77 Pa 221

[22]*Westmoreland & C Natural Gas Co* v *DeWitt,* 130 Pa 235, 5 L R A 731, 25 W N C 103, 18 Atl 724

[23]*Duffield* v *Hue,* 136 Pa 602, 20 Atl 526, *Duffield* v *Rosenzweig,* 144 Pa 520, 23 Atl 4

[24]*Acheson* v *Stevenson,* 146 Pa 228, 23 Atl 331, 396.

the grantor, and not to the entire thing or interest. So where the owner of a half interest conveyed the same subject to the right to a fourth of the oil, and then leased his remaining interest for an eighth of the oil produced, his interest is to be measured by a thirty-second of the oil produced on the half interest, and not a sixty-fourth of the oil produced on the whole premises.[25]

839. Options to lease or explore.—"An option is the right of choice, election, or selection; not a right in or to the thing, but the right to acquire it, or an interest in it on certain conditions. Not until the owner of an option elects to accept and enforce its terms does it become binding upon him.   Ordinarily (and in the present case), the grantor of an option has no power to compel the grantee to accept the right or privilege conferred or reserved; this remains wholly within the discretion of the grantee."[26]   So an offer to buy or sell, without more, is an offer in the present, to be accepted or refused when made, until this is done it may be withdrawn, and a subsequent acceptance will be of no avail. As the interest in an oil and gas leasehold is liable to sudden changes in value, time is of the highest importance in dealing with it and presumably the essence of all contracts in relation thereto.[27]   So where the option has been given to the lessee to take the remainder of the lessor's lands, provided terms can be agreed upon, in case the first exploration is successful, the offer of the lessor must be accepted immediately or the rights of the lessee will be forfeited.[28]

The oil and gas lease usually provides for the payment of a bonus to the lessor with a covenant on the part of the lessee to complete a well within a certain period, with the right to the les-

---

[25] *Ewing* v. *Fertig*, 9 Pa Dist R 756, 24 Pa Co Ct 301

[26] *Wiles* v *People's Gas Co* 7 Pa Super Ct 562   In this case a mechanic's lien had been filed against the interest of the alleged lessee, and the question arose as to whether or not any such interest existed

[27] *Vincent* v *Woodland Oil Co* 165 Pa 402. 30 Atl 991, *Kelly* v *Marshall*, 172 Pa 396, 33 Atl 690

[28] *Childs* v *Gillespie*, 147 Pa. 173, 23 Atl 312.

see to extend the period by the payment of a specified rental, otherwise the lease to be null and void   Such contracts give to the grantee the right to explore, and if no product is found after a well is drilled his obligation to continue ceases.[29]   But if the lessee has contracted to drill two wells, and abandons work because the first is a failure, he is not excused from liability.[30]   If no exploration is made, the lessee cannot consider the lease as forfeited, so as to relieve himself from the obligations imposed thereunder, without an express stipulation to that effect, for the reason that the option to forfeit is inserted for the benefit of the lessor, and must therefore be asserted by him.[31]   So where the option is "to drill a well or not or pay said rental or not as he may elect," the lessee is bound either to drill a well and pay no rental, or pay a rental and drill no well.[32]   But if there is no implied covenant on the part of the lessee to drill the well, then he may abandon at his option without liability.[33]

840. Successive leases.— The lessee is bound to take notice of a prior recorded lease, and the interest acquired by him is subject thereto, but, though a prior lease be outstanding, a subsequent lessee without notice will acquire a better title [34]   And where oil lands are leased with a term apparently outstanding, it is his duty to make inquiry of the prior lessee as to the facts as they exist.   If an abandonment by the first lessee is alleged, the risk of showing it is taken by the subsequent lessee, and the question of the intention is for the jury.[35]   Where notice of the

[29]*McKee* v *Colwell,* 7 Pa Super Ct 607, *McNish* v *Stone,* 152 Pa 457 note, *Cassell* v *Crothers,* 193 Pa 359, 44 Atl 446

[30]*Ahrns* v *Chartiers Valley Gas Co* 188 Pa 249, 41 Atl 739

[31]*Wills* v *Manufacturers' Natural Gas Co* 130 Pa 222, 5 L R A 603, 18 Atl 721, *Galey Bros* v *Kellerman,* 123 Pa 491, 16 Atl 474, *Ray* v *Western Pennsylvania Natural Gas Co* 138 Pa 576, 12 L. R. A. 290.

21 Am St Rep. 922, 20 Atl 1065, *Cochran* v *Pew,* 159 Pa 184, 28 Atl 219

[32]*McMillan* v *Philadelphia Co* 159 Pa 142, 28 Atl 220

[33]*Glasgow* v *Chartiers Oil Co* 152 Pa 48, 25 Atl 232

[34]*Aye* v *Philadelphia Co* 193 Pa. 457, 44 Atl 556

[35]*Bartley* v *Phillips,* 179 Pa. 175, 36 Atl 217.

outstanding title has been received the second lessee takes subject thereto   Thus a recital in a deed is notice to the purchaser
or lessee of the prior grant; and the mere declaration by the committee of a lunatic, that he has no interest in the land conveyed
to him by the unrecorded deed, cannot operate to deprive the
lunatic of his interest in the land in favor of the subsequent purchaser to whom the declaration was made.[36]   So the second lessee was held to be affected by the notice of the earlier lease
received by his law partner[37]   And knowledge on his part is
shown by his agreement with the lessor to protect him against
other claimants[38]   But no duty to inquire arises from the fact
that a well is being drilled on an adjoining farm, though in fact
such was being done by the first lessee in compliance with his
agreement with the lessor[39]

Though there be notice of the prior lease yet, if the same has
been abandoned, or a forfeiture declaied, or for other reasons it
is null and void, the second lessee will secure a good title,—thus,
where the first lease was abandoned,[40] or was forfeited,[41] or
was void because of improper execution of the instrument;[42] or
where one is in possession of the premises claiming the land as a
gift, when it can be shown that no such gift was executed[43]

841. Nature of oil and gas— Oil is a mineral substance obtained from the earth by a process of mining, and lands from
which it is obtained may with propriety be called mining
lands[44]   It is a mineral and being a mineral is part of the
realty.   In this it is like coal or any other mineral product,

[36]*Jennings* v *Bloomfield,* 199 Pa
638, 49 Atl 135, 204 Pa 123, 53 Atl
1127
[37]*Thompson* v *Christie,* 138 Pa
230, 11 L R A 236, 20 Atl 934
[38]*Stone* v *Marshall Oil Co* 188 Pa.
602, 41 Atl 748, 1119
[39]*Aye* v *Philadelphia Co* 193 Pa
457, 44 Atl 556
[40]*Bartley* v *Phillips,* 119 Pa 175,
36 Atl 217.

[41]*Jones* v *Stowell,* 42 Phila Leg
Int 92
[42]*Ibid; Enterprise Transit Co's
Appeal,* 9 W. N C 225
[43]*Kennedy* v *Forest Oil Co* 199 Pa.
644, 49 Atl 133
[44]*Gill* v *Weston,* 110 Pa 312, 1
Atl. 921.

which *in situ* formed part of the land [45] So gas is a mineral, but it is a mineral with peculiar attributes [46] Leases for oil and gas purposes are therefore in legal effect sales of a portion of the land.[47] Such being the case, life tenants have no right to lease the realty for oil and gas purposes, where no such operations have been commenced on the land before the estate for life has accrued. If such is done the lease cannot be enforced.[48] But the life tenants and the remaindermen may join as lessors, in which case the life tenants are entitled to the interest on the royalties during life, and at their death the corpus of the fund, made up of the aggregate royalties, goes to the remaindermen [49] Being practically a sale of the realty, the guardian cannot lease for such purposes without the consent of the orphans' court [50]

842. Interest conveyed by lease.— In determining the interest acquired by the lessee, the terms of the particular agreement must be considered Thus where the lease gave the right to mine "petroleum, rock, or carbon oil, or other valuable volatile substances," the question was for the jury to determine whether natural gas was included [51] So where the lease contemplated the mining for salt, and as a result oil was produced, which was separated and sold, the lessee could be compelled by bill in equity to account, though trover could not be maintained, since there was no right to possession in the lessor [52] So gas cannot be taken under a lease for oil [53] As has already been noticed a reservation may be made as to portions of the land upon which

"*Stoughton's Appeal*, 88 Pa 198, *Blakley* v *Marshall*, 174 Pa 425, 34 Atl 564

"Westmoreland & C Natural Gas Co v *DeWitt*, 130 Pa. 235 5 L R A 731, 25 W N C 103, 18 Atl 724

"*Blakley* v *Marshall*, 174 Pa 425, 34 Atl 564, *Marshall* v *Mellon*, 179 Pa 371, 35 L R A 816, 57 Am St Rep 601, 36 Atl 201 *Jennings* v *Bloomfield*, 199 Pa 638, 49 Atl 135, *Ridgway Light & Heat Co* v *Elk County*, 191 Pa 465, 43 Atl 323.

"Marshall v *Mellon*, 179 Pa 371, 35 L R A 816, 57 Am St Rep 601, 36 Atl 201

"Blakley v *Marshall* 174 Pa 425. 34 Atl 564 The so called lease was a sale of the oil and gas

"*Stoughton's Appeal* 88 Pa 198 ¹*Ford* v *Buchanan*, 111 Pa 31, 2 Atl 339

²*Kier* v *Peterson*, 41 Pa 357 ³*Kitchen* v *Smith*, 101 Pa 452

the lessee should have the right to drill wells   In case such a
provision appears, the lessee is bound thereby, and the rights of
the lessor will be protected by injunction.   But where land has
been conveyed with a restriction against the drilling of oil wells,
the vendor is not entitled to an accounting for the oil produced,
though he may restrain the erection which will operate to the
detriment of other property [54]

843. Interest retained by lessor —The same principle applies
to reservations made by a grantor, such however being construed
most strongly against him   Thus a reservation of "all minerals" does not include petroleum oil, and the grantors are liable
if they enter and take the same [55]   So where the conveyance reserved the oil and gas with the right of the grantor to enter upon
the land to secure the same, compensation however to be made
for the land used in and the damages caused by the mining operations, the reservation will be held to refer to the right to mine
for oil and gas, and not the coal, iron, or other substances not
named [56]

It has been said by reason of the vagrant character of oil and
gas, that a lease of these substances partakes of the character of
a lease for general tillage, rather than that of a lease for mining
or quarrying the solid materials,[57] that the estate in the lessee
was separate and independent from the estate in the owners of
the land.   The one was personal,—an estate for years; the other
was real,—a fee simple.[58]   Therefore where three tracts of land
were subject to the same oil and gas lease, and were devised respectively to the owner's three children, the royalties accruing
under the lease were divisible among the three devisees, although

[54]*Acheson* v *Stevenson*, 146 Pa
228, 23 Atl 331, 396
[55]*Dunham* v *Kirkpatrick*, 101 Pa
36, 477 Am Rep 696
[56]*Moody* v *Alexander*, 145 Pa 571,
23 Atl 161   The first hearing of this
case is to be found in 20 W N C.
283.

[57]*Wettengel* v *Gormley*, 160 Pa
559, 40 Am St Rep 733, 28 Atl.
934
[58]*Wettengel* v *Gormley*, 184 Pa
364, 39 Atl 1118, *Hanna* v *Clark*,
204 Pa 149, 53 Atl 758

all the wells were sunk on one only of the three tracts [59] And each child was entitled to receive such share of the total royalty as his or her share of the land bore to the whole tract covered by the lease. But the child upon whose land the wells were sunk was entitled to compensation for the decrease in the rental value of his part, caused by the presence of the wells.[60] The cost of repairing the injury to the realty caused by the sinking of the wells must be postponed until the termination of the lease, since that subject could not be intelligently considered until then [61] The lessor is bound to pay the taxes assessed upon the property unless otherwise agreed In case the lessee is compelled to do so he may recover from him [62]

844. Estate acquired.—A lease for oil and gas purposes is in legal effect a sale of a portion of the land.[63] The leasehold for a definite term of years is a chattel real [64] As such it is to be treated as an asset of a partnership, so as to be subject to its indebtedness [65] And is to be seized on execution and held only as real estate [66] But it is a chattel real in possession, and is not subject to the lien of a judgment,[67] as such is subject to the mechanic's lien law,[68] and to a lien for labor under the act of April 8, 1868 [69] By the act of April 27, 1855, P. L. 369, the leasehold may be mortgaged.[70] When the lease is executed, by which power is conferred upon the lessee to experiment for oil

[59]*Wettengel* v *Gormley*, 160 Pa 559, 40 Am St Rep 733, 28 Atl. 934

[60]*Wettengel* v. *Gormley*, 184 Pa. 354

[61]*Ibid*

[62]*Kitchen* v *Smith*, 101 Pa 452

[63]*Stoughton's Appeal*, 88 Pa 198, *Jennings* v *Bloomfield*, 199 Pa 638, 49 Atl 135

[64]*Duffield* v *Hue*, 129 Pa. 94, 18 Atl 566

[65]*Brown* v *Beecher*, 120 Pa 590, 15 Atl 608, *Chamberlain* v. *Dow*, 16 W. N. C 532

[66]*Titusville Novelty Iron Works' Appeal*, 77 Pa 103

[67]*Lefever* v *Armstrong*, 15 Pa Super Ct 565

[68]*McElvaine* v *Brown* (Pa) 9 Cent Rep 789, 11 Atl 453, *James Smith Woolen Mach Co* v *Browne*, 206 Pa 543, 56 Atl 43, *Wettling* v *Kelly*, 25 Pa Co Ct 33. See act June 4, 1901, P L 431

[69]*Harley* v *O'Donnell*, 9 Pa Co Ct. 56

[70]*Gill* v *Weston*, 110 Pa 305, 1 Atl 917.

or gas, the title is inchoate until oil or gas is found, in which case it becomes vested [71]

Since an estate vests in the lessee for years, such lessee is entitled to notice of a partition of the owners of the fee, whether such partition be by action at law or by amicable agreement, and the lessee will not be bound by such partition, if it divides the land to his injury, unless he has had notice thereof or been made a party thereto [72]

845 License — Where the grant is of the free and uninterrupted privilege to go upon land for prospecting, boring, and taking of oil from the earth, an incorporeal hereditament in fee is granted. It is a license merely to work the land for minerals, but it is not a mere permission conferred, revocable at the pleasure of the licensor. It gives to the grantee an estate which may be assigned to a third party. Even a parol license without consideration, on the faith of which the grantee expends money, cannot be revoked at the pleasure of the grantor, but will be enforced in equity.[73] But where the license is a personal one, it cannot be assigned, and such action by the licensee acts as a forfeiture.[74] The licensor may maintain ejectment against the licensee, if the land be used for other purposes than those contemplated, or if used to a greater extent than allowed, or when revocable, no improvements having been made as a result of it.[75] Such a license gives to the licensee the right to such possession as is necessary for the exercise of the privilege [76]

846 Tenants in common.— Where a lease is made to joint

[71]*Calhoon* v *Neely*, 201 Pa 97, 50 Atl 967, *Venture Oil Co* v *Fretts*, 152 Pa 451, 25 Atl 732, *McCarty* v *Mellon*, 5 Pa Dist R 425, *Barnhart* v *Lockwood*, 152 Pa 82

[72]*Duke* v *Hague*, 107 Pa 57 In *Hanna* v *Clark*, 204 Pa 149, 53 Atl 758 partition of oil under the land was refused where it appeared that the lands were subject to oil leases previously made and still in effect

[73]*Funk* v *Haldeman*, 53 Pa 229, *Dark* v *Johnston*, 55 Pa 164, 93 Am Dec 732

[74]*Dark* v *Johnston*, 55 Pa 164, 93 Am Dec 732

[75]*Rynd* v *Rynd Farm Oil Co* 63 Pa 397

[76]*Union Petroleum Co* v *Bliven Petroleum Co* 72 Pa 173.

lessees, they become joint grantees of the privilege conferred, and are jointly obliged to perform the covenants of the lease [77] When tenants in common jointly operate an oil well, no presumption of existence of partnership between them arises.[78] The lessor and the lessee are not to be considered tenants in common, and the lessor is entitled to the share of the product reserved by the lease without a deduction of a proportion of the expenditure necessarily made.[79]

847 Interest of lessee after termination of work — Where there is no covenant, express or implied, to develop land, the lease may be terminated by either the lessor or the lessee [80] But as has been noticed the provision for forfeiture for failure to comply with stipulations of the lease is ordinarily for the benefit of the lessor, and the forfeiture is at his option.

The lease may be terminated at the option of either party after the required exploration has been made and it becomes apparent that oil cannot be produced profitably.[81] Until this right is exercised, the lessee holds as a tenant at will.[82]

848 Exclusiveness of lessee's right.—Whether the lessee acquires the exclusive right to drill for oil is a question of the intention of the parties to be derived from their agreement [83] The grant of "all" of the oil was held to give such privilege [84] In *Rynd* v. *Rynd Farm Oil Co.*[85] the word "exclusive" was used in the lease, but the question as to the extent of the power conferred was not decided. In case the exclusive right is given, the lessor is also precluded from taking oil from the land leased [86] But

[77]*Hooks* v *Forst*, 165 Pa 238, 30 Atl 846

[78]*Neill* v *Shamburg*, 158 Pa 263, 27 Atl 992

[79]*Union Oil Co's Appeal*, 3 Pennyp 504

[80]*Glasgow* v *Chartiers Oil Co* 152 Pa 48, 25 Atl 232

[81]*McNish* v *Stone*, 152 Pa 457, note. *McKee* v *Colwell*, 7 Pa Super Ct 607.

[82]*Cassell* v *Crothers*, 193 Pa 359, 44 Atl 446

[83]*Funk* v *Haldeman*, 53 Pa 229

[84]*Westmoreland & C Natural Gas Co* v *DeWitt* 130 Pa 235, 5 L R A 731, 25 W N C 103, 18 Atl 724

[85] 63 Pa 397

[86]*Union Petroleum Co* v *Bliven Petroleum Co* 72 Pa 173

he may bore for oil on land which he has reserved from the operation of the lease.[87]   The exclusive right to produce the oil carries with it as well the privilege to use such land as is necessary for the proper enjoyment of the lease [88]

849. Construction of agreements —"The rule in regard to contracts is that where the parties have expressly agreed on what shall be done there is no room for the implication of anything not so stipulated for, and this rule is equally applicable to oil and gas leases as to other contracts   There is nothing peculiar about them in this respect."[89]   Where there is no latent ambiguity involved, the construction of the contract is for the court [90] But the court will not construe a written contract where the parts in dispute are expressed in words that have no well-defined meaning. Such words create an ambiguity and their construction becomes a mixed question of law and fact in which the court, if the facts are undisputed, and otherwise the jury, must have the aid of competent witnesses.[91]   Where the evidence is conflicting the question must be submitted to the jury.[92]   So where evidence is submitted to show an abandonment, the question should be passed upon by it,[93] or the determination of the question as to whether gas is included under the terms "volatile substances,"[94] or whether sufficient gas was produced to furnish the lessee gas in sufficient quantities to operate the lease, where the agreement provided that in such case the lessor should be entitled to a portion of the product for domestic purposes [95] Or where the contract provided for the casing of the well, and

[87]*Guffey* v *Deeds,* 9 Pa Co Ct. 449

[88]*Bronson* v *Lane,* 91 Pa 153

[89]*Aye* v *Philadelphia Co* 193 Pa 451, 74 Am St. Rep 696, 44 Atl 555

[90]*Duffield* v *Hue,* 129 Pa 94, 18 Atl 566

[91]*Ford* v *Buchanan,* 111 Pa. 31, 2 Atl. 339

[92]*Prindle & Co* v *Kountz Bros Co.* 15 Pa Super Ct 258

[93]*Aye* v *Philadelphia Co* 193 Pa. 451, 74 Am St Rep 696, 44 Atl 555, *Bartley* v *Phillips,* 165 Pa 325 30 Atl 842, 179 Pa 175, 36 Atl 217

[94]*Ford* v *Buchanan,* 111 Pa 31, 2 Atl 339

[95]*Fanker* v *Anderson,* 173 Pa 86, 34 Atl 434

the shutting off of water above any gas-bearing sand before drilling it, and after passing the last known gas-bearing sand the driller was to go to the contract depth, and if new sand were found, to recase the well, the question was for the jury to find whether the last known gas-bearing sand had been passed when the plaintiff ceased to drill, because of the refusal of the defendant to pay for the work unless the well below was cased, water having come in.[96]

850. Meaning of words.— Where a contract is partly printed and partly written, the written words are entitled to have greater effect given them in the interpretation of the contract, than those which are printed, for the written words are the terms selected by the parties themselves to express their meaning in the particular case [97] Words are to be taken in their legal meaning [98] And it is incompetent to show the uniform construction placed upon such leases by lessors and lessees, since such is a mere offer to reform an instrument upon evidence of popular error as to the law [99] If the words have no fixed technical meaning they should be taken in their natural and obvious sense, and where capable of two meanings, the term used is to be most strongly construed against him whose undertaking it is. Circumstances surrounding the parties when the contract is made, and affecting the subject to which it relates, form a sort of context that may be resorted to in doubtful cases to aid at arriving at the proper interpretation.[100] The contract should be considered as a whole, and the meaning given by the parties should be examined.[101] It is not admissible to show that one of the parties believed that a clause inserted meant a certain thing, since such is not a con-

[96]*Prindle & Co v Kountz Bros Co* 15 Pa Super Ct 258

[97]*Duffield* v *Hue*, 129 Pa 94, 18 Atl 566

[98]*Cochran* v *Shenango Natural Gas Co* 23 Pittsb L J N S 82

[99]*Jones* v *Western Pennsylvania Natural Gas Co* 146 Pa 204, 23 Atl. 386

[100]*Jamestown & F R Co* v. *Egbert*, 152 Pa 53, 25 Atl 151

[101]*Smith* v. *Hickman*, 14 Pa Super Ct. 46.

temporaneous agreement nor such mistake as to furnish ground for reformation or relief to the parties who inserted it.[102] The trade meaning or understanding of a technical term used in a contract between the parties engaged in a particular business may be shown by parol testimony, thus, where the phrase was, "a complete carpenter's rig of good quality," and an "outfit of drilling tools and lines"[103] The question of what is meant by "due diligence" in a lease may be shown by parol proof as to the understanding and agreement of the parties[104] So, where the lease provides for operation "as much longer as oil or gas is found in paying quantities," the meaning given by the parties must be considered So long as the wells drilled by the lessee continue to supply oil and gas in paying quantities the lease remains in force[105] A custom showing what is meant by "paying quantities" cannot be proven without offering to show in what oil producing country the custom controls, and that the usage was known to the plaintiff, or was so notorious that he was bound to be aware of it In any case the custom must appear to be certain, uniform, and notorious[106] If the gas is to be produced in paying quantities, it is immaterial whether such comes from an oil or from a gas well, the lease giving the right to drill for both[107] A lease containing a covenant to drill a well when the contract is assigned does not bind the covenantor until such transfer is made[108] Where the lease gives to the lessor a right to an attachment to secure gas for his own purpose, if sufficient for both parties, his right is confined to a well drilled on his own land, and he is not entitled to attach a pipe to a line which conveys gas from his well in common with others. It is immaterial

[102]*Cochran* v *Pew*, 159 Pa 184. 28 Atl 219

[104]*Glenn* v *Strickland*, 21 Pa Super Ct 88

[105]*Bartley* v *Phillips*, 165 Pa 325, 30 Atl 812

[106]*Smith* v *Hickman*, 14 Pa Super. Ct 46.

[103]*Collins* v *Mechling*, 1 Pa Super Ct 594

[107]*Burton* v *Forest Oil Co* 204 Pa 349, 54 Atl 266

[108]*Knupp* v. *Bright*, 186 Pa 181, 40 Atl 414.

in such case that originally he had been permitted to do so but, after notice, the pipe had been disconnected [109] A privilege to take gas for a mill, as now erected or built, is not lost by the changing of the building from an old fashioned mill to a new process one, provided no more gas is taken [110]

851. Understanding of the parties.—A certain, uniform, and notorious custom fixing the meaning of a specified word may be proven where the usage was known to the plaintiff or was so notorious that he may be held to be aware of it [111] So, though the legal meaning of words will usually control, yet a different understanding between the parties may be shown.[112] Parol evidence is receivable, in order to ascertain the nature and peculiar qualities of the subject-matter, and to show the situation of the parties.[113] And the circumstances surrounding the parties and affecting the contract may be resorted to in doubtful cases to aid in arriving at the true meaning.[114] So the evidence of experts is admissible to aid in the interpretation of the contract, though not to change, modify, or contradict the writing [115] But, if the meaning is not doubtful, parol evidence is not admissible [116] An alleged oral understanding can only affect the parties thereto, and not the assignee of the lease who took without knowledge of the arrangement.[117] If the lessee alleges a contemporaneous parol agreement, his evidence must be clear and precise [118] And the lease will not be reformed when the essential facts are testified to by one and denied by the other.[119] It is not

---

[109]*Pearce* v *Bridgewater Gas Co* 28 Pittsb L J N S 171

[110]*Pearce* v *Bridgewater Gas Co* 28 Pittsb L J N S 171

[111]*Collins* v *Mechling,* 1 Pa Super Ct 594

[112]*Cochran* v *Shenango Natural Gas Co* 23 Pittsb L J N S 82

[113]*Duffield* v *Hue,* 129 Pa 94, 18 Atl 566

[114]*Jamestown & F R Co* v *Egbert,* 152 Pa 53, 25 Atl 151.

[115]*Douthett* v *Ft Pitt Gas Co* 202 Pa 416.

[116]*Burton* v *Forest Oil Co* 204 Pa 349, 54 Atl 266

[117]*Springer* v *Citizens' Natural Gas Co* 145 Pa 430, 22 Atl 986, *Thompson* v *Christie,* 138 Pa 230 11 L R A 236, 20 Atl 934

[118]*Sanders* v *Sharp,* 153 Pa 555 25 Atl 524

[119]*Thompson* v *Christie,* 138 Pa 230, 11 L R A 236, 20 Atl 934

sufficient to show that the lessee, who signed individually, was acting as the agent of a proposed corporation, or of persons about to organize as such, unless he can show fraud, misrepresentation, or mistake [120] Nor in the absence of such proof that lands, not embraced in the description, were intended to be included [121]

852 Alteration.— It may be shown by parol that a second lease was made as a substitute for a former lease [122] Or a subsequent parol agreement may be proven by which the obligations of the lessee are changed, and the extent of the change intended may be shown.[123] Thus the lessee may prove that the rental provided for in the lease was waived in consideration of receiving gas from the well for domestic purposes [124] But where the lessor has agreed to reduce the rental to a certain amount, and the offer is refused by the lessee, the latter's liability is not decreased.[125] When a parol agreement changes or adds to a previously executed contract under seal and subsequently made, the whole becomes parol, and the remedy for a breach is assumpsit, and not covenant.[126]

853. Where lease lost.— Where the lease has been lost or destroyed its contents may be proven by parol. But where the destruction was by the defendant's agent, it was held to be improper to admit the form of a lease usually used by the defendant in that community, and the fact that he took many leases in that form, under an arrangement with the recorder of deeds, who had the same printed in his lease book, is immaterial [127]

854. Remedy for interference —*a By injunction.*—The lessee is entitled to protection against interference, while in possession

[120]*Ibid*

[121]*Duffield* v *Hue*, 129 Pa 94, 18 Atl 566

[122]*Vanderlin* v *Hous*, 152 Pa 11, 25 Atl 232

[123]*Hunter* v *Apollo Oil & Gas Co* 204 Pa 385, 54 Atl 274

[124]*Cranford* v *Bellevue & G Nat-* ural *Gas Co* 183 Pa 227, 38 Atl. 595

[125]*McClane* v *People's Light & Heat Co* 178 Pa 424 35 Atl 812

[126]*Stoddard* v *Emery*, 128 Pa 436, 18 Atl 339

[127]*Morris* v *Guffey*, 188 Pa 534, 41 Atl 731

of the leased premises, whether the same be by the lessor or by third parties The aid of the court may be secured by injunction where the bill shows actual possession in the plaintiff for a definite period, and prays that the defendant be restrained from the commission of a continuing trespass and the perpetration of wrongs alleged to be irreparable. In such case the bill should not be dismissed on answer and replication.[128] So the lessor may be enjoined from continued interference, a re-entry having been made in assertion of a disputed claim that the lessee had forfeited his rights.[129] And damages may be awarded against the lessor for the injury sustained, without prejudice to his rights to a share of the royalties[130] And he may be restrained from erecting works which would inconvenience the operation of the lessee and result in the destruction of his pipe line,[131] or from interfering with the agents of the lessee by ordering them from the land[132] Likewise the lessor will be restrained from drilling on land reserved and thereby injuring the wells of the lessee, and damages may be assessed for the injuries sustained[133] So the lessee of the land for farm purposes, who took with knowledge of the existence of the oil and gas lease, will be restrained from interference with the operation of it.[134]

The lessor may also invoke the aid of the court of equity to protect his rights, thus, where land was transferred under an agreement that no well for oil should be drilled thereon[135] And the lessee may be restrained from drilling beyond the "100 ft. sand," without testing it by shooting, where there are indications

[128]*Greensboro Natural Gas Co* v *Fayette County Gas Co* 200 Pa 388, 49 Atl 768

[129]*Poterie Gas Co* v *Poterie,* 153 Pa 10 25 Atl 1107

[130]*Poterie Gas Co* v *Poterie,* 179 Pa 68, 36 Atl 232

[131]*Consumers Heating Co* v *American Land Co* 31 Pittsb L J N S 24

[132]*Westmoreland & C Natural Gas*

Co v *DeWitt,* 130 Pa 235, 5 L R. A 731, 25 W N. C 103, 18 Atl. 724

[133]*Allison's Appeal* 77 Pa 221; *Duffield* v *Rosenzweig,* 144 Pa 520, 23 Atl 4

[134]*Snyder* v *Brown,* 197 Pa 450, 47 Atl 1135

[135]*Acheson* v *Stevenson* 146 Pa. 228, 23 Atl 331, 396

of the presence of oil, where the evidence shows that oil was found in this particular stratum of sand, if found at all, and it not being made to appear that such treatment would seriously jeopardize the further drilling of the well in case oil was not found.[136] But an injunction will not be granted to compel the burying of the pipe line as required by the lease, when the lessor has never demanded that such be done, and the tenants of the surface have been compensated for the injury sustained.[137] Equity has jurisdiction in a contest over the right to operate land for oil, where the lease under which the right is claimed does not grant a conveyance in fee, but merely an incorporeal hereditament.[138] But where the purpose of the bill is to secure a declaration of forfeiture of the lease, the action being possessory, the court will not interfere, the proceeding being an ejectment bill.[139] And the fact that prayers have been added asking for an account, will not change the rule, since such is incidental to the disputed title.[140] Since lack of jurisdiction may be taken advantage of at any time, so this objection may be.[141] Where a bill has been filed to declare a forfeiture of the lease, and the decree is in favor of the defendant, no relief can be granted to him in such decree in the absence of a cross-bill.[142]

A decree is bad when based upon a bill to declare a forfeiture, or to compel performance of covenants, when filed against the lessee and a large number of assignees and the judgment is entered against all without respect to the various interests.[143] Where the purpose of the bill is to secure performance of a covenant to drill additional wells, a decree may be entered declaring

---

[136]*Douthett* v *Ft Pitt Gas Co* 202 Pa 416

[137]*Pearce* v *Bridgewater Gas Co* 28 Pittsb L J N S 171

[138] *Carnegie Natural Gas Co* v *Philadelphia Co* 158 Pa 317, 27 Atl 951

[139]*Thomas* v *Hukill*, 131 Pa 298, 18 Atl 875, *Poterie Gas Co* v. *Poterie*, 153 Pa 13, 25 Atl 1107

[140]*Williams* v *Fowler*, 201 Pa 336, 50 Atl 969

[141]*Williams* v *Fowler*, 201 Pa 336, 50 Atl 969

[142]*Freeland* v *South Penn Oil Co* 189 Pa 54, 41 Atl 1000

[143]*Young* v *Forest Oil Co* 194 Pa. 243, 45 Atl 121

the leasehold abandoned, except as to the well already drilled and the space around necessary for its operation [144]

On appeal from a decree of the lower court awarding a preliminary injunction, the appellate court will not examine the merits of the case unless it appears that great injustice has been done [145]

b. By action of trespass —In an action of trespass for injuries sustained by the lessee through the lessor's interference with the operations, actual possession need not be shown.[146] But there must be actual or constructive possession. Where the land is improved this must be shown. But if not, then it follows from the paper title.[147] So the action may be maintained where it appeared that the plaintiff and defendant owned adjoining tracts of land, neither of which was improved in the ordinary sense, but upon both of which were oil wells; and where it also appears that the defendant, after having drilled and maintained a well on plaintiff's land for several years, abandoned the well and removed the machinery, and that thereupon the plaintiff re-entered and erected a wire fence along a portion of the boundary line,—since the possession of the plaintiff after re-entry is sufficient to support the action for the injury done by the boring of the well upon his premises. The plaintiff in such case is not estopped from recovering damages by his knowledge of the existence and operation of the well for many years, where neither plaintiff nor defendant knew where the boundary line was.[148]

Though the lessor will be liable to the lessee for damages resulting from his negligence, yet the injury is too remote to sustain a recovery by the lessee of a farm from his landlord, who

[144]*Kleppner* v *Lemon*, 176 Pa 502, 35 Atl 109

[145]*Snyder* v *Brown*, 197 Pa 450, 47 Atl 1135.

[146]*Union Petroleum Co* v. *Bliven Petroleum Co* 72 Pa 173
　　LAND & TEN. 47.

[147]*Enterprise Transit Co* v *Hazlewood Oil Co* 20 Pa Super Ct 127

[148]*Enterprise Transit Co* v *Hazlewood Oil Co* 20 Pa. Super Ct 127

has agreed to keep up fences for cattle, where the cattle got through the same and were injured by drinking from a stream polluted by the oil well, it not appearing how the fence was broken.[149]

c. By ejectment.—The right to possession is essential to the maintenance of the action of ejectment, and in case the right thereto is not given by the lease the lessee cannot maintain the same.[150] So, where possession is given of certain designated property, portions of which are reserved, ejectment will not lie against the lessor who drills wells upon the reserved parts The lessee is however entitled to the protection of the entire premises and equity has jurisdiction to restrain the lessor, or others acting under him, from drilling wells outside of the designated sites thereby lessening the protection of the wells drilled by the lessee.[151] A mere ordering of the agent of the lessee from the land is not such a dispossession or ouster of him as to make ejectment the proper remedy[152]

Where the lessor is entitled to possession he may maintain ejectment, thus, where the lease has been abandoned. But such abandonment is a question of intention for the jury to pass upon, and the declaration of the agents of the lessee employed to sink the well, as to the reason for the abandonment, is not binding upon the principal.[153] Where the right was given to experiment for oil, and in case such was found in paying quantities a perpetual lease to be granted and oil was found on a portion of the land, ejectment will not lie in favor of the lessor for that part on which it was not found.[154] But if the land is used by the lessee

---

[149]*Brimmer* v *Reed*, 23 Pa Super Ct 318

[150]*Dark* v *Johnston*, 55 Pa 164, 93 Am Dec 732.

[153]*Duffield* v. *Hue*, 129 Pa 94, 18 Atl 566; *Duffield* v *Hue*, 136 Pa. 602, 25 Atl 526, *Duffield* v *Rosenzweig*, 144 Pa 520, 23 Atl 4.

[152]*Westmoreland & C Natural Gas Co* v *DeWitt*, 130 Pa 235, 5 L R. A 731, 25 W N C 103, 18 Atl 724

[151]*Karns* v *Tanner*, 66 Pa 297

[154]*Rynd* v. *Rynd Farm Oil Co* 63 Pa 397.

for other purposes or to an extent greater than that permitted by the lease, it could be maintained [155]

855. Interference with third parties.— The lessee cannot maliciously or negligently interfere with the rights of third parties. So he is entitled to protection from similar acts by them. Thus he cannot permit gas to escape so as to injure his neighbor, where his act is malicious or negligent, but it is otherwise where such elements do not appear [156] And he may use a gas pump to increase the flow of oil where it appears that such pumps have been in constant use in all oil fields except one, to a greater or less extent, and that their cost is within the reach of all operators and, when used by all, none is injured. [157]

856. Account.— The right to compel an accounting by the lessee may be enforced by the lessor. Where the lease of an oil refinery extended to March 1, 1870, and it was provided that accounts should be rendered semi-annually from January 1, 1868, an accounting by bill in equity could not be compelled until the termination of the lease [158] Nor will an accounting be required for oil produced by the vendee of a town lot, who accepted the same with a restriction against the drilling of a well, though an injunction to restrain its continued operation will be granted [159] Nor will an accounting be granted where the lessee has sunk a well, and it subsequently appears that the same was upon the land of another, whereupon the lessee offered to surrender the premises. [160] An account will be required of tenants in common, who in fraud of other cotenants secured an agreement for a one-fourth royalty whereas an offer had been made to them, and accepted, on the basis of a one-half royalty. [161]

[155] Ibid

[156] Hague v Wheeler, 157 Pa. 324. 22 L R. A 141, 37 Am. St Rep 736, 27 Atl 714

[157] Jones v Forest Oil Co 194 Pa 379, 48 L R. A. 748, 44 Atl. 1074.

[158] Fleming's Appeal, 67 Pa 18

[159] Acheson v Stevenson, 146 Pa 228, 23 Atl 331, 396

[160] Mays v Dwight, 82 Pa 462

[161] Zahn v McMillin, 198 Pa 20, 47 Atl 976

857. Receivers.— In *Dunlap* v. *Riddell*,[162] a receiver was appointed after the filing of a bill in the nature of a proceeding to stay waste, pending an action of ejectment. This decision is apparently overruled by *Enterprise Transit Co.'s Appeal*[163] The same ruling is found in *Emerson's Appeal*[164] Provision was subsequently made by act of assembly for the appointment of a receiver in certain cases[165] This legislation provides:

"That whenever petroleum shall be produced from land in controversy in any action of ejectment hereafter commenced, the court in which said action is pending, or a law judge thereof at chambers, upon the application of the plaintiff or plaintiffs therein, may direct a writ of estrepement to issue against the defendant or defendants, and all parties claiming or acting under them, to prevent the further production of petroleum from the said land.

"Before an order directing the issuing of a writ of estrepement shall be made, under the first section of this act, the plaintiff or plaintiffs, or some one in his or their behalf, shall present, along with the application for said writ an affidavit setting forth the facts upon which the application is based, and also a bond with sufficient sureties to be approved by said court or judge, conditioned to indemnify the defendant or defendants for all damages that may be sustained by reason of said writ of estrepement.

"Upon the application of any party interested, the said writ of estrepement may be dissolved, by the said court or law judge upon such terms and conditions as may be deemed proper in the discretion of said court or law judge.

"In case there shall be, upon the land in controversy, an open well or wells producing petroleum at the time when said writ of estrepement shall be applied, or at any time subsequent there-

[162] 7 W. N C. 466

[163] 9 W N C 225.

[164] 95 Pa 258   See also *Chicago &*   *A Oil & Min Co* v *United States Petroleum Co* 57 Pa 83

[165] Act June 5, 1883, P. L 79.

to, the court or law judge thereof at chambers, may, unless the defendant or defendants shall give bond with sufficient sureties, and in a sum to the satisfaction of the court or law judge, conditioned to indemnify the plaintiff or plaintiffs, in addition to awarding said writ, on the application of any party interested, appoint a proper person to take charge of the said well or wells and of the petroleum produced therefrom pending said action of ejectment, to have like power and authority upon like conditions and accountability as receivers under the equity practice of this commonwealth."

Where a receiver has been appointed, and he pays out money upon the order of the court, in good faith, he will be protected even though the order was made improvidently. If, however, the decree was obtained by mistake or fraud, and the money is paid out thereon to one of the parties, the court, even after such payment, has power to rescind the decree, and require the payees to restore the money to the custody of the court or of its officers. But, if the decree was made in the presence, and with the knowledge and assent, of attorneys representing both parties, an order upon the payees for repayment will not be made, unless the petitioners present a strong equity, and show they will sustain an irreparable injury if it be not made.[166]

[166]*Palmer* v. *Truby*, 136 Pa. 556, 20 Atl. 516.

CHAPTER XL.

OIL AND GAS LEASES—CONTINUED.

858. Covenants to operate — "The discovery of petroleum led to new forms of leasing land   Its fugitive and wandering existence within the limits of a particular tract was uncertain, and assumed certainty only by actual development founded upon experiment   .   .   .   Hence it was found necessary to guard the rights of the landowner as well as public interest by numerous covenants, some of the most stringent kind, to prevent their lands from being burdened by unexecuted and profitless leases, incompatible with the right of alienation and the use of the land "[1] Of the express covenants, appearing in oil and gas leases, the two most common are those providing for forfeiture, and those providing for the payment of rent or royalties   As has been noticed, the clause providing that the lease shall be null and void upon failure to operate or to pay the rentals specified is for the benefit of the lessor, and can be exercised by him alone, unless the lessee is expressly given the same privilege

Where there is an express covenant on the part of the lessee to explore, he is bound to do so, unless relieved from his obligation by the lessor [2]   And this rule is not changed by a declaration that all rights under the lease are to cease and determine upon failure to comply.[3]   Or where the provision was that no right of action should accrue to either party.[4]   Nor can the lessee defend by showing that the drilling of the additional well would not

[1]Agnew, Ch J, in *Brown* v *Vandergrift*, 80 Pa. 142.
[2]*Gibson* v *Oliver*, 158 Pa 277, 27 Atl 961, *Springer* v *Citizens' Natural Gas Co* 145 Pa 430, 22 Atl 986, *Ogden* v *Hatry*, 145 Pa. 640, 23 Atl 334, *Wills* v *Manufacturers' Natural Gas Co* 130 Pa 222, 5 L R A 603, 18 Atl 721,

Ray v *Western Pennsylvania Natural Gas Co* 138 Pa 576 12 L R A 290, 21 Am St Rep 922, 20 Atl 1065
[3]*Cochran* v *Pen*, 159 Pa 184, 28 Atl 219
[4]*Leatherman* v *Oliver*, 151 Pa 646, 25 Atl 309.

benefit the covenantee, because of the lessening of the gas pressure [5] But the lessor may release the lessee from the obligations imposed by the contract.[6]

Where the lease merely gives the right to explore, without a covenant providing for operation, the failure to drill operates merely as an abandonment of the rights acquired, and no action will lie thereon [7] If an exploration be made and no product is discovered, the lease may be abandoned without further obligation on the part of the lessee.[8] But if the covenant has provided for the drilling of more than one well, such must be done by the lessee, though the first is a failure.[9] The remedy for the breach of such a covenant is by action thereon [10]

Ordinarily it is not a defense to an action upon the covenant that exploration upon adjoining land shows that no oil exists [11] But if the lease permits investigation of this character by the lessee, he will be protected by the agreement.[12] Such drilling, though in compliance with the lease, would not be sufficient to put a subsequent lessee upon inquiry as to the existence of an outstanding lease [13]

859. Implied covenant to operate — Where oil has been discovered by exploration, there is an implied obligation on the part of the lessee to put down so many wells as may be reasonably necessary to secure oil for the common advantage of both lessor and

---

[5]*Young* v *Equitable Gas Co.* 5 Pa Super Ct. 232

[6]*Nelson* v *Eachel,* 158 Pa 372, 27 Atl 1103.

[7]*Glasgow* v *Chartiers Oil Co* 152 Pa. 48, 25 Atl. 309, *Marshall* v *Forest Oil Co* 198 Pa 83, 47 Atl. 927, *Barnhart* v. *Lockwood,* 152 Pa. 82, 25 Atl 237

[8]*Venture Oil Co* v *Fretts,* 152 Pa. 451, 25 Atl. 732; *McNish* v. *Stone,* 152 Pa 457, note, *May* v *Hazelwood Oil Co* 152 Pa 518, 25 Atl 564; *Adams* v. *Stage,* 18 Pa Super. Ct 308

[9]*Young* v. *Equitable Gas Co.* 5 Pa.

Super Ct 232, *Iddings* v *Equitable Gas Co* 8 Pa Super. Ct 244, *Stoddard* v *Emery,* 128 Pa. 436, 18 Atl 339.

[10]*Blair* v *Peck,* 1 Pennyp 247, *Janes* v *Emery Oil Co.* 1 Pennyp. 242

[11]*Cochran* v. *Pew,* 159 Pa. 184, 28 Atl 219

[12]*Aye* v *Philadelphia Co* 193 Pa. 451, 74 Am St Rep 696, 44 Atl 555

[13]*Aye* v *Philadelphia Co* 193 Pa. 451, 74 Am St. Rep. 696, 44 Atl. 555.

lessee. But he is not bound to put down more wells than are reasonably necessary to obtain the oil of his lessor, nor to put down wells that will not be able to produce oil sufficient to justify the expenditure [14] And such implied obligation, or express, if appearing in the lease, is binding upon the assignee of the lessee, where such covenant is not personal, but runs with the land.[15] A distinction, however, has been drawn in the case of a gas lease from that for the production of oil. The duty imposed upon the lessee in such case cannot be measured by the same rule, applied in the same manner as in the case of a leasehold operated for oil, and it was held error to charge the jury that a failure to drill all such wells as could produce the gas in paying quantities was a breach of an implied covenant, imposing a liability for damages upon the lessee.[16]

Though there is an implied covenant to drill all wells necessary to properly develop the land, yet such must be done only where oil can be produced in paying quantities; and a court of equity will not enforce this obligation unless fraud upon the rights of the lessor appears [17] Nor in such case will the lease be forfeited, and the lessee ousted, so that the lessor may experiment.[18] But where it appears that the act of the lessee is in fraud of the rights of the lessor, the court may decree the leasehold abandoned if more wells are not sunk within a specified time, except those which are already drilled and a fixed space around the same necessary for their operation.[19] Where provision has been made for the drilling of a test well, and no pro-

---

[14]*Kleppner v Lemon*, 176 Pa 502, 35 Atl. 109, *Adams v Stage*, 18 Pa Super Ct 308; *McKnight v Manufacturers' Natural Gas Co* 146 Pa 185, 28 Am St Rep 790, 23 Atl. 164; *Cole v Taylor*, 8 Pa Super Ct 19

[15]*Bradford Oil Co v Blair*, 113 Pa. 83, 57 Am Rep 442, 4 Atl 218

[16]*McKnight v Manufacturers' Natural Gas Co* 146 Pa 185, 28 Am. St. Rep. 790, 23 Atl 164.

[17]*Young v. Forest Oil Co* 194 Pa. 243, 45 Atl 121, *Colgan v Forest Oil Co* 194 Pa 234, 75 Am St Rep. 695, 45 Atl 119

[18]*Colgan v Forest Oil Co* 194 Pa. 234 75 Am St Rep 695, 45 Atl 119

[19]*Kleppner v Lemon*, 176 Pa 502, 35 Atl. 109, 197 Pa 430, 47 Atl 353.

vision appears for meeting the contingency of the same proving
dry, an implied obligation exists after the well does become dry
to proceed further with due diligence. A failure to do so will
be considered as abandonment, and the lessor may re-enter the
premises.[20]

860. **Damages for failure to drill** — If there has been a failure
on the part of the lessee to comply with the covenant to drill, an
action upon the covenant will lie.[21] And the recovery on the
lease of the royalties provided for therein is no bar to a subsequent suit for damages during the same period for the breach of
the implied covenant for the proper and sufficient operation.[22]
Where the lessee refused to drill wells, the measure of damages
was held to be the value of the additional oil which the plaintiff
should have received, at the time at which it should have been delivered, less the cost of producing what should have been taken
out, with interest on the balance from the time that it should
have been produced [23] So, where the owner of a lease agreed to
convey five eighths of an oil lease to another, who agreed to drill
one well to sand rock before a day specified, and to carry one
fourth of the working interest in the well for the vendor, who
was to pay upon the one-eighth interest the one-eighth part of the
expense of drilling the well, the vendee to pay the share of the
other one quarter of the lease in drilling the wells; and it being
provided that the vendor was to own one eighth of the material
used for drilling put upon the premises in case the well did not
pay, it was held that the measure of damages for failure to drill
was seven eighths of the cost of drilling, less seven eighths of the
market value of the material put upon the premises for use in

[20]*Aye* v *Philadelphia Co.* 193 Pa
45, 74 Am St Rep 696, 44 Atl 555

[21]*Janes* v *Emery Oil Co* 1 Pennyp
242, *Blair* v *Peck*, 1 Pennyp 247;
Springer v *Citizens' Natural Gas
Co* 145 Pa 430, 22 Atl 986, *Gibson*
v. *Oliver*, 158 Pa 277, 27 Atl. 961,

Cochran v. *Pew*, 159 Pa 184, 28 Atl.
219

[22]*Hill* v *Joy*, 149 Pa 243, 24 Atl.
293

[23]*Bradford Oil Co* v *Blair*, 113 Pa.
83, 57 Am Rep 442, 4 Atl 218

drilling.[24] But damages for the breach of a contract for which compensation may be claimed and allowed must be such as may fairly be supposed to have been in contemplation of the parties when they made their contract, or such as, according to the ordinary course of things, might be expected to follow its violation. Therefore, when three persons agree that each shall drill an oil well on his own land, at his own expense, but that each shall share equally in the production, one of them, who drills on his own land an unproductive well, may not recover from another, who drills no well, damages to be measured by one third of the money expended in the experiment. Since the plaintiff was bound to drill his own well, he could not recover his share of the cost from the others, and no other damages appeared [25]

If the lessee fails to comply with his covenant to sink the well, he is liable for actual damages, and the value placed upon success may properly be deemed, prima facie, the just measure of compensation for the default [26]

If no obligation existed on the part of the lessee to drill a well, but a mere right to explore was granted, then the only penalty to be imposed for failure to so drill is a forfeiture of the lease.[27]

861. Rent and royalties.— Liability for rent or royalties is determined by the wording of the contract between the parties. An undivided half of land having been conveyed, reserving one fourth of the oil or gas therein the grantor subsequently leased this fourth, for the royalty of one eighth of the oil or gas produced. He became entitled to one eighth of one fourth, or one thirty second of the product of the one-half interest in the land, and not to one thirty second part of all the oil produced upon the entire property.[28] If the lease provides for

[24]*Knupp* v *Bright*, 186 Pa. 181, 40 Atl 414.

[25]*Hutchinson* v *Snider*, 137 Pa 1, 20 Atl 510

[26]*Iddings* v *Equitable Gas Co* 8 Pa Super Ct 244

[27]*Marshall* v. *Forest Oil Co.* 198 Pa 83, 47 Atl 927, *Glasgow* v. *Chartiers Oil Co* 152 Pa 48, 25 Atl. 232

[28]*Dickson* v *Fertig*, 21 Pa Super Ct 283 See *Ewing* v *Fertig*, 9 Pa Dist. R 756, 24 Pa. Co Ct. 301

a share of the oil produced, the lessor is entitled to his proportion of such as is raised to the surface at the expense of the grantee. And the measure of damages for the failure to deliver the grantor's share is the actual market value of the oil at the date of the refusal, with interest from that date.[29]

862. Time of payment.— The accruing of rights under the covenant depends upon the conditions set forth in the lease Thus, where the lessor was to designate the sites to be operated upon, and failed to do so, no action could be maintained.[30] So, where the obligation was to drill a well upon the assignment of a lease, the duty to do so did not begin until such assignment was made [31] Where it was stipulated that rent should be paid in case of delay in putting down a well, no time being specified when it should become due, it became payable by operation of law at the close of the year [32] If the rent is payable quarterly, in advance, the interpretation to be given to the contract is that each quarterly payment accrues in advance.[33] And when the payment is conditioned upon the production of oil or gas in paying quantities, the question as to whether such a condition has been fulfilled is for the jury, in case of conflict of testimony.[34] Where the lease stipulated for the payment of a bonus of $75.00, and, if oil was found in paying quantities, then the further sum of $600 00 to be paid in thirty days, the obvious meaning is that if, for the period of thirty days after its completion, the well continues to produce oil in such quantities as to make it profitable to operate it during that period, the $600.00 shall then be due and payable [35]

[29]*Union Oil Co's Appeal*, 3 Pennyp 504

[30]*McKnight* v. *Manufacturers' Natural Gas Co* 146 Pa 185, 28 Am St Rep 790, 23 Atl. 164

[31]*Knupp* v *Bright*, 186 Pa. 181, 40 Atl 414

[32]*Lynch* v *Versailles Fuel Gas Co* 165 Pa 518, 30 Atl 984

[33]*Wills* v *Manufacturers' Natural Gas Co* 130 Pa 222, 5 L R A 603, 18 Atl 721

[34]*Aye* v *Brown*, 178 Pa 291, 35 Atl 957

[35]*Collins* v. *Mechling*, 1 Pa Super. Ct 594.

863. For what rent liable.— The sum to be paid by the lessee is fixed by the lease. So, if rental is to be paid as long as the land is retained, the meaning is, until a formal surrender takes place, surrender could not be shown to have been made by the solicitor of the lessee, having control only of legal business, and no authority to do more appearing.[36] Where the lease and its supplement provided for the developing of an old well, and the payment of a certain bonus if it produced 5 barrels per day, as well as for a test well, and the payment of a certain sum if it produced a certain number of barrels per day for thirty days, the bonus is payable where the test well produces the amount stipulated for, though the development of the old well was a failure [37] If the stipulation is for the payment of a stipulated sum per year for each well from which gas is used off the premises, and there is no apportionment provided for in case of a failure of gas, the obligation arises at the beginning of the new year to pay for the whole of a year, subject to any stipulated right to annul by reassignment.[38] There is ordinarily no obligation to pay royalties for the drawing of oil from wells on adjoining lands, the wells upon the land of the lessor having proved valueless.[39] But where the lessee fails to develop the lands of his lessor, but does develop adjoining lands, to the injury of the lands of the lessor, and it appears to be the purpose of the defendant to take the oil of the lessor through the other wells, he will be held liable for royalties to the lessor on all of his oil produced by the well operated on the adjoining land [40] The measure of the lessor's damage in such case is the value of the royalties on a portion of the oil produced through the well, ascertained by comparing it with the total production through the well, in the same propor-

[36]*Jamestown & F R Co* v *Egbert,* 152 Pa. 53, 25 Atl 151

[37]*Brushwood Developing Co* v *Hickey,* 2 Monaghan (Pa.) 65, 16 Atl 70

[38]*Coulter* v. *Conemaugh Gas Co.* 14 Pa Super Ct. 553

[39]*Adams* v. *Stage,* 18 Pa Super Ct. 308

[40]*Kleppner* v *Lemon,* 197 Pa 430, 47 Atl 353. See also 176 Pa 502, 35 Atl. 109.

tion as the lessee's lands within the circle drained bear to the whole area of drainage, the oil-producing capacity of every part of the area being the same. In such a case the rule as to the wrongful confusion of goods should not be applied so as to give to the plaintiff royalties on all of the oil produced through the well, it being possible approximately to determine the amount of oil drawn from the lessor's land [41]

864. Who liable.— The assignee of the lease is liable for the rent or royalties which accrue while he holds the lease [42] And where one half of the lease is assigned to one company, and the other half to a second company, the operation being by the first assignee under an agreement with the second, the first is liable to the lessor for the whole of the royalties.[43] Where the lease was taken by one in his own name, who subsequently executed a declaration of trust that the money from the sale of the oil was the property of others, but the *cestuis que trustent* never had possession of the property, or control of the operation, they cannot be held personally liable for rents which the trustee fails to pay. He is not to be considered their agent, but the trustee of an active trust [44]

865. Recovery of rents or royalties.— The lessor can enforce the covenant to pay the rent or royalty by appropriate action. It is properly brought in the name of the lessor. If the wife is named as a party in the lease, but has not executed it, she need not be joined.[45] The amount stipulated in the lease fixes the liability. If it has been reduced for a valid consideration, such as the building of a pipe line, only such sum can be recovered.[46]

[41] *Kleppner* v *Lemon*, 198 Pa 581, 48 Atl 483.

[42] *MacDonald* v *O'Neil*, 21 Pa Super Ct 364; *Bradford Oil Co* v *Blair*, 113 Pa 83, 57 Am Rep 442, 4 Atl 218, *Coulter* v *Conemaugh Gas Co* 14 Pa Super Ct 553

[43] *Burton* v *Forest Oil Co* 204 Pa. 349, 54 Atl 266

[44] *Hartley* v *Phillips*, 198 Pa. 9, 47 Atl 929

[45] *Boal* v *Citizens' Natural Gas Co.* 23 Pa Super Ct 339

[46] *Consumers' Heating Co* v *American Land Co.* 31 Pittsb L. J N. S. 24.

So, a reduction of rental of a gas well in consideration of a covenant to put down casing, and to test the well for oil when abandoned for gas purposes, can be enforced. And upon failure of the covenantor to do so, actual damages may be recovered Oil having appeared in the gas well, evidence of the amount thereof is admissible on the question of the damages recoverable, and the cost of drilling the well at the time the gas company abandoned the property can be shown [47] And it is no defense on the part of the lessee, who has received the right to drill for oil and gas upon land the coal right of which had been conveyed, reserving oil and gas, that the owners of the coal right had refused to allow the lessee to drill.[48] Nor is it a defense that the wife of the lessor had failed to join in the lease, when she had agreed to sign the same upon its presentation by the agent of the defendant, who failed to do so, and where it appeared that there had been no interference by her with the lessee.[49] So, as has already been noticed, it is no defense to an action for rentals or royalties that the lease provides for its forfeiture upon failure to drill, since such provision is for the benefit of the lessor, who must take advantage of it.[50] Though the rule is otherwise where the right is given merely to explore, and there is no obligation to do so.[51] But under such a lease it is a defense where the oil or gas cannot be found in paying quantities, due diligence having been exercised in exploration for the same.[52] And by paying quantities is meant the power to produce without loss,[53] and where the evi-

[47]*McClay* v *Western Pennsylvania Gas Co* 201 Pa. 197, 50 Atl 978

[48]*Chambers* v. *Smith*, 183 Pa 122, 38 Atl 522

[49]*Kunkle* v *People's Natural Gas Co.* 165 Pa 133, 33 L R A. 847, 30 Atl 719.

[50]*Cochran* v *Pew*, 159 Pa 184, 28 Atl 219, *Miller* v *Logan*, 31 Pittsb L J N S 217

[51]*Glasgow* v *Chartiers Oil Co.* 152 Pa 48, 25 Atl 232, *Marshall* v. *Forest Oil Co* 198 Pa 83, 47 Atl. 927.

[52]*McConnell* v *Lawrence Natural Gas. Co* 30 Pittsb L J N S 346, *Williams* v *Guffy*, 178 Pa 342, 35 Atl 875, *Adams* v *Stage*, 18 Pa Super. Ct 308, *Colgan* v *Forest Oil Co* 194 Pa 234, 75 Am. St. Rep 695, 45 Atl 119

[53]*Young* v *Forest Oil Co* 194 Pa.

dence as to this is conflicting, the question is for the jury.[54]

866. To whom payable.— Where the lease has been made by the cotenant the rent may be validly paid to either of them, unless a notice to the contrary has been given. This rule is not changed because of the assignment by one cotenant of his interest to a stranger.[55] In case a secret contract is made by two tenants in common for one half of the product, and an agreement is secured by them from the other tenants in common to accept one fourth of the product, they will be compelled to account to them for the entire amount received.[56] The lessee is not liable to the plaintiff, who was a cropper upon the land of his father, and who joined in the lease, who alleged that the land was held by him under a promise of one half of the royalties, made by the father, when nothing was said at time of execution of the lease to show that he claimed a share.[57] As the lease of oil is practically a sale, the proceeds represent the respective interests of the parties. If the lessors are life tenants and remainder-men, the former are entitled to the interest on the royalties during life, and at their death the corpus passes to the remainder-men.[58] Where the life tenant and remainder-man have agreed that the former shall receive two thirds of the royalties during his life, and the latter shall receive one third of the royalties during his life, and all at his death, and the life tenant has received two thirds prior to his death, the remainder-man can have no claim on the sum so collected.[59] If the royalties have been collected by the husband on land leased by the wife, and used in support of the family, he cannot be compelled to account therefor by the administrator of the wife for the sum received

243, 45 Atl 121, *Iams* v. *Carnegie Natural Gas Co* 194 Pa 72, 45 Atl. 54.

[54]*Aye* v. *Brown*, 178 Pa. 291, 35 Atl 957.

[55]*Swint* v *McCalmont Oil Co* 184 Pa 202, 63 Am St Rep 791, 38 Atl. 1021.

[56]*Zahn* v *McMillin*, 198 Pa 20, 47 Atl 976.

[57]*Acklin* v *McCalmont Oil Co* 201 Pa. 257, 50 Atl 955

[58]*Blakley* v. *Marshall*, 174 Pa. 425, 34 Atl 564.

[59]*Agnew's Estate*, 17 Pa. Super Ct. 201

prior to her death. Nor can he be held liable for royalties collected after her death, inasmuch as he owns them in his own right as tenant by curtesy.[60]

Where the decedent owned land subject to an oil lease, the royalties becoming due prior to his death are to be treated as corpus of the estate. Such sums as accrue thereafter are to be treated as income of the estate in the hands of the executor.[61] Where the lands subject to oil leases have been devised, the royalties accruing are to be treated as personal estate, since the lease was practically a sale, and not rent running with the land. No specified disposition having been made of them, they fall into the residue.[62] Where the decedent, being the owner of three contiguous farms, subject in their entirety to an oil and gas lease for a fixed term, devised the three farms respectively to his three children, and wells were sunk upon only one of the farms, it was held that each child was entitled to receive such share of the total royalties as his or her share of the land bore to the whole tract covered by the lease, no matter on whose farm the wells were located. The child upon whose land the wells were sunk was entitled to compensation for the decrease in the rental value of his part, caused by the presence of the wells. The cost of repairing injuries to the realty caused by the sinking of the wells must be postponed until the termination of the lease, because this could not be intelligently considered until that time.[63]

867. Other covenants.— A covenant to put down casing and to test the well for oil when abandoned for gas purposes, in consideration of a reduction of rental of a gas well can be enforced. And upon failure of the covenantor to do so actual dam-

[60]*Bubb* v. *Bubb*, 201 Pa. 212, 50 Atl 759

[61]*Woodburn's Estate*, 138 Pa 606, 21 Am St Rep 932, 21 Atl 16

[62]*Brunot's Estate*, 29 Pittsb L. J. N S 105

[63]*Wettengel* v *Gormley*, 184 Pa 354, 39 Atl 57, and Following *Wettengel* v *Gormley*, 160 Pa 559, 40 Am St. Rep 733, 28 Atl. 934.

ages may be recovered   Oil having appeared in the gas well, evidence of the amount thereof is admissible on the question of the damages recoverable, and the cost of drilling the well at the time the gas company abandoned the property can be shown.[64] Where the lease contained a covenant to drill wells, and to furnish gas to the lessor for domestic purposes, the lessee cannot cease operations upon the failure of a single well, and the lessor may recover from him damages for the injury sustained. Where he has purchased gas from others to take the place of that which the lessee should have given, he may recover the price paid, unless it can be shown that he purchased gas which was not needed, or that the price paid was not reasonable.[65]

868 Denial of lessor's title — As in the case of other leases, the lessee is estopped from denying the title of the landlord under whom he claims. Thus, where a second lease is taken from one holding adversely, the lessee cannot refuse to pay the second lessor on the ground that the first had a better title [66]   Or, where a lease has been made after a sale of the land for taxes, but before the period for redemption has expired and the title of the vendee at the tax sale is consequently acquired.[67]   So, the lessee is estopped from denying the authority of the agent to sign the lease by which he agreed to drill two wells, after having opened and worked one of them.[68]   But where a father and son, who was a cropper upon the land of the father, had both signed the lease, the son claiming a one-half interest in the royalties, the lessee is not estopped from showing that the son had no interest, this not being a denial of the landlord's title, but merely showing that the son was not a landlord.[69]

[64] *McClay* v *Western Pennsylvania Gas Co* 201 Pa 197, 50 Atl 978

[65] *Boal* v *Citizens' Natural Gas Co* 23 Pa Super Ct 339

[66] *Hamilton* v *Pittock*, 158 Pa 457, 27 Atl 1079

[67] *MacDonald* v. *O'Neil*, 21 Pa. Super Ct 304.

[68] *Ahrns* v *Chartiers Valley Gas Co.* 188 Pa 249, 41 Atl 739

[69] *Snant* v *McCalmont Oil Co* 184 Pa 202, 63 Am St Rep. 791 38 Atl. 1021   See also *Acklin* v *McCalmont Oil Co.* 201 Pa 257, 50 Atl 955

869. Termination of lease. —*a. By abandonment.*—Where a lease has been made giving the right to explore for oil, the relationship may be terminated by the lessor where the premises have been abandoned. "The right of the lessee or grantee under its provisions was to explore for, and determine the existence of, oil or gas under the farm. . . . A vested title cannot ordinarily be lost by abandonment in a less time than that fixed by the statute of limitations, unless there is satisfactory proof of an intention to abandon. An oil lease stands on quite different ground. The title is inchoate and for purposes of exploration only until oil is found. If it is not found no estate vests in the lessee, and his title, whatever it is, ends when the unsuccessful search is abandoned. If oil is found, then the right to produce becomes a vested right, and the lessee will be protected in exercising it in accordance with the terms and conditions of his contract."[70] So, where no operation had been conducted for seven years, it was held that the premises were abandoned by the lessee[71] And for nine years.[72] Or after twelve years.[73] Or after eleven years, no possession as contemplated by the lease ever having been taken.[74] And the rights of the lessee will be lost by abandonment, though there be no provision in the contract for forfeiture for failure to comply with the covenants[75] So, if the lease fails to provide for the contingency of the test well becoming dry, the relationship will terminate by abandonment, if there is a failure on the part of the lessee to use reasonable diligence in sinking another well.[76]

"Abandonment is a question of fact, to be determined by the acts and intentions of the parties An unexplained cessation of

[70]*Venture Oil Co* v. *Fretts,* 152 Pa 451, 25 Atl 732

[71]*Venture Oil Co* v. *Fretts,* 152 Pa 451, 25 Atl 732

[72]*Calhoon* v *Neely,* 201 Pa 97, 50 Atl 967

[73]*McNish* v *Stone,* 152 Pa 457, note. 23 Pittsb. L. J N S 232.

[74]*Barnhart* v. *Lockwood,* 152 Pa. 82, 25 Atl 237

[75]*Marshall* v *Forest Oil Co* 198 Pa 83, 47 Atl 927

[76]*Aye* v *Philadelphia Co* 193 Pa 451, 74 Am. St. Rep 696, 44 Atl 555.

operations for the period involved in this case [four years], gives rise to a fair presumption of abandonment, and, standing alone and admitted, would justify the court in declaring an abandonment as matter of law."[77]   But, where there is a conflict of evidence as to the intention of the parties, the question is one for the jury.[78]   So, evidence may be offered to show that no intention to abandon existed when machinery was removed from the premises.[79]   But the declaration of an agent employed to sink a well as to the reason of the principal for ceasing operations is not admissible to show intention.[80]   Where the lessee has notified the lessor of his intention to abandon, but has refused to surrender the lease upon demand, he may show that the reason therefor was to protect a pipe line also provided for in the same writing.[81]

Though the abandonment may be complete as between the grantor and grantee before the passing of the statutory period, yet this is not true as to strangers.[82]   But where the first lessee claims the right to possession as against a subsequent lessee, he may offer testimony to show that there has been an abandonment, though he was aware of the outstanding lease.[83]   So, the purchaser of the interest of the lessee at a sheriff's sale will acquire only the interest of the lessee, and, if this has been abandoned, secures no interest.[84]   And the same is true of an assignee of the lessee.[85]

b. By acceptance of new lease.—If the lessor has notified the lessee of the termination of his interest by abandonment, and the

[77]*Aye* v *Philadelphia Co.* 193 Pa. 451, 74 Am St Rep. 696, 44 Atl. 555, *Calhoon* v *Neely,* 201 Pa 97, 50 Atl 967.

[78]*Bartley* v *Phillips,* 165 Pa 325, 30 Atl. 842, *Karns* v *Tanner,* 66 Pa 297

[79]*Bartley* v *Phillips,* 179 Pa. 175, 36 Atl 217

[80]*Karns* v. *Tanner,* 66 Pa. 297.

[81]*Stage* v *Boyer,* 183 Pa 560, 38 Atl 1035

[82]*Bartley* v *Phillips,* 165 Pa. 325, 30 Atl 842, 179 Pa. 175, 36 Atl 217.

[83]*Bartley* v *Phillips,* 165 Pa 325, 30 Atl 842

[84]*Karns* v *Tanner,* 66 Pa 297, *Christie's Appeal,* 85 Pa 463

[85]*Cole* v *Taylor,* 8 Pa. Super Ct 19.

lessee accepts from him a new lease, he waives all rights existing under the first.[86]

c. By forfeiture—It is true as a general statement that equity abhors a forfeiture; but this is when it works a loss contrary to equity; not when it works equity, and protects the landowner against the indifference and laches of the lessee, and prevents a great mischief, as in case of such leases [87] "Forfeiture for non-development or delay is essential to private and public interests in relation to the use and alienation of property.   In such cases as this equity follows the law."[88]

(1) *Where forfeiture clause.*—The ordinary oil lease provides for the payment of a bonus, with a covenant to drill a test well within a specified period, extending, however, the privilege upon the payment of stipulated rentals. Such a stipulation is inserted for the benefit of the lessor, and can be taken advantage of by him alone   The lessee cannot defend to an action for breach of the covenants, where the lessor has failed to declare the forfeiture.[89]   To give the lessee the same right the lease must provide that the forfeiture shall be at the option of either party or of the lessee.[90]   And this option of the lessor exists both as to the lessee and his assignee.[91]   Though it is ordinarily agreed that the lease shall be "null and void" upon default, the right to forfeit at the option of the lessor alone has been sustained where additional phrases have been added.   Thus, where it is provided that upon default there shall be an absolute forfeiture, but that this shall not prevent the collection of sums then due, no inten-

[86]*Carnegie Natural Gas Co* v. *Philadelphia Co.* 158 Pa 317, 27 Atl. 951

[87]*Brown* v. *Vandergrift,* 80 Pa. 142

[88]*Munroe* v *Armstrong,* 96 Pa 307.

[89]*Springer* v *Citizens' Natural Gas Co* 145 Pa 430, 22 Atl 986, *Sanders* v *Sharp,* 153 Pa 555, 25 Atl 524, *Ray* v *Western Pennsylvania Natural Gas Co* 138 Pa 576, 12 L R. A. 290, 21 Am. St. Rep 922, 20

Atl 1065; *Liggett* v. *Shira,* 159 Pa. 350, 28 Atl 218, *Jamestown & F R Co* v *Egbert,* 152 Pa 53, 25 Atl 151, *Phillips* v *Vandergrift,* 146 Pa 357, 23 Atl 347; *Galey Bros* v *Kellerman,* 123 Pa 491, 16 Atl 474

[90]*Cochran* v. *Pew,* 159 Pa 184, 28 Atl. 219

[91]*Jackson* v. *O'Hara,* 183 Pa 233, 38 Atl 624.

tion is manifested that the lessee may forfeit and defend to a
suit for rentals on the ground that the lease was forfeited by default before they accrued.[92]   Nor by the phrase that in case of
default the rights will only be renewed on mutual consent, and
no right of action should accrue to either party on account of the
breach.[93]   Nor by the phrase "can only be renewed by mutual
consent."[94]   Or by the declaration that all rights should be extinguished.[95]   Or by the words "neither party be held further."[96]   Or to "be no longer binding on either party."[97]

(2) *Facts warranting declaration of forfeiture.*—The existence of facts warranting the forfeiture must clearly appear.[98]
If there has been a failure to drill as required by the lease, or
to pay the rent due upon default, the forfeiture may be declared,[99] for time is ordinarily of the essence of such contract.[100]
And where a fixed period is given for the finding of oil, there is
not sufficient compliance with the agreement by beginning work
on the last day fixed.[101]   But where operations are to be commenced within a certain number of days, work may be begun
on the last one, the question as to whether or not lessee was acting in good faith being for the jury[102]   But where time is not
stipulated as an essential, the forfeiture for non-payment of

---

[92]*Wills* v *Manufacturers' Natural Gas Co* 130 Pa 222, 5 L R A 603, 18 Atl 721

[93]*Leatherman* v *Oliver*, 151 Pa. 646, 25 Atl 309

[94]*Jones* v *Western Pennsylvania Natural Gas Co* 146 Pa. 204, 23 Atl. 386, *Conger* v *National Property Co* 165 Pa 561, 30 Atl 1038, *Van Voorhis* v *Oliver*, 39 Pittsb L. J. 114, *contra*

[95]*Ogden* v. *Hatry*, 145 Pa 640, 23 Atl 334

[96]*Matheus* v *People's Natural Gas Co.* 179 Pa 165, 36 Atl 216

[97]*McMillan* v. *Philadelphia Co.* 159 Pa 142, 28 Atl 220; *Miller* v *Logan*, 31 Pittsb L J N S 217

[98]*Thompson* v *Christie*, 138 Pa 230, 11 L R A 236, 20 Atl 934

[99]*Brown* v. *Vandergrift*, 80 Pa 142, *Munroe* v. *Armstrong*, 96 Pa. 307.

[100]*Brown* v. *Vandergrift*, 80 Pa 142, *Heintz* v. *Shortt*, 149 Pa 286, 24 Atl 316, *Cryan* v *Ridelsperger*, 7 Pa Co Ct 473

[101]*Kennedy* v *Crawford*, 138 Pa 561 21 Atl 19

[102]*Henderson* v. *Ferrell*, 183 Pa. 547, 38 Atl 1018.

rent, or for other matters that admit of a full compensation, equity will relieve against.[103]

Where the lease provides for drilling test wells the covenant is not complied with by drilling upon adjoining land.[104] Unless the agreement of the parties distinctly provides that such shall be a compliance.[105]

If there has been a failure to operate, but the stipulated rental is paid, no forfeiture can be declared.[106] But there is no failure to pay where the rent is taken to the bank for the lessor, and is credited to his account by the cashier, he not being present.[107] Nor if there has been but a slight delay, due to an oversight.[108]

(3) *Where no forfeiture clause.*—Where the lease has failed to provide for forfeiture, such cannot be declared by the lessor, unless there is an abandonment of the premises. He can proceed for the collection of the rent,[109] or maintain an action for the breach of the covenant.[110] Though there be no provision for forfeiture in the lease, yet a subsequent parol agreement giving the right could be enforced between the parties, but not as against the innocent assignee of the lessee.[111]

(4) *For nonpayment of rent.*—Where the lease provides for forfeiture for nonpayment of rent, and the lessee fails to comply with the provision as to payment, the lease may be forfeited at the option of the lessor. But the mere failure to pay does not *ipso facto* have this effect.[112] But, if there be no provision for forfeiture for nonpayment, the lessor's only right is to proceed

[103]*Lynch* v. *Versailles Fuel Gas Co* 165 Pa. 518, 30 Atl 984

[104]*Carnegie Natural Gas Co* v. *Philadelphia Co* 158 Pa 317, 27 Atl 951

[105]*Aye* v *Philadelphia Co.* 193 Pa 457, 44 Atl 556

[106]*Brown* v. *Vandergrift,* 80 Pa 142; *Galey Bros* v *Kellerman,* 123 Pa 491, 16 Atl 474

[107]*Sayers* v. *Kent,* 201 Pa. 38, 50 Atl 296.

[108]*Lynch* v *Versailles Fuel Gas Co* 165 Pa 518, 30 Atl 984

[109]*Marshall* v *Forest Oil Co* 198 Pa 83, 47 Atl 927

[110]*Blair* v *Peck,* 1 Pennyp 247, *Janes* v *Emery Oil Co* 1 Pennyp 242

[111]*Thompson* v *Christie,* 138 Pa 230, 11 L R A 236, 20 Atl 934

[112]*Shettler* v. *Hartman,* 1 Pennyp 279.

for the collection of the rent.[113] Since forfeitures are not favored, such will not be declared where there has been a short delay in payment through oversight.[114] Particularly where work has progressed with the knowledge of the lessor, and without objection[115] Nor will such be done where the money due was paid to the cashier of the bank and credited to the lessor's account, the lessor having failed to appear at the time fixed.[116] As forfeitures must be strictly construed, a provision for the nonpayment of rent will be held to apply to a whole payment, and not to a balance of a running account, part of the sum due having been paid before the time fixed.[117] So, the bill to forfeit will not be sustained for the failure to pay rent for three months, where the lessee has paid during the previous three months double rent. Upon the dismissal of such a bill no relief can be granted to the defendant in the absence of a cross bill.[118]

(5) *For failure to produce.*—Where a lease of land is made for the purpose of exploration for oil, to be void if not found within a specified period, a forfeiture may be declared by the lessor at the end of a time if not found. The lessee in such case cannot extend his rights by the payment of rental after the time fixed has elapsed.[119]. Nor is the condition fulfilled by finding gas[120] Nor is he entitled to reimbursement for the expenses incurred from the proceeds of the gas found.[121] The lessor may waive the right to forfeit, or estop himself by allowing the lessee to continue to make expenditures thereafter.[122] Where a sufficient time has been given for the produc-

[113]*Marshall* v *Forest Oil Co.* 198 Pa 83, 47 Atl 927

[114]*Lynch* v. *Versailles Fuel Gas Co* 165 Pa 518, 30 Atl 984

[115]*McCarty* v *Mellon*, 5 Pa Dist. R 425

[116]*Sayers* v *Kent*, 201 Pa 38, 50 Atl 296

[117]*Westmoreland & C Natural Gas Co* v *DeWitt*, 130 Pa 235, 5 L R A 731, 25 W. N. C. 103, 18 Atl. 724

[118]*Freeland* v *South Penn Oil Co* 189 Pa 54, 41 Atl 1000.

[119]*Western Pennsylvania Gas Co* v. *George*, 161 Pa. 47, 28 Atl 1004

[120]*Truby* v. *Palmer*, (Pa) 4 Cent Rep 925, 6 Atl 74

[121]*Palmer* v *Truby*, 136 Pa 556, 20 Atl 516

[122]*Riddle* v. *Mellon*, 147 Pa 30, 23 Atl 241.

tion of oil in paying quantities, the tenancy of the surface after that time is in the nature of a tenancy at will, which may be determined by either party, or continued by mutual consent.[123]

(6) *Declaration of forfeiture* —There must be a formal declaration of the forfeiture by the lessor to be effective[124] This may be given by formal notice.[125] Or by the making of a second lease after the expiration of the period fixed for the first lease.[126] Or by the selling of one lot without a reservation of oil, where the oil covered two.[127] But a mere retention of possession of the premises by the lessor, which he has always had, is not sufficient.[128] Or the erection of a building upon one lot, where two had been leased for oil purposes.[129] Nor by the making of a second lease, in which the lessee agreed to stand between the lessor and all having claims to operate upon the land.[130] The declaration of forfeiture should be promptly made[131]

It may be by the lessor or by one acting for him. Where it is made by a brother, on behalf of himself and his minor sisters, who are tenants in common, the declaration as to the latter will be binding provided the jury find that he was authorized to act for them, and where it appears in addition, to be for their best interest.[132] A ward will not be bound by the declaration of the guardian, that he has no interest in the lease.[133] Nor will the

[123]*Cassell* v *Crothers*, 193 Pa. 359, 44 Atl 446

[124]*Shettler* v *Hartman*, 1 Pennyp 279, *Westmoreland & C Natural Gas Co* v *DeWitt*, 130 Pa. 235, 5 L R A. 731, 25 W. N O 103, 18 Atl 724

[125]*Carnegie Natural Gas Co.* v. *Philadelphia Co.* 158 Pa 317, 27 Atl 951, *May* v *Hazelwood Oil Co* 152 Pa 518, 25 Atl. 564

[126]*Wolf* v. *Guffey*, 161 Pa 276, 28 Atl 1117.

[127]*Mathews* v *People's Natural Gas Co* 179 Pa. 165, 36 Atl 216

[128]*Ray* v. *Western Pennsylvania*

Natural Gas Co 138 Pa 576, 12 L. R A 290, 21 Am St Rep 922. 20 Atl 1065

[129]*Mathews* v. *People's Natural Gas Co.* 179 Pa 165, 36 Atl 216

[130]*Stone* v *Marshall Oil Co* 188 Pa. 602, 41 Atl. 748, 1119

[131]*Thompson* v *Christie*, 138 Pa. 238, 11 L. R A 236, 20 Atl 934; *Lynch* v *Versailles Fuel Gas Co* 165 Pa 518, 30 Atl 984

[132]*Heinouer* v *Jones*, 159 Pa 228, 28 Atl 228, *Wilson* v *Goldstein*, 152 Pa. 524, 25 Atl 493

[133]*Springer* v *Citizens' Natural Gas Co* 145 Pa 430, 22 Atl. 986.

mere declaration by the committee of a lunatic, that the lunatic has no interest in the land, conveyed to him by recorded deed, operate to deprive the lunatic of his interest in the land in favor of a subsequent purchaser to whom the declaration was made.[134]

(7) *Who bound by forfeiture.*—The assignee of the lease takes the risk of its previous forfeiture.[135] So the purchaser at a sheriff's sale takes only the interest which the lessee has at the time [136] And the subsequent lessee from the lessor takes the risk as to whether rights under the first have been lost [137]

(8) *Waiver of forfeiture.*—Where the forfeiture has occurred merely through oversight, and the lessor permits work to continue, forfeiture will be considered waived.[138] Or where the conduct of the lessor has led to the belief that strict compliance was not required as to the date of payment of rent.[139] Or as to the time of the sinking of the wells provided for [140] But a waiver of the time fixed for commencing the well will not act as a waiver of the time for completing it.[141] So, if there has been a practical compliance with the conditions, by depositing the rent in the bank to the credit of the lessor, instead of paying directly to him [142]

(9) *Effect of forfeiture.*—Where a forfeiture has been declared, no rent thereafter becoming due can be recovered.[143] Nor is the lessee liable where there was no covenant to pay rent, although, the lease being assigned, the assignee pays some rent

[134]*Jennings* v *Bloomfield*, 199 Pa 638, 49 Atl. 135, 204 Pa 123, 53 Atl 1127

[135]*Carnegie Natural Gas Co* v *Philadelphia Co* 158 Pa 317, 27 Atl 951, *Cole* v *Taylor*, 8 Pa Super Ct. 19

[136]*Christie's Appeal*, 85 Pa 463, *Karns* v *Tanner*, 66 Pa 297.

[137]*Bartley* v. *Phillips*, 179 Pa 175, 36 Atl 217

[138]*Lynch* v. *Versailles Fuel Gas Co.*

165 Pa. 518, 30 Atl. 984, *McCarty* v *Mellon*, 5 Pa Dist R 425

[139]*Steiner* v. *Marks*, 172 Pa 400, 33 Atl 695

[140]*Duffield* v. *Hue*, 129 Pa. 94, 18 Atl 566

[141]*Cleminger* v *Baden Gas Co* 159 Pa 16, 28 Atl 293

[142]*Sayers* v *Kent*, 201 Pa 38, 50 Atl 296

[143]*Wolf* v *Guffey*, 161 Pa 276, 28 Atl 1117.

without his knowledge.[144] Payments which have accrued at time of forfeiture may be recovered [145] But it has been said in *Wheeling* v. *Phillips*,[146] that such could not be done where no such reservation appeared.

d. Termination by lessee.--Where the mere right to explore is given by the lease, and there is no covenant on the part of the lessee to do so, he may terminate at his option.[147] Or the lease may distinctly provide that the lessees may rescind [148] But, as has already been noticed, a mere provision that the lease shall be null and void upon failure to drill, or to pay rent, is for the benefit of the lessor, and can be taken advantage of only by him.[149]

(1) *Where no oil.*—If explorations be conducted with due diligence by the lessee, and no oil is found, the right exists on the part of the lessee to abandon the premises, and to terminate the contract.[150] But this right does not exist where the obligation is to sink more than one well [151] And the failure must appear as to all of the lands embraced in the lease, and not to a single tract [152] The determination of the failure of it is a matter for the lessee, in the exercise of his own judgment, so long as he acts in good faith [153] And he is relieved, though oil is produced, if it is not in paying quantities, by which is meant, more

[144]*McKee* v *Colwell*, 7 Pa Super Ct 607

[145]*Wills* v *Manufacturers' Natural Gas Co* 130 Pa 222, 5 L R A 603, 18 Atl 721

[146] 10 Pa Super Ct 634

[147]*Glasgow* v *Chartiers Oil Co* 152 Pa 48 25 Atl 232, *Marshall* v *Forest Oil Co* 198 Pa 83, 47 Atl 927, *McKee* v *Colwell*, 7 Pa Super Ct 607.

[148]*Hooks* v *Forst*, 165 Pa 238, 30 Atl 846, *Cochran* v *Pew*, 159 Pa 184, 28 Atl 219

[149]*Wills* v *Manufacturers' Natural Gas Co* 130 Pa 222, 5 L R A. 603, 18 Atl. 721.

[150]*Venture Oil Co* v *Fretts*, 152 Pa 451, 25 Atl 732, *May* v *Hazelwood Oil Co* 152 Pa 518, 25 Atl 564, *McConnell* v *Laurence Natural Gas Co* 30 Pittsb L J N S 346, *Balfour* v *Russell*, 167 Pa 287, 31 Atl 570

[151]*Gibson* v *Oliver*, 158 Pa 277, 27 Atl 961

[152]*Oil Creek & C Branch Petroleum Co* v *Stanton Oil Co* 23 Pa Co Ct.

153

[153]*Young* v *Forest Oil Co* 194 Pa. 243, 45 Atl 121.

than the cost of producing it.[154]   So, where the well does produce in paying quantities, but subsequently ceases to do so, the lessee may abandon, and is liable for rent only to that time [155]

(2) *Where lessee evicted* —Where the lessee is in possession, the mere ordering of his employees sent to drill an additional well from the land is not an ouster.[156]   But where two tracts of land have been leased, and one is sold by the lessor without the reservation of the right to drill, there is a constructive eviction which terminates the lessee's liability.[157]

(3) *Where lease for definite time* —Where the lease is for a definite period, and the time fixed passes, either party may determine the contract, or continue the same by mutual consent.[158]

(4) *Notice of termination* —The lessee is bound to notify the lessor in writing of his intention to abandon the premises, where his lease gives him the right to terminate.[159]   And he remains liable until the notice is given, mere cessation of the use of the premises not being sufficient [160]   Where the rental is payable annually in advance, it becomes due as of the date of the lease, and a notice given on that day is too late to affect the claim for rent for the succeeding year.[161]   So, when a new year is begun, the obligation to pay for that year exists, subject to the right to annul by reassignment.[162]

(5) *By surrender.*—The surrender may be made by the lessee, or one authorized to act for him.   A solicitor appointed

[154]*Young* v *Forest Oil Co* 194 Pa. 243, 45 Atl 121; *Cole* v *Taylor*, 8 Pa Super Ct 19; *Consumers' Heating Co* v *American Land Co.* 31 Pittsb L J N S. 24

[156]*Williams* v *Guffy*, 178 Pa 342, 35 Atl 875

[156]*Westmoreland & C. Natural Gas Co* v *DeWitt*, 130 Pa 235, 5 L. R A. 731, 25 W N C 103, 18 Atl. 724.

[157]*Mathews* v *People's Natural Gas Co.* 179 Pa 165, 36 Atl 216.

[158]*Consumers' Heating Co.* v *American Land Co* 31 Pittsb. L. J. N. S 24, *Cassell* v *Crothers*, 193 Pa 359, 44 Atl 446.

[159]*May* v *Hazelwood Oil Co.* 152 Pa 518, 25 Atl 564

[160]*Double* v *Union Heat & Light Co* 172 Pa 388, 33 Atl. 694

[161]*Nesbit* v *Godfrey*, 155 Pa 251, 25 Atl 621

[162]*Coulter* v. *Conemaugh Gas Co.* 14 Pa Super Ct 553.

to attend to legal business has no such authority.[163] But liability remains until the formal surrender [164] And the lessee who has never gone into possession of the land may surrender his rights by parol.[165] The surrender and the acceptance thereof may both be oral.[166]

As has been said, it is the duty of the lessee to surrender the lease or offer to; otherwise liability continues [167] And the vendee of the lessee's interests at sheriff's sale, who fails to surrender, is likewise bound.[168] And so surrender is too late if made after suit is brought.[169] Where the lease was for a definite period, it being provided that certain monthly payments should be made after that time until the lease was surrendered, or oil found in paying quantities, and the lessee never went upon the ground, or had further dealings with the lessor, it was held unnecessary to surrender the lease. In such a case no recovery could be had for the monthly payments falling due after the expiration of the fixed period, and until actual surrender.[170] So the lessee was excused from surrendering the lease, which gave the right to drill for oil and gas, and the additional right to construct a pipe line, where notice of an intention to abandon had been given to the lessor, since the retention of the lease was necessary to protect the pipe line.[171]

e. *Termination by court.*—Where the lease provides for the releasing of the property under certain conditions, the court may, by bill in equity, compel the specific performance of the contract, and direct the execution of the release. But such will

[163]*Jamestown & F R Co* v *Egbert*, 152 Pa 53, 25 Atl 151.

[164]*Jamestown & F. R Co.* v. *Egbert*, 152 Pa 53, 25 Atl. 151, *Ramsey* v. *White*, 21 Pittsb. L J. N. S 425.

[165]*Hooks* v *Forst*, 165 Pa. 238, 30 Atl 846

[166]*Cochran* v *Shenango Natural Gas Co* 23 Pittsb L J. N. S 82

[167]*Shettler* v. *Hartman*, 1 Pennyp.

279; *Ahrns* v *Chartiers Valley Gas Co* 188 Pa 249, 41 Atl 739

[168]*Aderhold* v *Oil Well Supply Co* 158 Pa 401, 28 Atl 22

[169]*Douthett* v *Gibson*, 11 Pa. Super Ct 543

[17]*Briggs* v. *Elder*, 22 Pa Super Ct 324

[171]*Stage* v *Boyer*, 183 Pa 560, 38 Atl. 1035.

not be done where the material terms of the agreement are in doubt.[172]

870. Property on termination.— Where the lease is terminated, the lessees may, within a reasonable time, remove the derricks, casing, and tools from the premises of the lessor. Such are trade fixtures, and belong to the tenant.[173] The lessor cannot prevent the removal on the ground that the lessee has failed to complete the work as required.[174] But the removal must be made within a reasonable time, unless a period has been fixed in the contract itself. So it is too late to do so four years after the termination of the lease.[175] But a failure of the lessee to remove for more than six years after notice, his right to possession in the meantime being questioned, in ejectment proceedings, will not bar his right, when ousted.[176] The lessee may recover in an action for conversion if the landlord refuses to deliver the chattels upon demand [177] Or an action in replevin may be maintained [178] But he cannot maintain ejectment to obtain possession of the premises in order to remove the personal property though the court will direct a judgment for the defendant without prejudice to the lessee's right to maintain an action against the lessor for taking and appropriating personal property.[179]

Where the lease has provided for the abandonment of an unproductive well, and gives to the lessor the gas upon paying the ordinary price for casing and rig, the lessor may, upon abandonment, take the same, if he so elects, by paying the stipulated

[172]*Cleland* v. *Aiken*, 23 Pa. Co Ct 1

[173]*Sattler* v *Opperman*, 14 Pa Super Ct 32, *Shellar* v *Shivers*, 171 Pa 569, 33 Atl 95, *Wick* v *Bredin*, 189 Pa 83, 42 Atl 17, *Williams* v *Guffy*, 178 Pa 342, 35 Atl 875

[174]*Patterson* v *Hausbeck*, 8 Pa Super Ct 36

[175]*Shellar* v. *Shivers*, 171 Pa. 569, 33 Atl 95

[176]*Sattler* v *Opperman*, 14 Pa. Super Ct 32

[177]*Sattler* v *Opperman*, 14 Pa. Super Ct 32

[178]*Forest Oil Co.* v *Hart*, 33 Pittsb. L J N S 17

[179]*Cassell* v *Crothers*, 193 Pa 359, 44 Atl 446.

price [180] If the lessee has agreed to put in an oil well, upon abandoning the premises for gas purposes, the lessor can recover actual damages for the failure to do so.[181]

871. Reimbursement for expenditures.— Where land has been leased for the production of oil, and gas is found in paying quantities, the lessee is not entitled to reimbursement for the cost of drilling the well from the proceeds arising from the sale of the gas [182] If a person, while in possession of oil land, believing he has a valid title thereto, in good faith drills an oil well thereon, he has the right, if the land be afterward recovered from him in ejectment, to retain out of the proceeds of oil produced during his occupancy a sum sufficient to reimburse him for the cost of drilling the well [183]

In such case, if, pending the action of ejectment brought, the court issues a writ of estrepement, and appoints a receiver under the act of June 5, 1883, P. L. 79, the defendant is entitled to compensation for the cost of putting down the well out of a fund in the receiver's hands arising from the sale of the oil therefrom produced.[184]

872. Sublease.— Where the rights of a lessee have been assigned to another, the assignee can acquire only such rights as the lessee had.[185] And the same is true where his interest passes to a sheriff's vendee.[186] Where the sublease is made subject to the reservation of the right to take gas upon paying the cost of drilling to the assignee, the lessee retains no present interest in the leasehold.[187]

Though no power is given by the contract to sublet, yet, if the lessor subsequently enters into a contract with an assignee,

[180] *Smith* v *Hickman*, 14 Pa Super. Ct 46

[181] *McClay* v *Western Pennsylvania Gas Co* 201 Pa 197, 50 Atl 978

[182] *Palmer* v *Truby*, 136 Pa 556, 20 Atl 516

[183] *Palmer* v. *Truby*, 136 Pa 556, 20 Atl. 516.

[184] *Phillips* v. *Coast*, 130 Pa. 572, 18 Atl 998

[185] *Cole* v. *Taylor*, 8 Pa Super Ct 19

[186] *Aderhold* v *Oil Well Supply Co* 158 Pa 401, 28 Atl 22

[187] *Wiles* v *People's Gas Co* 7 Pa. Super. Ct. 562.

by which it is agreed that the lease shall remain in full force, the lessor is estopped from objecting, and the assignee may recover from him damages for breach of a covenant contained therein.[188] Where the condition was that the lessees should manage the property, they may sublet the right to operate upon such terms as they see fit, regardless of the consent of the grantees.[189]

The assignee will be bound by the covenants in the lease, though he failed to sign the contract or an assignment of it.[190] And the fact that an assignment of the lease is in violation of a covenant therein does not prevent the passing of the title. It does not lie in the mouth of an assignee to set up such an irregularity while holding under an assignment which the assignor has ratified in any way.[191] Nor can the assignee aver that he came into possession under a lease from another and the lessor in question.[192] The assignee of the lease must notify the lessor of the transfer to him.[193]

873. Liability of assignee.— When the covenant is for the performance of some duty in connection with the possession of land, or in the nature of rent or royalties for use and enjoyment of the premises, it is a covenant running with the land.[194] So the assignee of the lease is liable upon the covenants contained in the original lease for breaches committed while the right of possession is in him.[195] And this is true whether there be one assignee or successive assignees.[196] But no liability exists for breach of the covenant which matures after the interest has

[188]Guffey v Clever, 146 Pa. 548, 23 Atl 161
[189]Thompson's Appeal, 101 Pa 225
[190]Williams v Short, 155 Pa 480, 26 Atl 662
[191]Oil Creek & C. Branch Petroleum Co v Stanton Oil Co 23 Pa. Co Ct. 153
[192]Ewing v Fertig, 9 Pa Dist R. 756, 24 Pa. Co. Ct 301
[193]Carnegie Natural Gas Co. v. Philadelphia Co. 158 Pa. 317, 27 Atl 951
[194]Stone v. Marshall Oil Co 188 Pa 602, 41 Atl 748, 1119.
[195]Oil Creek & C Branch Petroleum Co v Stanton Oil Co 23 Pa Co Ct. 153
[196]Washington Natural Gas Co v. Johnson, 123 Pa 576, 10 Am. St. Rep. 553, 16 Atl 799.

been parted with.[197] In order that liability attach to the assignee, there must be privity of contract or estate between him and the lessor. Where the lessee was a corporation, and was subsequently merged into another corporation, whose charter provided that the obligation of the constituent company should be assumed by the consolidated one, it was held that no action for breach of the covenant to pay rent could lie against the assignee.[198]

874. For rent or royalty — Covenants to pay rent or royalty run with the land, and the assignee is liable for the same which accrue while he holds the assignment[199] And so is the purchaser of the lessee's interest at sheriff's sale[200] And where there has been an assignment to one half of the interest to one company, and the other half to another, and the first company agrees to operate for both, it is liable for all of the rents and royalties[201] It is not necessary that the rent or royalty be payable in money The same rule applies where the covenant provides for the transfer of a share of the proceeds to the lessor[202]

The liability of successive assignees is for performances of covenants falling due during their respective ownerships only.[203]

875. For failure to drill.—The assignee is liable for the breach of the covenant to drill, if broken while he holds the lease; for such covenant runs with the land.[204] But he is not liable where the covenant matures after his interest has been

[197]*Watt* v *Equitable Gas Co* 8 Pa Super Ct 618

[198]*Acheson* v *Kittanning Consol Natural Gas Co* 8 Pa Super Ct 477

[199]*Fennell* v *Guffey*, 139 Pa 341, 20 Atl 1048, *Fennell* v *Guffey*, 155 Pa 38, 25 Atl 785, *Coulter* v *Conemaugh Gas Co* 14 Pa Super Ct 553, *MacDonald* v *O'Neil*, 21 Pa Super Ct 364

[200]*Aderhold* v *Oil Well Supply Co.* 158 Pa 401, 28 Atl 22

LAND & TEN 49

[201]*Burton* v *Forest Oil Co* 204 Pa 349, 54 Atl 266

[202]*Stone* v *Marshall Oil Co* 188 Pa 602, 41 Atl 748, 1110

[203]*Washington Natural Gas Co* v *Johnson*, 123 Pa 576. 10 Am St Rep 553, 16 Atl 799, *Stone* v *Marshall Oil Co* 188 Pa 602, 41 Atl 748 1119

[204]*Bradford Oil Co* v *Blair*, 113 Pa 83, 57 Am Rep 442, 4 Atl 218

transferred[205] And where an assignment of an oil and gas lease was made in consideration of a certain sum paid at the time of the assignment, "and the further consideration of the sum of $1,000 if oil is found in any well drilled on any of the territory herein described, and said well or territory be further operated by the said F B. T. [or assigns]," no covenant running with the land is created, and the assignor is not entitled to recover from an assignee of the assignee the $1,000 mentioned in the agreement[206]

876   Liability of lessee in case of assignment.—Owing to his privity of contract with the lessor, a lessee's liability in an oil and gas lease continues after his assignment of the lease[207] The liability of the assignee of an oil and gas lease for the rents and royalties which accrue to the lessor is found in privity of estate   He takes the lease with notice of its covenants, and is liable for all breaches thereof which occur while he holds title When the assignee executed a lease of the premises, reserving a larger rent or containing covenants more advantageous to the lessor than those found in the original leasehold, he reserved to himself a benefit derived under the original lease, and his privity of estate is thus continued   And an action may be brought against the assignor for the entire rental.[208]

Where there was no obligation on the part of the lessee to explore for oil, he cannot be affected by the payment of the rent and the continuing of the lease by his assignee, made without his knowledge, and not ratified by him[209]

877. Actions.—Where the reversion of lands let for oil and gas purposes has been sold by the lessor, no action will lie in the

[205]*Watt* v *Equitable Gas Co* 8 Pa Rep 553, 16 Atl 799, *Pittsburg* Super Ct 618, *Washington Natural Gas Co* v *Johnson*, 123 Pa 576, 10 Am St Rep 553, 16 Atl 799

[206]*Fisher* v *Guffey*, 193 Pa 393, 44 Atl 452

[207]*Washington Natural Gas Co* v *Johnson*, 123 Pa 576, 10 Am St

Consol Coal Co v *Greenlee*, 164 Pa 549, 30 Atl 489

[208]*McClaren* v *Citizens' Oil & Gas Co* 14 Pa Super Ct 167, *Drake* v *Lacoe* 157 Pa 17, 27 Atl 538

[209]*McKee* v *Colwell*, 7 Pa Super Ct 607.

name of the lessor, for the use of his vendee, for a breach of covenants by the lessee, where no breach had occurred before the sale of the reversion.[210]

The action may be maintained either against the lessee, who is liable, or his assignee   The landlord is not bound to sever his action, nor to bring it in such a form as to further the convenience of one who has attempted to make a profit for himself out of the estate by creating a new estate upon essentially different conditions.[211]   The action may be maintained jointly against the assignee of a part and the original lessee [212]   But a decree upon a bill to enforce a covenant of a lease against the lessee and many assignees, without designating the respective interests, or showing a joint possession, is bad [213]

878 Liability to lessee.— The assignee of the lease is liable to the lessee for breach of the covenants agreed to   But if he has agreed to pay in case product is found in paying quantities, and the assignee then takes a new lease from the landlord, with new conditions, he will not be liable to the original lessee until oil has been produced in paying quantities.[214]

879 Plugging wells.— One may permit gas to escape from a well on his land though it interfere with the product of a well on adjoining land, where his act is not malicious or negligent [215]   By the act of June 10, 1881, P. L. 110, the right is given to plug abandoned oil wells by adjoining owners as well as requiring the owners of such wells to plug when abandoned   This right to so act at the expense of the delinquent operator is appurtenant to the estate in the land   When one acquires title

[210]*Stoddard* v *Emery,* 128 Pa 436, 18 Atl 339

[211]*McClaren* v *Citizens' Oil & Gas Co* 14 Pa Super Ct 167

[212]*Jackson* v *O'Hara,* 183 Pa 233, 38 Atl 624

[213]*Young* v *Forest Oil Co* 194 Pa. 243 45 Atl 121

[214]*Smith* v *Munhall,* 139 Pa 253 21 Atl 735

[215]*Haque* v *Wheeler,* 157 Pa 325, 22 L R A 141, 37 Am St Rep 736, 27 Atl 714.

under a lease he becomes entitled, through privity of estate, for the protection of his property, to plug a well abandoned prior to his leasing the adjoining property, and to recover the cost from the delinquent operator.[216] In case an action is brought for the penalty for the failure to plug as required by the act of June 10, 1881, no affidavit of defense is required[217]

[216]*Steelsmith* v. *Aiken,* 14 Pa Super Ct. 226.

[217]*Bartoe* v *Guckert,* 158 Pa 124, 27 Atl 845.

INDEX.

(References are to pages).

A.

(*References are to pages*).

ACT DECEMBER 14, 1863—(continued)

evidence assumed to have been sufficient, 612.

when record shows absence of, 613

substantial conformity with statute enough, 614.

when record is incomplete, 614

execution from common pleas, 615

supersedeas of, 615

restoring tenant's possession 615

liability of landlord in damages, 616.

appeal, 616

time and mode of, 616.

the recognizance, 617.

affidavit 618

procedure 619

amendment 619

nonsuit, 620

trial, 620

proving tenancy, 621

proving end of term, 622

tenant's defenses, 623, 624.

prohibited 625

not a supersedeas 625

damages of tenant, 625.

landlord, 628

judgment of restitution, 628.

ACT FEBRUARY 28, 1865

lost lease in Philadelphia, 637

means of compelling tenant to reveal when term closes, 637.

conditions under which remedy exists, 637.

notice to tenant to give information, 638.

proceedings before justice, 639.

ACT OF GOD

tenant not liable for, 95.

ACTS OF ASSEMBLY

May	28, 1715, assigning choses in action, 525
March	21, 1772, frauds, 31, 367
March	21, 1772, § 1, appraisement of distrained goods 234 236, 239, 244, 261
March	21, 1772, § 2, pound breach, 196, 197 246
March	21, 1772, § 3, distress when no rent is due, 253
March	21, 1772, § 5, fraudulent and clandestine removal of goods, 196 217
March	21, 1772 § 6, distress on goods sold, 220
March	21, 1772, § 7, things subject to distress, 209
March	21, 1772 § 10, replevin, 263

(References are to pages)

ACTS OF ASSEMBLY—(continued)

(References are to pages)

LAN & TEN 50

(References are to pages).

COVENANTS OF LESSOR

    kinds of, 66

    to make repair, 67, 73, 74 75

    to erect building 68

    as to existing state of premises, 68

        measure of damages for breach of, 83.

    as to suitableness of premises, 68

    as to habitableness of house, 68

    that premises are perfectly dry, construction of, 70.

    as to changes to be made in neighborhood, 71.

    to reimburse tenant for repairs, 76

    to furnish steam, 81

    to procure a right to a railroad switch, 82.

    to furnish material for fencing, 85

    for quiet enjoyment, 332

    to allow the tenant to renew the term, 460, 461.

    implied, 68, 69, 71.

        as to stairway when floors are let to different tenants, 71.

    effect of breach of, on rent, 71, 72

    action for damages resulting from breach, 71.

        foreign attachment, 83.

CROPPER

    distinguished from tenant, 11.

        consequences of distinction, 14

        from employee, 13

        right of distress as respects 14, 170

    right to tenant's remedies, as against landlord, 14.

    right to share of crop, 14, 117

    no preference of, as to executions, 287.

CROPS

    lease for raising of two, interpretation of, 12.

    rent payable in share of, 115

        death of lessor, 525

    when owned by tenant, 116

    when landlord's share becomes specifically his, 116, 531.

    stipulation to be landlord's until division, 119.

    way-going, 507

        see WAY-GOING CROP

    in ground at commencement of term, 519

    when wholly the lessee's, notwithstanding sheriff's sale of reversion, 532

    when rent payable in share of, falls due after conveyance of reversion, 536

CULM

    personal property, 688.

(References are to pages).

DAMAGES—(continued)

respecting hay, fodder and straw, 521

detention of premises, act March 21, 1772, 569

December 14, 1863, 600

dispossession of tenant, act December 14, 1863, 625.

of landlord on appeal, act December 14 1863, 628

exemplary, for removal of surface support, coal lease, 693.

interest on damages, 693

for breach of contract to buy interest in oil lease, 721.

treble, for taking minerals from others' lands, 694

for breach of covenant to mine with diligence, 696

for failure to mine minimum quantity of coal, 701

for lessor's drilling oil wells within protected area, 735

for lessee's failure to drill proper number of oil wells 746.

to deliver to landlord his share of oil, 747

DEATH

of tenant, landlord's preference, as to rent, 296.

equivalent to notice to quit, 306

effect on duration of term, 327

transmission of term, 364

of lessor, to whom right to rent passes 525.

does not terminate lease, 710.

DECEIT

action for, in misrepresenting condition of premises, 43.

breach of warranty of purity of water, 83

DECLARATION

on covenant omitted from written lease, 46, 47.

in action for rent, 135

DEFALCATION

by justice against rent, prior to distress, 258.

DELIVERY.

of lease, necessity of, 26

DEMAND OF RENT

condition to forfeiture of lease, 410, 415.

where made, 416

when unnecessary, 417

condition to procedure under act April 3, 1830, 437.

DENIAL OF LESSOR'S TITLE

by lessee, implied conditions against, 398, 434, 754.

DISCHARGE

of surety, 62.

(Refei ences are to pages).

DISTRESS

right to, at common law, 154.

contractual right of, 154

modification of right to contract, 154, 155.

right to, as against cropper, 14, 170

right to, for penalty, 154 167

effect of, on liability of surety, 62

when rent is payable in kind, 117, 118

rent must be already payable, 155, 181.

computing time when rent is due, 156.

rent payable in advance, 157

when time of paying rent is hastened by act of lessee, 157

    retarded, 159

rent not due, because condition has not been complied with, 159.

spoliation of deed reserving rent, 160.

rent must be certain, 160

none for use and occupation, 160

for rent for holdover period, 162

lease contingently reduces rent, 163.

rent apportioned, 164 *et seq*

    divided, 165

    apportioned by division of fee, 165, 171.

lease contingently increases rent, 166

for taxes, gas, steam heat, 167

for water rent, 168

necessity of reversion in distrainer, 168, 179, 284.

by ground landlord, 168, 172, 180

kind of term to which right is incident, 169.

for dower, 169

things subject to, 186, 209.

    grain in ground, 209.

    building, 210.

    fixtures, 210.

    the term itself, 210.

    landlord's goods, 210

    exemption of, 210

        waiver of, 212

        by investment, 212.

goods of subtenant, 186

    who has paid rent, 188

    though tenant's goods are sufficient, 189.

goods both of tenant and subtenant, 189

goods of assignee of leasehold, 190

    lessee after assignment of term, 191.

    any one on premises, 191

    wife, daughter, mother, of tenant, 192.

    lent to tenant or wife, 193

    piano, melodeon lent to tenant, 194

(References are to pages).

EXECUTION SALE
 see LANDLORD'S PREFERENCE

EXEMPTION
 from execution for rent, 137.
  waiver of, 138
 from distress, 199, 210, 393
  joint property of joint lessees, 211
  waiver of, 212, 284
  tenant s methods for securing, 214, 262
   remedies for denial of, 214.
  landlord's preference as to goods exempt, 283
  when sublessee has no right to exemption, 393

EXPERTS
 testimony of, in construction of lease, 733

F.

FEE
 transfer of, during term, 523
 right of transferee of, to rent, 524

FENCES
 lessor's covenant to supply material to repair, 85, 98.

FIRE
 effect of, on right and duties of lessor and lessee, 77
  duty of paying future rent, 77
 insurance, duty to pay future rent, 77
 when tenant must pay insurance money to landlord, 78.
 when the thing demised is an upper story, 78
 duty to pay rent conditioned on nondestruction of fire, 79
 possession taken by lessor to rebuild, 80
 between the making of lease and commencement of term, 80
 lessee's duty to deliver in good condition, notwithstanding, 95.

FIXTURES
 when subject to distress, 210
 proceeds of, execution sale, 282
 right to remove, 485
  annexation not decisive, 486
  intention decisive, 486
  evidence of intention, 487
 other criteria than intention, 488
 what are, is question of law and fact, 489.
 usage as determining what are, 490
 whether a tramroad is, 490
 contractual modification of tenant's right to, 490, 714.

FURNACE
    lease of, includes right to take limestone, 41.

FURNISHED HOUSE.
    lease of, 43

G.

GAS,
    nature of, 724
    leases, 718
        see OIL AND GAS LEASES

GAS BILL
    distress for, as part of rent, 167
        when preferred, on death of tenant, 297.

GAS METERS.
    tenant not obliged to tolerate, 39

GRADING
    lessee's duty to pay assessments for, 108.

GRANT, BARGAIN AND SELL
    significance of, as indicating sale of minerals, 682.

GRATE IN PAVEMENT
    duty of lessee to repair, 93.

GROUND RENT
    distress for, 168
        by assignee of, for rent, 172.
    no landlord's preference for, 286

GUARANTOR
    difference between surety and, 53, 57.

GUARDIAN
    lease by, made valid by estoppel, 30.
        by ratification, 676
    as lessor, may distrain, 171
    landlord's preference, execution sale, 284.
    oil lease by, 718.

H.

HABIT
    of lessor, proof of, 49.

HABITABLENESS OF HOUSE
    implied covenant as to, 68

(*References are to pages*).

MANURE—(continued)

trespass in estrepement, 506.

violation of lessee's covenant, respecting hay, fodder, etc 521.

MARRIED WOMEN

lessee, liability of surety of, 59.

separate acknowledgment of lease by, 59, 719

husband occupies her land, duty to pay rent 129

distress of goods of, for husband's rent, 192

wife of tenant, may remove goods and avoid distress 196

effect of nonjoinder of, in lease, 719

liability of husband to for royalties belonging to her as lessor, but received by him, 752

MECHANICS' LIEN

when lease contains contract to convey, 9.

when tenant may put one on the fee, 22.

leaseholds in mines subject to, 686

on oil and gas leaseholds, 727

MELODEON

lent to tenant, exempt from distress, 194.

MERGER

of agreement to lease in lease afterwards made, 6.

of term in reversion, 328

when it will not occur, 329

MESNE PROFITS

when there is no contract for rent, 126.

tenant's liability for, effect on rent, 355.

MINE

what is, 673.

MINERAL

what the term embraces, 673.

MINER'S WEIGHT

meaning of phrase, 698.

MINING LEASES

option to lease, 674.

bond to bore coal treated as penalty, 697

contract to lease, liability for not accepting lease, 674.

offer of lease in a reasonable time 674

liability of lessor for not making lease, 675

certainty as to commencement and end of term, 678.

lease of one mineral, excludes other 677

(References are to pages).

MINING LEASES—(continued)

    meaning of "ton," 698

    proportioned to selling price, 698.

    meaning of screened coal, 698

    on coal lease, coal measured by bushel, 699

    varying according to sizes of coal, 699

    none for coal taken from lessor's land beyond the bounds of the
      lease, 699

    none, on coal used in the mining operations, 699.

    landlord s preference as to, 699

    eviction suspends, 700, 704, 711

    minimum royalty, 701

        when only conditionally payable, 705

        mining in one year, more than, 706

        damages for failure to mine minimum, 701

        cessation of operations no excuse, 702

        unprofitableness of operations no excuse 702

        poorness of quality of ore no excuse, 702

        nonexistence of ore as an excuse, 703, 704

        no defense that coal in place is more valuable than if it had
          been mined, 704

        defenses against action for, 704, 706

        eviction a defense, 704, 711

        eviction from one of several tracts, 704

        release from liability for, 705

        accounts rendered by lessee, 706

        conclusiveness of acceptance of payment, 706

        payment of royalty in excess of what is due, 707.

        payment of royalty to wrong person, 707

        interest on royalty, 707

        to whom royalty is payable, 707, 708

        contract a sale, royalty payable to whom 708

        right of life-devisee to royalties, 708

        royalties payable to trustee, his commission on them, 709.

        action to recover royalties, 709

            where brought, 709

            jurisdiction of justice of peace, 709.

        forfeiture of mining lease, 711

            time of, 711.

            for not properly working mine, 712

            notice of, 713

            effect on royalty subsequently accruing, 713.

            mode of enforcing, ejectment, 713

            mode of enforcing, equity, 714

        improvements and fixtures, 714

            when removable by contract, 714

            when removable without contract, 715

            setting off value of, against rent, 716.

(References are to pages).

(References are to pages).

OPTION—(continued).

    to buy the lease, given by the lessee, 670.

    to accept an oil lease, 722

ORGAN

    lent to tenant, exemption of, from distress, 194.

OYER

    of lease, 137.

P.

PAROL EVIDENCE

    to show lessor's misrepresentations, 42

        mistake in framing lease, 44, 45 79

        to show omissions of parts of actual agreement, 44, 68, 75

    omitted covenants must be declared on, 58

    to show duress, 45

        insanity 45

    of promise which induced acceptance of lease, 47, 48

    to explain the terms, 51, 731

    to show situation of parties, the state of the subject-matter, 733

    of later modification of lease, 51, 734

    of promise to make repairs, 75

    of release of surface support to the lessee of coal, 692

    to contradict lease as to amount of coal to be annually mined 696.

    modifying written lease as respects coal, 705

    of understanding of parties, not affecting assignee of lease, 733.

    degree of, necessary to modify a writing, 733

PARTITION

    between tenants in common, how it affects lessee, 541, 728.

PARTNER

    as distinguished from tenant, 12 17

    lease by one of several, 29

    authority of one, to make lease for all, 30.

    equity of, as respects leasehold, 369

    oil lease, asset of partnership, 727

PAVEMENT

    duty of landlord to lay, 90

    right of tenant of part of building, to use, 105.

    lessee's duty to pay assessment for, 133

PAYING QUANTITIES

    meaning of, in oil and gas leases, 751.

PAYMENT

    on account of rent by distress 143, 145.

    appropriation of, to rent, 143

RENT

(References are to pages).

RESERVATION.

> distinguished from exception, 721
> with respect to right to drill for oil, 725, 726.
> of "all minerals," not inclusive of oil, 726.

RESTITUTION, WRIT OF

> under act March 21, 1772, 571.
> under act April 3, 1830, 443
> under act December 14, 1863 602

RESTRICTION

> on tenant s use of premises, 40.

REVERSION

> change of ownership of, effect on surety's liability, 64.
> in distrainor necessary, 168, 179
> transferee of, may distrain, 171
> necessity of, to support landlord's preference as to executions, 284
> transfer of, during term, 523
> lessor's covenants run with, 523
>> covenant to let lessee purchase, runs, 523
> right of transferee of, to subsequent rent, 524, 533.
>> when there is no apportionment, 533.
> transfer of, by death of lessor, 525
>> rent a share of crop, 525
>> of lessor, a life-tenant, 526.
>> by sheriff's sale, 527
>>> purchaser affirming the lease, 528.
>>> prepayment of rent, 529
>>> assignment of rent, 529
>>> lessor's share of crop sold by sheriff, 531.
>> by other judicial sales, 532
>> when alienee's title begins, 534.
>> when rent payable in crop, falls due after grant of reversion, 536
>> of part of reversion, 539
>>> effect on recovery of possession, 541.
> right of transferee of, to sue for breaches of tenant's covenant, 771.

ROOF AND WALL.

> lease of, 20

ROYALTIES

> recovery of, when only an option to accept lease, 2.
> upon coal lease, 697 *et seq.*
>> see MINING LEASE

RUN WITH THE LAND

> covenants that, 92, 768
> covenants regulating manner of removing coal, 689.

(References are to pages).

STEAM
    covenant to furnish, 81

STEAM HEAT
    distress for charge for, as rent, 167.

STEREOPTICON VIEWS
    lease of roof for exhibition of, 20.

STONES
    when grant of right to take is a lease, 10, 19, 28
    lease of furnace, including right to take limestone, 41.

STRAW
    landlord's share of, as rent, 115.
    a part of way-going crop, 509
    lessee's covenant respecting, 520.

SUBJECT OF LEASE
    area defined, 37
    building, and not the soil, 38.
    water-right included, 39
    easements included, 39
    furnished house, 43
    different parts of same building, 104 *et seq.*

SUBLETTING.
    effect of, on liability of surety, 62
    right of distress, 173, 392
    goods of sublessee distrainable for primary rent, 187, 282.
    of all or part of premises, 188, 388
    landlord's preference, as respects sublessee's goods, 282
    sublessor entitled to landlord's preference, 288
    preventing sublessee's taking possession, on eviction, 337.
    effect of, on liability of assignee, 379
    by assignee of lease, 383, 390
    distinction between assigning and, 384, 387, 389.
    when transferee's right is restricted, 389
    the right to underlet, 390
    damages for, 390
    condition against, 391
        acquiring easement, not a violation of, 392
        sublessee about to be evicted, declines to pay rent, 392
        liability of sublessee for negligence, although sublease a breach
          of condition, 392
        duty of sublessee to pay rent to lessee, 392
        distress for rent due by sublessee, 392
    effect of tenant's surrender, on his sublessee's rights, 393.
    sublessee may assign the sublease, 394

SUBLETTING—(continued)

    acquire the reversion, 394

    right to way-going crop, 510

    not bound by lessee's covenants, 394

    subject to conditions affecting lessee, 395.

    right of, when eminent domain is exercised, 396.

    right to remove fixtures, 490

  conditions may be in a sublease, 399

SUITABLENESS OF PREMISES

  to particular use, no implied covenant for, 69.

SUNDAY.

  distress on, 225.

SURETY

  in constable's bond, liability to landlord, 267

  in recognizance for appeal, act April 3, 1830, 449.

    set-off by, 450, 456

  lessee as surety for his assignee of term, 382

  of assignee of term, rent falling due after another assignment, 368.

SURETY OF LESSEE

  distinction between guarantor and, 53, 57.

  becomes such, by writing only, 54, 56

  consideration necessary, 54, 56

  connection between his contract and the lease, 55.

  necessity of signature of lessee, 55.

    lessor, 55

  when jointly liable with lessee, 55

  when severally liable, 55

  liable on all the lessee's covenants, 56

  liable for taxes, 56, 58

  when he becomes such, after the making of lease, 56

  notice of lessor's acceptance of contract unnecessary, 58.

  not discharged by lessor's failure to seek payment from lessee, 58

  notice by, to lessor, to collect rent from lessee, 58.

  notice of refusal to continue, liable, 58

  effect of reducing rent, on liability of, 58

  effect of his death, a future liability, 59, 61, 62

  effect of surrender of term, on liability of, 59, 60, 63.

  liability of, when lessee a married woman, 59

    when lease is within statute of frauds, 59

    when renewals are made, or tenant holds over, 60.

    affected by conditions subsequent, 60.

  right of, to prevent renewal of term on his credit, 61.

  liability of, when lessor relinquishes means of paying rent, 62, 185, 267.

    when partial payment is refused, 65, 191.

(References are to pages).

(References are to pages)

(References are to pages).

TYPE-WRITING MACHINE
exemption from distress, 195

U.

USAGE OF TRADE.
determining what is a fixture, 490.

USE AND OCCUPATION
when lease is inchoate, 2.
assumpsit for, 122, 124
actual possession unnecessary, 122
when action for, is inapplicable, 123
when rent is precisely defined, 123
when lease provides for precise definition of rent, 123
when lease is voidable because of statute of frauds, 124.
when lease calls for a 'reasonable rent," 125
what constitutes occupation, 125
when contract to pay any rent is implied, not express, 126
when no contract can be implied and there is no express contract, 126, 127
liability for, of tenant to sheriff a vendee of reversion 128, 529
when occupation is permitted without expectation of compensation, 128
when relationship negatives expectation of rent, 129
when land belongs to several owners duty to pay to each, 131.
liability for, of tenants at sufferance, 131.
measure of compensation for, 132, 481
no right to distrain for compensation for, 160
landlord's preference, as against execution creditor, 287.
when tenant holds over, 481.

USE OF PREMISES.
restriction on, 40

V.

VIADUCT
for railroad, on leased premises, 39.

W.

WAIVER
by tenant, of defects of premises, 91
of exemption, 138, 212, 284
of sewing machines from distress, 206
of right to appeal from justice's judgment for rent, 139.
of appraisement in distress proceedings, 237.
of public notice of distress—sale, 241

CPSIA information can be obtained
at www.ICGtesting.com
Printed in the USA
BVHW042148150719
553553BV00006B/117/P

9 781376 870176